Exciting News!

Library of the Written Word

VOLUME 122

The Handpress World

Editors-in-Chief

Andrew Pettegree (*University of St Andrews*)
Arthur der Weduwen (*University of St Andrews*)

Editorial Board

Ann Blair (*Harvard University*)
Falk Eisermann (*Staatsbibliothek zu Berlin – Preußischer Kulturbesitz*)
Shanti Graheli (*University of Glasgow*)
Earle Havens (*Johns Hopkins University*)
Ian Maclean (*All Souls College, Oxford*)
Alicia Montoya (*Radboud University*)
Angela Nuovo (*University of Milan*)
Helen Smith (*University of York*)
Mark Towsey (*University of Liverpool*)
Malcolm Walsby (*enssib, Lyon*)

VOLUME 100

The titles published in this series are listed at *brill.com/lww*

Exciting News!

Event, Narration and Impact from Past to Present

Edited by

Brendan Dooley
Alexander S. Wilkinson

BRILL

LEIDEN | BOSTON

Cover illustration: 'Poy', 'Sausage for Tea', Poy's War Cartoons from 'The Evening News' (London: Simpkin, Marshall, Hamilton, Kent & Co., 1915). A cartoon on the great feat of the late Lieut. Warneford, V.C.

Library of Congress Cataloging-in-Publication Data

Names: Dooley, Brendan Maurice, 1953- editor. | Wilkinson, Alexander Samuel, editor.
Title: Exciting news! : event, narration and impact from past to present / edited by Brendan Dooley, Alexander Samuel Wilkinson.
Description: Leiden ; Boston : Brill, 2024. | Series: The handpress world; vol.100 | Includes index.
Identifiers: LCCN 2023059382 (print) | LCCN 2023059383 (ebook) | ISBN 9789004689824 (hardback) | ISBN 9789004689831 (ebook)
Subjects: LCSH: Journalism–History. | Journalism–Social aspects. | Mass media–History. | Mass media–Social aspects.
Classification: LCC PN4801 E79 2024 (print) | LCC PN4801 (ebook) | DDC 070.9–dc23/eng/20240123
LC record available at https://lccn.loc.gov/2023059382
LC ebook record available at https://lccn.loc.gov/2023059383

Typeface for the Latin, Greek, and Cyrillic scripts: "Brill". See and download: brill.com/brill-typeface.

ISSN 1874-4834
ISBN 978-90-04-68982-4 (hardback)
ISBN 978-90-04-68983-1 (e-book)
DOI 10.1163/9789004689831

Copyright 2024 by Koninklijke Brill NV, Leiden, The Netherlands.
Koninklijke Brill NV incorporates the imprints Brill, Brill Nijhoff, Brill Schöningh, Brill Fink, Brill mentis, Brill Wageningen Academic, Vandenhoeck & Ruprecht, Böhlau and V&R unipress.
All rights reserved. No part of this publication may be reproduced, translated, stored in a retrieval system, or transmitted in any form or by any means, electronic, mechanical, photocopying, recording or otherwise, without prior written permission from the publisher. Requests for re-use and/or translations must be addressed to Koninklijke Brill NV via brill.com or copyright.com.

This book is printed on acid-free paper and produced in a sustainable manner.

Contents

List of Figures and Tables IX
Notes on Contributors XII

Introduction 1

PART 1
Early Modern Origins

SECTION 1
The Force of News

1   1600: A Year to Remember 15
    Sara Mansutti, Wouter Kreuze, Carlotta Paltrinieri, Lorenzo Allori, Davide Boerio and Brendan Dooley

2   Information Shadows
    Meteorological Disaster and Misinformation across Europe in the Wake of the 1625 Raid on Cadiz 41
    Thom Pritchard

SECTION 2
Natural Disasters

3   Troubling News Travels Fast
    The Sannio Earthquake Ripples through the Spanish Monarchy 59
    Alessandro Tuccillo

4   Narratives and Media Ecology of the "Revolutions" of Naples of 1647–48 75
    Davide Boerio and Luca Marangolo

5   St Filippo Neri in the Spanish Press
    Earthquakes, Veneration and Wondrous Events 100
    Milena Viceconte

6   'Yet Once More I Shake Not Only the Earth'
    News of Earthquakes in Early Modern England   120
        Lena Liapi

   SECTION 3
   Rebellion and War

7   Reading the 1641 Irish Rebellion
    Nehemiah Wallington and the Cultural Construction of Violence   143
        Eamon Darcy

8   The Power of the Pen
    Huguenot Gazettes in the Pursuit of Information during the Last Quarter of the Seventeenth Century   162
        Panagiotis Georgakakis

   PART 2
   Eighteenth-Century Developments

   SECTION 4
   Circulation and Reception

9   Tadhg Ó Neachtain
    A Case-Study in Gaelic Media Reception in Eighteenth-Century Dublin   187
        Liam Mac Mathúna

10 MURDER! He Wrote
    The News as Reported by James Ryan in his Diary (1787–1809)   207
        Bláithín Hurley

11 News about Justice
    Telling Crime Stories in Eighteenth-Century Europe   224
        Pasquale Palmieri

12 The Imperial Crisis in the News, c.1760–1780
    News and Newspapers as a Source for Writing Transnational Histories   242
        Joel Herman

PART 3
The Media and the Masses

SECTION 5
The Politics of News

13 The Wars at Home
    Victorian Imperial Sieges and the Conscription of Public Opinion 261
        Brian Wallace

14 The Czechoslovak Media Landscape in 1938
    *A Lack of Media-Induced Anxiety, and the Origins of the
    'Munich Betrayal'* 281
        Johana Kłusek

15 All Quiet on the Domestic Front?
    Dealing with Anxiety in Late Socialist Czechoslovak Media 297
        Ondřej Daniel and Jakub Machek

16 The Media Portrayal of Radical Irish Republicans
    An Anthropological Perspective 310
        Aodhán (Maria-Valeria) Morris

SECTION 6
Trouble in the Headlines

17 Hyde and the Media—Friend or Foe? 329
        Máire Nic an Bhaird

18 The German Air Campaign against Britain, 1915–18, and British
    Cartoon Responses 353
        Chris Williams

19 'Every Night You Take Up the Paper You Find Someone Has Either Been
    Killed or Severely Injured'
    *The Irish Press's Portrayal of Road Traffic Accidents in the Early
    Motoring Era* 381
        Leanne Blaney

20   Making a Splash
       A Brief History of Headlines   396
         Daniel Carey

   PART 4
   Beyond the News

21   Challenges beyond the News
       Events, Neglected Voices and Collective Consciousness   415
         Jane L. Chapman

     Index   429

Figures and Tables

Figures

1.1 Newsletter dated 12 February 1600. ASFI, Mediceo del Principato (MdP) vol. 3087, fol. 1   16
1.2 Fortifications along the Sava river in Schiavonia. MdP 4578, fol. 45   27
1.3 Distribution of main hubs   28
1.4 Hubs and places of news   29
4.1 Title page of Alessandro Giraffi, *Le rivoluzioni di Napoli* ([Napoli: Presso Filippo Alberto, 1647]). Courtesy of Società Napoletana di Storia Patria   85
4.2 Title page of James Howell, *An Exact Historie of the Late Revolutions in Naples* (London: R. Lowndes, 1664). Courtesy of Società Napoletana di Storia Patria   86
4.3 Engraving of Masniello by Pieter Jode the Younger. Courtesy of Kislak Center for Special Collections, Rare Books and Manuscripts, University of Pennsylvania   91
4.4 Drawings of Masaniello from Pietro Bacchi's model. Courtesy of Kislak Center for Special Collections, Rare Books and Manuscripts, University of Pennsylvania   92
4.5 *El Maior Monstro del Mundo y Prodixio dela Italia Tomas Aniello d'Amalfi*. Courtesy of Società Napoletana di Storia Patria   95
4.6 Michelangelo Cerquozzi, The Revolt of Masaniello in 1647. Rome, Galleria Spada. Public domain image taken from Wikimedia Commons   97
5.1 *Relación del prodigio obrado por San Felipe Neri* (Barcelona: Rafael Figueró, 1688). Courtesy of Barcelona, Biblioteca de Catalunya   104
5.2 *Relación del prodigio obrado por San Felipe Neri* (Valencia: Antonio de Bordázar, 1724). © Valencia, Biblioteca Valenciana Nicolau Primitiu   107
5.3 *Prodigios obrados por el gran Patriarca San Felipe Neri en tiempo de terremotos* (Valencia: Joseph Thomás Lucas, 1748). © Valencia, Biblioteca Valenciana Nicolau Primitiu   109
5.4 Giovanni Girolamo Frezza (after Pier Leone Ghezzi), *Archbishop Orsini extracted from the rubble of the 1688 earthquake,* in Pietro Giacomo Bacci and Giacomo Ricci, *Vita di S. Filippo Neri Fiorentino, fondatore della Congregazione dell'Oratorio* (Rome: Bernabò and Lazzarini, 1745). © Los Angeles, Getty Research Institute   111
5.5 Augustin Bouttats, *St Filippo Neri's vision of the Virgin Mary*, in *Prodigios obrados por el gran patriarca San Phelipe Neri en tiempo de terremotos* (Madrid: Herederos de la viuda de Juan García Infanzón, 1755). © Madrid, Biblioteca Nacional de España   113

8.1	Van Swoll's first attack against the Capuchin order, *Gazette d'Amsterdam*, 5 September 1679	164
8.2	The end of the report from Turin and the report from camp Rivoli. Both praised the Duke of Savoy, in the *Nouvelles extraordinaires de divers endroits*, 7 June 1696. Image from delpher.nl	179
10.1	Entry detailing the marriage of Dr Younge and Miss English, Folio 4^r, *A Carrickman's Diary*, Image Courtesy of Waterford Libraries	210
10.2	Entry detailing the marriage of Miss Nancy Dalton and Mr Morrisey, Folio 5^r, *A Carrickman's Diary*, Image Courtesy of Waterford Libraries	211
10.3	Entry revealing the escape from Kilkenny Jail of Stephen Hearn, Folio 100^v, *A Carrickman's Diary*, Image Courtesy of Waterford Libraries	212
11.1	William Hogarth (1697–1794), *Industry and Idleness*, Plate 11; *The Idle 'Prentice Executed at Tyburn*	229
13.1	John Ritchie, 'A Summer Day in Hyde Park' (detail) (oil on canvas, 1858), Museum of London Collections, MOL 5636. © Museum of London / Bridgeman Images	264
13.2	Charles Gordon, *Journals*, 13 October 1884, p. 191	273
13.3	*The Mafeking Mail* siege newspaper masthead, 10 November 1899	277
17.1	Inside cover of Úna Ní Ógáin's album presented to Hyde at Christmas 1906. Image courtesy of the James Hardiman Library, Morrisroe-Connolly Collection, at NUI Galway, G37, Hyde Scrapbook	332
17.2	Cover of Douglas Hyde's 1904–1907 diary. Courtesy of the National Library Ireland, LS G 1047	336
17.3	Hyde's American tour schedule. Image courtesy of the National Library Ireland, NLI LS 18 253	337
17.4	Dr Douglas Hyde, A Distinguished Irish Orator addressing a large audience in the Massey Hall, Toronto (*The News*, Toronto, 18 May 1906)	338
17.5	Postcard sent by Douglas Hyde entitled *What the Earthquake did in Half a Minute*. It depicts a scene from the stark aftermath of the 1906 San Francisco earthquake and fire. Image courtesy of Aidan Heavey Collection, Athlone, Co. Westmeath, Ireland, DPC-AT-045	348
17.6	Filleadh an Chraoibhín—Hyde's return from America (June 1906)	352
18.1	Louis Raemaekers, 'The Wonders of Culture', *'Land and Water' Edition of Raemaekers Cartoons* (London: Land and Water, 1916), Part 8	357
18.2	Will Dyson, 'Wonders of Science!', *Kultur Cartoons* (London: Stanley Paul, 1915)	363
18.3	Louis Raemaekers, 'The Zeppelin Triumph', *'Land and Water' Edition*, Part 3. 'But Mother had done nothing wrong, had she, Daddy?'	365
18.4	Louis Raemaekers, 'The Zeppelin Raider', *'Land and Water' Edition*, Part 14	366
18.5	J. M. Staniforth, 'Gott Mit Uns', *Western Mail*, 27 December 1917. 'The year 1917, with its great battles, has proved that the German people has in the Lord of	

Creation above an unconditional and avowed ally, on Whom it can absolutely rely. Without Him all would have been in vain ... You have seen how in this last four years of war God's hand has visibly prevailed, punished treachery, and rewarded heroic perseverance'—Kaiser's address to his troops   367

18.6   Frank Townsend, 'Essence of Parliament: Funk-Holes for Ministers—designed for protection against raids by our air-experts', *Punch*, 29 March 1916   369

18.7   J. M. Staniforth, 'The Only Way To Stop It', *Western Mail*, 27 September 1917. John Bull: 'H'm! I shall be better satisfied when I read of my air-men taking reprisals on Essen and other German towns. Until then I must expect those raids on London to continue'   370

18.8   Frank Townsend, 'The Letter and the Spirit', *Punch*, 10 October 1917. Prime Minister: 'You young rascal! I never said that'. Newsboy: 'Well, I'll lay yer meant it'   371

18.9   'Poy', 'Sausage for Tea', *Poy's War Cartoons from 'The Evening News'* (London: Simpkin, Marshall, Hamilton, Kent & Co., 1915). A cartoon on the great feat of the late Lieut. Warneford, V.C.   373

18.10 Frank Townsend, 'A Wasted Life', *Punch*, 27 September 1916. Kaiser (to Count Zeppelin): 'Tell me, Count, why didn't you invent something useful, like the "tanks"?'   374

18.11 J. M. Staniforth, 'To The Vile Dust', *Western Mail*, 19 June 1917. 'To the vile dust from whence they sprung, Unwept, unhonour'd, and unsung'   375

18.12 Frank Townsend, *Punch*, 3 November 1915. 'By Jove! Isn't it low? I believe I could hit it with my gun!'. 'Oh, please, dear, don't do anything to irritate it!'   377

18.13 Frank Townsend, 'Echoes of the Air-Raids', *Punch*, 17 October 1917. First Souvenir-hunter: 'Found anyfink, 'Erb?' Second ditto: 'No; but that'll be all right. They're sure to come again termorrer night'   377

Tables

1.1   Word frequencies in 1600 corpus   17

8.1   Huguenot Gazettes: days of publication, publishers, and years of circulation   169

8.2   Numbers of advertisements appearing in the Huguenot gazettes during 1677–1687, 1688–1697 & 1698–1701, and the percentage of French notices within the total corpus of advertisements   175

16.1 Frequency of 'Provisional' tropes encountered in news narratives about radical Republicans, from a selection of 50 articles   317

17.1 Hyde's lecture locations in California from 21 February 1906 to 22 March 1906. Taken from National Library Ireland MS 18 253   339

18.1 Cartoons and publications assessed   359

Notes on Contributors

Lorenzo Allori

holds a Master's Degree in Cybersecurity at the University of Pisa and graduated in Media Studies and Business Communication at the University of Siena. As a postdoctoral research fellow on the EURONEWS project based in UCC, he was responsible for: data entry supervision, data modelling, and data transformation. He is the project manager for the MIA (Medici Interactive Archive) digital portal (https://mia.medici.org), which is used by the EURONEWS project to perform the data-entry process. He has worked also for Syracuse University and for several other firms, building ad hoc IT solutions. He has been a member of the The Medici Archive Project team since 2003, creating the entire MAP information technology infrastructure. He has been the project manager for MAP's digital platform BIA (http://bia.medici.org). He is also in charge of the Mediceo del Principato Digitization Project. His interests include Digital Humanities, Digital History, Data Curation, and developing opensource software using the latest web technologies.

Leanne Blaney

is currently based in Glasgow, where her research focuses on the historical interrelationship between the media, migrants and modernity. Her particular interests relate to the impact and influence of technology and transport on wider British and Irish society. Alongside her monograph *The Motorcar in Ireland: 1896–1939* (Liffey Press, 2019) she is the author and co-author of *Easter Rising 1916* (Willow Press, 2016) and *UCD Collegians* (UCD Press, 2017).

Davide Boerio

obtained a dual Ph.D. in early modern history from the University of Teramo and University College Cork with a thesis titled 'News, Network and Discourses during the Neapolitan revolution of 1647–48 and its Aftermath'. His research focuses on the production, circulation, reception and control of political information in the early modern period. He has participated in several conferences on this subject in England, Ireland, Italy, Germany, Spain, and his research has appeared in leading international publications. In 2013, he was a Samuel Freeman Charitable Trust Fellow at the Medici Archive Project. Since 2014 he has been a research fellow at the MAP, working on the Birth of News program, and also instructor for the palaeography course. He has held several post-doctoral research fellowships related to history of communication for both Italian and European research agencies. In 2018 he was Instructor of Early

Modern History at Temple University Campus in Rome. In January 2019 he joined the EUORNEWS project on the history of early modern news, sponsored by the Irish Research Council, where he is a post-doctoral research fellowship and research coordinator.

Daniel Carey

is the research project officer for community engagement on the CUPHAT (Coastal Uplands Heritage and Tourism) project and is based in the School of Geography at University College Dublin. A graduate of National University of Ireland, Galway, he completed his BA (International) in History, Sociology and Political Science in 2003, and his MA in Journalism in 2004. He worked full-time in journalism for thirteen years, most of them as a reporter with The Mayo News in Westport. His PhD, undertaken at the School of Communications in Dublin City University, took the form of an oral history project on the working lives of former journalists and editors in Ireland, in which he conducted in-depth, face-to-face interviews with thirty participants.

Jane L. Chapman

is Professor of Communication at Lincoln University, and a former Research Associate at Wolfson College Cambridge. Author of thirteen books, plus over thirty articles/book chapters, she is an editorial board member for the journal *Media History*. Previous awards include the Colby Prize for Victorian Literature (shared), and Emerald Publishing best academic article of the year. Jane specialises in content produced by neglected and disenfranchised voices in the comparative history of newspapers and cartoons. She has researched and published extensively on the theme of newspaper communications by women and ethnic minorities in the nineteenth and twentieth centuries. Her collaborative research on Comics and the World Wars was funded by the UK's Arts and Humanities Research Council, who also funded her four grants for the Centenary of World War One. Her monograph (Palgrave 2024) analyses secrecy, deception, and the growth of journalistic participation transnationally during the Second World War.

Ondřej Daniel

earned his PhD from Charles University's Faculty of Arts, with a dissertation published as *Bigbít nebo turbofolk: představy migrant z bývalé Jugoslávie* (Rock or Turbofolk: The Imagination of Migrants from the Former Yugoslavia, 2013). He is a co-founder of the Prague-based Centre for the Study of Popular Culture (cspk.eu) and works as an historian in the Seminar on General and Comparative History within the Department of World History at Charles

University's Faculty of Arts. Since 2016, he has published a series of works that have synthesised his research on the role of subcultures and violence in the development of post-socialist mainstream Czech culture and DIY subcultural practices. His current work covers different aspects of reception of popular and alternative music. His recent book *Ušima střední třídy: mládež, hudba a třída v českém postsocialismu* (Through the Ears of the Middle Class: Music, Youth and Class in the Czech Postsocialism, 2023) examines intersections of different social categories and music in contemporary Czech history.

Eamon Darcy

is editor of *Archivium Hibernicum* and an historian of early modern Britain and Ireland based at Maynooth University. Author of *The Irish Rebellion of 1641 and the Wars of the Three Kingdoms* (Boydell and Brewer, Woodbridge, 2013), he has published extensively on print culture and popular politics. He is also co-investigator of Ancient Woodlands Ireland, a €1.2 million project funded by the Irish Department of Agriculture, Food and Marine, which aims to identify and map ancient Irish woodlands.

Brendan Dooley

(PhD University of Chicago 1986), is currently Professor of Renaissance studies at University College Cork, having previously taught at Harvard, Notre Dame and Jacobs University Bremen. He works on the histories of culture and knowledge with reference to Europe and especially to Italy and the Mediterranean world. Publications include *Angelica's Book and the World of Reading in Late Renaissance Italy* (Bloomsbury, 2016) and *A Mattress Maker's Daughter, the Renaissance Romance of Don Giovanni de' Medici and Livia Vernazza* (Harvard, 2014), and, as editor (with Paola Molino), *Years of News: What the Early Moderns Knew About their World* (Brepols, in press).

Panagiotis Georgakakis

holds a doctorate degree in Early Modern European History from the University of St Andrews. In his thesis, he explored the development and the dissemination of the Huguenot newspapers in the Dutch Republic, 1670–1701. He is a graduate of the Department of History and Archaeology of the National and Kapodistrian University of Athens, where he also earned his master's degree in European History. He has published two journal articles to date on early-modern news, and has participated in numerous conferences. He was one of the three delegates elected by the University of Athens to participate in the UNHCR European conference 'Refugees, Migrants, undesirables' held in Perpignan in 2016.

Joel Herman

is a PhD Candidate in the School of Histories and Humanities at Trinity College Dublin. His thesis, 'Revolutionary Currents: The Imperial Public Sphere and the Destabilization of Empire, c.1760–1784', investigates the emergence of certain features of an imperial public sphere in the period of the imperial crisis, and describes how these features contributed to the destabilization of the British empire and revolutionary reactions in the American colonies and Ireland. He has previously published on the subject of patriotism in Ireland and early America and has other work forthcoming on the news, and newspapers, which flowed between Ireland, the American colonies, and Britain in the late eighteenth-century. He has been awarded visiting fellowships to carry out his research including most recently being named a 2022–2023 David Center for the American Revolution International Fellow at the American Philosophical Society.

Bláithín Hurley

has a PhD in the History of Art from the University of Cambridge (2016), an MA in the History of Art from the University of Warwick (2009) and a BA in the History of Art and Music from University College Cork (2008). She is currently studying for an MA in Library Information Services at the University of Aberystwyth. Bláithín is a Staff Officer and Local Studies Librarian at Waterford Library Services, Waterford, Ireland. She is also an Associate Lecturer with the Open University's Faculty of Arts and Social Sciences. Bláithín has previously published articles on the art and music of the Italian Renaissance and on Public Libraries in Ireland. At present her research centres around the art and architecture of the Church of Ireland Cathedrals in Waterford City and Lismore, Co. Waterford, Ireland.

Johana Kłusek

is a PhD candidate in Modern History at the Department of European Studies at Charles University in Prague. Her dissertation follows her previous research in the field of history of mentalities, for which she was awarded the Edvard Beneš Prize for Best Thesis in Modern History in 2017. The doctoral thesis deals with the Image of Britain in Czechoslovak Media Discourses between 1939 and 1948. In 2019 she participated in the Humboldt University's project 'London Moment' as a SYLFF fellow. In 2020 she was awarded a SYLFF Research Abroad Award for research in London. She studied Political Science at Le Moyne College in Syracuse, New York, and conducted an internship at the University of Oxford. Currently she is a Visiting Scholar at Jagiellonian University in Kraków, where she teaches the history of Europe from below.

Wouter Kreuze

completed his PhD at University College Cork while working for the EURONEWS project. His research involves the development of new digital methodologies for the study of manuscript newsletters, including building *avvisi* databases which draw from several European collections and then deploying tools to interrogate this information to uncover patterns in early modern news. Before starting his doctorate, he received BA degrees in History and Italian as well as an MA in History from the University of Leiden.

Lena Liapi

is an Honorary Research Fellow at Keele University, UK. Her research revolves around cultures of communication, crime and urban history. Her monograph *Roguery in Print: Crime and Culture in Early Modern London* examined a wide range of cheap print in order to analyse the multivalence of the figure of the rogue. She is currently working on a new project, 'Famous: News, Reputation and Public Opinion (1600–1720)'. This explores the ways in which fame was produced and circulated through words, texts, and images, and the ability of individuals to manage their reputation.

Jakub Machek

is a social historian. He lectures in the Media Studies Department, Metropolitan University Prague. He is the author of the monograph *Počátky populární kultury v českých zemích, The Emergence of Popular Culture in the Czech Lands* (2017) and has co-edited several collections of essays. His research covers the development of Czech popular culture, media, and society in the twentieth and twenty-first centuries. His latest research is focused on the function of music in Czech society, from brass band music to disco. He is a founding member of the Centre for the Study of Popular Culture in Prague.

Sara Mansutti

holds a master's degree in Italian Philology and Literature from the University of Udine and is currently a Ph.D. candidate in Digital Humanities at University College Cork. Her doctoral research started within the EURONEWS project, funded by the Irish Research Council and led by Professor Brendan Dooley, and focuses on the correspondence between Cosimo Bartoli, a Florentine agent in Venice, and the Medici family during the years 1562 to 1572. Specifically, she explores Bartoli's methods of acquiring information in Venice, reconstructs his network and examines how the information in his letters relates to the information in the handwritten newsletters. With a keen interest in Digital Humanities, her research interests extend to automatic text recognition, participatory editing, and digital editions, to explore new workflows to broaden accessibility to historical primary sources.

Liam Mac Mathúna
is Professor Emeritus of Irish at University College Dublin. He has published widely in Ireland and abroad on the lexicon, literature, and culture of Irish. He is editor of Éigse: A Journal of Irish Studies, published by the National University of Ireland. His recent publications include *Douglas Hyde: My American Journey* (co-edited, 2019), *The Ó Neachtain Window on Gaelic Dublin, 1700–1750* (2021) *and Douglas Hyde: Irish Ideology and International Impact* (co-edited with Máire Nic an Bhaird, 2023). He is collaborating with Dr Nic an Bhaird on research into the life and work of Douglas Hyde, with the first volume due in 2024.

Aodhán (formerly Maria-Valeria) Morris
was born in Chelyabinsk, Russia. After finishing his Cand.Sci. in Legal History in HSE (Moscow), he turned to Folklore Studies and wrote a master's thesis on early modern portrayals of Tuatha Dé Danann in the writings of Keating and Ó Cléirigh. Developing an interest in social anthropology, he then ventured into Troubles Studies, almost reaching the point of defending a further Cand.Sci. thesis on contemporary Irish rebel urban folklore. However, coming from a Ukrainian Jewish family and being pro-Ukraine and openly queer, he was forced to flee to Israel for fear of political repercussions after Russia invaded Ukraine. From there, he was awarded the 2023 Hardiman Scholarship at the University of Galway where he will now continue his research.

Luca Marangolo
is an Adjunct professor of Comparative Literature and History of literary criticism at the University of Naples, "Federico II". He received his doctorate in Comparative Literature at the university of Rome "Roma Tre" in 2016. He has lectured in a number of universities in Italy and Europe, and has served as a consultant on the project "Tales of Two cities" at the University of Naples. He is currently writing a book on tragedy in the Ancien Régime (1582–1744). He has written extensively on the relationship between literature and other media.

Máire Nic an Bhaird
is a lecturer in Irish Language and Literature and History of Education in Maynooth University, Ireland. Her main area of research is the life and work of Douglas Hyde, Ireland's first President. She is currently writing a book about the life and work of Douglas Hyde with An tOllamh Liam Mac Mathúna.

She has several publications relating to her research and has also presented her research interests on national and international television and radio programmes.

Pasquale Palmieri

is an associate professor of Early Modern History at the University of Naples Federico II. He holds a Ph.D. in the History of European Society (Naples, 2008) and Italian Studies (University of Texas at Austin, 2021). His research interests include early modern media and literary culture, with a particular emphasis on the relationship between politics and religion. He also works on the eighteenth-century Italian novel, print culture and book history. He directs the interdisciplinary project 'Tales of Four Cities. News/Legends between Print and Archive (Naples, Rome, Florence, Venice, 1571–1789)', and is now co-director of the NEH International Collaboration Grant 'Rethinking Eighteenth-Century Italian Culture and Its Transnational Connections". His recent publications include: *L'eroe criminale. Giustizia, politica e comunicazione nel XVIII secolo* (Bologna: Il Mulino, 2022) and *Le cento vite di Cagliostro* (Bologna: Il Mulino, 2023).

Carlotta Paltrinieri

received her doctoral degree in Italian Studies at Indiana University Bloomington in August 2018, with a specialization in early modern literature and art history. Her doctoral dissertation examined the changing status of visual arts between the fifteenth and sixteenth centuries, through the linguistic and stylistic analysis of the contemporary artistic literature. She has worked on the social and intellectual exchanges within the Accademia del Disegno of Florence, joining the research group *Tuscan Academies of the 17th century*, coordinated by the *Centro Internazionale di Studi sul Seicento* at the Università di Siena. Her recent publications include: 'Cosimo I, l'Accademia del Disegno, e 'il beneficio pubblico' (Pontecorboli, 2019); 'Alla riscoperta della sociabilité dell'Accademia del Disegno di Firenze: i Luogotenenti', (2020); and 'The celebrations of the canonization of Saint Andrea Corsini in San Giovanni dei Fiorentini: a Florentine saint in Rome' (forthcoming). As a post-doctoral researcher within the EURONEWS Project, Carlotta worked on the development of the language of the avvisi as a lingua franca.

Thom Pritchard

is a PhD researcher at The University of Edinburgh. His PhD project entitled 'The Bellicose Days: News, Memory and the Culture of the Stuart Intervention into the Thirty Years War 1624–1630', is a cultural history based upon the movement of people, soldiers, refugees and diplomats and information, news and ideas, between the Stuart kingdoms and a war-torn Continent. At Edinburgh, Thom founded the interdisciplinary and award-winning Edinburgh Early Modern Network which has organised many events for an international audience such as the four-day Enemies in the Early Modern World conference in March 2021. Thom was a visiting researcher at the University of Leiden and at the European University Institute in Florence and prior to the PhD completed a MA at the Centre for Renaissance and Early Modern Studies at the University of York. Thom has also been published by the *Journal for the Northern Renaissance* on the Valtellina Crisis.

Alessandro Tuccillo
is an Associate Professor in Early Modern History at the Department of Cultures, Politics and Society of the University of Turin. He has worked primarily on the intellectual and political history of the eighteenth and nineteenth centuries, especially on the debates about colonial slavery. As member of the DisComPoSE project (Disasters, Communication and Politics in Southwestern Europe: The Making of Emergency Response Policies in the Early Modern Age, ERC StG 2017, University of Naples Federico II), he deals with the ecclesiastical information networks and devotional practices in case of disasters caused by natural events (Hispanic Monarchy in the seventeenth and eighteenth centuries). He is the author of two monographs, *Il commercio infame. Antischiavismo e diritti dell'uomo nel Settecento italiano* (Naples 2013) and *Umanità contesa. L'apologetica di Giambatista Roberti contro il «filosofismo»* (Roma 2020), has edited two unpublished diplomatic briefs by patriot Matteo Galdi (1765–1821) (Naples 2008), and has published several essays in collective volumes and in international journals.

Milena Viceconte
obtained a PhD in History of Art in 2013, a joint degree between the University of Naples Federico II and the University de Barcelona. She took part in several research groups within the University of Barcelona, focused on artistic circulation between Italy and Spain in the early modern period. From 2018 she has been a postdoctoral fellow at the University of Naples Federico II in the framework of the ERC research project *DisComPoSE* (Disasters, Communication and Politics in Southwestern Europe), within which she deals with issues related to the imageries of disasters in the territories of the Spanish Monarchy through the analysis of figurative sources (16th–18th centuries). Among her recent publications, she edited together with Gennaro Schiano and Domenico Cecere the volume *Heroes in Dark Times. Saints and Officials Tackling Disaster* (Viella, 2023).

Brian Wallace

is a Leverhulme Early Career Fellow at the John Rylands Research Institute and Library, University of Manchester, working on technology and magic in nineteenth-century imperial encounters. His general research focus is the cultural history of imperialism and its legacies, and his previous project explored the impact of Victorian colonial sieges on British culture and national identity. His work has been published in the *Historical Journal*, *History Workshop Journal*, and *History Today*.

Alexander S. Wilkinson

is a Professor of Early Modern History at University College Dublin. Sandy was educated at the University of St Andrews and was employed there thereafter as a Postdoctoral Research Fellow from 2001–2006, serving as Project Manager of the St Andrews French Book Project. He is a Fellow of the Royal Historical Society, and the author of several studies of the early modern European book world, including: *Mary Queen of Scots in French Public Opinion* (Palgrave, 2004), *French Vernacular Books*, co-edited with Andrew Pettegree and Malcolm Walsby (Brill, 2007), *Iberian Books*, edited with Alejandra Ulla Lorenzo and Alba de la Cruz (Brill, 2010, and 2018), as well as articles in journals such as *French History*, *The Library*, *Quaerendo* and *Renaissance Studies*. He is currently working on a project deploying AI and image recognition to explore the ornamentation and illustration used in the book world of fifteenth and sixteenth century Europe.

Chris Williams

has been Head of the College of Arts, Celtic Studies and Social Sciences and a professor in the School of History at University College Cork since 2017. Educated at Balliol College, Oxford, and the University of Wales, his previous positions include Professor of Welsh History at Swansea University and Head of the School of History, Archaeology and Religion at Cardiff University. He edited the *Richard Burton Diaries* (Yale University Press, 2012). His work on political cartoons has been published in *War in History*, *Media History* and the *Journal of Religious History*, and in edited volumes including Brake et al., *The News of the World: Journalism for the Rich, Journalism for the Poor* (2016). He maintains three websites that hold digitised versions of over 5000 cartoons by the Welsh cartoonist J. M. Staniforth: Cartooning the First World War (cartoonww1.org), Cartooning the Road to War (roadtowarcartoons.org), and Cartooning the Post-War World (postwarworldcartoons.org).

Introduction

International tragedies! National disgraces! Local dangers! The news never ends, and reporting seems to magnify the trauma. How may we gain a deeper analytical understanding of episodes often too immediate for detached observation by our sources or even, perhaps, by ourselves? And more to the point, how may we measure short term and long-term impacts of what itself at times may appear unfathomable? Speakers from across the disciplines and from near and far posed these questions and more at the 2021 Irish Humanities Alliance annual conference, bringing together a broad range of current research in Europe and abroad. The resulting papers, integrated with others specially solicited, are gathered here with a view to shedding light on issues of crucial importance for understanding past cultures and our own. There are discussions about the ramifications of media-induced anxiety and anxiety-inflected media, engaging the humanities, including history, film studies, literature, folklore, creative writing and adjacent fields intersected by sociology, politology, psychology, anthropology. News media here include all means of mass communication impinging on daily experience, from books to music, from the social web to films, on multiple platforms and in multiple languages across municipal, state, and regional boundaries.

But what is news? We might be tempted to say, the concept has a long enough pedigree to make it self-explanatory. Consider for instance the 2021 Princeton *Historical Companion* to *Information*, where most of the entries concerning news, understandably enough, simply plunge into the means, modes and messages.[1] And yet, a look at historical usages of the various terms across time in the various relevant languages—Italian, French, English, Spanish, German, Dutch, Polish—brings us up against the inevitable social science dilemma between actors' categories and historians' categories—especially because we will often be letting our sources speak for themselves before launching into our detailed explanations. Take for example the discussions by Mario Infelise and others in the 2016 volume edited by Joad Raymond and Noel Moxham.[2] In the earliest stages of media development, we are told, 'avvisi' and 'news' are close

---

1 Ann Blair, Paul Duguid, Anja-Silvia Goeing, and Anthony Grafton (eds.), *Information: A Historical Companion* (Princeton: Princeton University Press, 2021). The entry on 'newsletters' by Joad Raymond on p. 628 comes the closest to a definition.
2 Paul Arblaster, André Belo, Carmen Espejo, Stéphane Haffemayer, Mario Infelise, Noah Moxham, Joad Raymond and Nikolaus Schobesberger, 'The Lexicons of Early Modern News', in Joad Raymond and Noah Moxham (eds.), *News Networks in Early Modern Europe* (Leiden: Brill, 2016), pp. 64–101.

friends but not twins. The Italian word does not automatically connote newness, which it may possess in certain circumstances, in regard to the information or 'informazione' of which it speaks. The English word on the other hand does not automatically involve the general idea of information at all, except as related to what the earliest dictionaries called 'affairs', or 'things that have been done or that have happened'.

In leaving the definition ultimately up to our authors, we suggest that the varieties of news experience gain clarity and accessibility by the application of interdisciplinary cross-cultural and cross-chronological perspectives. News media studies experts encourage us in this view. Michael Schudson, introducing *The News Media: What Everyone Needs to Know*, refers back to the early modern origins of the news business as a prelude to analysing the development of a profession at least nominally dedicated to reporting what happens, and a plurality of worldwide structures for diffusion.[3] Frédéric Barbier and Catherine Bertho Lavenir apply an array of social science methods to understanding the long transition from the advent of print to the arrival of the Internet, as do Peter Burke and Asa Briggs, and likewise Rudolf Stöber.[4] Other studies focus on explaining this temporal dynamic, or a portion of it, in particular regions.[5] Much work has already been done, as Andrew Pettegree's elegant summary in *The Invention of News* suggests, and the papers in our volume draw upon a long line of relevant prior research by our contributors and many others, including a particularly rich vein of studies in the last ten years.[6] What is not covered in

---

[3] Michael Schudson, *The News Media: What Everyone Needs to Know* (Oxford: Oxford University Press, 2016).

[4] Peter Burke and Asa Briggs, *A Social History of the Media* (3rd edition, Cambridge: Polity Press, 2009); Frédéric Barbier and Catherine Bertho-Lavenir, *Histoire des médias de Diderot à Internet* (Paris: Armand Colin, 1996); and Rudolf Stöber, *Mediengeschichte. Die Evolution "neuer" Medien von Gutenberg bis Gates. Eine Einführung* (Wiesbaden: Westdeutscher Verlag 2003).

[5] Bruce J. Schulman and Julian E. Zelizer (eds.), *Media Nation: The Political History of News in Modern America* (Philadelphia: University of Pennsylvania Press, 2017); Johannes Arndt and Esther-Beate Körber (eds.), *Das Mediensystem im Alten Reich der Frühen Neuzeit (1600–1750)* (Gottingen: Vandenhoeck & Ruprecht, 2010), Jürgen Wilke, *Grundzüge der Medien- und Kommunikationsgeschichte. Von den Anfängen bis ins 20. Jahrhundert* (Vienna: Böhlau, 2000), and Guillaume Pinson, *Culture médiatique francophone en Europe et en Amérique du Nord* (Montreal: Les Presses de l'Université Laval, 2016).

[6] Apart from Andrew Pettegree, *The Invention of News: How the World Came to Know About Itself* (New Haven: Yale University Press, 2014), and Roger Chartier and Carmen Espejo Cala (eds.), *La aparición del periodismo en Europa: comunicación y propaganda en el Barroco* (Madrid: Marcial Pons Historia, 2012), consider the following volumes: Jan Hillgärtner, *News in Times of Conflict: The Development of the German Newspaper, 1605–1650* (Leiden: Brill, 2021); Rosanne M. Baars, *Rumours of Revolt: Civil War and the Emergence of a Transnational News*

the general treatments has been voluminously elaborated in the many studies devoted to particular periods or genres.[7] Rather than a unified perspective regarding event and narration in the past and present mediascape we offer a plurality of case studies as well as broad surveys shedding light on the production, circulation and impact of exciting news in multiple contexts.

A recurring theme throughout the volume is the social psychology of news, which has gained still more attention in recent months for reasons no doubt connected with new or lingering world crises in national politics, international relations and public health. Already in 2016, in the wake of the US general election, Martha Nussbaum made reference to a 'monarchy of fear', stoked by populists and social media.[8] But the theme dates at least to the 1980s when the 'risk society' theorized by Ulrich Beck took root, referring to the combined effects of scientific and industrial development in the absence of constraints imposed by traditional structures, leading to a reliance on the media to tell about risks and how to handle them.[9] In 2000, Zygmunt Baumann introduced the concept of 'liquid modernity', to convey the interruption, incoherence, and surprise that had become ordinary conditions of life.[10] More recently, in 2005, Hartmut Rosa has added the element of 'acceleration' in work and life as a characteristic of late modernity.[11] Exciting news spreads within exhausted populations already expecting the worst.

Meanwhile historians have been tracing a climate of fear in the West back to the middle ages, although Jean Delumeau's striking interpretation in a trilogy begun in 1979 dealt mainly with superstition and religious dread.[12] These elements are replaced in the seventeenth century, according to Euan Cameron,

       Culture in France and the Netherlands, 1561–1598 (Leiden: Brill, 2021); as well as Simon Davies and Puck Fletcher (eds.), *News in Early Modern Europe. Currents and Connections* (Leiden: Brill, 2014); and Siv Gøril Brandtzæg, Paul Goring and Christine Watson (eds.), *Travelling Chronicles: News and Newspapers from the Early Modern Period to the Eighteenth Century* (Leiden: Brill, 2018).

7   For instance, Giovanni Ciappelli and Valentina Nider (eds.), *La invención de las noticias. Las relaciones de sucesos entre la literatura y la información (siglos XVI–XVIII)* (Trent: Università di Trento, 2017); Arthur der Weduwen and Andrew Pettegree (eds.), *News, Business and Public Information: Advertisements and Announcements in Dutch and Flemish Newspapers, 1620–1675* (Leiden: Brill, 2020).

8   Martha Nussbaum, *The Monarchy of Fear: A Philosopher Looks at Our Political Crisis* (New York: Simon & Schuster, 2018).

9   Ulrich Beck, *Risk Society: Towards a New Modernity* (1986), translated by Mark Ritter (London: Sage Publications, 1992).

10   Zygmunt Baumann, *Liquid Modernity* (Cambridge: Polity Press, 2000).

11   Hartmut Rosa, *Social Acceleration: A New Theory of Modernity* (2005), translated and introduced by Jonathan Trejo-Mathys (New York: Columbia University Press, 2013).

12   Jean Delumeau, *La peur en Occident, XIVe–XVIIIe siècles* (Paris: Fayard, 1978).

by fear of atheism, but we are still in the realm of religion and philosophical awareness.[13] The problem is recast in political terms in a 2004 contribution by Corey Robin, focusing on the usefulness of fear as a whip for the masses, reflecting on the tradition of political thought from Thomas Hobbes to now, when the convenient distinction between a civil society at home and a state of nature abroad seem equally called into question, all the more vehemently due to coverage in the news.[14]

Turning to the origins of regular news publications, any rapid rush through the sources reveals an impressive range of terrifying events, fearful spectacles, awful forebodings, recorded in regularly distributed writings. Sensationalism seemed to run rampant in every period. No wonder the critics, for instance Restoration writer Samuel Butler, sometimes blamed the news writers themselves for preferring the bad to the good.[15] And quite apart from the truth or falsehood of the accounts, the intrinsic negativity gave reason for concern. Already in 1572, Pope Pius V, tried to ban news outright, among other reasons due to the too-frequent effect of sowing "hate, hostility, insurrection, strife, and homicide".[16] News, in other words, according to this interpretation, was causing more news, not of the best kind.

Yet a historical perspective may serve also to soften the message of the prophets of doom. Even disasters have their usefulness, we have to say. So do revolts, regardless of the outcome. Not only because, as in the philosophical perspective of Martin Heidegger, human existence (Dasein) occurs within a context of care and concern (Sorge), which, extended to the social sphere, may include struggles of various sorts.[17] There are structural consequences too. A momentary rallying round the rebels in occasions of civil discord may induce a temporary sense of solidarity among a portion of the population, of which the memory, as in the case of the Neapolitan revolution, could have widespread consequences at home and abroad. In the past or the present, for good or for ill, the habit of checking in on what is going on in the world has created a global community of readers and viewers. The full consequences are yet to be made

---

13 Euan Cameron, *Enchanted Europe: Superstition, Reason, and Religion 1250–1750* (Oxford: Oxford University Press, 2010).
14 Corey Robin, *Fear: The History of a Political Idea* (Oxford: Oxford University Press, 2004).
15 The note regarding 'The Newsmonger' appears in Samuel Butler, *Characters and Passages from Note-Books*, edited by A. R. Waller (Cambridge: Cambridge University Press, 1908) p. 126.
16 Francisco Gaude (ed.), *Bullarium Romanum* (Turin: Franco et Dalmazzo, 1862), vol. 7, p. 969. Thanks to Sara Mansutti for the indication.
17 Martin Heidegger, *Being and Time*, translated by Joan Stambaugh (Albany: SUNY Press, 2010), chap. 6.

manifest. Vicarious experience joins real experience to form event awareness and encourages the involvement of individuals. The narration occurs as a necessary consequence of the situation of being human and living in the world.

To be sure, in the best circumstances information can be a force for positive change, not only by naming the micro and macro aggressors at home and abroad, flagging violations of human rights, pointing to the perpetrators of atrocities, and even celebrating the doers of good. Unquestionably, a better-informed society is better able to resist challenges and face uncertainties. We may hope that a kind of inverse Gresham's law could apply, where in the end, quality news chases out the inferior type. In the best of all possible worlds, the instruments of communication serve to gather public support for worthy causes. No wonder Michael Schudson suggests that the media make democratic government possible. A powerful role indeed, and one that challenges all the institutions involved—political, economic and educational. Too optimistic? Too dismissive of the antagonistic forces at work, of class, of discourse, of mentalities? We will allow the assessment to stand, as we delve into the thick of news, analysed by our authors, and we defer to our readers to draw their own conclusions.

Our volume begins in the early modern period, where we are impressed by the thick texture of multimediality in evidence here. Rather than a society given over to orality, handwriting, or print we find a deep context of all three, each mode assuming particular roles among given audiences. Also importantly, we find stories where all Europe was involved, one way or another, in a vast multilingual performance of narration. Chapter One, researched by the EURONEWS Project team, gives an account of the momentous year 1600, as conveyed in the earliest forms of regular news transmission, through a vast network of handwritten news distribution, linking Europe to areas beyond. Next, Thomas Pritchard studies news about the 1625 Anglo-Dutch raid on Cadiz, rife with fantastic rumors partly due to serious blockages to information flow that encouraged speculation.

In the subsection on organized violence, Eamon Darcy shows how particular interpretations of events during the Irish rebellion of 1641 shaped perceptions in England. The focus is on an extraordinary record left by the London artisan Nehemiah Wallington regarding his reading of the relevant news, giving evidence of sentiments of compassion regarding the supposed targets of Catholic violence, mixed with anger and hopes for divine retribution in regard to the supposed perpetrators. Other narratives of victimhood as justifications for violence will be a common theme in these pages. In the case of the Neapolitan revolution of 1647, studied here by Davide Boerio and Luca Marangolo, we have an event with worldwide repercussions and widespread coverage that fed into the lasting literary and cultural legacy, with inevitable variations in the narrative along the way. Panagiotis Georgakakis studies the circulation of news about the Franco-Dutch war of 1672–78 by way of the Dutch French language press, conjecturing about readership and impact. The war reports, framed from an exclusively Dutch point of view, reached an international audience.

A set of chapters on disaster begins with Alessandro Tuccillo's account of reporting about the 1688 earthquake in Naples, based on some of the closest sources to the events, namely, diplomatic correspondence. Discussing the same 1688 event, Milena Viceconte focuses on a widely reported miracle of St Filippo Neri in Benevento, where the archbishop was saved from the rubble of his palace by intervention of the Saint, an event perhaps more widely discussed than the earthquake itself, at least in Southern Italy and Iberia. While paying the closest attention to reporting about late seventeenth century earthquakes, Lena Liapi discusses factuality and truth claims, as well as appeals to the emotions. The overall effect of such reporting could have been the formation of a virtual global community of suffering.

As we move into the eighteenth century we delve more deeply into the literary side of things, showing how interest and emotion could be engaged by astute manipulation of the materials at hand. Brendan Twomey's account of Jonathan Swift's polemical engagement with current events shows the use of satire, ridicule and creative exaggeration on both sides of the Anglo-Irish divide. Liam Mac Mathúna studies a remarkable and unique testimony regarding the impact of news in early eighteenth-century Dublin, namely, the commonplace books of Tadhg Ó Neachtain written in Irish. Bláithín Hurley takes us across the turn of the eighteenth century with an account of the diary of James Ryan in Carrick-on-Suir, on the Waterford-Tipperary border, describing current events as reported in the available sources and showing how rich was the store of information that seeped into the relatively remote location. Joel Herman looks at Irish, American, and British newspapers from 1765–1780, to grasp the global media environment of the British Empire in a period of intense conflict, observed and experienced by a global public.

Next, the section on media and the masses takes us deep into the modern and contemporary predicament, with reflections on events as fresh as now. We begin with the politics of news as examined by Brian Wallace, based on reporting about uprisings against the British Empire at Lucknow (1857), Khartoum (1884–5), and Mafeking (1899–1900). The battles there, and the way they were portrayed in terms of heroic defenders against Indian attackers, transmitted by numerous media consumed by the British masses, are viewed as part of the development of a national community beyond party interests, harbouring particular beliefs regarding whiteness and the world. Johana Kłusek studies the Czech media in 1938 in the lead-up to the Munich Agreement, pointing out how a failure to convey persuasively the realities of German threats and aggression, and Europe's unwillingness to take these seriously, contributed, unintentionally, to an anxiety-ridden and misinformed public. Jakub Machek brings in evidence of media activity in socialist Czechoslovakia in the 1970s and 1980s, showing a deliberate tendency to avoid disturbing news while conveying a sense of social peace and stability at home, amid chaos abroad, until the final years of perestroika in the 1980s, when problems were more freely discussed, with fingers being pointed at local perpetrators. Aodhán Morris looks at the interaction between media portrayals of violent Irish republicanism and performances of contemporary Irish rebel music, exploring the ways in which particular contexts including the traditional music revival may impinge on the musical message, whereas the music scene including performers may seek greater incisiveness to add to the republican message.

In the final group of papers devoted to trouble in the headlines, Máire Nic an Bhaird examines a particular case of media impact, namely Douglas Hyde's 1905–1906 fund-raising tour of America for the Gaelic League, as evidenced in an extraordinary document: the scrapbook compiled by a colleague of Hyde using material from this tour, evidencing the movement from place to place, the media attention, the significance in Ireland. Hyde himself hones his own public speaking skills, on the way to a significant career in Irish public affairs. Chris Williams shows how visual journalism was used to move public opinion in the context of the German air campaign against Britain, 1915–1918. While engaging audience emotions and expressing public outrage, he argues, cartoons performed and reflected civilian stoicism and resilience. Leanne Blaney looks at reporting of road accidents, and the impact this had on public perceptions at the beginning of widespread automobile traffic in Ireland. As different actors, including media outlets, car companies and the Catholic Church chimed in, public opinion could be swayed this way and that. Andrea di Carlo considers T. S. Eliot's engagement with current events, including journalism per se, as well as the reflections by Hermann Hesse upon that period which followed the First World War, especially in terms of analysing the site of a disaster (Europe), showing how Hess's idea of the downfall of Europe and the decay into chaos influenced poetical reflections by Eliot in 'The Waste Land'. Daniel Carey studies the creation and diffusion of attention-grabbing headlines in tabloids and other mass media, by looking at the production aspects from within the industry, drawing on numerous interviews, and taking into account the occasionally unexpected reactions of readers and regulators.

In widening the gaze to encompass the whole field and its significance for individuals and societies, Jane Chapman reflects on the promise shown by news media from time to time in giving voice to neglected and/or disempowered groups, in terms of class, race and gender. Although the focus is on the early twentieth century, the conclusions apply to current media as well, whereas events, framed in certain ways, can be exciting and inspiring, as well as adding to the collective unconscious that moves to effect change. Likewise applicable to different circumstances are such theoretical reference points, mentioned here, as Jacques Derrida, for the theory of traces, Robert Darnton for the notion of collective consciousness, and William H Sewell for the logic of history.

Numerous indeed are the general insights among our contributors, regarding the ultimate impact and functioning of the media within societies. The formation of a public sphere is often implied rather than explicitly stated (except by Herman, referring to Habermas), perhaps in view of the practical mainstreaming of these ideas, stripped of the chronological and conceptual aporia. Pressures placed on public reasoning may include the use of propaganda for manufacturing consent. Machek, Morris, and Nic an Bhaird speak of the phenomenon in the modern context; Darcy, Tucillo and Georgakakis use the term for earlier examples. An intuitive understanding here overrides the need to refer back to well-known theoretical reference points such as Noam Chomsky or Harold Lasswell.[18]

Methodological approaches obviously vary according to the questions posed, the disciplines engaged and the sources being examined. For instance, an account of the year 1600 based on numerous handwritten newsletters utilises corpus analysis to discover the news horizon of readers in a given time and place. A corpus of another kind, composed of a wide range of political cartoons, forms the basis of Williams' study of Victorian Age visual journalism. Survey approaches occur where subjects are still living and the material is fresh, as in the account of media portrayals of radical republicanism in Ireland (Morris); likewise oral history interviews are the instrument of choice for the latter part of Carey's study of headlines.

Adding extra depth to the broader chronological lines sketched out from chapter to chapter, case studies abound, often based on the rediscovery of a special source. Based on the Carrickman's diary, preserved at the Central Library in Waterford, and concerning events in eighteenth to nineteenth-century

---

18   Harold Lasswell, *Propaganda Technique in World War I* (Cambridge, Mass.: M.I.T. Press, 1971), and Noam Chomsky and Edward S. Herman, *Manufacturing Consent: the Political Economy of the Mass Media* (New York: Pantheon Books, 1988). In general, including bibliography, see Brendan Dooley, 'Media History. Cultural Considerations', *International Encyclopedia of the Social and Behavioral Sciences* (2nd edition, Amsterdam: Elsevier, 2015), vol. 15, pp. 11–18.

Carrick-on-Suir, County Tipperary, Hurley shows for instance the juxtaposition of Marie Antoinette's beheading in Paris and, on the same page, the local murder by Bryan Murphy of his wife, thus illustrating the effect of distance on perspectives forming everyday experience. Revealed in a unique scrapbook consulted by Nic an Bhaird in the Hardiman library at the University of Galway, is the moment in 1906, when Douglas Hyde, president of the Gaelic League (and later President of Ireland), during a fundraising tour of North America widely covered in journalistic prose and image, stops in Toronto and holds his audience in Massey Hall spellbound with songs and tales of great appeal not only to the mostly Irish audience but also to sympathizers, managing to collect a good sum of money during the occasion.

How is news related to other forms of discourse? Marangolo and Boerio show examples of news genres becoming the basis for literary imagination, whereas Twomey shows general literary engagement with the news. Science and nature come into the picture in Tucillo and Liapi, in regard to the transition from a providential to a humanistic framework, with disasters occurring not because of divine planning (at least from the standpoint of what can be verified by observation and experiment) but due to the workings of natural laws of causation. On the other hand, Carey reminds us that appeals to the divine have still been very much at work in modern times.

Although we have already covered a good deal of ground we are aware of the challenges ahead, for our disciplines and our specific projects. How to deal with what is not there? Absent evidence, due to intractable media transmission issues, implies presences of another kind, Pritchard suggests, pointing to the space left open to conjecture and imagination. But the question could extend to the endeavours of media history in general. Abundantly noted among our authors and also among often-cited works on our topic, is that the libraries and archives upon which we rely will inevitably fail to yield a vast amount of what is no longer available for us to analyse, because it simply does not exist except in principle, however important such material may be.[19] Nonetheless, we close here with the assurance that we have attempted to base our conjectures and hypotheses on the best knowledge we have, reserving the right to correct ourselves if necessary should the library of the missing some day once more become available for us to view.

But at this point let us close this very schematic discussion of the road ahead, and begin the journey through four hundred years of exciting news!

---

19 Andrew Pettegree and Arthur der Weduwen, *The Library: A Fragile History* (New York: Basic Books, 2021).

PART 1

Early Modern Origins

∴

SECTION 1

The Force of News

CHAPTER 1

1600: A Year to Remember

Sara Mansutti, Wouter Kreuze, Carlotta Paltrinieri, Lorenzo Allori, Davide Boerio and Brendan Dooley

A newsletter from Graz dated 17 January 1600 carried the following story:

> There is a report that Ibrahim Bassa, after having strangled the chief of the Tatars, as was already known, headed from Belgrade to Constantinople, where exactly at that time there arrived another Tatar from the same family, claiming to be the successor of the deceased.[1]

The murder of the Tatar chief was only one of many violent episodes reported in this and other handwritten newsletters available in Italy in the year 1600, along with court intrigue, major celebrations, religious devotions, and much else, offering readers plenty of material for reflection and even emotional involvement. No wonder the writings in the same genre elsewhere would form the basis of the first printed newspapers five years later.[2] Until now such writings have been more often cited than read, largely due to the difficulties of combing through a vast amount of manuscript material never before indexed or transcribed. In their time, they offered the only regularly issued news in a media context involving printed broadsheets, pamphlets and other occasional items. To understand how they circulated and what they said about contemporary times, and in what terms, we have chosen a sample drawn from the Medici papers at the State Archive in Florence. And after submitting these to an analysis involving five main themes and a number of sub-themes we have been able to show that, although somewhat one-sided, they offered a surprisingly

---

1   Florence, Archivio di Stato (hereafter ASFI) Mediceo del Principato (hereafter MdP), vol. 4578, fol. 3ʳ. The Medici Archive Project (hereafter MAP), DocId 50842. Responsibilities in this a co-written chapter were divided as follows: data curation, Lorenzo Allori; power and commerce, Brendan Dooley and Davide Boerio; diffusion, Sara Mansutti; regions, Wouter Kreuze; language and rhetoric, Carlotta Paltrinieri.
2   For a general orientation, Andrew Pettegree, *The Invention of News: How the World Came to Know About Itself* (New Haven: Yale University Press, 2014), pp. 107–116; Mario Infelise, *Prima dei giornali: Alle origini della pubblica informazione* (Bari: Laterza, 2002), chapters 1–3; Johannes Weber, 'Straßburg 1605. Die Geburt der Zeitung', in H. Böning, A. Kutsch, & R. Stöber (eds.), *Jahrbuch für Kommunikationsgeschichte*, vol. 7 (2005), pp. 3–26.

FIGURE 1.1 Newsletter dated 12 February 1600.
ASFI, Mediceo del Principato (MdP)
vol. 3087, fol. 1

comprehensive picture of a European world struggling for security in the midst of threats from inside and outside, replete with expressions indicating worry, fear, anxiety and occasionally elation that suggest provisional conclusions regarding impact in the first century of news.

The 96 newsletters we will be discussing here, pertaining to the year 1600 and now conserved in the Medici papers, bear the typical traits of the genre. Mostly anonymous, with place and date of compilation heading the first of one or more bifolios, followed by a dense concatenation of stories located and dated separately, their basic form followed a pattern basically unchanged across three centuries. Some examples are divided according to numerous places and dates of compilation indicating where and when the relevant stories were collected. Others, such as Figure 1.1 above, simply include the different places of news among the stories from the main location, in this case, Venice, where in the first line we read of news brought by 'letters from Vienna' reporting about the ill health of Giorgio Basta, the governor of Transylvania.

Nonetheless, there are some peculiar features in our newsletter corpus. We are particularly struck by the small number of examples from Rome and Venice.[3] Instead we find an abundance of newsletters from Flanders, testimony to the well-developed trade relations between Flanders and Florence, as well as to the dynastic connections between the House of Medici and leading elements of the House of Austria, with the consequent sharing of private and strategic interests, including a massive contingent of Florentine soldiers in the army of Flanders.[4]

---

3 For a useful contrast with a comparable volume, see Urbinati Latini Collection 1068, held in the Vatican Library, https://digi.vatlib.it/view/MSS_Urb.lat.1068 (accessed 18 December 2022).

4 For an overview of the political situation, Samuel Berner, 'Florentine Society in the Late Sixteenth and Early Seventeenth Centuries', *Studies in the Renaissance*, 18 (1971), pp. 203–246.

For the following account we have analysed our corpus of fully transcribed and annotated documents around the five major themes of: power, commerce, regions, diffusion, and rhetoric. There are transversal subthemes that cross all categories and require treatment in each, such as, for instance religion, disease, natural disaster, gender, family, and society. These themes and subthemes will serve to convey the substance of weekly news as evidenced in this source.

1 Power

We begin with the exercise of power, arguably the main material of news. Not surprisingly, the first ten items in a frequency table (see Table 1.1) of the most-used words in our corpus are mainly about this. Personages whose actions are worth recounting belong to courts or various sorts of governing bodies capable of turning actions into events and events into news.

Major stories on this theme generally involved war, diplomacy and negotiations, matters at court and in other official institutions, as well as internal issues of law and order. Ongoing problems included the Eighty Years' War between the United Netherlands and its allies on the one hand, with the Spanish Empire and its allies on the other. There was continuing conflict between France and the duchy of Savoy regarding control over the Marquisate of Saluzzo. Meanwhile, the Long Turkish War persisted between the Habsburg Monarchy and the Ottoman Empire. Diplomacy, such as there was, often concerned one or another of these three areas. Internal affairs included the punishment of crimes and the regulation of religious life. Reports on ceremonial events focused on the local, aimed at building respect and loyalty in regard to church and state authorities.

Some reports delved deeply into early modern warfare, including practices such as mutinies of soldiers, notoriously difficult to take from the field

TABLE 1.1 Word frequencies in 1600 corpus

Term	Frq	DocFrq	Term	Frq	DocFrq
signor (lord)	134	82	parte (part)	84	56
duca (duke)	112	81	lettere (letters)	84	64
maestà (majesty)	93	72	conte (count)	78	61
mila (thousand)	93	61	re (king)	73	52
altezza (highness)	89	60	pace (peace)	73	55

to the page.[5] In 1600 trouble developed in Flanders when soldiers protested pay arrears by damaging lands and rebelling against the pro-Spanish regime. According to the item in the news, no solution was likely until sufficient funds could be found to pay what was owed (all translations our own unless otherwise indicated):

> The mutineers from Tilimon and Dist … well armed took over a town called Mons Enao [i.e., Mons Hainaut], which threw the whole country into confusion … seeing themselves perplexed by the very people supposed to defend them against the others, and various conclusions are being drawn, whereas Their Highnesses are said to be very displeased, and are doing everything to remedy the situation, but the great sum necessary for payment impedes and will impede any good intentions for many weeks and months, since getting money together for daily needs is becoming every day more difficult.

The complexities of the situation appear in the last line, suggesting that the (enemy) United Provinces could get involved, but 'the estates do not want to take on such a burden'.[6]

A particularly important engagement in the ongoing Eighty Years' War was the battle of Nieuwpoort with Archduke Albert of Flanders on the Spanish side fighting against Maurice of Nassau leading the Dutch.[7] Here is the first account we get of the events of 2 July 1600:

> On the second of July His Highness left Bruges to go and follow the said Prince Maurice, who was said to have gone toward Ostend and Nieuwpoort, and to have turned … as though going toward Dunkirk, hoping to fight him with good hopes of putting him to flight, but this did not happen, because His Highness having caught up with the said Prince between Nieuwpoort Castle and Ostend; although at first he had the advantage, and practically destroyed the enemy's rearguard, nonetheless attempting to engage, ran into the battle which had stalled, and having thrust forward with his cavalry followed by many thousands of

---

5 Compare Miguel Martínez, 'Narrating Mutiny in the Army of Flanders: Cristóbal Rodríguez Alva's *La inquieta Flandes* (1594)', in Raymond Fagel, Leonor Alvarez Frances and Beatriz Santiago Belmonte (eds.), *Early Modern War Narratives and the Revolt in the Low Countries* (Manchester: Manchester University Press, 2020), pp. 89–106.
6 ASFI, MdP 4256, fol. 26ʳ, MAP DocId 50868.
7 For context we used among others Luc Duerloo, *Dynasty and Piety: Archduke Albert (1598–1621) and Habsburg Political Culture in an Age of Religious Wars* (New York: Routledge, 2012).

mutineers, the said cavalry reversed itself on the mutineers, and the mutineers reversed onto the rest of the infantry, so the whole army was put to flight and then was so hotly pursued by the said Prince Maurice that most were cut to pieces, and His Highness was forced to retreat to Bruges with three horses and then to Ghent, where he now is. The battle was very bloody due to the lengthy combat, and they say ten thousand men were killed on both sides. His Highness was slightly injured in two places on his face. The admiral of Aragon was killed; the Duke of Umala was injured, and all his retinue including the pages was killed; don Luigi di Velasco, the Count of Berleymont, and La Barlotta were saved. His Highness lost all his weapons and baggage, along with all his family.[8]

The piling of clause upon clause contributes to the breathless thrust of the narrative, seeming to emphasise the rapid developments being described, and possibly first communicated by an eyewitness to the build-up before the siege of Ostend, which would later prove to be one of the most discussed events in the war.[9] We are reminded that this genre of writing stands close to the oral transmission of information, not only because newsletters were often read to an audience, but also because the so-called 'wars in ottava rima' (*guerre in ottava rima*), rhymed accounts of particularly interesting battles, were a notorious popular tradition on Italian streets and squares in the preceding century and probably later.[10] In closing, the writer establishes a stake in the regular unfolding of the event, while setting up reader expectations: 'Other details are not known for certain, but we will be informed in two days, and I will report'. Whether he kept his word or not is still under study.

Only the benefit of hindsight would permit directing attention to the innovation, considered by Geoffrey Parker to have been the fourth 'revolution in military affairs' of early modern times, which saw the use of infantry volley fire, involving lines of soldiers shooting at once and then falling back to load while another line took their place, supposed to have first occurred at Nieuwpoort

---

8   ASFI, MdP, 4256, fol. 43^r. MAP DocId 50810.
9   Werner Thomas, 'How a Defeat became a Victory: the Siege of Ostend in Contemporary Dutch War Coverage and Post-war Chronicles (1601–15)', in Fagel et al. (eds.), *Early Modern War Narratives*, pp. 125–45.
10 Massimo Rospocher, 'La miscellanea del cardinale: la battaglia della Polesella tra stampa, manoscritto e oralità', in Giovanni Ciappelli and Valentina Nider (eds.), *La invención de las noticias: Las relaciones de sucesos entre la literatura y la información* (Trent: Università degli Studi di Trento, 2017), pp. 31–50, and bibliography. For oral reading of newsletters, see Brendan Dooley, 'Art and Information Brokerage in the Career of Don Giovanni de' Medici', in Hans Cools, Marika Keblusek and Badeloch Noldus (eds.), *Your Humble Servant: Agents in Early Modern Europe* (Hilversum: Uitgeverij Verloren, 2006), pp. 81–95.

in July 1600.¹¹ Perhaps this is what the writer is suggesting when he says that elements in the army fell back; but his understanding does not seem to include the particularities of the action, at least in regard to this development, later so highly touted. An account in Spanish transmitted through the same Medici court network, entitled 'Relación de lo sucedido en el Ejército hasta 3 de julio de 1600', offers no further insight.¹² Evidently, the revolution in question was not yet recognized, or perhaps some scholarship is close to the mark in suggesting that the military innovation in question was more in the general area of discipline than any specific practice.¹³

Religion appears in our documents in cases of the expansion of Christendom by the proposed creation of a church in Peru, as for example: 'Yesterday morning a very long Consistory was held in which, after the audiences, Cardinal Deza proposed a church in the Indies of Peru …'.¹⁴ That the same line of text went on to say, 'Cardinal d'Ossat proposed a monastery in France …' underlined the importance of internal and external proselytizing within Catholicism, a central theme in discussions among religious orders.¹⁵ Elsewhere we are alerted when beliefs or structures are under threat. The fallout from the French Religious Wars continued in spite of the Edict of Nantes and the Peace of Vervins in 1598, and relevant events, such as an anti-Huguenot riot in Lyons in April 1600, become news.¹⁶ Likewise, the battles against Ottoman expansion in south-eastern Europe occasionally adopted the character of a crusade, with the Holy Roman Emperor assuming a role, at least in principle, as defender of the faith.¹⁷ Confessional actions and disputes within countries, as viewed here, speak to the political significance of religion and its power as an instrument of order rather than to religion's essential hold on consciences. Other genres of writing than news were more suited to dealing with the latter.

---

11   Geoffrey Parker, 'The Limits to Revolutions in Military Affairs: Maurice of Nassau, the Battle of Nieuwpoort (1600), and the Legacy', *The Journal of Military History*, 71/2 (2007), pp. 331–372.

12   ASFI, MdP, 4256, fol. 44ʳ-45ᵛ. MAP DocId 50899.

13   Consider Bouko de Groot, *Nieuwpoort 1600. The First Modern Battle* (Oxford: Osprey, 2019) and Enrique F. Sicilia Cardona, *Batalla de Nieuport 1600. Los Tercios de Flandes en la "batalla de las dunas"* (Madrid: Almena, 2013).

14   ASFI, MdP, 4028, fol. 7ʳ.

15   Gigliola Fragnito, 'Gli ordini religiosi tra Riforma e Controriforma', in Mario Rosa (ed.), *Clero e società nell'Italia moderna* (Rome and Bari: Laterza, 1992), pp. 115–205.

16   ASFI, MdP, vol. 4028, fol. 2ʳ. Background in Michel De Waele (ed.), *Lendemains de guerre civile: réconciliations et restaurations en France sous Henri IV* (Paris / Québec: Hermann / Éditions du CIERL, 2015).

17   Minutely detailed in Karl Vocelka, *Rudolf II. und seine Zeit* (Wien: Böhlau, 1985).

On the other hand, court ceremonial and intrigues among those near the pinnacle of power are as evident in Rome, and therefore in our documents, as anywhere in Europe, exemplified in an account dealing with the assignment of ecclesiastical offices, referring to the duke of Parma's wedding to a cardinal's relative (personally officiated by Pope Clement VII) and the minutiae of Roman social and religious protocol.[18] The same document narrates a curious case perhaps meant to suggest ironies in regard to the Church's apostolic mission in the context of its institutional structure. The Bishop of Augsburg, travelling incognito on a tour of the charitable works in the Eternal city, dined among the congregation at the church of Trinità dei Monti, and only after he revealed his true identity, was he led up to the separate dining space dedicated to the church hierarchy. Which setting reflects the true character of the Church, the reader might ask: the first dinner or the second, or both?

Women occupied a number of roles of power, which were mentioned in the newsletters, including Maria de' Medici as queen of France, the archduchess Maria Anna von Wittelsbach of Inner Austria, and the princess and margravine Sibylle of Jülich-Cleves-Berg and Burgau. Decisive functions may be performed, as revealed in single episodes, such as the one which occurred in Constantinople, reported in a Venice newsletter of 12 February 1600:

> They write from Constantinople that in the Porte there arrived an ambassador who turned out to be a very astute and wise Persian woman, sent by the King of Persia to tell the Grand Turk that he and his whole empire were currently ruled by women, and that her King on the other hand was ruled by Counsellors and very prudent persons full of judgment, demanding Tauris and other places or there would be war.[19]

For this and similar occurrences there is little confirmation so far from other kinds of documents, but the general tenor gives an impression of prevailing ideas about women in the Turkish context, as well as a certain sentiment of exoticism. Women ambassadors, the account seems to imply, were far from commonplace in Europe. In any case, power and precariousness, force and fragility, roles and refashioning, characterise the lives and structures we observe here, far from the categorical rhetoric of the treatises on the absolute state.

---

18   ASFI, MdP, vol. 4028, fols. 3ʳ–8ᵛ. MAP DocId 50843. Relevant here is Klaus Jaitner, 'Der Hof Clemens VIII (1529–1605). Eine Prosographie', *Quellen und Forschungen aus italienischen Archiven und Bibliotheken*, 84 (2004), pp. 137–331.

19   ASFI, MdP, 3087, fol. 2ʳ. MAP DocId 50847.

2   Commerce

There was a difficult relationship between commerce and the state. 'Nervos belli, pecuniam infinitam' (endless funds are the sinews of war), said Cicero, and the costs of properly waging war rose steeply as the invention of new armaments and artillery kept pace with the design of new fortifications from one end of Europe to the other and likewise in the Middle East, placing such huge burdens on economies as to drive smaller powers into the periphery.[20] Developing absolutisms depend for survival on encouraging trade as well as on extracting from it, while at the same time increasing taxable surface through marriage, annexation and conquest.

State information systems intersected significantly with commercial ones in the 1600 documents, evidencing the emergence of a world in which private and public mail routes were becoming established features, while information itself had become a commodity in exchange.[21] Not surprisingly, the news often concerned tangible things, in the form of possessions or goods, mentioned in a context comprising the relevant persons who are found to be moving, owning, distributing or acquiring them. Our period seems to lie near the advent of a commodity-filled world, although specialized studies have long debated whether the circulation of goods may in itself serve as an index of economic prosperity, or not.[22] The documents suggest a new side to the question, incorporating the diffusion of knowledge about objects in motion at both ends of a spectrum whose extremes were defined by luxury products such as gold medals and artworks at one end, and, at the other, ordinary merchandise in exchange, from simple clothing to common foodstuffs.

The emergence of a world (or global) economy is much in evidence here, confirming the theses laid out in such painstaking detail by Fernand Braudel

---

20   Cicero, Philippics 5.5. A general treatment of the themes in this paragraph is Gregory Hanlon, *European Military Rivalry, 1500–1750: Fierce Pageant* (Abingdon: Routledge, 2020).

21   Concerning the development of public mail routes in general, see Jay Caplan, *Postal Culture in Europe, 1500–1800* (Oxford: Voltaire Foundation, 2016); and work on specific areas includes for instance Clemente Fedele and Mario Gallenga, *Per servizio di nostro Signore : strade, corrieri e poste dei papi dal Medioevo al 1870* (Modena: Mucchi, 1988); Bruno Caizzi, *Dalla posta del re alla posta di tutti. Territorio e comunicazione in Italia dal XVI secolo all'Unità* (Milan: Angeli, 1993); and Wolfgang Behringer, *Im Zeichen des Merkur: Reichspost und Kommunikationsrevolution in der Frühen Neuzeit* (Göttingen: Vandenhoeck & Ruprecht, 2003).

22   Lauro Martines, 'The Renaissance and the Birth of Consumer Society', *Renaissance Quarterly*, 51/1 (1998), pp. 193–203.

and later by Emmanuel Wallerstein and others.[23] New world discoveries came into play, as well as colonies around the globe. Brazil received mention, if only as an embarkation point.[24] Movements of the Spanish treasure fleet were of universal interest due to the impact of Spanish royal finances on everything from the banking industry to international relations. More in general, port city news, as for instance from Genoa, delved into the minutiae of loading and unloading cargo (in other years, occasionally including full or partial bills of lading or even lists of sailors).[25] New products came to market—apart from the new genres of news themselves. We find traces of these here, as well as of standard fare. Apart from sugar, in various forms, we find mention of cloth of various kinds, raw wool, foodstuffs, salt and more—not to mention gold (in forms rarely specified).[26] Apart from the seasonal and cyclical topicality of news, a part of our story has to do with what Europeans thought they discovered about the tangible things in the world from week to week, and how that discovery was articulated within different cultures.

Commerce most explicitly becomes news when some impediment occurs. And our themes of commerce and power overlap with particular effect in cases of attacks on shipping. The Uskok pirates were notorious in the Adriatic Sea, bothering anyone who crossed their path out of sight of Venice. In addition, fishing fleets and cargo ships were easy prey to belligerents in the various wars. For instance, in January 1600 we read, 'The two ships that were recently seen in England have now arrived in the Netherlands, richly laden with spices, and have left two other vessels behind ... full of the same merchandise, and their arrival is expected by the hour. Furthermore they write that two Dutch vessels have left their fleet and gone forth on their own, such that they encountered some Portuguese ships coming from Brazil, full of cases of sugar, and they seized and plundered them'.[27] Likewise, public health had a powerful impact on commerce, as we are reminded in a document from Lisbon dated 24 June, where we find an account of how the bubonic plague was making deep inroads into Iberian society, including among the 'nobility', such that transit was

---

23 I. Wallerstein, *The Modern World-System* (New York: Academic Press, 1974–80), volumes 1, 2 and 3; Fernand Braudel, *La Méditeranée et le monde méditeranéen à l'époque de Philippe II* (2 vols., Paris: Armand Colin, 1966); Fernand Braudel, *Civilisation matérielle, économie et capitalisme : XVe–XVIIIe siècle*, vol. 1: *Les structures du quotidien* (Paris: A. Colin, 1979); and synthesis and updating by Michel Wieviorka, 'From Marx and Braudel to Wallerstein', *Contemporary Sociology*, 34/1 (2005), pp. 1–7.
24 ASFI, MdP 4256, 20^r.
25 ASFI, MdP 2860, 490^r.
26 ASFI, MdP 2860, fol. 512^v.
27 ASFI, MdP 2860, fol. 482^r.

'suspended' to and from not only Lisbon, but also Seville.[28] No news is not necessarily good news; in fact in cases of dearth the worst is regularly feared before the best is hoped. In January 'where is the Spanish fleet?' was being asked with anticipation of shipwreck and catastrophic loss.[29]

War and commerce are also connected by the devastating effect of the former on the latter. Consider the case of Maurice of Nassau's rampage through the Flemish countryside in late June and early July. 'He headed toward Sluis burning and sacking villages and houses', although 'the destruction by [Federico] Spinola of all the munitions boats, scattering of the armada and imprisonment of some 1000 sailors and soldiers left him lost', whereupon he sought refuge with his forces in the forts around Ostend, only to be 'cut to pieces' by the enemy Archduke Albert.[30] The laying waste of entire regions by soldiers in the various wars was a regular feature of life in the period, interrupting the flow of goods, the provision of services, the distribution of food, even interfering in public health by the spread of disease, thus constituting a major threat to already precarious early modern economies.

How the unequal distribution of power and prosperity may have impacted regional relations and even identities raises questions meriting a separate treatment.

3   Regions

Geography features prominently in newsletter discourse, and regions turn up in multiple contexts as writers attempted to convey where and how events were occurring.[31] A list of the hundred most frequent substantive terms in our corpus includes Spain, Transylvania, Holland, France, and Flanders, as well as key cities such as Vienna and lesser-known ones such as Canissa (Nagykanizsa), not just as places of compilation in a heading, but as places where important events were occurring. Of course, regions can also be indicated in many other ways, such as by adjectives for the inhabitants or things pertaining to them, in this case 'Wallachian' or 'Turkish'—this last attested both in the form of 'turco' and 'turchesco'.

---

28   ASFI, MdP 2860, fol. 496^r.
29   ASFI, MdP 4256, fol. 1^r.
30   ASFI, MdP 4256 fol. 47^v.
31   Concerning time as a challenge, especially in regard to calendar abnormalities, Miranda Lewis, Arno Bosse, Howard Hotson, Thomas Wallnig, and Dirk van Miert, 'Time', in H. Hotson and T. Wallnig (eds.), *Reassembling the Republic of Letters in the Digital Age* (2019), https://doi.org/10.17875/gup2019-1146, pp. 97–119.

Wherever they happen to be, newsletter writers also often referred to the geographical origin of the news, by naming the city or region whence the original source or people in their milieu have received letters, or by naming the place of departure of couriers. In this sense regions appear not merely as locations of news, but also as indicators of the actual origin and possibly of the trustworthiness of the account. Some place names are familiar and would have been well-known to readers, such as state capitals and locations of great cultural importance. Others could be rather more bewildering.[32] These may be in improvised Italian translations by the writer, such as 'Zachmar' and 'Bobozesse'. Others pertained to small towns that were once of greater importance than later, or that happened to be the accidental scene of a battle. Sometimes a modern equivalent of such places is impossible to find, as languages have changed or even because the news writer himself might have misunderstood.

Naturally, not all proper names of geographical locations appear equally often in the different hubs of newsletter production. They are invoked in those stories where they are relevant, broadly following the general pattern of newsletter diffusion. Sometimes, these are very straightforward. The name of Holland, one of the provinces involved in the rebellion against the Spanish monarchy, appears most often from Antwerp and Brussels, that were themselves within the theatre of war, as well as from Cologne, just outside the provinces. References to the Turk are most commonly found in the newsletters from Graz, Vienna and Prague, where news about new Ottoman threats would arrive sooner. Almost all cases of 'Transilvania' were reported from Graz, not directly bordering that region, but still one of the closest major hubs. Political connections also played a role, such that reports emanating from the Republic of Genoa often speak of the Spanish monarchy, a close ally, although mentions of Milan, a nearby state directly under Spanish rule, in the same Genoese reporting, are not very frequent.[33]

Soldiers are often named for their region of origin, such as Italians, Germans, French, Flemish or whoever else in Europe and beyond, in another instance of the use of place names in contexts of conflict. In these cases, they often appear in large numbers, such as 'four thousand Swiss'.[34] At times, the specific characterizations do not necessarily refer to the birthplace of the soldiers in question. When a newsletter talks, for example, about 'due terzi de Lombardi'

---

32 On the challenges of geographical fixity, we note the discussion by Arno Bosse, 'Place', in Hotson et al. (eds.), *Reassembling the Republic of Letters*, pp. 79–96.

33 Giuseppe Galasso, *Alla Periferia Dell'impero: Il Regno Di Napoli Nel Periodo Spagnolo (Secoli XVI–XVII)* (Turin: Einaudi, 1994), p. 201.

34 ASFI, MdP 3256, fol. 17ʳ MAP DocId 52066.

this seems to indicate the place where the soldiers were stationed rather than where they were born.³⁵

There are, however, more ways to portray differences among groups of people. There appears, for instance, a clear idea of the Catholic world, bordering in the north on the Protestant areas, such as the United Provinces and England, with the Turks in the east. Through language, newsletters writers usually distance themselves from these latter groups, aligning themselves with the Catholic world instead.³⁶ The armies under Catholic authority in both of these areas, were generally regarded as fighting for the right side of Christendom. Not rarely, these are identified as 'our army', and victories or setbacks are described as 'ours', portrayed as being involved in various struggles against 'heretics' and 'rebels'. Neutrality and objectivity, two frequently asserted values in manuscript news writing, are obviously intended in relation to a particular confessional world view considered to be not only only reasonable and correct but also obligatory.

Other clues reinforce the distinct impression of bias toward the Catholic world. In speaking of the peace negotiations in Bergen op Zoom between representatives of the King of Spain and those from the provinces in revolt, the report remains clearly in favour of the former.³⁷ There are exceptions, especially where a newsletter aims to give a balanced account of the whole current state of affairs. Another example reports on an interesting argument made by the deputies of the rebelling states, who claimed that their natural prince, i.e. originally Philip II in his hereditary function as Count or Duke of the various provinces, had wronged them by placing many cities and fortresses in the hands of Spanish noblemen. Instead, they argued, he should have left the country in the hands of its 'natural masters', 'li signori naturali del paese'.³⁸ As things stood, they added, the utterly useless royal authorities did not even recognise them as legitimate negotiators. Therefore, the only possible alternative to continued warfare was to be more subjected to Spain than ever before. Although the perspective of the Spanish monarchy almost always dominated the description of important events such as the battle of Nieuwpoort, there could nonetheless be criticism of the conduct of the battle. An *avviso* from

---

35   ASFI, MdP 3256, fol. 7ʳ, MAP DocId 52281.
36   Nina Lamal, 'Promoting the Catholic Cause on the Italian Peninsula: Printed Avvisi on the Dutch Revolt and the French Wars of Religion (1562–1600)', in Joad Raymond and Noah Moxham (eds.), *News Networks in Early Modern Europe* (Leiden: Brill, 2016), pp. 675–94; Vincenzo Catani, *Roma, l'Italia e l'Europa durante il pontificato di Sisto V*, vol. 1: *Gli 'Avvisi' dal 1585 al 1586*) (Teramo: Palumbi, 2020), p. 18.
37   ASFI, MdP 4256, fol. 57ʳ, MAP DocId 50856.
38   ASFI, MdP 4256, fol. 57ᵛ, MAP DocId 50856.

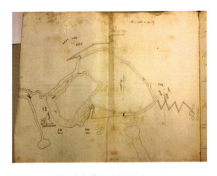

FIGURE 1.2
Fortifications along the Sava river in Schiavonia. MdP 4578, fol. 45

as far away as Prague, for example, set out to assess who among the Catholics should be blamed for the debacle.[39]

One graphic illustration of where place and conflict meet occurred in a battle map sent to accompany one of the newsletters.[40]

In Figure 1.2, we find indicated (among other things) Turkish fortifications along the Sava river in Schiavonia, under attack by the Marquis Savorgnan, showing the location of the allied camp and various batteries of cannon. However, the newsletters provided a map of another kind, a mental map, realized through language, indicating distinctions between named entities that can be as vital in daily life as they are in the recounting of what happened. The spatial consciousness of early modern Europe was partly built by news.

4   Diffusion

The 96 newsletters found in the Medici collection for the year 1600 were mostly either written or acquired by grand ducal residents, representatives, and correspondents abroad, such as Giovanni Niccolini in Rome, Cosimo Bartoli in Venice, Cosimo Concina in Prague, Francesco Guicciardini in Madrid, Baccio Giovannini in Paris and many others, and forwarded to the court in Florence. Figure 1.3 visualises this geography by looking at the distribution of news hubs and the relationship between the hubs and the places where the news items came from.

The main hub in this collection was Graz, followed by Genoa, Cologne, Antwerp and Milan, establishing beyond doubt the wide reach of Medici curiosity. Various conjectures are possible in regard to the loss of documents,

---

39   ASFI, MdP 4578, fols. 19ʳ-21ʳ, MAP DocId 51225.
40   ASF, MdP, vol. 4578, fol. 45ʳ MAP DocId 51251.

FIGURE 1.3   Distribution of main hubs

which we will not pursue here.[41] Instead we advance to a representation in Figure 1.4 of the data collected for 1600 in terms of news hubs where newsletters are compiled and places where the information is sourced, as follows.

Places of news in this representation are situated around the most important hubs, forming three clusters, showing that each European area only sends information into the closest hub or hubs belonging to the same cluster. Austria, Hungary, Bohemia, Poland, and Transylvania communicated with Graz, and to a lesser extent, with Prague and Vienna. Genoa and Milan gathered information from the Italian States, Switzerland and France, whereas news from the Netherlands, Flanders, France, England and the German cities flowed into Cologne, Antwerp and Brussels. Newsletter news circulated widely in Europe but always via the hub, which functioned like a funnel: usually the information was not sent directly to Florence from the battlefield in Hungary, but was collected in a major city, for example Graz or Vienna.

---

41   For relevant information, Antonio Panella, 'Introduzione', in Marcello Del Piazzo (ed.), *Archivio Mediceo del Principato: Inventario Sommario* (Roma: Ministero dell'Interno, 1966), pp. v–xxviii.

1600: A YEAR TO REMEMBER

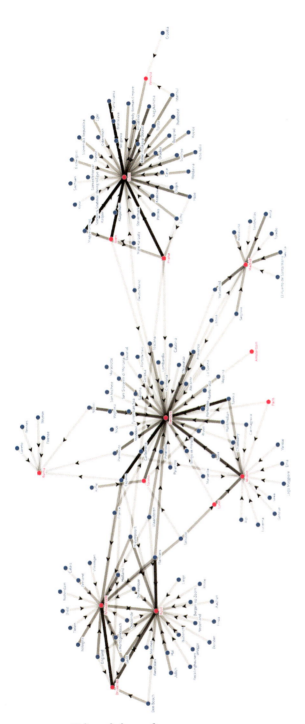

FIGURE 1.4 Hubs and places of news

Within these hubs, merchant networks were often important bearers of news as well as consumers of newsletters. True, the newsletters rarely reported about themselves, and the persons who mailed them out were reticent in regard to who wrote the news, who collected it and how. However, some excerpts do give insight into how the dissemination of information occurred. For instance, a newsletter from Genoa written on 8 January 1600 reported information from Spain received through letters, as well as what was being talked about in the port city: 'They say that also Prince Doria will go to Rome this Holy Year'.[42] The means of communication whereby the news item was transported does not affect it being news, and for this reason it is included in the newsletter. Receiving information from outside the diplomatic network was not unusual, since merchants as well as rulers utilised the information constantly in their activity, as evidenced in the remarkable collection of newsletters gathered by Octavian Secundus Fugger (1549–1600) and his brother Philipp Eduard (1546–1618).[43] The merchants were often bearers of news as well as consumers of newsletters, as another paragraph of the Genoa newsletter reveals: 'Among some of these German merchants there seem to be letters from Amsterdam that say the Dutch armada in the sea of the Indies encountered the fleet and fought it, sinking 7 ships and taking 3, rich in many crimsons and much gold, but at this point it is not very much believed, however if it is true there must appear some confirmation'.[44] The uncertainty of the source, i.e. the letters from Amsterdam in the hands of the German merchants, combined with the dubious content makes this news item tentative, requiring further confirmation. True news is often juxtaposed with uncertain, perhaps false, information, perhaps awaiting some kind of verification, which may or may not occur.

The news was also brought by couriers, as 'This week there arrived a courier sent by the Grand Duke to This Most Serene Prince with the news of the marriage between the Princess his niece and the king of France', or spies, 'We hear from spies and secret information that the Grand Turk borrowed a multitude of ships for the particular needs of his House, so that this city is experiencing a shortage of ships for the ongoing war'.[45] In these examples it is difficult to

---

42   ASF, MdP, vol. 2860, foll. 482^r-v, MAPDocId 50740.
43   On which, Karin Keller and Paola Molino, *Die Fuggerzeitungen im Kontext. Zeitungssammlungen im Alten Reich und in Italien* (Vienna: Böhlau, 2015); in addition, Nikolaus Schobesberger, 'Mapping the Fuggerzeitungen: The Geographical Issues of an Information Network', in Raymond & Moxham (eds.), *News Networks in Early Modern Europe*, pp. 216–40.
44   ASF, MdP, vol. 2860, fol. 482^r-v, MAPDocId 50740.
45   ASF, MdP, vol. 4578, fol. 16^r-v, MAPDocId 51147; ASF, MdP, vol. 4578, fol. 3^r-v, MAPDocId 50842.

understand whether these persons were mere carriers of letters and newsletters written by others, or if they also played a role in writing and reporting information viva voce.

In some cases, the distinction between letter and newsletter is unclear and the latter may be written starting from the content of the former. Indeed before the newsletter genre becomes fully consolidated, the information content is often simply copied from a letter, ignoring the initial and final formulas typical of ordinary correspondence.[46] Even in the 1600 corpus of newsletters analysed for this study, a newsletter from Cologne, dated 12 March, concerning the discovery of rebellious Protestants preaching in the city, presents some features that suggest this is taken from a letter. It is written in the first person, an uncommon gesture in a genre which attempts to protect anonymity. Moreover, the link to a member of the Cologne Senate, the request made to the Pope and the content make it plausible that the original is a letter of Coriolano Garzadori (1543–1618), Apostolic Nuncio in Cologne. Though the original has not been found, the conclusion of the newsletter shows the presence of a recipient and the use of a letter as source for the newsletter: 'I wanted to inform Your Illustrious Lordship about this event, so when the order comes from Rome you will know what happened'.[47]

The manuscript newsletters not only reported news from written sources, but also rumours that spread in a city, across a region, on a battlefield.[48] Compared to letters and written reports, oral transmission is more often defined as uncertain, to such an extent that this newswriter warned his reader before reporting the piece of news: 'Recently there was talk (though uncertain) about the Turks getting ready near Canissa [Nagykanizsa]'.[49] Though often inaccurate, rumours tend to spread. Only rarely are we informed about the person who reports them. An example: 'Here we have nothing certain about the peace negotiations, except a rumour that circulates regarding some hopes for a good result, and a Frenchman who came through here testified to this, but from what one sees the rumour seems unfounded'.[50] More often the reference is generic, as for instance, 'a rumour was spread', 'fu sparsa voce'. In this

---

46 Mario Infelise, 'From Merchants' Letters to Handwritten Political Avvisi', in Francisco Bethencourt and Florike Egmond (eds.), *Correspondence and Cultural Exchange in Europe, 1400–1700* (Cambridge: Cambridge University Press, 2007), pp. 33–52, especially pp. 35–38.
47 ASF, MdP, vol. 4256, fol. 9ʳ–11ᵛ, MAPDocId 50807.
48 John M. Hunt, 'Rumour, Newsletters, and the Pope's Death in Early Modern Rome', in Simon Davies and Puck Fletcher (eds.), *News in Early Modern Europe—Currents and Connections* (Leiden: Brill, 2020), pp. 143–144.
49 ASF, MdP, vol. 4578, fol. 32ʳ, MAPDocId 51240.
50 ASF, MdP, vol. 3256, fol. 17ʳ-ᵛ, MAPDocId 52066.

newsletter from Graz, dated 30 October 1600, the news item is a rumour, and therefore uncertain, and thus clearly opposed to the news story, believed to be true, that arrived by letter to the Archduke of Austria in Graz:

> From Canissa a rumor spread that there was a surrender to the Turk, but the rumor got no further, nor do we know anything else for certain, except that Hermestain, the general of Schiavonia, writes to this Archduke that he got from a spy from the Turkish camp that Paradaiser, the general of Canissa, having sent two soldiers from the fortress, a German and a Hungarian, with letters, both were taken by the Turks, whereas it was certain that these would have described the true situation of the city and of the besieged people.[51]

The news item is therefore considered to be reliable because it came in writing; and because it was addressed to the Archduke, it arrived in the same city where the newswriter was situated, while the fact that the primary source was a spy is not given any weight. But why bother to report news that was not confirmed? In some cases, a rumour, although still dubious at the time of writing, could prove to be true. At the end of this newsletter, indeed, an update confirming the loss of Canissa (Nagykanizsa) was added with a darker ink, proof that this latter information came in only at a later time. The rumour therefore turned out to be true, but the newsletter primed the reader for what might have been.

A major feature that the newswriters emphasise to highlight the quality of their writings is the novelty of the information reported. For instance, a newsletter from Graz, dated 24 April 1600, opens with the words 'With very fresh news [freschissimo aviso] from Vienna, brought by a qualified person, we hear that the Turk is making very great preparations for going into Hungary[…]'.[52] The term 'aviso' means both the document and the information.[53] Here the meaning is ambiguous, because the qualified person could have brought from Vienna the physical newsletter or the mere information regarding the Ottoman army. What is notable is the use of the superlative 'freschissimo' to stress the novelty of the news story, because the nouns 'notizia' and 'aviso' in Italian mean information and do not always imply something recent, unlike the English word 'news'. The adjective 'fresco' in this context means recent,

---

51 ASF, MdP, vol. 4578, fol. 44^{r}-v, MAPDocId 51249.
52 ASF, MdP, vol. 4578, fol. 10^{r}-v, MAPDocId 50872.
53 Sheila Barker, '"Secret and Uncertain": A History of Avvisi at the Court of the Medici Grand Dukes', in Raymond & Moxham (eds.), *News Networks in Early Modern Europe*, p. 717, note 4.

just happened, and this meaning has a long tradition.[54] Fresher news may confirm news already written in the newsletters, confirming that the writing of these documents was not a one-act process but a continuous enrichment of the text in time between one newsletter and the next, due to the continuous arrival or collection of new information. Another newsletter from Graz, dated 7 August 1600, announces news having come via Vienna about the death of the imperial general Adolf von Schwarzenberg in Pàpa, Hungary, on 29 July. The news travelled from Pàpa to Vienna to Graz, around 270 kilometres, in ten days; however, after two other news items, the newsletter writer announced that 'by other fresher information', probably coming directly from Pàpa, the death of Schwarzenberg has been confirmed and Ferencz Nádasdy has been appointed his successor.[55] The arrival of more recent news confirming prior reports makes the story of the event more reliable and credible, while confirming the quality and seriousness of the anonymous news writer. When instead the news is old, it loses importance and attractiveness in the eyes of the writer and of the readers. A newsletter from Genoa, 12 December 1600, ends with a mention of the arrival of a ship from Valencia which, having been long enroute, reported nothing new.[56] The news items, then, before being included in the newsletter, are evaluated by the writer according to how 'fresh' or 'old' they were.

The source and therefore reliability of the news also plays an important role. It is in the newswriter's interest to write that the news comes from a qualified person, for two reasons: both to confirm the truthfulness of what he writes and to show the value of his work. Introducing the news item about the Archduke Mathias with 'As far as can be understood from a very reliable and well informed person', the writer suggests a personal connection with someone close to the court, making his report more secure than an anonymous rumour spread throughout the city or a piece of news reported without stating the source.[57] However, even uncertain or only whispered news could interest the newsletters' readers. The Medici, for instance, in their letters to ambassadors and agents, asked to be informed about every news story in circulation, whether false or true. Even what we call today fake news had an informative and political role because it could allow administrators to explore the moods of the population and compare information arriving from other

---

54 Consider this quote from Petrarch: 'né d'aspettato ben fresche novelle' (nor fresh news of some hoped-for good) in sonnet 312 of the *Canzoniere*.
55 ASF, MdP, vol. 4578, fol. 30^r-v, MAPDocId 51239.
56 ASF, MdP, vol. 2860, fol. 511^r-512^v, MAPDocId 50879.
57 ASF, MdP, vol. 4578, fol. 50^r-v, MAPDocId 51255.

hubs.[58] Concerning this theme, a news item in a newsletter from Cologne, dated 11 September 11 1600, led to a reflection: 'One reasons but without any author, and with very little foundation that between the States of Holland and Zeeland and Count Maurice necessarily there are differences and difficulties, if the war with France does not progress the Dutch won't last long'.[59] For its importance, the piece of news is reported even if uncertain; it is also conveyed without an author, probably meaning the news item reached the writer's ear but the source was unknown. The use of the word 'autore' evokes authorship and raises questions about who were considered to be the authors of the news. This example and the previous ones suggest that the writer of newsletters did not consider himself the author of the news, but gave this authoritative role to the person who provided him with the news, i.e. the reliable and well informed person of the above mentioned newsletter from Graz. Whoever provided the newswriter with information therefore had a role of his own, but, as we have shown, also the newsletter's writer has a particular weight, since he chooses the news items to be included in the newsletters, evaluating the relevant ones even when uncertain or discarding those too old to be of any use.

The time of travel and the diffusion of news are certainly also linked to material conditions. The establishment and organisation of postal systems that connected Europe from North to South played a crucial role in the diffusion of news as told by the couriers themselves, and as published in the handwritten newsletters sent out regularly to subscribers once or twice a week from the major information centres.[60] Reading the texts of the newsletters gives a sense of how fast these news items travelled. For example, in September 1600, information of the 20th from Vienna took five days to reach Graz, from whence a newsletter dated 25 September departed. Other newsletters may be even more specific about the journey followed by the news: between 16–17 September 1600, a battle took place between the imperial troops and the Voivode of Wallachia in Turda, 50 kilometres away from Alba Iulia, while the imperials managed to enter Alba Iulia itself. On the 19th letters reporting these news items were sent from Transylvania and reached Graz before 2 October, which is the date of the newsletter. Although the letters from Transylvania were sent immediately after the events, it is necessary to take into account the typical travel times prevalent in the period. There were faster channels of communication, such as sending

---

58 Sheila Barker, "'Secret and Uncertain': A History of Avvisi at the Court of the Medici Grand Dukes," p. 733.

59 ASF, MdP, vol. 4256, fol. 67ʳ, MAPDocId 50816.

60 Nikolaus Schobesberger et al., "European Postal Networks." *News Networks in Early Modern Europe*, ed. Raymond and Moxham, pp. 19–63.

an extraordinary courier, but a normal news item concerning events happening in Transylvania took about a month to reach Florence, not by a direct route, but passing through Graz first. Analysing a large number of newsletters, not only at the hub level, but at the capillary level of the individual pieces of news that make them up, thus reveals the network and infrastructure required for dissemination as well as the reasons for the durability of the genre.

Regarding the impact of news, the manuscript newsletters are very reticent. However, scattered sentences and brief comments made by the writers reveal how people talked about the news that arrived in their cities. For instance, 'Here it is held to be true, and nothing else is talked about except for the peace between France and Savoy, to the great displeasure of the Heretics'.[61] We learn about how people were affected by local crime, which caused great concern, as in a report 'that in the Milanese region and state thieves have begun to rob houses using explosives [...] such that in Cremona they knocked down the door of a goldsmith who had reinforced it as much as he could, and after taking 12,000 scudi they killed the wife and child [...] so among the people [there is] much murmuring about such events'.[62] Between such comments and the evidence of curiosity among the news writers themselves, we feel safe in supposing the presence of an avid news public. Other sources, such as letters, diaries, iconographic sources, will eventually give a more complete picture of the real impact of news and newsletters inside and outside the courts.

5   Rhetoric

While there are several studies on the language and rhetoric of manuscript newsletters and printed newspapers (the latter especially concerning the English-language examples), much remains to be done.[63] Our investigations

---

61   ASF, MdP, vol. 4256, fol. 4^r, MAPDocId 50813.
62   ASF, MdP, vol. 2860, fol. 483^r-486^v, MAPDocId 50741.
63   Jérôme Hayez, 'Avviso, informazione, novella, nuova: la notion d'information dans les correspondances toscanes vers 1400', in *Information et société en Occident à la fin du Moyen Âge. Actes du colloque international tenu à l'Université du Québec à Montréal et à l'Université d'Ottawa (9–12 mai 2002)* (Paris: Publications de la Sorbonne, 2004), pp. 113–134; Johann Petitjean, 'Mots et pratiques de l'information. Ce que aviser veut dire (xvie–xviie siècles)', *Mélanges de l'École française de Rome—Italie et Méditerranée modernes et contemporaines*, 122/1 (2010), pp. 107–121; Paul Arblaster, André Belo, Carmen Espejo, Stéphane Haffemayer, Mario Infelise, Noah Moxham, Joad Raymond, and Nikolaus Schobesberger, 'The Lexicon of Early Modern News', and Mario Infelise, 'The History of the Word Gazzetta', both in Raymond & Moxham (eds.), *News Networks in Early Modern Europe*, respectively, at pp. 64–101 and 243–60. For the English side, Roberta Facchinetti,

here focus on the self- and meta-references within our corpus, revealing much about the purposes and expectations of the writers, as well as about broader underlying themes such as linguistic changes influenced by newsletter culture. We find explanations of delays, excuses for not bringing the most up-to-date news, and expressions particularly crafted for a certain kind of content. Curiously, although some types of information were clearly more sought-after than others, this does not seem to have affected the register deployed by their compilers. Instead, the newsletters' linguistic variations and changes in form appear to depend on the vicinity and reliability of the source, the vagaries of transmission, the use of imagination and poetic license, and above all, on the level of literacy and knowledge available to the writer. Although the majority of newsletters are in Italian, there are a few examples in Spanish.[64] Still to be determined is whether our corpus contains translations from other idioms.

A characteristic 'opening' accompanies each piece of news in a newsletter, indicating the relationship between the source, the news writer and the reader. Here are some of our findings, indicating where relevant, the location of the story and the Medici Archive Project DocId:

a) Openings using the verbs *to say* (and similar reporting clauses). Examples: 'Come altro dettosi' (Flanders, DocId#50837); 'Si dice che li Spagnoli ...' (Rome, DocId#50866); 'Di Spagna dicono che ...' (Rome, DocId#24161); 'Qua si dice che ...' (Milan, DocId#52069); 'Sono alcuni che dicono ...' (Germany, DocId#51248).

b) Opening *in medias res*, indicating that the reader already has a knowledge of the events, or relating to something already discussed in previous exchanges. Examples: 'Il giorno sequente alli 2 del mese essendosi risoluto l'archiduca ...' (Flanders, DocId#25874); 'In Fiandra la moneta non avea fatto variazione ...' (Flanders, DocId#25873); 'Il signor Giovan Francesco Aldobrandini si trova ...' (Rome, DocId#24161).

c) Openings expressing a wish, usually in the future tense. Example: 'Si spera che S.A. uscirà ...' (DocId#25872/Flanders); 'Si spera una straordinaria provisione di denari di Spagna ...' (DocId#50855, Flanders); 'Si spera che l'Arciduca ...' (DociID#50813, Flanders).

Nicholas Brownlees, Birte Bös, and Udo Fries (eds.), *News as Changing Texts: Corpora, Methodologies and Analysis* (Cambridge: Cambridge Scholars Publishing, 2015); Nicholas Brownlees, *The Language of Periodical News in Seventeenth-Century England* (Cambridge: Cambridge Scholars Publishing, 2011).

64 These are: Fiandra: DocId#50899; DocId#50811; Madrid: DocId#52368; DocId#52067; DocId#51649; DocId#14925; DocId#963; DocId#14924.

d) Openings using *believe, think, assume, seem like* (...), expressing a lesser degree of certainty. Examples: 'Si crede che alcuni mercanti ...' (Germany, DocId#50840); 'Pare che ultimamente ...' (Germany, DocId#50838); 'Pare che il contante ...' (Genoa, DocId#50850).
e) Openings voicing the public opinion. Examples: 'opinione comune ...' (Flanders, DocId#50868); 'Si dice pubblicamente ch'i ...' (Germany, DocId#51225).
f) Openings expressing certainty. Example: 'Si tiene per certo ...' (Flanders, DocId#9622); 'Si conferma che ...' (Fiandra, DocId#50816); 'Qui si tiene per ferma che ...' (DociID#50813, Fiandra); 'Fu vero che morì ...' (Germany, DocId#50840); 'Non è stato vero che ...' (Rome, DocId#50866); 'Si ha la confirmatione ...' (Rome, DocId#24161).
g) Openings expressing uncertainty or lack of information. Example: 'Non s'e' per anco inteso ...' (Flanders, DocId#50868); 'Non si ha per anco aviso ...' (DocId#50851, Flanders); 'Per lettere di Spagna delli 18 e 26 passato non s'intende nuova alcuna ...' (DocId#50839, Flanders); 'Si ragiona ma senza authore, et con non molto fondamento ...' (Flanders, DocId#50816); 'Qui non v' è nova che ...' (Milan, DocId#52064); 'Non habbiamo qui alcuna cosa di certo ...' (Milan, DocId#52066); 'Ultimamente s'è sparsa voce (se ben incerta) che ...' (Germany, DocId#51240).
h) Openings expressing freshness or trustworthiness of news. Example: 'Con freschissimo aviso di Vienna, portato da persona qualificata ...' (Germany, DocId#50875); 'Ci è avviso di Vienna da buona parte ...' (Germany, DocId#50865); 'Per quello che s'intende di persona assai sicura et ben informata ...' (Germany, DocId#51255); 'Con altri avvisi piu freschi ...' (Germany, DocId#51239).
i) Openings with direct reference to the courier who carries the news. Example: 'L'ultimo messaggiero, che fu spedito d'Inghilterra ...' (DocId #50818, Flanders); 'L'ordinario di Vienna ha portato avviso che ...' (Rome, DocId#50866); 'Per il Corriero straordinario di Parma ...' (Rome, DocId #24161); 'L'ordinario di Spagna giunto Domenica ...' (DocId#50843).

These openings convey important information to the readers at the time, and also to us.

Due to the composition of our corpus, that is to say a series of accounts of events happening in a single year, we are not surprised to find that the general tenor of these openings stresses the derivative nature of the information being conveyed. The writer of the newsletter is not necessarily the author of the ideas being expressed and takes some care to indicate the provenance of a story. Looking more deeply, we find that the *in medias res* openings are the most frequent. Out of 96, all but 6 sheets of newsletters contain 80 per cent or more news items opening *in medias res*. A feature of this opening is the lack of a reporting clause: this could imply that the compiler is taking for granted that the reader will know that this is reported news; or that the piece of news they are reporting comes directly from their knowledge (there is no specific case in this corpus in which the compiler makes this direct knowledge explicit). Out of all the newsletters in the 1600 corpus, only one opens in the first person.[65] Forty-five per cent (42 out of 96) of the sheets of newsletters include reporting clauses, followed by indirect speech (there is no example of direct speech). These reporting clauses include several types of verbs, as specified above, which carry different meanings and express different degrees of certainty about the news reported.[66] Out of the newsletters presenting a reporting clause, 20 use verbs such as *to say, to tell*; 3 express wish or hope; 2 used the verbs *to think, to seem like*; and 2 channelled the public opinion. Overall, the distribution of openings was even across the different news hubs, indicating that the 'reporting style' in 1600 was basically homogeneous. There seems to be no significant correlation between the topic and the way it is reported.

Apart from the value for understanding the business of reporting, news conveyed in these terms constitutes an important episode in the wider movement of codification and standardisation of the Italian vernacular. Begun in the early sixteenth century with Pietro Bembo's *questione della lingua*, and culminating in the first dictionary of the Italian language published by the *Accademia della Crusca* in 1612, the movement eventually comprising the foundation of early modern language academies represented, as Peter Burke points out, a 'desire for fixity' that could bring about the codification of language.[67] Newsletters compiled between the 1590s linguistic debates that resulted in the first *Vocabolario della Crusca*, and the 1650s decline of interest in codification and standardisation, can be viewed in the context of the emergence of regional dictionaries and the rediscovery of local dialects. Echoes of codification can be traced especially in the use of technical vocabularies (medical, mercantile, and legal) and of idiomatic expressions (particularly frequent in news). Terminologies and idioms in the newsletters bear comparison with the

---

65   DocId#52281—Avvisi di Milano.
66   7 expressed a degree of uncertainty, often caused by lack of further information, while 5 expressed absolute certainty of the truthfulness of the news.
67   Paul Oskar Kristeller, 'The Origin and Development of the Language of Italian Prose', in Paul O. Kristeller, *Renaissance Thought II* (New York: Harper & Row, 1965). Peter Burke, *Languages and Communities in Early Modern Europe* (Cambridge: Cambridge University Press, 2004).

Vocabolario and its precursors, post-Bembian treatises on the Italian vernacular and its use, and contemporary treatises on diplomatic language.[68]

Newsletters possessed significant advantages as vehicles for linguistic change. Unlike other diplomatic outputs, such as ambassadorial correspondence, pamphlets, and official *relazioni*—reserved to the high ranks of European courts—they were meant for a wider geographic and social circulation, and were available to whoever could afford the service.[69] This was seen, both from below and above, as an opportunity to establish the Italian vernacular as a lingua franca, as was already the case among scholars and artists. Although outside the date range of our corpus, English newsletters in the Medici collections show the translation and gradual assimilation of Italian idioms, suggesting that the Italian texts may be the linguistic scaffolding for the composition and diffusion of news in other languages.[70] Comparing the level of codification and standardisation of such documents, as well as their re-use of Italian expressions, confers insights into the ongoing effort, well under way in the year 1600, to achieve cultural hegemony through language.[71] Further analysis of the evolution of language and style in the newsletters will reveal the extent of this enterprise over the years, and the resultant shifts in the intended audience.

At this point, leaving a number of important lines of inquiry still open, we can say without equivocation that members of the grand ducal court and others in the original distribution network of the Archivio di Stato's newsletters for the year 1600 were treated to an extraordinarily rich selection of material. To be sure, our mostly macro analytic approach here has left out many precious details that would have drawn this contribution out to impossible lengths.

---

68   On the Vocabolario and its precursors, see Francesco Alunno's *Della fabrica del mondo* (Venice: Stamp. al segno della Luna, 1575) (USTC 808925); and Pergamini's *Il Memoriale della lingua italiana* (Venice: Gio. Battista Ciotti, 1602) (USTC 4031210). On post-Bembian treatises, see, for instance, Vincenzo Borghini's unpublished history of the Italian language; Benedetto Varchi's *L'Hercolano* (Florence: nella stamperia di Filippo II Giunta & fratres, 1570) (USTC 862030); Celso Cittadini's *Le origini della volgar toscana fauella* (Siena: Silvestro Marchetti, 1604) (USTC 4033457). On treatises on diplomatic language, see, for instance, Francesco Sansovino's *Il Secretario overo formulario di lettere missive e responsive; Idea del perfetto ambasciatore* (Venice: Francesco Sansovino, 1575) (USTC 854817), the Italian translation from the French of Juan Antonio de Vera y Zúñiga's *El Embaxador*.

69   Isabella Lazzarini, *Communication and Conflict. Italian Diplomacy in the Early Renaissance* (Oxford, Oxford University Press, 2015); Chiara De Caprio, 'Lingua, testi e discorsi della negoziazione politica e della prassi amministrativa', unpublished paper.

70   Brownlees, *The Language of Periodical News*.

71   Gianfranco Folena, *Il linguaggio del caos: studi sul plurilinguismo rinascimentale* (Turin: Bollati Boringhieri, 1991); Louis-Jean Calvet, *Language Wars and Linguistic Politics* (Oxford: Oxford University Press, 1998).

Apart from a more exhaustive examination of specific cases, the comparative framework could potentially be extended to other sources from other archives in Italy and elsewhere, to understand the news narratives fully in their context of historical narratives, then and now. Then the analysis could include numerous events of the year not reported in our documents such as Tyrone's invasion of Munster in Ireland against the English, the Dutch excursion to Japan, and moving more into the realm of culture, the burning of Giordano Bruno, the performance in Florence of the first lyric opera, and the meeting between Johannes Kepler and Tycho Brahe. However, our documents cover a surprisingly wide range of human experience just in the five thematic areas outlined in this chapter. Maligned at the time for being foolish, biased and inaccurate, the handwritten newsletters were always of interest to readers, and for this reason alone they illuminate an important corner of the early modern episteme. Furthermore they bear witness to an increasingly widespread awareness of the wider world beyond the visible horizon, agitated by the ever-present element of change that may be taken as a characteristic of news per se: in the news, for better or for worse, there is almost always something to get excited about.

CHAPTER 2

Information Shadows

Meteorological Disaster and Misinformation across Europe in the Wake of the 1625 Raid on Cadiz

Thom Pritchard

There are occasions when the flow of news is profoundly slowed, diverted or halted altogether.[1] Extreme weather, the movement of armies and censorship can hinder the movement of information creating a phenomenon we define as an 'information shadow', a spatial zone covering regions and even entire states where news cannot easily travel. This multi-causal phenomenon impedes and strains the processes of receiving and understanding news of a pivotal event; a hindrance which could in turn cloud the judgement of kings, diplomats and generals. Writing in the early nineteenth century the Prussian veteran of the Napoleonic wars Carl von Clausewitz warned that fog upon a battlefield slowed reports reaching a general, obscured the movement of enemy troops, and challenged the judgement of artillery commanders.[2] Information shadows behave much like their acoustic counterparts, where sound from a particular source might be heard only faintly or might be imperceptible altogether. The diaries of Samuel Pepys and John Evelyn offer a curious instance of this phenomenon. In 1666, the guns of the Four Day's Battle between the English and Dutch fleets in the North Sea were heard in London, whilst residents on the south coast, though closer to the action, heard nothing.[3] Acoustic shadows have influenced the outcome of battles. In his study of this phenomenon during the American

---

1 I would like to thank Brendan Dooley and Sandy Wilkinson for their kind support in developing this article as well as the organisers and participants at the Exciting News Conference for their questions. My interest in the perceptions of Cadiz was piqued following a conversation with Nadine Akkerman on Elizabeth Stuart's reaction to the calamity whilst at Leiden University. I also acknowledge the respective financial and intellectual generosity of my funding body, the Scottish Graduate School for the Arts and Humanities and my supervisors at Edinburgh, Catriona Murray and James Loxley.
2 Carl Von Clausewitz, *On War*, translated by J. J. Graham (London: N. Trübner, 1873), p. 40.
3 R. J. Peters, B. J. Smith, and Margaret Hollins, *Acoustics and Noise Control* (London: Routledge, 2011), p. 46. See *The Diary of John Evelyn Vol II*, ed. William Bray (London: Walter Dunne, 1901), p. 15, and *Diary and Correspondence of Samuel Pepys Vol III*, ed. Richard Baybrooke and Mynors Bright (London: Bickers and Son, 1876), p. 461.

Civil War, Charles D. Ross argued that these shadows impaired a commander's judgement of an unfolding fight.[4]

Information shadows were manifestly present during the Thirty Years War through the brutal interplay between the Little Ice Age and widespread conflict. If an information shadow occurred during a campaign overseas, it would hinder the comprehension of diplomats across Europe, of a state's ability to provide provisions for hypothermic survivors instead of treasure-laden victors, for the architects of foreign policy to defend or retaliate accordingly. On the more personal micro level, the families of sailors and soldiers anxiously waiting for news of their loved ones at sea would be forced to read and hear conflicting wild rumours in lieu of the sails of the returning ships, and the reputation of officers could be ruined by their inability to deliver timely testimonies.

The beginning of King Charles I's reign brought the Stuart kingdoms directly into the Thirty Years War, for the recovery the lost Palatinate of his sister Elizabeth Stuart and brother-in-law Frederick V by force of arms. As part of a wide campaign against Spain, the army of Count Ernst von Mansfeld was diverted to the siege of Breda, and months later an Anglo-Dutch fleet was launched to raid cities on the Iberian coast and capture the Spanish silver fleet returning from the New World. In the middle of November 1625, Sir James Bagg the vice admiral of the south of Cornwall received exciting and momentous news.[5] According to the letters, the King of France had sent a ship to Penryn to convey tidings that Lisbon had been captured.[6] Weeks later, writing from Dover Castle, Sir John Hippisley reported to Secretary of State Sir Edward Conway with further news from Flanders. These dispatches suggested that the fleet had stormed Cadiz and the surrounding forts, put its defenders to the sword and were now awaiting a Spanish counterattack; reports from Calais corroborated this account and added that the Spanish silver fleet was expected in the bay at any moment.[7]

Such reports would prove wildly unfounded. What in fact had ensued when the storm-battered fleet entered the Bay of Cadiz in early November was

---

4 Charles D. Ross, *Civil War Acoustic Shadows* (Shippensburg: White Mane Books, 2001), pp. 27–32.
5 The raid on Cadiz took place between 1 and 7 November 1625. Some of the footnotes below from the state papers and calendars of state papers reflect the Julian calendar, whilst those composed on the continent reflect the Gregorian. As such, on first glance, some offer impossible dates. Therefore, any mention of the date in the main body reflects the Gregorian for clarity.
6 Richard Rickman to Sir James Bagg, 31 October 1625, *Calendar of State Papers Domestic* (hereafter CSPD), 16/7/72.
7 Sir John Hippisley to Sec Conway, 23 November 1625, CSPD 16/7/18.

nothing short of a tragicomedy, characterised by dramatic irony, drunken farce and a shocking loss of life. The Spanish ships in the harbour were to escape to safety, while the English forces disembarked only to discover that Cadiz was protected by formidable modern fortifications.[8] Without adequate supplies of water from the ships, the expeditionary force gorged itself on 600 tons of wine from a nearby vineyard. Inebriated, the English force was then slaughtered by a disciplined Spanish counterattack as it attempted to beat its retreat back to the ships.[9] Due to battle, winter storms and disease, the fleet that would eventually return to England was reduced to just two thirds of its original size—a considerable loss of lives and ships.[10] Neither Lisbon nor Cadiz had been captured. Charles I and George Villiers, 1st Duke of Buckingham may have had ambitions to relive Elizabethan blue-water foreign policy in which the 1597 Sack of Cadiz stood amongst its brightest triumphs. Yet, by 1625, the Spanish were better prepared and had learned their lesson; they were primed for the English onslaught.

This chapter seeks to trace the flow of news from the Bay of Cadiz during an information shadow, through Spain, France and the Low Countries, as it traversed the arteries of Europe's major news networks before its staggered arrival in the Stuart kingdoms. It will attempt to locate the reasons behind the misinformation linked to this event, especially the complex interplay between military and meteorological factors. We will also seek to explore how Caroline authorities on the south coasts of England and Ireland interpreted and negotiated disparate narratives.

1   Tracing an Information Shadow

Climatic conditions exerted a profound influence on the flow of information from the Bay of Cadiz. The tempestuous autumn weather created an information shadow covering the west Atlantic's storm-ridden seaboard. Bad weather—storms at sea and flooding on land—could temporarily disrupt or divert routes of information, so that news was received only gradually compared with other locations in the topography.

---

8   Peter H. Wilson, *Europe's Tragedy: The Thirty Years War* (Cambridge Massachusetts: Belknapp Press, 2011), p. 369.
9   Charles Carelton, *This Seat of Mars: War and the British Isles 1485–1746* (New Haven: Yale University Press, 2011), p. 83.
10 Ibid., pp. 83–84.

Substituting acoustic waves for news and information, the information shadows of the Thirty Years War were not only a result of the limitations of Europe's news networks but also of particularly challenging meteorological conditions which occurred from the late sixteenth century onwards. The Grindelwald Fluctuation (1560–1630) named after a contemporaneous Swiss glacier, caused what Evan T. Jones, Rose Hewlett and Anson W. Mackay would describe as 'some of the worst weather of the last millennium'.[11] Their examination of chronicles written in the city of Bristol reveal severe frosts and flooding, storms and droughts and unseasonably bad summers.[12] The early seventeenth century witnessed bizarre weather events on a global scale which ran parallel to the tumultuous series of political, religious and economic crises. Between 1614 and 1621, sub-Saharan Africa suffered a particularly severe drought, snow fell in Fujian, and Europe's winter of 1620–1621 was bitterly cold.[13]

During the campaigning season in the immediate aftermath of the fall of the fortified city of Breda in the Low Countries to Spanish forces (1624–1625), the weather in the Channel—reportedly the worst in nearly half a century—prevented news of its surrender from reaching the Caroline kingdoms. Writing under the imprint *Mercurius Britannicus*, the prolific London publishers Nathaniel Butter and Nicholas Bourne described the multiple conflicts with the Habsburgs from Brazil to Breda in *The Continuation of Our Weekely Newes, from the 21. Of June, unto the 28*.[14] The editors began apologetically, excusing the absence of information heralding Breda's fall due to extreme weather patterns: 'we have received none [news] from the United Provinces in the space of 5 or 6 weeks by reason of contrary wind, which was not seen in the space of 30 years'.[15] Although news had previously seeped through the blockades of the besieged city to inform individuals and printers across Europe of the conditions endured by its inhabitants, the worst weather in living memory created an information shadow which stifled news of the fall of Breda from reaching England's south coast for weeks. According to Joad Raymond, news was 'more plentiful during the summer when travel was easier and sparse during the

---

11 Evan T. Jones, Rose Hewlett, and Anson W Mackay, 'Weird Weather in Bristol During the Grindelwald Fluctuation (1560–1630)', *Weather*, 76/4 (2021), p. 104.
12 Ibid., p. 4.
13 Geoffrey Parker, *Global Crisis: War, Climate Change and Catastrophe in the Seventeenth Century* (New Haven: Yale University Press, 2014), p. xxvii.
14 Jayne E. E. Boys, *London's News Press and the Thirty Years War* (Aldershot: Boydell and Brewer, 2011), p. 101. Butter and Bourne would write under this imprint from 1625–1627.
15 Nathaniel Butter and Nicholas Bourne, *The Continvation of Our ustri Newes, from the 21. Of June, vnto the 28* (London: Printed for Mercurius Britannicus, 1625) (USTC 3011956), A2v.

winter'.[16] Whilst certainly true, these seasonal patterns are complicated by the increased frequency and violence of storms of the Grindelwald Fluctuation, hindering flow of an otherwise abundance of news during the summer months.

Information shadows could and did exacerbate normal processes of news-gathering and news dispersal. They sat at the extreme end of patterns of news reporting in the period. For publishers and the recipients of newsletters, contradictory reports were to be considered alongside each other, validated or proven incorrect by the arrival of subsequent news. Even for privileged diplomats, reports were frequently confirmed, corrected or contradicted, 'all without apology or embarrassment'.[17] Butter and Bourne reminded their demanding readership of this news-reading process:

> And I hope that none that haue any sense or judgement will blame us if either hee, or I, or any other shall receive or publish hereafter anything contrary to this newes, for I translate merely the News verbatim out of the tongues and languages in which they are written (...) I leavue therefore the judgement of the Reader (...) especially when there are tidings which contradict one another.[18]

David Randall, in his reconstruction of Elizabethan and Stuart military news, looked to the letter writer John Chamberlain's narrative of how news was consumed by Londoners, an environment in which 'credibility and uncertainty are leitmotifs'.[19] According to Randall, 'in the 1620s English military news was unstable in medium, uncertain in credibility, contradictory in content, and never to be read in blind faith'.[20] This raises the question, with a series of conflicting reports often arriving, when does a period of 'every-day' uncertainty end and an information shadow begin? In the case of the fall of Breda and as this chapter on news from Cadiz will argue, an information shadow warranted a far lengthier process of collation and scrutiny than was typical. Considering the expedition operated in Cadiz and the nearby waters for around two weeks in the beginning of November, misinformation was still circulating in the

---

16   Joad Raymond, *The Invention of the Newspaper: English Newsbooks 1641–1649* (Oxford: Oxford University Press, 1996), p. 5.
17   Noah Millstone, 'Seeing Like a Statesman in Early Stuart England', *Past and Present*, 223 (2014), p. 94.
18   Butter and Bourne, *The Continvation of Our ustri Newes, from the 21. Of June*, p. 5.
19   David Randall, *Credibility in Elizabethan and Early Stuart Military News* (London: Routledge, 2016), p. 2.
20   Ibid., p. 2.

Stuart kingdoms and Dutch Republic in early January due to the effects of the shadow.

Whereas Breda was a colossal media event in print and manuscript as 'news' travelled from the hinterland of the Rhine Delta to Amsterdam, Paris and London, flowing from the mouth to the quill to the printing press, the 1625 raid upon Cadiz left no such printed paper trail in English. We cannot look to cheap print for the immediate aftermath of the raid on Cadiz. Even when we consider the very low survival rate for early modern print, a rate which worsens when applied to serials and other cheap print that could constitute a 'vast shadow army' of lost publications, Cadiz is still an anomaly.[21]

Nevertheless, we can trace the movement of news from Cadiz from across Spain, through France and to the Low Countries to find how Hippisley received misinformation of the capture of Cadiz. The arrival of news from the epicentres of Europe's news networks, such as Antwerp, Amsterdam, Venice, Paris and Cologne ordinarily provided crucial sources of news for the Stuart kingdoms. Yet in an information shadow, with bad weather hindering the return of ships from the Anglo-Dutch fleet, translated information travelling through these arteries of Europe's news networks became the sole sources of the success or failure of this Stuart entry into the Thirty Years War. With a lacuna of English-language print, we must turn to manuscript sources to see how, as the information shadow abated, when the storm-battered ships gradually arrived in English and Irish ports, the Council of War assembled narratives of how the catastrophic failure unfolded in an autopsy in ink. Furthermore, by examining the correspondence of the most famous painter of his generation and occasional diplomat, Peter Paul Rubens in Antwerp, and through the vast correspondence of the exiled Winter Queen Elizabeth Stuart writing from The Hague, we can see how conflicting sources slowly spread outwards.

Reconstructing the Cadiz expedition is complicated by a plethora of considerations, not least the timeline of our sources, with the dates of the letters written by the participants aboard the storm-battered fleet reflecting the time of their composition, not their reception on England's south coast. The officers who wrote these dispatches naturally dated their letters according to the Julian calendar, whereas news received in Antwerp reflected the Gregorian calendar giving a surreal discrepancy of a full 10 days. Europe was splintered between two calendars. Although much of Catholic Europe adopted the Gregorian

---

21   Andrew Pettegree, 'The Legion of the Lost. Recovering the Lost Books of Early Modern Europe', in Andrew Pettegree and Flavia Bruni (eds.), *Lost Books: Reconstructing the Print World of Pre-Industrial Europe* (Leiden: Brill, 2016), pp. 1–4.

calendar in the 1580s, Protestant countries resisted this change until the eighteenth century.[22]

This is not to say that information shadows were solely the result of meteorological conditions. The interplay between the weather, ongoing naval warfare, political expectations and the nature of Iberian news networks, all played their part. These obstacles were to impede the task of the officers and administrators of the Council of War waiting in Plymouth from ascertaining an accurate sequence of the failure. King Charles might have told Parliament that 'the season of the yeare was far spent, yet the time not unseasonable for the Design', yet the conditions in the North Atlantic into which his fleet sailed were to prove otherwise.[23] The letters written aboard the fleet relate a harrowing passage. Writing aboard the flagship, the Anne Royal, the commander of the expedition Sir Edward Cecil's letters mention great losses of life during a huge storm that scattered the fleet, forcing it to regroup near the Bay of Cadiz.[24] Also huddled aboard the Anne Royal, Sir Thomas Love's letters reported that enroute to Cadiz the Long Robert sank claiming the lives of her 175-strong crew, and at the moment of searching for the Spanish treasure fleet, the weather and ageing and leaky ships inspired little confidence.[25] With the fleet engaged in bombarding the fortifications surrounding Cadiz and later in charting an ultimately futile pursuit of the Spanish silver fleet, those ships that did manage to survive and return north were slowed and scattered by winter storms.

Therefore, the testimonies of officers aboard the fleet, those eyewitness accounts which related farce and rivalry, reached the south coast only in mid-December. These delayed reports were themselves overtaken by news arriving from France and Flanders—an overland trail complicated by Spain's curious position in pan-European news networks. In contrast to Central Europe where a sophisticated postal network was in place, Spain was far less well served. At the onset of the Thirty Years War, Spain's position in Europe and its many conflicts contributed to 'the partial failure of the postal and communicative flow' of information when fledgling news publications were on the

---

22 Sara Barker, 'Time in English Translations of Continental News', in Raymond and Moxham (eds.), *News Networks in Early Modern Europe*, p. 333.
23 John Rushworth, *Historical collections of private passages of state* (London: printed by Thomas Newcomb for George Thomason, 1659), p. 194.
24 Sir Edward Cecil to Buckingham, 8 November 1625, CSPD 16/6/8.
25 Sir Thomas Love to Nicholas, 2 November 1625, CSPD 16/6/9.

rise across Europe.[26] Subsequently, news of Spanish affairs was often relayed through 'other intermediaries, mostly Italian, French and Flemish'.[27]

2   Spectating Cadiz from under the Shadow

With this plethora of complications in mind, we now look at how news from Cadiz slowly moved over land, across Spain, through France and the Low Countries to the Stuart kingdoms beyond during this information shadow. Bundled amongst the collections of reports the Council of War collated in the aftermath of Cadiz, we find Spanish handwritten sources. News in manuscript form, that may have arrived from Antwerp before the first remnants of the Anglo-Dutch fleet returned to England's south coast. Presumably obtained during mid to late December, an 'Account of attack on Cadiz, and another copy' is a translated Spanish narrative of the raid, 'Dedicated to the Infante Don Fernando' dated 'On Saturday the first of November of all Saints'.[28] This manuscript newsletter attests to Jason Peacey's reminder that 'English diplomats read European gazettes in order to keep themselves apprised of developments across the continent'; the ambassador Sir Dudley Carleton was furnished with news from Venice and Sir Thomas Roe subscribed to French mercuries.[29] In these remarkable conditions, however, for those nervously waiting on the south coast, these Spanish documents may have provided the first accurate narrative of the disaster at Cadiz.

The first document described a fatal error in the Anglo-Dutch fleet's judgement.

In a miscalculation the Spanish authors ascribed to the kindness of providence, the invaders bombarded the fort of El Puntal at the harbour's mouth instead of immediately attacking the vulnerable Spanish ships who escaped

---

26   Nikolaus Schobesberger, Paul Arblaster, Mario Infelise, André Belo, Noah Moxham, Carmen Espejo and Joad Raymond, 'European Postal Networks', in Joad Raymond and Noah Moxham (eds.), *News Networks in Early Modern Europe* (Leiden: Brill, 2016), pp. 39–40.

27   Ibid., p. 39.

28   Anon, 'Account of attack on Cadiz, and another copy', November 1625, SP 94/33 f.137. The pencil marks of the curator attributes this mistakenly to the 1596 raid. We can infer from the November dates and the unfolding narrative of drunken slaughter, that the Spanish writer was narrating events in 1625.

29   Jason Peacey, '"My Friend the Gazetier": Diplomacy and News in Seventeenth-Century Europe', in Raymond and Moxham (eds.), *News Networks in Early Modern Europe*, pp. 421–422.

to safety.[30] The second translated copy captures a sensation of the confusion inside the city of Cadiz, for when the fleet entered the harbour, its citizens mistook the enemy for their own returning 'galleons of the Indies fleet'.[31] It is here we find the first mention of the drunken farce. On Friday morning, with Cecil's forces, unable to enter Cadiz marauding around the city's hinterland, it was 'reported that the enemy had done much spoyle spilling the wine and firing of some houses'.[32] We also find an allusion to the very conditions that would slow the dispersion of news from Cadiz: 'the weather grows foul'.[33]

This Spanish manuscript may have accurately recorded the drunken farce and bad weather, but its contents are the result of a process of nervous and jubilant newsgathering conducted between Cadiz and Madrid. Despite its veracity, this translation must also be located alongside a wider corpus of 'news' travelling into the information shadow across continental Europe, containing wild rumour, misinformation and echoes of the truth. The arrival of the Anglo-Dutch fleet in the Bay of Cadiz sparked a frantic endeavour to ascertain the fate of the city and the progress of the enemy. The letters of Venetian ambassador Lunardo Moro attest that on 9 November, a week after the arrival of the fleet, uncertain news reached Madrid. Moro condensed conflicting reports to assemble a narrative of events and significances. The newly arrived eighty galleons had purportedly stormed El Puntal, putting all but two to the sword. Those spared had been ordered to relay the message that the fleet had arrived under the flag of the Palatinate, not to wage war with the King of Spain but to leverage the restoration of the lost state.[34] Moro also examined a letter by none other than the city's commander Don Fernando Giron who was nevertheless confident that Cadiz would be safe behind its fortifications.[35] Three days later, on the evening of the 12 November, decisive news arrived at court. Giron's courier had ridden hard, bearing news of a heavy defeat for the English in weather so torrid that musketeers had been unable to use the weapons.[36] However, like the storms, danger had not yet abated. Prevented from leaving the harbour by

---

30 Anon, 'Account of attack on Cadiz, and another copy', p. 1.
31 Ibid., p. 3.
32 Ibid., p. 3.
33 Ibid., p. 3.
34 Lunardo Moro to the Doge and Senate, 9 November 1625, Calendar of State Papers Venice, vol. 19, 1625–1626, letter 302.
35 Ibid., letter 302.
36 Lunardo Moro to the Doge and Senate, 12 November 1625, Calendar of State Papers Venice, vol. 19, 1625–1626, letter 306.

a winter tempest, Moro stated that the English lay in wait for the imminently anticipated fleet from Brazil.[37]

With Cadiz unscathed, presses in Córdoba, situated roughly between Cadiz and Madrid, printed a *Relacion verdadera del suceso de la armada inglesa, su llegada a Cadiz*. This 'true Relation of the events of the English Armada, on its landing at Cadiz', celebrated the victory of the elderly veteran Giron, bringing the events of the calamitous retreat from the circles of diplomats and soldiers to wide public consumption.[38] Although by 12 November the fate of the city of Cadiz, if not the returning fleet had been verified by royal couriers in Madrid, we can see in the letters of Rubens in Brussels that the first reports arriving in the Low Countries were rife with speculation, uncertainty, rumour and wild misinformation. Sixteen days later, on 28 November, Rubens wrote to Valavez that the first news about Cadiz:

> had first to pass through France: namely, that the English fleet had seized land at Cadiz, and put ashore 12,000 men? Some people write that they had taken the fortress by storm, but this is denied by others. In short, all Spain is in arms.[39]

As news travelled overland, the taking of El Puntal apparently become conflated and confused for the taking of Cadiz. Especially in times of war, distance is a fundamental principle in the instability and reception of early modern news. Fillipo di Vivo's case study of an inconclusive battle between Venetian and Spanish in the Adriatic in 1617 is a case in point. For both sides, the distance of the event was an opportunity to distort its narrative, aggrandising the size of the enemy, omitting losses altogether, creating in effect 'a flurry of antithetical reports'.[40] Therefore, in the conflated rumours emanating from Cadiz, wild optimism, diplomatic spin and even outright manipulation cannot be ruled out, nor can accident. Theoretically, if news travelled overland from one city to another with many points in between (towns, taverns and so on) the opportunities for news to metamorphose increase. Passing through spaces where the contents of the news may transition between textual and oral forms

---

37   Ibid., letter 306.
38   Anon, *Relacion verdadera del suceso de la armada inglesa, su llegada a Cadiz* (Córdoba: por Salvador de Cea Tesa, 1625) (USTC 5035287), p. 1.
39   Peter Paul Rubens to Valavez, 28 November 1625, letter 70. *The Letters of Peter Paul Rubens*, translated and edited by Ruth Saunders Magurn (Cambridge Massachusetts: Harvard University Press, 1955), p. 119.
40   Filippo di Vivo, 'Microhistories of Long-Distance Information: Space, Movement and Agency in the Early Modern News', *Past and Present*, 242, Supplement 14 (2019), p. 180.

increases the potential for what would colloquially be called Chinese Whispers in English, or Stille Post in German. The likelihood of rumours both accurate and inaccurate fusing together decreases if this news travelled overseas with fewer stops and opportunities for the information contained to metamorphose. The information shadow slowed and even prevented this latter route across the margins of the Atlantic. The rumour of Cadiz's capture received by Hippisley in early December might have stemmed from the same source Rubens recorded. An evening dispatch from Antwerp could arrive in England in only eight days via the mercantile news network of the Dover Road, run by the Flemish Matthew de Quester by royal appointment.[41] Therefore, if we convert Hippisley's date to the Gregorian, he received the misinformation about Cadiz on 5 December, making this connection all the more plausible.

Strange news continued to arrive in the Low Countries. Rubens was alarmed by reports that as part of the assault on Cadiz, 'the Moors of Algiers have threatened to join the English and the Dutch'.[42] This troublesome scenario provoked the painter to wonder, and to interrogate the rumour. Was Buckingham simply displaying brash 'bravado' in his assault on Spain? Or, more sinisterly, was this alleged alliance between reformed Protestants and Muslims 'an extreme, unheard of act of desperation (...) to ally themselves with Turks and Moors for the overthrow of Christians'.[43] In the conditions of an information shadow, definitive news from Cadiz would not arrive in the Low Countries for another fortnight. The prolonged period of uncertainty subsequently created a liminal period where anxieties arising from misinformation could not easily be verified or dispelled.

Paul Arblaster's extensive studies of the news epicentre of Antwerp casts more light onto the shadow affecting the flow of news from Cadiz. Writing for the prolific Antwerp publisher Abraham Verhoeven, the English Catholic émigré Richard Verstegan contributed towards no fewer than three editions of *Nieuwe Tijdinghen* on 3 December, each issue containing more details of the raid on Cadiz than the last.[44] 50 miles away in Brussels, Rubens' letters relate the moment when Cadiz's fate was received on 12 December. News sent on behalf of King Philip IV to the 'Most Serene Infanta' confirmed that the 'captain of seventy years Don Fernando Gryon made a sortie from the fortres with only 500 musketeers' and repelled the English force from Spanish shores.[45]

---

41   Schobesberger et al., 'European Postal Networks', p. 58.
42   Rubens to Valavez, 28 November 1625, letter 70, p. 119.
43   Ibid., p. 119.
44   Paul Arblaster, *Antwerp and the World: Richard Verstegan and the International Culture of the Catholic Reformation* (Ithica: Cornell University Press, 2004), p. 148.
45   Rubens to Valavez, 12 December 1625, letter 71, p. 120.

Only by Christmas did the arrival of accurate news overcome the stifling effects of the shadow, allowing spectators in the Low Countries to build a richer and more holistic narrative. In letters dated 26 December and 9 January respectively, Rubens summarised conversations with the Count-Duke of Olivares who confirmed the fact that the returning Spanish treasure fleet narrowly missed the marauding English fleet. It 'seems almost a miracle' the Count had exclaimed, 'that they could have passed so close to one another without having met'.[46] Speaking to the architect of Breda's fall, Ambrogio Spinola was perplexed that the English had landed by a desolate, heavily defended Cadiz. Displaying confusion or dry humour the general had concluded: 'The English apparently thought they could take all of Spain [with] 12,000 infantry and a few horsemen (...) the only prudence the English showed in their enterprise was retiring as speedily as possible'.[47]

However, if we move north to the United Provinces, it appears that remnants of the shadow had not yet fully dissipated. The letters of the Winter Queen Elizabeth Stuart in exile in The Hague to the Bohemian general Count Jindřich Matyáš Thurn confirm that intelligence in the Dutch Republic had only partially untangled accurate relations from misinformation. Stuart wrote:

> The fleet has returned; it was at Cadiz where they took a small fort, but the town was too strong to take it by siege and the unpredictable winter weather was not reliable enough (...) they returned with the loss of no more than fifty men.[48]

In a carefully crafted conversational syntax, the epistolary equivalent of the 'oh wait', Stuart made a dramatic revelation of the success of the expedition and the capture of the silver fleet: 'That is all new here. I forgot to tell you that the fleet captured a great many very rich ships belonging to the King of Spain'.[49] Stuart's misplaced optimism may have stemmed from a wildly exaggerated capture of three ships from Hamburg who had been unfortunate enough to be near Sanlúcar de Barrameda when Cecil's fleet was desperately trying to intercept the returning treasure fleet.[50] Or, perhaps Stuart was participating in diplomatic spin. Events off the Spanish coast were still sufficiently murky

---

46   Rubens to Valavez, 26 December 1625, letter 72, p. 121.
47   Rubens to Valavez, 9 January 1626, letter 73, p. 123.
48   Elizabeth to Thurn, The Hague, 5 Jan 1626, letter 399. The *Correspondence of Elizabeth Stuart, Queen of Bohemia*, Nadine Akkerman, Lisa Jardine, and Steve Murdoch (eds.) (Oxford: Oxford University Press, 2011), p. 573.
49   Ibid., p. 573.
50   Sir Thomas Love to Nicholas, 2 Nov 1625 CSPD 16/6/9.

for Lord Falkland, the Lord Deputy of Ireland to collate information obtained from Iberian boats taking shelter in harbours across Ireland. Falkland wrote to Conway with news that a ship from Lisbon had taken refuge inside Waterford harbour; according to the crew the plate fleet had arrived safely with only a small escort barely three days after Cecil had abandoned the expedition.[51] News from Cadiz and the bellicose direction in Caroline foreign policy was also followed avidly by Stuart émigrés and their supporters in the Low Countries, its outcome signifying the direction of the fortunes of Catholics in the Caroline kingdoms. In the first days of 1626, we find conversations in convents and monasteries in Ypres about the arrest of 300 Catholics in London, about hopes the new Queen Henrietta Maria might intercede on their behalf, and the momentous news that the English fleet had returned with the loss of nearly 5,000 men.[52]

3 An Autopsy in Ink: Overcoming the Shadow?

As the survivors of the expedition slowly made their way back to Plymouth, the Council of War conducted their own autopsy in ink, collating the testimony of newly arrived officers to understand the tragic farce, an endeavour previously impossible due to the effects of the information shadow. Yet this process was once again slowed and frustrated as storms forced many ships to divert to Ireland's south coast, creating in effect another information shadow across the Celtic Sea. In 1596, aboard the victorious English fleet, many senior officers had sent dispatches ahead of their return to disseminate their own gallant actions in the sack.[53] In 1625, we see the same practice occurring for very different reasons. With Buckingham addressed as the recipient of many of these letters written from the Bay of Cadiz, it is almost certain that the authors witnessing and orchestrating the disaster wished to acquit themselves of blame as much as they wished to send a stream of military intelligence to the Duke. Sir William Leger wrote to the Duke from the Bay of Cadiz. According to Leger, whilst the Earl of Essex had eventually taken the fort of El Puntal, Cadiz was judged impregnable, and the Marshal, possibly an obtuse reference to Cecil, had let his provisioned men drink wine, which rendered them unruly and necessitated their shameful withdrawal. Leger was keen to stress that he had suggested marching

---

51 Lord Falkland to Lord Conway, 11 Jan 1626, SP63/242/f.51.
52 Fr. Beda of the Barefooted Carmelites to Silvester Pardo of Ypres, 26 December 1625, CSPD 16/12/57.
53 Anthony Payne, 'Richard Hakluyt and the Earl of Essex. The Censorship of the Voyage to Cadiz in the Principal Navigations', *Publishing History* 72 (2012), p. 10.

upon Sanlúcar de Barrameda, but had been overruled; if the silver fleet could not be captured, Leger dramatically confessed he did not wish to survive the return voyage for shame.[54]

We need to take heed of the verisimilitude of these letters. As Yuval Noah Harari cautions, few early modern testimonies written by the eyewitnesses of war, which stress the veracity of their narrative 'had the production of truth as its supreme aim'. Some employed the convention of a truthful relation 'as a means of gaining credibility and authority, which they then employ in the service of more'.[55] If 'the service of more' equates to the patronage equivalent of 'saving ones own skin', then Harari's formulation is applicable to the series of letters and testimonies written aboard ships and by those newly arrived in Plymouth. There is a careful subjective selection of certain truthful events which firstly almost always cites another officer's poor judgement or inadequate conduct, and secondly, if possible, valorises one's own conduct in an otherwise disastrous event. In these epistolary testimonies of failure, social juxtaposition is essential. Take one letter written by Cecil aboard his flagship in the immediate aftermath of the farcical retreat. Cecil was careful to blame Sir Samuel Argoll as the officer who reconnoitred Cadiz and judged the city impregnable. Cecil also complained that the men he was given to command were so poorly trained that they killed more of their own than the enemy in combat. To compound matters, the ships were leaky and poorly victualled from the start, logistical problems Cecil had foreseen but tolerated to prosecute the Duke's orders.[56]

It is difficult to discern when these letters reached Plymouth. The returning fleet's voyage to its homeport was hampered by the continued extreme winter weather. Many ships, including the Anne Royal were forced to divert to Kinsale harbour in Ireland to see out the winter. According to Sir Thomas Love, as the flagship approached the Scilly Islands, its hold was flooded by six feet of seawater; they therefore sailed west to avoid a looming storm off the English coast and watery graves.[57] From Sir Michael Geere's letters we can see just how far the ships were scattered. Writing from Ventry, over a hundred miles west of Kinsale, Geere wrote an account of Cadiz; the troops had been withdrawn too soon, and the survivors were dying horribly through disease and a lack of supplies on the ships.[58]

---

54 Sir William Leger to Buckingham 29 October 1625, CSPD 16/8/93.
55 Yuval Noah Harari, *Renaissance Military Memoirs: War, History and Identity, 1450–1600* (Woodbridge: Boydell and Brewer, 2004), p. 31.
56 Sir Edward Cecil to Sec Conway, 9 November 1625, CSPD 16/9/39.
57 Sir Thomas Love to Sec Conway, 11 December 1625, CSPD 16/11/48.
58 Sir Michael Geere to his son William Geere, 11 December 1625, CSPD 16/11/49.

Cecil was right to be anxious. In Plymouth, those officers who arrived sporadically through the winter storms were putting experiences of disaster to paper. Arriving in Plymouth in late December 1625, Sir William St. Leger wrote to Buckingham, defending the Duke's strategy as a brave business, but one pathetically performed by Cecil who lacked the abilities required of a general. In the 'Journal of the Expedition to Cadiz, written by someone who was in the division of the fleet which arrived at Plymouth this day', a chaotic retreat is fashioned into an action in which only a few individual gentlemen are acquitted. The logistical nightmare and the failure of judgement to let the men drink from captured vineyards resulted in slaughter: '100 of our Drunkards' were left behind to have their 'throats cut before they were sober'.[59] In this testimony, the heroes are the commanders of the rear-guard, Lord Essex, Colonel Harwood, Lord Valentia who fought outnumbered and undersupplied, especially Sir Thomas Morton who bravely halted the Spanish onslaught with a counterattack of pikemen.[60] Absent from this narrative of a brave few, blamed for a humiliation in foreign policy, and physically absent from Plymouth, Cecil's reputation was tarnished as an information shadow prevented his own account from crossing the Celtic Sea.

There is undoubtedly a multitude of information shadows throughout history. Yet the increased frequency of storms during the Grindelwald Fluctuation which coincided with both Europe's Wars of Religion and the rise of Europe's news networks, created more occasions when the pivotal news of battles, sieges, massacres, and the death of kings was delayed by information shadows. News of the death of the Swedish king Gustavus Adolphus at the Battle of Lützen in November 1632 was slowed by the same phenomenon. In the new year, John Russell composed an uncertain elegy 'immediately after the first rumours of his death' arrived.[61] Russell recorded a scene of confusion with conflicting reports of the fate of the Lion of the North circulating and still no authoritative conclusion drawn during a winter shadow: 'Sure he's not dead! Swethlands grief would roar/ And make their groans heard to our English shore'.[62] Almost paradoxically, though an event might be past and its outcomes uncertain, an information shadow fosters a sensation of contemporaneity,

---

59　Anon, 'Journal of the expedition to Cadiz, written by someone who was in the division of the fleet which arrived at Plymouth this day', 14 December 1625, PRO SP16/11/f.135.

60　Ibid., f.135.

61　John Russell, *An elegie upon the death of the most illustrious and victorious Prince Gustavus Adolphus King of Swethland &c. Composed immediately after the first rumours of his death, and now published and dedicated to the memoriall of so renouned a prince* (Cambridge: Thomas Buck and John Buck, 1633) (USTC 3017029), p. 1.

62　Ibid., p. 1.

what Brendan Dooley defines as 'participating in a shared present, of existing in a length of time called "now"', as contemporaries across Europe collected, discussed and debated uncertain, troublesome and momentous news.[63] The profound interplay between climate change and war during Europe's Wars of Religion serve as a key source of, and temporary obstacle to, the growth of early modern European news.

63 Brendan Dooley (ed.), *The Dissemination of News and the Emergence of Contemporaneity in Early Modern Europe* (Abingdon: Routledge, 2016), p. xiii.

SECTION 2

Natural Disasters

∴

CHAPTER 3

Troubling News Travels Fast

The Sannio Earthquake Ripples through the Spanish Monarchy

Alessandro Tuccillo

On the evening of 5 June 1688, the apostolic nuncio to the Kingdom of Naples, Giovanni Muti Papazzurri, must have been in a state of some distress.[1] This was not the consequence of one of the many intractable issues with which he was confronted as part of his important diplomatic role within the Spanish Monarchy, a post to which he had been appointed some six years earlier. Rather, there was a far more immediate and disturbing crisis to be faced. An earthquake had struck at 'twenty hours' Italic time, around half past three in the afternoon. Muti recounted the event in one of the regular despatches he sent to Cardinal Alderano Cybo in Rome, Pope Innocent XI's Secretary of State. We can imagine how terrified Muti must have been while composing the letter at his desk in the nunciature, a building that still stands today in the Via Toledo, albeit with its seventeenth-century baroque façade now replaced with one in the neoclassical style.[2] The tremors may have been brief but they were to cause significant damage, in particular to the Jesuit church. There was only slight damage to the nunciature, but a few nearby buildings collapsed entirely, causing multiple injuries and deaths. Along with the people of Naples, the nuncio understood the earthquake to be divine retribution, a case of *flagellum dei* whose effects could only be mitigated by pleading for God's mercy through public acts of penitence and confession.[3]

---

1 This work was supported by the DisComPoSE project (Disasters, Communication and Politics in Southwestern Europe), which has received funding from the European Research Council (ERC) under the European Union's Horizon 2020 research and innovation programme (grant no. 759829).
2 The Via Toledo is a key thoroughfare named after Viceroy Pedro Álvarez de Toledo y Zúñiga (1532–1553), who had it built as part of a vast urban redevelopment plan. On the urban history of Naples in the early modern age, see Giovanni Muto 'Urban Structures and Population' and Gaetana Cantone 'The City's Architecture' in Tommaso Astarita (ed.), *A Companion to Early Modern Naples* (Leiden-Boston: Brill, 2013), pp. 35–61, 331–358. On the architectural history of the nunciature, see Paola Zampa, 'Il palazzo della Nunziatura di Napoli: la fabbrica sistina e le trasformazioni del XVII e XIX secolo', in Maurizio Caperna & Gianfranco Spagnesi (eds.), *Architettura: processualità e trasformazione* (Rome: Bonsignori, 2002), pp. 393–402.
3 *Archivio Apostolico Vaticano* (AAV), *Segreteria di Stato, Napoli*, 103, letter from Muti to Cybo, Naples, 5 June 1688, cc. 420^r–420^v.

It is hardly surprising that news of the earthquake was communicated to Rome so quickly. Timely and reliable information was crucial to the exercise of political power, and there was much to report. For the effects of the earthquake were felt on many levels. Above all, there was the destruction of the city and other populated areas, with large numbers left dead or injured. There was also the destabilisation of society and its institutions. The imagined potential for social chaos within this environment generated as much fear as the actual material damage and loss of human life. That such troubling if exciting news of the earthquake would be widely reported within the political area of the Spanish Monarchy was to be expected in the circumstances.[4] Yet, interest in the event would spill out far beyond the political sphere, spreading throughout society itself, and straining that limited space available for open debate which existed under the *Ancien Régime*. News events have the capacity to resurrect and inflame conflicts between powerful individuals and groups.[5]

Much recent work has been devoted to the politics of information in early-modern Europe.[6] But research into news of disasters due to natural events such as earthquakes or volcanic eruptions has its own particular historiographical dynamic; it is a rich topic, and one especially well-suited to interdisciplinary investigation, from environmental and climate historical approaches, to methodologies employed across a range of different humanities and social sciences,

---

4 See Arndt Brendecke, *Imperio e información. Funciones del saber en el dominio colonial español* (Madrid-Frankfurt: Iberoamericana-Vervuert, 2012); S. Sellers-García, *Distance and Documents at the Spanish Empire's Periphery* (Stanford: Stanford University Press, 2013); Fernando Bouza, 'Entre archivos, despachos y noticias: (d)escribir la información en la edad moderna', *Cuadernos de Historia Moderna*, XLIV (2019), pp. 229–240; and Filippo De Vivo, 'Microhistories of long-distance information: space, movement and agency in the early modern news', *Past and Present*, 242 (2019), pp. 179–214.

5 See Massimo Rospocher (ed.), *Beyond the Public Sphere. Opinions, Publics, Spaces in Early Modern Europe* (Bologna: il Mulino, 2012) and Filippo De Vivo, *Patrizi, informatori, barbieri. Politica e comunicazione a Venezia nella prima età moderna* (Milan: Feltrinelli, 2012).

6 Brendan Dooley & Sabrina A. Baron (eds.), *The Politics of Information in Early Modern Europe* (London-New York: Routledge, 2001); Brendan Dooley (ed.), *The Dissemination of News and the Emergence of Contemporaneity in Early Modern Europe* (Farnham: Ashgate, 2010); Andrew Pettegree, *The Invention of News. How the World Came to Know about Itself* (New Haven-London: Yale University Press, 2014); Massimo Rospocher, 'L'invenzione delle notizie? Informazione e comunicazione nell'Europa moderna', *Storica*, 64 (2016), pp. 95–116; Id., 'Per una storia della comunicazione nella prima età moderna. Un bilancio storiografico', *Annali dell'Istituto storico italo-germanico in Trento*, 44 (2018), pp. 37–62. On disasters due to natural events see Carlos H. Caracciolo, '*Natural Disasters and the European Printed News Network*', in Joad Raymond, Noah Noxham (eds.), *News Networks in Early Modern Europe* (Leiden-Boston: Brill, 2016), pp. 756–778; Domenico Cecere (ed.), *Disastri naturali e informazione negli imperi d'età moderna, Studi storici*, 60, 4 (2019) and his *Calamità ambientali e risposte politiche nella Monarchia ispanica (secc. XVII–XVIII)*, *Mediterranea. Ricerche storiche*, 51 (2021).

such as: philology, synchronic and diachronic linguistics, the history of art, anthropology, sociology and economics.[7] Disasters and their social impact can and have been explored using a full range of evidence, from official state documents, to narrative accounts, and works of art.[8]

Adoption of methodologies and concepts borrowed from the social sciences has contributed to a cultural history of disasters that emphasises the way in which disasters have been represented within society.[9] This approach has led to a fresh examination of persistence, discontinuity, overlap and fusion in the history of human fear.[10] This approach has had the effect of blurring the seeming dichotomy implicit in the shift of interpreting disasters away from the earlier paradigm based on providentialism which understood disasters as the manifestation of the presence of God and an instrument with which to punish mankind, towards a naturalistic/rationalist paradigm where

---

7   With reference to the Spanish Monarchy, see Armando Alberola Romá (ed.), *Clima, naturaleza y desastre. España e Hispanoamérica durante la Edad Moderna* (Valencia: Publicaciones de la Universidad de Valencia, 2013); Armando Alberola Romá & Luis A. Arrioja Díaz Viruell (eds.), *Clima, desastres y convulsiones sociales en España e Hispanoamérica, siglos XVII–XX* (Alicante, Zamora: Publicaciones de la Universidad de Alicante, El Colegio de Michoacán, 2017); Armando Alberola Romá (ed.), *Riesgo, desastre y miedo en la península Ibérica y México durante la Edad Moderna* (Alicante, Zamora: Publicaciones de la Universidad de Alicante, El Colegio de Michoacán, 2017); Armando Alberola Romá & Virginia García Acosta (eds.), *La Pequeña Edad del Hielo a ambos lados del Atlántico. Episodios climáticos extremos, terremotos, erupciones volcánicas y crisis* (Alicante: Publicaciones de la Universidad de Alicante, 2021).

8   On narrative accounts, see in particular: René Favier, Anne-Marie Granet Abisset (eds.), *Récits et représentations des catastrophes depuis l'Antiquité* (Grenoble: CNRS, MSH-Alpes, 2005); Françoise Lavocat (ed.), *Pestes, Incendies, Naufrages. Écritures du désastre au dix-septième siècle* (Tournhout: Brepols, 2011); Françoise Lavocat, 'Narratives of Catastrophe in the Early Modern Period: Awareness of Historicity and Emergence of Interpretative Viewpoints', *Poetics Today*, XXXIII (2012), pp. 253–299; Domenico Cecere, Chiara De Caprio, Lorenza Gianfrancesco & Pasquale Palmieri (eds.), *Disaster Narratives in Early Modern Naples. Politics, Communication and Culture* (Rome: Viella, 2018); Gennaro Schiano, *Relatar la catástrofe en el siglo de oro. Entre noticia y narración* (Berlin: Lang, 2021). On works of art, see Marco Folin & Monica Preti (eds.), *Wounded Cities: The Representation of Urban Disasters in European Art (14th–20th Centuries)* (Leiden, Boston: Brill, 2015); Carmen Belmonte, Elisabetta Scirocco & Gerhard Wolf (eds.), *Storia dell'arte e catastrofi. Spazi, tempi, società* (Florence, Venice: Max-Planck-Institut für Kunstgeschichte, Marsilio, 2018).

9   Gaëlle Clavandier, *La mort collective. Pour une sociologie des catastrophes* (Paris: CNRS, 2004).

10 François Walter, *Catastrophes. Une histoire culturelle (XVIe–XXIe siècle)* (Paris: Seuil, 2008); Gerrit Jasper Schenk & Jens Ivo Engels (eds.), *Historical Disaster Research. Concepts, Methods and Case Studies*. Special issue of the *Historische Katastrophenforschung. Begriffe, Konzepte und Fallbeispiele / Historical Social Research*, 121 (2007), pp. 9–334.

such events could be attributed to natural causes that science could probe and test. The rift between the two positions emerged during the debate following the 1755 Lisbon earthquake, in which the incisive words of Voltaire's *Poème sur le désastre de Lisbonne* (1756) and *Candide* (1759) undermined the optimistic theodicy of Leibniz and Pope, as well as faith in the efficacy of devotional practices. The naturalistic/rationalist paradigm first found favour in the educated urban elite, and eventually became the only rational explanation of disasters.

The difference between the two interpretations and the paradigm shift resulting from the eighteenth-century debate remain relevant today to an understanding of the history of the relationship between human beings and the destructive forces of nature. However, cultural history approaches to disasters have shown that society's religious symbols, the irrational elements of how disasters are interpreted, persisted for quite some time. Today, the objectivity of the natural sciences is undoubtedly key to how disasters are managed and how their risk is mitigated. Nevertheless, this does not eliminate the influence of social or cultural attitudes as filters that make some risks more acceptable than others.[11] Moreover, the coexistence of the two paradigms within the same social context predated the eighteenth-century shift to rationalism. There were also different interpretations of providentialism across the *Ancien Régime*. For example, from the early modern age, the dichotomy between the naturalistic and the providentialist interpretation of earthquakes could be resolved by distinguishing between 'natural' earthquakes that were determined by nature and 'non-natural' ones that represented divine punishment of sin-ridden societies.[12]

Research undertaken over recent years no longer views disasters simply through the lens of natural event itself, but instead encompasses consideration of the effect of the event on a given society. The humanities and social sciences can work together with the natural sciences and engineering in the field of disaster studies.[13] This interdisciplinarity has firm foundations. In Italy, the National Institute of Geophysics and Volcanology (*Istituto Nazionale di Geofisica e Vulcanologia*—INGV) has undertaken historical research into earthquakes for decades, producing the *Catalogue of Strong Earthquakes in Italy*

---

11 Walter, *Catastrophes*.

12 Emanuela Guidoboni & Jean-Paul Poirier, *Quand la terre tremblait* (Paris: Jacob, 2004) and the more recent enlarged version in Italian *Storia culturale del terremoto dal mondo antico a oggi* (Soveria Mannelli: Rubettino, 2019).

13 See, for example, Ronald Perry & Enrico L. Quarantelli (eds.), *What is a Disaster? New Answers to Old Questions* (Bloomington: International Research Committee on Disasters, 2005).

(*Catalogo dei Forti Terremoti in Italia (461 a.C.–1997) e nell'area Mediterranea (760 a.C.–1500)*)), which covers more than 2,000 years; this contains an impressive amount of research data and research and tools which have been made available freely online.¹⁴

The *Catalogue* is also valuable for our case study, as it includes transcriptions of printed texts, archive documents, maps, as well as a wealth of information on the earthquake that the apostolic nuncio Muti experienced on 5 June 1688. The Catalogue estimates the earthquake's intensity in Naples to have been at level VIII on the Mercalli-Cancani-Sieberg (MCS) scale—a scale developed in in the first decades of the twentieth century to estimate the impact of an earthquake on people, the environment and on the Earth's surface. In fact, Naples was actually some 70 kilometres from the earthquake's epicentre in Sannio, where the towns of Cerreto Sannita, Civitella Licinio and Guardia Sanframondi were almost completely destroyed (level XI on the MCS scale); the cities of Benevento and Avellino also suffered extensive damage (levels IX and VIII–IX on the MCS scale respectively).¹⁵

The 1688 earthquake has been the subject of major recent research which has focused on two main elements: how the authorities of Naples handled the emergency, and on the dynamics of political communication and the dissemination of news.¹⁶ Domenico Cecere has proposed combing a cultural approach to the study of disasters with a socio-institutional approach that also takes social issues and the interests of a range of secular and religious bodies into account, focusing on communication, the dissemination of information and the emergency measures triggered by a disaster. In particular, in 1688, such bodies showed a very keen interest in publications such as *vere relationi* (true relations), poems and short accounts that filled the news market the day after the earthquake. These publications were often short and of poor quality, but they were formulated in a register that attracted readers interested in such an

---

14   Emanuela Guidoboni, Graziano Ferrari, Dante Mariotti, Alberto Comastri, Gabriele Tarabusi, Giulia Sgattoni & Gianluca Valensise (eds.), *Catalogo dei Forti Terremoti in Italia (461 a.C.-1997) e nell'area Mediterranea (760 a.C.-1500)*—*CFTI5Med* (Rome: The National Institute of Geophysics and Volcanology (INGV), 2018), doi: https://doi.org/10.6092/ingv.it-cfti5, http://storing.ingv.it/cfti/cfti5/; Id., 'CFTI5Med, the New Release of the Catalogue of Strong Earthquakes in Italy and in the Mediterranean Area', *Nature. Scientific Data*, 6/80 (2019), https://doi.org/10.1038/s41597-019-0091-9.

15   http://storing.ingv.it/cfti/cfti5/quake.php?01108IT#. A large part of the correspondence of the apostolic nuncio in Naples on the 1688 earthquake is reported and transcribed in the *Catalogue of Strong Earthquakes in Italy*. All the documents used or cited in this paper were consulted in the *Archivio Apostolico Vaticano*.

16   Gaia Bruno, 'Fronteggiare l'emergenza: le reazioni delle istituzioni del regno di Napoli di fronte ai sismi del XVII secolo', *Mediterranea. Ricerche storiche*, 51 (2021), pp. 119–150.

exceptional and sensational event. They could spread news of the damage sustained by the city of Naples and other populated areas, and of the responses of local people, as well as the secular and religious authorities. Viceroy Francisco de Benavides Dávila y Corella, conde de Santisteban and Archbishop Antonio Pignatelli were therefore eager to ensure that the news reports showed them in a good light. Managing the emergency was clearly not simply a case of suspending tax payments or organising acts of veneration. In the Kingdom of Naples, as elsewhere under the *Ancien Régime*, those who wielded political power paid very close attention to political messaging and to the elaboration of consensus-building strategies and tactics.[17]

Let us apply these methodologies in greater depth. Rather than focusing on the relationship between the authorities and those they governed, we can look at the internal correspondence of the different bodies tasked with managing the emergency resulting from the Sannio earthquake, and the disputes that arose between them. In particular, we will focus on the diplomatic correspondence between Cardinal Cybo, Pope Innocent XI's Secretary of State in Rome, and the apostolic nuncio Muti in Naples and his Madrid counterpart, Cardinal Marcello Durazzo. Muti's despatch of 5 June 1688 detailing the troubling news of the earthquake was the harbinger of a flood of information that spread from Naples to the seat of Christianity in Rome, and from there to the heart of the Spanish Monarchy in Madrid. Between 5 June and 31 August, Muti sent 42 despatches to Rome about the earthquake, some of which were transcriptions of *Avvisi*, hand-written or printed bulletins used to transmit news swiftly. Between 12 June and 7 August 1688, Secretary of State Cybo sent 7 despatches in reply to Muti's. Copies of letters and documents written by key figures in the Papal States were sometimes attached to the despatches sent from Rome. The exchanges between Rome and Madrid were fewer in number but just as intensive. Between 13 June and 19 September 1688, the earthquake was mentioned in 7 despatches sent by Cardinal Cybo to the nuncio Durazzo in Madrid,

---

17 Domenico Cecere, 'Informare e stupire. Racconti di calamità nella Napoli del XVII secolo', in Alfonso Tortora, Domenico Cassano, Sean Cocco (eds.), *L'Europa moderna e l'antico Vesuvio. Sull'identità scientifica italica tra I secoli XVII e XVIII* (Battipaglia: Laveglia & Carlone, 2017), pp. 63–67; Id., 'Moralising Pamphlets: Calamities, Information and Propaganda in Seventeenth-Century Naples', in Cecere, De Caprio, Gianfrancesco & Palmieri (eds.), *Disaster Narratives in Early Modern Naples*, pp. 129–145; Domenico Cecere,'"Subterranea conspiración". Terremoti, comunicazione e politica nella Monarchia di Carlo II', *Studi storici*, 60 (2019), pp. 811–843; Domenico Cecere, 'Dall'informazione alla gestione dell'emergenza. Una proposta per lo studio dei disastri in età moderna', *Storica*, 77 (2020), pp. 9–40.

who replied in 5 despatches that referred to the disaster between 8 July and 19 August.

The spread of information about the earthquake via the channels of the papal diplomatic service reveals an interesting aspect of the Church's approach to disasters. Documents reveal that the approach was not limited to attending to people's needs or undertaking charitable work. Bishops, religious orders, and to some extent even the lower ranks of the clergy were political agents in the full sense of the term, in that they could engage with secular authorities and thus affect the effectiveness of their actions. Their influence was particularly powerful in the Kingdom of Naples, which depended on the diplomatic network of the Papal States within the Spanish Monarchy, both in Naples and in Madrid.[18] The apostolic nuncios sent information to the Roman Curia and received instructions on how to respond politically. It might even be said that they wielded executive power over the diplomatic relations of the Papal States as well as over the coordination and organisation of the Church's activities, from the powerful dioceses of the capital cities, to rural areas, and even down to individual parishes.[19] Four main themes emerge from the surviving correspondence: the response of the Church to the earthquake; the funds provided to victims and for reconstruction work; the political and diplomatic pressure applied to abolishing a significant lottery (the *beneficiata*); and the disputes over the Church's prerogatives in the territories of the Spanish Monarchy. Examining these aspects sheds light on the political backdrop to the 1688 Sannio earthquake and, more generally, on the links between politics, religion and science in the management of disasters under the *Ancien Régime*.[20]

1 The Church's response: earthquakes as divine wrath

It took several days for news from remoter regions of the kingdom to reach Naples. It was only then that it became clear that the devastation extended well beyond the capital. This delay influenced very significantly how the disaster was perceived, especially in the first few days. The fact that Sannio was the epicentre appears to be of secondary importance in accounts of the earthquake, as they focused on Naples as the capital city and on its role in the

---

18 Maria Antonietta Visceglia, *Roma papale e la Spagna. Diplomatici, nobili e religiosi tra due corti* (Rome: Bulzoni, 2010).

19 Alexander Koller (ed.), *Kurie und Politik. Stand und Perspektiven der Nuntiaturberichtsforschung* (Tübingen: Niemeyer, 1998).

20 Andrea Janku, Gerrit Jasper Schenk & Franz Mauelshagen (eds.), *Historical Disasters in Context: Science, Religion, and Politics* (London: Routledge, 2012).

collection and propagation of news. It was seen primarily as a Naples earthquake. It was only on 19 June, some two weeks after the first tremors were felt, that Muti informed Cardinal Cybo that 'dire news' was beginning to emerge about other parts of the kingdom. There was widespread dismay at reports of 'extermination' in 'the wretched city of Benevento'.[21] This was, in fact, understandable, as Benevento was an enclave of the Papal States within the Kingdom of Naples, so its residents were expecting intervention from the Pope, not only as head of the Catholic Church but also as their highest political authority.

The Church's initial response to the emergency was primarily religious in nature. On 8 June, Muti provided Secretary of State Cybo with further details of the 'great fear and terror' felt throughout the city as it experienced aftershocks in the days following 5 June. He provided first-hand accounts of how the people of Naples were reacting, such as engaging in private and public prayer, holding processions, going to confession and taking Holy Communion in large numbers, including even 'those who had not done such things for a very long time'.[22] Similar accounts reached Cybo from Archbishop Pignatelli, bemoaning the fact that there were too few confessors to meet the requirements of the faithful, and rejoicing in the conversion of prostitutes and inveterate sinners reminiscent of events he had witnessed on the occasion of the eruption of Mount Vesuvius.[23]

These devotions were set against the backdrop of a providentialist view of disasters which saw the earthquake as divine wrath brought down on the people of Naples. Only pleading for mercy could bring the earthquake to an end and reduce the severity of its consequences. Cybo swiftly informed Pope Innocent XI, who expressed support for Muti and solidarity with all of the victims of the earthquake, noting his profound sadness at the news that he had wished never to hear of 'a divine scourge of such gravity', and his hope that 'mercy' had 'softened the blow' of the 'irate hand of God'. The Pope's greatest fear, which was shared by the general public, was that the abrupt deaths caused by the earthquake might have caught victims in a state of sin, thus condemning them to eternal damnation. This could only be addressed by pleading for 'Compassion and Clemency'.[24] This interpretation of the earthquake, including the emotions it generated, was reflected in the texts published

---

21 AAV, *Segreteria di Stato, Napoli*, 103, letter from Muti to Cybo, Naples, 19 June 1688, cc. 482^r–482^v.

22 Ivi, letter from Muti to Cybo, Naples, 8 June 1688, cc. 431^r–431^v.

23 AAV, *Segreteria di Stato, Cardinali*, 52, letter from Pignatelli to Cybo, Naples, 5 June 1688, cc. 173^r–174^r. Ivi, letter from Pignatelli to Cybo, Naples, 15 June 1688, cc. 194^r–195^r.

24 AAV, *Segreteria di Stato, Napoli*, 340, letter from Cybo to Muti, Rome, 12 June 1688, cc. 122^v–123^r.

immediately afterwards. Gennaro Sportelli's poem *Napoli flagellata da Dio* (Naples Flagellated by God), as well as the most significant of the *vere relationi* (true relations) of the earthquake—the *Vera e distinta relatione* of the publisher Domenico Parrino, which became almost the official account of the earthquake by political powers in Naples—expressed the hope that the 'innocent tears' of the people of Naples might 'calm the divine outrage expressed by so severe a punishment'.[25]

The foundations of this providentialist paradigm lie in the Old Testament, where earthquakes were a theophany of Yahweh, a manifestation of the presence of God to the Israelites. This divine source of earthquakes was not the only interpretation available. Aristotle's *Meteorology* postulated that pneuma, the 'vital breath' produced by the sun warming the earth, could accumulate not only on the surface of the earth but also below it. On the surface, it produced winds, while beneath the surface it produced tremors. This model persisted for over two millennia and became an intractable problem for Christianity, which vacillated between refuting and accepting it. Christianity's refutation of this interpretation prompted some of its apologists to see as heretical any theory that diminished the exclusive power of God as the source of earthquakes. This was formalised by Philastrius, Bishop of Brescia in the fourth century, who inserted *De terræ motu hæresis* in his *Liber de hæresibus*. This uncompromising adherence to the letter of the Bible was not an isolated event and was a key factor in doctrinal opposition to any interpretation based on natural phenomena.

Thomism subsequently influenced Catholic orthodoxy. Thomas Aquinas framed Aristotle's theory of subterranean winds as a hierarchy of causes where the forces of nature that caused disasters were derived from God, the first cause of everything. This became the cornerstone of the Christian interpretation not only of earthquakes but also of other disasters well into the modern age. This providentialist paradigm saw disasters as the *flagellum dei* inflicted on mankind to punish sinners and to warn of the dangers of perdition. This view was supplemented over the years by a different interpretation where disasters might be seen as the work of the Devil, or even as gifts from God. That is, God had in fact intervened to find good in evil, such as the destruction of a city, deaths, injuries, and so on, in order to assure people of eternal beatitude or to enhance the cosmos of the Creator, such as the emergence of mountains

---

25   *Napoli flagellata da Dio con l'horribilissimo terremoto accaduto a cinque di giugno* [...] *nell'anno 1688, composta in verso sdrucciolo dal dottor Gennaro Sportelli* (Naples: Francesco Benzi, 1688). *Vera e distinta relatione dell'horribile e spaventoso terremoto accaduto in Napoli & in più parti del Regno il giorno 5 giugno 1688* (Napoli: Domenico Antonio Parrino, 1688). Nuncio Muti attached a copy to his despatch to Cybo dated 29 June 1688: AAV, *Segreteria di Stato, Napoli* 103, cc. 509^r, 513^r–516^v.

or the increased fertility of fields after a volcanic eruption. Moreover, in the face of the innocence of some of the victims, and in order to evade the blasphemy of attributing injustice to divine intervention, the interpretation of disasters saw them as unfathomable events that transcended human reason and were understood by God alone.[26] This view was expressed clearly in the opening lines of the *Vera e distinta relatione* noted above. Earthquakes were the manifestation of the wrath of God, but it was futile to examine their causes further, as the 'mysteries of Divine Judication [...] cannot be penetrated by human intellect'.[27]

The Church's response to the emergency was to stoke this established providentialist interpretation of the exciting and troubling news through the activities of its clergy at all levels. Secretary of State Cybo received correspondence not only from the nuncios but also from bishops and cardinals, which made this information-gathering network much more extensive than the diplomatic network. This was already evident in the correspondence with Archbishop Pignatelli, but the letters he received from Vincenzo Maria Orsini, Archbishop of Benevento, are also illuminating. Orsini was a key figure in the religious mobilisation that was mounted in response to the Sannio earthquake. He had survived the disaster, attributing this to the intervention of St Filippo Neri. He recounted the event in a well-received pamphlet that laid the foundation of Filippo Neri's canonisation as a saint who could offer protection against earthquakes.[28] There was also the direct intervention of Pope Innocent XI, who granted a plenary indulgence to all repentant victims of the earthquake, an event that Archbishop Pignatelli rejoiced over in a letter to Cybo.[29]

---

26 Guidoboni, Poirier, *Storia culturale del terremoto*. See also Christian Rohr, 'Writing a Catastrophe: Describing and Constructing Disaster Perception in Narrative Sources from the Late Middle Ages', *Historical Social Research*, 32/3 (2007), pp. 88–102; Gerrit Jasper Schenk, 'Dis-astri. Modelli interpretativi delle calamità naturali dal Medioevo al Rinascimento', in Michael Matheus, Gabriella Piccinni, Giuliano Pinto & Gian Maria Varanini (eds.), *Le calamità ambientali nel tardo Medioevo europeo. Realtà, percezioni, reazioni* (Florence: Firenze University Press, 2010), pp. 23–75.

27 *Vera e distinta relatione*.

28 *Narrazione de' prodigii operati dal glorioso S. Filippo Neri nella persona dell'Eminent. Sig. Cardinale Orsini arcivescovo di Benevento. In occasione, che rimase sotto le rovine delle sue stanze nel tremuoto, che distrusse quella città a' 5 di giugno 1688* (Naples: de Bonis, 1688). Muti attached this work to a despatch sent to Cybo dated 3 July 1688: AAV, *Segreteria di Stato, Napoli*, 104, letter from Muti to Cybo, Naples, 3 July 1688, c. 4. On Orsini's experience and the veneration of St Filippo Neri as protector against earthquakes, see Monica Azzolini, 'Coping with Catastrophe. St Filippo Neri as Patron Saint of Earthquakes', *Quaderni storici*, 156 (2017), pp. 727–750.

29 AAV, *Segreteria di Stato, Cardinali*, 52, letter from Pignatelli to Cybo, Naples, 19 June 1688, cc. 196^r-197^r. This letter also contains Pignatelli's account of Orsini's arrival in Naples and refers to St Filippo Neri's miraculous intercession.

The Papal States, a political body that mirrored and complemented the structure of the Church, was the driving force of these activities. In particular, the role of the representative of the Papal States in Naples was crucial to formulating the Church's religious and political response to the earthquake emergency. Muti supported the archbishop and the acts of veneration, for example by making Saint Michael the Archangel the patron and protector of Naples, in line with the wishes of the city's civil bodies, ensuring that his activities showed the Church's solidarity with the people and their torment.[30] The requirement to show solidarity made the nuncio a direct vehicle for the Pope's interventions and those of the Roman Curia, as clearly demonstrated by the financial assistance provided to the victims and the conflicts with the political authorities of the Spanish Monarchy. It is at this political level that we see the emergence of a more complex situation lurking beneath the generalisation of the disaster as a manifestation of the power of divine retribution. The providentialist paradigm was predicated on cause and effect, with its scope limited to appeals for mercy. However, it could be forged into a more flexible tool to wield power.

2   Financial Support and Reconstruction Work

On 26 June 1688, Muti notified Cybo that he had received an instruction from the treasurer of the Papal States to send two thousand ducats to the governor of Benevento. Pope Innocent XI had earmarked these funds to alleviate the 'suffering of these his subjects'. The nuncio arranged with the governor that the funds would be provided in cash. The two thousand ducats were consigned into the hands of trusted men who were accompanied by armed horsemen 'who served to protect the money en route', as there were evident dangers along the 70-kilometre journey from Naples to Benevento.[31] The nuncio had become a key post-earthquake figure in the running of Benevento, which was part of the Papal States. Reconstruction was the primary responsibility of the governor, but the role of the nuncio allowed Rome to intervene and to control events on the ground. For example, Muti not only transferred the two thousand ducats, but also sent an emissary to report on the damage sustained by the Santa Sofia abbey in Benevento in order to plan reconstruction work.[32] Moreover, the governor received assistance from the nuncio in terms of the relationship

---

30   AAV, *Segreteria di Stato, Napoli*, 104, letter from Muti to Cybo, Naples, 23 October 1688, cc. 299^r–301^r.
31   AAV, *Segreteria di Stato, Napoli*, 103, letter from Muti to Cybo, Naples, 26 June 1688, cc. 503^r–504^r.
32   Ivi, letter from Muti to Cybo, Naples, 24 June 1688, cc. 491^r–492^r. Damage to the abbey is mentioned frequently in subsequent correspondence between Muti and Cybo.

with the Kingdom of Naples. Apparently minor issues such as authorisations to gather firewood in woods beyond the enclave became even more important after the earthquake.[33]

The nuncio also took steps to safeguard the Benevento pig fair against the potential threat of a rival fair to be held at Atripalda, a town within the Kingdom of Naples some 30 kilometres from Benevento. The Atripalda fair had the support of the 'prince of Avellino', on the grounds that the damage caused by the earthquake would not allow the traditional Benevento fair to take place.[34] The pressure exerted by Muti on the viceroy to cancel the Atripalda fair was successful, also because it emerged that the required authorisations had not been obtained. However, the arguments used by the nuncio were even more interesting than the outcome. If the Atripalda fair had taken place, the fiefs of the 'prince of Avellino' would no longer be beneficiaries of the funds that Innocent XI had allocated to 'the most needy and wretched of the poor people who had endured' the earthquake.[35] This is evidence that financial relief was not being provided by the Pope exclusively to the residents of Benevento as subjects of the Papal States. The considerable sum of fifty thousand ducats had been allocated for distribution also in affected areas that were part of the Kingdom of Naples.[36]

Muti was assigned the task of delivering the funds to Archbishop Pignatelli, who would then distribute them to the victims. The importance and political significance of an intervention of this nature is clear, as it would have demonstrated that the activities of the Church were not limited to a religious response to the earthquake. In a matter of weeks, the Naples nunciature received a flood of imploring letters from the dioceses and parishes of the devastated areas. The letters detailed the damage sustained by Church properties and the needs of the local people. Similar letters were also sent to the episcopal palace and to the Curia in Rome, and they became a valuable compendium of information

---

33 AAV, *Segreteria di Stato, Napoli*, 340, letter from Cybo to Muti, Rome, 24 July 1688, cc. 133^v–137^r; Ivi, 104, letter from Cybo to Muti, Naples, 27 July 1688, cc. 82^r-83^r, 7 August 1688, cc. 112^r–112^v, 31 August 1688, c. 159^r.

34 The matter was raised by Cybo in his despatch of 17 July, and troubled Muti for some time: AAV, *Segreteria di Stato, Napoli*, 340, letter from Cybo to Muti, Rome, 17 July 1688, cc. 127^v–128^r.

35 AAV, *Segreteria di Stato, Napoli*, 104, letter from Cybo to Muti, Naples, 20 July 1688, cc. 51^r–51^v. The 'prince of Avellino' that Muti refers to is probably Marino III Caracciolo, fifth prince of Avellino (1668–1720).

36 Cybo tells Muti of the allocation of fifty thousand ducats in his despatch of 26 June: AAV, *Segreteria di Stato, Napoli*, 340, letter from Cybo to Muti, Rome, 26 June 1688, cc. 125^r–125^v.

that laid the foundations for planning the Church's economic response to the disaster.[37]

3 Diplomatic pressure to abolish the *beneficiata*

The exciting and troubling news of the Sannio earthquake had further consequences. A controversy arose over a lottery introduced in Naples in 1682, known as the *beneficiata*. This type of lottery first appeared in Genoa in 1644, with 5 numbers being drawn from a pool of 80 or 90 numbers and prizes going to those who matched 1, 2 or 3 numbers.[38] The lottery attracted the moral and religious condemnation of the Church, in line with its stance on all forms of gambling. Thomism held that games of chance were to be condemned as they were motivated by greed and led to vice and sinning. However, the lottery based on the Genoa model had turned out to be an excellent source of revenue for the public purse. It was therefore introduced in several Italian cities, including Naples, at the end of the seventeenth century. The lottery was made morally acceptable by linking it to charitable work. In Naples, each of the 90 numbers was assigned to an impoverished damsel who received a sum based on total receipts if her number was drawn.

The importance of the *beneficiata* was noted from the earliest despatches exchanged between Muti and Cybo on the 1688 Sannio earthquake. The attention it merited might seem curious or anecdotal, but it was in fact a particularly delicate matter and clearly pertinent to the earthquake. Rumours spread in Naples about a link between the *beneficiata* and sinning in general, and superstitious, magical or even satanic practices. It was said that people would sometimes worship the head of a demon in order to guess winning numbers. The divine retribution represented by the earthquake might therefore actually have been prompted by the *beneficiata*. The longstanding religious and moral condemnation of gambling was thus integrated into the providentialist

---

37   This 'bureaucratic' approach is in sharp contrast to how earlier disasters were managed, such as the 1631 eruption of Mount Vesuvius or the 1656 plague, where the Church's activities were mainly religious and devotional in nature. These changes, which did not, however, diminish the predominance of the providentialist view of the 1688 Sannio earthquake, are discussed in Pierroberto Scaramella, 'Chiesa e terremoto. Le reazioni ecclesiastiche al sisma del 1688 in Campania', *Campania sacra*, 23 (1992), pp. 229–274, a paper that includes a substantial appendix of transcriptions of letters written by Muti, and by cardinals and bishops, which are preserved in the Vatican Apostolic Archive, extracts from some of which have been cited in this chapter after consulting the original manuscripts.

38   Giovanni Assereto, *Un giuoco così utile ai pubblici introiti. Il lotto di Genova dal XVI al XVIII secolo* (Treviso, Rome: Fondazione Benetton, Viella, 2013).

interpretation of the earthquake. This view was held not only by the clergy and the Roman Curia; the causal relationship between the *beneficiata* and the earthquake was also beginning to gain ground amongst the general public. Although the viceroy did not share this view, he also saw the abolition of the lottery as a valuable move, in concert with the *Consiglio Collaterale*, the council with political and juridical powers that assisted the viceroy in the exercise of his responsibilities. Muti and Cybo also favoured its abolition. However, this required the approval of king Charles II. Moreover, Madrid would have had to cover the consequent losses to the public purse.

In the summer of 1688, the issue of whether to abolish the *beneficiata* in Naples was deliberated in Madrid at the highest political levels of the Spanish Monarchy, at two sessions of the *Consejo de Estado* and one of the *Consejo de Italia*. The diplomatic pressure applied by Cardinal Marcello Durazzo, the apostolic nuncio to Madrid, was decisive. One of his memoranda was in fact considered at the session of the *Consejo de Italia* that decided that the *beneficiata* should be abolished. This completed the success of the Church's intervention. The lottery was only reintroduced in 1712, a few years after the Kingdom of Naples had passed into the domain of Austria. The providentialist position had served as an effective political tool, but its objectives were only achieved when there was substantial harmony between secular and religious authorities. Indeed, the political authorities in Naples and Madrid accepted, albeit with some vacillation, that the *beneficiata* had led to the earthquake, and above all saw as valuable the abolition of a game of chance that was associated with behaviours and practices that had already disrupted social order in Naples well before the emergency.[39]

4   The Conflict between Church and State in the Spanish Monarchy

The final issue that emerges from the diplomatic correspondence of the day, in particular that between the Secretary of State and the Madrid nuncio, concerns the efforts of papal diplomacy to exploit the Naples earthquake to revive the old issue of the Spanish Monarchy's interference in the affairs of the Church. Prompted by Secretary of State Cybo, the nuncios implied that the earthquake

---

[39] For a more detailed account of the complex matter of the abolition of the *beneficiata*, based on sources in the Vatican archives, Simancas and Naples archives, see Alessandro Tuccillo, 'Abolire il gioco per placare l'ira divina. La diplomazia pontificia e il terremoto del 1688 a Napoli', *Mediterranea. Ricerche storiche*, 51 (2021), pp. 181–206.

was a manifestation of divine wrath at how the Church's prerogatives had been diluted by the king and his ministers.

This was about the rights of the royal rulers to nominate bishops and other Church authorities, and about the activities of the Spanish Inquisition. For Pope Innocent XI and the Roman Curia, the Sannio earthquake and other calamities were a clear demonstration of divine wrath at how the Church had been treated by the rulers of the Spanish Monarchy. The calamities cited were the revolt in Catalonia, the corsair attacks in the Caribbean, the Barbary threat in the Mediterranean and the 1687 Lima earthquake. To placate this divine wrath, a request was made to abolish the authority of the Spanish Monarchy over ecclesiastical matters in the Kingdom of Sicily as wielded by the *Regia Monarchia*.[40] This court of law, which had been formed in the sixteenth century under Philip II, drew its legitimacy from the medieval privileges granted by the Pope to the King of Sicily. The *Regia Monarchia* was a problem for the autonomy of the Church as its powers stretched to being able to examine cases that had been adjudicated by ecclesiastical courts, as well as to suspend or even annul ecclesiastical censure and excommunication. Despite the strong links between the Catholic Church and the Spanish Monarchy, and the pervasive presence of the clergy in state bodies, the specifics of the situation in Sicily made it an enduring jurisdictional dispute.[41]

This attempt to exploit the earthquake and other crises was consistent with the overall political agenda of Innocent XI's pontificate and its focus on the defence of papal jurisdiction. The issue of the *Regia Monarchia* weighed heavily on the enduring dispute between the Holy See and the *Monarquía*.[42] In 1687, the dispute even led to the excommunication (later withdrawn) of the officials in charge of defending their prerogatives. A year later, the Sannio

---

40   AAV, *Segreteria di Stato, Spagna*, 357, letter from Cybo to Durazzo, Rome, 13 June 1688, cc. 343v–344v and Rome, 5 September 1688, cc. 382v–383v.

41   José Martínez Millán, Manuel Rivero Rodríguez, Gloria Alonso de la Higuera, Koldo Trápaga Monchet & Javier Revilla Canora (eds.), 'La doble lealtad: entre el servicio al Rey y la obligación a la Iglesia', *Revista libro de las Cort.es*, 6 (2014); Elisa Novi Chavarria (ed.), 'Ecclesiastici al servizio del Re tra Italia e Spagna (secc. XVI–XVII)', in *Dimensioni e problemi della ricerca storica*, 2 (2015); R. Valladares (ed.), *La Iglesia en Palacio. Los eclesiásticos en las cortes hispánicas (siglos XVI–XVII)* (Rome: Viella, 2019). Maria Teresa Napoli, *La Regia Monarchia di Sicilia. 'Ponere falcem in alienam messem'* (Naples: Jovene, 2012); Fabrizio D'Avenia, *La Chiesa del re. Monarchia e Papato nella Sicilia Spagnola (secc. XVI–XVII)* (Rome: Carocci, 2015); Daniele Palermo, 'Nel gioco delle giurisdizioni: il Tribunale della Regia Monarchia di Sicilia nel XVII secolo', *Mediterranea. Ricerche storiche*, 50 (2020), pp. 697–716.

42   Maria Antonietta Visceglia, 'Convergencias y conflictos. La Monarquía católica y la Santa sede (siglos XVI–XVIII)', *Studia historica. Historia moderna*, 26 (2004), pp. 155–190.

earthquake became an opportunity to revive the demand to abolish this old privilege, as the wrath of God had come down on the Spanish Monarchy as a result of the violations it had committed against the Church. This diplomatic papal initiative did not end well. The king's ministers simply declared that they would, in general, respect the Church and the clergy, but the powers of the *Regia Monarchia* would remain intact in Sicily.[43] This led to several further crises in the eighteenth century.

In 1688, therefore, the providentialist position had served to abolish the *beneficiata* lottery, but was ineffective in making substantial changes to the balance of power between State and Church in the Spanish Monarchy. Irrespective of the outcomes of the Church's endeavours, what emerges from this case study is the relevance of disasters to historical research. The troubling news of the Sannio earthquake captured by Muti in Naples on the evening of 5 June 1688 offers a powerful insight into how emergencies were handled in Naples, Rome and Madrid, with consequences for the enduring unresolved issues between the Church and the Spanish Monarchy. Research into other disasters may shed further light on such matters.

---

43   AAV, *Segreteria di Stato, Spagna*, 167, letter from Durazzo to Cybo, Madrid, 19 August 1688, cc. 532^r-533^r.

CHAPTER 4

Narratives and Media Ecology of the "Revolutions" of Naples of 1647–48

Davide Boerio and Luca Marangolo

This chapter is an account of the media ecology surrounding the Neapolitan revolution of 1647–1648.[1] This event had strong political resonance throughout Europe and led to a significant change in the perceived relationship between the rulers and the ruled within the *Ancien Régime*, shifting the paradigm of media communication from crossmedia to transmedia. The revolution was the result of a concatenation of political, social, economic, institutional, and natural crises that spanned the seventeenth century and found its most tangible manifestation in the transformation of the public sphere or, in other words, in the complex narrative articulations of the event within the contemporary media ecology.[2]

Evaluating this moment's historical implications requires consideration of the communications system as a whole, as well as how that system influenced perceptions of the revolution. In the first part of our chapter, we offer an analysis of the *crossmedia* system of communication of the Kingdom of Naples. By providing a model of the development of the public sphere, we examine how the contemporary news network experienced the revolutionary events as a shock, and how the media system reacted to the resultant social changes. We define crossmedia communication as a top-down form of message

---

[1] This paper is the result of dialogue between different perspectives on the same problem. The first part on crossmedia narrative was written by Luca Marangolo; the second, on the riddle of revolutions and rise of trasmediality, by Davide Boerio. The introduction and the conclusions were co-authored. On the Neapolitan revolution, see Rosario Villari's *Un sogno di libertà. Napoli nel declino di un impero 1585–1648* (Milan: Mondadori, 2012) and *La rivolta antispagnola a Napoli. Le origini (1585–1648)* (Rome-Bari: Laterza, 1967). For the English version see *The Revolt of Naples* (London: Polity Press, 1993). See too Alain Hugon, *Naples insurgée. 1647–1648. De l'événement à la mémoire* (Rennes: Presses universitaires de Rennes, 2011); Francesco Benigno, *Mirrors of revolutions: conflict and political identity in early modern Europe* (Turnhout: Brepols, 2010), pp. 233–324; Giuseppe Galasso, *Storia del Regno di Napoli*, vol. III, *Il Mezzogiorno spagnolo e austriaco, 1622–1734* (Turin: UTET, 2005–2006); and Aurelio Musi, *La rivolta di Masaniello sulla scena politica barocca* (Naples: Guida, 1989).

[2] Geoffrey Parker, *Global crisis: war, climate change and catastrophe in the seventeenth century* (New Haven: Yale University Press, 2013).

transmission that tends to bring all channels of communication into line with a similar world view. Events were framed and codified as a crisis. The second part of this chapter takes a *transmedia* approach, exploring the long-term impact of the revolution on the media system. It analyses elements such as media cross-fertilisation, by exploring visual and textual networks within their historical context. The event gave rise to a diversity of media forms such as letters, dispatches, handwritten newssheets, printed gazettes, pamphlets, diaries, histories, chronicles, proclamations, engravings, drawings, portraits, medals, poems, and songs, which reached regional, national, and transnational audiences.[3] The revolution produced a multiplicity of viewpoints not only of actors on the ground but also of distant observers. The event was riven by a constant interchange between the historical experience and the mediatization process. This section deals with the communicative and symbolic dimension of the Neapolitan revolution of 1647–1648, while questioning the discursive canon through which the story has been handed down from one generation to the next. Such an inquiry involves comparing and problematising a heterogenous and wide-ranging corpus of sources produced both *in medias res* and *ex post facto*. If structural causes have a decisive influence on the outbreak of revolutions, both individual deeds and collective choices will contribute to the outcome. Here we will provide a detailed account of some of the most interesting cases of mediatic communication during the revolutionary period, showing how the writers, empowered by the contemporary evolution of the news media, produced a new point of view on the events, questioning a single, traditional political interpretation.

1 Crossmedia Narrative and The Emergence of the Public Sphere

This part of our chapter confronts the classic conception of the transformation of the public sphere, conceived by Jürgen Habermas *via* Reinhardt Koselleck, with a more media-aware conception of such a transformation. The traditional interpretation does not address many historiographical problems. Indeed, while in the background the emergence of the public sphere and freedom of opinion, *à la* Habermas, is a subject which looms large, the way in which the media amplifies a ground-breaking event such as the Neapolitan revolution of 1647–1648 in altering the communicative paradigm still has not received due

---

3   Davide Boerio, 'Texts, publics, and networks of the Neapolitan Revolution of 1647–1648', *Histoire et civilisation du livre. Revue internationale*, 14 (2018), pp. 218–219.

weight.[4] Here we propose to revise the dialogic approach of Habermas and his school for this purpose; events such as those which occurred in Naples and in the *Mezzogiorno* in 1647–1648 ought to be viewed from the perspective of their mediatic resonance as well as their impact on innovations in the media system and in political communication.

This is a key analytical point to understand how the *avvisi* network reacted to unprecedented events; they expressed a worldview that appeared to be universal.[5] In fact our thesis is that the consequences of the revolutions were reflected with difficulty by the crossmedia forms of communication in Naples, and that they might be better understood if we turn to what is, according to Luhmann, a nondialogic form of communication. In fact, not having the ability to include the unprecedented political events of the revolution, the crossmedia system registered it as an undecipherable complexity not easy to be elaborated, something that fell beyond its conceptual framework.[6]

The interaction between innovative forms of communication used during the Neapolitan events of 1647–1648 created a strong influence between different environments of communication. Far from interacting with each other in a dialogical way, these forms of communication interfered with each other, which in turn opened up the possibility of transformation and evolution of the political system. As has been noted recently, the evolutionary process that outlines the affirmation of the "new" bourgeois discursiveness, inevitably brings us back to the picture elaborated by Koselleck, and shared by Jürgen Habermas, falling in an analogous theoretical domain.[7] The urban spaces in which Habermas situates the progressive emergence of the public sphere are not properly political gathering spaces, such as squares or public market places, but rather milieux of intellectual elaboration and cultural exchange such as private salons and coffee houses. If this traditional model tends to exclude any form of direct political conflict in favour of a more cultural, dialectical, and rather quiet evolution, it does not properly account for the political changes that *produced* the change in question. This transition may

---

4   Jürgen Habermas, *The Structural Transformation of the Public Sphere: An Inquiry into a category of Bourgeois Society*, (Cambridge: Polity, 1989), see in particular 'On the genesis of the public sphere', pp. 14–21.

5   This is, of course, if we define crossmedia as a single message (and its implied worldview) that occupies all public space, by analogy with the contemporary sense of the word, which uses it to identify the practice of communicating the same content across different communication means.

6   Grom Harste, *The Habermas-Luhmann debate* (New York: Columbia University Press, 2021), p. 22.

7   M. Rospocher, 'La voce della piazza. Oralità e spazio pubblico nell'Italia del Rinascimento', in M. Rospocher (ed.), *Oltre la sfera pubblica* (Bologna: Il Mulino, 2020), pp. 77–91.

be better understood in all its complications and contradictions if we change the heuristic paradigm from the dialogical and dialectical vision, to a more media-based emergence of the public sphere; if by "media" we mean not just a way of *spreading* information, but rather, following Niklas Luhmann, a way of *representing* it. Andreas Gestrich has tried to elaborate a model of the public sphere from this standpoint:

> There is (…) also a large-scale society, or, to use Luhmann's words, the generalized exterior of all functional systems, which forms their environment. (…) It is in this exterior that Luhmann placed a general public sphere (*Öffentlichkeit*). This is, for the German sociologist, the "intrasocial environment", potentially open to all subsystems and arguments.[8]

In Luhmann's view the evolution of the public sphere might not simply be a dialogical process by which the social system enriches itself by the dialectical opposition of different points of view which seem more and more radically critical of the dominant *doxa*, but rather a more *complex* and problematic mutual observation between forms of self-referential systems which have to learn how to *represent* each other, as what appears distant from their mediatic domain seems indecipherable. In this theoretical framework, there is a word to define the way social systems represent both what is internal in the self-referential perspective of the social systems and what is outside it. As Claudio Beraldi pointedly characterises it:

> in Old-European cosmology, the world was conceived as an aggregate consisting of the set of visible and invisible things (*universitas rerum* or *aggregatio corporum*). In the functional differentiated society this concept loses reference to "things" and instead refers to the indeterminacy of meaning … Against this background, the world can be grasped as the ultimate horizon, that transcends all … the dimensions of meaning, as well as a formless correlate of the operations that are carried out in it.[9]

The mediasphere, or the media environment is rather an *aggregation* of known and unknown things, seen and represented from a specific point of

---

8 A. Gestrich, 'Lo stato premoderno e l'ascesa della sfera pubblica. Un approccio fondato sulla teoria dei sistemi', in M. Rospocher (ed.), *Oltre la sfera pubblica*, p. 312. The translation is by Luca Marangolo.
9 C. Beraldi 'World (Welt)', in C. Beraldi, E. Esposito, G. Corsi (eds.), trans. by K. Walker, *Unlocking Luhmann, a keyword introduction to systems theory* (Bielefeld: Bielefeld University press, 2021), p. 253.

view. Information, coherently, is not something that is simply transmitted, but is rather a *representation* of things of the outside world by instruments specifically belonging to a social system in a particular moment that are stimulated by external impulses of the environment.[10]

Our standpoint is that this critical approach to the progressively evolving conception of the world (*Welt*) is, indeed, *per* Luhmann's media conception, extensible to all the other systems of communication, and that the evolution of the public sphere is, therefore, a progressive mediatization of what is known as "complexity" in Luhmann's terms, that is something that interferes with our natural, typical and self-referential representation of the world, as our vision of it interferes with new environment *stimuli*, such as political turmoil, in a paradigm that diverges from a dialogical model of the evolution of the public sphere. From this standpoint, which prefers a vision of the public sphere unfolding as a progressive elaboration of complexity, we could see also the paradigm shift from crossmedia to transmediality.

This interference impacts a crossmedia world view with regard to the narrative surrounding the historical events of great consequence that took place in the city and Kingdom of Naples in 1647–1648. These major traumatic events had significant cultural effects on contemporary society. In order to explain how the transmedia narrative of the Neapolitan uprisings can illustrate some of the limits of Habermasian public sphere theory, we can look at news reports from networks across Europe, characterised as they were by a stilted, almost procedural prose. This can be seen, for example, in the following extract taken from the accounts produced in Naples the day before the outbreak of the revolution:

---

10   A good epistemological case study of the evolution of the social system is, for example, the progress of cartography. It is an historical fact that cartography, between the sixteenth and seventeenth centuries, was moving progressively, as Giorgio Mangani has written, from 'the myth of Hercules' to the 'myth of Atlas'; that is from the idea of the feudal state, similar to a "collection" of territories, to another more organic and structured model, which reveals some characters of the modern nation state. The ways Mercator revolutionised cartographic production, not only from the technical and projective point of view, show this same passage, in which the new political power builds an organic synthesis of morality, science and religion, deeply modifying the power of the state, and making use of the representation and the geographical/astronomic knowledge as 'divine sciences'. See G. Mangani, *'Nation and Collection, Hercules, Atlas and the Origin of Modern State'* in *Geotema*, 58 (2018), pp. 25–58. For the epistemological value of the Mercator revolution, see also John Brian Harley, *The new nature of maps. Essays in the History of Cartography*, Paul Laxton (ed.) (Baltimore and London: The Johns Hopkins University Press, 2001).

> After the celebration of the procession of the Daughters of Santissima Annunziata, the persons assigned to the government of that Holy House, and elected to the new government of the present year Sigr. Don Fabrizio Silva, with others of the People, all wealthy persons, and among theme mr. Felice Basile, who the day of his nomination, donated thirty proposed wooden pipes to this Holy House ...[11]

This form of prose conforms to the typical representation of semi-public figures and tended to present a heavily standardised perspective of events. In a dialogical conception of the public sphere, the evolution of the public social system—in a Habermasian sense of the word—would be simply a confrontation between critical notions of the socio-political events, in a process that progressively evolves into a bourgeois system. From a Luhmaniann standpoint, the evolution of the public sphere is rather a progressive elaboration of complexity, as different representations of the world enter the picture:

> On Tuesday with another ban that ordered again to all the soldiers to retire to their own places, that no one should have been bothered, under pain of death, since the People wanted to reach an agreement with the Viceroy, that [order] would have been followed if another unpredictable event did not bewilder it, and it was that in Piazza del Mercato where the Archbishop was dealing with the new Head of the People, a group of armed people started shooting suddenly many arquebus shots while crying 'kill, kill'.[12]

---

11   'Dopo la celebrazione della processione delle figliole della Santissima Annunziata, riunitesi quei Deputati al governo di quella Santa Casa, elessero al nuovo governo del presente anno il Sigr. Don Fabrizio di Silva, con altri del Popolo, tutte persone facoltose, e fra questi il sig. Felice Basile, che nel giorno della suo possesso donò con larga mano all'Ospidali di detta santa casa proposta 30 canne di legno ...'; Biblioteca Apostolica Vaticana, Ottoboniani Latini, Ms. 2449, pt. 3, Avvisi from Naples 6 July 1647, f. 522^r.

12   'Martedì con altro bando che di nuovo ordinava che le soldatesche tutte si ritirassero ai loro Posti che non desse fastidio a nissono sotto pena della vita, volendo quel Popolo aggiustarsi col Sig. Viceré che sarebbe seguito se un impensato accidente non gli havesse sconcertato, e fu che capitando questa mattina all'improvviso nella Piazza del Marcato dove stava trattando il Cardinale Arcivescovo col nuovo Capo del Popolo l'aggiustamento di una quantità di huomini armati cominciarono subito a sparare diverse archibugiate gridando ammazza, ammazza'; Archivio di Stato di Firenze, Mediceo del Principato, Filza 4146, Avvisi from Naples from 7 to 16 July 1647, f. 237^r.

The lack of a ritual organisation in the distribution of the information makes it clear that this form of communication is different from the documentary description shown above. The problem was not so much at a semantic or syntactic level, but rather at a referential one. The concatenation of revolutionary events lay, at least partially, outside the world picture of the one who was narrating them. What is more, one could argue that the correlative conjunctions that are introduced with the word *che* [that] or with gerunds represent a desire to present the events in a non-static fashion. This is, therefore, indicative of a narrative exigency, in line with the narrative characteristics defined by the narratologist David Herman, in spite of the fact that the writer does not yet have full command of this new communicative language.[13] This is most clearly shown by the use of the term 'e fu' [and it was] to stress the imbalance between the two parts of the world in flux, that prior to the start of the rebellion and that after. We would seem to be dealing with a desire on the part of the author to describe the event by employing particular narrative skills, but without having fully developed the narrative culture necessary to do so. It can be synthesised in the cognitive function that David Herman calls *worldmaking/world disruption*: the world of the characters must constantly be reconstructed as it gradually becomes more complex, that is as it gradually diverges from being simply an abstraction of the medieval public sphere, as found in the first news report cited above. Herman correlates, indeed, this kind of instability in narrating an event, to the non-canonicity of the event itself.

We can look at further examples:

> The aforementioned Masaniello having begun to know his strength, being obeyed by all the people at such a beginning sign of zealous and humble that he was to become proud, even despising the same Don Giulio Gienovino who had put him in that position not wanting any more advice, not even by the elect of the people governing himself according to his whim, going through the city alone and with a few others, running furiously stopping carriages and other people to render him obedience with harsh words, by issuing bans on disproportionate things, and immediately having the heads cut off by many at the simple lawsuit that was brought in loud voice with new gallows raised in very many places gossiping as a drunkard, of the Cardinal, of the Viceroy, and of the Pope.[14]

---

13   D. Herman, *Basic Elements of Narrative* (Hoboken: Wiley-Blackwell, 2009), pp. 133–136.
14   'Il sudetti Masaniello havendo cominciato a conoscere la sua forza essendo da tutto il Popolo obbedito ad un tal cenno cominciato di zelante, et humile ch'era adiventarsuperbo, disprezzando anco il medesimo D. Giulio Gienovino che l'haveva messo in quel posto non

The repetiton of various gerundive forms here, such as havendo ("having"), despising "disprezzando", volendo ("willing"), in an unnatural and rhythmic fashion, suggests how the linear interpretation of facts by the reader is challenged by the ongoing revolutionary process.

As we can see, in contrast with the description of canonical events, which are all circumscribed by the frame of a *Weltanschauung*, the event of the riots connected to the revolutions are described as a collection of disparate facts that aggregate in the perception of the narrator, who is not able to relate them. In the final example, from 16 July 1647, we see the same syntactical structure we have appreciated in the first ones:

> The following Monday the riot grew, and they abducted the houses of those who administered gabels, starting with that of Gironimo Letitia, and then of Felice Basile, of counselor Tonno d'Angelo, of the elected of the People Andrea Naclerio and the day after that of Cesare Lubrano, of Giovanni Zavaglios, of Ciommo Naccarella, of Bartolomeo Blasamo, of the counsellor Mirabello, of the President Cennamo, of the Duke of Caivano and his son Antonio Barrile, of Giovanni Battista Buzzacarino, and that of Bartolomeo d'Aquino in Chiaia, throwing in the streets all the robes that constituted the Treasury, and abusing them without keeping anything, except the weapons, and in the cellars they poured the bottles of wine, and would have continued the outrage had not a printed proclamation been issued by order of the People on pain of death that all the soldiers of the city should retreat, each to his own neighbourhood.[15]

---

volendo più consigli, nemeno dal eletto del popolo governandosi a suo capriccio andando per la città solo e con pochi altri correndo infuriato fermandocarrozze, et altre persone a renderli obbedienza con parole aspre, con far bandi in cose sproporzionati, e far tagliar subito la testa a molti alla semplice querela che gli veniva portata in voce con far alzar nuove forche in moltissimi luoghi sparlando come mbriaco, del Cardinale, del Viceré, et del Papa', Avvisi from 7 to 16 July 1647, f. 237ʳ.

15 'Lunedì seguente s'ingrosso il tumulto, et si diede ad abrugiarele case di quei tali che hanno amministrato gabelle, cominciando da quella di Gironimo Letitia, e poi di Felice Basile, del consigliere Tonno d'Angelo, del eletto del Popolo Andrrea Naclerio et il dì appresso a quella di Cesare Lubrano, di Giovanni Zavaglios, di Ciommo Naccarella, di Bartolomeo Balsamo, del Consigliere Mirabello, del Presidente Cennamo, del Duca di Caivano, e di D. Antonio Barrile suo figlio, di Giovan Battista Buzzacarini, e quella di Batolomeo d'Aquino a Chiaia, buttando in strada tutte le robbe che sono state un Thesoro, et abrugiandole senza ve tenersi cosa alcuna, ecceto l'armi, et nelle cantine spilavano le botte del vino, et habessero continato l'incendi se non fusse uscito bando stampatd'ordine del Popolo sotto pena della vita che tutte le soldatesche della città dovessero retirarsi ciascuna nel proprio quartiero', ibid., 7–16 July 1647, f. 237ʳ.

See in particular the anaphoric and jarring succession of the preposition "of" and of the conjunction "and", all along the phrasing, that transmits a sense of urgency which shakes up the narrative worldview, and follows the long list of people whose lives were impacted by the riots.

From the Luhmann social systems theory perspective, the evolution of the public sphere might be seen as the progressive learning of each system to narrate and represent what is outside its cognitive space, rather than an actual dialogue between different actors. The political event such as the Neapolitan revolution of 1647–1648 becomes of relevance, then, because it reveals—from the point of view of the narrator—a lack of ability to give account of what is perceived as complex and inconceivable, because it lies outside of its media sphere.

It is worth nothing that by means of this kind of sociological analysis, we might recover much of the socio-political value of the revolution, which was understated traditionally by historians, who relegated the nature of the outbreak to a form of ritual anthropological phenomenon, perhaps not perceiving the novelty of the event for the socio-communicative system as such.[16]

The example of the mediatic narration of the event shows a second way of representing the passage to the public sphere. Narrative, in itself, is something that tackles transformation instead of simply registering the transformative political and historical riddle *post hoc*.

2   The Riddle of the Revolution

'One of the most memorable popular commotions that has ever occurred anywhere …'; these words are the incipit of a manuscript written by a certain Gaetano Stefani, an observer who found himself caught up in one of the most radical political episodes of early modern times.[17] Another eyewitness, Tommaso De Santis, showed his inconsolable sorrow for the terrible upheavals that had afflicted his native homeland: 'Although the tumult of the plebs of Naples (which for nine uninterrupted months miserably afflicted the city and filled the kingdom with havoc and ruin) should more easily make a compatriot weep than renew in writing the bitter memory of those times'.[18]

---

16   See, for example, Peter Burke, 'The virgin of the Carmine and the revolt of Masaniello', *Past & Present*, 99/1 (1983), pp. 3–21.

17   'Una delle più memorabili commotioni popolari che siano già lungo tempo accadute in alcuna parte …'; University of Pennsylvania Kislak Center for Special Collections, Rare Books and Manuscripts, Ms. Codex 403, Gatetano Stefani, *Historia della revolutione di Napoli seguita nel tempo di Masaniello*, f. 4ʳ.

18   'Avvengachè il tumulto della plebe di Napoli (che per lo spazio di nove mesi continui ha miseramente afflitta la Città e ripieno il Regno di strage, e di ruine) dovria piu tosto

All eyewitnesses and contemporaries of the events in the city and the Kingdom of Naples of 1647–1648 agreed in recalling its popular character. A wide variety of terms were employed in describing the events: *sollevazioni, tumulti, ribellione, rumori, commotioni, guerre civili, rivolutioni* [uprising, tumult, rebellions, commotions, troubles, civil wars, revolutions]. However, "revolution"—or "revolutions" in its plural version—was one of the most often employed to narrate the Neapolitan and Southern Italian uprisings.[19] The word always encompassed a wide variety of meanings, ranging in subject matter from moral doctrines all the way to natural phenomena, but it acquired a new significance during the seventeenth century in reference to political forces uniquely characteristic of modernity.[20] Major shifts were recorded in a series of Italian books concerning the upheavals which tore apart the Spanish Empire throughout the 1640s. Several publications displayed the term on their title pages, such as Luca Assarino's *Delle Rivolutioni di Catalogna* [Of the Revolutions of Catalonia], Andrea Pocile's *Delle rivoluzioni della città di Palermo* [Of the Revolutions of the city of Palermo] and Alessandro Giraffi's *Le Rivolutioni di Napoli* [The Revolutions of Naples] (see Figure 4.1).[21]

However, Giraffi's book is the key title here. Despite the still undiscovered identity of its author, the book enjoyed immediate success. At least eight different Italian editions were printed in 1647 and 1648, while the revolution was still unfolding, while many other editions followed in the centuries to come, a testament to the curiosity and interest which the events aroused from the outset.[22] The wide circulation of this text was facilitated by the small format.

muovere un Compatriota a piangere, che a rinnovar scrivendo l'amara memoria di quei tempi', in Tommaso De Santis, *Historia del Tumulto di Napoli: nella quale si contengono tutte le cose occorse nella città, e Regno di Napoli, dal principio del governo del Duca d'Arcos, fin il dì 6 Aprile 1648* (Leiden: Elsevir, 1652), p. 1.

19 Aurelio Lepre, 'La crisi del XVII secolo nel Mezzogiorno d'Italia', *Studi Storici*, 22, 1 (1981), p. 68 (pp. 51–77).

20 Ilan Rachum, *"Revolution": the Entrance of a New Word into Western Political Discourse* (Lanham: University Press of America, 1999).

21 Luca Assarino, *Delle rivolutioni di Catalogna* (Genoa: per Gio. Maria Ferroni, 1644); Adrea Pocili [Placido Reina], *Delle rivolutioni della citta di Palermo avvenute l'anno 1647* (In Verona: per Francesco de' Rossi, 1648); Alessandro Giraffi, *Le rivolutioni di Napoli ... Con pienissimo ragguaglio d'ogni successo, e trattati secreti, e palesi* (Napoli: Presso Filippo Alberto, 1647).

22 Two editions were published in Naples and Venice in 1647: ([Naples]: s.n., 1647) (USTC 4020216); (Venezia: per il Baba 1647) (USTC 4020365). Another six were published in 1648: (Ferrara: per Giuseppe Gironi, 1648) (USTC 4020373); (Genève: presso Philippe Albert conforme la copia di Venezia, 1648) (USTC 6701054); (Gaeta [=Venezia]: appresso Aniello Pistone, 1648) (USTC 4019132); (Venezia: s.n, 1648) (USTC 4048526); (Padova: per Sebastiano Sardi, 1648) (USTC 4020290); (Padova: per Vincenti, 1648) (USTC 4048492).

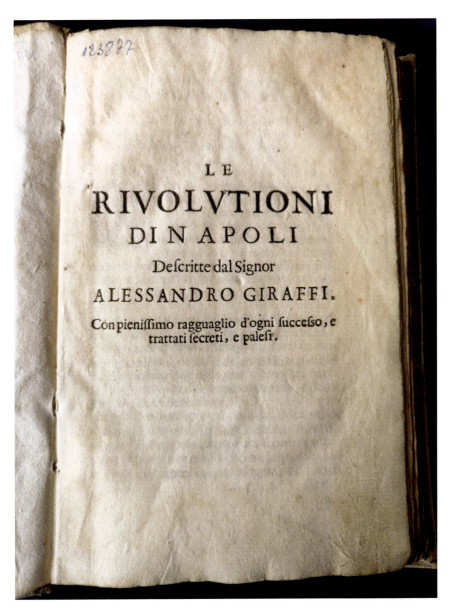

FIGURE 4.1   Title page of Alessandro Giraffi, *Le rivoluzioni di Napoli* ([Napoli: Presso Filippo Alberto, 1647])
COURTESY OF SOCIETÀ NAPOLETANA DI STORIA PATRIA

Another five were published in the eighteenth century: (In Ferrara: per Bernardino Pomatelli impress. episcop., 1705 and 1706); (In Venezia: presso Cristoforo Zane, 1732 and 1733).

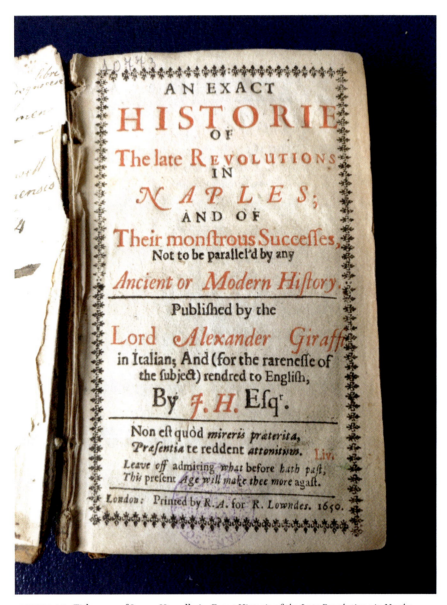

FIGURE 4.2 Title page of James Howell, *An Exact Historie of the Late Revolutions in Naples* (London: R. Lowndes, 1664)
COURTESY OF SOCIETÀ NAPOLETANA DI STORIA PATRIA

Also, the quality of the paper and the simple layout suggest that the book was essentially intended for the mass-market. The small size facilitated a wider circulation since it could be easily carried in a pocket and read out loud or used in a variety of social and cultural settings as it was the case for other genres pertaining to popular literature. It is not surprising that the book was then translated by the British polymath James Howell with the original English title *An exact Historie of the Late Revolutions in Naples*, opening another important chapter for the dissemination of the word in Western political discourse.[23] The title page of this work can be seen in Figure 4.2.

The radical nature of the event produced a transformation of the idea of revolution itself, which acquired a pluralistic dimension, and involved a paradigm shift in the public domain, while the political arena underwent an abrupt widening to include traditionally excluded subjects and witnessing the emergence of nascent forms of popular representation.[24] As David Como has aptly written:

> the word, and the amorphous and shifting set of concepts attached to it, spread back and forth through Europe by way of a series of borrowings, appropriation and refashioning that cannot be understood in any single national context ... this sort of transnational lexical drift was enabled by the emergence of a robust culture of news and information that had gradually over the previous decade come to knit Europe together in an ever tighter discursive community.[25]

---

23 James Howell, *An exact Historie of the Late Revolutions in Naples; and of Their monstrous Successes, not to be parallel'd by Any Ancient or Modern History. Published by the* OK *Lord Alexander Giraffi in Italian and (for the rarenesse of the subject) rendered to English by J. H. Esq.* (London: Robert Austin for Richard Lowendes, 1650) (USTC 3062059); (London: Richard Lowendes, 1650) (USTC 3062460); and (London, printed by J. G., for John Williams, 1650) (USTC 3062448). A continuation of the story was published a few years later as James Howell, *The Second Part of Massaniello: His Body Taken Out of the Town-Ditch, and Solemnly Buried, with Epitaphs Upon Him. A Continuation of the Tumult; the D. of Guise Made Generalissimo; Taken Prisoner by Young Don John of Austria. The End of the Commotions. By J. H. Esquire.* (London: Printed by A. M. for Abel Roper at the sign of the Sun, and T. Dring at the George near St Dunstans Church in Fleetstreet, 1652). On James Howell's translation career see Giovanni Iamartino, 'Translating behind Bars: James Howell's Alternative Space for Political Action during the English Civil Wars', in Sara Laviosa, et al. (eds.), *Recent trends in translation studies: an Anglo-Italian perspective* (Newcastle upon Tyne: Cambridge Scholars Publishing, 2021), pp. 20–42. On the reception of the Neapolitan revolution in England see Davide Boerio, 'The "Trouble of Naples" in the Political Information Arena of the English Revolution', in J. Raymond et al. (eds.), *News Networks in Early Modern Europe* (Leiden-Boston: Brill, 2016) pp. 779–804.

24 On the connection between political and scientific revolutions, see Thomas S. Kuhn, *The Structure of Scientific Revolutions*, 2nd ed. (Chicago: University of Chicago press, 1970), pp. 92–3.

25 D. Como, 'God's Revolutions: England, Europe, and the Concept of Revolution in the mid-Seventeenth Century', in K. M. Baker et al. (eds.), *Scripting revolution: a historical approach to the comparative study of revolutions* (Stanford: Stanford University Press, 2015), p. 48.

As Thomas Kuhn has explained masterfully, in particular socio-cultural conditions, a shift of paradigm occurs, so that traditional protocols of knowledge and social interaction are modified, altered and intensified.[26] These paradigm shifts are triggered by crises, such as the failure of a previously accepted theory to explain new observations or the discovery of a new phenomenon that cannot be explained by the existing paradigm. Such an epistemic rupture occurred with the revolution of Naples in 1647–1648, driven by latent tensions that had a profound impact on the transformation of the political and communication fields.

Whether or not the title of Giraffi's book contributed to a re-semanticisation of the word "revolution", its narrative helped to establish a symbiotic link to the identification of revolution with the last ten days of the life of the young Neapolitan fishmonger Tommaso Aniello D'Amalfi, better known as Masaniello, who led the first phase of the revolution before being brutally murdered by his own followers.[27] As in a baroque drama, the book presented the words and deeds of its protagonist, a young commoner, who rose from anonymity and hardship to the pinnacle of power before falling back into the abyss of madness and appalling tragedy. The division of the plot into ten days responded to a necessity for narrative order and systemisation, a literary expedient probably drawn from the Boccaccio novelistic tradition of the *Decameron*.[28] The plot thus brought about a further transformation by operating a *reductio ad unum*, in which the personal story of one man would absorb the twists and turns of a collective tragedy, representing the *pars pro toto* of an extraordinary historical episode. This figure of speech however has fuelled both its past and contemporary memory, giving shape to a historiographical canon, the so-called 'Revolt of Masaniello'. This pervasive image has been the main device through which the Neapolitan revolution of 1647–1648 has been passed down across the centuries, eventually distorting its historical significance which had a far longer and more complex gestation.[29] This trope has operated on many levels, fostering a stereotypical view which emphasises folkloric aspects rather

---

26   T. S. Kuhn, *The Structure of Scientific Revolutions*.
27   Silvana D'Alessio, *Masaniello: la sua vita e il mito in Europa* (Rome: Salerno, 2007).
28   Silvana D'Alessio, 'Un'esemplare cronologia: Le rivoluzioni di Napoli di Alessandro Giraffi (1647)', *Annali dell'Istituto Italiano per gli studi storici*, 15 (1998), pp. 287–340 (p. 288). See also Silvana D'Alessio, 'Una nuova aurora. Su un manoscritto de "Le rivoluzioni di Napoli" di Alessandro Giraffi', *Il Pensiero Politico*, XXXII, 3 (1999), pp. 383–403.
29   Rosario Villari, 'Masaniello: contemporary and recent interpretations', *Past & Present*, 108, 1 (1985), pp. 117–132.

than a more historically rounded reading of events and boosting a traditional paradigm which put emphasis on the "failure" and the "minority", when seen from the point of view of the central thrust of Western political culture.[30] Such commonplaces stem from what Perez Zagorin defined as 'the charismatic myth of revolution', which 'restricts its meaning to something total, grand, and monumental'.[31] According to him, the ghosts of the great revolutions—the American, French and Russian—hovered in the background of any analysis:

> This results in the exclusion of various kinds of revolutionary occurrences from the field of revolution because they are held to lack the requisite amplitude of scale, although the standard for determining the latter is purely arbitrary in accordance with the predilections of the observer.[32]

These remarks also fit the political and historical debate which followed the events in Naples and in the *Mezzogiorno* in 1647–1648. From time to time, the event has produced divergent interpretations, manifesting its intrinsic irreducibility to any simplification and definitive discourse.

3   The Rise of Transmediality

Soon after his death, the feats of Masaniello were recounted and re-enacted in a wide variety of texts and genres transcending the narrow bounds of Southern Italy.[33] The Neapolitan fisherman became a ubiquitous symbol embodying both positive and negative features of his constituency: the plebs, the commoners, the underdogs, the subaltern classes.[34] As Jacques Rancière noted

---

30 A. M. Rao, 'Missed Opportunities' in the History of Naples', in M. Calaresu et al. (eds.), *New Approaches to Naples c.1500–1800: The Power of Place* (London-New York: Routledge, 2013), pp. 203–23.

31 Peter Zagorin, 'Prolegomena to the Comparative History of Revolution in Early Modern Europe', *Comparative Studies in Society and History*, 18, 2 (1976), p. 156 (pp. 151–174). This article was later included in P. Zagorin, *Rebels and Rulers, 1500–1660* (Cambridge: Cambridge University Press, 1982), vol. 1, pp. 3–27.

32 Zagorin, 'Prolegomena', p. 156.

33 Vittorio Dini, *Masaniello. L'eroe e il mito* (Roma: Newton Compton, 1995); Aurelio Musi (ed.), *Protagonisti nella storia di Napoli: grandi napoletani*, vol. 2: *Masaniello* (Napoli: Elio De Rosa, 1994).

34 Martin Breaugh, *The Plebeian Experience: A Discontinuous History of Political Freedom*, translated by L. Lederhendler (New York: Columbia University Press, 2013).

aptly, 'the symbol is a detached part of a whole, a static moment in a movement that both presents and signifies this movement at the same time'.[35]

The drawings of Masaniello played a crucial role in this process of mediatisation.[36] Tommaso De Santis recounts the tragic and astonishing scenes which followed Masaniello's death. The following day, some bakers reduced the weight of the loaf of bread and increased the price going against the orders of the deceased Masaniello who had put political control over the price of foodstuffs. In the grip of unrelenting remorse, people stitched Masaniello's head back to the rest of his body, which they afterwards adorned with a rich robe and displayed in the Church of Carmine.[37] During the wake, De Santis noted:

> Many painters made his portrait, and some were made in wax in a very natural fashion, everyone wanted one, without caring about the price. While he was seated in the posture of portraying him, a rumour spread that he had been resurrected and that with a smiling face he had publicly blessed the people.[38]

Like the wax in this account, the plasticity of these images moulded the mimetic texture of the story of the Neapolitan revolution of 1647–1648. Many of these drawings are included in manuscripts found in Italian, European and American libraries, demonstrating not only the cross-mediatization process produced by the event, but also the complex sedimentation of its memory together with the spatial and material dispersion of texts.[39] In this latter

---

35 Jacques Rancière, *Figures of history*, translated by Julie Rose (Cambridge: Polity, 2014), p. 83.
36 Joana Maite de Ribereite de Fraga, *Three revolts in images: Catalonia, Portugal and Naples (1640–1647)* (unpublished Ph.D. thesis, Universitat de Barcelona, 2012–2013); Alain Hugon, *Naples Insurgeé 1647–1648—De l'événement à la mémoire* (Rennes: Presses Universitaires de Rennes, 2019); Roberto de Simone, et al. (eds.), *Masaniello nella drammaturgia europea e nella iconografia del suo secolo* (Napoli: Gaetano Macchiaroli Editore, 1998); Bartolommeo Capasso, *Masaniello et alcuni di sua famiglia effigiati nei quadri nelle figure, e nelle stampe del tempo: note storiche* (Naples: R. Tipografia Giannini & figli, 1897).
37 De Santis, *Historia del Tumulto di Napoli*, pp. 149–150.
38 'Molti pittori fecero il suo ritratto, e ne furono formati anche alcuni in cera molto al naturale: ogn'uno ne cercava, ogn'uno ne voleva uno, senza guardare à prezzo. Mentr'era accomodato in postura di ritrarlo, eccoti sparsa una voce d'essere resuscitato, e che con faccia ridente avesse benedetto pubblicamente il Popolo', ibid., p. 151.
39 As example of transmediality of a text see Francesco Moratti, '"Sollevazione di Tommaso Aniello di Napoli". Il manoscritto di Alessandro Molini (BUB, ms 2466)', *Storicamente*, 13 (2017), no. 10. DOI: 10.12977/stor665; See also Piero Ventura, 'Dai codici al cinema: note sulla memoria iconografica della rivolta antispagnola di Napoli', *Visual History: rivista internazionale di storia e critica dell'immagine*, IV (2018), pp. 43–64 (pp. 43–46). For the

FIGURE 4.3
Engraving of Masniello by Pieter Jode the Younger
COURTESY OF KISLAK CENTER FOR SPECIAL COLLECTIONS, RARE BOOKS AND MANUSCRIPTS, UNIVERSITY OF PENNSYLVANIA

regard, a typical example is codex 403 by Gaetano de Stefani held at the Kislak Center for Special Collections, Rare Books and Manuscripts at the University of Pennsylvania.[40] At the beginning of the codex, there are two images of Masaniello that would have had wide international appeal.

The first engraving, seen in Figure 4.3, depicts the figure of a young man with a moustache and wavy long hair. In a half-length framed portrait, facing forward, Masaniello wears a bonnet over his head, and wears an open shirt. In the background, birds-eye view of Naples can be glimpsed. A net on his right shoulder recalls to a repertoire drawn from religious discourse, connecting the fishmonger of Naples with the more famous fisherman, St Peter. This analogy is also present in a manuscript text which circulated during the revolution, a reinterpretation of the Second Psalm of David where Masaniello is compared to the vicar of Christ: 'Who was from the net Peter by God loosed \ Holding in the Vatican as his deputy on earth \ Mas' Anello from selling fish removed', 'che fu dalla rete Pietro da Dio sciolto \ Reggendo in Vatican suo vice in terra \ Mas'Anello

      manuscripts in the Neapolitan collections, see Saverio Di Franco, *Le rivolte del Regno di Napoli del 1647–48 nei manoscritti napoletani* (Napoli: Società napoletana di storia patria, 2017).

40   Rudolf Hirsh and Norman P. Zacour (eds.), *Catalogue of manuscripts in the libraries of the University of Pennsylvania to 1800* (Philadelphia: University of Pennsylvania Press, 1965).

FIGURE 4.4
Drawings of Masaniello from Pietro Bacchi's model
COURTESY OF KISLAK CENTER FOR SPECIAL COLLECTIONS, RARE BOOKS AND MANUSCRIPTS, UNIVERSITY OF PENNSYLVANIA

da vender pesce tolto'.[41] Both Masaniello and St Peter were united by having given up their previous work to devote themselves to a greater cause. Drawn by the Flemish painter Pieter de Jode the Younger, the image represents an idealised version of Masaniello, possibly similar to one that Spinoza, according to his biographer Johannes Colerus, used to portray himself in the guise of the young Neapolitan.[42] Ultimately, the revolution in Naples of 1647–1648, as Jonathan Israel has noted, became the symbol of a popular insurrection against monarchical absolutism.[43]

However, at the bottom of the engraving there is a Latin epigraph which offers an opposing interpretation to the one suggested so far:

---

41 Joahnnes Colerus, Spinoza's biographer, recounts that the philosopher owned 'un pècheur dessiné en chemise, avec un filet sur l'épaule droite, tout à fait semblable pour l'attitude au fameux chef de rebells de Naples, Massanielle … Ce crayon ou portrait ressemblait à Spinoza et c'était assurément d'après lui-méme qu'il l'avait tire', Johannes Colerus, *Vie de Spinosa* (La Haye: 1706), p. 60. For the circulation of this image in the Dutch context, see Roberto De Simone, et al. (eds.), *Masaniello nella drammaturgia europea* (Napoli: Macchiaroli, 1998), p. 180.
42 The text is published in Aurelio Musi and Saverio Di Franco (eds.), *Mondo antico in rivolta* (Napoli 1647–48) (Manduria: Laicata, 2006), p. 56 (pp. 54–58).
43 Jonathan Israel, *Enlightenment Contested: Philosophy, Modernity, and the Emancipation of Man (1670–1752)* (Oxford: Oxford University Press, 2006), p. ix.

Quis sim queris! Masaniello: sortis documentum exemplar omnibus credula quid fortuna possit; populo gratus piscatorio genere oriundus ad diadema regium euectus mox temeritate et superbia inflatus, mole laborans mea obrutus miserrima morte sublatus, canibus dilaniandis proiectus.

You ask who I am, Masaniello; an example of chance, a model for all of what gullible fortune is capable of, dear to the people, born in the class of fishermen I was raised to the diadem of kings, inflamed then by rashness and haughtiness, falling by my own weight, I was crushed, full of pride, by a miserable death, thrown as food for dogs.

The epigraph indicates the instability of human fortune and serves as a reminder of the end reserved for all those who dared to oppose the existing political authorities and to challenge the divine right to rule. This *topos*, deeply embedded in medieval and early modern political culture, served as a primary means of delegitimating rebellions and the rationality of popular agency in the eyes of the political and social elite.[44] Examples of this discourse of order reverberated throughout the Atlantic world as shown by several medals depicting Masaniello, on one side, and Oliver Cromwell, on the other, as well as by the appropriation of his name by North American insurgents, since they identified themselves as "Masanielli" during the 1680s uprisings.[45] Hence, the image of the Neapolitan fishmonger underwent several metamorphoses, subsuming a multiplicity of meanings. It is an amalgam composed of several discourses and representations blended together. The symbol switches from negative to positive depending on the interpreters' viewpoints. It was both a warning against the fury of the lower classes and an emblem of the desire for the liberation of human beings throughout all epochs. The richness of its semantic elements offers ongoing remoulding. The hat worn by Masaniello, for instance, recalls the traditional headgear used by his fellow fishermen in many port cities of early modern Europe. In other depictions, the same hat is coloured in red, predating by almost a century and a half the symbolism of the Phrygian cap of the French revolutionaries. Such iconology however has a long gestation and goes back to Ancient Rome; in particular, it is linked to the ritual of manumission when former slaves wore a hat as a sign of regained freedom.[46]

---

44 R. Villari, 'The Rebel', in Id, (ed.), *Baroque Personae*, trans. Lydia Cochrane (Chicago: University of Chicago Press, 1995), pp. 100–25.
45 Villari, 'Masaniello', pp. 125–26; David. S. Lovejoy, *The Glorious Revolution in America* (Middeltown, Conn.: University Press of New England, 1987), pp. 294–311.
46 F. Benigno, 'Simboli della politica: lo strano caso del berretto della libertà', *Storica*, 46, XIV (2010), pp. 1–25.

The second image, seen in Figure 4.4, also offers several interesting insights. Attributable to Pietro Bacchi (latinised as Petrus Bacchus), the drawing brings to life one of the numerous verbal descriptions of Masaniello's appearance and character which spread throughout Europe:

> A Young man about twenty four yeers old happen'd to be in a corner of the great Market place at Naples, a spritefull man, and pleasant, of a middle stature, black-ey'd, rather lean then fat, having a small tuff of haire; he wore linnen slops, a blew wastcoat, and went barefoot, with a Mariners cap, but he was of a good countenance, stout and lively as could be, as the effects will shew.[47]

Apart from representing Masaniello in the typical fisherman costume, wearing shirt and trousers of rough fabric according to his low social standing, and a sailor hat, the image portrays him standing barefoot with his right arm raised, pointing ahead, while his left arm is bent. The pose recalls the portraits of military chiefs of more noble lineage.[48] This representation epitomises the subversion of social and political hierarchies, as also shown by the bare feet which symbolise the condition of the poorest and most derelict members of society.[49]

Forged in such a volcanic repertoire blending religious suggestions with social and material circumstances, the body of Masaniello becomes a powerful medium representing restive popular aspirations, lending its shape eventually to a huge and nameless mass of the dispossessed and exploited. The following image, Figure 4.5, shows more than any other the political significance of this symbolism.

This print appears at the beginning of the book entitled *Napoli Sollevata* (Naples Risen Up). Like the other representations analysed previously, Masaniello is once again dressed in humble robes that recall his low social status. In the background, however, a large group of young men appears brandishing sticks. This anonymous mass represents his acolytes who, under his leadership, held the stage during the first acts of the uprisings. The image points to the charismatic power of the leader, who, with the simple gesture of his finger in front of his mouth, silences an agitated and shouting mass, thus exercising the power to give and take away the voice. On the upper and lower margins there is an

---

47 Howell, *An exact historie*, p. 11.
48 J. M. de Ribereite de Fraga, *Three revolts in images*, p. 262.
49 Virtus Zallot, *Con i piedi nel Medioevo: gesti e calzature nell'arte e nell'immaginario* (Bologna: Il Mulino 2018).

FIGURE 4.5 *El Maior Monstro del Mundo y Prodixio dela Italia Tomas Aniello de Amalfi*
COURTESY OF SOCIETÀ NAPOLETANA DI STORIA PATRIA

inscription in Spanish: 'El Maior Monstro del Mundo y Prodixio dela Italia Tomas Aniello de Amalfi', 'The greatest monster in the world and prodigy of Italy Tomas Aniello de Amalfi'. Apart from the strangeness of events, the reference evokes the semantic universe of representations of the multitude involving a monster, namely, the many-headed hydra.[50] This process of zoomorphism is a durable leitmotif that can be found in a sonnet *On the Plebs* (*Sulla Plebe*) by Tommaso Campanella in which the people are described as 'a beast diverse and large that ignores its strength'.[51] The theme of bestiality thus alluded to the irrationality of popular agency, traditionally described in the public and political discourse in derogative and moralising terms. A case in point is the pro-Spanish author Giovan Battista Buragna who describes the plebs:

> as under the generic name of animal, both the rational and the irrational correspond, but under the name of Plebs, it only includes that meaner sort, which is a species called Lazarina, that has neither roof nor cover, and that because it has neither art nor industry, it continually lives with the cowardice and ambition of the state and goods of others.[52]

The name of this particular species of men, "Lazarina", derives from the word "Lazzari", which in turn stems from the story of Lazarus of Bethany, the leper who was resurrected by Jesus as narrated in the New Testament, thus pointing to a condition of physical and social infirmity. The term was then appropriated by one of the most hardliner units of the revolution. Over the centuries this representation would undergo continual transformations, cementing a stereotypical reading of the common people shifting from the "Lazzaroni" siding with the counter-revolutionary forces against the Neapolitan republic of 1799 to subsequent representation as a "dangerous class".[53]

And yet, the lower classes constituted the largest fraction of the population of Naples which, by the mid-seventeenth century, reached the monstrous figure of around 300,000 inhabitants, making the city the greatest capital of

---

50 Peter Linebaugh, and Marcus Rediker, *The Many-Headed Hydra: sailor, slaves, commoners and the hidden history of the Revolutionary Atlantic* (Boston: Beacon Press, 2000).
51 'Il Popolo è una bestia varia e grossa che ignora la sua forza …', Tommaso Campanella, *La Città del Sole e Poesie*, edited by Adriano Seroni (Milan: Feltrinelli, 1962), p. 144.
52 '… como baxo de nombre generico de animal se corrisponden tanto lo racionales, como lo irrçionales, pero baxo el nombre de Plebe solamente inciue à quella genete menuda, que es una specie llamada Lazarina, que no tiene techo, ni cubierta, y que por no tener arte, ni industria, biue continuamente con la cobdiçia y ambiçion delos estado y bienes agenos …'. Giovan Battista Buraña, *Batalla peregrina entre amor y fidelidad* (Madrid: s.n., 1651) (Iberian Books, 69926), p. 5.
53 Francesco Benigno, 'Trasformazioni discorsive ed identità sociali: il caso dei lazzari', *Storica*, 31 (2005), pp. 7–44, and 'Tra storia e scienze sociali: la costruzioni sociale del male', *Merdiana*, 100 (2021), pp. 97–118.

the Spanish Empire and the second largest city in Europe after Paris.[54] The bustling urban life and the vital energy emanating from this true early modern Mediterranean metropolis favoured the dissemination of information, symbols, and discourses about the revolutionary events. The city became a magmatic laboratory of images, an open-air stage on which the dramatic nature of historical events was enacted by the theatricality of human life—wonderfully captured by the Roman painter Michelangelo Cerquozzi, who portrays the market square during the first phase of insurrection. Cerquozzi presents a wide scene filled with human bodies and colours, set within the architectural perimeters of the *Piazza del Mercato*, with Vesuvius standing at a distance, showing all its terrible force. As a member of the school of Bambloccianti—which had at the heart of its artistic agenda the representation of popular life, landscapes, as well as battles, using naturalistic tones and life-like traits, and influenced by the lesson of Caravaggio which, by the mid-seventeenth century, many artists had in mind as an ideal worthy of emulation—Cerquozzi puts a popular insurrection on the stage of art history (Figure 4.6). As aptly noted by Wassying Roworth, the painting was perceived as news; it was acquired by Virginio Spada on 28 February 1648 for forty scudi.[55]

FIGURE 4.6   Michelangelo Cerquozzi, The Revolt of Masaniello in 1647.
Rome, Galleria Spada
PUBLIC DOMAIN IMAGE TAKEN FROM WIKIMEDIA COMMONS

54   Claudia Petraccone, *Napoli dal Cinquecento all'Ottocento: problemi di storia demografica e sociale* (Naples: Guida, 1974).
55   Wendy Wassyng Roworth, 'The Evolution of History Painting: Masaniello's Revolt and Other Disasters in Seventeenth-Century Naples', *The Art Bulletin*, 75, 2 (1993), p. 227 (pp. 219–234).

Roworth further suggests a link between the subject on the canvas and a printed letter of the Archbishop of Naples, Cardinal Ascalnio Filomarino which had widespread circulation.[56] The text recounts the appearance of Masaniello on the stage of the revolution: 'Masaniello, a fisherman and youth of twenty years, who was also present, made himself leader of these boys, and of others who rushed to join them, and mounted on a horse which was on the piazza, cried: remove the tax on fruit. And in a twinkling of an eye thousands upon thousands of people joined them …'.[57]

The interdependence between different handwritten, printed, and pictorial texts is a feature of the transmedia dimension of the Neapolitan revolution of 1647–1648. This phenomenon determined the transformation of symbols and discourses, but also the production of new audiences both within and beyond the event, which reveal themselves through the sharing of messages.[58]

The impact of the Neapolitan revolution of 1647–1648 on *Ancien Régime* media ecology was variously articulated and multi-layered. At the crossmedia level of the *Avvisi* news network system, there was a very formalised communication protocol that, in narrating the revolution, faced a complexity very difficult for it to grasp; this phenomenon can be linked to longer-lasting trends in the evolution of media within society. On the other hand, we documented a great deal of transmedia communication. This was characterized by a peculiar multiplicity of aesthetic and performative strategies that reflected the moment of creativity, favoured by both communicative and political innovation. All of these vivid forms of transmedia communication provided new means of political expression, not predominantly based on rational critique, but rather on a new way of self-representing and self-observing political subjects. Such epistemic fractures cannot be understood fully with traditional political analysis. The impact of transmediality on the socio-political process can be seen as a paradigm shift in the communicative and political fields, spreading the revolutionary message to a plurality of users. Ultimately, the interaction between innovative forms of communication at a particular moment of media history that embraces the Neapolitan revolution of 1647–1648 created a tremendous collision between different environments of communication, so that they interfered with one another, opening up possibilities of transformation and evolution of the political system. Evaluating the meaning of this transformation involves combining contextual analysis with the diachronic projection of

---

56 The letters are transcribed in Francesco Palermo (ed.), 'Narrazione e documenti sulla storia del regno di Napoli dall'anno 1522 al 1667', *Archivio Storico Italiano*, IX, 1846, pp. 379–393.
57 Wassyng Roworth, 'The Evolution of History Painting', p. 226.
58 Michael Warner, 'Publics and Counterpublics', *Public Culture*, 14/1 (2002), p. 51 (pp. 49–90).

media history, deploying not only classical political categories such as revolt and revolution, but also cultural definitions of the history of thought such as the kuhnian notion of mutation of paradigm. The *long durée* approach, which looks at phenomena from a crossmedia perspective, registers the evolution of the whole social system, and the material and contextual analysis of the proliferation of the transmedia perspective in an evanescent, though fertile moment; they were two sides of the same historical phenomenon, with outcomes yet to be considered. As the single transmedia forms of communication may seem ephemeral from the point of view of the media system, the shift of paradigm to transmediality in itself is the most long-lasting of socio-political ruptures. Ultimately, analysis of historical experience cannot therefore be separated from the study of the media and the discursive dimensions of events.

CHAPTER 5

St Filippo Neri in the Spanish Press
Earthquakes, Veneration and Wondrous Events

Milena Viceconte

One of the most significant religious phenomena to emerge in Spain in the seventeenth century was the rise of the veneration of St Filippo Neri, a figure who would become vital to the Catholic Reformation.[1] The first congregations of the oratory of Filippo Neri were founded following his canonisation in 1622: in Valencia in 1645, Madrid in 1660, and in Granada in 1671.[2] These congregations were to launch the promotion of the Florentine saint, but his appeal would soon grow throughout the Iberian peninsula as a whole. The movement was boosted substantially in 1688 as news began to emerge of a prodigious event in Italy during the earthquake that hit the Sannio area on 5 June of that year. An eminent friar, Cardinal Vincenzo Maria Orsini, (b. Gravina in Puglia 1649, d. Rome 1730)—also Archbishop of Benevento, and who would go on to become the future Pope Benedict XIII—was trapped under the rubble of what remained of his Benevento residence.[3] Orsini, it was alleged, was rescued thanks to the divine intervention of St Filippo Neri.

News of Orsini's miraculous escape spread through the press, reinvigorating the saint's appeal. Neri came to be called upon routinely not only for his own spiritual qualities, but also for his intercessional power over earthquakes. Over the course of the eighteenth century, Neri's popularity grew alongside the

---

1   This work was supported by the DisComPoSE project (Disasters, Communication and Politics in Southwestern Europe), which has received funding from the European Research Council (ERC) under the European Union's Horizon 2020 research and innovation programme (No. 759829).
2   Ángel Alba Alarcos, *Los españoles y lo español en la vida de San Felipe Neri. Raíces históricas de la devoción a San Felipe Neri en España* (Alcalá de Henares: Abel, 1992). On Valencia, see Emilio Callado Estela, 'Origen, progreso y primeras tribulaciones del oratorio de San Felipe Neri en España. El caso valenciano', *Libros de la Corte*, 3 (2015), pp. 51–72; Massimo Bergonzini, *Storia della fondazione della Congregazione dell'Oratorio di San Filippo Neri di Valencia* (Porto: CITCEM, 2017).
3   Giacomo de Antonellis, *Il Papa beneventano: Vincenzo Maria Orsini—Benedetto XIII* (Naples: Edizioni Scientifiche Italiane, 2014).

number of earthquake-related events credited to him.[4] This chapter will outline the circumstances that led to the veneration of St Filippo Neri as a divine agent against seismic events, with particular reference to the Spanish press, and how it disseminated news of Orsini's rescue and other similar incidents in both text and image.[5]

1   Press Coverage of the Earthquake and the Prodigious Event

The Sannio earthquake was one of the most devastating of the second half of the seventeenth century. The destructive force of the shocks that hit Benevento and Cerreto Sannita, the earthquake's epicentre, on the evening of 5 June 1688 were also felt in and around Naples. Very swiftly, the Naples press published news of the tragic event which so had badly afflicted the local population.[6] Two anonymous accounts published by the printers Camillo Cavallo and Domenico Antonio Parrino were to enjoy particular success.[7] The pamphlets were reprinted even beyond the bounds of the Kingdom of Naples, and were translated into French, English and Spanish, highlighting the interest that the event had generated across Europe.[8]

---

4   On the proliferation of devotional rites specifically against earthquakes in the early modern period, see Emanuela Guidoboni & Jean-Paul Poirier, *Storia culturale del terremoto dal mondo antico a oggi* (Soveria Mannelli: Universale Rubbettino, 2019), pp. 131–157.

5   An important work which begins serious research on this topic, though limited to the situation in Spain, is Carlos Santos Fernández, 'El terremoto de Nápoles (1688) y la protección del Cardenal Orsini (Papa Benedicto XIII) por San Felipe Neri: testimonios hispanos de la pervivencia de una relación', in S. López Poza (ed.), *Las noticias en los siglos de la imprenta manual: homenaje a Mercedes Agulló, Herny Ettinghausen, Mª Cruz García de Enterría, Giuseppina Ledda, Augustín Redondo y José Simón* (A Coruña: SIELAE, 2006), pp. 201–221. For a more general approach, see Monica Azzolini, 'Coping with Catastrophe. St. Filippo Neri as Patron Saint of Earthquakes', *Quaderni storici*, 156/3 (2017), pp. 727–750.

6   Domenico Cecere, 'Estrategias de comunicación y de intervención frente a desastres en la Monarquía Hispánica bajo Carlos II', *Revista de Historia Moderna*, 39 (2021), pp. 8–43.

7   *Vera, fedele e distintissima relazione di tutti i danni, così delle fabriche come delle persone morte per cagione dell'occorso terremoto accaduto alli 5 di giugno 1688 tanto in questa città di Napoli, quanto nel suo Regno* (Naples: Camillo Cavallo, 1688); *Vera, e distinta relatione dell'horribile, e spauentoso terremoto accaduto in Napoli, & in più parti del Regno il giorno 5 Giugno 1688. Co'l numero delle cittá, terre, & altri luoghi rouinati. Come anco delli morti, e feriti rimasti in cosí compassioneuole tragedia* (Naples: Domenico Antonio Parrino, 1688).

8   Details of these reprints and of other works cited in this paper are provided in the appendix. For an overview of the dissemination of news about disasters in the press, see Henry Ettinghausen, *How the Press Began. The Pre-Periodical Printed News in Early Modern Europe* (A Coruña: SIELAE, 2015), pp. 173–208.

The two pamphlets had a similar narrative structure. The first part detailed the consequences of the earthquake on the city of Naples, where the principal places of worship had suffered damage severe enough to render them unsafe, including the Gesù Nuovo church, the Santi Apostoli convent, the royal chapel of Santa Chiara, and the Cathedral.[9] The second part provided accounts of the religious ferment of the people of Naples as crowds gathered to implore divine clemency, spurred on by the clergy and local officials as they led prayers through the streets of the city. Pamphlets of this kind were designed not only to inform but also to make the reader reflect upon the causal relationship between people behaving badly and seismic phenomena, based on a fatalistic view of disaster as divine punishment. These considerations also emerged in more sophisticated literature, and especially in certain poems that reflected the suffering caused by the unrelenting divine retribution brought down on the city.[10]

In their description of the damage to suburban Naples and the surrounding towns, the two accounts refer, albeit briefly, to Archbishop Orsini's inexplicable escape from certain death. The English version recounts: 'His Eminency, Orsini the Archbishop, was at that time discoursing with a Gentleman of Apice, named John Baptist Regina, a great Confident of his Eminency'.[11] The floor of the elegant upper-storey residential quarters of the episcopal palace then fell through when the earthquake hit, crashing down onto the lower levels of the archbishop's home. Both Orisin and the gentleman who was with him at the time:

> fell together, both being buried, tho' the second after an hour and half, was found dead at the feet of his Eminency, and the Cardinal was saved miraculously, there falling upon him an Image in paper of St Phillip Nery, to whom he is a very great Devotist; he not having receiv'd any other hurt than a few slight Wounds in his Head, and bruises in his Body.[12]

---

9   Massimo Visone, 'A European View on Ruins in Naples and Messina during the 17th and 18th Centuries', *Archistor*, 9 (2018), pp. 68–107.

10 Carlo Barra, *Partenope languente per l'accaduto terremoto à 5 giugno 1688* (Naples: Camillo Cavallo, 1688); Domenico Andrea de Milo, *Per lo tremuoto, succeduto in Napoli ne' 5 di giugno del corrente anno 1688; Ode* (Naples: Antonio Gramignani, 1688); Pietro Sigillo, *Partenope dolente. Ode* (Naples: Carlo Porsile, 1688); Gennaro Sportelli, *Napoli flagellata da Dio* (Naples: Francesco Benzi, 1688), and the verses written by Giacomo Lubrano and published a few years after the earthquake in the collection *Scintille poetiche, o poesie sacre, e morali di Paolo Brinacio napoletano* (Naples: Andrea Poletti, 1692), pp. 130–137.

11 *A true and exact relation of the most dreadful earthquake which happened in the city of Naples* (London: Rendan Taylor, 1688), p. 12.

12 Ibid. See also *Vera, e distinta relatione*, n.p.; *Vera, fedele e distintissima relazione*, p. 33.

The extraordinary event was also recounted in other press reports published in 1688, such as that written by Pompeo Sarnelli, who had also fled the collapsing building, as well as a remarkable poem from the pen of Giovanni Canale.[13] However, the most important testimony was provided by Orsini himself. A few days after the event, he expressed a wish to validate his account of it before Antonio Cirillo, a notary public of Naples, in the form of a letter he had written in his own hand on 22 June 1688 while at the Convent of Santa Caterina a Formello in Naples. His document attributes not only his lucky rescue from the rubble to the supernatural intervention of Father Filippo but also the rapid healing of the wounds he had sustained on his head, hands and other parts of his body.

His intention was probably to establish a link between this event and other rescues that occurred after Filippo Neri's canonisation in 1622, initially reported in the press and then updated in his official hagiographies.[14] The first such event occurred in 1623 and involved a certain Paolo de Bernardis, a resident of Treviso, who suffered a neck wound that healed very rapidly, prompting him to make a formal statement to an official that this was due to the saint's intercession. The extraordinary nature of the circumstances immediately made them newsworthy, and the word spread in a pamphlet that included not only his deposition but also declarations by doctors to the effect that there was no medical explanation for the rapid healing of the wound.[15]

The Orsini incident soon reached the printing presses, primarily those of Naples. Less than a week after he had made his formal declaration, the printing works of the archiepiscopal printer Novello de Bonis issued the first copies of *Narrazione de' prodigii operati del glorioso S. Filippo Neri*, a pamphlet that

---

13 Pompeo Sarnelli, *Memorie dell'insigne Collegio di Santo Spirito della città di Benevento* (Naples: Giuseppe Rosselli, 1688, ed. Cesena: P. P. Ricceputi, 1688), pp. 72–74. Part of his testimony can also be found in Vincenzo Magnati, *Notitie istoriche de' terremoti succeduti ne' secoli trascorsi, e nel presente, indirizzate alla serenissima real maestà di Carlo 2* (Naples: Antonio Bulifon, 1688), pp. 351–353. Giovanni Canale, 'Per la caduta del cardinale Orsini nel terremoto di Benevento', in *Poesie del sig. Giovanni Canale divise in morali, di lode, varie, funebri, eroiche, sagre* (Naples: Parrino & Mutii, 1694), pp. 113–114. See also Basilio Giannelli, *Orazione panegirica All' Eminentissimo signor cardinale Orsini Arcivescovo di Benevento* (Benevento: s.n., 1693).

14 Marcella Bruno, 'Da Gallonio a Cistellini: le biografie di San Filippo', in *Messer Filippo Neri, Santo: l'Apostolo di Roma* (Rome: De Luca, 1995), pp. 217–225.

15 *Miracolo insigne che fra molti altri ha operato S. Filippo Neri, fondatore della Congregatione dell'Oratorio dopo la sua Canonizatione in Roma alli 7 di nouemb. 1622* (Rome: Alessandro Zanetti, 1623). A similar event is reported some time later in the pamphlet *Miracolo insigne operato in Roma per intercessione di S. Filippo Neri, fondatore della Congregatione dell'Oratorio alli 5. di gennaio del corrente anno 1644. Nella persona di suor Maria Eletta Radi di Cortona* (Florence: Filippo Papini, 1644).

FIGURE 5.1
Relación del prodigio obrado por San Felipe Neri (Barcelona: Rafael Figueró, 1688)
COURTESY OF BARCELONA, BIBLIOTECA DE CATALUNYA

included both Orsini's letter and, once again, certificates from doctors who had examined the wounds testifying to their prodigious healing.[16] The last page showed a small image of the divine saviour Filippo, clearly inserted both for commercial reasons and to provide the reader with visual reinforcement of the exceptional event.[17] A second edition, based on the first, came out in Naples, and both were very soon being reproduced and put on sale in major cities including Rome, Florence, Turin and Lisbon—the latter in Portuguese.

Orsini's letter was also distributed widely in Spain, with six editions translated into Spanish and distributed in major cities including Madrid, Salamanca, Barcelona (reproduced in Figure 5.1), Valencia, Granada and Seville.

There were many reasons for this publishing boom. Firstly, a story about a priest being saved from the effects of a terrible earthquake and recovering in record time had intrinsic appeal, especially in Spain, where there was a keen

---

16   Vincenzo Maria Orsini, *Narrazione de' prodigii operati del glorioso S. Filippo Neri. Nella persona dell'Eminent. Sig. Cardinale Orsini Arcivescovo di Benevento. In occasione che rimase sotto le rouine delle sue stanze nel Tremuoto che distrusse quella Città à 5 di Giugno 1688* (Naples: Novello de Bonis, 1688).

17   Marco Santoro & Maria Gioia Tavoni (ed.), *I dintorni del testo: approcci alle periferie del libro: atti del Convegno internazionale (Rome, 15–17 November 2004; Bologna, 18–19 November 2004)*, (2 vols., Rome: Edizioni dell'Ateneo, 2005).

appetite for sensationalist news.[18] Secondly, the reader was drawn into the event through the first-hand account provided in the form of a letter.[19] Thirdly, the event itself had significant religious and spiritual implications, as it corroborated yet again that salvation came to those who, like Orsini, tirelessly practiced their faith and devoted themselves to prayer in the hope of God's mercy, and in particular when they turned to one of His most authoritative intermediaries.

Spanish oratory communities certainly benefited from the popularity of Orsini's letter and could use the account to stimulate local veneration of the saint. Indeed, he soon became the protagonist of rituals and prayers conducted to ward off divine retribution such as the violent earthquakes and other natural disasters.[20] In particular, his intervention was called for vigorously in collective supplication and litanies, as demonstrated by transcriptions in the press of sermons given in Toledo and Valencia in 1688 in which the Sannio earthquake was linked to another that had hit the distant city of Lima a year earlier.[21]

2   Rekindling the News and the Good Fortune of an Image

News of the Sannio earthquake was disseminated in Spain's main cities by a thriving publishing market which connected with a population eager to learn

18   Henry Ettinghausen, 'Hacia una tipología de la prensa española del siglo XVII: de "hard news" a "soft porn"', in I. Arellano Ayuso, C. Pinillos Salvador, M. Vitse, & F. Serralta (eds.), *Studia aurea: actas del III Congreso de la AISO (Toulouse, 1993)* (3 vols., Navarra: Universidad de Navarra-GRISO, 1996), vol. 1, pp. 51–66. For an overview of Spanish news networks, see Javier Díaz Noci, 'The Iberian Position in European News Networks: A Methodological Approach', in J. Raymond & N. Moxham (eds.), *News networks in early modern Europe* (Leiden-Boston: Brill, 2016), pp. 193–215.
19   Abel Iglesias Castellano, 'La interpretación de las catástrofes naturales en el siglo XVII', *Ab Initio*, 8 (2013), pp. 87–120: 93.
20   Armando Alberola Romá, 'La natura desfermada. Al voltant de manuscrits, impresos i imatges sobre desastres naturals en l'Espanya del segle XVIII', in A. Alberola Romá & J. Olcina Cantos (eds.), *Desastre natural, vida cotidiana y religiosidad popular en la España moderna y contemporánea* (Alicante: Publicaciones de la Universidad de Alicante, 2009), pp. 17–76.
21   Mathias Fernández de Consuegra, *Relacion sucinta de la solemne, quanto devota procession de rogatiua, que por el estrago de Lima, y Napoles ha celebrado la piedad de los fieles imperiales de la muy catholica, y nobilissima ciudad de Toledo* ([Madrid], s.n., 1688); Vicente Noguera, *Sermon de rogativas por los terremotos sucedidos en las ciudades de Napoles, y Lima* (Valencia: Jaime de Bordázar, 1688). Domenico Cecere, '"Subterranea conspiración". Terremoti, comunicazione e politica nella monarchia di Carlo II', *Studi storici*, 60/4 (2019), pp. 811–843.

of Orsini's extraordinary rescue, as well as of the tragic consequences of the disaster. The level of public interest in St Filippo Neri and his miraculous powers mirrored to some extent the interest that had been generated half a century earlier by another saint who also specialised in disasters, namely San Gennaro (St Januarius), whose popularity soared as a result of his heroic deeds during the 1631 eruption of Mount Vesuvius.[22] Yet, Neri's reputation would far eclipse that of St Januarius, bolstered during the eighteenth century thanks to the spread of news about another extraordinary event, once again disseminated by the press. During the night of 14 January 1703, an earthquake hit the central Italian town of Norcia, in Umbria. The shocks damaged the buildings of a community of oratorians, trapping them inside. The timely intervention of St Filippo Neri, called upon vociferously by the trapped priests, provided them with an escape route, once again averting certain tragedy.[23]

This drew a very similar reaction from the Italian press to the 1688 event.[24] The news spread to Spain quickly in the now-standard *relaciones de sucesos* format, and was seen as a clear repetition of the supernatural intervention that had saved Orsini.[25] This account, like Orsini's letter, had won the hearts of the Spanish public as a second great demonstration of the saint's powers against earthquakes. This enthusiasm was a clear incentive for the Spanish press to produce more newssheets addressing both events over the course of the century, as well as devising a specific editorial format for them: an evolving compendium of news about the wonders performed by the saint when earthquakes struck.

The first opportunity came in 1724 when Orsini became Pope Benedict XIII. His elevation to the pontificate was the perfect moment to remind the general public of how he had survived the Sannio earthquake. Indeed, as well as being mentioned in brief biographies of the new Pope, Orsini's letter was once again published separately, as evidenced by editions printed in Madrid, Barcelona, Seville, Valencia (see Figure 5.2) and Murcia. News of the earthquake, and Orisin's survival, proved a commercial hit once again.

---

22   Gennaro Schiano, *Relatar la catástrofe en el Siglo de Oro. Entre noticia y narración* (Berlin: Peter Lang, 2021), pp. 109–139.

23   Azzolini, *Coping with Catastrophe*, p. 739.

24   *Relatione d un miracolo fatto dal glorioso S. Filippo Neri in preseruatione di tutta la Congregatione dell'oratorio di Norcia, cioè sette padri, & un fratello di essa Congregatione nelle presenti ruine de terremoti sentiti in quest'anno 1703* (Rome: Giuseppe Monaldi [1703]). The pamphlet was published simultaneously in Viterbo, Perugia, Naples and Milan. An additional reprint was documented a year after the event, in Bologna.

25   *Relación de un milagro, que obro Nuestro Señor por medio del glorioso patriarca San Felipe Neri, en la preservacion de toda su congregacion del Oratorio de Norcia* (Seville: Juan Francisco de Blas, 1703).

RELACION
DEL PRODIGIO OBRADO POR SAN FELIPE
Neri, en la Perſona del Eminentiſsimo Señor Cardenal Vicente Maria Orſini, Arçobiſpo de Benavento, en ocaſion que ſe halló baxo las ruìnas de ſu quarto, en el Terremoto que arruinò aquella Ciudad à 5. de Junio de 1688.

Signada, y firmada de ſu propria mano.

Venida de Genova à eſta Ciudad, y mandada traducir de Italiano en Eſpañol por un Devoto de S. Felipe Neri, para mas gloria de Dios, honor del Santo, y conſuelo de ſus Devotos.

El qual Eminentiſ.ᵐᵒ Señor Cardenal ha ſido exaltado à la Suprema Dignidad del Pontificado en 29. de Mayo 1724. con el nombre de BENEDICTO XIV.

CON LICENCIA:

In Valencia, por Jayme de Bordazar, en la Plaça de las Barcas. Año 1688. Y reimpreſſa por Antonio de Bordazar, año 1724.

FIGURE 5.2 *Relación del prodigio obrado por San Felipe Neri* (Valencia: Antonio de Bordázar, 1724)
© VALENCIA, BIBLIOTECA VALENCIANA NICOLAU PRIMITIU

There were two further occasions on which the account was reactivated, when earthquakes in Spain struck Montesa (Valencia) on 23 March 1748, and Lisbon on 1 November 1755.[26] Apart from the intensity of the earthquakes and their material and personal consequences, each event created the right moment to republish accounts of the saint's powers and to rekindle veneration of him. Orsini's letter, the account of the rescue of the oratorians of Norcia, and other news on the same theme were reprinted verbatim with the eloquent title *Prodigios obrados por el gran patriarca San Felipe Neri en tiempos de terremotos* (The Prodigious Works of the Great Patriarch St Filippo Neri in Times of Earthquakes). The earliest known edition was published in Valencia by the printer José Tomás Lucas in 1748, under licence from Pedro Albornoz y Tapies, a canon and archdeacon. The title page of this edition can be seen in Figure 5.3.

Other editions appeared in 1755 in Madrid, and in particular in Granada, Córdoba and Seville, which had all been affected by the Lisbon earthquake. The format became a best-seller in Spain, providing readers with a regularly updated compendium of the saint's latest interventions against earthquakes; it continued to be produced throughout the second half of the eighteenth century and even into the early nineteenth century.

Returning to Orsini's account of the supernatural event, an interesting aspect is its precise description of the paper image that came to rest on his body like a heavenly shield during the earthquake, protecting him from certain death. It was part of a collection of images depicting the life of St Filippo Neri that Orsini assiduously conserved in his office, in a 'walnut cabinet filled with writings'.[27] The image depicted the well-known event of 1576, when the then Father Filippo held up a timber beam that was threatening to fall onto the chapel housing the Holy Sacrament and the much-venerated painting of the *Madonna della Vallicella*.[28]

Indeed, this event was seen as central to Neri's biography and had spawned a specific iconography, starting with Pietro da Cortona's fresco (1664–1665) on the vault of the Congregation of the Oratory founded in 1650. One of the more

---

26 Armando Alberola Romá, 'La huella de la catástrofe en la España moderna. Reflexión en torno a los terremotos de 1748 y 1755', in M. D. Lorenzo, M. Rodríguez & D. Marcilhacy (eds.), *Historiar las catástrofes* (Mexico City: Universidad Nacional Autónoma de México – Sorbonne Université, 2019), pp. 67–92.

27 Orsini, *Narrazione de' prodigii*, n.p. The engravings were kept in folders, and were intended for Orsini's new residence in Benevento, near the church of Santa Maria della Pace (which was also destroyed by the earthquake). According to Orsini's account, the shocks had knocked over all the furniture, including the cabinet. The cabinet doors had flown open, strewing out the precious illustrations.

28 Ivi. See also Sarnelli, *Memorie dell'insigne Collegio*, p. 73.

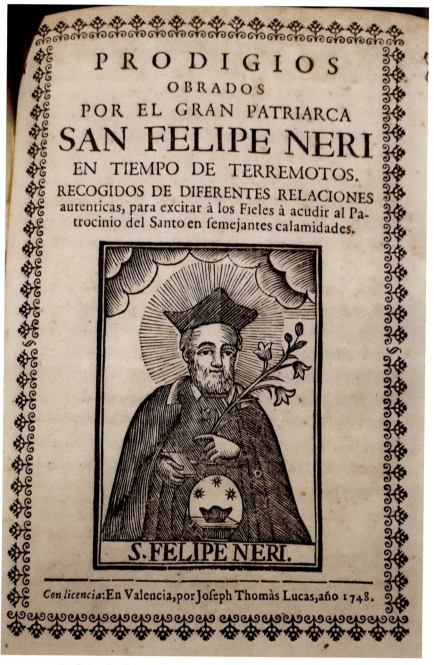

FIGURE 5.3 *Prodigios obrados por el gran Patriarca San Felipe Neri en tiempo de terremotos* (Valencia: Joseph Thomás Lucas, 1748)
© VALENCIA, BIBLIOTECA VALENCIANA NICOLAU PRIMITIU

famous versions of this image is the work of Giuseppe Maria Mitelli, produced in 1666.[29] However, we have no way of knowing whether the engraving in Orsini's collection was based on this work or some other version of the scene. Some clues can be gleaned from the official images depicting Orsini's rescue from the rubble, all of which were based on Pier Leone Ghezzi's 1725 canvas for St Filippo Neri's living quarters at the church of Santa Maria in Vallicella, and then reproduced in the church of St Filippo Neri in Macerata in 1725–1730.[30] In both, as in Giovanni Girolamo Frezza's exquisite engraving of the scene, which can be seen in Figure 5.4, the image shown next to Orsini does not appear to match the scene of the perilous beam devised by Pietro da Cortona.[31]

Technical issues related to the production of small-format engravings might have influenced the decision to use a simple representation of the saint in a state of ecstasy, with or without an accompanying Madonna and Child. The reference appears to refer more closely to Guido Reni's 1614 version for the Vallicella church. This was popularised through a number of *stampe di traduzione*, engraved prints of works of art with a brief description, starting with the earliest works of Luca Ciamberlano and Johann Friederich Greuter.[32] This image was already in use as a generic depiction of St Filippo Neri's post-canonisation interventions in press reports.[33] This perhaps contributed to it becoming the preferred visual element illustrating written accounts of Orsini's authoritative testimony of his extraordinary rescue. It can frequently

29   Evelina Borea, 'Le cupole nelle stampe', *Prospettiva*, 93/94 (1999), pp. 213–224: 223, fig. 12.
30   Anna Lo Bianco, *Pier Leone Ghezzi pittore* (Palermo: ILA Palma, 1995), pp. 204–205.
31   The *Archivio della Congregazione dell'Oratorio di Roma* houses an anonymous reproduction of Ghezzi's painting. See Sofia Barchesi, 'San Filippo Neri salva dal terremoto Vincenzo Maria Orsini arcivescovo di Benevento', in Antonella Pampalone, Sofia Barchiesi, *Iconografia di un Santo. Nuovi studi sull'immagine di San Filippo Neri* (Rome: Edizioni Oratoriane, 2017), pp. 242–244, cat. 18. A third version, also anonymous, can be found in *Das Ruhm- und Wunderwürdige Leben und Thaten Pabsts Benedicti des Dreyzehenden* (Frankfurt: Christoph Riegel, 1731), p. 34.
32   For more on engraved prints in the *stampe di traduzione* format, see the recent works published in Francesca Mariano & Véronique Meyer (eds.), *'Invenit et delineavit'. La stampa di traduzione tra Italia e Francia dal XVI al XIX secolo* (Rome: UniversItalia, 2018). Francesca Candi, *D'après le Guide. Incisioni seicentesche da Guido Reni* (Bologna: Fondazione Federico Zeri—Università di Bologna, 2016), pp. 118–119, 245. On Guido Reni's successful approach to iconography on San Filippo Neri, see Olga Melasecchi, 'Nascita e sviluppo dell'iconografia di S. Filippo Neri dal Cinquecento al Settecento', in A. Costamagna (ed.), *La Regola e la fama: San Filippo Neri e l'arte* (Rome: Museo di Palazzo Venezia, 1995), pp. 34–49: 38. For an overview, see Pampalone-Barchiesi, *Iconografia di un Santo*.
33   See, for example, the images in the frontispiece of *Miracolo insigne che fra molti altri ha operato S. Filippo Neri* and *Miracolo insigne operato in Roma per intercessione di S. Filippo Neri*, published in 1623 and 1644, respectively.

FIGURE 5.4 Giovanni Girolamo Frezza (after Pier Leone Ghezzi), *Archbishop Orsini extracted from the rubble of the 1688 earthquake*, in Pietro Giacomo Bacci and Giacomo Ricci, *Vita di S. Filippo Neri Fiorentino, fondatore della Congregazione dell'Oratorio* (Rome: Bernabò and Lazzarini, 1745)
© LOS ANGELES, GETTY RESEARCH INSTITUTE

be found in the frontispiece of many of the editions circulating in Italy and Spain cited above, whether they also include the Madonna with Child or only the figure of the saint in a state of ecstasy (see Figure 5.5). However, they were always cheaply-produced publications, in line with the requirements of a commercial product in general circulation or designed to be used during orations and canticles against earthquakes.[34]

The events examined in this chapter demonstrate how the diffusion of accounts of a disaster like the 1688 Sannio earthquake can launch a specific news event which can far outlive more conventional news stories. The popularity of Italian accounts in the Spanish publishing sector, reprinted so frequently, show that the focus of local printers immediately turned to the story of Archbishop Orsini's rescue by St Filippo Neri, as it was seen as a more viable commercial proposition than descriptions of the tragic consequences of the earthquake for the people and places directly affected by it.

Orsini's testimony gained great favour in this publishing sector, given its avidity for sensational news. His letter enjoyed particularly wide and enduring editorial success, circulating extensively in the main cities of Spain throughout the eighteenth century. The story also gave rise to the production of a specific form of publication recounting other wonders performed by Filippo Neri, the great divine agent against earthquakes. It was reprinted regularly whenever earthquakes struck to call upon the saint's divine powers. This led to the spread of a broad range of images that drew on the most eminent iconographic and compositional approaches in the repertoire of works depicting Filippo Neri. These spread across Spain as engravings and in newssheets to provide visual sustenance to the faithful.

---

34 For more on the use of religious imagery in the press, see Pierre Civil, 'Iconografía y relaciones en pliegos: la exaltación de la Inmaculada en la Sevilla de principios del siglo XVII', in H. Ettinghausen, V. Infantes, A. Redondo & M. C. García de Enterría (eds.), *Las relaciones de sucesos en España 1500–1750* (Alcalá de Henares: Servicio de Publicaciones Universidad de Alcalá, 1996), pp. 65–78. See too Henry Ettinghausen, 'The Illustrated Spanish News: Test and image in the Seventeenth-Century Press', in C. Davis & P. J. Smith (eds.), *Art and literature in Spain: 1600–1800: studies in honour of Nigel Glendinning* (London-Madrid: Támesis, 1993), pp. 117–134; Ettinghausen, *How the Press Began*, pp. 267–281. On orations and canticles, see Gennaro Angiolino, 'San Filippo Neri nelle immaginette religiose', in *Messer Filippo Neri, Santo: l'Apostolo di Roma* (Rome: De Luca, 1995), pp. 53–54; Ángel Alba Alarcos, *San Felipe Neri en el arte español* (Alcalá de Henares: Ballesteros, 1996), pp. 131–143.

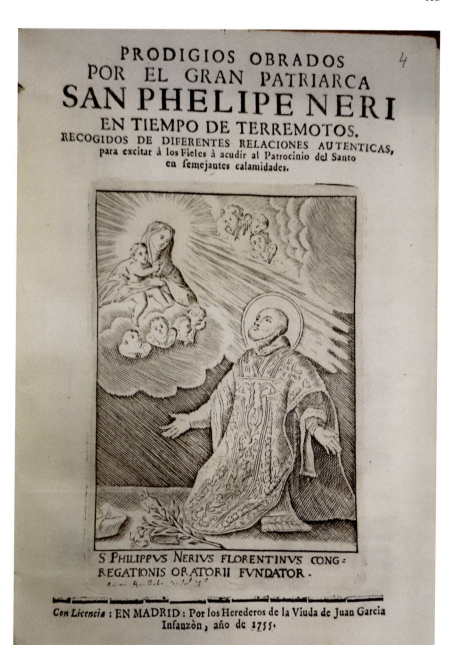

FIGURE 5.5 Augustin Bouttats, *St Filippo Neri's vision of the Virgin Mary*, in *Prodigios obrados por el gran patriarca San Phelipe Neri en tiempo de terremotos* (Madrid: Herederos de la viuda de Juan García Infanzón, 1755)
© MADRID, BIBLIOTECA NACIONAL DE ESPAÑA

Appendix: A Bibliography of News Items Related to St Filippo Neri and Earthquakes, 1623–1829

Miracolo insigne che fra molti altri ha operato S. Filippo Neri, fondatore della Congregatione dell'Oratorio dopo la sua Canonizatione in Roma alli 7 di nouemb. 1622 (Rome: Alessandro Zanetti, 1623). [Rome, Biblioteca Casanatense, VOL MISC. 2687 22]

Miracolo insigne operato in Roma per intercessione di S. Filippo Neri, fondatore della Congregatione dell'Oratorio alli 5. di gennaio del corrente anno 1644. Nella persona di suor Maria Eletta Radi di Cortona (Rome & Florence: Filippo Papini, 1644). [Florence, Biblioteca Nazionale Centrale, V.MIS 75.19]

A true and exact relation of the most dreadful earthquake which happened in the city of Naples (London: Rendan Taylor, 1688). [London, British Library, 444.b.29]

Copiosissima e distinta relatione dell'horribile, e spauentoso terremoto accaduto in Napoli [...] E con altre particolarità cospicue messe in questa seconda impressione, delle quali non si hauea notizia alla prima (Naples & Todi: Vincenzo Galassi, 1688). [Rome, Biblioteca Nazionale Centrale, MISC. B.499.15]

Declaracion authentica, que hizo el eminentissimo senor Cardenal de Ursini [...] (Naples & Seville: Juan Francisco de Blas [1688]). [IB: 69129; Santos Fernández, *El terremoto de Nápoles*, p. 207, n. 2]

Declaracion fielmente traduzida del idioma italiano en el nuestro castellano publicada por el Emmo. senor cardenal Vrsini, arcobispo de Benevento, de los prodigios obrados por el glorioso patriarca S. Phelipe Neri en su persona en la ocasion de quedar sepultado en las ruinas de su mismo Palacio en el terremoto que asolo aquella ciudad en 5 de Iunio de 1688 (Madrid: Julián de Paredes [1688]). [IB: 74289; Santos Fernández, *El terremoto de Nápoles*, p. 208, n. 3]

Declaracion fielmente traduzida del idioma italiano en el nuestro castellano, publicada por el cardenal Ursini, arçobispo de Benevento, de los prodigios obrados por el glorioso patriarca s. Felipe Neri en su persona, en la ocasion de quedar sepultado en las ruinas de su mismo palacio, en el terremoto que assolo aquella ciudad en 5 de junio de 1688 (Granada: Imprenta del Convento de la Santísima Trinidad por Antonio de Torrubia, 1688.). [IB: 74288]

Fernández de Consuegra, Mathias, *Relacion sucinta de la solemne, quanto devota procession de rogatiua, que por el estrago de Lima, y Napoles ha celebrado la piedad de los fieles imperiales de la muy catholica, y nobilissima ciudad de Toledo* ([Madrid]: s.n., 1688). [IB: 106413; Santos Fernández, *El terremoto de Nápoles*, p. 210, n. 6]

Individual y verdadera relacion del horrible y espantoso terremoto sucedido en Napoles, y mas partes del Reyno el dia 5 de Junio de 1688, con el numero de las ciudades, tierras, y otros lugares arruinados, como tambien de los que quedaron muertos, y heridos en tan lastimosa tragedia (Seville: Tomás López de Haro, 1688). [IB: 123041; Santos Fernández, *El terremoto de Nápoles*, pp. 206–207, n. 1]

La Déplorable désolation générale, arrivée au royaume de Naples, le 5 et 6 juin 1688 veille et jour de Pentecôte, à onze heures du matin ; qui a abimé plusieurs villes, bourgs, villages et châteaux. Avec le tremblement de terre arrivée au Pérou. Traduit d'italien en françois (Turin: A. Giannelli, 1688). [Paris, Bibliothèque nationale de France, K-14768]

Magnati, Vincenzo *Notitie istoriche de' terremoti succeduti ne' secoli trascorsi, e nel presente, indirizzate alla serenissima real maestà di Carlo 2* (Naples: Antonio Bulifon, 1688). [Naples, Biblioteca della Società Napoletana di Storia Patria, SISMICA 07.B. 039]

Noguera, Vicente, *Sermon de rogativas por los terremotos sucedidos en las ciudades de Napoles, y Lima* (Valencia: Jaime de Bordázar, 1688). [IB: 115254; Santos Fernández, *El terremoto de Nápoles*, p. 211, n. 7]

Nuoua, e vera relatione del grandissimo terremoto seguito nella città di Napoli, e suoi luoghi circonvicini. Seguito alli cinque di giugno à hore vent'una 1688 (Naples and Genoa: Anton Giorgio Franchelli, [1688]). [Genoa, Biblioteca Universitaria, SALA 2 /B /9bis 1 5]

Noticias generales del Imperio; y con entera relacion de los terremotos que han sucedido en Napoles, y Lima. Venidas à Barcelona à 9 de julio de 1688 (Barcelona: Rafael Figueró, 1688). [IB: 115451]

Orsini, Vincenzo Maria, *Narrazione de' prodigii operati del glorioso S. Filippo Neri. Nella persona dell'Eminent. Sig. Cardinale Orsini Arcivescovo di Benevento. In occasione che rimase sotto le rouine delle sue stanze nel Tremuoto che distrusse quella Città à 5 di Giugno 1688* (Naples: Novello de Bonis, 1688). [Naples, Biblioteca Nazionale, V. F. 162 E 40 (0003]

Orsini, Vincenzo Maria, *Narrazione de' prodigii operati del glorioso S. Filippo Neri* [...] (Naples: Novello de Bonis, reprinted by Michele Monaco, 1688). [London, British Library, 444.c.41.(8.)]

Orsini, Vincenzo Maria, *Narrazione de' prodigii operati del glorioso S. Filippo Neri* [...] (Naples & Rome: per Francesco Buagni, 1688). [Florence, Biblioteca Nazionale Centrale, 34. 7.F.21.15]

Orsini, Vincenzo Maria, *Narrazione de' prodigii operati del glorioso S. Filippo Neri* [...] (Naples & Florence: Eredi degli Onofri, 1688). [Florence, Biblioteca Nazionale Centrale, V.MIS 1001.30]

Orsini, Vincenzo Maria, *Prodigii operati da S. Filippo Neri nella persona dell'Eminent.mo Orsino Arcivescovo di Benevento in occasione, che rimase sotto le ruine delle sue stanze nel terremoto che distrusse quella città a 5. giugno 1688* (Turin: Gio. Battista Zappata, 1688). [Biella, Biblioteca del Santuario di Nostra Signora di Oropa, OROPA 17 O 010]

Relaçam dos prodigios obrados pelo glorioso S. Felippe Neri na pessoa do ... Cardeal Ursino, Arcebispo de Benevento, quando ficou debaixo das ruinas do seu palacio no terremoto, que assolou aquella cidade a 5. de Junho de 1688 (Lisbon: Domingos Carneyro, 1688). [IB: 123691]

Relatione dell'orribile terremoto seguito nelle Città di Napoli, Benevento, et altri luoghi (Naples & Bologna: s.n., 1688). [Catalogue of Strong Italian Earthquakes http://storing.ingv.it/cfti/cfti4/quakes/01108.html#]

Relacion de el prodigio obrado por s. Felipe Neri, en la persona del eminentissimo señor d. fr. Vicente Maria Orsini, cardenal de la s. iglesia romana, de el titulo de s. Sixto, de la orden de predicadores, arçobispo de Benavento (Salamanca: Lucas Pérez, 1688). [IB: 69092]

Relacion del prodigio obrado por San Felipe Neri [...] (Barcelona: Rafael Figueró, 1688). [IB: 69128; Santos Fernández, *El terremoto de Nápoles*, pp. 208–209, n. 4]

Relacion del prodigio obrado por San Felipe Neri [...] (Valencia: Jaime de Bordázar, 1688). [IB: 69130; Santos Fernández, *El terremoto de Nápoles*, pp. 209–210, n. 5]

Sarnelli, Pompeo, *Memorie dell'insigne Collegio di S. Spirito della città di Benevento* (Naples: Giuseppe Rosselli, 1688, ed. Cesena: P. P. Ricceputi, 1688). [Florence, Biblioteca Nazionale Centrale, MAGL. 4.1.65]

Terza relatione dell'horribile, e spaventoso terremoto accaduto in Napoli, & in più parti del Regno il giorno 5. Giugno 1688. Co'l numero delle città, terre, & altri luoghi rouinati. Come anco delli morti, e feriti rimasti in così compassionevole tragedia (Naples & Genoa: Antonio Casamara, [1688]). [Genoa, Biblioteca Universitaria, SALA 2 /B /9bis 1 6]

Vera, e distinta relatione dell'horribile, e spauentoso terremoto accaduto in Napoli, & in più parti del Regno il giorno 5 Giugno 1688. Co'l numero delle città, terre, & altri luoghi rouinati. Come anco delli morti, e feriti rimasti in cosí compassioneuole tragedia (Naples: Domenico Antonio Parrino, 1688). [Rome, Biblioteca Casanatense, VOL MISC.387 20]

Vera e distinta relazione dello spauentoso terremoto occorso nelle citta di Napoli, Benevento e Salerno con la sua castelli e terre circonvicine. Seguito il di 5, 6 e 7 giugno 1688 [...] (Florence: S.A.S. alla Condotta, 1688). [Naples, Biblioteca della Società Napoletana di Storia Patria, SISMICA 07.D. 014 (19)]

Vera, fedele e distintissima relazione di tutti i danni, così delle fabriche come delle persone morte per cagione dell'occorso terremoto accaduto alli 5 di giugno 1688 tanto in questa città di Napoli, quanto nel suo Regno (Naples: Camillo Cavallo, 1688). [Modena, Biblioteca Estense, E 063 G 042 002]

Giannelli, Basilio, *Orazione panegirica All' Eminentissimo signor cardinale Orsini Arcivescovo di Benevento* (Benevento: s.n., 1693). [Benevento, Biblioteca Provinciale—Museo del Sannio, SEZ. RARI B 120]

Capece, Angelo, *Orazione panegirica per le glorie di S. Filippo Neri fondatore della Congregazione dell'Oratorio in Roma* [...] (Rome: Luca Antonio Chracas, 1703) [Azzolini, *Coping with Catastrophe*, p. 747]

Relación de un milagro, que obro Nuestro Señor por medio del glorioso patriarca San Felipe Neri, en la preservacion de toda su congregacion del Oratorio de Norcia (Seville: Juan Francisco de Blas, 1703). [Munich, Bayerische Staatsbibliothek, Rar. 4554]

Relatione d un miracolo fatto dal glorioso S. Filippo Neri in preseruatione di tutta la Congregatione dell'oratorio di Norcia, cioè sette padri, & un fratello di essa Congregatione nelle presenti ruine de terremoti sentiti in quest'anno 1703 (Rome: Giuseppe Monaldi, [1703]). [Cremona, Biblioteca Statale, FA.Ab.3.24/10]

Relatione d un miracolo fatto dal glorioso S. Filippo Neri [...] (Rome & Naples: Novello de Bonis, 1703). [Naples, Biblioteca della Società Napoletana di Storia Patria, SISMICA 03.A. 056 (46)]

Relatione d un miracolo fatto dal glorioso S. Filippo Neri [...] (Rome & Perugia: Desideri, 1703). [Perugia, Biblioteca Augusta, ANT I.I 2521 (24)]

Relatione d un miracolo fatto dal glorioso S. Filippo Neri [...] (Milan: Giuseppe Pandolfo Malatesta, 1703). [Milan, Biblioteca Nazionale Braidense, XM.+ 04. 0014/10]

Relatione d un miracolo fatto dal glorioso S. Filippo Neri [...] (Viterbo: Stamperia di Giulio de' Giulii, 1703). [Rome, Biblioteca Vallicelliana, S.BOR Q.V 238(18)]

Relatione d un miracolo fatto dal glorioso S. Filippo Neri [...] (Bologna: Manolessi, 1704). [Bologna, Biblioteca Universitaria, A.5.Tab. 1.K.2. 118/5]

Breve relacion de la vida dell'Emin.mo Señor Cardenal Fr. Vicente Maria Orsini [...] (Valencia: Joseph Pablo ciego, [1724]). [Santos Fernández, *El terremoto de Nápoles*, pp. 211–212, n. 8]

Breve relacion de la vida dell'Emin.mo Señor Cardenal Fr. Vicente Maria Orsini [...] (Madrid: Juan Pérez, [1724]). [Santos Fernández, *El terremoto de Nápoles*, pp. 2012–2013, nn. 9–10]

Declaracion authentica, que hizo el eminentissimo senor Cardenal de Ursini [...] (Madrid: s.n., 1724). [IB: 123424; Santos Fernández, *El terremoto de Nápoles*, pp. 214–215, n. 12]

Declaracion authentica, que hizo el eminentissimo senor Cardenal de Ursini [...] (Seville: s.n., 1724). [Santos Fernández, *El terremoto de Nápoles*, pp. 213–214, n. 11]

Prodigio de San Phelipe Neri obrado en 5. de junio de 1688 (Barcelona: Francisco Guash, [1724]). [Barcelona, Universitat de Barcelona, Biblioteca de Reserva, 07 B-39/4/9–19]

Relacion del prodigio obrado por San Felipe Neri [...] (Valencia: Jaime de Bordázar, 1688, reprinted by Antonio de Bordázar, 1724). [Santos Fernández, *El terremoto de Nápoles*, pp. 215–216, n. 13]

Relacion de un milagro que obró el P. S. Felipe Neri [...] (Murcia: s.n., 1724). [Santos Fernández, *El terremoto de Nápoles*, p. 216, n. 14]

Prodigios obrados por el gran patriarca San Felipe Neri en tiempo de terremotos. Recogidos de diferentes relaciones authenticas, para excitar à los Fieles à acudir al Patrocinio del Santo en semejantes calamidades (Valencia: Joseph Thomás Lucas, 1748). [Santos Fernández, *El terremoto de Nápoles*, pp. 216–217, n. 15]

Patrocinio admirable del glorioso patriarcha, y perfectissimo modelo del Estado Eclesiastico San Phelipe Neri, segundo Thaumaturgo, y especial auogado en tiempo de terremotos. Sacanlo a la luz publica la deuocion de sus hijos, para excitar al pueblo sevillano (Seville, imprenta de los Recientes, [1755]. [IB: 118295]

Prodigios obrados por el gran patriarca San Felipe Neri [...] (Madrid: Herederos de la viuda de Juan García Infanzón, 1755). [Santos Fernández, *El terremoto de Nápoles*, pp. 217–218, n. 16]

Prodigios obrados por el gran patriarcha San Felipe Neri [...] (Cordoba: Gonzalo Serrano por Francisco Vallón [1755]). [IB: 120215; Santos Fernández, *El terremoto de Nápoles*, p. 219, n. 18]

Prodigios obrados por el gran patriarcha San Felipe Neri [...] (Granada: Joseph de la Puerta, 1755). [Santos Fernández, *El terremoto de Nápoles*, pp. 218–219, n. 17]

Prodigios obrados por el gran patriarcha San Felipe Neri [...] (Granada: Imprenta Real, 1785). [Santos Fernández, *El terremoto de Nápoles*, pp. 219–220, n. 19]

Oracion muy devota al gran padre y patriarca San Felipe Neri, en tiempo de terremotos, junto con algunos prodigios obrados por intersecion del mismo santo, recogidos de diferentes relaciones autenticas (Barcelona: Francisco Suriá y Burgada, 1790). [Valencia, Biblioteca Valenciana Nicolau Primitiu, XVIII F-974]

Prodigios obrados por el gran Patriarca San Felipe Neri, en tiempo de terremotos: Recogidos de diferentes relaciones autenticas, para excitar à los Fieles à acudir al Patrocinio del Santo en semejantes calamidades (Cordoba: Luis Ramos, 1804). [Cordoba, Biblioteca Municipal]

Oracion, muy devota, al grande Padre y Patriarca, San Felipe Neri, en tiempo de terremotos, junto con algunos prodigios obrados por instercesion del mismo Santo, recogidos de differentes relaciones auténticas, para escítar, á los fieles á acudir al patrocinio del, Santo en semejantes calamidades (Barcelona: Valero Sierra y Martí, 1829). [Barcelona, Biblioteca de Catalunya, 24–12-C 15/13]

CHAPTER 6

'Yet Once More I Shake Not Only the Earth'
News of Earthquakes in Early Modern England

Lena Liapi

On 24 May 1688, the *London Gazette* led with the news that 'on the 20th of October last, at 4 a Clock in the morning, there happened an Earthquake at Lima in the Kingdom of Peru'.[1] It may have taken a long time for this news to reach London, but readers were at last able to learn all about this disaster that shook a faraway land. Satirists unceasingly mocked the populace's thirst for foreign news.[2] Echoing earlier criticisms, Caspar Stiele satirised Germans for always seeking to learn the latest news, claiming that it was folly to care about events as remote as the eruption of volcanoes in Italy or the safe arrival of ships in harbours worldwide. Such occurrences were of as little relevance to German audiences as 'knowing whether or not men or spirits live on the moon'.[3] Despite such claims, unusual events were of prime interest to readers, judging by how often they were presented in newspapers and other news media. Partly due to restrictions in reporting domestic occurrences, news about incidents taking place in increasingly remote areas proliferated.[4] News of earthquakes was part of this trend: in the seventeenth century the rise of serial publications accompanied by increased international trade and colonisation made news of earthquakes more easily accessible and more significant, even when such news took a long time to reach Europe.

This chapter will examine the reportage of earthquakes in seventeenth-century newspapers. Recent scholarship has argued that newspapers were an innovative news medium, since they reported matter-of-fact. In particular, Barbara Shapiro has analysed newspapers as discourses of fact, arguing that they sought to bolster their credibility by emphasising the reliability of their

1 *The London Gazette* 2349, 24 May 1688.
2 André Belo, 'News Exchange and Social Distinction', in Joad Raymond and Noah Moxham (eds.), *News Networks in Early Modern Europe*, (Leiden & Boston: Brill, 2016), pp. 375–393.
3 Eileen Reeves, *Evening News: Optics, Astronomy, and Journalism in Early Modern Europe* (Philadelphia: University of Pennsylvania Press, 2014), p. 5.
4 S. K. Barker, 'International News Pamphlets' in A. Kesson & E. Smith (eds.), *The Elizabethan Top Ten: Defining Print Popularity in Early Modern England* (Farnham: Ashgate, 2013), pp. 145–157.

sources (using 'credible witnesses') and trumpeting claims of 'truth telling and impartiality' in their title and contents. Editors supported such claims by employing a 'plain style' of reporting, giving specific details, such as the time and place of an event, and by using tentative language for unverified reports. In Shapiro's words, newspapers stressed 'the rejection of fiction and the distinction between a relation of matters of fact and commentary or conjecture on those facts'.[5] According to Shapiro, but also historians of science, in the same period natural sciences also articulated fact-based discourses. Vladimir Jankovic, summarising the field, has claimed that the new sciences from the mid-seventeenth century were 'marked by the socially informed practices of epistemological censoring. Through these practices, the new sciences declared illicit the discourses—such as "popular technique"—which failed to dissociate "nature" from "politics", psychology from objectivity—in other words, which failed to make "nature" the subject of disinterested fact gathering and specified literary technologies of reporting'.[6] Both scholars show that newspapers and natural sciences emphasised matter-of-fact and disinterested observation as the main methods for information gathering and presenting. As Rienk Vermij has argued, in the reportage of natural phenomena such as earthquakes, these methods of presenting information intersected, as newspapers 'collected and released the bare facts' of earthquakes.[7]

Newspaper editors employed a range of rhetorical strategies in order to make their news more relevant and, by consequence, more saleable. These strategies were not limited to presenting events as matter of fact. On the contrary, even though newspaper reportage claimed to be matter-of-fact, credible, and disinterested, these claims were often undermined by the use of anonymous witnesses whose credibility could not be checked, by adopting what D. R. Woolf called the 'common voice', and by employing language and styles of description from 'strange news' pamphlets, which foregrounded human suffering. This sensational reportage, which focused on the reactions of onlookers and painted vivid images of desolation, was intended to provoke a stronger emotional response, by allowing readers to vicariously experience the catastrophe wrought upon distant communities. This sensationalism should not be separated from newspapers' 'matter of fact' reportage: both made the impact of such news more profound. By constantly reporting natural disasters, by

---

5 Barbara J. Shapiro, *A Culture of Fact: England, 1550–1720* (Ithaca & London: Cornell University Press, 2000), pp. 86, 121.
6 Vladimir Jankovic, 'The Politics of Sky Battles in Early Hanoverian Britain', *Journal of British Studies*, 41/4 (October 2002), p. 445.
7 Rienk Vermij, *Thinking on Earthquakes in Early Modern Europe: Firm Beliefs on Shaky Ground* (London: Routledge, 2020), p. 161.

relating such news to the personal interests and religious viewpoints of readers, and by appealing to their emotions, newspapers elicited a sense that the world was shrinking both cognitively and emotionally. Contrary to the claims of satirists, newspapers stressed that readers had reason to care about news of earthquakes.

1 Witnesses and Credibility

Newspaper claims of truth-telling and trustworthiness, according to Shapiro, hinged on the existence of credible witnesses.[8] In the seventeenth century, however, credibility was often dependent upon social status. Members of the upper orders were more likely to be believed than commoners, even in a legal setting, when testimony was given under oath.[9] Historiographical work on credit has modified this picture, by arguing that it depended on the standing of individuals in the community and was also contingent on their interactions with others.[10] Newspaper sources, however, were for the most part anonymous, thus not allowing any gauging of the individual's credit. With few exceptions—more often details of a ship passing by a stricken area—the reports included in newspapers bore no authenticating name.[11]

Newspapers presented reports as correspondence by claiming that they had 'advice' or a 'relation' from nearby cities.[12] Implicit in the use of this technique was the assumption that correspondents were credible. Traditionally, they were diplomats or other officials: their account could be seen as authoritative, even if they often reported rumours or the mood of a city rather than verified events.[13] Newspapers, however, kept the appearance of correspondence without specifying who their sources were. In this, they were imitating newsletters, manuscript news which were sent to subscribers. Newsletter readers relied on the credibility of the newsletter writer rather than the sources themselves; readers could assume that Henry Muddiman—one of the most famous newsletter writers of the period—would have reliable information. Similarly, newspapers could reinforce their credibility when their editor was known,

---

8   Shapiro, *A Culture of Fact*, p. 121.
9   Steven Shapin, *A Social History of Truth: Civility and Science in Seventeenth-Century England* (Chicago & London: The University of Chicago Press, 1994), pp. 65–125.
10 Craig Muldrew, *The Economy of Obligation: the Culture of Credit and Social Relations in Early Modern England* (Houndmills: Macmillan, 1998).
11 *The London Gazette* 1571, 9 December 1680.
12 *The London Gazette* 693, 8 July 1672.
13 Raymond and Moxham, *News Networks in Early Modern Europe*, p. 9.

such as *Dawk's Newsletter* or John Dunton's *The Athenian Mercury*, or when the newspaper was connected to official sources, such as the *London Gazette*. Even in these cases, however, trustworthiness lay with the editors or newspapers themselves and could be debated, but not in witnesses. Most readers were aware that news writers often depended on rumour and hearsay as sources for news.[14] In the case of earthquake reportage, no credible witnesses were employed; newspapers relied on the status of their editor to be seen as trustworthy. This required a significant leap of faith on behalf of the reader, given that there was no way to ascertain where such news came from.

Newspapers navigated the issue of credibility by presenting reports of earthquakes as eyewitness accounts. As David Randall has argued 'Newspaper rhetoric, written by an unknown writer to an unknown reader, substituted logical argument, embedded in the narrative, for the rhetoric of personal knowledge', with the aim to lend credence to the reports.[15] When reporting on earthquakes happening in Naples in June 1688, the *London Gazette* included a first-person description: 'The 7th Instant we had here another Earthquake ... The 10th we again perceived a trembling of the Earth; and on the 14th felt a more violent Shock ... so that we fear the Earthquake will continue all this Moon, as that did which happened in December 1456'.[16] Even though the account is coming—readers are left to assume—from an eyewitness, no attempt is made to evaluate their social credit.

In order to make anonymous reports more reliable, newspapers resorted to the 'common voice' or 'common fame': this was a consensual view of events which was agreed upon by local inhabitants. D. R. Woolf uses this concept to talk about the memory of a community and argues that this 'common voice' was accepted as credible by antiquarians and historians in early modern England. Information gained by the consensus of inhabitants could be suspect or distorted, but in the absence of other sources it could be taken as an authoritative source of information.[17] Vladimir Jankovic has employed Woolf's concept of the 'common voice' to discuss how pamphleteers writing on prodigies and miracles used local inhabitants almost exclusively as witnesses.[18]

---

14   Brendan Dooley 'News and Doubt in Early Modern Culture' in Brendan Dooley & Sabrina A. Baron (eds.), *The Politics of Information in Early Modern Europe* (London & New York: Routledge, 2001), p. 278.
15   David Randall, 'Epistolary Rhetoric, the Newspaper, and the Public Sphere', *Past & Present*, 198 (2008), p. 27.
16   *The London Gazette* 2365, 16 July 1688.
17   D. R. Woolf, 'The "common voice": History, folklore and oral tradition in early modern England', *Past & Present*, 120 (1988), pp. 26–52, p. 30.
18   Jankovic, 'The Politics of Sky Battles', p. 438.

The same emphasis on the 'common voice' can be seen in newspaper reportage of earthquakes. For example, in 1652 the *Severall Proceedings in Parliament* reported from the Island of Scilly: 'On the 25 instant about ten at night the people of these Islands were terrified with an Earthquake, that they feared the falling downe of their low Houses ...'.[19] Here, the phrasing of the news report suggests that we hear the experiences of local inhabitants. This was also the case with an earthquake in Lyon in 1681: 'they write ... that an Earthquake has lately happened in those parts, continuing very terrible for the space of half an hour, to the great consternation of the Inhabitants'.[20] Invoking local memory also implied that the information was coming from the local community, with such expressions as 'the like [earthquake] has not been known within the memory of Man'or 'we had such a violent Earthquake here, as the oldest Man alive does not remember the like'.[21] An account from Naples found in the *London Gazette* starts by providing information in the third person, but then moves to the first, implying that this was also taken from local eyewitnesses: 'On Saturday last the 5th Instant about the 22th hour, hapned here a Dreadful Earthquake (though it lasted not long) which frightning the Inhabitants out of their Houses' they fled. The same report continues 'this day we have felt nothing of it'.[22] The slippage from the third to the first person frames this as an eyewitness account. With no way of knowing the identity of this source, its credibility rests on assuming it represents what local inhabitants experienced.

There was no way to verify that the accounts of earthquakes presented in newspapers were given by eyewitnesses, let alone that such witnesses were credible. Since newspapers could not rely on having reliable witnesses, they resorted to presenting their anonymous sources as the consensus of local inhabitants. This meant, however, that people who were not traditionally seen as trustworthy gained a podium, while readers had to accept the fidelity of the newspaper. For all the talk of examining their sources or presenting news as 'matter of fact', newspapers' information had to be taken on trust. Joad Raymond identifies some of the same issues and claims that the veracity of news could be found in the nexus between the impartial reader and the impartial intelligencer. Impartiality was contingent on editors presenting reports without interpretation and on readers piecing news together from fragmented

---

19   *Severall Proceedings in Parliament*, 121, 15 January 1652, p. 1870.
20   *The Domestick Intelligence, or News both from City and Country Impartially Related* 11, 30 June 1681.
21   *The Domestick intelligence, or News both from City and Country Impartially Related* 132, 28 August 1682; *The Flying Post* 685, 28 September 1699.
22   *The London Gazette* 2358, 21 June 1688. The same can be seen in the earthquakes of Sicily, see *The London Gazette* 2847, 23 February 1693.

weekly reports.[23] Nonetheless, the impartial editor and the impartial reader are idealised versions of what took place in the interplay between news presentation and news reading. As we will see, the reports themselves included editorial material and the selection of which sources to present as credible was an act of interpretation. Eyewitnesses could also be discredited by editors when it suited them.

2   Natural and Providential Understandings of Earthquakes

In the seventeenth century, explanations of earthquakes ranged from the natural—influenced by classical writers but also the development of natural sciences—to the supernatural. A common compromise between the two positions was to accept that God was the primary cause for the earthquake, but also investigate the natural phenomena which surrounded seismic activity and establish causal links between the ground and the skies.[24] Newspapers were sensitive to natural explanations of disasters but also engaged with providential understandings of them. Newspapers often borrowed the language and styles of description from 'strange news' pamphlets, which dealt with unusual phenomena such as earthquakes, floods, storms, and monstrous births.[25] This complicates recent scholarship on newspapers by both Shapiro and Vermij, who claim that newspapers sought to strengthen their claims of accuracy by presenting events as matter-of-fact. In the case of earthquakes, this 'objective' style included emphasis on specific details, an analysis of the causes of the earthquakes based on natural phenomena, and the use of non-committal language when information was uncertain.

Newspapers typically presented the same details: the exact time of an earthquake and its duration, the extent of damages caused, both to people and property. However, they occasionally provided observations of natural phenomena, which could be associated with earthquakes, such as the rise of 'black Vapors and Flames like to those of Mount Vesuvius', or the fact that four days before an earthquake in Naples, 'the Sun appeared at 17 Hours with a Flame about

---

23 Joad Raymond, 'Exporting Impartiality', in Kathryn Murphy & Anita Traninger (eds.), *The Emergence of Impartiality* (Leiden & Boston: Brill, 2014), p. 163.
24 Gerrit Jasper Schenk, 'Disastro, Catastrophe, and Divine Judgment: Words, Concepts and Images for "Natural" Threats to Social Order in the Middle Ages and Renaissance', in Jennifer Spinks & Charles Zika (eds.), *Disaster, Death and the Emotions in the Shadow of the Apocalypse, 1400–1700* (London: Palgrave Macmillan, 2016), p. 49.
25 Alexandra Walsham, *Providence in Early Modern England* (Oxford: Oxford University Press, 1999), pp. 167–224.

it'.²⁶ Even though no causal link between these phenomena was presented, the implication was that they presaged the motion of the earth. This was especially the case with descriptions of weather. An earthquake in Lyon in June 1681 was also accompanied by 'a Storm of Hail and Rain, that the like has not been known in that Kingdom, for it rather seemed the falling of a water spout than a Shower'.²⁷ A report of the earthquake in Ferrara in June 27 1681, highlighted that there was 'a great Storm, attended with Thunder Lightning, and Hail-Stones of an exceeding bigness, which did great dammage in these parts, and scarcely was the Storm ended, but a very Terrible Earthquake began'. This report also proffered an explanation for these events, stating that 'some think it was occasioned by the dryness of the weather, which letting in abundance of heat, upon the suddain, whereupon the heat and cold fighting together, forcing the Earth, caused her to Tremble'.²⁸ This naturalistic description of earthquakes was becoming more common in the seventeenth century and echoed natural philosophers' theories.²⁹ Before we take the turn to empirical observation too far, it is worth noting that the same issue of *The Domestick Intelligence* also featured a story of a sea monster sighting 'Reported for a certain truth'.

The choice to highlight natural or supernatural explanations for earthquakes seems to have been made on a case-by-case basis, problematising Jankovic's claim that they engaged in 'disinterested fact gathering'.³⁰ Even though newspaper editors often had to rely on oral reports of dubious provenance, they could also choose to reject reports as hearsay. This is evident in the case of prodigies, which include any event that was considered inexplicable, or to have a supernatural explanation, such as monsters or monstrous births. Earthquakes could also be described as 'prodigious', and analysed as an expression of God's wrath. Due to the brevity of newspaper reports (often a few lines long), they did not often present providential accounts. When they engaged in such questions, they showed an ambivalent stance towards prodigies, which reflected some of the criticisms of seventeenth-century thinkers. For example, the *Domestic Intelligence* on 22 July 1679 mentions:

---

26   *The London Gazette* 2365, 16 July 1688; *The London Gazette* 2368, 26 July 1688.
27   *The Domestick Intelligence or News both from City and Country Impartially Related* 11, 30 June 1681.
28   *Domestick intelligence, or News both from City and Country Impartially Related* 15, 14 July 1681.
29   Vermij, *Thinking on Earthquakes*, p. 168. See also Gerrit Jasper Schenk, 'Disastro, Catastrophe, and Divine Judgment', p. 49.
30   See p. 121.

> There is a Relation from Scotland of which we must expect the Confirmation, that on Thursday the Tenth day of this Instant July there happened a Terrible storm of Thunder and Lightning accompanied with an Earthquake, which shook the Houses in a dreadful manner, after which it is said that there were appearances of several shapes and Figures and several Persons that were in the Fields do affirm that before the beginning of the Tempest they heard a Terrible noise like the bellowing of a Bull.[31]

Here, the newspaper opts for non-committal language when talking about the experiences of eyewitnesses: 'we expect confirmation', 'it is said', 'several persons do affirm'. The claims of eyewitnesses, elsewhere taken as fact, are here viewed with ambivalence, presumably because they relate to the common providential sign of figures in the sky.[32] The same newspaper was even more cautious in 1681, when presenting news of an earthquake in Lyon on 30 June 1681: 'several people affirm, that they saw Flames of Fire ascending out of the Earth, but it is imagined they might be deceived by the flashes of Lightning that ran along the ground'.[33] Here we see a clearer example of the rejection of prodigies as hearsay. Again, the same eyewitnesses who had been credible enough when it came to a description of the earthquake are seen as deceived when they claim to have seen something miraculous. The editor foregrounds his scepticism and provides an explanation rooted in natural history.

The *True Protestant Mercury* is more direct in February 1681, mentioning that 'There is likewise a noise of an Earthquake near Uxbridge, but we are sparing to Credit Visions and Prodigies'.[34] Here, however, it could be suggested that it was politically expedient to reject prodigies: in the same paragraph, the *True Protestant Mercury* reports that the Maid of Hatfield (a female prophetess) had tried to see the King, driven by an apparition advising her to warn the King against moving Parliament to Oxford.[35] The newspaper editor noted that 'most conclude it the Transport of a Melancholy Imagination'. The rejection of 'Visions and Prodigies' connects the two events (the earthquake and the apparition), implying that the sources for the earthquake had also employed

---

31 *The Domestick Intelligence, or News both from City and Country Impartially Related* 5, 22 July 1679.
32 Walsham, *Providence*, pp. 181–186.
33 *The Domestick Intelligence, or News both from City and Country Impartially Related* 11, 30 June 1681.
34 *True Protestant Mercury, or Occurrences Forein and Domestick* 12, 5 February 1681.
35 H. T. Swedenberg (ed.), *The Works of John Dryden, Volume II: Poems, 1681–1684* (Berkeley: University of California Press, 1972), p. 390.

providential themes. This suggests that the categoric refutation of prodigies was motivated by political rather than 'scientific' considerations.[36]

At the same time, there are examples of newspapers which presented earthquakes with language that harked back to providence and to 'strange news' pamphlets and ballads.[37] Describing earthquakes as 'prodigious' and 'ominous' or focusing on the miraculous salvation of individuals was a way to tacitly acknowledge that these natural catastrophes were shaped by divine will.[38] *Modern History or a A monthly account of all considerable Occurences*, a monthly newspaper, mentioned that in the Naples earthquake in 1688 'several Ladies that were there were Miraculously taken out alive from under the Ruines'.[39] In the same publication, the earthquake that struck Lima is said to 'execute God's justice upon us'.[40] The *Athenian Gazette*, which aimed at answering the questions of its readers in literary, religious, scientific or historical matters, also ventured into this field. On the issue of 11 October 1693, a reader asked the *Athenian Gazette*'s editor John Dunton his opinion about the recently published book *A practical discourse on the late earthquakes: with an historical account of prodigies and their various effects*, whose author is identified as a 'reverend divine'. Dunton answers favourably, claiming that in this book there is 'the most Elaborate Discourse of Prodigies, and the best Observations on the late Earthquakes we have yet seen'. Here Dunton sees no tension between prodigies and observations.[41] Pettegree argues that the *Athenian Gazette* was 'very different from the science of the Philosophical Transactions, but on the other hand it was also a far cry from the news-books and their monstrous births'.[42] Dunton's stamp of approval to a discourse on

36   For more examples of using providential signs for political or religious purposes, see Walsham, *Providence*, pp. 225–280.
37   Sara Barker, 'Translating Tempests and Tremblements: Natural Disasters, News, and the Nation in Early Modern England and France', *Renaissance and Reformation*, 43/2 (2020), pp. 183–212.
38   *The London Gazette* 2376, 27 August 1688; *The London Gazette* 1757, 21 September 1682; *The Flying Post, or the Post-Master* 233, 10 November 1696. Using the term 'prodigious' to talk about earthquakes was also popular in pamphlets, such as Anonymous, *A True and Exact Relation of the late Prodigious Earth-quake and Eruption of Mount Aetna, or Monte-Gibello* (London: T. Newcomb, 1669).
39   *Modern History or a A monthly account of all considerable Occurences* 9, June 1688, p. 10. More on the *Athenian Gazette* in Urmi Bhowmik, 'Facts and Norms in the Marketplace of Print: John Dunton's Athenian Mercury', *Eighteenth-Century Studies*, 36/3 (2003), pp. 345–365.
40   *Modern History or a A monthly account of all considerable Occurences* 9, June 1688, p. 12.
41   *The Athenian Mercury* 13, 11 October 1693.
42   Andrew Pettegree, *The Invention of News: How the World Came to Know About Itself* (New Haven & London: Yale University Press, 2014), p. 273.

prodigies and the religious meaning of earthquakes suggests a blurring of the distinction between science and prodigies.

A less clear-cut case of the interplay of newspapers and providential readings of earthquakes was *The General History of Earthquakes* (1694). Even though this was a pamphlet, it employed almost exclusively newspaper excerpts in its presentation of recent earthquakes. Additionally, it included signed certificates, which verified that prodigious signs such as the singing of psalms in the sky had been witnessed. This pamphlet employed credible witnesses more effectively than newspapers, albeit to prove a providential understanding of seismic activity.[43]

This section shows the problems with employing eyewitness accounts as a way to bolster the credibility of newspapers. The claims of onlookers did not necessarily agree with the viewpoint of the editor or their imagined audience. Editorial comments disqualifying the sources they presented could also undermine the credibility of the newspaper. Additionally, distinguishing between 'disinterested' observation and belief in wonders was not automatic in newspapers, as some also chose to record visions and providential signs. Providential understandings of earthquakes were less pronounced in newspapers than in other media, but mentions of miraculous salvation or providential signs suggest that newspapers reflected broader cultural understandings of earthquakes, which vacillated between viewing them as natural phenomena and prodigious events. The multivalence of earthquakes made them more relatable to readers interested in establishing causal links between events. Newspapers could and did imitate pamphlets and ballads about natural catastrophes; this was also the case with sensational descriptions of earthquakes.

3   Sensationalising Human Suffering

'Sensationalism' has been discredited in discussions of news in the early modern period.[44] This was a process that begun in the seventeenth century, when the term 'news' was discredited because it was used in sensational pamphlets whereas newspaper editors tried (initially at least) to present their news as 'serious records of matters of fact'.[45] In order to achieve this, newspapers

---

43   R. B., *The General History of Earthquakes* (London: Nath Crouch, 1694), p. 134.
44   Joy Wiltenburg, 'True Crime: The Origins of Modern Sensationalism', *The American Historical Review*, 109/5 (2004), pp. 1377–1404.
45   Paul Arblaster et al., 'The Lexicons of Early Modern News', in Raymond & Moxham (eds.), *News Networks in Early Modern Europe*, p. 92.

often employed a 'plain style' of reporting: clear, brief, and presenting specific information.[46] This was fast becoming not only a way to court a broader audience, but also to stake a claim of truth-telling: 'Plain language, unsophisticated but informative' according to David Randall, 'was coming to be perceived as an indicator of truth in and of itself'.[47] By consequence, Shapiro argues, it was appropriate for 'discourses of fact'.[48] These statements need to be balanced with the sensational style of writing employed for descriptions of earthquakes. Scholars are used to thinking that newspapers contained 'little snippets of news', but presenting scenes of misery and destruction was also common in newspapers and was therefore not entirely limited to pamphlets, songs, or histories.[49] The detailed depictions of devastation and fear, as well as the first-person narrative often employed, invited readers to put themselves in the victims' place and vicariously experience the catastrophe and the feelings of fear and helplessness.[50]

Evoking the terror that a seismic event caused was an important part of the description of earthquakes. Of 151 earthquake reports between 1645–1696, 30 use the adjective 'terrible' to describe seismic activity.[51] This is by far the most common adjective to describe earthquakes—with a few mentions of 'great' or 'most dreadful'. This was not just about the words used: newspapers often depicted the terrified reactions of those caught in the midst of the earth shaking and everything collapsing. For example, when reporting an earthquake on 27 August 1679, *The Friendly Intelligence* reported: 'From Scotland it is advised there hath been a terrible Earthquake … which continued a very considerable season to the great amazing and affrigthment of those people'.[52] This sense of surprise and terror is also evident in the *True Protestant Mercury* of May 1681, which brought tidings of an earthquake in Candia (Crete): 'a great Earthquake lately happening there, which hath struck the whole Island with very great

---

46   Joad Raymond, *The Invention of the Newspaper: English Newsbooks, 1641–1649* (Oxford: Oxford University Press, 1996), pp. 128–9.

47   Randall, 'Epistolary Rhetoric, the Newspaper, and the Public Sphere', *Past & Present*, 198 (2008), p. 28.

48   Shapiro, *A Culture of Fact*, p. 94.

49   Henry Ettinghausen, 'International Relations: Spanish, Italian, French, English and German Printed Single Event Newsletters Prior to Renaudot's Gazette', in Raymond & Moxham (eds.), *News Networks in Early Modern Europe*, p. 279.

50   For similar findings in other printed materials, see Alexandra Walsham 'Deciphering Divine Wrath and Displaying Godly Sorrow: Providentialism and Emotion in Early Modern England' in *Disaster, Death and the Emotions*, pp. 28–29.

51   This figure is based on a search of mentions of earthquakes in seventeenth-century newspapers within the Nichols and Burney Newspaper collections.

52   *The Friendly Intelligence* 1, 7 September 1679.

Terror and amazement, and hath done a great deal of mischief'.[53] In both newspapers, the editors foregrounded the fear caused by the earthquake, providing little other information. Even accounts of earthquakes which did not cause damage focused on fear. *The Flying Post* reported in 1697 that 'The terror was very much increased at Naples, because of an earthquake that was felt there, but without any damage' while the 1682 earthquake in France was said to 'more fright people than hurt them'.[54]

Most newspapers sought to shock their readers not only by enumerating the loss of human life, but also by depicting the feelings of helplessness experienced by the victims. In an earthquake reported in the *London Gazette* in 1680, it is described how the shaking of the earth in Madrid caused a 'terrible desolation' and details of the stricken individuals are included: '112 persons were wounded, and 40 known to be killed, besides others, who it's feared may lye buryed under the Ruines; the like was never heard of before in these Parts'.[55] Here, it is not just the death count, but also the fear of people being buried alive that is being highlighted. Reports of the earthquake at Peru also stressed how this catastrophe levelled the town 'burying many of the Inhabitants under the Ruins' and due to the resulting flooding of the sea 'great numbers of People and Cattle were drowned'.[56] Many newspapers followed this pattern, such as the report of an earthquake in Lorrain, which related 'a Terrible Earthquake' that 'continued to shake the Earth very furiously for the space of half an hour' resulting in 'several persons being Killed and Wounded, both in their Houses and as they Fled through the Streets, to their no small consternation'.[57] 'Consternation', a term that combined amazement and terror, was also frequently evoked in newspaper reports of earthquakes.[58] The emphasis on the inhabitants' reactions is also evident in the newspaper reportage of the earthquake in Naples in 1688 (mentioned earlier): this 'Dreadful Earthquake … frightning the Inhabitants

---

53   *The True Protestant Mercury* 34, 4 May 1681. See also *The London Gazette* 2566, June 16 1690; *The London Gazette* 3017, 11 October 1694.

54   *The Flying Post, or the Post-Master* 381, 21 October 1697; *The London Gazette*, 15 May 1682.

55   *The London Gazette* 1563, 8 November 1680.

56   *The London Gazette* 2349, 24 May 1688. See also *The London Gazette* 2630, 26 January 1691.

57   *The Domestick intelligence, or News both from City and Country Impartially Related* 24, 15 August 1681.

58   About the 'consternation' of inhabitants see also *The Domestick intelligence, or News both from City and Country Impartially Related* 80, 27 February 1682; *The London Gazette* 2528, 3 February 1690, p. 2; *The London Gazette* 2851, 9 March 1693; *The Flying Post* 111, 30 January 1696; *The Post Boy* 114, 30 January 1696; *The Post Boy* 130, 7 March 1696; *The Domestick intelligence, or News both from City and Country Impartially Related* 127, 10 August 1682; *The Post Man and the Historical Account* 377, 30 September 1697; *The Post Man and the Historical Account* 384, 16 October 1697.

out of their Houses with the terror of an inevitable Destruction, they betook themselves to the Piazzaes and the open publick Places of the City'.[59] These relations invite the reader to imagine how such individuals must have felt running in fear of their lives.

The London Gazette's depiction of the earthquake in Arpaia also painted a vivid picture of the devastation and fear of the inhabitants:

> the Town of Arpaia was quite destroyed by an Earthquake, and that a Mountain near Ceretto was split asunder. The Earth has likewise opened in several places about this City, out of which did arise black Vapors and Flames like to those of Mount Vesuvius. These new Accidents do so terrifie the Inhabitants that they daily retire from hence in great numbers insomuch that there is hardly left in this City a third part of the People that were here before we fell under this publick Calamity.[60]

The splitting of the earth and the eruption of fires is the background against which the terror of the inhabitants is etched.

In order to maximise the emotional impact of such scenes of destruction, newspapers often tapped into the language of sensorial perception. In the earthquake of Ferrara, the focus is on sight: 'a very Terrible Earthquake began, which continued about a quarter of an hour, the Earth opening on the foot of an Hill about five miles hence, and swallowed up several high Trees, leaving a great gapp in the Earth, which several hundreds have been since to take a view off'.[61] The reader can virtually insert themselves into this picture by following the gaze of onlookers. Many of the images presented relied on vision for their emotional effect, but other senses were also marshalled. For example, in 1688, *The Orange Gazette* gives a 'dismal Relation' of the Smyrna earthquake adding that the earthquakes' death toll could also lead to increased morbidity, since 'the Physitians judge the Air to be infected, through the putrefaction of 20000 Bodies, by a modest Computation, that are Inhum'd by the Earthquake, the Stench passing through the Clefts and Crannies of the Ground that were occasioned by the Distaster'.[62] Imagining the smell of the dead bodies, readers vicariously experience the effects of earthquakes.

---

59   *The London Gazette* 2358, 25 June 1688.
60   *The London Gazette* 2365, 16 July 1688.
61   *The Domestick Intelligence* 15, 14 July 1681.
62   *The Orange Gazette* 1, 31 December 1688.

In the descriptions of the earthquake in Lima, in 1687, the *Monethly Account* presents graphically the sounds (human and natural) surrounding the earthquake:

> The next day at five in the Morning there was another Shaking and Noise almost as big as the first, at which the People were in so great a Consternation, that there was nothing to be heard but Clamours and Voices to the Heavens, all People publickly confessing their Sins in the Streets and Places. At six in the Morning, when all People were quieted, there was another most Stupendious Earthquake, which came with so great fury and Noise that it seemed the Heavens were falling upon us, and the Earth full of fury ready to Bury us; also the Sea with its lofty Waves and horrible noise, did pass its accustomary Limits to Execute God's Justice upon us; and finally, according to these Chastisements so was the Repentance of all, so as that it seemed the day of Judgment. The very Bells ringing of themselves, it was so horrible a Ruine that there is not left one entire Structure standing; the greatness of this Noise caused the very Beasts in the fields to roar, and to joyn one with another as it were to ask help and assistance.[63]

Noise and voices are the focal points of the description, which conjures a nightmarish image punctured by the 'horrible noise' of the earthquake and flood, the bells desperately calling for repentance and the cries of those helpless to save themselves. In the description of the 1682 Naples earthquake, the sound itself is meant to intimidate: '[the earthquake] continues to Roar so loud that in a still Night it is heard of those that Inhabit 40 Miles distance'.[64]

This emphasis on sound is mirrored in a letter about the Jamaica earthquake of 1692, which was transcribed by the diarist Narcissus Luttrell. Even though it has not been possible so far to locate the source of this letter, Luttrell usually transcribed news taken from newspapers and newsletters. The letter presents an eyewitness's account, with language which very closely resembles the one by newspapers:

---

63 *Modern History or a A monethly account of all considerable Occurrence*, June 1688, p. 12. See also *The Domestick intelligence, or News both from City and Country Impartially Related* 103, 18 May 1682.

64 *The Domestick intelligence, or News both from City and Country Impartially Related* 141, 28 September 1682.

> I cannot sufficiently represent the terrible circumstances that attended it; the earth swelled with a dismal humming noise, the houses fell, the earth opened in many places, the graves gave up some of their dead, the tomb stones rattled together; at last the earth sunk below the water, and the sea overwhelmed great numbers of people, whose shreiks and groannes made a lamentable echo.[65]

The sensationalist descriptions of earthquakes did not necessarily undermine the truth claims of newspapers. On the contrary, the combination of a style of writing focused on precise details with passages highlighting the feelings of victims and asking readers to mobilise their senses in order to vicariously experience the effects of earthquakes had the potential to make these tragedies relevant to readers far away.

4 Reading News of Earthquakes

Newspaper coverage of earthquakes changed the volume of accounts of catastrophes rather than the way in which they were reported. Such news of earthquakes made people aware that similar phenomena were commonplace.[66] As Joop W. Koopmans, examining Dutch newspapers, has also shown, many of the reports of earthquakes were about minor tremors.[67] Such minor incidents existed side-by-side with tales of horror about earthquakes which devastated cities or countries. The plethora of earthquakes reported highlighted their relevance to readers. These phenomena could affect readers' interests, feelings, or sense of the world. Scholars working on news media have concluded that the emphasis on international news and their effects produced a 'community-building sense of participation in widely dispersed occurrences'.[68]

---

65 Narcissus Luttrell, *A brief historical relation of state affairs from September 1678 to April 1714* (Oxford: University Press, 1857), p. 539.
66 Vermij, *Thinking on Earthquakes,* p. 160.
67 Joop W. Koopmans, 'Coverage in Dutch Newspapers of Earthquakes in Italy and Beyond before Lisbon 1755' in Lotte Jensen and Hanneke van Asperen (eds.), *Dealing with Disasters. Cultural Representations of Catastrophes, 1500–1900* (Amsterdam: AUP, 2023).
68 Tony Claydon, 'Daily News and the Construction of Time in Late Stuart England, 1695–1714', *Journal of British Studies,* 52/1 (2013), p. 56, summarising the work of scholars in Brendan Dooley (ed.), *The Dissemination of News and the Emergence of Contemporaneity in Early Modern Europe* (Farnham: Ashgate, 2010).

We cannot say with certainty how readers would react to such news. Nonetheless, the emphasis on both the casualties and the suffering caused, as well as on the feelings of surprise, terror, and helplessness experienced by the victims were probably intended to maximise the emotional impact of this news on readers. Susan Broomhall, analysing how French diarists recorded and interpreted natural catastrophes in the early modern period has argued: '[e]ven though the events and experiences that these printed texts described were often physically distant from their authors, emotionally they occurred at close hand. News stories recounting tales of death, disaster and divine intervention clearly made a profound impact on contemporary readers and viewers, warranting reproduction within their own personal accounts of the world they perceived they lived in'.[69] The frequency with which earthquakes were framed as terrifying events and the focus of reportage on the feelings of victims suggests that editors expected reactions of pity.

The accounts of earthquakes recorded by Narcissus Luttrell and John Evelyn indicate how some English readers understood earthquakes. Luttrell showed special interest in the Port Royal earthquake of 1693, probably because it affected English trade. Luttrell not only bought the pamphlet *A true and perfect relation of that most sad and terrible earthquake, at Port-Royal in Jamaica* (1692) but also noted the earthquake in Jamaica in his 'A brief historical relation of state affairs'.[70] Luttrell presented information about the destruction in Port Royal and the attempts by Jamaica merchants to petition the queen. As we saw earlier, he also transcribed an eyewitness account providing a disturbing image of the catastrophe. Even though Luttrell did not record his reactions to this news, the inclusion of this letter suggests an interest in how victims felt.[71] This could have been voyeuristic, but as Charles Zika has argued, collecting reports of natural disasters could also be a product 'of intense uncertainty and anxiety', a way of coping with such concerns.[72] The diarist and public servant John Evelyn showed a greater interest in earthquakes even when they did not directly affect England. In his diary written between 1665 and 1699, he includes news of eleven earthquakes. He also employs the same adjectives in order to

---

69 Susan Broomhall, 'Divine, Deadly or Disastrous? Diarists' Emotional Responses to Printed News in Sixteenth-Century France', in *Disaster, Death and the Emotions*, p. 332.

70 From the Harvard Library website: 'Narcissus Luttrell's copy, priced & dated in his hand: 1d. 27. Sept. 1692. No. B96 of the Marquess of Bute broadsides', Houghton Library p EB65 A100 B675b v.4.

71 Narcissus Luttrell, *A brief historical relation of state affairs*, p. 539. The other mentions of the Port Royal earthquake are in pp. 533–536.

72 Charles Zika, 'Disaster, Apocalypse, Emotions and Time in Sixteenth-Century Pamphlets' in *Disaster, Death and Emotions*, p. 70.

describe earthquakes as newspapers, dubbing them 'prodigious', 'dreadful', 'dreadful and astonishing', 'deplorable', and 'strange'.

The act of recording such events suggests interest and an emotional connection; nonetheless, this does not mean that there was a uniform emotional reaction to such news. For example, it seems that the English showed more interest in the Port Royal earthquake of 1692 because it was an English colony. Economic interests could influence the way such news was received, and newspapers seemed to cater to the different needs of their readers: for example, the coverage of the earthquake in Smyrna focused on human suffering, but it also made extensive mentions to the fates of the English merchants and their fortunes.[73] Others read such events as providential, confirming their view that earthquakes were ominous warnings of future troubles. John Evelyn, for example, viewed the 1688 earthquakes in Smyrna, Italy, and west Indies as 'forerunners of greater calamities'.[74] The reportage of earthquakes, both great and minor, forced readers to conceptualise the world as more interconnected. Even if readers did not necessarily know where such places were, as newspapers did not provide explanatory notes, they were bombarded with information about disasters taking place in faraway places.[75] This highlighted the relevance of such reporting: earthquakes happening in distant lands could still influence readers in England.

This had more theoretical implications as well. Newspapers and readers, following natural philosophers, started to acknowledge the possibility that earthquakes were not as localised as classical philosophy had claimed. In 1688, judging by English newspaper reports alone, 10 earthquakes in different places were made known to readers. Thus, it should not surprise us that there was concern about such pan-European (or broader) phenomena. This period saw a change in the way that people thought about earthquakes, by seeing them less as very localised phenomena and emphasising that such events were interconnected. This is evident in Evelyn's diary, which draws connections between earthquakes happening in different places. On 12 October 1690, Evelyn noted 'Spencer wrote me word from Althorpe, that there happened an earthquake the day before in the morning, which, though short, sensibly shook the house. The "Gazette" acquainted us that the like happened at the same time, half-past seven, at Barnstaple, Holyhead, and Dublin. We were not sensible of it here'.

---

73   *Publick Occurrences Truely Stated* 31, 18 September 1688. Also see *The London Gazette* 2383, 20 September 1688; *The Orange Gazette* 1, 31 Dec. 1688.

74   John Evelyn, *The Diary of John Evelyn* Volume II, edited by William Bray (Washington & London: W. Walter Dunne, 1901), p. 277.

75   Pettegree, *The Invention of News*, pp. 209–10.

Here, Evelyn cross-checks the information he received from a familiar letter with that from the *London Gazette* and establishes that the earthquake was more widespread. In the same vein, in the big 1692 earthquake in Europe, Evelyn wrote: 'There happened an earthquake, which, though not so great as to do any harm in England, was universal in all these parts of Europe. It shook the house at Wotton, but was not perceived by any save a servant or two'.[76]

Evelyn's comments were precipitated by newspapers' suggestions that this was the case. For example, the *Domestic Intelligence* commented in 1679:

> It is remarkable that about the same time when that Terrible Whirlwind and Earthquake happened in the Empire, of which we gave an Account in our last, it appears to be near that time wherein the Earthquake happened in Scotland, which did some dammage there, by rending some part of the Walls of Starling Castle in that Countrey; as also the time of that dreadful Thunder and Lightning which we had in England, the like whereof hath been seldome seen, which Demonstrates that the Tempest was very large and General throughout Europe.[77]

The True Domestic Intelligence of the same date repeated the comment, adding only that it was 'some ingenious Observers' who made this connection.[78] Natural philosophers could also use newspapers to publicise their theories about the connections between different earthquakes: John Ray had an article published in the *Athenian Mercury*, where he suggested that 'vapours dispersed from [the earthquake] in Jamaica' could have caused the earthquakes in Flanders and Holland.[79]

The sense that earthquakes could be connected did not need to be based on natural philosophy; wading through a deluge of news about earthquakes, readers could also view them as global instances of misery. A good example of this reaction was the editor's commentary in *A True and Impartial Account of the Remarkable Accidents, Casualties and other Transactions of the like Nature* of 1688:

> I cannot conclude Paper better, than by giving God thanks for the blessings of this Climate of England, that when all the other parts of the World

---

76 Evelyn, *The Diary of John Evelyn*, pp. 307, 318.
77 *The True Domestick Intelligence, Or, News both from city and country* 23, 23 September 1679.
78 'Ingenious' is also the term used for members of the Royal Society, see *Philosophical Transactions; giving some account of the present Undertakings, Studies and Labours of the Ingenious.*
79 Vermij, *Thinking on Earthquakes*, p. 211.

are more of less subjected to the miseries of Innundation, Hurricanes, Eruptions of Fire, and terrible Earthquakes, we are seldome or never exposed to those Calamities; as we have heard of terrible Earthquakes in Peru, and the like lately at Naples; To instance only in the late Devastation at Smyrna, whereof by Letters of fresh date, we receive a very mellancholly Account, they write that the Earthquake there, hath not only greatly defaced and ruined that flourishing place, but destroyed many of the Factorys, together with the Lives and Estates of sundry eminent Persons, turning that famous Trading City into a heap of Ruin and Devastation.[80]

The editor here enumerates some of the most spectacular and terrifying natural catastrophes which took place in that year. His conclusion may be a pat on the back, congratulating his country for its climate, but it is also an acknowledgement of others' pain and suffering. Even though it is impossible to know if his readers agreed with this assessment, it seems a likely reaction to expect, judging by the newspapers' emphasis on the painful consequences of earthquakes.

Newspapers employed a plain style and often reported laconically on earthquakes. These were techniques of presenting their news as 'truth'. Shapiro's claim that they did so by using credible witnesses and employing an objective tone is more difficult to support. As we have seen, newspaper editors used any witness accounts they could get their hands on and most often than not did not specify where their information came from. They implied that their information came from eyewitnesses by presenting their perspective or using the first person in descriptions of earthquakes. Even though they used oral testimonies, they were ready to gloss over any reports that did not agree with their worldview. This should not make us think that it was a fact versus interpretation battle, however. Not only were editors happy to provide their own interpretations of events but they could also include (or at least accept) providential discourses. It seems that whether a description of an earthquake would be dismissed as 'hearsay' or accepted as the 'common voice' depended on each editor and on the particular circumstances surrounding the seismic event.

This constant reportage of earthquakes, minor or significant, did not lead to consistent reactions to them. Some readers likely read such news to check how their lives would be affected by earthquakes: interest in English trade and colonies was significant, while for others, earthquakes presaged God's judgement against humanity. Newspapers also sought to make such news relevant

---

80 *A True and Impartial Account of the Remarkable Accidents, Casualties and other Transactions of the like Nature, Happening in City and Country, &c* 11, 25 August 1688.

by maximising its emotional impact. The use of vivid images of catastrophe and the emphasis on the victims' feelings of fear created a sense of dread but also a possibility to empathise with others. This may have been even more impactful to an English audience, unused to devastating earthquakes.[81] The emphasis on the fear and surprise of victims also suggested that editors expected reactions of shock, awe, and pity. The constant reportage of earthquakes and the attempt to make them relatable to readers was likely to drive home that the world was shrinking.[82] Newspaper reportage of earthquakes familiarised readers with faraway lands and could lead to a sense of belonging to a broader imagined community.

---

81 Matthew Mulcahy, 'The Port Royal Earthquake and the World of Wonders in Seventeenth-Century Jamaica', *Early American Studies: An Interdisciplinary Journal*, 6/2 (2008), p. 410.

82 Sara Barker also finds that news pamphlets 'gave a sense of collective European identity', while still prioritising national concerns, 'Time in English Translations of Continental News', Raymond & Moxham (eds.), *News Networks in Early Modern Europe*, p. 328.

SECTION 3

Rebellion and War

CHAPTER 7

Reading the 1641 Irish Rebellion
Nehemiah Wallington and the Cultural Construction of Violence

Eamon Darcy

News that a rebellion had erupted in the north of Ireland on 23 October 1641 reached London in early November, circulating by word of mouth, scribal publications and, in time, printed news. The London puritan artisan Nehemiah Wallington recorded the prevailing sense in the English houses of parliament after letters were read out describing the event: 'vnlese the parliament did not svpply them with svdden forces, they [Irish Protestants] had none or very small hopes of defending their lives'.[1] The rebellion was primarily led by Catholic 'rebels' who sought, among other things, to reclaim lands and political privileges lost at the hands of 'upstart' New English Protestant settlers in Ireland. Yet, contemporaries immediately interpreted events within a sectarian framework. The subsequent outbreak of popular violence led to the murders of many hundreds, possibly thousands, of Irish Protestants as well as assaults, lootings, and strippings.[2] Refugees from Ulster soon arrived in Dublin where a 'commission for the despoiled subject' was established to record their testimonies and inventories of losses incurred. About 8,000 statements were gathered and are now known as the 1641 depositions.[3] Considerable attention has been given to the fact that the 1641 depositions were soon cited as evidence for claims that the rebellion was a popish conspiracy led by the English king, Charles I. Thus, the Irish rebellion of 1641 became embroiled in a broader

---

1 Nehemiah Wallington, 'A bundel of marcys', British Library (hereafter BL), Add MS, 21,935, f. 164v.
2 Nicholas Canny, *Making Ireland British 1580–1650* (Oxford: Oxford University Press, 2001), pp. 476–478; Eamon Darcy, *The Irish rebellion of 1641 and the wars of the three kingdoms* (Woodbridge: Boydell and Brewer, 2013), pp. 52–67; Michael Perceval-Maxwell, *The outbreak of the Irish rebellion of 1641* (Québec: McGill-Queen's University Press, 1994), pp. 227–233; John Walter, 'Performative violence: patterns of political violence in the 1641 depositions', in Jane Ohlmeyer and Micheál Ó Siochrú (eds.), *Ireland 1641: contexts and reactions* (Manchester: Manchester University Press, 2013), pp. 134–152.
3 Aidan Clarke, 'The commission for the despoiled subject, 1641–7', in Brian Mac Cuarta (ed.), *Reshaping Ireland 1550–1700: Colonization and its consequences* (Dublin: Four Courts Press, 2011), pp. 241–60.

political crisis that engulfed the Three Kingdoms.[4] It is also well known that at this time of heightened politico-religious tension polemicists shaped their narratives in specific ways to promote a range of agendas.[5] What has not been subject to scrutiny to any great detail, however, is the extent to which contemporary English readers picked up on these messages.[6] The purpose of this chapter, therefore, is to analyse the portrayal of news from Ireland in contemporary pamphlets printed in London and, by using Nehemiah Wallington's surviving notes, to investigate how Londoners understood this news. It will argue that biblical allusions embedded within news publications provided literary cues that shaped readers' interpretations. Audiences well versed in Scripture and godly literature drew meaning from these cues and contextualised the Irish rebellion within a broader Foxean framework of Protestant martyrdom. Wallington then supplemented his notes of this literature with other biblical references suggesting that he wanted to lay a path for his family and wider community to follow in their own reading of news from Ireland.

1   Cultural Constructions of Violence

Space precludes a detailed investigation of how English pamphleteers disseminated news from Ireland ranging from the mundane to the mythological. Yet, Wallington's notebooks offer a keyhole through which we can view the circulation and reception of news from Ireland in London. Admittedly, Wallington was, in the words of his biographer, 'an exceptional Englishman' in terms of the scale of evidence he left behind, but historians still gain a valuable insight into the content and circulation of news describing the Irish rebellion regardless

---

4   Joseph Cope, *England and the 1641 Irish rebellion* (Woodbridge: Boydell and Brewer, 2009), pp. 89–118; Joseph Cope, 'Fashioning victims: Dr. Henry Jones and the plight of Irish Protestants, 1642', *Historical Research*, 74/186 (2001), pp. 370–391; Darcy, *The Irish Rebellion*, pp. 77–101.

5   Eamon Darcy, *The Irish Rebellion of 1641 and the Wars of the Three Kingdoms* (Woodbridge: Boydell and Brewer, 2013); Jason Peacey, *Politicians and pamphleteers: Propaganda during the Civil Wars and Interregnum* (London: Ashgate, 2004); Joad Raymond, *Pamphlets and pamphleteering in Early Modern Britain* (Cambridge: Cambridge University Press, 2003).

6   Heidi Brayman Hackel, *Reading material in Early Modern England* (Cambridge: Cambridge University Press, 2005); Kevin Sharpe, *Reading Revolutions: The Politics of Reading in Early Modern England* (London: Yale University Press, 2000); Kevin Sharpe and Steven Zwicker (eds.), *Reading Society and Politics in Early Modern England* (Cambridge: Cambridge University Press, 2003).

of how unusual a reader/writer Wallington was.[7] While we do not know what influenced Wallington's selection of pamphlets, a number of tentative statements can be made. First, it appears that Wallington read a wide range of materials from sensationalist news to more official pronouncements disseminated by Irish politicians to English audiences. Secondly, he made little attempt to determine the veracity of what he read.[8] Thirdly, he was uninterested in more mundane reports about troop movements and the course of battles. Finally, Wallington clearly preferred reading pamphlets that provided lurid details on the atrocities committed by Irish 'rebels' as opposed to newsbooks for news about the Irish rebellion. This section, therefore, will focus on the pamphlet literature that described news from Ireland during the 1640s with a particular focus on the cultural construction of violence.

English pamphleteers circulated two different narratives about the Irish rebellion, as illustrated by Ethan Shagan. Some publishers (mostly with royalist sympathies) tended to portray the rebellion as an example of social anarchy, describing it as an attack on the king's authority.[9] Another interpretative model, the focus of this section, was rooted in John Foxe's *Acts and Monuments* (1563) and offered graphic, titillating, moralistic accounts replete with lurid violence committed by seemingly barbaric Irish rebels against Protestant settlers. As Shagan has noted, the English reading public had already been polarized at this point. Readers of this Foxe-inspired narrative could, therefore, locate the deaths of innocent Protestants in Ireland within a broader providentialist framework and chronology of religious martyrdom thanks to the widespread availability of Foxe's work in English parishes. This provided further justification for supporting parliament instead of Charles I. In effect, news of the Irish rebellion was deliberately spun to English audiences to promote a range of agendas and was carefully stage-managed over the course of the 1640s.[10]

Wallington read sensationalist news about the Irish rebellion within a broader Foxean framework but with an awareness of recent events.[11] By the

---

7   Quotation from Paul Seaver, *Wallington's world: A puritan artisan in seventeenth-century London* (London: Meuthen, 1985), p. 1. See also: Kathleen Lynch, 'Extraordinarily ordinary: Nehemiah Wallington's experimental method', in Matthew C. Augustine (ed.), *Texts and readers in the age of Marvell* (Manchester: Manchester University Press, 2018), pp. 75–91.
8   Cope, *England and the 1641 Irish rebellion*, pp. 80–81.
9   Roger Puttocke, *An abstract of certain depositions* (London: Robert Baker, 1642); Darcy, *The Irish Rebellion*, pp. 93–95.
10 Darcy, *The Irish Rebellion*, pp. 77–101; Jason Peacey, *Politicians and pamphleteers: propaganda during the English civil wars and interregnum* (Burlington, VT: Ashgate, 2004); Ethan Shagan, 'Constructing discord: ideology, propaganda and English responses to the Irish rebellion of 1641', *Journal of British Studies*, 36/1 (1997), pp. 4–34.
11 Joseph Cope, *England and the 1641 Irish Rebellion* (Woodbridge: Boydell Press, 2009), p. 90.

mid-seventeenth century, decades of religious wars in Europe meant that Londoners were regularly exposed to particularly gruesome news of violent events replete with vivid, titillating images. Such 'discursive structures' were heavily influenced by John Foxe's *Book of Martyrs*, which provided a literary scaffold for English authors.[12] We know less about the literary cues embedded in these publications that helped readers to understand the significance of what they read. A father and son publishing team, whose publications Wallington read, were John Rothwell junior and senior. Based at the 'Sign of the sun' in St Paul's Churchyard, the Rothwells gradually aligned with the Presbyterian cause and published mostly anti-prelatical and theological works from 1631 until John senior's death in 1649.[13] One of the more sensationalist items printed by the Rothwells was a cheaply produced pocketbook by Philip Vincent called the *Lamentations of Germany* (1638), which Wallington read. Vincent witnessed parts of the Thirty Years' War having travelled to Germany between 1633 and 1635. He was in Heidelberg when it was besieged by Spanish forces.[14] Biblical allusions were embedded as deliberate literary cues in Vincent's account of the Thirty Years' War, providing a godly framework for readers to interpret events. For example, in his preface, Vincent exclaimed: 'Behold here, as in a Glasse, the mournefull face of a sister Nation, now drunke with misery; according to what God threatened by the Prophet *Ieremy* [Jeremiah]'.[15] The pamphlet's opening captured a sense of shared identity between English puritans and German victims of Catholic atrocities. Furthermore, this biblical allusion linked the title of the pamphlet to the Book of Lamentations and provided a biblical context to German Protestants' suffering. In the Book of Lamentations, Jeremiah weeps for the children of Israel after prophesying the destruction of Jerusalem as a consequence of the sins of the Israelites and their failure to heed his warnings.[16] Much like Jeremiah's warning to the Israelites, Vincent's account of the Thirty Years' War encouraged English readers to consider their own sinning and how it contributed to the political crises that slowly engulfed England at this time:

---

12   Shagan, 'Constructing discord', p. 7.
13   Sharon Achinstein and Benjamin Button, 'Who printed Milton's *Tetrachordon* (1645)?', *The Library*, 14/1 (2013), pp. 18–44, p. 20; William R. Parker, 'Milton, Rothwell, and Simmons', *The Library*, 4/18 (1937), pp. 89–103, pp. 90–91.
14   Tony O. Bickham, 'Vincent, Philip', *Oxford Dictionary of National Biography*. Available online: https://doi-org.jproxy.nuim.ie/10.1093/ref:odnb/28313 (consulted 28 October 2021).
15   Philip Vincent, *The Lamentations of Germany* (London: John Rothwell, 1638), Sig A3.
16   Jeremiah 13:17.

do as Nehemiah did, when he heard of the state of Ierusalem and the Termple therein. He sate downe and wept, mourned and fasted certaine daies, and prayed before the Lord God of Heaven, *Neh.* 1.4.[17]

To further emphasise this interpretative structure a woodcut by Wenceslaus Hollar depicted Lady Germany as Rachel mourning the loss of her dead children, with the inscription: 'Have pity upon me, have pity upon me, o ye my friends for the hand of the lord has touched me', an unattributed line from the Book of Job.[18] Such literary cues infused with biblical imagery were commonplace in contemporary descriptions of violence and provided neat interpretative hooks for contemporary readers.

Another publication by the Rothwells that described violence against Protestant civilians committed during the 1641 Irish rebellion was James Cranford's *Teares of Ireland* (1642). Unlike Vincent, who had experienced parts of the Thirty Years War, Cranford had not witnessed events in Ireland personally, but he determined they were further evidence of the Catholic threat that encircled London and her parliamentary defenders.[19] The *Teares of Ireland* provided an anthology of publications and information about the Irish rebellion, most of which had previously circulated in print, replete with gory woodcuts of unknown provenance (which may also be the work of Hollar). Like many of the Foxean narratives that appeared at this time, readers were reminded of the threat posed by popery. In Cranford's preface to the 'Courteous Reader' he warned his audience that the papal Antichrist was responsible for the rebellion and that Irish Protestants were being slaughtered like their co-religionists during the French wars of religion and the Thirty Years War. Like the *Lamentations of Germany*, Cranford used subtle biblical allusions to encourage his readers to be empathetic toward the plight of Irish Protestants. Using an unattributed reference to Judges 9:2 he evoked a personified Ireland crying to her English brethren 'I am your bone and your flesh'.[20] Cranford also alluded to the Book of Lamentations in his attempts to provide a suitable biblical interpretative framework. Lady Ireland mournfully asks 'was there ever sorrow like my sorrow'? another uncited biblical passage this time from Lamentations 1:12.[21] Such

---

17 Vincent, *Lamentations of Germany*, 'Preface exhortatory' [last page].
18 Vincent, *Lamentations of Germany*, [p. 69]; Job 19:21.
19 E. C. Vernon, 'Cranford, James', *Oxford Dictionary of National Biography*. Available online: https://doi-org.jproxy.nuim.ie/10.1093/ref:odnb/6610 (consulted 28 October 2021_.
20 James Cranford, *Teares of Ireland* (London: John Rothwell, 1642), 'Ireland's warning to England' [no pagination]; Judges 9:2.
21 Cranford, *Teares of Ireland*, 'Ireland's warning to England' [no pagination]; Lamentations 1:12.

biblical allusions, images and references helped invest texts with context and meaning for readers to draw upon.

Cranford's account of the Irish rebellion offered a narrative that mixed verifiable events with more sensationalist news. Warning his readers of 'false and idle pamphlets' he assured his audience that the *Teares of Ireland* offered 'the truth of things that all men may behold what bloudy Tigres and Vultures these popish spirits are'.[22] In London news circles a pertinent debate had emerged about the duties of printers in circulating news. Both John Greensmith and John Thomas were reprimanded for 'seditious' printing, having hired two Cambridge University students to fabricate news, including accounts of sectarian atrocities allegedly committed in Ireland and Norwich, stoking the fires of anti-popery.[23] An anonymous letter writer reported from Ireland how 'many idle rumours divulged among you, concerning the present condition of Ireland, some of which are improbable, other [sic] are so doubtfull, that men have just cause of suspition not to believe'.[24] The anonymous author of *The Poets Knavery Discouered* argued that such fantastical works were a product of 'roving fancies'. Now, London was 'embroydred with nothing but incredible lyes, that jars so much in the wearied eares of the World'.[25] The Poets Knavery denounced thirty-seven publications related to Ireland. Others shared the sentiment; *No pamphlet, bvt a Detestation against all such Pamphlets As are Printed, Concerning the Irish Rebellion* (1642) noted how many would 'for a small gaine endeavour with opprobrious lines to abuse God and Man'.[26] Whether this was an appeal for greater journalistic integrity or a critique of rival publications is unclear. Despite this (rhetorical?) abhorrence of the circulation of fabricated news from Ireland, much of what appeared in the pamphlet literature contained a mix of sensationalised accounts alongside tracts describing troop movements or political machinations among the colonial elite in Ireland.

---

22 Cranford, *Teares of Ireland*, p. 4.
23 'Person committed', 25 Jan 1642 in *House of Commons Journals* (13 vols, London, 1802), ii, p. 396. Available at: https://www.british-history.ac.uk/commons-jrnl/vol2/pp392-396#h3-0044 (accessed 10 April 2020); 'Obnoxious publication', 8 March 1642, in *House of Commons Journals* (13 vols, London, 1802), ii, p. 472. Available at: https://www.british-history.ac.uk/commons-jrnl/vol2/pp471–472 (accessed 10 April 2020); *Bloody Newes from Norwich* (London: John Greensmith, 1641); *Joyfull News from Ireland, Being a Relation of a Battell which was fought between the Protestants, and the Rebels of Ireland, where the Protestants got the victory* (London: John Greensmith, 1641).
24 *The most blessed and truest Newes from Ireland, shewing the fortunate successe of the Protestants, And Gods just vengance on the Rebels* (London: J. Harton, 1642), Sig A2.
25 *The Poets Knavery Discouered, in all their lying Pamphlets* (London: T.H., [1642?]), Sig A2.
26 *No pamphlet, bvt a Detestation against all such Pamphlets As are Printed, Concerning the Irish Rebellion* (London: [anonymously printed], 1642), Sig A2.

Their accuracy did not trouble Wallington, at least in what he recorded in his notebooks.

Irish political figures disseminated news for London audiences to influence debates within the English parliament. In March 1642, desperately seeking aid to fund an army to suppress the rebellion, the head of the 'commission for the despoiled subject', Henry Jones, compiled a dossier for the English parliament. It contained evidence gleaned from the 1641 depositions about the aims, actions and intentions of the Irish rebels. It was ordered to be printed the following month.[27] As demonstrated by Joseph Cope, Jones carefully fashioned Irish Protestant victimhood to elicit greater relief for the Irish Protestant war effort.[28] Throughout the English civil wars key military and political figures in Ireland disseminated news publications to influence English political debates, particularly concerning the English parliament's strategic plans for suppressing the rebellion. After the passage of the Adventurer's Act, for example, more positive news emanated from Ireland highlighting the potential of English armies to crush the rebellion in order to encourage investment in the scheme at a popular level.[29] After the decision by Charles I to cease hostilities with the Irish 'rebels' in 1643 and again in 1644, key figures in Dublin attacked this policy, most notably the parliamentarian Chidley Coote. Coote, preying on fears of a Catholic fifth column in England, warned English audiences that Irish rebels would 'imbrew their wicked hands in the innocent blood of the inhabitants of England'.[30] Wallington sympathised with Coote's plight as news from Ireland further justified his support for the English parliament as he now believed that Charles had abandoned his Protestant subjects in favour of popery.

Henry Jones's portrayal of Protestant victims of Catholic atrocities was not unique. Numerous publications of the period accentuated the vulnerability of victims of Catholic atrocities, especially in Ireland and Germany, and highlighted the barbarity of their Catholic assailants. In order to compound the sense of misery they suffered, many pamphleteers used specific examples as the basis for sweeping generalisations that Wallington did not challenge. James Cranford, for example, offered detailed descriptions of the violence suffered by Irish Protestants such as Sir Patrick Dunston who was forced to watch as his wife was raped. Then the rebels:

---

27 Darcy, *The Irish rebellion*, pp. 92–5.
28 Cope, 'Fashioning victims', pp. 370–91.
29 Darcy, *The Irish rebellion*, pp. 119–23.
30 Childey Coote, *Ireland's lamentation for the late destructive cessation* (London, 1644), p. 7; Darcy, *The Irish rebellion*, pp. 124–125.

slue his Servants, spurned his Children till they died, bound him with roules of Match to a board, that his eyes burst out, cut off his eares and nose, teared off both his cheeks, after cut off his arms and legs, cut out his tongue, after run a red hot iron into him.[31]

From this Cranford inferred that:

> Many Gentlewomen have they ravished before their husbands faces, stripping them first naked to the view of their wicked companions, taunting and mocking them (after they have spoiled them) with bitter and reproachfull words.[32]

There were widespread allegations of similar home invasions and sexual violence committed by Irish rebels, a particular concern of Wallington's.[33] Victims were defenceless and vulnerable, according to Cranford. 'All their cruelties have been usually committed on disarmed men in small villages, where [there] was no strength to resist them'.[34] In a semi-official 'history' of the rebellion written in 1646, Sir John Temple, the Irish Master of the Rolls, echoed the defenceless nature of Irish Protestant victims:

> Their servants were killed as they were ploughing in the fields, Husbands cut to pieces in the presence of their Wives, their Childrens [sic] brains dashed out before their faces ... and all as it were at an instant before they could suspect the Irish for their enemies ...[35]

The Foxean construction of Protestant victimhood emphasised that they were martyrs for their faith in the face of international conspiracy against God's

---

31 Cranford, *The Teares of Ireland*, p. 30.
32 Cranford, *The Teares of Ireland*, p. 32.
33 *Doleful nevves from Ireland sent in a letter* (London: T. Bates, 1642); *Irelands tragical tyrannie* (London: T.L., 1643); *The Kings maiesties speech on the 2 day of December 1641 to the honourable houses of parliament* (London: John Greensmith, 1641); *The victorious proceedings of the protestants in Ireland* (London: John Wright, 1642), p. 15; Cope, *England and the 1641 Irish rebellion*, p. 81. see also: Diane Hall and Elizabeth Malcolm, '"The Rebels Turkish Tyranny": Understanding sexual violence in Ireland during the 1640s', *Gender & History*, 22/1 (2010), pp. 55–74.
34 Cranford, *The Teares of Ireland*, p. 65.
35 John Temple, *The Irish Rebellion: or, An History of the Beginnings and first Progresse of the Generall Rebellion raised within the Kingdom of Ireland, upon the three and twentieth day of October, in the Year 1641* (London: Samuel Gellibrand, 1646), p. 40.

elect that spanned centuries. Yet, that the assailants were now Irish suggested that greater depths of barbarity were now at work.[36]

In contrast to the innocence of Irish Protestant victims, the portrayal of Irish Catholic rebels drew upon generations of English colonial accounts of Irish people as well as Foxean constructions of popish deviants. *Late and Lamentable News from Ireland* claimed 'Protestants' had been cut down with swords, 'without any distinction of Sexe with Cruell Tyranny'. The anonymous author then deployed melancholic rhetoric to show how the extent of Irish Catholic cruelty could not be truly related: 'wofull relations of the Rebels diabolicall dealings, which are so cruell, that my pen cannot express to the full'.[37] Despite this, readers were informed:

> They spare not the Protestants, whersoever they come, taking away their lives, and estates, utterly extirpating whole families. Those that escape with their lives, come strake naked (great ladies of noble bloud, not being excused) to this place, where they have the best relief we can give them, both of food and rayment.[38]

This was a stark warning for English audiences as it was widely claimed in contemporary print that the rebellion would spread into England; further evidence was provided by the 'commission for the despoiled subject'. Thus, printers and polemicists alike tapped into wider English fears of popish conspiracies and plots and preyed upon established stereotypes of Irish people. In time, pamphlets offered help on how to identify Irish people should they surface in England. 'Many of the Irish who come to England claim to be Scots' one pamphleteer warned, urging his audience to ask suspected Irish people to pronounce English words with the letter h or to say a prayer in English, 'which they cannot do'. If neither of those tests proved satisfactory readers were instructed to 'vncover their bosomes, most of them weare Crucifixes, especially the women'.[39]

---

36 Kathleen Noonan, '"The cruell pressure of an enraged, barbarous people": Irish and English identity in seventeenth-century policy and propaganda', *Historical Journal*, 41, 1 (1998), pp. 151–177.
37 *Late and Lamentable News from Ireland, Wherein are truly related, the Rebellious, and Cruell proceedings of the Papists there* (London: Joseph Hunscott, 1641), p. 3.
38 *Late and Lamentable News*, p. 3.
39 Thomas Emitie, *A New Remonstrance from Ireland* (London: George Tomlinson, 1642), p. 5; Robin Clifton, 'The popular fear of Catholics during the English Civil Wars', *Past & Present*, 52/1 (1971), pp. 23–55.

Cultural constructions of violence, rooted in Foxe's *Book of Martyrs*, shaped the portrayal of news from Ireland. Biblical references, regardless of whether a verse was supplied, helped to provide an interpretative framework around these accounts that those considered literate in Scripture could draw upon.[40] The contrast between the innocence of Protestant victims and their Irish Catholic assailants heightened the sense of hopelessness Irish Protestants faced. This was recognisably Foxean to contemporary audiences. It provided further evidence of the extent of Protestant martyrdom and suffering in an era of widespread fears of an international Catholic conspiracy that threated England's very existence, a concern felt in a visceral way by Nehemiah Wallington.

2 Nehemiah Wallington's Reading of the 1641 Rebellion

Wallington read pamphlets on the 1641 rebellion within this immediate national context. He feared for the future of England and his fellow English elect, whom he believed were contemporary Israelites.[41] Aggrieved at the rise of Laudian reforms or 'popish' traditions in the Church of England, the Spanish menace as evidenced in the Armada of 1588, and the 'hellish gunpowder plot' of 1605, Wallington was wary of 'the plotts and designes of the wicked papists'.[42] This belief in the eternal struggle between the Popish Antichrist and the true Church coloured Wallington's understanding of international events.[43] Thus, the outbreak of the Wars of the Three Kingdoms, which pitted king against parliament across Ireland, England and Scotland, was also interpreted within this ideological framework.

We know a significant amount about how Wallington read contemporary news from his notebooks. Between 1618 (when he bought his first Bible) and his death in 1654, Wallington wrote fifty notebooks of which seven survive.[44] It is clear that he intended his notes to serve a two-fold purpose. First, they served as intimate journals of his life and his encounters with divine

---

40   Kate Narveson, *Bible readers and lay writers in early-modern England: Gender and self-definition in an emergent writing culture* (London: Routledge, 2016), pp. 101–130.

41   Nehemiah Wallington, 'A record of marcyes continued or yet God is good to Israel' in David Booy (ed.), *The Notebooks of Nehemiah Wallington, 1618–1654: A Selection* (Aldershot: Ashgate, 2007), pp. 215–34.

42   Nehemiah Wallington, 'A bundel of marcys', B.L., Add Ms, 21,935, f. 9; Seaver, *Wallington's World*, p. 161.

43   Cope, *England and the 1641 Irish Rebellion*, pp. 76–77; Seaver, *Wallington's World*, pp. 165–166.

44   David Booy, 'Introduction' in Booy (ed.), *The Notebooks of Nehemiah Wallington*, pp. 1–28, see esp 7–8; Seaver, *Wallington's World*, pp. 2–6.

providence. As David Booy argued, by constantly reflecting on his actions and feelings, Wallington became more spiritually disciplined thereby enhancing his spiritual relationship with God.[45] Referring to his excessive reading and note-taking habits, Wallington recorded how 'I doe all that I doe to the glory of God'.[46] Indeed, the effect of puritan theology on Wallington was so strong that 'he could only construct his life and self in their terms'.[47] Secondly, Wallington wished to instruct his family, friends and neighbours 'to walke in the ways of God'. He encouraged his family and the 'generation to come' as he termed it, to take comfort and 'hang on to God's promises for he hat sayd I will not leaue thee nor forsake thee'.[48] Here Wallington referred to, but did not cite, Hebrews 13:5—'I will not fail thee, nor forsake thee'. Such sentiments comforted him while he attempted to take meaning from accounts of massacres of Protestants in Ireland and Germany during the 1630s and the 1640s. As Kate Narveson has recently shown, Wallington noted key excerpts from what he read as a means of structuring meaning from the texts.[49] Yet, he was aware that his writings would be read by others. Consequently, he provided a biblical framework for other readers of his notes to draw upon, hence the frequent supply of sometimes unattributed biblical references. The purpose of this section is to build upon the work of Joseph Cope, Kathleen Lynch, Kate Narveson, and Paul Seaver on Wallington's extensive notes to show how his biblical allusions drew upon literary cues embedded in contemporary publications that shaped his interpretation. Wallington also supplied his own biblical references as key moments to act as a map to future generations to assist their understanding of his own reading and as a means to demonstrate to his audience how they could read godly material and follow the cues set out by authors in their texts.

Wallington's reading was extensive. He claimed to have read the Bible several times and over two hundred books get special attention in his notes. His note-taking was an instructive process whereby he and his children could 'stand vp & praise the Lord'.[50] Wallington believed the world witnessed God's divine

---

45   Booy, 'Introduction', p. 16; see also: Kathleen Lynch, 'Extraordinarily ordinary: Nehemiah Wallington's experimental method' in Matthew C. Augustine (ed.), *Texts and readers in the age of Marvell* (Manchester: Manchester University Press, 2018), pp. 75–91.
46   Diary of Nehemiah Wallington, B.L., Add Ms, 40,883, f. 15v.
47   Booy, 'Introduction', p. 19.
48   Diary of Nehemiah Wallington, B.L., Add Ms, 40,883, ff 4v, 16, 25v.
49   Narveson, *Bible readers*, pp. 101–130. See also John King, *Foxe's Book of Martyrs and Early Modern Print Culture* (Cambridge: Cambridge University Press, 2006), pp. 232–42, 284–320; Andrew Chambers, *Godly reading: print, manuscript and puritanism in England, 1580–1720* (Cambridge: Cambridge University Press, 2011), pp. 91, 99, 221–227.
50   Diary of Nehemiah Wallington, B.L., Add Ms, 40,883, f. 15v.

will daily, in the home, locally and internationally.[51] This providential framework shaped his reading of English politics. Prior to the execution of Thomas Wentworth, earl of Strafford, Wallington was part of a crowd that shouted 'Justice! Justice!' at members of the English House of Lords.[52] Wallington distrusted Strafford because of rumours that Strafford falsely accused the owner of land he coveted of stealing one of his horses. The accused was found guilty and executed thereby releasing the land for Strafford's personal gain. Wallington commented simply: 'You may read of the like cruell wicked act of Ahab towards Naboth for his vineyard in 1 Kings xxi ver 1 to 20'.[53] The role of Puritan theology and providentialism, therefore, had a more subtle influence on Wallington's writings. As Booy has painstakingly shown in the scholarly apparatus applied in his edition of Wallington's notebooks, biblical phrases not only shaped Wallington's political outlook but also his careful choice of words which invested his reading with a meaningful and godly interpretation.[54]

Although Wallington's sympathies lay with the English parliament, he still struggled to justify with appropriate biblical references his distrust for the king. Over the course of the 1630s and 1640s, Wallington grew suspicious of prelates and papists whose malevolent dealings with Charles I threatened English Protestantism.[55] For example, he blamed Strafford for the growth of popery in Ireland and across the Three Kingdoms. His execution served as a potent reminder to Wallington of the need for unity among Protestants.[56] Later, Wallington claimed that Strafford's policies had jeopardised Irish Protestants after the outbreak of rebellion, leaving them short of arms to defend themselves.[57] As the rebellion in Ireland evolved into the Irish confederate wars, Irish Catholics allied with royalist forces in England. Understandably, Wallington preferred to read news that condemned the Cessation of Arms between the Confederates (the Irish Catholic government formed after the rebellion) and Charles I. Wallington transcribed a significant portion of two notable anti-Cessation tracts, Chidley Coote's *Irelands lamentation for the late destructive cessation* and *Irelands misery since the Late Cessation*.[58] These

---

51   Diary of Nehemiah Walington, B.L., Add Ms, 40, 883, f. 7v; Folger Shakespeare Library, V.a.36, f. 38.
52   Seaver, *Wallington's world*, p. 151.
53   Nehemiah Wallington, 'A bundel of marcys', B.L., Add Ms, 21,935, ff 133–9v, f. 139v.
54   Booy (ed.), *The Notebooks of Nehemiah Wallington*.
55   Seaver, *Wallington's world*, p. 161.
56   Nehemiah Wallington, 'A bundel of marcys', B.L., Add MS, 21,935, ff 141-v.
57   Nehemiah Wallington, 'A bundel of marcys', B.L., Add MS, 21,935, ff 168, 181v.
58   Chidly Coote, *Irelands Lamentation For the late Destructive Cessation, Or, A Trap to catch Protestants* (London: R.C., 1644); Richard Harrison, *Irelands Misery Since the Late Cessation* (London: Henry Shephard, 1644).

selections led Wallington to the conclusion that Irish Catholics were not true subjects and that Charles had now turned his back on Irish Protestants. Now, Wallington feared that a popish conspiracy to murder Protestants had taken hold across the Three Kingdoms.[59] This alliance seemed to heighten the barbarity of Irish Catholics in Wallington's mind for they 'vsed all the Protestants with most barbarous and hellish cruelties killing murthering & slaying all that came into their powers'.[60] But he took solace in the thought that their suffering was not in vain: 'The Lord is holy in all his wayes and iust in all his workes repaying the wicked according to their deserts as Iudg 1 5 6 7'.[61] At this point, Wallington had already justified his support for parliament by referring to Psalm 72, which showed irrefutable evidence that due to his support for Catholicism and popish innovations in religious practice, Charles I was not acting as a divine agent in the mould of King Solomon.[62] This belief that Charles was implicated in the loss of innocent Protestants persisted for the rest of Wallington's life; unlike many other Londoners, he did not turn to royalism after the king's imprisonment and execution.[63] The provision of these biblical references as evidence for his thought process presumably benefitted Wallington's wider reading community who combed through his writings, occasionally alongside Wallington.

Part of Wallington's attempt to draw meaning from the cataclysmic events of the 1640s involved the scouring of news for evidence of divine intervention. Drawing upon Philip Vincent's *Lamentations of Germany*, Wallington noted the similarities between the sins of Germany in the 1630s and those of England in the 1640s.[64] Wallington copied considerable portions of Vincent's work into his notebooks. He feared, as Vincent intended, that England would be punished for similar sins as revealed in his reference to Zachariah 5:3, a passage that warned of God's curse against sinners. As Vincent wrote, 'we are not ignorant of our own indeserts', Wallington too confessed that he was 'somewhat senchable of my owne sinnes in haueing a iontstocke in the sins of the time'.[65] Vincent's desire that the reader should:

---

59 Nehemiah Wallington, 'A bundel of marcys', B.L., Add MS, 21,935, ff 241v–8v.
60 Nehemiah Wallington, 'A bundel of marcys', B.L., Add MS, 21,935, f. 232.
61 Nehemiah Wallington, 'A bundel of marcys', B.L., Add MS, 21,935, f. 232.
62 Nehemiah Wallington, 'A bundel of marcys', B.L., Add MS, 21,935, f. 12; Seaver, *Wallington's world*, pp. 161–165.
63 Seaver, *Wallington's world*, pp 168–169.
64 Nehemiah Wallington, 'A bundel of marcys', B.L., Add MS, 21,935, ff. 2v, 81; Seaver, *Wallington's World*, pp. 160–161.
65 Vincent, *Lamentations of Germany*, [p. 2], 'Preface to the Reader'; Nehemiah Wallington, 'A bundel of marcys', B.L., Add MS, 21,935, f. 82v.

not forget to bee thankfull for this unto the God of peace, and withall to shunne those provocations, for which hee maketh a fertile land barren, a populous Land desolate, even the iniquity of them that dwell therein.

prompted Wallington to do as instructed. Wallington noted:

> Oh now let vs reprent heartily, and cry unto him mightily to spare vs to be mercifull vnto vs vncessant praiers repentant teares are most powerfull to procure Gods mercy to diuert his iudgements: he is he is [sic] mercifulll and will receiue our praiers, he is petifull and will reward our teares.[66]

Wallington's lamentation for those afflicted in Germany, and his introspection, followed the cues outlined by Vincent's use of biblical passages.[67]

As mentioned earlier, an unattributed quotation from Lamentations that adorned the title page of Vincent's work further shaped Wallington's reading of the text and other news publications.[68] Upon reading Tristram Whetcombe's *The rebels turkish tyranny* Wallington imagined the plight of Protestant sufferers in Ireland.[69]

> They Lye Lingquishing and crying to vs saying Haue you no pitty of me O you in England (oh Haue yee no regard al you that here of my mesryes. Behold and see if their be any sorrow like vnto my sorrow which is don vnto mee wherewith the Lord hath afflicted me in the day of his f[i]erce wrath.[70]

Thus, Wallington's reading of the cruelties committed by Irish rebels was influenced by his understanding of the Book of Lamentations, as well as Philip Vincent's *Lamentations of Germany* (1638) thanks to literary cues embedded in the latter. In this way, the plight of German and Irish Protestants were located on a convenient timeline which outlined the persecution of the godly from a broader chronological perspective. Wallington consoled himself that their

---

66 Vincent, *Lamentations of Germany*, [p. 2], 'Preface to the Reader'; Nehemiah Wallington, 'A bundel of marcys', B.L., Add MS, 21,935, f. 82v.
67 Vincent, *Lamentations of Germany*, [p. 1], 'Preface to the Reader'; Matthew 2: 17–21, Nehemiah Wallington, 'A bundel of marcys', B.L., Add MS, 21,935, ff 82v–84v.
68 Vincent, *Lamentations of Germany*, titlepage; Lamentations 1:12.
69 Tristram Whetcombe, *The rebels turkish tyranny* (London: W.R., 1641).
70 Nehemiah Wallington, 'A bundel of marcys', B.L., Add MS, 21,935, f. 169.

suffering provided a glimpse of God's will.[71] The afflictions of Irish Protestants were portrayed within the broader Protestant culture of consolation:

> As for his people to fly to him in holy prayer So likewise God many times bring his peopl into great troubles & straits eyen to a very low ebbe so that he might haue the mor honour and praise in their deliueranc.[72]

Martyrdom, therefore, was a necessary part of the propagation of the true Church Wallington argued.[73]

The failure of both king and parliament to deal adequately with the Irish rebellion during the early days of the rising prompted Wallington to warn of God's vengeance. He spoke of the punishment sent by God to the town of Meroz who refused to help the Israelites.

> O how shall England escape that Cvrse in Iudges v 23 Cvrse yee Meroz (saith the Angel of the Lord) cvrse the inhabitants thereof because they came not to helpe the Lord, to helpe the Lord against the Almighty.[74]

This reflected the general concern of pamphleteers and preachers alike in the winter of 1641–2 when they feared for the loss of Ireland unless swift action was taken, using the curse of Meroz as warning of the dire consequences Englishmen faced if they stood idly by.[75] Consequently, in Wallington's mind, Irish Protestants were slightly different to their German counterparts in that there was a greater sense of solidarity between English and Irish Protestants because Ireland was a *de facto* colony of England. He noted the sibling relationship between Ireland and England and argued 'we see how Caine did hate Abel to the death'.[76] Fearing for the safety of England Wallington argued that

> Now all these plots in Ireland are but one plot against England ... these bloode thirsty papists doe heere among vs in England plott what may

---

71 Jan Frans van Dijkhuizen, '"Never better": Affliction, consolation and the culture of Protestantism in early modern England', *Journal of Early Modern Christianity*, 5/1 (2018), pp. 1–34.
72 Nehemiah Wallington, 'A bundel of marcys', B.L., Add MS, 21,935, f. 169.
73 Nehemiah Wallington, 'A bundel of marcys', B.L., Add MS, 21,935, f. 169; Luke 11: 50–51; Revelations 16:6.
74 Nehemiah Wallington, 'A bundel of marcys', B.L., Add MS, 21,935, f. 169.
75 Jordan S. Downs, 'The curse of Meroz and the English Civil War', *The Historical Journal*, 57/2 (2014), pp. 343–368.
76 Nehemiah Wallington, 'A bundel of marcys', B.L., Add MS, 21,935, f. 180v.

> be for our ouerthrow to bring in their damnable svperstion and idolatry among vs.[77]

A warped form of ethnic cleansing by the Irish rebels horrified Wallington who described how

> the papists in Ir[e]land must be inforced to kill their own wiues that they had marryed of the English great with childe, because they had English blood in them as they sayd and all those English allyed vnto them by their wiues.[78]

This extended to claims that English animals were tortured by the Irish rebels 'if the beasts either roare or groane for misery or paine they would in detestation & mockery of the English cry out that they vnderstood not their English language'.[79] Wallington ended his notes with a reminder of the importance of maintaining Ireland firmly under the control of Parliament: 'It is an old saying Hee that will England win with Ireland first begin, they haue already fowly done too faire for that Kingdom, take timely heed oh England, Scotland'.[80] Thus, concerns over the godly as well as the military security of the English nation further shaped Wallington's reading of news about the Irish rebellion.

Wallington also drew upon a Foxean framework in order to understand the extent of cruelty enacted by Irish rebels. Their barbarous actions dominated much of what he recorded about the Irish Rebellion. Borrowing from Chidley Coote, Wallington spoke of the loss of 154,000 Protestants in Ireland, although earlier he maintained that 200,000 were killed.[81] He had a macabre fascination with rebel violence:

> they inflicted strang kinds of death vpon them, as stabbing drowning staruing ye English vntill they forced them to eate pieces of their own flesh cut off & broiled on the coales and many such horrid deaths as these.[82]

Wallington also incorporated some of John Greensmith's fabricated news from Ireland with a particular emphasis on the fictitious rebel 'Vaul'. Wallington

---

77   Nehemiah Wallington, 'A bundel of marcys', B.L., Add MS, 21,935, f. 185.
78   Nehemiah Wallington, 'A bundel of marcys', B.L., Add MS, 21,935, f. 256.
79   Nehemiah Wallington, 'A bundel of marcys', B.L., Add MS, 21,935, f. 256v.
80   Nehemiah Wallington, 'A bundel of marcys', B.L., Add MS, 21,935, f. 281v.
81   Nehemiah Wallington, 'A bundel of marcys', B.L., Add MS, 21,935, ff 232, 267v.
82   Nehemiah Wallington, 'A bundel of marcys', B.L., Add MS, 21,935, f. 256.

recorded the titillating description of Vaul descending upon Irish Protestants like a 'violent sea', ravishing virgins and stabbing a pregnant woman 'till the poore Infant in his Mothers bloud fell out of the macerated wombe'.[83] Protestant abhorrence of the treatment of their dead was also shared by Wallington who bitterly noted how

> neither did their rage extend onely to the liuing but most in humanly conueyed it selfe to the dead they haue disinterred the bodies of the innocent protestants sleeping in their graues and haue exposed them to be a prey either to beasts to birds.[84]

This echoed descriptions of cruelty towards German Protestants published by Philip Vincent.[85] Wallington's transcriptions of pamphlets that detailed rebel cruelty towards Irish Protestants suggests his sympathy for their cause and his desire for revenge as he mentioned through numerous allusions to passages of the Bible.[86]

Wallington's reading of godly literature combined news from Ireland and his knowledge of Scripture consequently provided the framework he drew upon in order to understand what happened to his in-laws who were based in Fermanagh. His sister-in-law, Dorothy Rampaigne, lost her husband, Zachariah, when he was killed upon the outbreak of rebellion. There is a curious disparity between the account that Dorothy recorded as part of the 1641 depositions and Wallington's portrayal of her suffering which he incorporated in his notes about the crisis of the 1640s. In her deposition, Rampaigne noted her losses as result of the rebellion and claimed that she had been expelled from her home. Shortly afterward, her husband and others were murdered 'vpon a wyld mountaine'. She, her four children, and her maid were stripped of their clothes but nonetheless managed to escape to Dublin. Two of her children, however, starved to death *en route*. Dorothy's account lacks the sort of godly framework that other deponents, many of whom were Protestant clergy, incorporated into their depositions.[87] Yet, Wallington's retelling of her experience shows clear signs that his interpretation was heavily influenced by his reading of godly literature and pamphlets that described the rebellion. The starkest instance of

---

83 Nehemiah Wallington, 'A bundel of marcys', B.L., Add MS, 21,935, f. 166; *More Happy Newes from Ireland of a battell fought betwixt the Scottish volunteers against the Irish rebels* (London: John Greensmith, 1641), Sig A3.
84 Nehemiah Wallington, 'A bundel of marcys', B.L., Add MS, 21,935, f. 256.
85 Vincent, *Lamentations of Germany*, p. 37.
86 Nehemiah Wallington, 'A bundel of marcys', B.L., Add MS, 21,935, ff 167–8.
87 Deposition of Dorothy Rampaigne, 4 Sept 1643, Trinity College Dublin, MS 835, f. 247.

this is Wallington's portrayal of the treatment of Dorothy and her family which closely resembles that of 'Mr Dabnet' in Whetcombe's *Rebels Tvrkish Tyranny* whose family were attacked in their home.[88] Wallington, furthermore, added signs of divine providence that were absent from Rampaigne's narrative. He claimed that 'five paire' of her husband's greyhounds (which she never mentioned as part of her possessions in her deposition) returned to the site of their owner's murder every day 'and did make such an howling and yeeling that they were a terror and a horrow to the Enemy'.[89] Once again, Wallington reassured himself, his sister-in-law, and his readers that Dorothy's suffering was not in vain by referring to a well-known biblical verse: 'Dorothy wee are here by the Lords permission in these Rebels hands, led as sheepe to the slaughter, but let us not feere them for they can only take away this life'.[90] Much like the consolation Wallington drew from the suffering of other Irish Protestants, Wallington took comfort in the fact, supported from Scripture, that Zachariah's death was not in vain.

While we do not know Wallington's exact views on the range of measures proposed during the 1640s in the English parliament concerning the suppression of the Irish rebellion, he did call for the 'rooting out and destruction of those wicked Rebels and bloody papest there & heere'.[91] This suggests that the Foxean narratives swayed his views considerably and that Wallington's understanding of the Irish rebellion was heavily influenced by contemporary news publications, godly literature, anti-popish tracts, and Scripture. What we have little evidence for, however, is how Wallington's conversations with members of his family and local community, including preachers, may have contributed to this.[92] Yet Wallington's notes, comprising a careful structuring of excerpts from news publications contextualised by carefully chosen biblical references, provides tentative evidence of how Wallington wanted others in his community to understand the significance of the Irish rebellion.

Wallington's scriptural knowledge and reading of Foxean-inspired news shaped his reading of the 1641 rebellion. The outbreak of the 1641 rebellion in Ireland occurred at a key moment on the path to the English civil wars, adding

---

88 Booy (ed.), *The Notebooks of Nehemiah Wallington*, pp. 142–4; Whetcombe, *The rebels turkish tyranny*, pp. 1–5.

89 Booy (ed.), *The Notebooks of Nehemiah Wallington*, p. 144.

90 Booy (ed.), *The Notebooks of Nehemiah Wallington*, p. 144; the reference is probably to Psalms 44:22 in light of how Wallington interpreted the deaths of the 'innocent': 'Yea, for thy sake are we killed all the day long; we are counted as sheep for the slaughter'.

91 Nehemiah Wallington, 'A bundel of marcys', B.L., Add MS, 21,935, f. 169v.

92 Lucy Busfield, 'Doubt, anxiety, and Protestant epistolary counselling: the letter-book of Nehemiah Wallington', *Studies in Church History*, 52 (2016), pp. 298–314.

further fuel to the English parliament's campaign against the Personal Rule of Charles I. Pamphlets containing news from Ireland suited the particular interests and information needs of English audiences. It appears that the more sensationalist, cheaper, Foxean-inspired works had a particular appeal to readers like Nehemiah Wallington who consequently interpreted the various crises of the mid-seventeenth century within a broader Foxean and anti-popery framework. The 1641 rebellion fitted into Wallington's sense that evil councillors like Strafford controlled the English court and that an international Catholic menace threatened the existence of English Protestantism. Wallington readily recognised the biblical allusions within these publications. They provided literary cues through which he could shape his reading of events while drawing upon his knowledge of godly literature and Scripture. Presumably these were well known to readers who also drew upon similar interpretative frameworks. This allowed Wallington to draw connections between the plight of German and Irish Protestants. It also facilitated Wallington's attempts to show his family and wider community an epistemological pathway to understand events. News from Ireland confirmed to Wallington that Charles I had abandoned his Protestant subjects across his Three Kingdoms, but his referral to Psalm 72, which celebrated the wisdom of King Solomon, highlighted the disparity of esteem between an ideal king and a contemporary reprobate (in Wallington's eyes). The rationale behind Wallington's unwavering parliamentarianism was evident for those who read his notebooks and, presumably, those who spoke to him. Cultural constructions of violence and Foxean narratives, however, had a much stronger impact than simply shaping Wallington's political allegiances. They framed Wallington's understanding and retelling of his sister's experience of the Irish rebellion for his own benefit and that of the future generations of readers of his notebooks. In a very intimate but publicly accessible way, Wallington's writings, which captured his reading of the 1641 rebellion and the wars of the three kingdoms, helped him to construct his own meaning of events. By providing biblical references to invest his notes with meaning, Wallington offered guidance to his family and wider community on how to interpret news from Ireland in the appropriate godly way. Much like the pamphleteers of the mid-seventeenth century, it is probable that Wallington too had an acute sense of what his audience demanded, expected and liked, and that he wrote his notes with this purpose in mind. Thus, his notebooks also provide a useful insight into what many in his community might have thought having read the latest news about the wars of the three kingdoms.

CHAPTER 8

The Power of the Pen

Huguenot Gazettes in the Pursuit of Information during the Last Quarter of the Seventeenth Century

Panagiotis Georgakakis

On 23 March 1690, an advertisement in the *Nouveau journal universel*—an Amsterdam gazette published by the Huguenot Claude Jordan—informed its clientele that:

> Claude Jordan, the editor of the Nouveau Journal Universel and former editor of the Gazette de Leyde, has been authorised by the city magistrates to print the Gazette d'Amsterdam as well.[1]

Seven days later, the first issue of this historic newspaper, the *Gazette d'Amsterdam*, circulated again, now with a Huguenot publisher at the helm. The *Gazette d'Amsterdam* had been published by Dutch publishers since 1655, and until 1677 it was the only Francophone gazette circulating in the Dutch Republic. However, during the 1680s it was often banned because of its hostile reports against Dutch officials. It was for this reason that Claude Jordan would become the first Huguenot to publish the gazette.

Huguenot newspapers published in the Dutch Republic during the seventeenth and eighteenth centuries continued a long tradition of French-language newspaper publishing. The first French newspapers appeared in the Dutch Republic as early as 1620. This was only fifteen years after Johann Carolus of Strasbourg printed the very first newspapers. Soon, many would follow his example. Newspapers began to make their appearance in many cities, first in Germany and then throughout Europe. Every country, however, took different attitudes to newspapers, and followed different regulatory policies. In the Dutch Republic, newspapers flourished, transforming Amsterdam into the most competitive news market in Europe. The avid news reader could buy fresh newspaper issues on five days of the week. For the first half of the seventeenth century, Amsterdam newsmen supplied not only local customers, but readers

---

1 Bibliothèque Nationale de France (hereafter BnF) M 11707: XXIV. *Nouveau Journal Universel*, *23.03.1690, ad.*, p. 96. All translations are my own unless otherwise stated.

throughout the Dutch Republic. On the other hand, France employed newspapers primarily as a tool of propaganda. Cardinal Richelieu understood the power of the newspaper as a means to control public information. Richelieu took one gazetteer, Théophraste Renaudot, under his close protection, eliminating the rest of the competition. Renaudot established his newspaper, the *Gazette de Paris*, on 30 May 1631. Soon the *Gazette* was granted a monopoly to publish serial news throughout France; it was an instrument of propaganda of the French court.[2]

In the seventeenth century, France supported a population of around twenty million. Officially at least, this population was serviced by a single bi-weekly newspaper, offering only news favourable to the French crown. French-language gazettes published in the Dutch Republic, however, offered an alternative source of news. Their reports could be very hostile against France or against *La Gazette*, but it was a relationship that was far from straightforward; indeed it could be highly nuanced. On 5 September 1679, as Figure 8.1 indicates, Cornelis van Swoll, the editor of the *Gazette d'Amsterdam* and a stern Calvinist, attacked the Capuchin order in one of his reports. Swoll accused the friars as frauds who tried to get rich selling false remedies—exploiting the faith of a gullible people; his attacks continued across several issues.[3] The Count of Avaux, the French ambassador to the Dutch Republic, complained to the States General in an attempt to protect the reputation of the Capuchin fathers against such accusations. It had been only a year since the Franco-Dutch war (1672–1678). The Dutch authorities, concerned by France's reaction, immediately banned the gazette. The French demand, however, was far milder than the reaction of the States. On 21 September, Count Avaux de Pomponne wrote to the King:

> I have made complaints, sir, against the gazetteer of Holland as you have asked me, but the States have made a greater punishment than the King apparently desired, because they absolutely forbade the gazetteer of Amsterdam to print any other gazette in the future. If the intention of His Majesty was to ban the French gazetteer as we have done to all the

---

2   Gilles Feyel, *L'Annonce et la Nouvelle. La Presse d'information en France sous l'Ancien Regime (1630–1788)* (Oxford: Voltaire Foundation, 2000), p. 131. The exact title of the French newspaper was *Relation des nouvelles du Monde*. In other scholarship, the titles *Gazette de France*, *Gazette de Renaudot*, and *La Gazette* are more commonly used. In this chapter the title *La Gazette* will be used.
3   University Library Amsterdam O 62–2478: *La Gazette d'Amsterdam*, *05.09.1679; 14.09.1679; 19.09.1679*. The issues can also be found in www.delpher.nl.

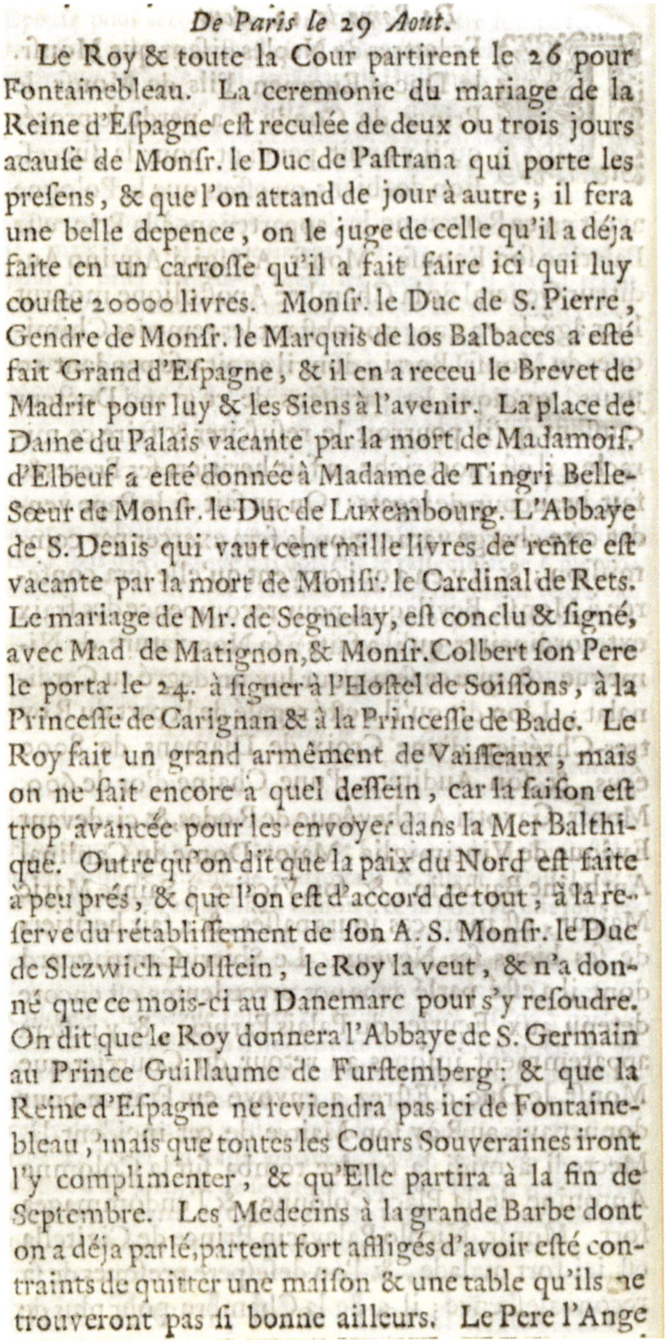

De Paris le 29 Août.

Le Roy & toute la Cour partirent le 26 pour Fontainebleau. La ceremonie du mariage de la Reine d'Espagne est reculée de deux ou trois jours acause de Monsr. le Duc de Pastrana qui porte les presens, & que l'on attand de jour à autre ; il fera une belle depence, on le juge de celle qu'il a déja faite en un carrosse qu'il a fait faire ici qui luy couste 20000 livres. Monsr. le Duc de S. Pierre, Gendre de Monsr. le Marquis de los Balbaces a esté fait Grand d'Espagne, & il en a receu le Brevet de Madrit pour luy & les Siens à l'avenir. La place de Dame du Palais vacante par la mort de Madamoisf. d'Elbeuf a esté donnée à Madame de Tingri Belle-Sœur de Monsr. le Duc de Luxembourg. L'Abbaye de S. Denis qui vaut cent mille livres de rente est vacante par la mort de Monsr. le Cardinal de Rets. Le mariage de Mr. de Segnelay, est conclu & signé, avec Mad de Matignon, & Monsr. Colbert son Pere le porta le 24. à signer à l'Hostel de Soissons, à la Princesse de Carignan & à la Princesse de Bade. Le Roy fait un grand armement de Vaisseaux, mais on ne sait encore à quel dessein, car la saison est trop avancée pour les envoyer dans la Mer Balthique. Outre qu'on dit que la paix du Nord est faite à peu prés, & que l'on est d'accord de tout, à la reserve du rétablissement de son A. S. Monsr. le Duc de Slezwich Holstein, le Roy la veut, & n'a donné que ce mois-ci au Danemarc pour s'y resoudre. On dit que le Roy donnera l'Abbaye de S. Germain au Prince Guillaume de Furstemberg : & que la Reine d'Espagne ne reviendra pas ici de Fontainebleau, mais que toutes les Cours Souveraines iront l'y complimenter, & qu'Elle partira à la fin de Septembre. Les Medecins à la grande Barbe dont on a déja parlé, partent fort affligés d'avoir esté contraints de quitter une maison & une table qu'ils ne trouveront pas si bonne ailleurs. Le Pere l'Ange

FIGURE 8.1 Van Swoll's first attack against the Capuchin order, *Gazette d'Amsterdam*, 5 September 1679
IMAGE FROM DELPHER.NL

others, I would be glad to have it done, but I dare not speak of it until you did me the honour to ask me.[4]

Avaux answered that the king would prefer an apology from the gazetteer, rather than a ban on the publication of the gazette. The French answer to the Dutch authorities demonstrates the complexity of the relationship between the French authorities and the Francophone press of the Dutch Republic. *La Gazette d'Amsterdam* was circulated in large numbers throughout France, and especially amongst the French Court. It gave French courtiers the opportunity not only to receive information from a different source besides *La Gazette*, but also to monitor the shifting reputation of the French monarch. The French Court was extremely sensitive about the image of France and its King abroad. Moreover, the *Gazette d'Amsterdam* paid a significant fee to allow its circulation in France; this fee was made over to the Secretary of the State for foreign affairs, Colbert de Torcy. Any ban on *La Gazette d'Amsterdam*, therefore, may have favoured Eusèbe II Renaudot, the editor of *La Gazette*, as it reduced the competition in the news market, but it would also financially hurt Torcy, his political master.

This chapter will document the attitude of the Huguenot gazettes published in the Dutch Republic during the last quarter of the seventeenth century, using reports appearing both in times of peace and war. It is noteworthy that even though these gazettes had Huguenot refugees as editors or as publishers, their attitude was not always as hostile to France as we might have supposed.[5]

1   The Emergence of the Huguenot Gazettes

From 1620, the Dutch Republic published and circulated Francophone gazettes. At least one Francophone gazette circulated during the first half of the seventeenth century, but the majority would appear following 1685 and the Revocation of the Edict of Nantes. There was an influx of some 50,000 to 75,000 Huguenots into the Northern Netherlands in the years following the Revocation, making it easier for Huguenot publishers to establish their own gazette with a ready-made market.[6] Moreover, booksellers and printers were

---

4   Cited in Feyel, *L'Annonce et la Nouvelle*, p. 512.
5   The gazette that was published in Leiden has two titles: *Traduction libre des gazettes flamandes et autres*, and after 1679, *Nouvelles extraordinaires de divers endroits*. This chapter uses both titles.
6   Els. M Peters, 'England as Halfway House and Final Homeland for Huguenots', *Refugees and Emigrants in the Dutch Republic and England, Papers of the annual Symposium* (22 Nov. 1985)

prominent amongst the stream of Huguenot refugees who settled in the Dutch Republic—a useful asset.

However, the first specifically Huguenot (as opposed to simply Francophone) gazette published in the Dutch Republic appeared a little before the Revocation. In 1677, the Huguenot Alexandre de la Font resigned from his post as an editor of *La Gazette d'Amsterdam* and moved to Leiden. There, he established his own venture, together with the Dutch publisher Johannes van Gelder. His gazette entitled *Nouvelles extraordinaires de divers endroits* was the first French-language gazette of the Dutch Republic published outside Amsterdam. La Font was a key figure in the advancement of Huguenot gazettes in the Dutch Republic during the second half of the seventeenth century. He started his career as a newsman writing reports for Smient's *Gazette ordinaire d'Amsterdam*. After the merger of the papers of Van Swoll and Smient, La Font was hired as editor by Van Swoll. La Font was productive during his service as editor in *La Gazette d'Amsterdam*. Every time that *La Gazette d'Amsterdam* was banned, La Font published clandestine gazettes covering the information vacuum left by *La Gazette d'Amsterdam*. One of these clandestine publications, entitled *Memoires qui servir a la composition de La Gazette d'Amsterdam,* was also the first Huguenot gazette ever published. Alexandre died in 1685, and his son, Anthony de la Font became the editor and the publisher of the newspaper until his death in 1738.[7]

La Font was not the only Huguenot who worked under the guidance of Dutch newsmen, later establishing his own venture. His example was followed by Gabriel de Ceinglen, a former captain in the service of the States of Holland, who collaborated as a journalist with *La Gazette d'Amsterdam*. He transferred news from the camp of the Prince of Orange to the gazette. Ceiglen probably resigned from *La Gazette d'Amsterdam* at the same time that La Font moved to Leiden. In 1682, he established his gazette entitled *Nouvelles solides & choisies* in Amsterdam, which became the competitor of *Nouvelles extraordinaires de divers endroits*. Ceiglen was a strict Calvinist who had no love for the French King. The French ambassador often protested against the aggressive reports appearing in his gazette. Ceiglen died in 1684, and his wife, Marie Patoillat, continued the publication of his gazette until 1686. She was banned

---

(Leiden, 1986), p. 57.; David van der Linden, *Experiencing Exile, Huguenot Refugees in the Dutch Republic, 1680–1700* (Farnham: Ashgate, 2015), pp. 16, 34–35; Jan and Leo Lucassen (eds.), *Migration, Migration History, History: Old Paradigms and New Perspectives* (Bern: Lang, 1997), p. 16.

7 For more on the clandestine Huguenot gazettes, see Panagiotis Georgakakis, 'Huguenot clandestine papers published in the Dutch Republic', in Jason McElligott (ed.), *Elia Bouhereau and the World of the Huguenots* (forthcoming).

from Amsterdam, and she was fined for publishing unauthorized short reports. *Nouvelles solides & choisies* was circulated for three more years, until 1689, by Noël Aubert de Versé and Genevois. Patoillat, on the other hand, moved to Rotterdam establishing her own newspaper there in 1691. Either alone, or with the help of her son, Simeon Antoine published the *Gazette de Rotterdam* until 1713.[8]

After the ban of the *Nouvelles solides & choisies*, Amsterdam remained with only one Francophone gazette, the *Nouveau journal universel*. The *Nouveau journal universel* was a brief venture, established by Claude Jordan in Amsterdam, which circulated from 1688 to 1690. Claude Jordan had fled to the Dutch Republic in 1681. He was a bookseller, printer, and a journalist. Soon after arriving in the country, Anthony de la Font recognised his talents, and Jordan became the editor of the *Nouvelles extraordinaires de divers endroits* from 1686 to 1688. In 1688 he settled in Amsterdam starting his own venture. The *Nouveau journal universel* must have impressed the magistrates of the city of Amsterdam, as they asked Jordan to become the editor and the publisher of the new edition of the *Gazette d'Amsterdam* in 1690. Jordan would launch the new *Gazette d'Amsterdam* together with Jean Tronchin Dubreuil. The first issue of this new *Gazette d'Amsterdam* was published on 23 March 1690. At the same time with the circulation of the *Gazette d'Amsterdam*, Jordan published another gazette entitled *L'Histoire abrégée de l'Europe*. It was also a biweekly newspaper circulating every Monday and Thursday, making Jordan the only Huguenot who was publishing two Francophone gazettes. Nevertheless, Claude Jordan did not stay long in the Dutch Republic. He fell into the disfavour of the Dutch authorities and was forced to leave the country. In April 1691, the Amsterdam authorities would force him to abandon his privileges in publishing newspapers. He immediately returned to France and became Louis XIV's historiographer. The publication of the *Gazette d'Amsterdam* subsequently became the responsibility of Jean Tronchin Dubreuil.

Dubreuil was a famous humanist, political historian, and scholar. He became friends with Jean-Baptiste Colbert and Jacques-Bénigne Bossuet during the time he spent in Paris. He entered the service of Colbert in 1660 and he remained in this post until 1682. Dubreuil rejected Catholicism while Colbert's efforts to persuade him failed; he left Paris and France two years before the Revocation. His political connections, however, did not stop at the French court. Dubreuil had frequent correspondence with Anthoine Heinsius (1641–172), a prominent figure in Dutch politics and key adviser to William III. At the same time as

---

8   Jean Sgard (ed.), *Dictionnaire de la presse: 1600–1789. 2* [...]: *Dictionnaire des journalistes: 1600–1789 K–Y* (Oxford: Voltaire Foundation, 1999), pp. 205–206.

the publication of the *Gazette d'Amsterdam*, Dubreuil also circulated another French-language gazette entitled the *Recueil des nouvelles*. This venture continued for a short period, from August 1691 to 22 October 1693.[9]

All the Huguenot gazettes mentioned above were printed in quarto, and every issue consisted of four pages. Each page was divided into two columns. The gazettes had a biweekly circulation, as Table 8.1 highlights. However, there were some subtle differences in presentational style. The *Nouvelles extraordinaires de divers endroits*, *Nouvelles solides & choisies*, and the *Gazette de Rotterdam* printed headlines with the name of the city from where the reports emanated along with the dates these reports reached the Netherlands. On the other hand, the *Nouveau journal universel*, *L'Histoire abrégée de l'Europe*, *Gazette d'Amsterdam*, and the *Recueil des nouvelles* adopted a slightly different approach. These gazettes used countries as headlines, with reports organised below by city. The gazettes presented diplomatic, military, and political news from across the major cities of Europe. Each piece of news coming from the same city was separated from the next by a small space after the full stop. The reports which appeared in these gazettes were dense.

The number of Huguenot gazettes published in the Dutch Republic increased during the last decade of the seventeenth century. The Huguenot refugees who settled in the Dutch Republic swelled the domestic readership, yet they could not sustain the establishment of more Francophone gazettes alone.

This raises questions regarding the survival of these newspapers. How could these ventures survive in a Francophone news market too small to sustain all of them? Survival depended on targeting a larger news market beyond the Huguenot refugee community in the Republic. This news market was France, which had just one gazette in circulation. *La Gazette* was the constitutional gazette of the state, and it had tight connections with the French court. The Renaudot family had run this venture since 1631 and their privilege depended upon the King himself. Thus, *La Gazette* was more often a propagandist paper of the French court than a newspaper, a fact of which its readers were very aware. Huguenot gazetteers could sense opportunity.

---

9 For more information about the emergence of the *Nouvelles extraordinaires de divers endroits*, the *Gazette d'Amsterdam* and the *Gazette de Rotterdam*, see Panagiotis Georgakakis, 'Delivering the News from abroad: French-language gazettes published in the Dutch Republic during the second half of 17th century', in Sebastien Drouin (ed.), '*Edition et réception de la presse hollandaise*', *University of Toronto Quarterly*, 89/4 (2020), pp. 657–674.

TABLE 8.1   Huguenot Gazettes: days of publication, publishers, and years of circulation

Gazette	Days of publication			Publisher	Years of publication
	Monday	Tuesday	Thursday		
Nouvelles extraordinaires de divers endroits		x	x	Alexandre de la Font (1677–1685); Anthony de la Font (1685–1738)	1677–1793
Nouvelles solides & choisies		x	x	Gabriel de Ceinglen (1682–1684); Marie Pattoilat (1684–1686); Noël Aubert de Versé and Genevois (1687–1689)	1682–1689
Nouveau journal universel	x		x	Claude Jordan (1688–1690)	1688–1690
L'Histoire abrégée de l'Europe	x		x	Claude Jordan (1690–1691)	1690–1691
Gazette d'Amsterdam	x		x	Claude Jordan (1690); Jean Tronchin Dubreuil (1691–1720)	1690[a]–1796
Recueil des nouvelles	x		x	Jean Tronchin Dubreul (1690–1693)	1690–1693
Gazette de Rotterdam	x		x	Marie Pattoilat (1691–1720)	1691–1720

a The table deals with the gazettes published by Huguenots. Therefore, it does include the previous circulation of the *Gazette d'Amsterdam*.

2   The Role of Advertisement in the Circulation of the Huguenot Gazettes

It remains difficult to estimate the circulation figures for each gazette, or even how they were distributed between domestic and foreign readers. One piece of evidence, though, that can provide some indirect evidence can be found within paid advertisements. The sale of a newspaper was more complicated than the sale of other forms of commercial news, because the periodicity of a newspaper required a continuous flow of money; expenditures of gathering news and maintaining correspondence were high. A well-informed correspondent required a substantial salary. As a result, most newspaper publishers battled against bankruptcy for several years after the establishment of their enterprise. If they were lucky, they turned some profit a few years later, when they had built their credibility and created a reliable customer base.

However, Dutch publishers were the pioneers of a new source of income beyond subscription, and that was advertising. While never the backbone of their ventures, publishers found it extremely profitable to advertise goods.[10] Soon, Dutch newsmen placed advertisements in almost every issue of their newspapers, and while we do not have any precise information on how lucrative this revenue stream was for publishers in the seventeenth century, it is clear that such additional income would have been very welcome indeed.

Advertisements placed in several issues of Huguenot gazettes provide us with indirect information about the geographical distribution of each issue. An advertiser would prefer to place his goods or services in a paper that had a wide circulation among his potential clients. Revealingly, Huguenot gazetteers targeted the lucrative Parisian market. Their principal competition, *La Gazette*, did not place any advertisement in its issues, as it had no need to do it; it was financially controlled by the crown.

Huguenot publishers, to different extents, managed to build an international network of advertising, which extended from Amsterdam to Rome, from Strasbourg to London and from Leiden to Bordeaux. Most of the advertisers were based in France, but there were others too further afield. Such networks were dependent, however, on the political situation in Europe, thriving during peace, but all but collapsing during periods of war. Between 1677–1687, the two Huguenot gazettes then being published included no fewer than 432 advertisements. The *Nouvelles extraordinaires de divers endroits* printed 393 advertisements in its issues, while the *Nouvelles solides & choisies* included 39. La Font's

---

[10]   Arthur der Weduwen and Andrew Pettegree, *The Dutch Republic and the Birth of Modern Advertising* (Leiden & Boston: Brill, 2020), pp. 12–13.

gazette had a wide publicity among the Francophone readership, as the advertisers preferred it to draw attention to their wares. That does not mean necessarily that the *Nouvelles solides & choisies* did not circulate in France; it did, but it was risky for the French advertisers to put notices of their goods in a gazette that was clearly hostile to the King. Interestingly, the Parisian advertisements constituted 50 per cent of the total advertisements, 217 in all, while the advertisements from the Dutch Republic constituted less than 30 per cent. In other words, the French market was the main target of the Huguenot gazetteers.

The *Nouvelles extraordinaires de divers endroits* was the Huguenot gazette that dominated the Parisian advertising market until the eve of the War of the Grand Alliance. This control, however, affected the presentation of news. La Font did not confront reports appearing in *La Gazette*; on the contrary, he often used information, especially the diplomatic news, that first appeared in Renaudot's gazette to present different details about the same event. La Font was a clever man. He wanted to provide his readership with the latest news without provoking any French reaction that could damage his appeal within the Parisian market and, inevitably, diminish the flow of advertisements to his gazette. Reports, for instance, which outlined French cruelties against Huguenots during the time of the Revocation of the Edict of Nantes remained broadly neutral. He showed of course his sympathy to his fellow Huguenots, referring to the violence and the torments against them, but remained restrained in not offering any details of this violence. The issue published on 13 September 1685 featured a report from Paris dated 11 September:

> Finally, we will soon have only one religion in the realm. The violence of the [Catholic] soldiers who are lodged in the Protestants' houses and the torments that they are suffering helped move them to the Catholic faith more in one hour than the Catholic priests had been able to accomplish in a year.[11]

Although there was a reference to cruelties against the Huguenots, the report noted them without further comment. It was the first time that La Font referred to the violence that the Huguenots had suffered at the hands of the French troops. This was not the case, however, with the *Nouvelles solides & choisies*. Its publisher Ceiglen had died in 1684, but his wife Marie Pattoilat had immediately taken charge. The *Nouvelles solides & choisies* featured reports with a clear anti-French attitude. Even during peacetime, the gazette attempted to

---

11 BnF G-4275–4390 4279: *Nouvelles extraordinaires de divers endroits, du Jeudi 13 Septembre 1685*.

find fault with any act of Louis XIV which might be deemed in any way positive. This position became even more overt following the Revocation of the Edict of Nantes. Contrary to La Font, Pattoilat had chosen who she would support. Pattoilat used rumours and stories from Huguenots who managed to flee, alongside news coming from those French cities which had suffered violence. Thus, most of the reports featured in the *Nouvelles solides & choisies* evoked feelings of sympathy, despair, and pain for the Huguenots, as well as hatred for the French King.

The difference between the two Huguenot gazettes is clear if we compare the issue of the *Nouvelles solides & choisies* published on 13 September to the *Nouvelles extraordinaires de divers endroits* we have described above. The *Nouvelles solides & choisies* presented far more detail on the violence perpetrated by the French soldiers. The report outlined how Catholic bishops reacted to this violence, and the pleasure they had taken at the success of the soldiers; the bishops 'praised them by using the most disgusting words against those poor people [Huguenots]'. Holding Huguenots as prisoners in their own houses, the soldiers succeeded in cutting them off from their coreligionists, not attending their congregation and, inevitably, 'filling their hearts with despair'.[12]

On 22 October 1685, the Edict of Fontainebleau was signed. That political decision was the last blow against French Protestants. The *Nouvelles extraordinaires de divers endroits* remained faithful to its previous approach of presenting the news in neutral terms. The issue dated 30 October included news of the Revocation. The Paris report stated that:

> Mr. Chaucelier signed the Edict which ended the Edicts of Nantes and Nîmes, and all that had been granted to the Protestants; the same Edict also orders the demolition of all the temples of the Kingdom and the general prohibition of the exercise of the reformed religion. All Protestant ministers have orders to leave the Kingdom within two weeks, or else they will be punished in the galleys.[13]

On the other hand, *Nouvelles Solides & Choisies* published on the same date as the *Nouvelles extraordinaires de divers endroits*, expressed far more pronounced indignation. The Parisian report opened by stating that:

---

12   BnF G-4390 : *Nouvelles solides et choisies. Du Jeudi 13 Septembre 1685.*
13   BnF G-4275–4390 4279 : *Nouvelles extraordinaires de divers endroits, du Mardi 30 Octobre 1685.*

They have just struck the last blow against the Protestants of this kingdom. A declaration of the King revokes, breaks and cancels in all points the Edict of Nantes, prohibits the exercise of religion throughout the kingdom, without exception. It orders the demolition of all the temples, and that those ministers who will not renounce their faith should leave the kingdom in just a few days or else they will be sent to the galleys. It declares that those ministers who will become Catholic, their wages will be increased by a third, which will also pass to their widows. That they will pass all kinds of charges without undergoing an examination and that those who want to be clergymen will be able to have degrees and be Doctors in Universities.

The report continued by presenting further details. In Lyon, Huguenots were forced to renounce their faith due to the cruelties they sustained, cruelties which 'make people shudder in horror'. In La Rochelle, the desolation of entire neighbourhoods was spoken of. Dragoons and fusiliers came at night, surprising the inhabitants and taking all their goods by force which they then sold in public. As the report mentioned, many of the citizens in La Rochelle fled using dangerous escape methods and routes.[14]

Serious questions are raised by the way that the news of the Revocation of the Edict of Nantes, as well as the French policy against the Huguenots before the signing of the Edict of Fontainebleau, was communicated in the two gazettes. Although the aggressiveness of *Nouvelles solides & choisies* against the French decision was not a surprise, this was not the case with *Nouvelles extraordinaires de divers endroits*. Alexandre de la Font was a member of the Huguenot congregation in Leiden and the former copywriter and editor of the *Gazette d'Amsterdam*, which was hostile to France. Why would such a strict Calvinist use a neutral tone towards Louis XIV and his policies during the most significant threat against his fellow Huguenots? How can we explain this change in attitude? This is particularly interesting as the *Nouvelles extraordinaires de divers endroits* would become one of the most anti-French gazettes during the War of the Grand Alliance several years later.

There are many potential answers to this. Alexandre de la Font died in November 1685, passing the gazette to his son Anthony. Alexandre de la Font was considered by his contemporary Pierre Bayle as one of 'the greatest gazetteer(s) of his era', though Claude Bellanger described him as an 'unscrupulous

---

14   BnF G-4390 : *Nouvelles solides et choisies. Du Mardi 30 Octobre 1685.*

character'.[15] If we take at face value Bellanger's opinion about the personality of Alexandre de la Font, then we could understand his stance towards the Revocation of the Edict of Nantes. Alexandre de la Font was indeed a faithful Huguenot, but first and foremost he was a businessman. Gazetteers during the seventeenth century struggled to keep their ventures profitable, and Alexandre was no exception. His gazette dominated the French news market during the 1680s; it circulated in many French cities without facing any serious competition. It would have been unwise for La Font to have taken a hostile stance against France; he had to be as diplomatic as he could to secure the dominance of his gazette within the French news market.

This stance continued after Alexandre de la Font's death. At the beginning of 1686, Claude Jordan became the editor, while Anthony de la Font became the owner and the publisher of the gazette. Claude Jordan was also a Huguenot, but he was friendly towards France. He believed that the Revocation of the Edict of Nantes was likely a sinister plan advocated by the King's advisors rather than a decision taken by the King himself. In 1688, Jordan abandoned his post as an editor of the *Gazette de Leyde* and established his own venture. This was not a coincidence. It was at this time that the *Gazette de Leyde* changed attitude towards France, as the French King was once again engaged in war against several European states.

Thus, Anthony de la Font was faced with a dilemma; should he continue to support the French crown or adopt a more critical position? The choice was easy. The Dutch authorities would not be happy if a gazette published in the Dutch Republic had supported the enemy, and the risk of a ban on the gazette was increasing rapidly. Moreover, a considerable number of Huguenots had fled France and settled in states that were hostile against France. Much of this readership shared no love for the French King, and it was a potential clientele that could cover some of the losses of readers in France. At the same time, new Huguenot gazettes had appeared in the Dutch Republic, and some of them had editors and publishers like Dubreuil who already had good contacts at the French court. Thus, the French news market was not secure at all. La Font would not take such a risk; it was the time to abandon his neutral or indeed friendly attitude towards France and become its opponent.

La Font's strategy seemed to be the correct one. If we study the placement of advertising notices in Huguenot gazettes during the time of the War of the Grand Alliance, some interesting observations can be made. Eight Huguenot gazettes circulated during the war, and they featured 565 advertisements in total. The *Gazette d'Amsterdam* printed the majority of these advertisements,

---

15   Claude Bellanger et al. (eds.), *Histoire Générale de la Presse Française* (Paris: Presses Universitaires de France, 1969), vol. 1, p. 514.

with 295 notices in all. The *Nouvelles extraordinaires de divers endroits*, on the other hand, accounted for only forty-nine, holding fourth place behind the *Gazette de Rotterdam* and the *Recueil des nouvelles*. The *Nouvelles extraordinaires de divers endroits* accounted for only twelve advertisements from Paris; most importantly, these notices were placed in the gazette during 1688, on the eve of the War of the Grand Alliance. In contrast, the *Gazette d'Amsterdam* contained 107 advertisements placed by Parisian merchants and booksellers. If we add to these 107 notices and the 49 Parisian advertisements which appeared in the *Recueil des Nouvelles*, we get some sense of the dominance of Dubreuil within the Parisian market.

The new era of advertising for the Huguenot gazettes had arrived. During 1688–1697, Paris lost its dominant position as the city with the most advertisements in Huguenot gazettes. From its 50 per cent share during the period 1677–1687, the percentage dropped to almost 30 percent in the following decade. The same happened during the years of truce. The number of notices that were placed in the Huguenot gazettes during 1698–1701 increased to 727. The French advertisements constituted only the 24 per cent of this corpus. Thus, the importance of the French market to the Huguenot gazetteers diminished. This reduction affected the attitude of the reports towards France. We can chart these shifts in Table 8.2.

TABLE 8.2   Numbers of advertisements appearing in the Huguenot gazettes during 1677–1687, 1688–1697 & 1698–1701, and the percentage of French notices within the total corpus of advertisements

Gazette	1677–1687 advertisements (ads)	French ads %	1688–1697 ads	French ads %	1698–1701 ads	French ads %
Nouvelles extraordinaires de divers endroits	393	51%	49	24%	16	19%
Nouvelles solides & choisies	39	41%	14	50%	x	x
Gazette d'Amsterdam	x	x	295	36%	374	6%
Gazette de Rotterdam	x	x	92	1%	102	14%
Recueil des nouvelles	x	x	60	82%	x	x

3 Huguenot Reports during the War of the Grand Alliance

The war of the Grand Alliance between France and a coalition of European states including England, the Dutch Republic, Spain, the Holy Roman Empire, and small German states closed the last decade of the seventeenth century. Circulated during a turbulent period in European history, the Huguenot gazettes were at the forefront of information, providing readers with an alternative news source of events that took place during the war. This scope often contradicted the reports of *La Gazette*, especially when the outcome of events was negative for the French side.

On 25 March 1692, French forces began the siege of Namur. Louis XIV headed a French army which numbered no fewer than 120,000 men. On the other hand, the defenders under the command of the Spanish Duke of Barbancon and the Dutch Baron Menno van Coehoorn, numbered just 6,000 men. The siege lasted for thirty-seven days, and on 1 July, the city surrendered to the French.

Tronchin Dubreuil was very interested in the outcome of the siege since both of his gazettes, the *Gazette d'Amsterdam* and the *Recueil des nouvelles*, covered it extensively. On 7 July, the *Gazette d'Amsterdam* brought the first news of the capitulation of Namur. The Brussels report dated 3 July stated: 'The news from Namur and the allied camp do not allow us to say any more than that the castle has fallen; what happened there is not clear as yet'. The report continued by presenting the unsuccessful French assaults on the castle in the preceding days, before then revealing the capitulation. The next issue dated 10 July presented the news from the French side. The Paris report included news about the capitulation of Namur; yet this news was not at the beginning of the report but rather in the middle, between the news from St Malo and Marseille.[16] Dubreuil tried to present the reports of the capitulation of Namur in a neutral tone; however, it soon became clear that he was not very excited about the outcome. Dubreuil did not make any comment in his issues about the French victory. He presented the events by following the chronological timeline without any sign of emotion. His true beliefs, though, would become clear later.

On 2 July 1695, it was the allies' turn to besiege Namur. Two days after the start of the siege, the *Gazette d'Amsterdam* presented the number of English forces that would participate in that siege. The rest of the Huguenot gazettes would follow with their reports. The siege lasted for three months,

---

16 St. Geneviève Library, France CD 39 RES: LIV. *Avec Privilege de Nosseigneurs Les Etats de Hollande & de West-Frise. Du Lundi 7. Juillet. 1692.*; LV. *Avec Privilege de Nosseigneurs Les Etats de Hollande & de West-Frise. Du Jeudi 10. Juillet. 1692.*

and its development was the first concern of the gazettes. The reports coming from different and rival camps agreed about the outcome of battles outside Namur. Finally, the supplement of *Gazette d'Amsterdam* on 5 September was the first Huguenot paper that brought the news of the allied victory. The supplement stated:

> We have just been fully made aware of this great event, which kept all of Europe enthralled. It was God's pleasure to grant victory to the fair arms of the allies in a time of crisis, where all minds were divided between fear and hope. It was a time of vows and prayers, which is fortunately changed for the common cause into a happy time of thanksgiving. This important fortress that the French believed they had made impregnable [...] defended inside by an elite army headed by a Marshal of France, and outside by an army of more than one hundred thousand men, was held only as long as it took so the conquest would be more glorious.[17]

Again, Dubreuil's different tone on presenting this news was apparent. The way he expressed the capitulation of Namur was completely at odds with the way he had reported the similar news just three years earlier.

On 8 September, the *Gazette de Rotterdam* also confirmed the outcome of the siege, praising William III of England, and the allies for this victory. The *Gazette de Rotterdam* spent two pages presenting the news from this 'glorious expedition'. On the other hand, the *Gazette*, in its issue published on 10 September 1695, admitted the loss of the city in only a few words; nevertheless, Eusèbe II Renaudot claimed that this was only a Pyrrhic victory for the allies, as they lost virtually their entire army. In the issue published on 10 September 1695, Renaudot wrote at the end of the Dinant report:

> Their army was reduced during the siege by about 30,000 men. Almost all the regiments which took part in the attacks have been entirely ruined. And the officers who remain are desperate to re-establish their regiments.[18]

---

17 St. Geneviève Library, France CD 39 RES : *LXXI. Avec Privilege de Nos-Seigneurs Les Etats de Hollande & de West-Frise. Du Lundi 5 Septembre 1695.*

18 Municipal Archives, Rotterdam: *No. 36 Gazette de Rotterdam Du Jeudi 8. Septembre. 1695.* The issue can be found also in www.delpher.nl; BnF 4-LC2–1: *N. 36. Gazette, 10.09.1695.* The issue can be found in www.gallica.fr.

At the beginning of June 1696, French armies deployed in Savoy and besieged Turin. News from Piedmont appeared in many reports in the *Gazette d'Amsterdam*, the *Nouvelles extraordinaires de divers endroits* and the *Gazette de Rotterdam*. Every gazette, however, presented this information in a different tone.

The issue of the *Gazette de Rotterdam* published on 7 June 1696 reported that the French army had settled down in three different camps, preparing for the siege of Turin. The report came from the French camp of Rivoli on 23 May. The Turin report also contained information about the size of the Spanish army. Additionally, it presented rumours that the French army needed more than fifteen thousand mules to transfer oats and hay for the horses. The tone of the reports attempted to be neutral, as the main goal was not to provoke any reaction from either side. Nevertheless, the *Gazette de Rotterdam* showed a slight preference for the French side. In the report that came from the French camp in Rivoli, for instance, readers learned that peasants provided the camp with food. The report just mentions French deserters, not giving any other information whatsoever.

The same news was also presented in the Leiden paper that was published the same day as *Gazette de Rotterdam*. The *Nouvelles extraordinaires de divers endroits*, however, presented the news from Turin's perspective. Figure 8.2 presents this different approach of the Leiden gazette. In that issue, readers were informed that the Duke of Savoy 'showed his royal superiority as he distributed his own powder and lead to his subjects [...] he is ready to defend it [Turin] well'. The Duke also brought his guards into Turin and ordered women and children to leave the city. The Paris report placed far more emphasis on the bravery of the Duke, informing readers that 'The Duke took every precaution imaginable to counter the effect of the bombing'.[19]

Not surprisingly, the *Gazette* presented the news differently. In the issue published on 9 June 1696, we learn that the Duke of Savoy could not inspire his subjects, since the latter abandoned their homes without following his orders. Thus, it was more a decision of the people of Turin to leave the city rather than any adherence to the duke's order. The *Gazette* does not refer to any news about the number of deserters in the French army, unlike the other two gazettes. On the other hand, *Gazette d'Amsterdam* tried to be neutral. It presented the same news as the *Nouvelles extraordinaires de divers endroits* and the *Gazette de Rotterdam*, without showing any preference.

---

19   Rome, Vatican Library, ASV No. 38. *Gazette de Rotterdam Du* 07.06.1696; *Nouvelles extraordinaires de divers endroits*, 07.06.1696. The issues can be found also in www.delpher.nl.

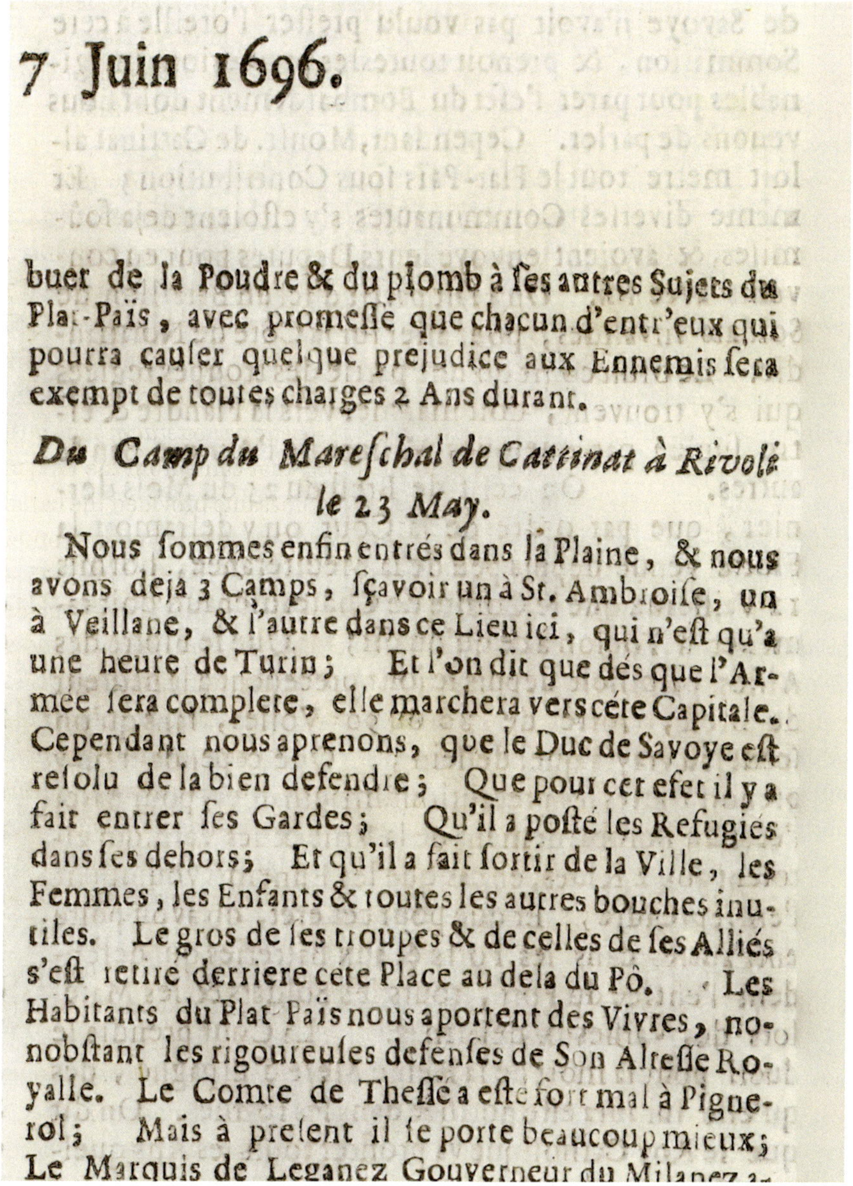

7 Juin 1696.

buer de la Poudre & du plomb à ſes autres Sujets du Plat-Païs, avec promeſſe que chacun d'entr'eux qui pourra cauſer quelque prejudice aux Ennemis ſera exempt de toutes charges 2 Ans durant.

Du Camp du Mareſchal de Cattinat à Rivoli le 23 May.

Nous ſommes enfin entrés dans la Plaine, & nous avons deja 3 Camps, ſçavoir un à St. Ambroiſe, un à Veillane, & l'autre dans ce Lieu ici, qui n'eſt qu'à une heure de Turin; Et l'on dit que dés que l'Armée ſera complete, elle marchera vers céte Capitale. Cependant nous aprenons, que le Duc de Savoye eſt reſolu de la bien defendre; Que pour cet efet il y a fait entrer ſes Gardes; Qu'il a poſté les Refugiés dans ſes dehors; Et qu'il a fait ſortir de la Ville, les Femmes, les Enfants & toutes les autres bouches inutiles. Le gros de ſes troupes & de celles de ſes Alliés s'eſt retiré derriere cete Place au dela du Pô. Les Habitants du Plat-Païs nous aportent des Vivres, nonobſtant les rigoureuſes defenſes de Son Alteſſe Royalle. Le Comte de Theſſé a eſté fort mal à Pignerol; Mais à preſent il ſe porte beaucoup mieux; Le Marquis de Leganez Gouverneur du Milanez a

FIGURE 8.2 The end of the report from Turin and the report from camp Rivoli. Both praised the Duke of Savoy, in the *Nouvelles extraordinaires de divers endroits*, 7 June 1696
IMAGE FROM DELPHER.NL

So, how can we explain this diversity in the reports? And what about the different attitude that the same editors showed during the years? Though the answer is complex and multifaceted, the religious beliefs of the editors were critical. After the Revocation of the Edict of Nantes, the majority of Huguenots became hostile to Louis XIV. The Huguenot editors were no exception, though their political beliefs diverged. Already from the 1670s, the French expansion policy had been accepted by the Huguenots first with scepticism and then with open hostility. Alexandre de la Font and Gabriel de Ceiglen were two of the Huguenots who lead this opposition with their clandestine papers. The same political beliefs were shared by Jean Tronchin Dubreuil who corresponded frequently with Heinsius, the Grand Pensionary of the Dutch Republic. Dubreuil's detailed knowledge of the financial status of France was extremely helpful for Heinsius and the allies in the war with France.[20]

Financial circumstances also played a major role. Alexandre de la Font was a strict Calvinist who had no love for Louis XIV. Yet, during the Revocation of the Edict of Nantes, he had no problem holding a neutral attitude towards the aggressiveness of the French crown against his coreligionists, in order to maintain the circulation of his gazette in France. His son Anthony continued in his father's footsteps, until the domination of the *Nouvelles extraordinaires de divers endroits* in French advertisements collapsed. Then, Anthony de la Font changed tack. The reports that appeared in the *Nouvelles extraordinaires de divers endroits* often answered those in the *Gazette* by presenting exactly the opposite information. The brave French army was transformed into the brave allies in La Font's paper. La Font probably changed the original reports coming from the French side by adding admiring words about allied personalities, as in the example of praising the bravery of the Duke of Savoy. Moreover, La Font exaggerated French losses, deaths, or deserters. It would not be unreasonable to argue that the *Nouvelles extraordinaires de divers endroits* tried to be the equivalent of the *Gazette* for the allies. This aggressive tone against the *Gazette* and against France in general was also one of the reasons why so few French advertisements appeared in the *Nouvelles extraordinaires de divers endroits* during the War of the Grand Alliance. The circulation of the newspaper in France became problematic, as these polemical reports conflicted so clearly with official French propaganda. Since the French authorities could not ask the Dutch to restrain La Font's paper in wartime, they had no other choice but to reduce its circulation in France.

---

20   Marion Brétéché, *Les Compagnons de Mercure: Journalisme et Politique Dans l'Europe de Louis XIV, Époques* (Ceyzérieu: Champ Vallon, 2015), pp. 153–157.

Less aggressive but still critical was the attitude of the *Gazette d'Amsterdam*. Tronchin Dubreuil tried to be neutral, though expressing his favouritism for the allies when events gave him the opportunity. Thus, the *Gazette d'Amsterdam* praised allied victories with reports deviating from the neutral tone or made comments about the French reactions in communicating their losses. However, Dubreuil's reactions against the *Gazette* were delicate. He did not want to lose the acceptance that he still had from his friends in the French Court, an acceptance which favoured his gazette.

On the other hand, Marie Pattoilat adopted the opposite strategy of La Font. She started her career as an editor and publisher of a Huguenot gazette following the anti-French attitude of her husband, Gabriel de Ceiglen. However, when she established her own venture, she reported the French news with some neutrality. This neutrality became clearer during the war. It was no coincidence that the *Gazette de Rotterdam* was the second gazette which accounted for the highest number of French advertising notices after the *Gazette d'Amsterdam* between 1698–1701, the years of truce. Pattoilat did not share any information that did not seem objective. She neither used the propagandistic tactics of the *Gazette* nor the exaggerations of the *Nouvelles extraordinaires de divers endroits*. On the contrary, Pattoilat concentrated only on presenting the news in its most neutral form.

French newspapers printed in the Dutch Republic between the second half of the seventeenth century and the two first decades of the eighteenth century provide diverse and interesting perspectives on the political, diplomatic, and military events which took place in Europe in this period. Many of these gazettes, however, were short ventures, as it was extremely difficult for them to survive in a highly competitive market.

In order to survive, Huguenot editors had to balance their political and religious beliefs on the one hand with financial security on the other. The reception of the Huguenot newspapers was significant; many circulated among the upper classes of French society, including the French court. As a result, Huguenot gazettes circulated in France in large numbers. Advertising revenues gave them a financial boost. French booksellers, merchants, doctors, apothecaries, and lotteries all advertised their goods and services in the Huguenot gazettes. This economic benefit of this advertising, however, was not without cost. Huguenot editors were cautious not to provoke any direct French reaction with their reports, as they feared French retaliation against their gazettes. When they had less to lose, as the example of La Font indicates, then the publishers had no problem expressing their political and religious beliefs; usually hostility against France.

PART 2

Eighteenth-Century Developments

∴

SECTION 4

Circulation and Reception

CHAPTER 9

Tadhg Ó Neachtain
A Case-Study in Gaelic Media Reception in Eighteenth-Century Dublin

Liam Mac Mathúna

1   The Ó Neachtain Circle

Seán Ó Neachtain (c.1647–1729) and his son Tadhg (1671–1752) were at the centre of the Gaelic scholarly community in Dublin in the first half of the eighteenth century. Originally from Co. Roscommon, Ó Neachtain senior seems to have settled in Dublin with his wife Úna Ní Bhroin about the year 1670, and their son Tadhg was born there in 1671. The city was undergoing rapid growth at the time. While this was especially true with regard to the area north of the river Liffey, it was also the case in relation to the Earl of Meath's liberty, situated west of the city walls and St Patrick's Cathedral, the locality where Seán Ó Neachtain had come to live. Although both father and son earned their living as teachers, they were tireless scholars and scribes as well. The numerous extant manuscripts, which the Ó Neachtains and their learned colleagues wrote, bear testimony to that circle's industry, not only in preserving the literature of earlier periods but in creating new works. The Ó Neachtains were unusual in Irish in their readiness to express their personal feelings and record domestic events. Responding to the rise of the individual alongside the traditional sense of community of the native Irish Catholics, much of their work is infused by the impulses of modernity and sensibility, which permeated the city's intellectual life at the time. They attained a high degree of sophistication and sensibility in their compositions, especially in the many poems they wrote for family and friends. Illustrative of the novel concerns and emphases of their approach is a fondness for personal lists and records. Tadhg, in particular, regularly noted contemporary happenings in the domestic and public spheres.[1] Three of his texts are central to an understanding of the Ó Neachtains' general

---

1 For consideration of the role of listing and categorisation in Tadhg's work, see Emma Nic Cárthaigh, 'Tadhg Ó Neachtuin: a man of lists', in John Carey et al. (eds.), *Cín Chille Cúile. Texts, saints and places. Essays in honour of Pádraig Ó Riain* (Aberystwyth: Celtic Studies Publications, 2004), pp. 208–224, and Liam Mac Mathúna, 'A Gaelic scholar's approaches to recording and tabulation in early eighteenth-century Dublin', in Dafydd Johnston et al. (eds.), *'Yn llawen iawn, yn llawn iaith': Proceedings of the 6th International Colloquium of Societas*

family and scholarly circumstances. The first is a list of obits and other major family events which Tadhg started to compile in 1715.[2] The second is a comprehensive and informative poem composed c.1726–8, in which he celebrates the circle of almost thirty Gaelic scholars which had formed around his father and himself in the early decades of the eighteenth century.[3] The third composition is the elegy he wrote on his father's death in March 1728/9, which outlines much of the latter's corpus.[4]

The Ó Neachtains were also keen observers of the public sphere. Of particular interest in this connection, is the fact that Tadhg compiled a number of commonplace volumes, in which he entered Irish translations and English versions of items from the Dublin newspapers of the day. These are now held in King's Inns Library (KIL), the National Library of Ireland (NLI), the Royal Irish Academy (RIA) and Trinity College Dublin (TCD). He also recorded accounts of contemporary happenings in the city, which he witnessed personally. Thus, in addition to traditional material such as genealogies, place-name lore and bardic poetry, Tadhg Ó Neachtain was keenly interested in the wider world and current affairs. Reflecting his profession of schoolteacher, he composed a world geography, *Eólas ar an domhan* ('Knowledge about the world'), and wrote histories of individual countries such as Poland, Hungary, Turkey and Canada in the form of dialogues with his father Seán.

In all Tadhg entered 150 news-items in six commonplace manuscripts over a period of forty-five years, from 1707 to 1752. The manuscript volumes concerned and the number of entries which each contains are as follows: KIL MS 20 (5 entries), NLI MS G 132 (12 entries), NLI MS G 135 (42 entries), NLI MS G 198 (12 entries), RIA MS 24 P 41 (1404) (15 entries) and TCD MS 1361 (H.4.20) (62 entries). The majority of the news items were short pieces and translations into Irish. Although Tadhg's interests were broad, he tended to focus on the following topics: extreme weather events and unusual meteorological phenomena,

---

Celto-Slavica. Studia Celto-Slavica 7 (Aberystwyth: University of Wales Centre for Advanced Welsh and Celtic Studies, 2015), pp. 163–180.

2   British Library MS Eg. 198, f. 2; cf. Robin Flower, *Catalogue of Irish manuscripts in the British Library [formerly British Museum].* Vol. II. (Reprint ([Dublin]: School of Celtic Studies, Dublin Institute for Advanced Studies, 1992), pp. 98–99.

3   *Sloinfead scothadh na Gaoidhilge grinn* ('I shall name the best scholars of the keen Irish language'), in T. F. O'Rahilly, 'Irish scholars in Dublin in the early eighteenth century', *Gadelica* 1 (1912–13), pp. 156–162, 302–303.

4   Cathal Ó Háinle, 'Ar bhás Sheáin Uí Neachtain', *Éigse* 19/2 (1982–83), pp. 384–394. These three lists have provided a contextual framework for the author's study of the extent and impact of the work of the Ó Neachtains in the Dublin of their day: *The Ó Neachtain window on Gaelic Dublin, 1700–1750* (Cork: Cork Studies in Celtic Literatures, 2021).

natural disasters, periods of shortage and famine, sectarian-cum-political unrest in Dublin, and European high politics, especially stories concerning the exiled Stuarts. He also kept a close eye on the wider world, no matter how distant geographically. Be it a major storm in Bengal in India (1707), the state of health of 76-year-old Pope Benedict XIII in Rome (1725), a huge fire in St Petersburg (1727), or an earthquake in Lima, Peru (1746/7), Tadhg was on the case. Sometimes, as for example, during the severe and protracted frost and famine endured by Ireland and Britain in 1740–41, the news-items he selected are integrated into a larger body of material. In this particular case, his account includes two new poems, expressing his own emotional response to the societal ravages of the famine.

That Tadhg's news interests were at one with the temper of the times is clear from some light-hearted doggerel verse sent in the 1720s by way of *Letter from the Quidnunc's at St. James's Coffee-House and the Mall, London, To their Brethren at Lucas's Coffee-House, in Dublin*, and addressed to 'Mr. S—th, Inquisitor General, and President of the Arch'd-Seat, and the Athenian Corner, at Lucas's Coffee-house':

> Sir, having nothing else to do,
> We send these empty Lines to you:
> To you, these empty Lines we send,
> For want of News, my worthy Friend:
> In hopes e'er long, some Spirit kind
> Will, either raise a Storm of Wind,
> Or cause an Earthquake, or, in the Air,
> Embattled Troops will make appear:
> Or produce, somewhere, something new:
> Cause Stories, whether false or true,
> To flie about: For without News,
> Our Ears and Tongues are of no use;
> And when there's nothing to be said,
> Tis better, sure, that we were dead.[5]

---

5 See facsimile no. 10 in Robert Munter, *The history of the Irish newspaper 1685–1760* (Cambridge: Cambridge University Press, 1967), part of an inset between pp. [208] and 209. Lucas's coffee-house was situated on Cork Hill, not far from Dublin Castle.

2   Newspapers

The publication of newspapers spread to Dublin from Britain early in the eighteenth century. Given the socio-political circumstances of the time, and the ongoing exclusion of the native Irish—mostly Irish-speakers, Catholics and adherents of the Stuarts—from active participation in the public sphere, this is no surprise.[6] The newspapers were entirely in English and originally they were aimed at the Protestant upper echelons of society. However, Munter notes that the picture was changing as early as 1717: 'it appears that readers of the lower social strata were starting to subscribe in large numbers to the periodical press and ... were beginning to make their needs known as subscribers and as advertisers'.[7] Interestingly, the importance of Dublin's eighteenth-century newspapers' contribution to the history of the city was adverted to by Douglas Hyde and D. J. O'Donoghue some fifty years before Munter's studies.[8]

One might assume that the newspapers published in Dublin would deal largely with local affairs, but this was not the case. These papers did not concern themselves exclusively, or even predominantly, with matters Irish. The Dublin Protestant elite were anxious to be kept abreast of political developments in Britain. But in addition to secondary reporting about events in Britain, the papers paid considerable attention to international affairs. In this regard too, they were largely dependent on London as the source of their reports. The process and timeline was explained by Cornelius Carter, who gave notice 'that the Paris Gazette as 'tis English'd in London, will be reprinted in Dublin by Cornelius Carter; it being large, it can't be Publish'd till the next day after it comes in'.[9] The range of material which the papers carried is broadly indicated by the subtitle of *The Dublin Intelligence*, 'Containing a Full and Impartial Account of the Foreign and Domestick News'.[10] Furthermore, it was customary at the time to summarise the overall contents on the front page, and

---

6   For the general background, see Tony Crowley, *War of words. The politics of language in Ireland 1537–2004* (Oxford: Oxford University Press, 2005) and Liam Mac Mathúna, 'From Early Modern Ireland to the Great Famine', in Raymond Hickey (ed.), *Sociolinguistics in Ireland* (Basingstoke, Hampshire: Palgrave Macmillan, 2016), pp. 154–175.

7   Munter, *The history of the Irish newspaper*, p. 132.

8   See Douglas Hyde and D. J. O'Donoghue (eds.), *Catalogue of the books and manuscripts comprising the library of the late Sir John T. Gilbert* (Dublin: Browne and Nolan, Limited, 1918), p. vi.

9   Quoted in Munter, *The history of the Irish newspaper*, p. 76.

10 Facsimile reproduction of front page of issue of 'Saturday, January the 30th, 1714 [1713–4]', Munter *The history of the Irish newspaper*, no. 7 of inset between pages [208] and 209; cf. Breandán Ó Buachalla, *Aisling ghéar. Na Stíobhartaigh agus an t-aos léinn 1603–1788* (Baile Átha Cliath: An Clóchomhar Tta, 1996), p. 370.

the wide-ranging international concerns of these newspapers is illustrated for instance by the following extract from *Whalley's News-Letter*, dated 13 June 1716:

> From Dantzick, Hamburgh, The Hague and Paris of the King of Sweden's Progress, his Continuance, and being Reinforced in Norway. The dismal State of Affairs in Poland. The Death of the Elector Palatine. The Miseries and Poverty of France. The late Lord Bolingbroke's being still in Paris, in Disgrace with the Pretender. The Reducing of the Rebels in Scotland, and the Indightment Tryals and Conviction of several more of 'em at London, and his Friends. Recalling the British Seamen from Foreign Services. The Confinement of the Imperial Envoy by the Turks, and a Battle in Hungary with the Turks. The Names of the Commissioners for the Forfeited Estates. The Disposition of the Pretender &c.[11]

The general context of newspaper publishing in Ireland is considered by Munter.[12] He stresses the fact that newspapers were circulated in extremely limited numbers and states that prior to 1760 it was only the Dublin newspapers which flourished, the reading public at the beginning of the eighteenth century being limited to a small literate minority. Although there were some Catholic printers, there was no Catholic newspaper as such. Significantly, however, by the 1730s and 1740s a few Protestant publishers such as George Faulkner and Ebenezer Rider had adopted a less bigoted stance, with Faulkner being described by Charles O'Conor as the first Dublin printer '... who stretched out his hand to the prostrate Christian Catholic, recognizing him as a fellow Christian and a brother, and endeavoured to raise him to the rank of a subject and a Freeman'. Nonetheless, Munter acknowledges that there were undoubtedly Catholic subscribers in Dublin.

It is not known whether or not Tadhg Ó Neachtain subscribed to newspapers himself, but given the variety of titles he drew on, the probability is that he read them in coffee-houses or the like. On a visit to Dublin in 1696 John Dunton, the London bookseller, noted that the coffee-houses were already being served by nine newspapers weekly, all English imports.[13] Apart from subscribers *The Dublin Daily Advertiser* was sent 'gratis to all the most noted Inns, Taverns and Coffee-houses throughout the Kingdom, and to the chief Ale-houses of

---

11 Munter, *The history of the Irish newspaper*, p. 116; cf. Ó Buachalla, *Aisling ghéar*, pp. 370–371.
12 See especially Munter, *The history of the Irish newspaper*, pp. 67–69.
13 Munter, *The history of the Irish newspaper*, p. 17.

the City of Dublin'.[14] When Ebenezer Rider launched his *Dublin Daily Post, and General Advertiser* at the beginning of 1738/9 his prospectus announced that, in addition to supplying the usual inns and houses, the paper would be posted up every day '(that it might be read by all Degrees of People) on the Gates of our University, the Custom-House, the Tholsel, the Market-House, and other Public Places'.[15] The fact that Tadhg Ó Neachtain went to the trouble of translating many of the news items of interest to him suggests strongly that he did this for the benefit of others, in other words, in order to pass on the information to an audience who would not have easily comprehended the original English-language versions.[16]

The city of Dublin had been continuously served by newspapers since the launch of the *Flying Post* by Cornelius Carter in 1699 and a large number of newspapers was published in the first half of the eighteenth century.[17] Newspapers were usually published twice a week, on Tuesdays and Saturdays.[18] Continuity was fitful, however. Newspapers frequently changed title, were often short-lived and transient or prone to breaks in their runs and issued by a succession of printers.[19] Twomey summarises their general format:

> The newspaper normally took the form of a single sheet printed on both sides although addendums were not uncommon. Foreign and British news provided at least 75% of the copy and Irish news and advertisements/notices usually less than 25%. Core themes of the coverage included political events and celebrations such as the arrival/departure of the lord lieutenant, celebration of the queen's birthday and other key Protestant anniversaries. The newspapers also included reports of shipping movements, crime reportage, accounts of the privations of French privateers and desertion from the army, items lost usually with a reward, property for sale, and a miscellany of personal advertisements, personal notices and weather reports.[20]

---

14 *The Dublin Daily Advertiser*, 7 October 1736, quoted in Munter, *The history of the Irish newspaper*, 61.

15 *Dublin Daily Post*, 11 January 1738/9: see Munter, *The history of the Irish newspaper*, 62.

16 For discussion of some of the evidence for this practice of reading aloud, albeit at a later period, see Niall Ó Ciosáin, *Print and popular culture in Ireland 1750–1850* (Dublin: The Lilliput Press, 2010), pp. 214–219.

17 Brendan Twomey, *Dublin in 1707. A year in the life of the city* (Dublin: Four Courts Press, 2009), p. 58.

18 Twomey, *Dublin in 1707*, p. 58.

19 See R. L. Munter, *A hand-list of Irish newspapers 1685–1750* (London: Bowes and Bowes, 1960).

20 Twomey, *Dublin in 1707*, pp. 58–59.

Tadhg drew on sixteen newspapers in all. In the case of five of these he provided Irish versions of their titles.[21] They are:

> *Castle Courant*: Luas an Disirt .i. Castle Curant Dia Luain. Nov. 21. 1726.[22]
> *Faulkner's Dublin Journal*: 1725. Bealt. 11. Seorse Falcner ionna Nuadhuigheacht.
> Leopal Ab. 25.[23]
> Áth Cliath Dia Sathurn Dec. 18. 1725, Seorsa Falcnar an clodhuighthe;[24]
> Dia Mairt Ian. 25 1725/6 Nuadhuigheacht Duibhlinne;[25]
> Duibhlinn Diamairt Iuil. 9. 1728. Falcner.[26]
> *Faulkner's Dublin Postboy/The Dublin Postboy*:
> Diniosach Athacliath .i. Dubhlinn Post Boy 1726 Diardaoin Nov. 24.[27]
> *Harding's Dublin Impartial News Letter*:
> Seon Harding na Nuadhuigheacht. Dia Máirt, Iún 23, 1724;[28]
> Eoin Harding ionna Nuadhuigheacht. Dia Sathuirn, Iuil an 11, 1724.[29]
> *Walsh's Weekly News-Letter*:
> Ath Clíath Dia Lúain Febh. 28 1725. Tomas Vailis a Scinner Row.[30]

As can be seen, Tadhg regularly uses the word *nuadhuigheacht*, modern *nuaíocht* (*nuacht*) 'news', when referring to specific newspapers. Interestingly, it was only later in the century that the word 'newspaper' became an accepted generic term, replacing the various titles employed—'Intelligence', 'Occurrences', 'News-Letter', 'Post-Boy'—which had hitherto functioned essentially as common nouns.[31] It is therefore no surprise that Conchobhar O Beaglaoich's *The English Irish dictionary: An focloir Bearla Gaoidheilge*, published in Paris in 1732, has no specific entry 'Newspaper'. Rather, it renders 'News' by *Nuaidhsgéala*, 'Printed

---

21 The other eleven are: *The Dublin Intelligence, The Dublin Gazette, The Flying-Post, Whalley's News-Letter, Needham's Post-Man, The Dublin Journal, Dublin Journal, Dublin Weekly Journal, Old Dublin Intelligence, Dublin Evening Post, Weekly Gazette.*
22 TCD MS 1361 (H.4.20), p. 526.
23 RIA MS 24 P 41 (1404) (c), p. 207.
24 RIA MS 24 P 41 (1404) (c), p. 221.
25 RIA MS 24 P 41 (1404) (c), p. 224.
26 TCD MS 1361 (H.4.20), p. 529.
27 TCD MS 1361 (H.4.20), p. 526.
28 RIA MS 24 P 41 (1404) (a), p. 74.
29 RIA MS 24 P 41 (1404) (a), p. 74.
30 RIA MS 24 P 41 (1404) (c), p. 229.
31 See Munter, *A hand-list of Irish newspapers*, p. viii and Munter, *The history of the Irish newspaper*, p. 97.

News' by *Nuaidhsgéala curtha agclódh, clódh-churtha*, and uses the word *Nuaidheacht* to translate 'Newness'.[32] Interestingly, there is an Ó Neachtain Dublin link here, as the Clare poet Aodh Buidhe Mac Cruitín, who assisted O Beaglaoich in compiling his dictionary,[33] was a member of the Ó Neachtain circle, being accorded a quatrain of his own in Tadhg's celebratory roll-call poem, *Sloinfead scothadh na Gaoidhilge grinn*, mentioned above.

3   News Entries from 1707

Tadhg Ó Neachtain's first entries from newspapers relate to the year 1707, coincidently the one chosen by Brendan Twomey as the focus for his book entitled *Dublin in 1707. A year in the life of the city*. This allows us to contrast a number of accounts of a weather event in December of that year. From Twomey we learn that Robert Bryan, writing in 1726 on the reverse side of the *Dublin Gazette* of 27 December 1707, has the following note: 'December the 5th & 6 a great storm of wind' (*Dublin Gazette*, 6–9 December 1707), while the newspaper itself has:

> On Friday and Saturday last happened as terrible a storm of wind as has been known for some years past which has blown down Houses, several stacks of Chimnies, and done great damage throughout this City and Suburbs.[34]

Tadhg's own eye-witness account has a different focus:

> 1707 Dec. 5. Oidhche readhorchadh ó uair an se do deich bha néaltaibh fuildhaiteadh roidhiomadamhuil san aer, 7 an oidhche codhsoillseach et sin go bhfhaicfidh na sleibhte ós cathair Atha Cliath, so bhus fiadhnuisidh me féin air. Tadhg O Neachtuin.

> 1707 Dec. 5 A moonless night, from six until ten there was a great number of blood-coloured clouds in the sky, and the night was so bright that the

---

32   Conchobhar O Beaglaoich, *The English Irish dictionary. An focloir Bearla Gaoidheilge* (Paris: Seamus Guerin, 1732), pp. 492–493.

33   The title page states that the dictionary was 'edited by Conchobhar Ó Beaglaoich together with the help of Aodh Buidhe Mac Cruitín' (*ar na chur a neagar le Conchobhar O Beaglaoich mar aon le congnamh Aodh bhuidhe mac Cuirtin*).

34   Twomey, *Dublin in 1707*, p. 66. For text of *Dublin Gazette*, 9 Dec. 1707, see Nessa O'Sullivan, *Tadhg Ó Neachtain agus na nuachtáin*. Unpublished thesis, University College Cork (Corcaigh: Unpublished thesis, Roinn na Gaeilge, Coláiste na hOllscoile, 1990), pp. 104–105.

mountains over the city of Dublin could be seen, which I am witness to. Tadhg Ó Neachtain.[35]

Two of Tadhg's 1707 entries are of wonders reported from England: a great fish, 53 feet in length seen in Essex and a lamb born in Somerset with one head, but two bodies, including four ears, four eyes and eight legs. On 27 June a letter had arrived in London recounting all the damage inflicted by a great storm in Bengal in India—a French ship had been blown aground by the great violence of the wind. But in this account there is also a link to the fascination with wondrous creatures. A number of men were let down into the ship in order to retrieve objects from the wreck, but one after another they failed to return. A light was then carried to look down into the depths of the ship and they found *Alligator .i. crocadil anmhor* ('An alligator, i.e. a great crocodile') which they shot and 'on opening it found the bodies of the three men aforementioned. Some of these creatures are 40 feet in length'.[36]

4   Earthquakes and Landslides

Tadhg took a keen interest in earthquakes. Reviewing them chronologically, we find firstly one centred on Palermo in Sicily in 1726. On 1 September 1726, Tadhg tells us that a really terrible earthquake shook Palermo, the capital of Sicily, destroying a third of the city and burying alive about 5,000 people in a great crater, which opened up in the earth. Many English and Sicilian ships were lost in the bay.[37] Then on 5 March 1727/8 Tadhg noted a report from Nevis in the Caribbean, regarding an earthquake which had occurred on the island of Martinique on 9 November. He tells us that it had almost totally destroyed the fort of St Peter, had levelled one mountain and split a second in two, had destroyed 200 sugar houses and a great number of churches and other buildings and the people within.[38] Interestingly, the Irish term which Tadhg uses for 'earthquake' is not *crith talún* as would be usual today, but rather *fonnchreathadh*, a compound combining *fonn* 'ground' and *creathadh* 'shaking'. On 10 October 1728 it was Peking's turn to be struck by a great earthquake,

---

35   NLI MS G 135, p. 19, translation by the author.
36   NLI MS G 135, p. 19. The Irish original reads *ar na fosgladh doibh fuaireadar cuirp in tríar shuas ann. Bíodh cuid de na duilibh si 40 troith a bhfad*; see O'Sullivan, *Tadhg Ó Neachtain agus na nuachtáin*, p. 85.
37   TCD MS 1361 (H.4.20), p. 522, O'Sullivan, *Tadhg Ó Neachtain agus na nuachtáin* p. 61; cf. pp. 92–3 for *Castle Courant* accounts, dated 3 and 15 October 1726.
38   TCD MS 1361 (H.4.20), p. 529, O'Sullivan, *Tadhg Ó Neachtain agus na nuachtáin*, p. 69.

which destroyed half the royal quarter and all the dwellings and the people living there ... and affected other cities.³⁹ A lull of twenty years follows this cluster of seismic events 1726–28, before Tadhg records an earthquake which devastated Lima, the capital of Peru in South America. April 1747 contains three entries in all regarding the earthquake in Lima, which had taken place in October 1746. Tadhg writes that the city no longer exists, that everything was sucked into the earth at half past ten at night, the carnage amounting to 15,000 deaths and the destruction of a great variety of buildings.⁴⁰

Much nearer to home, we are told that there was an earthquake in Co. Wicklow on 28 May 1726, but there is no mention of damage.⁴¹ Ironically, the report of a landslide cum moving bog in Co. Limerick in 1727 was more spectacular and it generated much public interest. Tadhg relates that on 25 June 1727, while a group of workers was cutting turf on a bog three miles from Charleville, the bog moved beneath them and did not stop till it rested a mile distant from where they were on the side of a hill, and strange to say, it then only moved a few feet every day and meadows and gardens were hidden and houses knocked down as the bog travelled. We are told that this is according to a letter from Seamus Leuuis (James Lewis) to Eoin Mac Caithil (John Cahill) in Dublin, and another sent by Uilliam a Burc (William Bourke), a solicitor from Cúilín in Co. Limerick, to Tomas a Burc (Thomas Bourke, his cousin) in St Michael's Lane in Dublin, 7 July 1727.⁴² *The Flying Post* of 17 July 1727 includes the interesting detail that both letters were to be seen in the Three Tons hostelry in Wine-Tavern-Street. The strange phenomenon itself attracted sightseers, as we learn from the second letter which ended with the interesting note: 'They tell me there were more People there Yesterday than at a Fair', and adds: 'There are Tents built on purpose, for to Entertain all the Spectators which comes [sic] in great Multitudes all round the Country, to view this strange and Wonderful Bog'.⁴³

5   Fire and Plague

Major events of tabloid quality like great fires and conflagrations also attracted Tadhg's attention. For instance, there was a major fire in Reitling (Reutlingen)

---

39   TCD MS 1361 (H.4.20), p. 532, O'Sullivan, *Tadhg Ó Neachtain agus na nuachtáin*, p. 74.
40   NLI MS G 135, p. 169, O'Sullivan, *Tadhg Ó Neachtain agus na nuachtáin*, p. 90.
41   NLI MS G 132, p. 33, O'Sullivan, *Tadhg Ó Neachtain agus na nuachtáin*, p. 78.
42   TCD MS 1361 (H.4.20), p. 527, O'Sullivan, *Tadhg Ó Neachtain agus na nuachtáin*, p. 67.
43   O'Sullivan, *Tadhg Ó Neachtain agus na nuachtáin*, pp. 97–98.

in the province of Swabia in Germany on 6 October 1726 and Tadhg writes that the great church, the free school and the hospital and 600 other houses were burned down.[44] The effects of the fire are to be seen to this day. The following year St Petersburg was hit by an even greater calamity. A report of 12 August 1727 carried by the *Dublin Journal*, 29 Aug.–2 Sept., stated that a dreadful fire started in a warehouse storing hemp, flax, oil, pitch and tar and soon spread to the other warehouses. In all, 130 houses were destroyed and many people were killed. Then the flames spread to the ships in the harbour, three English, two Dutch, two German as well as forty-two Russian vessels. Up to 500 sailors who jumped overboard, hoping to make it to the side of the harbour, were burned to death by the flaming oil and pitch which floated on the water.[45] In June 1731 Tadhg reported on fires which occurred in England, in London, Blanfort, Tiverton in Devonshire, Hoborn Turnstile in London and Cari in Somersetshire,[46] while individual occurrences in Ireland were regularly mentioned.

Tadhg Ó Neachtain took a keen interest in the affairs of the Stuarts on the Continent, and Breandán Ó Buachalla has shown that one news item has been translated almost word for word from Faulkner's *Dublin Journal*.[47] This is an account of an audience granted on 14 November 1725 by Pope Benedict to the Pretender, i.e. *don treas Seamus righ Sacson* ('to James III, king of the English') who was accompanied by his son, *oighre an tSeamuis* ('heir to James', *viz.* Bonnie Prince Charlie):

> His Holiness continues constant in his devotion, watchings and fastings and on all occasions seems sensible of the nothingness of this world; and tho' the clergy here, as well as in other parts, are wishing for a new conclave, yet his Holiness is in as good a state of health as can be expected for one who is upwards of 76 years of age ... The Chevalier de St. George, his spouse and eldest son, had lately an audience of the Pope ...[48]

Tadhg related an outbreak of plague in Constantinople in August 1726, reporting that at least 7,000 people were dying of the plague in the city every day, with the result that the dead remain unburied for many days and the air

---

44   TCD MS 1361 (H.4.20), p. 523, O'Sullivan, *Tadhg Ó Neachtain agus na nuachtáin*, p. 62.
45   TCD MS 1361 (H.4.20), p. 528, O'Sullivan, *Tadhg Ó Neachtain agus na nuachtáin*, pp. 68 and 98–99 (*Dublin Journal*).
46   KIL MS 20, p. 177.
47   Ó Buachalla, *Aisling ghéar*, pp. 380–381.
48   *Faulkner's Dublin Journal*: 18 December 1725, quoted in Ó Buachalla, *Aisling ghéar*, p. 697, n. 96. Tadhg's Irish translation, which signs off with the ascription, *Seorsa Falcnar an clodhuighthe* ('George Faulkner the printer') is to be found in RIA MS 24 P 41 (1404) (c), p. 221.

became so foul that the birds fell down dead from flying above the place.⁴⁹ This was followed six months later by an update: 'There perished in the recent plague in this city 180,000 people' (*do thuit a ttámh deighionach na cathrach so 180000 pearsa*).⁵⁰

6 International Conflict

In the international, geopolitical arena, Neil Buttimer has undertaken a close study of Tadhg's reactions to the largely maritime War of Jenkin's Ear which broke out between England and Spain in October 1739 and continued until October 1748. Indications of Tadhg's own feelings may be gleaned from the fact that he treats of Spanish successes at some length, but has little to say about English victories. As Buttimer puts it:

> The Irish source concentrates almost exclusively on Spanish seizures of English ships. ... From Tadhg Ó Neachtain one might infer that England made no headway in military matters during the hostilities. However, the periodicals convey a different impression. From the beginning of the conflict onwards they report English successes in detail alongside the type of losses instanced in the Irish document.⁵¹

The contrast between Tadhg's own narrative and the accounts he was reading in the pro-ascendancy, pro-establishment newspapers points to the steadfastness of the Catholic Irish in their allegiance to the Stuart cause.

7 Civil Tensions and Repression

The cruelty and harshness of the times are frequently in evidence in Tadhg's accounts, of which the following are a few representative extracts:

---

49 TCD MS 1361 (H.4.20), p. 523, O'Sullivan, *Tadhg Ó Neachtain agus na nuachtáin*, p. 62. O'Sullivan provides a range of original newspaper accounts from *Castle Courant* and *Dublin Weekly Journal* on pp. 93–94.

50 Report of 27 Jan. in TCD MS 1361 (H.4.20), p. 526; see O'Sullivan, *Tadhg Ó Neachtain agus na nuachtáin*, pp. 66, 93–94.

51 C. G. Buttimer, 'An Irish text on "The War of Jenkins' Ear"', *Celtica*, 21 (1990), pp. 75–98 (at p. 79 and n. 15).

> 1722 Ab. 18. Do roine ceathramhán do Eoin Mac Gearailt 7 do Éinrígh Mhac in Bhaird a gCorcuidh 7 do cuire a gcinn for spícidh mar do iomlatadar Gaoidhil ógáin chum in Pretender ionna a long chum na Fraingce.

> 1722 April 18. Eoin Fitzgerald and Henry Ward were quartered in Cork and their heads were put on spikes because they ferried youths to the Pretender in their boats to France.[52]

There were many other tensions, especially religious ones. From Dublin, 20 April 1727, one has the very succinct report:

> Ag seisiún Luimnídh, do diotáladh an tAthair Raghalluigh ar son Catoiliceach 7 Protestant do phósa. Do curruigheadh an sagart, 7 do crochadh é.

> At the Limerick sessions, Fr O'Reilly was indicted for marrying a Catholic and a Protestant. The priest was condemned, and he was hanged.[53]

In Dublin itself public executions were quite frequent. The extremes to which the authorities went in their efforts to suppress political opposition are described in the following translation from the Irish—one of several such accounts—where viciously cruel punishment was meted out publicly, combining suppression and spectacle:

> 1726 July 6. Moses Nowland was quartered and his entrails were burned in Dublin because he was sending new soldiers overseas to the Pretender i.e. *An Tagarach* who was by this time in exile in Rome. And by the time this poor captive had suffered death (although the day was basking in the sun until then) there fell flashes of lightning together with terrible thunder which knocked down the smokestack or chimney in a house near Bloody Bridge in Dublin. And after that there came or fell the most awful shower of rain that I myself ever saw, as the shower fell as if a river should descend in a sieve or colander.[54]

---

52   NLI MS G198, p. 299.
53   TCD MS 1361 (H.4.20), p. 526, O'Sullivan, *Tadhg Ó Neachtain agus na nuachtáin*, p. 66, with original passage from the *Dublin Weekly Journal* of 6 May 1727 [sic leg.].
54   NLI MS G 132, p. 104, cited in Ní Shéaghdha, *Catalogue of Irish Manuscripts in the National Library of Ireland. Fasciculus IV. Mss. G 115–G 160* (Dublin: Dublin Institute for Advanced Studies, 1977), p. 62.

Pathetic fallacy comes into play here in Tadhg's account, as the heavens themselves blazed forth the death of the courageous Jacobite.

Perhaps even more remarkable, however, was another occasion when nature's reaction to a king's death was interpreted as one of celebration rather than mourning. The event in question also marks the meeting of international and domestic affairs, of high politics and Tadhg's everyday activities. In this account Tadhg mischievously juxtaposes two events, news of the sudden death of King George I of England in Hanover on 19 June 1727, and an outline of a successful fishing and fowling expedition in Dublin Bay between Howth and Dalkey Island with his companions the following day. Tadhg's laconic account is a mixture of second-hand reporting and first-hand diary-keeping. At any rate, the cheery tone is a long way from pathetic fallacy. Again, the following piece is translated from the Irish:

> 1727. June 19. Dublin. News from London in the city of Osnabruck. June 14. George the first, king of England, died suddenly in his main dwelling of Hanover and he now 68 years of age, and his son, George the second, was proclaimed king. On the 20th here Tadhg Ua Neachtain, Uilliam Aeirs and twenty others along with them were fishing in the sea between Howth and Bullock or Dalkey and killing birds in Dalkey island.[55]

Tadhg took a lively interest in infrastructural development in Dublin. He clearly appreciated that the city's public services needed to keep abreast of the requirements of its growing population. He noted the steps taken in 1721 to improve Dublin's water supply by building the city basin reservoir, beside James's Street, close to the Liberties. The basin was said to cover six acres of ground.[56] This urban reservoir is still recalled today in the street names, *Basin Street Upper* and *Basin Street Lower*. It did not take long for this basin reservoir to become a popular and fashionable gathering spot, evidently rivalling St Stephen's Green, for Tadhg informs us in August 1727 (in translation):

> At the beginning of this month there was beautiful autumn weather, ... and the favourite place for gathering for Dublin's citizens for their night of

---

55 TCD MS 1361, p. 524, cited in Ó Buachalla, 'Seacaibíteachas Thaidhg Uí Neachtain', *Studia Hibernica* 26 (1991–92) 31–64 (at p. 49). The point being made here appears to be the opposite of pathetic fallacy: the elements were out of sympathy with the fortunes of the House of Hanover; see the discussion by Ó Buachalla, ibid., pp. 49–50.

56 NLI MS G 198, p. 299. This improvement was first proposed at the April 1707 meeting of the Corporation assembly, where it was noted that 'it would considerably augment the city revenue to have a main laid from James Gate to Newgate to supply the inhabitants with water and likewise to Francis street'; see Twomey, *Dublin in 1707*, pp. 20–21.

music was at the city's water basin, every second night, and other nights at St Stephen's Green and no one was allowed except they were clothed in black, in mourning for king George, and it seemed that the inlets and sea harbours were altogether abundantly laden with every kind of fish from the night the report came of the death of George.[57]

What we have here is a fine instance of Tadhg's subversive textual messaging. Officialdom is enforcing a show of mourning on Dublin's citizenry. But nature knows otherwise and is out of sympathy with the royal bereavement and fish are abundant.

8   Use of English

As already observed, whether they are attributed explicitly to a particular source or whether it is merely clear from the content, the vast majority of Tadhg Ó Neachtain's news items are versions in Irish of English language originals. Although Tadhg's manuscripts include references to various English language publications, printed in both England and Ireland, there is little evidence of familiarity with the literary works of Jonathan Swift and his associates. However, Tadhg does quote eight lines by the Dean, which he has taken from a city newspaper:

> Your Mouldering walls are mending still
> yr. churches Empty lye
> And yet ye. scripture you fulfill
> by walking circumspectly
> The Church & Clergy they are both
> Here very near a kin
> Both weather beaten are without
> And Empty both within.

To these he subjoined the following note: 'Falkner's new's letter. 1726. Ap. 26, says yt. Dean Swift Entering Chester wrote these Verses w. a Diamond Pencil On a pane of Glass in a Church there'.[58]

Otherwise, direct English extracts from newspapers seem to date from 1738/9. In this context, Ó Buachalla provides us with Ó Neachtain's interesting

---

57   TCD MS 1361 (H.4.20), p. 527, O'Sullivan, *Tadhg Ó Neachtain agus na nuachtáin*, p. 67.
58   NLI MS G 132, p. 25; cf. O'Sullivan, *Tadhg Ó Neachtain agus na nuachtáin*, pp. 77–8, who cites the *Dublin Journal*.

abridgment of the following passage which appeared in *The Dublin Journal* of 7 June 1726:

> Dublin, June, 7th. This Morning the following men were taken by two Tide Waiters, on the long Strand and delivered into the Custody of two Serjeants, and 24 Men, between 3 and 4 o' clock, this morning and now lie Prisoners in the Castle. They had several things about them, as for a Voyage viz. Shirts, Stockings &c. a Pistol was Fir'd by some of 'em late last Night, on each side of the Water as a Signal, by which they were suspected and apprehended. Their Names are as follows
>
> | Brion Cavenoch, | Patrick Duggan, Piper, |
> | Den. Coul. | Patrick Kennion, |
> | James Hand, | James Doyle, |
> | Mathew Brown, | John French |
> | John Hurly, | Mathew Duggan |

It is noteworthy that Tadhg (who himself had no compunction about using Naghten, anglicised forms of his surname) provides Irish originals (or at least re-gaelicised versions) of all the names in his somewhat briefer rendering:

> 1726 Iún 7. Do gabhadh ar chaladh Átha Cliath Brian Caomhánach, Donnchadh Ó Cothbhuidh, Séamus Ó Láimhe, Matha Brún, Eoin Hurleidh, Pádruic Ó Dubhagán píobuire, Pádruic Ó Cíonán, Séamus Ó Dubhghaill, Eoin Frenc, Matha Ó Dubhagán tré a mbeidh ag dul tar sáile re cathaibh Gaoidhuil san bhFraingc do líona nó do mhéadughadh.[59]

As to language medium, entries directly transcribed from English (or composed by Tadhg himself in that language) are comparatively late:

> 1738–9. Feb. 1 London, there was taken [by] Preston ferry a Monstrous fish with four Eyes its head like a Jack two Arms like a child, paw'd Like a Bear, claw'd like an Eagle ... like an Eel, a cross (?) on its nose, and the creature six foot long.[60]

---

59   NLI MS G 132, p. 115. See Ó Buachalla, *Aisling ghéar*, p. 382 for the Irish version and see O'Sullivan, *Tadhg Ó Neachtain agus na nuachtáin*, p. 104 and Ó Buachalla, 'Seacaibíteachas Thaidhg Uí Neachtain', for the original *Dublin Journal* account of 7 June 1726.

60   TCD MS 1361 (H.4.20), p. 557. The animal in question is thought to have been a seal.

Miscellaneous, ref. to 'the Jurnall 1742':[61]

> 1743/4 Jan. about the 7, or eight of the new Moon or the 9th. or 10th. of the month was seen in the county of Dublin a Blazeing Star or commet with a tail Like the Rainbow, ... it continued a month or six weeks in the evening in the west and in morning in the East.[62]

> 1743/4 Feb. the 10th. the Romane clergy was taken up and imprisoned and two days before, the ffrench ships in the River Dub: was arrested ...[63]

> 1749 May 23 two suns was plainly seen (about 4 a clock in the morning) by those in Dublin.[64]

Otherwise, much of the English material transcribed directly is literary in nature, typical pieces being 'Notes in English on Chaucer followed by poems by Leland, Thomas Occleve, John Lidgate, Spenser, John Hardin, Robert Fabian, Robert of Gloucester, Francis Quarlos, Robert Herick. Thomas Randolph',[65] and B. Jonson's verses on the Countess of Pembroke.[66] However, they can also be more popular in nature, e.g. a English drinking song in praise of October ale: 'How void of ease / He spends his days'.[67] The interplay of the two languages, along with Latin, in the scientific sphere is also noteworthy; see, for instance, a glossary of plant and herb names, arranged alphabetically by Latin names, with the corresponding name in English and Irish based on Caleb Threlkeld's *Synopsis stirpium hibernicarum alphabetice dispositarum* ... (Dublin 1727).[68] This confirms how aware Tadhg was of the works being published in Dublin, be it in English or Latin. Compare his list of 'The Names in English, Irish, and Latin; of Birds, Beasts, Fishes, Reptiles, or Insects, which are known and propagated in Ireland. Alphabetically', which is arranged in three columns in English, Irish, and Latin.[69]

---

61 NLI MS G 135, p. 187. No doubt *Faulkner's Dublin Journal* is in question.
62 NLI MS G 135, p. 8, O'Sullivan, *Tadhg Ó Neachtain agus na nuachtáin*, p. 83.
63 NLI MS G 135, p. 8, O'Sullivan, *Tadhg Ó Neachtain agus na nuachtáin*, p. 83.
64 NLI MS G 132, pp. 56, O'Sullivan, *Tadhg Ó Neachtain agus na nuachtáin*, p. 79.
65 Summary in Pádraig de Brún, *Catalogue of Irish manuscripts in King's Inn Library Dublin* (Dublin: Dublin Institute for Advanced Studies, 1972), p. 61 of KIL MS 20, pp. 169–76, from c.1730.
66 TCD MS 1361 (H.4.20), p. 7.
67 TCD MS 1361 (H.4.20), p. 4.
68 KIL MS 20, pp. 151–169.
69 KIL MS 20, pp. 221–236.

Evidence for the use of English by Catholics in Dublin is of particular interest, as indication of the participants, context, progress and timing of the language shift from Irish to English in the city:

> Passion Sunday, 11 April 1736, English sermon delivered by Fr Bonra Boylan, Bonaventura Ua Baoidhillean in response to sermon delivered on same by Anglican bishop, as explained in Irish.[70]

9 Societal Cooperation

However, there was also societal cooperation. The nationwide famine which accompanied the great frost of 1740–41 prompted cross-community collaboration. Tadhg Ó Neachtain's own testimony is particularly significant with regard to the bitter weather and subsequent famine of 1741, which many historians feel may have surpassed even the Great Famine of 1846–49 in its devastation.[71] The dire situation was described by Tadhg as follows:

> 1741 Tug cruatan ar an iomad ar feadh iomlán na hÉireann bás dfhagháil et go mórmhór san Mumhain 7 a gConnachtaibh, a gCorcadh amháin do feartadh a i naonchlais 160 pearsaibh ... a gConnacht ... bhá an tinneas fiabhrasach codh ainspiadhantadh sin 7 codh coitcheann go ndruidfuídh na toitheibh ionna mbí amhuil aimsir plághadh.

> Hardship caused very many to die throughout all of Ireland, and especially in Munster and in Connacht, in Cork alone 160 people were buried in a single pit ... in Connacht the fever sickness was so dreadful and so common that the houses in which it occurred were shut as in the time of plague.[72]

However, treating each news item as a discrete entry in Tadhg's manuscripts does not do justice to the complexity of their integration into his narrative. Tadhg's news accounts are interwoven with two poems of his own composition in Irish. This mingling of poems among prose narrative is characteristic of

---

70   KIL MS 20, pp. 203–219.
71   For a comprehensive account of this famine, see David Dickson, *Arctic Ireland. The extraordinary story of the great frost and forgotten famine 1740–41* (Belfast: White Row Press Ltd, 1997).
72   NLI MS G135, p. 28, Ó Buachalla, *Aisling ghéar*, p. 373.

the Irish tradition. Verse serves as the medium which gives voice to heightened emotion. The last quatrain of the second poem reads as follows:

> Croídh cruadh mar shioc atá
> sa dhaonnacht a bhfhuacht sneachta
> charrannacht nir imigh thráth
> os fuireann Eireann algadh.
>
> A hard heart is like frost
> and its humanity in coldness of snow
> charity never departed at any time
> from the people of noble Ireland.[73]

Were it not for the help organised by people on all sides, vast numbers of the poor would have starved to death, as the suffering was so great. Charity was shown by all sides, as Tadhg himself witnessed:

> mar is feasach mé féin, do chonairc deighirc laothamhuil Gaill 7 Gaedhil do bhochtain Atha Clíath 7 na gcrioch coimhneas oir thugadar go deontach ór 7 airgead, min 7 gual re cothughadh truaghain gan fheachaint do Protastun na Papis acht do reir a chéile 7 tug feilmeoiribh cead sceachadh a gcloidheachadh do ghearra 7 do losgadh. Ó carrannacht os gach carranacht.
> Misi Tadhg O Neachtuin
>
> as I myself know, who saw the daily charity of Englishman and Irishman to the poor of Dublin and the neighbouring districts, for they voluntarily gave gold and silver, meal and coal to nourish the wretched without enquiring whether Protestant or Papist, but in their turn and farmers gave permission for bushes and fences to be cut and burned. O charity above all charity.
> I am Tadhg Ó Neachtain.[74]

---

73 Cf. Cormac Ó Gráda and Diarmuid Ó Muirithe, 'The Famine of 1740–41: representations in Gaelic Poetry', *Éire-Ireland* 45/3–4 (2010), pp. 41–62 (at p. 59).
74 NLI MS G 135, p. 28; cf. Nessa Ní Shéaghdha, *Catalogue of Irish Manuscripts* IV, p. 71 and Ó Buachalla, *Aisling ghéar*, pp. 373–374. See also the discussion in Meidhbhín Ní Úrdail and Cormac Ó Gráda, 'Tadhg Ó Neachtain agus Muiris Ó Conaill ag trácht ar Bhliain an Áir, 1739–42', in John Cunningham and Niall Ó Ciosáin (eds.), *Culture and society in Ireland since 1750. Essays in honour of Gearóid Ó Tuathaigh* (Dublin: The Lilliput Press, 2015), pp. 33–43.

In many ways this quotation sums up Tadhg Ó Neachtain's worldview. He was someone who felt great empathy for others, be they the poor of his own city and country or those suffering a great disaster far away, at the ends of the earth. As well as that, he was capable of rising above the sectarian strife which permeated Irish life and European politics during his lifetime.

The final line we have in Tadhg's hand is simple, succinct and written in English. Characteristically, it relates to the process of modernisation, in this case to the abstract reckoning of time. It implicitly acknowledges that Britain had just embraced the Gregorian calendar, long since in use in the countries of mainland Europe. Tadhg wrote: 'September Thursday 1752. The new stile commenced'.[75] This record of the advance of modernity provides the last words we have from his quill. It affirms that, above all else, Tadhg Ó Neachtain was a man of the world, a man of the moment, a man fascinated by breaking news, by exciting news!

---

75   NLI MS G 135, p. 186 (last item, entered towards the bottom of the page). The date in question was Thursday, 14 September 1752 (new style). The change from the Julian to the Gregorian calendar involved an adjustment or 'loss' of eleven days: Wednesday, 2 September was followed by Thursday, 14 September 1752.

CHAPTER 10

MURDER! He Wrote

The News as Reported by James Ryan in his Diary (1787–1809)

Bláithín Hurley

How do individuals ascertain what 'news' is and, more importantly, which news is interesting enough to be worthy of recording? The answer to this is wide-ranging and fluid; everyone's idea of news, or of exciting news, is different. This chapter will examine a single case study, a late eighteenth and early nineteenth-century manuscript known as the *Carrickman's Diary*. It will explore how, for the writer of this diary, noteworthy and exciting news could be local, national or international.

1 The Manuscript

The *Carrickman's Diary* first came to public notice a little over one hundred years ago when the Free Public Library (now the Central Library) in Waterford City, Ireland received a donation from Miss Power of Newtown House, Tramore, Co. Waterford. The donation was of a manuscript which had come into Power's possession through her great-grandfather; she felt the library a more fitting place for the work to be held than her private residence.[1] The Central Library in Waterford is where that manuscript remains to this day. Known as the *Carrickman's Diary*, the manuscript is a surviving witness to how living in a small town in eighteenth-century Ireland proved no hindrance to someone wishing to discover and report on the news of the day.

---

1 The first time this diary was brought to the attention of the public was through the articles written for the *Journal of the Waterford and South East of Ireland Archaeological* Society, by the Waterford historian the Reverend Dr Patrick Power in the early part of the twentieth century. In the first of these articles Power details how he managed to gain access to the diary through his friendship with Miss Power. Some years following the publication of the Rev. Power's articles, the diary was donated to the Central Library, Waterford City, by Miss Power. The original manuscript, and a microfilm copy, are now held in the library's Local Studies Department. See Patrick Power, 'A Carrickman's Diary—1787–1809', *Journal of the Waterford and South-East of Ireland Archaeological Society*, IX (1911), pp. 97–102.

The work was written by James Ryan, a resident of Carrick-on-Suir, a town on the border of the counties of Waterford and Tipperary, between 1787 and 1809. We know nothing about Ryan outside scant references within the diary itself. In 1911 a Waterford historian, the Reverend Canon Patrick Power, described Ryan as a land surveyor in his article on the *Carrickman's Diary* which appeared in a volume of the *Journal of the Waterford and South East of Ireland Archaeological Society*.[2] This claim is based on an entry in the *Diary* which lists one 'James Ryan, L. Surveyor' among the subscribers to the 'new Chapel of ___ ___ [sic] Carrick; 1st July 1804'.[3] As the diarist took the trouble to transcribe the names of all the subscribers to the chapel from the Treasurer's books, it would seem likely that he had a particular interest in the project. Therefore, as there is only one James Ryan listed, one could conclude, as Power did, that this is the diarist himself.

The circuitous route the *Diary* took following Ryan's death before its arrival in the Central Library Waterford, is worthy of mention. The last entry in the diary is dated 6 November 1808, wherein he details an occasion of the 'savage sport' of bull-baiting.[4] This is followed by an entry by one William Hayes dated 14 September 1809, which includes a hand-written copy of Ryan's obituary taken from an unnamed Waterford newspaper. Hayes' entry tells us of the close friendship enjoyed by both gentlemen and of the terms under which he agreed to take on the diary.[5] There is also reference made to Ryan's will and another book which is described as a memorandum or common-place book, though now sadly lost.[6]

Hayes continued to keep the diary, as best he could, in honour of Ryan's memory. However, Ryan had instructed Hayes that should the latter ever move away from Carrick-on-Suir, the diary should pass to someone resident in the town. On 1 November 1809, Hayes wrote that he had moved away from Carrick-on-Suir, and was therefore unable to carry out Ryan's wish that he continue to record events in and affecting that town. Accordingly, he handed the volume to Francis Doyle, a mutual friend of his and Ryan, with the proviso that if Hayes should return to live in Carrick-on-Suir, then Doyle was to hand

---

2 Reverend Power held the position of Professor of Archaeology in University College Cork from 1915–1934. For more on the academic life and work of Power see, Twohig, Elizabeth Shee 'Devoted to archaeology: Professor (Canon) Patrick Power (1862–1951)', *Journal of the Cork Historical & Archaeological Society*, Ser. 2, Vol. 118, (2013), pp. 109–134. 118, pp. 109–133.
3 Central Library, Lady Lane, Waterford City, MSS *Carrickman's Diary* (hereafter *Diary*), p. 237.
4 *Diary*, p. 252.
5 *Diary*, p. 253.
6 *Diary*, unnumbered page which lies between the inside cover and the diary's index.

it back to him again.[7] Hayes does not provide an explanation as to why he left the town, or where he moved to, but we can only conclude that he never returned because Francis Doyle bequeathed the diary to his own nephew Patrick Hayden. Patrick Hayden was the great-grandfather of Miss Power, who was later to donate the manuscript to the library.[8]

Over a period spanning twenty years, James Ryan recorded a series of events that he believed newsworthy and, therefore, merited inclusion in his diary—more of a record of news, than any series of personal reflections. Instead of following daily events in any logical chronological order, especially those which impacted directly on the author, Ryan approached his task differently. The events he recorded were a mixed bag of social, political, municipal and ecclesiastical incidents and events. Together these provide an unprecedented view of life in Ireland at the end of the eighteenth century, along with how well-informed one could be of the news of the day. The diary consists of 265 handwritten folio pages, exclusive of 200 blank pages; it is bound in vellum, measures 30cm x 18cm, and is inscribed on the cover: 'JAMES RYAN 1787 TO WILLIAM HAYES 1809'.

Ryan's arrangement of his notes is somewhat peculiar, lending further weight to the fact that this is not a traditional diary. Ignoring the usual journal order he adopts a method of record by subject, and so we have the headings—Accidents, Deaths, Phenomenon, and so on. Interspersed throughout the diary are occasional recipes, calculations, and cures for various medical ailments. Unsurprisingly for someone who relied very heavily on his writing implements, Ryan includes instructions on how to prepare quills and inks. Apparently, one should cut the tops off the quills, boil them for two hours and ensure them 'well-dried before a fire'.[9] He provides recipes for black ink, red ink, ink powder and marking ink.[10] Ryan often added asides on the information he received, as seen in Figure 10.1, wherein he states that a 'match greatly admired!' has been entered into between Dr Younge and Miss English, the Post-Mistress. The writer, however, appears less enthusiastic about Miss Nancy Dalton's choice of husband. Indeed, he would seem to cast doubt as to the validity of the claim that the marriage did indeed take place, as can be observed in Figure 10.2. Occasionally Ryan makes a note or observation in Irish. One example of this is when the diarist is writing under the heading

---

7   *Diary*, p. 263.
8   Power relates the relationships between the previous owners of the *Diary* in Power, 'A Carrickman's Diary', pp. 97–102.
9   *Diary*, p. 24.
10 *Diary*, p. 26.

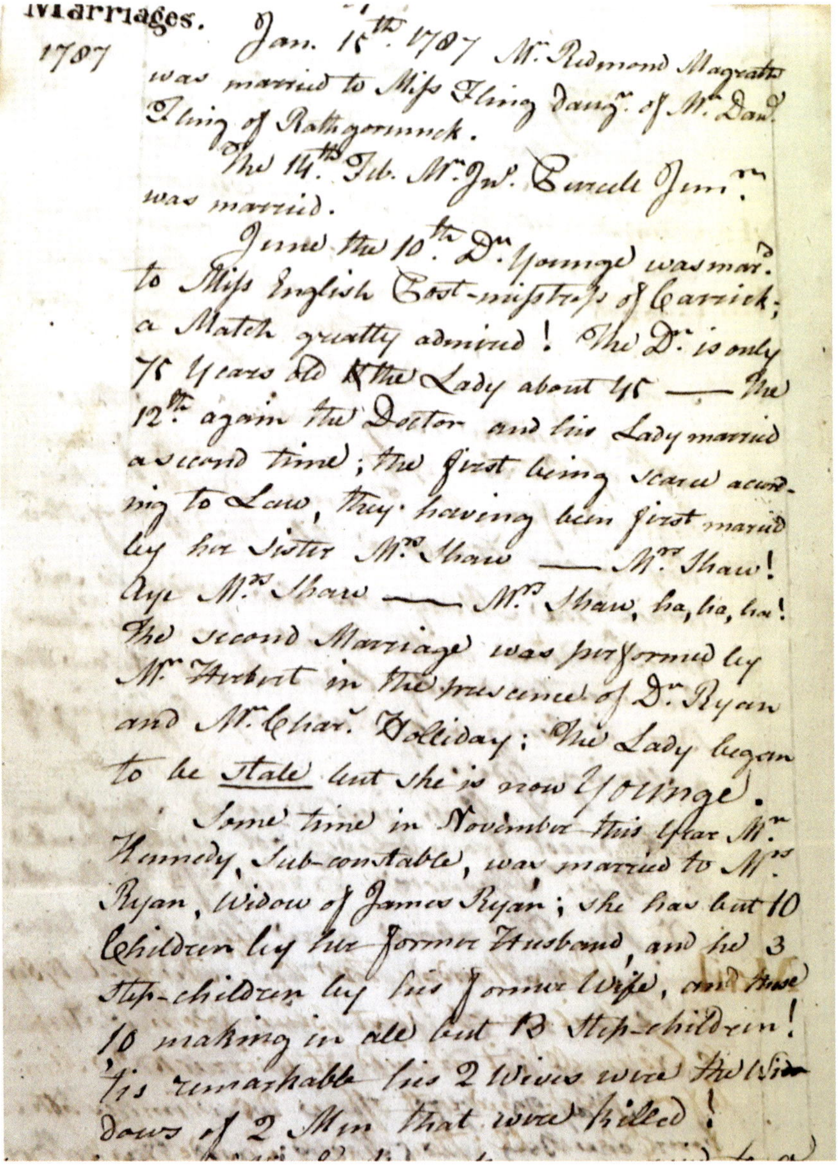

> Marriages.
> 1707
>
> Jan. 15.th 1707 Mr. Redmond Magrath was married to Miss Fling daugr. of Mr. Dand. Fling of Rathgormuck.
>
> The 14.th Feb. Mr. Jn.o Purcell Junr. was married.
>
> June the 10.th Dr. Younge was marrd. to Miss English Cost-mistress of Carrick; a Match greatly admired! The Dr. is only 75 years old & the Lady about 45 — The 12.th again the Doctor and his Lady married a second time; the first being scarce accord-ing to Law, they having been first married by her Sister Mrs. Shaw — Mrs. Shaw! Aye Mrs. Shaw — Mrs. Shaw, ha, ha, ha! The second Marriage was performed by Mr. Herbert in the presence of Dr. Ryan and Mr. Char. Holliday: The Lady began to be stale but she is now Younge.
>
> Some time in November this Year Mr. Kennedy, Sub-constable, was married to Mrs. Ryan, Widow of James Ryan; she has but 10 Children by her former Husband, and he 3 Step-children by his former Wife, and those 10 making in all but 13 Step-children! 'tis remarkable his 2 Wives were the Wid-ows of 2 Men that were killed!

FIGURE 10.1   Entry detailing the marriage of Dr Younge and Miss English, Folio 4r, *A Carrickman's Diary*
IMAGE COURTESY OF WATERFORD LIBRARIES

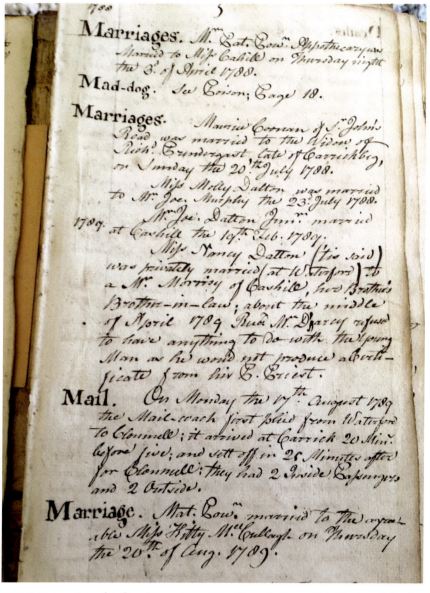

FIGURE 10.2 Entry detailing the marriage of Miss Nancy Dalton and Mr Morrisey, Folio 5ʳ, *A Carrickman's Diary*
IMAGE COURTESY OF WATERFORD LIBRARIES

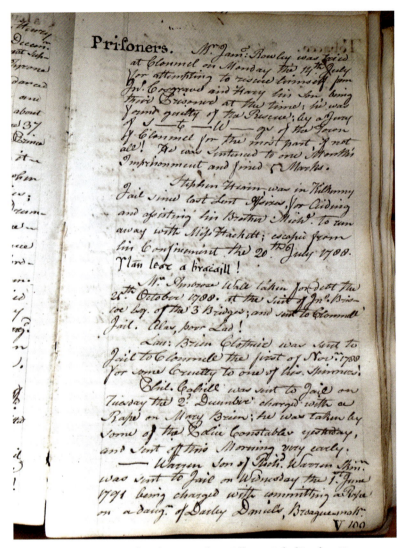

FIGURE 10.3   Entry revealing the escape from Kilkenny Jail of Stephen Hearn, Folio 100ᵛ, *A Carrickman's Diary*
IMAGE COURTESY OF WATERFORD LIBRARIES

'Prisoners'. Among the entries can be found one dated July 1788, which relates the tale of young Stephen Hearn, from Carrick-on-Suir, who was arrested for his role in helping his brother Michael run away with Miss Hackett. Stephen managed to escape from jail in Kilkenny and Ryan ended his entry with *'Slán leat a buachaill'* (Figure 10.3), which today translates as—'Good-bye boy', but in Ryan's time could equally have been used to wish someone good luck.[11] The diarist writes Irish in a good scribal hand in the script which was in use at the time, and which would not be familiar to the modern Irish language scholar.[12] For scholars of eighteenth-century Ireland, on the other hand, the *Carrickman's Diary* is an invaluable resource.

2   Bridges, Boats and Business

All of Ryan's entries are written in his own inimitable style, and through a unique combination of compassion and melodrama we learn of events of which we might otherwise have remained unaware. Sometimes these seemingly inconsequential entries offer fascinating insight into life in eighteenth-century Carrick-on-Suir. For example, in Ryan's entry under the heading 'Accidents', he states that on, 'This day (15th Nov. 1787) one of Cornelius Ryan's Boats was wrecked against the Bridge. (The Old Bridge, of course)'. of a crew of seven hands, three were drowned: Thomas Woods, John Ryan and Martin Quin. John Ryan's body was found at Clonmore, and Thomas Woods' at Mount Bolton—both locations about 20 kilometres downstream from Carrick-on-Suir. The diarist completes his entry on this tragic event with the poignant note that 'poor Woods when found was still wearing his hat and wig'—a reminder of the prevailing men's fashion.[13] What is interesting about this seemingly average entry is the amount of information it contains. We learn for example that Cornelius Ryan had a business of several boats, and the one which was lost must have been of a substantial size, given that it had a crew of seven hands. This entry serves to remind us that in the eighteenth century, despite its small size, Carrick-on-Suir was a busy port on the River Suir and many boats operated out of it.[14] The importance of Carrick-on-Suir as a port is further emphasised by the diarist when, under the heading 'SHIP' he writes:

---

11   *Diary*, p. 39. For a history of the etymology of the Irish language and how its direct translation into English has been a fluid occurrence over the centuries see Aidan Doyle, *A History of the Irish Language: From the Norman Invasion to Independence* (Oxford: Oxford University Press, 2015).

12   For more on the reasons for the standardisation of the Irish language in 1958 and its impact on how the language is now written see *Gramadach na Gaeilge* AN CAIGHDEÁN OIFIGIÚIL (Dublin: Arna Fhoilsiú ag Seirbhís Thithe an Oireachtais, 2017), especially, 'AN RÉAMHRÁ LEIS AN GCÉAD EAGRÁN, pp. xxi–xxiv.

13   *Diary*, p. 1.

14   P. C. Power, *Carrick-on-Suir and its People* (Dun Laoghaire: Anna Livia Books, 1976), p. 58. Carrick-on-Suir is frequently mentioned by visitors to Ireland in the eighteenth and

> This day (27th Sept. 1787) a Brig of Mr. Cardiff's from Dublin arrived at Mr. Hays's Quay, being the first that ever came up here: the 13th of October she ran ashore upon a sandbank below Mr. Sausse's new Ware-house (sic), in attempting to go down the river, laden with Timber, where she remained 'till the 27th of November. After taking out 12 or 13 Ton of her load she floated ... on Sunday the 2nd December she went off down the River with her Cargo with all her sails sett (sic). I wish her safe.[15]

By 1791, along with the many boats calling to Carrick-on-Suir from Clonmel and Waterford, we also learn of brigs arriving from Belfast, Liverpool and the French port of Bordeaux.[16] This underlines Carrick-on-Suir's important role in conveying goods from larger towns in the surrounding counties of Tipperary, Waterford and Kilkenny to ports in other parts of Ireland and Europe. The town was also a destination for goods imported from abroad which were then transported via the River Suir or the road network to elsewhere in the country. This led inevitably to the need for the construction of a quay in Carrick-on-Suir in 1792. Predictably, Ryan documents this event, which got underway with the 'blasting [of] the Rocks' at the riverside. The enterprise was the brainchild of local businessman and warehouse owner James Sausse, for which a subscription was organised to provide the necessary finance. The diarist believed it to be a worthy venture for which the town should be eternally grateful and of which he wrote, 'May his name [James Sausse] never be forgotten while there remains any trace of a Quay at Carrick-on-Suir'.[17] The need for a quayside in Carrick-on-Suir for the mooring, loading and unloading of watercraft, reminds us just how newsworthy the 1787 accident was, not least because of the potential impact incidents had on local business.

In his entry relating to the accident which saw Cornelius Ryan's boat wrecked, the diarist makes special mention of the fact that the bridge against which the boat was wrecked was the one known as the 'old bridge'. To this day, Carrick-on-Suir has a bridge called the 'old bridge'. There were, and still are,

---

nineteenth centuries, and the usual mode of transport by which these visitors arrived in the town was by boat. See Arthur Young, *A tour in Ireland; with general observations on the present state of that Kingdom: made in the years 1776, 1777, and 1778. And brought down to the end of 1779* (London: T. Cadell and J. Dodsley, 1780), vol. 1, p. 515; J. Luckcombe, *Tour through Ireland wherein the present state of that kingdom is considered; and the most noted Cities, Towns, Seats, Buildings, Loughs, &c. described* (London: T. Lowndes, 1780), p. 105.

15 *Diary*, p. 2.
16 *Diary*, p. 3.
17 *Diary*, p. 25.

two bridges across the Suir in the town.[18] The 'old bridge' was built in 1447, although the structure we see today was strengthened in the 1920s.[19] What is notable, however, is that this was the first bridge above the estuary of the River Suir and was a strategically important link between South Leinster and East Munster. The city of Waterford downstream had no bridge until 1794.[20] Therefore, any traffic that wanted to make its way from Dublin to Waterford, the only city in the south-east of the country; or from Dublin to Cork (Ireland's second largest city), often found that the only way this could be achieved was by travelling through Carrick-on-Suir. This further meant that the town was on the direct route for news from the capital city and, by extension, its population learned of news, both national and international, often before those living in Cork or Waterford.

3   Post, Coach and Steam

As one who had a voracious appetite for news—local, national and international—we can appreciate Ryan's excitement at the appointment of a new postmaster in the town, wherein he writes 'Mr. Will Hutchinson appointed Postmaster ... November 1788'.[21] He makes the comment 'bad enough it has been kept for some time past', which relates to how badly served Carrick-on-Suir had been for mail deliveries prior to this appointment. In 1789, following the postmaster's appointment one year earlier, to Ryan's relief a new post route was opened which brought mail directly to Carrick-on-Suir from Dublin. In his entry relating this news the diarist writes of the introduction of the relatively new system of 'cross-posting', when he states:

---

18   By the 1770s, there were two bridges across the River Suir in Carrick-on Suir, and the remains of what appeared to have been a third bridge according to an account by Charles Smith in his *The Ancient and Present State of the City and State of Waterford. Containing a Natural, Civil, Ecclesiastical, Historical and Topographical Description Thereof.* (Dublin: W. Wilson, No. 6 Dame-Street, 1774), p. 233.

19   For more on the history of the building of the bridge in the fifteenth century see C. A. Empey and Katharine Simms, 'The Ordinances of the White Earl and the Problem of Coign in the Later Middle Ages', *Proceedings of the Royal Irish Academy: Archaeology, Culture, History, Literature*, 75 (1975), pp. 161–187.

20   R.H. Ryland, *The History, Topography and Antiquities of the County and City of Waterford; With an Account of the Present State of the Peasantry of that Part of the South of Ireland* (London: John Murray, Albemarle Street, 1824), pp. 175–178.

21   *Diary*, pp. 18–19.

A Cross Post appointed to receive the Mail for Carrick, at Ballypatrick [12 kms away and mid-way between Carrick-on-Suir and Clonmel, the main town in County Tipperary] began the 7th of July 1789. Procured by Mr. James Sausse [the businessman who spearheaded the building of the quay in Carrick-on-Suir]. It expedites the arrival of Letters from Dublin considerably.[22]

An example of Carrick-on-Suir's central role in the exchange and transportation of news, goods and travellers, is given when Ryan states that on 8 June 1789, a post coach began, for the first time, to ply between Waterford and Cork. Having departed Waterford at '4 in the morning', it arrived in Carrick-on-Suir at '25 Minutes after 7 o'clock'.[23] It already had one passenger and took on another in Carrick-on-Suir before continuing its journey. This new service was closely followed by another when we read that 'On Sunday the 17th August 1789 the Mail-coach first plied from Waterford to Clonmell (sic)'. We further learn that 'it arrived at Carrick 20 Minutes before five; and sett (sic) off in 28 Minutes after for Clonmell'. It carried 2 passengers inside and 2 outside.[24] These mail coaches not only carried news within their cargo of letters, but they also transported passengers who also frequently carried news with them.

All told, 1789 was a momentous year for travel and communication, especially for those living in Carrick-on-Suir. Along with the inauguration of the passenger mail coach from Waterford to Clonmel, Sunday 17 August also witnessed the arrival of another coach, this time travelling between Kilkenny and Waterford, stopping at Carrick-on-Suir. Two years earlier, in 1787, a mail packet service had been established between Milford Haven in Wales and Waterford City. The combination of the mail packet service and the mail coach services from Waterford meant that mail, newspapers and news from abroad arrived in Carrick-on-Suir sooner than it ever had previously. To quote Ryan on the mail packet service 'this business ... is expected to be of great use and advantage to the Southern parts of Ireland in general'.[25]

---

22 Prior to this, all the mail for Carrick-on-Suir from Dublin had to go to Clonmel first, *Diary*, p. 19. In the early eighteenth century in the UK, a system of crossroads to connect two post roads was introduced. This meant a larger distribution of mail, faster, and this system of 'cross-posting' was introduced to Ireland by the late eighteenth century—see William Lewis, *Her Majesty's Mails: A History of the Post Office and an Industrial Account of its Present Condition* (London: Sampson Low, Son and Marston, Milton House, Ludgate Hill, 1865), p. 24.
23 *Diary*, p. 19.
24 *Diary*, p. 5.
25 *Diary*, p. 20. Ryland also refers to the steam packet service between Milford Haven and Waterford City and states it to be a 'cheap and expeditious conveyance'. The time it took

4 Players, Music and Revels

But it is not just news and gossip that made its way to Carrick-on-Suir ahead of Waterford or Cork. Travelling players when journeying from Dublin to these two cities often stopped off in Carrick-on-Suir on the way, and while there they entertained the townsfolk with plays, concerts and operettas. They also introduced the latest fashions in musical entertainment to the little town of Carrick-on-Suir. Players, Ryan tells us, came to town in October 1788 where they 'played to great houses'.[26] The regular access to plays put on by travelling players ensured that the local actors were completely up-to-date on the kind of dramatic fare which attracted audiences in the Irish cities of Dublin, Cork and Waterford, as well as further afield in London. Therefore, not to be outdone by these outsiders, on 20 April 1790, Ryan wrote that the 'young gentlemen of Mrs Dineen's, Carrick Academy' performed the *Siege of Damascus* to a 'full house and great applause'.[27] *The Siege of Damascus* was written in 1720 by the British playwright John Hughes and relates the events of the 634 siege of that city.[28] The play itself had premiered at the Theatre Royal, Drury Lane, before becoming a regular choice of dramatic groups across Britain and Ireland. Carrick-on-Suir, in spite of its size and distance from London, had its finger on the pulse of popular entertainment.

Dramatic and musical events were also used to collect funds for the needy. One such instance of this is the benefit, performed by Mr O'Neill's Company. This was run on 19 October 1795 in aid of the Sick-Poor of the locality. The musical choice of the night was the ballad opera *Love in a Village* by Thomas Arne. This operetta had premiered at the Royal Opera, Covent Garden in 1762.[29] Once again, the little town of Carrick-on-Suir was keeping abreast of international musical tastes and offered an engaged audience for the travelling players.

Plays and operas were not the only entertainment on offer at this time, and Ryan informs us that on 15 May 1798 a ball was given by Thomas McCarthy to celebrate the building of his new house.[30] In attendance, 'There were about

---

for mail to travel from London to Waterford rarely exceeded 48 hours, see Ryland, *The History, Topography and Antiquities*, pp. 242–243.
26 *Diary*, p. 20.
27 *Diary*, p. 20.
28 John Robert Moore, 'Hughes's Source for the "Siege of Damascus"', *Huntington Library Quarterly*, 21/4 (August 1958), pp. 362–366; Malcolm Boyd, 'John Hughes on Opera', *Music & Letters*, 52/4 (October 1971), pp. 383–386.
29 Julian Herbage, 'Thomas Augustine Arne (1710–1778)', *The Musical Times*, 101/1412 (October 1960), pp. 623–625.
30 *Diary*, p. 23.

TWO HUNDRED present, out of 300 asked!' Nevertheless, despite one hundred fewer revellers than expected being in situ, the lower, middle and upper floors of the house were all fully occupied: the lower and upper for tea, coffee and dancing and the middle floor for, what the writer describes as—'SQUELSH-ING!'. This he emphasises with an exclamation mark. Ryan further writes that there had never been 'such a FANDANGO in Carrick before. Plearacha na Ruairceach!'.[31] Which roughly translates as 'High Jinks a Plenty!'.

These entries paint a picture of a busy, colourful, exciting, cultured, well-connected, mercantile town in the middle of Ireland at the end of the eighteenth century. However, 1798, the year in which Thomas McCarthy's ball took place, was also the year in which a bloody rebellion occurred. And although Carrick-on-Suir was not known as a town which played a central role in this revolt, it was not immune to the rebellion's effects either.

5   Rebellion, Aftermath and News

Soon military movement became the order of the day, and under the heading 'Army' we learn that every road leading to Carrick-on-Suir resounded to the tramp of marching troops.[32] On 'Sunday the 3rd June 1798 were marched into Carrick the Roscommon Militia on their way to the County of Wexford, to quell the Insurrection raging there'. They had with them forty one prisoners condemned as United Irishmen and were taking them to the prison ship at Duncannon in Wexford for transportation.[33] This reference relates directly to one of the bloodiest battles of the 1798 Rebellion which took place at Vinegar Hill in Wexford, and its aftermath.[34] A report which appeared in the *Freemans Journal* on 5 June 1798, describes the battle as detailed in a letter received from Colonel L'Estrange, of the Crown Forces.[35] Although the validity of all the claims made in L'Estrange's letter have since been questioned, the report in the *Journal* coincides closely with the date of the entry made by Ryan. Ryan's entry also serves to remind us that no-one in Ireland was unaffected by the Rebellion, even those not directly involved.

31   *Diary*, p. 23.
32   *Diary*, p. 129.
33   *Diary*, p. 101.
34   For more on the Vinegar Hill battle see Ronan O'Flaherty and Jacqui Hynes (eds.), *Vinegar Hill: The Last Stand of the Rebels of 1798* (Dublin: Four Courts Press, 2021).
35   L'Estrange, Robert Taylor, John Beevor, and Hardwicke. 'Some Letters Relating to the Battle of Bunclody, 1 June 1798.', *The Past: The Organ of the Uí Cinsealaigh Historical Society*, 21 (1998), pp. 39–44.

The sense of panic that the events at Vinegar Hill caused in Carrick-on-Suir is described clearly to us through the diarist's entry under the heading 'ALARM'. This Alarm turned out to be a false one, but for a time the population thought that 'the Town of Carrick was to be destroyed!'.[36] A rampart was formed on one end of the bridge and the necessary preparations were made at the military barracks to repel any attackers. Stationed in the barracks at that time were the North Cork Militia. Ryan states that they had been quartered in Carrick-on-Suir since 26 June 1798, but the Militia marched off on 26 August of the same year. They were under the command of the notorious Lord Kingsborough, the man who is generally credited with the invention of the pitch cap torture. This involved placing caps of tar on victims' heads, which were then set alight, in order to extract confessions and information.[37] When the Militia left, we are told 'the people of Carrick did not feel much afflicted for this loss', a statement which speaks volumes. The North Cork Militia was replaced the same day by about 1,200 Guards whom Ryan describes as being 'remarkably well behaved'. This final remark leaves us in no doubt as to how badly behaved the North Cork Militia had been when contrasted with their successors. On the 12 September 1798, the Dorsetshire Militia arrived in Carrick, only to be replaced two weeks later by the Devonshire Militia. All in all, between September and December 1798, Ryan informs us that five English regiments were quartered in the town at various times.[38] This is a good indicator as to the level of military and rebel activity in the country. Along with being a centre point for news, trade and cultural exchange, Carrick-on-Suir was now very clearly on a core military axis.[39]

In spite of the immediate distractions of local troop and prisoner movements, Ryan was still very much aware of events happening nationally. He writes that on 26 August 1798, the same day the North Cork Militia left Carrick-on-Suir, and before their replacements had arrived, news had already filtered through to the town that the French were landing at Sligo.[40] Therefore, when some of the Guards newly quartered in Carrick-on-Suir were sent to Sligo, the reason for this cannot have come as any surprise to the residents of the town. Further accounts, as related by Ryan, stated that one of the French transports had been taken by the English and was being brought into Cork with 250 prisoners. The diarist continues, saying that the French ship was said to have had 50 guns and

---

36 *Diary*, p. 128.
37 J.M. Barry, *Pitchcap and Triangle: The Cork Militia in the Wexford Rising* (Cork: Sidney Publishing, 1998).
38 *Diary*, p. 129.
39 *Diary*, pp. 148 and 159.
40 *Diary*, p.p. 142 and 157.

1,000 men onboard. The French had marched to Castlebar, which they attacked with some success. But by 10 August, news was received in Carrick-on-Suir that the French had surrendered, and those rebels who had joined with them were cut to pieces and dispersed.[41] One might also surmise from the date of these entries that the moving of the North Cork Militia out of Carrick-on-Suir, was related to the French events. Ryan, unfortunately, does not state where he received such detailed information, especially regarding the precise numbers of men and guns. It is possible, however, that some of it filtered through from the barracks. The mail coach, too, would have brought news by way of newspapers and the coach passengers themselves.

News did not always travel smoothly. The non-arrival of the Dublin mail coach on 24 and 25 May 1798 would cause Ryan enormous irritation. It would not arrive until 31 May. Ryan records that this was due to a 'rising of insurgents at Naas and Carlow', when 'at Naas more than an hundred, and upwards of 400 [rebels] at Carlow' were killed.[42] Though he seems to talk about such a large number of deaths in a neutral, offhand manner, we must remember that these were turbulent times. As Ryan kept an almost daily record of local, national and international events, it did not do to make one's personal affiliations too clear lest the diary fall into unfriendly hands. But we can also sympathise with Ryan and understand his dependence on the mail coach as this was his gateway to the world, and news, outside of Carrick-on-Suir.

Yet, despite all upheaval, Ryan certainly managed to keep himself well informed. One example of this is when Ryan writes about the ongoing war between England and France. Interestingly, it is not just skirmishes between English and French forces which took place off the coast of Ireland that came to Ryan's notice. He was also aware of the battles between these nations which were occurring further afield. On 'Saturday the 6th October' the diarist writes of a 'defeat of the French Fleet by Admiral Nelson, first of August, at the mouth of the Nile!'.[43] We further learn that Nelson captured nine ships, and set two alight. This demonstrates that throughout the disturbances in Ireland, news still managed to make its way to Carrick-on-Suir, albeit delayed at times. Once again, Ryan shows his interest in recording statistics and ensures we know not just the fate, but also the number of the French ships involved in the battle.

The Irish Rebellion extended beyond 1798; skirmishes continued to occur, and the rebels continued to fight on for some years come.[44] The years following the Rebellion also brought deprivations and worries, outside of insurrection, to the

41   *Diary*, p. 159.
42   *Diary*, P. 125.
43   *Diary*, p. 68.
44   O'Flaherty and Hynes (eds.), *Vinegar Hill*, pp. 268–275.

people of Carrick-on-Suir. On 20 November 1799, Ryan writes of a notice being given to the bakers of the town 'not to make any White Bread 'til further orders', due to the shortage of flour. Interestingly, the Argyll Fencibles, who were stationed in Carrick-on-Suir at that time, had got notice a few days before to 'discontinue the use of Hair-powder'.[45] Whereas being unable to use hair powder would have been little more than an annoyance, the lack of bread was a very real burden for many, due to the difficulty in making and distributing flour around an unstable country.[46] The difficulties securing flour led to an increase in prices and hardships for everyone, not just the residents of Carrick-on-Suir.

There was also the political fallout of the Rebellion. The passing of the Act of Union in 1801 saw the end of the Irish Parliament in Dublin and the formation of the United Kingdom of Great Britain and Ireland.[47] Unsurprisingly, an event of this magnitude occurring in the Irish political landscape merits a mention by Ryan:

> Union with England proposed and carried with a Vote in the Irish Parliament LORDS & COMMONS. Strange indeed!—And very strange that the Lords could be prevailed on to sign their own DEGREDATION—their DEATH-WARRANT! If that is not compleat IRISH BLUNDERING, it remains yet undiscovered what, in fact, ought to be called so! Time will tell all ... All's well that ends well!!! To commence 1st January 1801.[48]

This was a very telling comment indeed, written by a man who had lived through some profoundly unsettling times, and who was now passing comment on the end of one era and the beginning of another.

6 Revolution Abroad

As has already been established, news, its acquisition, digestion, and circulation, was of paramount importance to Ryan. He documented and remarked upon events which occurred in Carrick-on-Suir, other parts of Ireland, and

---

45 *Diary*, p. 162.
46 William Shaw Mason, *A statistical account; or parochial survey of Ireland*, vol. 2 (Dublin: Faulkner Press, 1819), p. 123; L.A. Clarkson, 'The Demography of Carrick-on-Suir, 1799', *Proceedings of the Royal Irish Academy: Archaeology, Culture, History, Literature, 1987*, 87, (1987), pp. 13–36 (p. 33).
47 For more on the Act of Union of 1801 and its consequences for Ireland see Patrick M. Geoghan, *The Irish Act of Union: A Study in High Politics 1798–1801* (Dublin: Gill & MacMillan, 1999).
48 *Diary*, p. 109.

even other parts of the world. Yet Ryan never privileged national or international news over more local events, believing that all news was equally important and equally exciting. The Irish Rebellion, when it came in 1798, was not the first bloody insurrection on which Ryan had reported. Under the heading 'REVOLUTION', we are informed that 'The Revolution of France so celebrated throughout Europe commenced the 17th June 1789.'[49] The diarist makes no further comment on the revolution at this stage, turning immediately to the movements between houses being made by his neighbours in Carrick-on-Suir. 'Mr. Wilson, moved to New Lane', 'Mr. Spencer removed to John Purcell's former house', and 'Mr. Will Hayes sett (sic) up the Hardware business at Bridge Lane'. But events in France return to the diary when, under the heading 'Murder!', Ryan tells us that on '10 August 1792 the King of France's Swiss Guards and several Officers of the Court at Paris, were assailed by the Mob, and butchered'. He further writes that 'several of the Heads [were] carried on poles thro' the City in triumph!'. Ryan follows this by informing us that on 2 September the prisoners, 'not excepting Clergymen and Ladies', were confined for 'crimes of State, as they are pleased to call them!' At once we can sense Ryan's shock and dismay at the violence he had heard and read about. There is little doubt too as to how shocked the diarist was by the reports he had received, especially when he interjects with words such as 'horrid'. This may not necessarily be because the diarist supported the French royal family, but more that his source of information came from English newspapers and journals. These would have been invariably royalist and anti-revolutionary in tone and would not have held back in their descriptions of the atrocities taking place in Paris.[50]

Ryan continues to write of French events and relates that Louis XVI was 'removed from the Palace the 10th of August 1792', found 'guilty of a conspiracy against the liberty of the Nation,', by the French National Assembly, and 'beheaded on a public scaffold on Monday the 21st January 1793! Horror! Horror!'.[51] This entry is followed with the news that 'the French Queen, Marie Antoinette, was murdered on 16 October' of the same year. However, to put the French Revolution into context, on the same page that Ryan broadcast the news of the execution of Marie Antoinette, he writes of the killing of another woman. 'Bryan Murphy's wife', he stated, 'was murdered on Friday night! And her husband sent to jail for the murder'. Bryan Murphy, we learn, was hanged

---

49   *Diary*, p. 67.
50   Hugh Gough and David Dickson (eds.), *Ireland and the French Revolution* (Co. Dublin: Irish Academic Press (1990).
51   *Diary*, p. 110.

for his crime.[52] For Ryan, the murder of Mrs. Murphy was every bit as horrific and worthy of reporting as the brutalities of the French Revolution. He saw no difference between the wife of the French king and the wife of a local Carrick-on-Suir man.

The French Revolution was not the only uprising outside of Ireland to come to Ryan's notice. In January 1795 he wrote that the 'Revolution of the United Provinces (Dutch)' had taken place when the French entered Amsterdam. He continues by stating this to be the third revolution within a few years—'America, France and Holland!'.[53] Ryan, and the residents of Carrick-on-Suir were as well-informed as anyone, at this time, about the various rebellions, uprisings and revolutions which were occurring in the late eighteenth century.

James Ryan had a voracious appetite for news, and for recording it in his diary. He never saw the fact that he lived in a small town in a small country on the edge of Europe as a problem. Instead, he regarded living in Carrick-on-Suir as an advantage; he was in the centre of the Irish road and river network. Although he was often reliant on the possibly skewed news of events which occurred outside of his own immediate area from newspapers and travellers, he still determined what he would record in his diary and how it would be recorded. A product of his time, James Ryan was also ahead of his time. The valuable legacy he has left us is a tribute to his ability to locate, distil and narrate sometimes mundane, sometimes remarkable events. For Ryan, though, all news—whether local, national or international—was exciting news.

---

52 *Diary*, p. 114.
53 *Diary*, p. 111.

CHAPTER 11

News about Justice

Telling Crime Stories in Eighteenth-Century Europe

Pasquale Palmieri

During the early modern age, news narratives about famous court cases allowed the European governing elite to demonstrate the singular effectiveness of the judicial system in punishing criminals and affirming the rule of law. The theatre of the courtroom, as we might call this form of propaganda, had been the product of a dominant culture that sought to deliver a highly-controlled, self-serving message about its right to exercise juridical power over a passive and receptive audience.[1] However, in the central decades of the eighteenth century, thanks to a booming information market, that same dominant culture could no longer control the narratives emerging from the traditional theatre of the courtroom, and the formerly passive and receptive audience grew active and contentious. The representation of justice became all the more conspicuously mediated by competing modes of communication. Those modes, which gave space to contradictory versions of the same story, thrust the public into a new socio-political reality in which the repressive apparatus of the State produced controversial outcomes, and criminals' guilt or innocence was now open for debate. The theatre of the courtroom joined a transmedia and participatory information culture, in which non-experts made use of a range of media to take part in the transformation of circulating narratives.

These writings about trials, which proved to be popular among both ordinary people and social elites, helped foster a new form of sociability in mid-eighteenth century. Their widespread revision and circulation all over Europe—often translated and reworked—impacted on different social groups. This impact is all the more evident in the context of the criminal figure, for often enough the authors represented the criminal by borrowing expressions and definitions from hybrid narratives that may not have been fully literary, but

---

1 Recent overviews of early modern representations of justice include: Marco Bellabarba, *La giustizia nell'Italia moderna* (Roma-Bari: Laterza 2011); D. Lemmings (ed.), *Crime, Courtrooms and the Public Sphere in Britain, 1700–1850* (London-New York: Routledge, 2012); D. Lemmings & A. May (eds.), *Criminal Justice during the Long Eighteenth Century. Theatre, Representation, Emotion* (London-New York: Routledge, 2018); Lisa Roscioni, *La badessa di Castro. Storia di uno scandalo* (Bologna: Il Mulino, 2017).

typically relied on hybrid formulas, genres, and rhetorical strategies. Scholars therefore need to bear in mind that the media shaped perceptions about criminal actions and behaviours through the use of literary conventions, whether those perceptions originally derived from established powers (governmental agencies), cultural industries and sociable spaces (such as print shops, book shops, coffee shops, and barber shops), or the participatory impulses of the public (gossip, street theatre, and the like).[2] In visual terms, we might say that the criminal became a privileged blank screen on which society projected its key concerns. In other words, the drives and emotions that ran through society lodged in the collective, but hardly uniform, representations of criminals.

These crime stories attracted a large readership from a large part of the population, that cut across the social hierarchy. Thus the flow of information gave rise to a creative interaction between individuals and groups, by also allowing them to take advantage of a growing participatory culture.[3] By the same token, narratives of famous trials and sensational events did not so much inform people about how the government enacted justice. Rather, they established a 'folklore' about criminals in general and their role in society. For this reason, narratives of the type discussed in this chapter 'shaped reality itself', as Robert Darnton has pointed out, 'and helped to determine the course of events'.[4] Accordingly, what matters is not only the origins of the messages delivered through these narratives (namely, who wrote what to whom and why at a particular moment in history), but also the amplification and assimilation of these polyvalent messages, 'the way [they] reverberated through society and became meaningful to the public'.[5] In anthropological terms, it is important

---

2 See Francesco Benigno, *La mala setta. Alle origini di mafia e camorra (1859–1878)* (Turin:, Einaudi, 2015); and his 'La questione delle origini: mafia, camorra e storia d'Italia', *Meridiana*, 87 (2016), pp. 125–148 and 'Ancora la mafia e la Spagna. Realtà e finzione nella costruzione sociale del male', *Between*, 9–18 (2019), pp. 2–19. See too J. Caro Baroja, *Realidad y fantasia en el mundo criminal* (Madrid: C.S.I.C., 1986). On the 'social construction of evil', see J. C. Alexander, *The Meanings of Social Life: A Cultural Sociology* (Oxford: Oxford University Press, 2003).
3 See Filippo De Vivo, *Information and Communication in Venice: Rethinking Early Modern Politics* (Oxford: Oxford University Press, 2007).
4 Robert Darnton, *The Forbidden Best-sellers of Pre-Revolutionary France* (New York: Norton, 1996), p. XXII.
5 Ibid., p. 190. According to Roger Chartier, narratives often played upon 'a well-established repertory of plots and motifs', but we have to discern 'the bitter conflicts, polemical motivations and political designs that led to their writing and publication': Roger Chartier, *The Culture of Print, Power and the Uses of Print in Early Modern Europe* (Princeton: Princeton University Press, 2014), p. 8.

to examine the broad cultural field in which these messages operated, not just their content.

Additionally, following the thoughts of Melissa Calaresu, Filippo De Vivo, and Joan-Pau Rubiès, we need to bear in mind that 'audience response is no less important than authorial intentionality', especially if we consider that the names of most of the authors are often unknown.[6] The study of representations, as is well known, has been revitalised as part of a history that 'sees the social *imaginaire* as crucial not only to the quality of life experience but also to political action'.[7] By taking into account the complex and multifarious exchanges between different people in a given cultural context, it is possible to find continuities, discontinuities, and overlaps in the perceptions and representations of reality. A close reading of the primary sources be they published or unpublished, written or visual sheds important light on the circulation of news, knowledge, and experiences about criminals. Produced as they were by people from different social environments such as bureaucrats or 'professional' writers, legates, clerics, lawyers, artisans, forensic memoires (legal writings to support defendants or accusers), and narratives of famous trials bring to light a complex world open to the circulation of conflicting beliefs and ideas related to events of keen public interest. They thus offer testimonies to the movement of themes, images, and cultural practices, which move back and forth between elite and popular culture.

By the same token, we should not be surprised to discover that criminals described within the burgeoning transmedia culture of the old regime resembled heroes of the epic-chivalric poem or the picaresque novel, even though they are not specifically rooted in these genres.[8] As mentioned, these same criminals seem to resemble fictional characters rather than real believable people, and this slippage mattered in terms of readerly expectations.[9] Sometimes, for instance, the public sympathised with these crime celebrities,

---

6 M. Calaresu, F. de Vivo, and J.-P. Rubiés (eds.), *Exploring Cultural History. Essays in Honour of Peter Burke* (London: Ashgate, 2010), p. 3.

7 Ibid., p. 6.

8 See Marina Roggero, *Le carte piene di sogni. Testi e lettori in età moderna* (Bologna: Il Mulino, 2006); Giovanni Levi, 'Microhistory and Picaresque', in B. de Haan, K. Mierau (eds.), *Microhistory and the Picaresque Novel* [...], (Newcastle upon Tyne: Cambridge Scholars Publishing, 2014), pp. 19–28; Konstantin Mierau, *Capturing the Pícaro in Words* [...] *in Early Modern Madrid* (London-New York: Routledge, 2018). On transmedia culture, a concept borrowed from media studies, see Henry Jenkins, *Convergence Culture. Where Old and New Media Collide* (New York: New York University Press, 2006); Paolo Bertetti, *Che cos'è la transmedialità* (Rome: Carocci, 2021).

9 See Adriano Prosperi, *Dare l'anima. Storia di un infanticidio* (Turin: Einaudi, 2005); Edward Muir & Guido Ruggiero, 'Introduction: The Crime of History', in E. Muir & G. Ruggiero (eds.),

viewing them as marginal subjects in search of redemption and as capable of upsetting relations of power, and even repairing abuses perpetrated by unfair authorities—in essence, of speaking truth to power.[10] Other times, felons appeared in these writings to mediate between different ethnic, religious, or linguistic groups, as well as between different social conditions, thus upsetting economic and cultural norms.[11] Either way, the government and the emergent media industries delivered different messages about the criminals. On the one hand, narratives about criminal punishment aroused pity and contrition. On the other, narratives about their adventures evoked empathy, envy, or a desire to imitate what these outlaws did, how they behaved, and what they stood for. These narratives had no one social function; they delivered no one message, served to elicit no single emotion, were grounded in no one genre, adopted no literary convention, and appealed to no one rational explanation of the events described.

1 François Gayot de Pitaval and his Collection of Famous Trials

Crimes, trials, and punishments were at the centre of a wave of texts that met with enormous success by updating the paradigms of the relationship between verbal communication and justice. However, something began to change in the early decades of the eighteenth century. A collection of *Causes Célèbres et intéressantes avec les jugements qui les ont décidées* [Famous and Interesting Trials with the Final Judgments] was first published in 1734 in several volumes.[12] The author was François Gayot de Pitaval (1673–1743), an ambitious French lawyer who found little gratification in the tribunal, and in his fifties turned into an anomalous picaresque figure, halfway between a gentleman and an adventurer.[13] Endowed with good writing skills, Pitaval tried his luck at literary activity. His early crime-stories were mostly addressed to legal professionals, but later also became popular amongst a wide public. Within a few decades,

---

History from Crime: Selections from the Quaderni Storici (Baltimore and London: The Johns Hopkins University Press, 1994), pp. I–XVIII.
10   See M. Harris, 'L'omicidio e la stampa: rappresentazioni del crimine e della legge (1660–1760)', in R. De Romanis & R. Loretelli (eds.), *Il delitto narrato al popolo [...] in età moderna* (Palermo: Sellerio, 1999), pp. 19–3.
11   See Mierau, *Capturing the Pícaro*.
12   F. Gayot de Pitaval, *Causes Célèbres et intéressantes avec les jugements qui les ont décidées* (Paris, G. Cavelier, 1734), vol. 1.
13   Aldo Mazzacane, 'Letteratura, processo e opinione pubblica: le raccolte di cause celebri', in M. Marmo & L. Musella (eds.), *La costruzione della verità giudiziaria* (Naples: ClioPress, 2003), p. 55 (63–70).

the *Causes Célèbres* were part of the generative moment of the crime novel, able to stimulate conspicuous imitations and variations, contributing to the construction of an unprecedented imaginary of justice, shaping new mental categories, or dismantling the old ones.[14]

The *Causes Célèbres* broke into an already rich publishing market, in particular with regard to matters related to justice. The most accessible products were *canards* and *colportage* books, sold at low prices in fair-stalls, assembled using fragile bindings and cheap paper. Together with other popular prints, these small volumes also contained pieces of 'gallows literature'. These writings consisted of 'whole-sheet' broadsides, in one or two columns of wretched, aging type, with a woodcut at top, to be sold in shops and hawked at the foot of the gallows. They often included biographies, 'last speeches', and 'dying verses' of celebrated burglars or murderers, along with pamphlets, anecdotes, tales of renowned trials, and judicial acts, which were reworked to become attractive to the public, especially *decisiones* and *consilia*, or sentences.[15] These 'instant books' helped the public understand the reasons for the sentence. They had a similar structure in different countries, including a brief biography of the offender, a detailed description of the crime, an exposition of the sentence, and the farewell words of the condemned or his abjuration.[16]

These writings were usually aimed at highlighting the efficiency of the justice system and the State's ability to provide security to the subjects by punishing bad behaviour. In the Holy Roman Empire, France, and England, a key role was played by texts usually defined as *complaintes* (laments) and *récits* (orally transmitted stories, similar to dramatic monologues), which had almost the same characteristics as the last speeches, dying verses, and crime anecdotes, with a marked link to oral culture. In these countries, the printing industry tried to anticipate the magistrates by selling these writings even before the execution of the sentence (see Figure 11.1).[17]

14 Ibid., pp. 63–70. For the methodological framework, see I. Ward, *Law and Literature* (Cambridge: Cambridge University Press, 1995).
15 Mazzacane, 'Letteratura, processo', p. 73; De Romanis, 'Identità camuffate, scritture criminali', in R. De Romanis & R. Loretelli (eds.), *Il delitto narrato al popolo. Immagini di giustizia e stereotipi di criminalità in età moderna* (Palermo, Sellerio, 1999), pp. 62–94.
16 Bellabarba, *La giustizia*, p. 154; Holger Schott Syme, '(Mis)representing Justice on the Early Modern Stage', *Studies in Philology*, 109 (2012), pp. 63–85; Lisa Roscioni, 'L'omicidio funesto del principe Savelli', in S. Luzzatto (ed.), *Prima lezione di metodo storico* (Rome-Bari: Laterza, 2010), pp. 85–104; Roscioni, *La badessa*, pp. 105–113; Alberto Natale, *Gli specchi della paura. Il sensazionale e il prodigioso nella letteratura di consumo (secoli XVI–XVIII)* (Rome: Carocci, 2008).
17 This is depicted in William Hogarth's engraving 'The Idle Prentice Executed at Tyburn', see Ian A. Bell, 'Cartoline di un'impiccagione: La rappresentazione del crimine nella serie

FIGURE 11.1   William Hogarth (1697–1794), *Industry and Idleness*, Plate 11; *The Idle 'Prentice Executed at Tyburn*

These cheap and widely-circulated texts coexisted with more cultured books, inspired by the models of Italian Renaissance *novellas*, collections of curious anecdotes, and narratives of extraordinary events ('histoires admirables', 'histoires prodigieuses', 'notables', 'singulières, mèmorables', etc). In seventeenth-century France, the preacher Jean-Pierre Camus enjoyed a great success with his *Spectacles d'horreur* (1630), and the translator François de Rosset managed to have his *Histoires tragiques de nostre temps* (1614) reprinted several times.[18] The authorities allowed only reports of the final parts of the trials and of the capital sentences to be published, keeping secret within the courts of justice all debates about the case.[19] Even the titles (*Distinta relazione della gran giustizia* [Detailed Relation for the Great Justice], *Il lamento e la morte* [Lament and Death], *Relazione degli enormi delitti commessi dai condannati* [Account of the Crimes Committed by the Convicts], *Succinta relazione del processo e sentenza*

    Industry and Idleness di William Hogarth', in R. Loretelli, R. De Romanis (eds.), *Il delitto narrato al popolo. Immagini di giustizia e stereotipi di criminalità in età moderna* (Palermo: Sellerio, 1999), pp. 173–198.

18   Jean-Pierre Camus, *Les Spectacles d'horreur* (Paris, André Soubron, 1630) (USTC 6032305); François de Rosset, *Les histoires tragiques de nostre temps* (Cambray: Jean de la Rivière, *1614*) (USTC 1119735).

19   Roscioni, *La badessa di Castro*, pp. 109–110.

[Short Account of the Trial and Sentence]), illustrated how the pedagogical aim came first in these texts, in order to show how effective and inflexible was the power in punishing criminals. More detailed accounts of famous trials circulated only in manuscript form, evading censorship and other limitations, staying within the exclusive channels of patrician and ecclesiastical reception. The reason for this phenomenon is ostensibly simple: the most contentious texts were frowned upon by the authorities since they displayed controversial procedures and aroused doubts about the validity of the judge's resolution.[20]

Pitaval merged all of these literary traditions—both the fictional and the nonfictional ones, with all their subtle distinctions—in his *Causes Celebres*, promoting the meeting of the True with the Marvellous by simultaneously satisfying the claims of verisimilitude and fancy.[21] While offering an enjoyable reading and aiming to reach a heterogeneous audience, the author also endeavoured to provide the reader with some legal information, teaching him how to move through the labyrinths of justice, making the *arcana* [mysteries] of jurisprudence more intelligible. Each story was accompanied by documents, namely judicial records, reinforcing the text's claim to credibility. The apparent historicity of the accounts helped create a higher degree of suspense and surprise in the texts. Nevertheless, as Pitaval clarified in his introduction, the pleasure of this camouflaged fiction could turn into poison for the readers. He thus gave priority to reality, which itself was marvellous enough to provide the public with amusement, reliable information about justice, and useful moral teachings. Conversely, we should also observe that this pedagogical effort remained incomplete. Pitaval weakly clarified the chronology of his plots, and he sometimes forgot to display the social identity of the characters. It was not easy for the reader to understand if they were nobles, bourgeois, or peasants, if they were rich or poor.[22]

An Italian translation of the *Causes Celebres* was printed in Naples in 1755, after a Venetian edition dated 1749, and an analysis of this publication is crucial here in order to understand how trial stories were evolving and gaining popularity. It was edited by Domenico Moro, a lawyer by profession, who some years

---

20 Ibid., p. 110. See for example, Harry Ransom Centre (University of Texas at Austin), Ranuzzi Collection, *Raccolta di diverse Vite, Morti e Processi e Casi Curiosi*. On the handwritten accounts of criminals' adventures, see Mario Infelise, 'Criminali e "cronaca nera" negli strumenti pubblici di informazione tra '600 e '700', *Acta Histriae*, 15-2 (2007), pp. 507–520.
21 Mazzacane, *Letteratura, processo e opinione pubblica*, p. 75.
22 Ibid., pp. 82–84.

later would circulate his own treatise on 'criminal practice'.²³ In the preface, the editor offered important suggestions on how readers constructed meaning over Pitaval's work. Public interest in the accounts of famous trials was very high in the Italian peninsula, and it sparked new energy within a more general expansion of the print market, which had recently come 'to its peak'.²⁴

The French edition of the *Causes* had enjoyed a wide circulation, so booksellers took advantage of the situation by raising the price. The *Famous Trials* provided court insiders with useful legal materials, but also attracted the attention of a non-specialised public. The aim of the Italian translation was therefore to make the text readable and understandable for 'all Italians'.²⁵ The 'learned' took pleasure in reading, thanks to contents that the author proposed 'very subtly, and with profound erudition'.²⁶ However, 'other sorts of people' enjoyed the stories without any moral commitment, including 'non-learned women', who found a way to 'satisfy their curiosity, for the vagueness of the events, and for the amazingness of the facts themselves, all great, and wonderful'.²⁷

The success of the collection convinced publishers to invest in similar products, which offered both 'very good examples of the principles of Law' and 'luminous images' of 'rare and sensational facts'.²⁸

> Nor could his Work have met with such approval from the Public, if [the author] had not taken the certain path of combining utility and pleasure, the importance of legal articles and the enjoyment of plots, which entice people's curiosity, and even teases the spirit of the most shy people, and of those who do not like to read very much.²⁹

---

23 François Gayot de Pitaval, *Cause celebri e interessanti. Tomo Primo* (Naples: Vincenzo Pauria, 1755); Domenico Moro, *Pratica Criminale* (4 vols., Naples: Eredi Moro, 1782–1783). The first edition was published in 1749.
24 Pitaval, *Cause Celebri*, p. IV, 'in questa Città dove l'uso della stampa è giunto al suo colmo'.
25 Ibid., p. VI, 'renderla universal a tutti gl'Italiani'.
26 Ibid., 'sottilissimamente, e con profonda erudizione'.
27 Ibid., 'ognaltra sorta di persone', 'fino le donne, non erudite', 'troveranno nella lettura di che appagare la loro curiosità, per la vaghezza degli avvenimenti, e per la sorprendenza de' fatti istessi, tutti grandi, e meravigliosi'.
28 Ibid., 'dare ottimi principJ della Giurisprudenza', 'luminose immagini', 'fatti strepitosi e rari'.
29 Ibid., p. 7, 'Né per altro avrebbe potuto la sua Opera incontrar tanto applauso presso il Pubblico, s'egli non avesse presa questa sicura strada di unire all'utile il piacevole, ed al grande degli articoli legali il dilettevole degli avvenimenti, che invogliano l'altrui curiosità, e solleticano lo spirito anche de' più schivi, e di quegli, a cui meno piaccia leggere'.

The accounts of the trials included 'all of the things that had happened before the judgment was delivered'.[30] Each account consisted of a 'foreword', a narrative of the trial 'with all its circumstances', a 'description of the evidence or of the clues', an explanation of the lawyers' strategies, and a review of interlocutory decrees, arguments, and final sentences.[31]

Nevertheless, it was necessary to consider the possibility that some 'weak-minded' readers did not manage to develop a familiarity with 'history', 'mundane events', and the issues of the 'criminal forum'.[32] Those readers who could easily fall into misunderstandings, believing that the *Famous Trials* were nothing more than 'novels'.[33] In the end, criminal narrative and fictional works lived within a common territory, facing the same problems of interpretation: the main task of the writer was to teach the reader how to manage complexity, grasp the right messages, reject the dangerous ones, maintain a solid morality, and move in the 'Theatre of this world'.[34]

The innovative character of Pitaval's collection was undeniable; its innovation ended up increasing the anxieties connected with the reception of the text. A substantial distance lay between the *Famous Trials*' view of justice and the *ancien régime* way of representing it. Significantly, the French lawyer displayed part of the procedure alongside the crime narrative, offering the reader not only certainties, but also a conspicuous variety of doubts. Pitaval's collection showed the reader how complex the judicial search for truth was and how rhetorical tricks and overloaded concepts were capable of undermining the judge's impartiality. Ultimately, the great problems of *ancien régime* justice appeared even more evident, and added to those that the population already perceived in a consolidated way. Justice therefore had to protect itself from the intrusiveness of noble and ecclesiastical privileges, but it also had to defend itself from the lies of court storytellers and maintain its own credibility in dealing with impostors and swindlers.

The success of the *Famous Trials* allowed publishers to use the author's name to identify a literary genre; along with other popular genres, in the second part of the eighteenth century, they started selling 'Pitavals'. Given their wide circulation, scholars are still investigating the effect of these narratives on the public sphere. Many have asserted that the impact of the *Causes* went far beyond the intentionality of the author, who for his part kept a mild conservatism, at least

---

30   Ibid., 'le cose tutte, che avvennero fino al fine de' loro Giudizi'.
31   Ibid., 'proemio', 'con ogni sua circostanza', 'descrizione della pruova o degli indizj'.
32   Ibid., p. IX, 'mente debole', 'storia', 'avvenimenti del mondo', 'foro criminale'.
33   Ibid., 'romanzi'.
34   Ibid., p. VIII: 'il Teatro di questo mondo'.

on a formal level. That said, his plots highlighted the weight of corruption, the ability of the deceivers to escape the law, a great deal of unpunished transgressions, the frequency of unjust and hasty sentences, and how criminals could be protected by both local and central authorities.

In a nutshell, these crime stories ended up exposing the weakness and the inefficiency of the judicial system. They possessed a hidden subversive energy, because they surreptitiously, or almost unconsciously, stimulated the public to lose confidence in the authorities. Often without meaning to, Pitaval displayed the hidden aspects of the trials by highlighting their internal contradictions. By doing so, he opened the texts to multiple uses, not necessarily linked to obedience to the rules of common morality, religion, or the State. By taking control of the stories, the public easily transformed convicted criminals into models to imitate, or into victims of arbitrary justice. Consequently, a great deal of blame was attributed to judges, who did not preserve their reputation as custodians of the truth, but rather seemed at the mercy of uncertainties, unreliable, ready to change their mind at every whim and fancy, and more attentive to their personal interests than to the public good. Legitimate doubts begun to grow about the use of torture and about the condition of jails as well.[35]

Starting from the 1750s and 1760s, publishers and authors began to complement the vintage fashion of the *Famous Trials* with accounts that gave a new importance to contemporaneity, focusing on recent trials and proposing novelistic accounts of real stories. Forensic *memoires* started being sold along with gazettes and broadsheets at public halls, squares, and street markets. Readers identified with the characters, who increasingly belonged to lower classes.[36] Sentences rarely turned out to be predictable. The public was asked to take part in the search for truth by examining the documents and was expected to pronounce its own reasonable sentence. Private and public affairs became the objects of open debate in saloons and cafés, as well as in squares and courtyards. This explosion of shorter and longer narratives ended up stimulating the development of critical reflection on justice.

Scholars now recognize the importance of the press in constructing the image of justice in a variety of contexts, and sometimes with divergent orientations. On the one hand, printed and manuscript accounts of trials contributed to the growth of a critical spirit about the functioning of justice. On the other

---

35 See Mazzacane, *Letteratura, processo e opinione pubblica*; Michael Harris, 'L'omicidio e la stampa: rappresentazioni del crimine e della legge (1660–1760); , in De Romanis & R. Loretelli (eds.), *Il delitto narrato al popolo*, pp. 19–35; Giancarlo Baronti, *La morte in piazza [...] in età moderna* (Lecce: Argo, 2000) and *Vita volant, scripta manent. Vicende criminali nella letteratura di piazza* (Foligno: Il Formichiere, 2020).

36 Mazzacane, 'Letteratura, processo e opinione pubblica', pp. 88–95.

hand, these documents were often meant to reassure the public, legitimise the government, and celebrate the role of the monarchs in punishing the guilty while ensuring the safety of the subjects. Nevertheless, these two purposes were not distinct.

The *Select Trials* published in London in 1764, for example, showed 'a noticeable trend towards a more complex rendering of the criminal courts'. They reached 'a complex market, including lawyers and legal officials', as well as a variety of non-specialist readers. These texts were 'both useful and entertaining' in representing the complicated issues involved in producing judgments, 'while at the same time maintaining an uncompromising general image of justice'.[37] Although they continued to portray crime as a matter of serious offenses and severe punishment, they were sometimes inclined to stimulate in the public the development of empathy toward those who had broken the law. The visions proposed by criminal records do not always faithfully mirror hegemonic ideologies; they sometimes show nuanced traces of dissonant values or subversive impulses.[38] In the accounts of justice and possibly in the perception of the public, the criminal could easily become a courageous picaro [rogue] who disrupted the social order by implicitly questioning hierarchies and power relations.[39]

News about trials stimulated social interactions and communicative practices, they reshaped the public space and revealed unknown aspects of the functioning of justice to a wide public, to some extent breaking the secrecy

---

37   Ibid., p. 22. Robert Shoemaker suggests that, in the last thirty years of the eighteenth century, publishers stimulated a more open engagement between authorities and the public; see Robert Shoemaker, 'Representing the Adversary Criminal Trial: Lawyers in the Old Bailey Proceedings, 1770–1800', in D. Lemmings (ed.), *Crime, Courtrooms and the Public Sphere in Britain*, pp. 71–92. Simon Deveraux, on his side, highlights the performing attitudes of lawyers, often recognised as powerful storytellers, with a great ability in strengthening the dramatic tone of their dialogues and in embellishing their plots with colourful inventions; see Simon Deveraux, 'Arts of Public Performance: Barristers and Actors in Georgian England', in D. Lemmings (ed.), *Crime, Courtrooms and the Public Sphere in Britain*, pp. 93–119.

38   According to Malcolm Gaskill, we have to be careful about the 'danger of equating representations of power with its efficacy'. Messages originating in the dominant cultures were often appropriated in a popular way, 'bypassing intended meanings and thus limiting the extent of acculturation'. Print allowed the centre to communicate with peripheries, the elites to address the lower classes. But it would be misleading to think it was a hegemonic process imposed from above. Indeed, learned ideas in print passed 'through a screen of oral knowledge' and 'were reinterpreted to fit popular parameters of understanding'; see Malcolm Gaskill, *Crime and Mentalities in Early Modern England* (Cambridge: Cambridge University Press, 2000), p. 26.

39   See De Romanis, 'Identità camuffate, scritture criminali'.

that had marked the old regime system. In the middle decades of the eighteenth century, the circulation of news on such cases increased exponentially. The defendants became the heart of a complex media landscape, contributing to the growth of new verbal, visual, and performative representations. At once, the mediatization of justice favoured a mutual-exchange relationship between different literary genres, sometimes relying on stereotyped representations of reality, which facilitated public understanding of the text. The accounts competed with each other, claiming veracity and relying on weak evidence or uncertain testimonies—sometimes purely fictional products—linked to masterpieces of the literary tradition. The texts showed their malleability in the hands of lawyers, priests, friars, members of the State administration, merchants, printers, booksellers, and manual workers. All these actors used them, from time to time, to pursue their own purposes, such as defending or increasing their social status, earning money, seeking fame, or satisfying their cultural interests or religious needs.

2 Crime Stories and Novels

In order to understand how accounts of famous trials impacted on the media and cultural landscape of the eighteenth century, we should observe how the texts worked within a literary system. For instance, popular trial publishing bears affinities to other literary genres, which enjoyed great success in the publishing market. As scholars have recognised, there is a reciprocal relationship between fictional works and narratives of real sensational events. This relationship is even more pronounced if we consider that the reciprocal influence existing between accounts of criminal cases and the emerging genre of the novel is now widely recognised by scholars. The two styles borrowed repeatedly and strategically from each other. For instance, novels met their readers, in Lennard J. Davis's words, as 'an ambiguous form—a factual fiction which denied its fictionality' by claiming its own historicity.[40] Criminal biographies and diverse narratives of the later seventeenth century reflected how the boundaries between fiction and nonfiction were tenuous. It also often happened that judicial documents, factums (statements of the facts of a case), and memoirs offered material to build dramaturgical works and to improve the mythicization of *picari* and criminals. The 'news/novel discourse' was 'a kind

---

40 Lennard J. Davis, *Factual Fictions: The Origins of the English Novel* (New York: Columbia University Press, 1983), p. 36.

of undifferentiated matrix' out of which factual narratives found their distinction from fictional ones.[41]

In his *Criminality and Narrative in Eighteenth-Century England* (2001), Hal Gladfelder has provided a counter-reading to both J. Bender's *Imagining the Penitentiary* (1987) and D. A. Miller's *The Novel and the Police* (1988), by 'shifting the focus of discussion from the institutions of law (the prison, the police) and the law's strategies of surveillance and control to the experience of the outlaw: the social forces and forms of identity that violate the boundaries of legality'.[42] Examining constructions of the criminal underworld—picaresque and providential fictions, crime reports and gallows writing, accounts of trials and biographies of offenders—Gladfelder unearths fascinating tales of criminality. He detects the close connection between these narratives and the fictions of early novelists. According to Gladfelder, writers like Defoe and Fielding compelled their readers into a sympathy with their heroes and heroines. Gladfelder claims that 'the reader's complicity with criminal voices is implicit in the form of Defoe's mock-autobiographical texts', soliciting identification with the 'experience of transgression and the guilty pleasure of fear that grows out of it'.[43] Similarly, Fielding's *Amelia* 'evokes the allure of the transgressive acts and desires whose dangers it wishes' to denounce, involving the public in 'unsuspected sympathies'.[44]

This trend was evident all over Europe, and was probably one of the keys of the success of crime news, as it was capable of incorporating different languages and styles into captivating plots. The first objective of the *memoires* produced by lawyers and journalists was to provide the public with models of behaviour, but they also aimed to engage readers' and listeners' emotions. The Italian case study is enlightening; it is likely that the success of the novel in the Italian states through the 1740s and the 1750s (in translations from French and English) stimulated the authors of trial accounts to devise strategies of emulation.[45] In a comparable manner, we also have good reason to believe that

---

41   Ibid., p. 67. See also Paul Hunter, *Before novels. The Cultural Contexts of 18th-century English Fiction* (New York: Norton and Comp., 1990).

42   Hal Gladfelder, *Criminality and Narrative in Eighteenth-Century England* (Baltimore: JHU Press, 2003), p. 8; See also Philip Rawlings, *Drunks, Whores and Idle Apprentices. Criminal Biographies of the Eighteenth Century* (London-New York: Routledge, 1998).

43   Gladfelder, *Criminality and Narrative*, p. 131.

44   Ibid., p. 188.

45   Tatiana Crivelli, *"Né Arturo né Turpino né la tavola rotonda". Romanzi del secondo Settecento italiano* (Rome: Salerno, 2002). From 1748 to 1798, 136 editions of Italian novels were published, without taking into consideration the translations. See also Lynn Hunt, *Inventing Human Rights. A History* (New York: Norton and Company, 2007), p. 40: 'In France, 8 new novels were published in 1701, 52 in 1750, and 112 in 1789. In Britain, the number of new

these same accounts provided sources of inspiration for the emerging novelists of the eighteenth century. In the same years, mainstream publishers flooded the market with titles like Richardson's *Pamela*, Fielding's *Tom Jones*, Lennox's *Henrietta*, almost all of Carlo Goldoni's plays, and a considerable number of pirated versions of the works of Pietro Chiari (1712–1785), a best-selling novelist from Brescia, whose popularity had increased on the Venetian market during the 1750s.[46] In his successful books, Chiari offered a wide *repertoire* of wandering characters who struggled to give meaning to their lives, were tempted by adventure, but who also made mistakes. It is therefore not surprising that these stories were based on binaries such as crime and punishment, damnation and redemption, sin and fear. The idea of justice that emerged from these writings was ambiguous; despite learning from the mistakes of their transgressive literary heroes, the readers often ended up desiring to imitate them.

Chiari's writings in particular provide a clear understanding of the literary context within which the various accounts of famous trials operated. Consider, for instance, Chiari's best-seller *La filosofessa italiana* [The Italian Woman Philosopher], which was repeatedly reprinted in Naples under a different title, *La filosofante italiana*, from the beginning of the 1750s to the end of the 1760s, and with some changes, in order not to incur penalties from the original producers from Venice.[47] Through the words of the protagonist, enigmatically called N.N., Chiari explains the complexity of the narrative. He did not expect readers to take the *Woman Philosopher* as a model, but rather to learn from her mistakes:

> I have seen from experience that all the precautions of human prudence end up being in vain, that fate plays an important role at the expense of prudence, and that most often perfidy and deception triumph over her fate. ... I do not need fictions, whatever is the outcome of my undertaking, since it is aimed at teaching ... with pleasure. My life is a continuous weave of extravagances, which would seem incredible to me if they

---

novels increased sixfold between the first decade in the eighteenth century and the 1760s. About 30 new novels appeared every year in the 1770s, 40 per year in the 1780s, and 70 per year in the 1790s'.

46 On Chiari and the publishing market of the Italian peninsula, see Cristina Cappelletti, '"Un diluvio di romanzi perniciosi". Per una storia editoriale dell'abate Chiari', *Studi sul Settecento e l'Ottocento, Rivista internazionale d'Italianistica*, IV (2009), pp. 39–54.

47 See Mario Infelise, 'Gli scambi librari veneto-napoletani. Fonti e tendenze', in A.M. Rao (ed.), *Editoria e cultura a Napoli nel XVIII secolo* (Naples: Liguori, 1998), pp. 237–250; Clotilde Bertoni, 'Editoria e romanzo fra Venezia e Napoli nella seconda metà del Settecento', in A.M. Rao (ed.), *Editoria e cultura*, pp. 697–722. The first edition is Pietro Chiari, *La filosofessa italiana, o sia le avventure della marchesa N.N.* (Venice: Pasinelli, 1753).

hadn't really happened to me. ... Here is the only favour I ask from my readers; that is, to be pitied for my frivolities. ... Being human is enough to be prone to make mistakes; nor do I claim that I have never failed; but it would be enough for me to have drawn from my mistakes the great profit of detesting them, in order to never fail again.[48]

It soon became clear to educated readers of the time that novels like Chiari's, although inspired by famous European models, gave space to a narrative 'crowded with episodes' and marked by 'a heap of doubtful and sometimes illogical situations'.[49]

Even the theoretical reflections of the critics on novelistic genres met with many embarrassments. Censors and reviewers continued to put recent production on an equal footing with ancient epic poems, although the former aimed primarily at constructing verisimilar plots, while the latter were based on supernatural and spectacular action. For their part, Catholic thinkers turned the initial doubts about the novel into a univocal orientation: they argued that, being centred on characters without judgment and inclined to follow their passions, the new tales in prose had the power to corrupt values. Novels were bad reading because they stimulated bad behaviour.[50]

The Modenese scholar Ludovico Antonio Muratori addressed the problem in the treatise *Della forza della fantasia umana* [On the Strength of Human

---

48   Pietro Chiari, *La Filosofante italiana* (Naples: Manfredi—Venaccia, 1763), pp. 6–7: 'Ho veduto per esperienza, che vane bene riescono tutte le precauzioni dell'umana prudenza, che ad onta sua molto opera il caso, che sopra di lei il più delle volte trionfa la perfidia, e l'inganno. ... Qualunque sia l'esito di questa mia impresa per insegnar [...] con diletto, non ho bisogno di fingere. La mia vita è un intreccio continuo di stravaganze, le quali se non fossero accadute a me, parrebbero a me stessa incredibili. ... Ecco l'unica grazia che io domando da' miei leggitori; cioè d'essere nelle leggerezze mie compatita. ... Per esser soggetti ad errare, basta essere uomini; né pretendo io già di non aver mai fallato; ma mi basterebbe aver trattato da' falli miei il gran profitto di detestarli, e di non fallare mai più'.

49   Carlo Alberto Madrignani, 'Il romanzo, catechismo per le riforme', in R. Loretelli & U.M. Olivieri (eds.), *La riflessione sul romanzo nell'Europa del Settecento* (Milan: Franco Angeli, 2005), pp. 77–101: 'affollato di episodi', 'un cumulo di situazioni poco probabili e pochissimo coerenti'. See also the important studies by Luca Clerici, *Il romanzo italiano del Settecento* (Venice: Marsilio 1997); Rosa Maria Loretelli, *L'invenzione del romanzo. Dall'oralità alla lettura silenziosa* (Rome-Bari: Laterza 2010); Valeria Tavazzi, *Il romanzo in gara. Echi delle polemiche teatrali nella narrativa di Pietro Chiari e Antonio Piazza* (Rome: Bulzoni, 2010); and Daniela Mangione, *Prima di Manzoni. Autore e lettore nel romanzo del Settecento* (Rome: Salerno 2012).

50   See Patrizia Delpiano, *Il governo della lettura. Chiesa e libri nell'Italia del Settecento* (Bologna: Il Mulino, 2007).

Fantasy], published in 1740.[51] He emphasised that novels proposed plausible stories with strong claims for truthfulness. Readers believed they were learning about historical facts, and they identified strongly with the characters. Thus, those stories had great persuasive power and could stimulate in the readers dangerous attempts at imitation. The Venetian playwright Carlo Gozzi expressed similar doubts on several occasions, fearing that novels would give rise to examples of moral degeneration. He wrote in 1761: 'Please take care of the morality ... Do not fill them [the novels] with wicked people, because you will make a bad mirror of the baseness of your soul'.[52]

Abbot Giambattista Roberti's *Del leggere libri di metafisica e divertimento* [Of Reading Books of Metaphysics and Entertainment, 1769], focused on the effects that the new literary genres had on the public. According to Roberti, novels proposed 'a certain bizarre blend of the sincere and the fake'.[53] Their dangerousness derived from the fact that they ended up in the hands of people unable to manage the contents or to orient themselves in this confusion, eventually falling into the temptations of fantasy:

> Fragile men, vain women, cheerful labourers, free soldiers, idle worldly people read [novels], and they find in the book the passion they experienced in their own life, and they identify the true story of their heart with that of fictional lovers; and they read with the whimsy of youth, under the force of their own temper, with the warmness of feelings, with the blindness of frivolity.[54]

---

51 L.A. Muratori, *Della forza della fantasia umana* (Venice: G. Pasquali, 1740).

52 Lodovica Braida, *L'autore assente. L'anonimato nell'editoria italiana del Settecento* (Rome-Bari: Laterza, 2019), p. 168: 'Vi raccomando il costume. ... Non gli empiete di scellerate persone, perocché farete uno specchio cattivo della bassezza dell'animo vostro'. The source is *Fogli sopra le massime del 'Genio e costumi del secolo' dell'abate Pietro Chiari e contro a' poeti Nugnez* (Venice: Appresso Paolo Colombani con licenza de'superiori, 1761). He was responding to Chiari, *Il genio e i costumi del secolo corrente. Riflessioni critiche e filosofiche tradotte dal francese ed accresciute dall'abate Pietro Chiari* (Venice: Giambattista Novelli, 1761).

53 Braida, *L'autore assente*, pp. 178–179: 'un certo bizzarro mescolamento del sincero e del finto'. The quotation is from the first offical edition of Roberti's book *Del leggere libri di metafisica e divertimento* (Bologna: Stamperia del Sant'Uffizio, 1769), p. 176. Nevertheless, a printed version without the city of publication and the name of the printer was already circulating in 1766.

54 Braida, *L'autore assente*, pp. 178–179: 'Leggonle uomini fragili donne vane garzoni festevoli liberi militari, mondani ozziosi, che riscontrano la propria passion sentita colla letta nel libro, e ravvisano la storia vera del loro cuore in quella de' finti amanti; e leggonle nell'estro della giovinezza nell'urto del temperamento nel bollor degli affetti nell'accecamento de' capricci'.

Roberti emphasised that the public, which now wanted to enjoy their emotions by getting deeply involved in the stories told by novelists, imitated the wicked actions of the heroes and ignored respect for hierarchies and traditional values.[55] Accordingly, he regarded the uncontrolled enjoyment of novels as a danger to established order, religion, and morality.

Ultimately, the novel had an internal contradiction, insofar as it served two different purposes. On one hand, authors and publishers sought a wide audience by promising pleasure. On the other hand, they sought appr[56]oval from an educated public, who wanted the utility of the text to take priority over the pure pleasure of reading.[57] Consequently, the moral question remained unsolved.[58] The novel aimed to entertain the audience and, at the same time, to build an 'exemplum', a new pedagogy, an alternative to hagiographies or edifying texts, traditionally monopolised by ecclesiastical authorities. This literary genre encouraged a desire for knowledge, fun, or adventure, but it also suggested ways of redemption, leading readers to amend transgression.

The potential of the novel was widely recognised all over Europe. In his famous *In Praise of Richardson*, Denis Diderot showed how the famous author of *Pamela* did not wander through the realm of fairy tales, but focused on the world he lived in, drawing on cases that dealt with the customs of civil nations. Richardson told of common passions and pains, recognizing the dangers that everyone had to face, encouraging practices of autonomy and empathy, stimulating the elaboration of new forms of organization of individual and social life.[59] The famous Neapolitan jurist Giuseppe Maria Galanti—who argued against the uncontrolled diffusion of legal texts—continued on the path traced by Diderot, considering the novel as a powerful media tool with which people could exercise civil virtues. From the late 1770s, Galanti engaged in the book market, publishing famous foreign novels in Naples. He wanted to instil principles of morality in a community that did not recognize the true values of progress, and that buried those values under a mountain of prejudices.[60] Novelists were expected to represent human weaknesses and vices in order to

---

55   Ibid., pp. 43–65. On Roberti's work, see Madrignani, 'Il romanzo, catechismo per le riforme', pp. 77–101, 77–101.
56   Denis Diderot, *Eloge de Richardson* (Lyon: Perisse, 1762).
57   Giacomo Mannironi, 'Un genere per pochi? Pubblico e mercato del romanzo a Venezia nel secondo Settecento', in L. Braida & S. Tatti (eds.), *Il libro. Editoria e pratiche di lettura nel Settecento* (Rome: Edizioni di Storia e Letteratura, 2016), pp. 279–290; Mario Infelise, 'L'Utile e il piacevole. Alla ricerca dei lettori italiani del secondo Settecento', in *Lo spazio del libro nell'Europa del XVIII secolo* (Bologna: Patron, 1997), pp. 113–126.
58   Madrignani, 'Il romanzo, catechismo per le riforme', p. 215.
59   Giuseppe Maria Galanti, edited by D. Falardo, with an essay by S. Martelli, *Osservazioni intorno a' Romanzi* (Naples: Istituto Italiano per gli Studi Filosofici, 2018), pp. XLII–XLIII.
60   Madrignani, 'Il romanzo, catechismo per le riforme', pp. 77–101.

teach readers how to reject moral corruption and how to take the right path. More than any treatise on jurisprudence or morals, Galanti maintained, the novel promoted deeper understanding of political and social justice.[61]

All of these works—novels, forensic memoirs, briefs, accounts of famous trials—inspired a profusion of transmedia storytelling, characterised by a dense circulation of news from hand to hand. The participation of different subjects in this exchange allowed the messages to quickly transform and acquire new appearances, thus widening the narrative universes revolving around famous trials or other sensational events. Different sectors of society—usually distant from each other economically, politically, and culturally—found common ground on which to share their different worldviews and, more specifically, their way of experiencing justice. Obscure and hidden as they were, the secrets of the procedure ended up being displayed to a much wider range of people, who began to perceive contradictions, inaccuracies, and even abuses.

More generally, we should observe how criminal tales moved across the media landscape, sometimes offering a vague image of the dominant classes and throwing shadows on the fairness and truthfulness of judicial procedures in their reconstructions of the facts. These texts were not at all linear. They were often suspended between gossip and licentious entertainment, but they still kept the appearance of a chronicle, based as they were on the pretence of truthfulness. They built on the traditional dialectic between transgression and punishment, but they also hid beneath their surface a destabilizing interpretation of reality, and created subversive effects in their impact on the public.[62]

In this changing scenario, the public could no longer place criminals within the usual framework of guilt and punishment and began to have mixed feelings concerning those who broke social rules. The same criminals sometimes came across as victims of an archaic system, prone to torture or other violence, garnering the solidarity of a part of the public. Not infrequently, their wrongdoings could even acquire a positive connotation, caught up as they were in their ability to question consolidated social structures and cultural paradigms. In other words, the figures of the criminals—thanks to the mutual influence between novelistic and legal plots—gradually lost their reputation for wickedness, thus becoming controversial, suspended between good and evil. In more extreme cases, people started cultivating solidarity and admiration for their actions, and ended up turning them into heroes.

---

61 Galanti, *Osservazioni intorno a' Romanzi*, pp. LV, and Hunt, *Inventing Human Rights*, p. 31. According to the author, what is relevant is 'the influence of new kinds of experiences, from viewing pictures in public to reading the hugely popular epistolary novels about love and marriage. Such experiences helped spread the practices of autonomy and empathy'.
62 Roscioni, *La badessa di Castro*, pp. 110–112.

CHAPTER 12

The Imperial Crisis in the News, c.1760–1780

News and Newspapers as a Source for Writing Transnational Histories

Joel Herman

The Imperial Crisis that broke apart the first British Empire in the late eighteenth century is best understood as a transnational event. This has become clear as historians, building on Palmer's influential age of revolutions thesis, have begun to uncover connections and reciprocities previously obscured by traditional national historiographies.[1] Along these lines this chapter investigates how 'the news' facilitated these connections.[2] Individuals, communities, and publics in Britain, Ireland, and the American colonies, and eventual republic, were often reading the very same news, but this is something that national histories, by their very parameters, fail to take into account.[3] On the other hand, practitioners of imperial history have focussed primarily on a binary metropolitan-periphery model of empire—something a new school of imperial history has complicated by thinking about multiple peripheries and how colonial and other communities related to one another rather than solely with the metropole. In examining how 'the news' allowed discursive, and in some cases revolutionary currents to travel between communities and reading publics, this chapter contributes to these strands of history by reinserting pieces of the puzzle ignored by historical practices of the past, which

---

1 For the original work, see R. R. Palmer, *The Age of Democratic Revolution: A Political History of Europe and America, 1760–1800* (2 vols., Princeton: Princeton University Press, 1959–64). For more recent works that emphasize, revise, and build on the transnational elements of Palmer's argument, see David Armitage and Sanjay Subrahmanyam, *The Age of Revolutions in Global Context, C. 1760–1840* (New York: Macmillan, 2009); David Armitage, *The Declaration of Independence: A Global History* (Cambridge: Harvard University Press, 2007); Jonathan Israel, *The Expanding Blaze: How the American Revolution Ignited the World, 1775–1848* (Princeton: Princeton University Press, 2017); Janet Polasky, *Revolutions without Borders: The Call to Liberty in the Atlantic World* (New Haven: Yale University Press, 2015).
2 Andrew Pettegree, *The Invention of the News: How the World Came to Know about Itself* (New Haven: Yale University Press, 2014); Brendan Dooley (ed.), *The Dissemination of News and the Emergence of Contemporaneity in Early Modern Europe* (Farnham: Ashgate, 2010).
3 See the Letters of Junius in the *London Chronicle*, 19 September 1769; *Hibernian Chronicle*, 30 October 1769; *New-York Journal*, 11 January 1770. See also Steven Pincus, et al., 'Thinking the Empire Whole', *History Australia*, 16 (2019), pp. 610–37 (pp. 4–7).

took the nation-state to be the primary object of inquiry and as a consequence addressed a transnational crisis in national terms.[4]

In what follows, news reports of Irish, American, and British newspapers from 1760–1780, will be used to access three significant episodes during the imperial crisis. Analysis of these episodes will be multi-layered in the sense that it will not only focus on how events were reported by local newspapers, but also how these local news reports were disseminated more widely. This will reveal the interplay 'the news' allowed between political communities and reading publics. The episodes that will serve as examples, in making a case for the need to reassess certain national versions of the past from another angle, include the furore surrounding the Stamp Act in the North American Colonies in 1765–1766, the issuing of the Declaration of Independence in 1776 by thirteen of those colonies, and the Free Trade Crisis of 1779 in Ireland.[5] These three examples have been chosen as key episodes within an imperial crisis that was to sunder old world from new and suspend Ireland somewhere in-between until the Act of Union in 1801.[6]

The first section of the chapter will outline the importance of investigating political and other news as a transnational force in the British Atlantic. This theory will provide the basis for an argument that will then be demonstrated through case studies using newspapers to access these three episodes. At the same time the reading of newspapers appearing in Ireland, the American colonies, and Britain will help to reveal how this line of inquiry can provide a fuller picture of the transnational nature of events that have to some degree remained trapped in national narratives.

1   The Rise of the Press and Public Spheres

In thinking about the transnational nature of political news in the eighteenth-century British Empire, it might seem odd to turn to one of the key texts on

---

4   Zoë Laidlaw, 'Breaking Britannia's Bounds? Law Settlers and Space in Britain's Imperial Historiography', *The Historical Journal*, 55 (September 2012), pp. 807–830 (pp. 809–17); Kathleen Wilson, *A New Imperial History: Culture, Identity and Modernity in Britain and the Empire, 1660–1840* (Cambridge: Cambridge University Press, 2004), pp. 1–26.
5   For the Stamp Act, see Edmund S. Morgan and Helen M. Morgan, *The Stamp Act Crisis: Prologue to Revolution* (Chapel Hill: UNC Press Books, 1962). For the Declaration of Independence see Armitage, *The Declaration of Independence*. For the Free Trade Crisis, see Vincent Morley, *Irish opinion and the American Revolution, 1760–1783* (Cambridge: Cambridge University Press, 2002).
6   Martyn Powell, *Britain and Ireland in the Eighteenth-Century Crisis of Empire* (London: Palgrave Macmillan, 2002), pp. 231–35.

nationalism, Benedict Anderson's *Imagined Communities: Reflections on the Origins and Spread of Nationalism*.[7] Yet, Anderson's incredibly influential description of the rise of print capitalism, which focussed particularly on the newspaper, came packaged within a larger interpretation of how early modern communities evolved into their modern national forms.[8] Anderson's account simultaneously illuminates aspects of this process and obscures others. In his account, he described the ways in which the periodical form of print facilitated the formation of imagined communities and shared conceptions of identity in representing the world through a medium that could be read by those communities at a similar time on a regular basis.[9] In this way, the press offered a kind of synchronised communal narrative and in its act of continually representing a common, but also constantly changing world, introduced newly imagined and constructed identities, and at the same time reinterpreted old ones allowing them to gain new features, be strengthened, or wither away.

The influence of Anderson's account has been felt in a number of fields, and rightly so, but the sweeping interpretive nature of Anderson's approach resulted in certain complexities being left undefined or neglected.[10] This neglect is understandable, due to the proportions of these changes and the shifts in consciousness and behaviour he set out to describe in a relatively slender book. However, with its analysis of the development of early national movements being focused primarily on former colonies of the Spanish Empire, *Imagined Communities* gives North America more of a sideways glance, while Ireland hardly features at all.[11] This is no criticism as one of the stated goals of the work was to make an argument using more than English language sources and anglo- or euro-centric examples, but it does leave certain questions unanswered.[12]

One such question that is critical to the theoretical argument of this chapter is this: how did the news, and the development of newspapers and a press in the different locations and contexts of the British Empire lead new identities to emerge alongside older local, regional, national, and imperial identities, and

---

7   Benedict Anderson, *Imagined Communities: Reflections on the Origin and Spread of Nationalism* (3rd ed., London and New York: Verso, 2006).
8   Anderson, *Imagined Communities*, pp. 9–36. See also the work that heavily influenced Anderson's account, Tom Nairn, *The Break-Up of Britain: Crisis and Neo-Nationalism* (London: Verso, 1977).
9   Anderson, *Imagined Communities*, pp. 32–36.
10 For the reach and impact of *Imagined Communities*, see John Breuilly, et al., 'Benedict Anderson's Imagined Communities: A Symposium', *Nations and Nationalism*, 22 (2016), pp. 625–659.
11 Anderson, *Imagined Communities*, pp. 47–65.
12 Ibid., p. xiii.

how did these identities overlap or conflict?[13] Prevailing practices of national historiography have led to a situation in which this question has, for the most part, been set aside in favour of other reductionist national interpretations of this process. In the American case this led to a tenuous exercise of searching for the roots or causes of an 'American' Revolution.[14] On the other hand, in Ireland, the pursuit of a national past led to the raising of a patriot pantheon that included eighteenth-century figures who may not have assumed any 'Irish' identity at all.[15] Such reductionist approaches to, and investigations of, national identity and national narratives may result in these identities being read further back into the past than they necessarily appeared or were adopted in reality.[16]

National historiographies that have emerged over time with the development of the nation-state and corresponding inventions of 'national traditions' and a 'national past' have obscured the process by which a shared imperial culture developed in the British Empire in the eighteenth century, one in which Anglo-Irish and Anglo-American settler and colonial populations dominated indigenous and enslaved peoples.[17] This is only made more confusing by the fact that this shared culture was expressed in different ways, by different peoples, in different locations, but nonetheless it is identifiable through a reading of the development of an eighteenth-century press in each context and

---

13 See Benjamin Bankhurst, *Ulster Presbyterianism and the Scots Irish Diaspora* (New York: Springer, 2013), pp. 31–58.

14 John Murrin, *Rethinking America: From Empire to Republic* (Oxford: Oxford University Press, 2018), pp. 187–204. T. H. Breen, 'Ideology and Nationalism on the Eve of the American Revolution: Revisions Once More in Need of Revising', *Journal of American History*, 84 (1997), pp. 13–39. See also David Armitage, 'Greater Britain: A Useful Category of Historical Analysis', *American Historical Review*, 104 (1999), pp. 427–45 (pp. 431–38).

15 R. F. Foster, *Paddy and Mr. Punch: Connections in Irish and English History* (London: Penguin Books, 1993), pp. 1–20. See also Ian McBride, '"The Common Name of Irishmen"': Protestantism and Patriotism in Eighteenth-Century Ireland', in Tony Claydon and Ian McBride (eds.), *Protestantism and National Identity: Britain and Ireland, c.1650–c.1850* (Cambridge: Cambridge University Press, 1998), pp. 236–262.

16 See Nicholas Canny and Anthony Pagden, *Colonial Identity in the Atlantic World, 1500–1800* (Princeton: Princeton University Press, 1987).

17 Jack P. Greene (ed.), *Exclusionary Empire: English Liberty Overseas, 1600–1900* (Cambridge: Cambridge University Press, 2009); S. J. Connolly, 'Varieties of Britishness: Ireland, Scotland and Wales in the Hanoverian State', in Alexander Grant and Keith Stringer (eds.), *Uniting the Kingdom? The Making of British History* (London: Routledge, 1995), pp. 193–207; Thomas Bartlett, '"A People Made Rather for Copies than Originals": The Anglo-Irish, 1760–1800', *The International History Review*, 12 (February 1990), pp. 11–25.

analysis of how this press helped to expand a 'British' or 'Imperial' public sphere outwards from London.[18]

A narrative of the development of this British press in Ireland and the American colonies in the eighteenth century is complicated by the fact that even as much of its content was taken directly from metropolitan sources and newspapers, it was also gradually infused with a distinctiveness derived from a variety of factors including the place in which it was reproduced, the printers doing the reproducing, and also eventually their own producing, as well as the contingency of events.[19] This was the result of ongoing urbanization, as the growth of cities and towns across empire allowed the formation of new political publics and even as these publics engaged with and reproduced a metropolitan print culture they also gradually made up their own.[20]

In reading newspapers printed in Britain, Ireland and the American colonies from the beginning of the eighteenth century, it becomes clear that the expansion of imperial and other information infrastructure is central to this process in that it was through these channels of communication that metropolitan political news and other print culture could find its way into the hands of individuals, communities, and publics across empire.[21] These ever-expanding and connecting structures of information interchange, whether postal systems or less formal arrangements facilitated by trade, enabled those outside of the capital to imagine themselves as participants not only in local and regional political events, but also in debates arising as a direct result of these events at

---

18   For the first and most influential description of the public sphere, see Jurgen Habermas, *The Structural Transformation of the Public Sphere: An Inquiry into a Category of Bourgeois Society* (Cambridge: MIT Press, 1989). However, his and other studies have failed to extend analysis of the public sphere beyond the nation-state despite Britain's expansion into an imperial state in the eighteenth century.

19   For the Irish newspaper, see Robert Munter, *The History of the Irish Newspaper 1685–1760* (Cambridge: Cambridge University Press, 1967). For the late eighteenth century, see Padhraig Higgins, *A Nation of Politicians: Gender, Patriotism, and Political Cultures in Late Eighteenth-Century Ireland* (Madison: University of Wisconsin Press, 2010), pp. 28–55. For newspapers in the American colonies see Joseph M. Adelman, *Revolutionary Networks: The Business and Politics of Printing the News* (Baltimore: John Hopkins University Press, 2019); Charles E. Clark, *The Public Prints: The Newspaper in Anglo-American Culture, 1665–1740* (Oxford: Oxford University Press, 1994).

20   David Dickson, *The First Irish Cities: An Eighteenth-Century Transformation* (New Haven: Yale University Press, 2021); Gary Nash, *The Urban Crucible: Social Change, Political Consciousness, and the Origins of the American Revolution* (Cambridge: Harvard University Press, 1979); Benjamin L. Carp, *Rebels Rising: Cities and the American Revolution* (Oxford: Oxford University Press, 2007).

21   Ian K. Steele, *The English Atlantic 1675–1740: An Exploration of Communication and Community* (Oxford: Oxford University Press, 1986).

the very centre of empire.[22] In the individual's ability to assume both local and imperial political identities through mediums such as the news, it is clear that an imperial public sphere had come into being. This sphere operated alongside, and in certain ways incorporated, other regional and local public spheres that grew in definition with the gradual development of a local press and representative forms of government in each context. Further developments such as the consolidation of postal systems and the introduction of new, and more regular, packet boats increased the flow of news and information and brought the political publics active in Britain, Ireland, and the American colonies closer together in certain ways.[23] This is evident in the way local news reports of public protests taken from provincial newspapers began appearing in metropolitan newspapers with greater frequency in the 1760s, which in turn led the provincial press where these reports originated to reflect metropolitan political comment back again on those publics involved. The clearest example of this novel news phenomenon is the way newspapers in London, Dublin and the American colonies reported the events of the Stamp Act.[24]

2 The Stamp Act, c.1765–1766

The Stamp Act of 1765 was introduced by the British Parliament in order to raise revenue in the American colonies. The revenue that was raised through this new tax was to contribute to an imperial state that had run up a staggering debt in the recently concluded war with France.[25] The Seven Years War ended when terms of peace were agreed with the signing of the Treaty of Paris in 1763, and though the terms of the treaty left Britain as the dominant force in North America, imperial agents still needed to find ways to extract resources and revenue from new and old territories to fund what was increasingly becoming

---

22 One good example of this is non-importation agreements in which men and women participated patriotically. For the Irish context, see Higgins, *Nation of Politicians*, pp. 82–88. For the American context see T. H. Breen, *The Marketplace of Revolution: How Consumer Politics Shaped American Independence* (Oxford: Oxford University Press, 2005).
23 *Pennsylvania Gazette*, 15 September 1763. See also Steele, *The English Atlantic*, pp. 168–188. For the post office see Howard Robinson, *The British Post Office: A History* (Princeton: Princeton University Press, 1948); John, R., *Spreading the News: The American Postal System from Franklin to Morse* (Cambridge: Harvard University Press, 1995).
24 *Boston Gazette*, 10 February 1766; *Boston Gazette*, 17 Feb. 1766.
25 Gautham Rao, *National Duties: Custom Houses and the Making of the American State* (Chicago: University of Chicago Press, 2016), pp. 34–42.

a fiscal-military empire.[26] The new stamp tax was to come in the form of stamped paper that was to be used for all paper goods and as a result, perhaps somewhat unsurprisingly, American newspapers had much to say about it. The introduction of a tax that threatened the livelihood of printers in the American colonies created the circumstances for stiff resistance and something more than events based reporting.[27] This can be seen in the response of the *Pennsylvania Journal* and its famous 'Tombstone Edition', which featured a skull and crossbones on the masthead, an emblem that was copied by other newspapers.[28] However, even more important than the inclusion of such images, and temporary changes in newspaper design, this hostile reaction of American printers, anonymous patriot contributors to newspapers, and the population of the colonies more generally, can be found in the content that was beginning to appear in newspapers in reaction to the tax.[29]

This content was not limited to reports of protests and collective action colonists took against the imposition of stamp duties in 1765 and 1766, but also included much ideologically charged material from American patriots describing the injustice of taxation without consent, or 'taxation without representation', which has become the historical tagline.[30] These news reports and opinion pieces were widely reprinted, and their appearance in Dublin and London newspapers and the corresponding reaction of patriot publics in each place demonstrates the power of the periodical 'news' to connect these publics across space through the reporting of events of political significance, though of course with some delay.[31] However, despite this delay, which in the American case was quite significant, the flow of information was constant which meant a kind of time-lag rather than any major dearth or gap in the arrival of news. This offered greater parts of the population in each location a kind of imagined participation or agency in the reported actions of patriot publics, especially in events of protest or reaction to imperial policy. This development suggests the possibility that the press that had developed in each place had become a kind

---

26 Fred Anderson, *The Crucible of War: The Seven Years War and the Fate of Empire in British North America, 1754–1766* (New York: Knopf Doubleday, 2007). See also Aaron Graham, 'The Colonial Sinews of Imperial Power: The Political Economy of Jamaican Taxation, 1768–1838', *The Journal of Imperial and Commonwealth History*, 45 (2017), pp. 188–209.
27 Adelman, *Revolutionary Networks*, pp. 51–80.
28 *Pennsylvania Journal*, 31 October 1765.
29 *Pennsylvania Gazette*, 5 December 1765; *Pennsylvania Gazette*, 2 January 1766.
30 *New-York Journal*, 30 October 1766.
31 For this delay in the early to mid-eighteenth century see Steele, *The English Atlantic*, p. 158. The delay continued to lessen over the course of the eighteenth century and was commonly under two months by the 1760s. For examples of this fact, see the *New-York Journal*, 24 November 1768; *New-York Journal*, 29 June 1769.

of 'alternate structure of politics' by the mid- to late-1760s; while this alternate structure emerged most prominently in London, it was also at some level coming into being in urban centres and towns across the empire.[32]

In his account, Brewer explained how the Stamp Act allowed ideas of representation to filter back into a London public sphere through arguments articulated by the American Colonists. He claimed that these arguments informed the demands of those groups that strove for parliamentary reform later in the century.[33] But the news and the proliferation of newspapers also allowed for something more immediate—something that becomes clear when reading newspapers appearing in Britain, Ireland, and the American colonies printed within a few days of each other at the time. In exploring the content of these newspapers that were printed simultaneously, the importance of assessing the Stamp Act, as well as other connected events on a transnational level is readily apparent, as one may quickly notice that the medium of the newspaper was perhaps the swiftest route for the flow of political ideas to publics over borders and across the expanse of the Atlantic.

On the 8 February 1766, the *London Evening Post*, a leading opposition paper printed thrice weekly, included news of the situation in New York from the previous December:

> Such are the unhappy times occasioned by the Stamp Act, that scarce any business is carried on. Our port is shut, no vessels cleared out; no law and no money circulating; in short, all traffick and trade seems to be at an end. ... The People of the Province seem to have such an aversion to taking the Stamp Papers, that they will sooner die than take them. What the event will be is really to be dreaded.[34]

Along with this news report of the deteriorating state of affairs in New York, which was joined by similar reports printed in the *London Chronicle*, the newspaper also described events of a political nature occurring in Boston.[35] However, these were given far greater coverage in a patriot newspaper printed that very same day in Dublin.

The front page of the *Freeman's Journal* was dominated by a series of clippings detailing unfolding events in the capital of the Massachusetts Bay Colony.

---

32   John Brewer, *Party Ideology and Popular Politics at the Accession of George III* (Cambridge: Cambridge University Press, 1976), pp. 137–160.
33   Ibid., pp. 201–216.
34   *London Evening Post*, 8 February 1766.
35   *London Chronicle*, 4 February 1766; *London Chronicle*, 6 February 1766.

But the paper did not stop there, also making space for news of political action taken in protest against the Stamp Act in the colonies of Maryland, Virginia, and Connecticut, as well as in the city of Philadelphia.[36] Just two days later a piece of news taken from another Philadelphia newspaper was reprinted in the *New-York Gazette* referencing the opinion of the 'people of Ireland'.[37] The paper, which stressed cooperation rather than dissension on its cover, carried information shared by a 'Captain Ashmead, from Cork, but last from Cove, which place he left the 12th of December'. In the reprinted report featuring in the gazette, the ship's captain informed a New York public 'that the Ministry in England held councils twice every week, on affairs of this continent' and that 'the people of Ireland are highly pleased at the opposition the Stamp Act meets with in America' and 'their general tosts are *Destruction to the American Stamp Act* ...'.[38]

The three perspectives offered here only scratch the surface of the types and kinds of news reports that were printed in reaction to the Stamp Act, but they have been selected with a reason in mind. In offering content printed within a few days of each other but many miles apart we are allowed to see how people in each place viewed the political world and consumed political information and news in similar ways whether they picked up a newspaper in London, Dublin, or New York. Although the news reports and newspapers did not carry the same information nor did they appear at precisely the same time, they are intriguing in the way that they report similar events happening in different locations at different times, and more importantly in the way that they connect these events and describe them in a shared political language. This shared language is representative of the common political culture that had developed through the imperial public sphere in the British Empire by the second half of the eighteenth century. At the same time, it reveals how this political culture had come under pressure due, in some part, to the development of a distinct press in each context, and the ability of the press to criticize, and bring public opinion to bear against, imperial policy. It was a development that contributed to the eventual rupture of the first British Empire, something our next example directly addresses.

---

36   *Freeman's Journal*, 8 February 1766.
37   *New-York Gazette*, 10 February 1766.
38   Ibid.

3   The Declaration of Independence, 1776

If our first episode has gone some way in accessing and demonstrating a common political culture and thinking about the workings of an imperial public sphere, through analysis of transnational news reports describing political events and opinion inspired by the Stamp Act, the appearance and reprinting of the Declaration of Independence may perhaps allow comment on the distribution of news at the time. The declaration was ratified at the Second Continental Congress in Philadelphia on 4 July 1776. Although conflict had already begun in the Colony of Massachusetts Bay in April 1775, it was the signed document that formally stated the colonies' intentions and explained the reasons they were declaring independence from Great Britain.[39] There were in total 27 colonial grievances listed in the declaration and much has been written about what exactly pushed the colonists over the edge. Here, though, we are concerned with how the declaration was disseminated and what the War it started meant for the distribution of the news and the printing of newspapers.[40]

In London, the declaration was reprinted first in the *Public Advertiser* on 16 August 1776 over a month after it had first appeared in the *Pennsylvania Evening Post* on the 6 July.[41] The newspaper included further revolutionary news carried by a ship arriving in Dublin from Virginia as well as reports of the strategy of the provincial and British forces brought with other New York papers by a 'Captain Maher ... arriving at Corke'. In Dublin, the *Freeman's Journal* called the declaration 'the best explanation of the rights of the people, which has been published this age'.[42] While, on the same day, the 24 August, the *Dublin Journal* offered predictions on which side the Native Americans would join in the ongoing conflict.[43]

Just a week earlier on 17 August, the day after the declaration was first printed in London, the *New-York Gazette and Weekly Mercury* recounted the celebrations of the provincial troops at the reading of the declaration at Ticonderoga, NY, claiming 'every Man's countenance was, now we are a People! We have a name among the States of the World'.[44] On the other hand, the *New-York*

---

39   Armitage, *The Declaration of Independence*, pp. 25–36.
40   *The Declaration of Independence*, 4 July 1776.
41   *Public Advertiser*, 16 August 1776; *Pennsylvania Evening Post*, 6 July 1776. For the appearance of the Declaration in London newspapers see Emily Sneff, 'When Independence was Declared' (Unpublished PhD Dissertation, William and Mary, 2023).
42   *Freeman's Journal*, 24 August 1776.
43   *Dublin Journal*, 24 August 1776.
44   *New-York Gazette, and Weekly Mercury*, 17 August 1776.

Journal referenced comments by the Lord Mayor Sawbridge at the common council of London, a constant source of radicalism in the city, in which he moved a resolution asking that 'his Majesty's subjects in America be continued upon the same footing of giving and granting money as his subjects in Ireland are, by their own representatives ...'.[45]

Reports of attempted reconciliation, and other more gloomy assessments, multiplied in the imperial capital, and Dublin. However, newspapers in the American colonies, already reliant on fewer sources, were beginning to see the impact of the onset of conflict on the flow of information. This is demonstrated by the increased overlap of news reports in New York, Boston, and Philadelphia at the time. Some newspapers named the Lord Hyde Packet Boat as their source, such as the *New England Chronicle*, but even when this was not the case, it is easy to identify many of the same reports reprinted verbatim.[46]

These problems with the distribution of news grew during the war years, resulting in an increased delay in certain news appearing in American newspapers. This was particularly true in those areas devastated by the war as a number of printers were forced to flee. In areas occupied by the British, some patriot newspapers were forced to cease printing altogether, while others, like the *Boston Spy* were forced to relocate.[47] In certain cases, royalist newspapers were established in occupied cities. *Rivington's Royal Gazette* was established by James Rivington, a loyalist printer who had originally fled to London but returned when the city was under British rule. In other cases, already established newspapers changed their line and came to occupy a position more favourable to that of the occupying force.[48] Even as war disrupted news, and transformed the information landscape of the colonies, it served as a constant in newspapers in Dublin and London. Newspapers there reported on all aspects of the conflict including details of battles, potential strategy, and much information on the progress of the war and the condition of the forces on each side.[49]

---

45 *New-York Journal*, 15 August 1776.
46 *New England Chronicle*, 22 August 1776; *Continental Journal*, 22 August 1776; *Pennsylvania Journal*, 21 August 1776; *New-York Journal*, 15 August 1776.
47 Adelman, *Revolutionary Networks*, pp. 139–146; Bernard Bailyn and John B. Hench (eds.), *The Press and the American Revolution* (Boston: Northeastern University Press, 1981), pp. 8–10.
48 *Rivington's New-York Loyal Gazette*, 4 October 1777. After only a few issues, Rivington changed the name of his newspaper to *The Royal Gazette*.
49 *London Chronicle*, 17 October 1776; *London Chronicle*, 9 November 1776; *London Chronicle*, 21 December 1776; *Freeman's Journal*, 7 September 1776; *Freeman's Journal*, 12 October 1776; *Freeman's Journal*, 28 November 1776.

Although the consequences of the declaration, and the War of Independence, meant very different things for news coverage, newspapers, printers, and political publics in Ireland, Britain, and the fledgling American Republic, it changed and redirected the flow of news and information into the colonies rather than stopping it completely.[50] This is evident in the many newspapers that continued printing throughout the war period, and in the ability of the printers of these papers to continue to include reports of events such as the Irish Free Trade Crisis of 1779.[51] Newspapers were quick to compare events in Ireland to those of the ongoing American war.[52]

4   The Irish Free Trade Crisis, 1779

If news reports of the Declaration of Independence have allowed comment on the distribution of 'the news', our next episode will enable us to think about how the news can be used to investigate events on a transnational level. The Irish Free Trade Crisis of 1779 has often appeared in Irish historical studies as an event that was mobilized to some degree by certain transnational circumstances within the British Empire such as the American War, but less has been said about the impact of the news on this movement, and even less on the representation of the Free Trade Crisis in the news elsewhere.[53]

An Irish movement for free trade began to grow in April 1779 when several county Grand Juries declared resolutions to boycott British goods. Other counties followed and eventually as many as 15 had joined together in a non-importation agreement.[54] At the same time, another phenomenon was taking hold in that a volunteer militia was rapidly growing in numbers. The Irish Volunteers were first established as a force to protect against possible French invasion, but they quickly turned their attention towards other political objectives.[55] The two movements were to merge over the course of 1779 and at the first sitting of the Irish House of Commons, a group of patriot MPs,

---

50   Adelman, *Revolutionary Networks*, pp. 139–140.
51   *New-York Gazette*, 20 March 1780; *Pennsylvania Journal*, 29 March 1780; *Boston Gazette*, 3 April 1780.
52   *Independent Chronicle*, 16 March 1780.
53   Morley, *Irish Opinion*, pp. 223–37; Higgins, *Nation of Politicians*, pp. 70–81.
54   Maurice R. O'Connell, *Irish Politics and Social Conflict in the Age of the American Revolution* (Philadelphia: University of Pennsylvania Press, 1965), pp. 135–36.
55   James Kelly, '"Disappointing the boundless ambition of France": Irish Protestants and the Fear of Invasion, 1661–1815, *Studia Hibernica*, 37 (2011), pp. 27–105 (pp. 83–91). See also Thomas Bartlett, *The Fall and Rise of the Irish Nation: The Catholic Question 1690–1830* (Dublin: Gill and Macmillan, 1992).

many of whom were serving in the Volunteers, proposed that they raise the issue of Free Trade in their address to the King.[56] The address was given much attention in Irish newspapers, but the event that was to capture even more space in newspapers in Ireland, and elsewhere, was the shift in the Volunteers arena of protest from within parliament to the streets outside. In Dublin, on the 4 November, the Volunteers spurned tradition by turning the annual celebration of the birthday of William III into something more radical and dramatic, a patriotic protest for Free Trade. Only a few weeks later, a further popular protest rocked the Irish House of Commons.[57] A month after these heavily reported protests, the British Parliament and the British Prime Minister Lord North would concede to Irish demands for a 'Free Trade'.[58] The view of the *Dublin Evening Post*, appearing on the 9 December, the same day the concessions were announced in London newspapers, is undeniably transnational: 'Had not these associations taken place, or had not America been humbled to an unconditional submission to Britain, our application for a free trade would probably have been heard, as a sounding brass and tinkling cymbal ...'.[59]

The situation dominated the newspapers of the metropole that month with the *London Evening Post* weighing in on the imperial crisis: 'Let it teach us wisely to grant IRELAND all she asks-a Trade-free as the winds of Heaven ... for once at least, profit from Experience-by letting her seem to receive from, our Justice-what, otherwise, she will force from us by, the Sword'.[60] This obvious reference to the ongoing conflict in the American colonies allows us to reflect on reporting of the Crisis there. The *Independent Chronicle*, a Boston newspaper, reprinted an account of the Volunteer protest first appearing in the *Freeman's Journal* with a few discrepancies.[61] The most notable being the famous signs they placed on each side of the statue of William the III in College Green, the last of which read a 'Free Trade or Else?' was instead rendered as 'A Free Trade: if not-----?'.[62]

The news of the concessions of the British parliament arrived around St Patrick's Day and celebrations and toasts to the Irish were reported in

---

56 Joel Herman, 'Imagined Nations: Newspapers, Identity, and the Free Trade Crisis of 1779', *Eighteenth-Century Ireland*, 35 (2020), pp. 51–69.
57 *Freeman's Journal*, 6 November 1779; *Freeman's Journal*, 16 November 1779.
58 *London Evening Post*, 11 December 1779.
59 *Dublin Evening Post*, 9 December 1779.
60 *London Evening Post*, 11 December 1779; *London Evening Post*, 25 December 1779; *London Evening Post*, 28 December 1779.
61 *Freeman's Journal*, 6 November 1779.
62 *Independent Chronicle*, 16 March 1780.

the *Pennsylvania Journal*, the *New-York Gazette*, and elsewhere in the month of March.[63] The news was also greeted with curiosity and conjecture as to what the Irish response would be with the *Connecticut Courant* claiming on 14 March: 'Under their protection the Commons dare to speak in a language of an independent nation, and voted solemn thanks to the companies of the associated volunteers'.[64] In contrast, the *New-York Gazette* offered far more dire analysis of hopes for an Irish republic in writing of the 'exhausted Hopes of the Republican Politicians'.[65]

The transnational significance of the Irish Free Trade Crisis becomes clear when exploring news reports printed in urban centres across the Atlantic world. Those involved in the crisis were aware of this fact as well as those who watched on from afar. In this way, we can begin to see how a transnational angle may open past events to new perspectives allowing them to be rediscovered and reassessed. When viewed from this angle, the Free Trade Crisis resurfaces as an event of Irish history that ties in other histories including British, Imperial, American and transnational histories. In this process 'the news', and the newspapers in which it took material form, may serve as a prism through which we can access narratives too often hidden from view by layers of national history built up over time.

This chapter has analysed news reports of three significant episodes that occurred during the imperial crisis. In the first, a common political language and culture was identified, which allowed us to think about how the news allowed an imperial public sphere to take shape. In the second, that sphere was fractured as the Continental Congress severed ties with the British Empire when it issued its Declaration of Independence and declared war—a war that would to some degree strangle the flow of information and news. In the third, the Irish Free Trade Crisis allowed us to analyse the transnational nature of news reports and investigate how newspapers distilled information and shaped perspectives of political events and the imperial crisis.

By bringing news of revolutionary and other events to greater numbers of people, and wider publics, in urban entrepots in Ireland and across the British Empire, the newspaper allowed increasing informational exchange, and facilitated the emergence of new identities and new conceptions of the place of the individual and the ethnic, religious, and national community in the world. Questions remain, including how individuals were reading the paper, who was

---

63 *Pennsylvania Journal*, 29 March 1780; *New-York Gazette*, 20 March 1780.
64 *Connecticut Courant*, 14 March 1780.
65 *New-York Gazette*, 20 March 1780; *New-York Gazette*, 27 March 1780.

reading the paper, and indeed who was excluded from the discourse of the news? However, it can clearly be said that the news, and information more generally, was not broken into national parts, but rather passed through webs of sociability, information networks, institutions of empire, and less formal structures of trade and commerce.

PART 3

The Media and the Masses

∴

SECTION 5

The Politics of News

CHAPTER 13

The Wars at Home
Victorian Imperial Sieges and the Conscription of Public Opinion

Brian Wallace

In early December 1857, an indignant Londoner wrote to *The Times* complaining of a new menace on the city's streets. He warned that 'mendacious itinerant newspaper vendors' were peddling old editions of the daily papers in the streets with loud cries falsely claiming that they were breaking news from the war in India—'Melancholy news from India! Defeat of General Havelock at Lucknow!'. The letter-writer himself had not been fooled by such pessimistic fantasies, he hastened to add, but he was deeply concerned by the possible effect of such cries on the health of any delicate ladies awaiting news of loved ones in India.[1] These opportunistic street hawkers were capitalising on an intense public anxiety aroused by the ongoing Indian Rebellion, which centred on the besieged garrison of Lucknow. Sepoy troops across northern India had rebelled against their East India Company officers in early summer, joined in many areas by local nobles and the wider population, and since the end of May the British soldiers and civilians in Lucknow had been beleaguered in a barricaded neighbourhood of the city centred on the British Residency. For months, the home public had been following the plight of this garrison through the uncertain, infrequent despatches which took roughly six weeks to arrive from India. The tenor of public feeling in this period was described in familiar terms by the *Illustrated London News*: 'The accounts from the East by the last mail left us very much in the condition of feeling which the terminations of the monthly pages of the serial works of our best modern novelists leave their readers'.[2]

Following Lucknow and sieges like it through the columns of the daily press was a formative collective experience in shaping attitudes towards imperial warfare for successive Victorian generations. Defences like those of the Indian Rebellion, with far-flung garrisons beleaguered and relief columns struggling to reach them, would become the defining imperial military set-piece for the Victorian home public across the second half of the nineteenth century. This

---

1 *The Times*, 10 December 1857.
2 *Illustrated London News*, 28 November 1857.

chapter will examine the role of the press in reporting on such sieges, in generating a sense of common peril and mission between the home public and the besieged garrisons, and in implicitly or explicitly conscripting public opinion in support of imperial wars. The relationship between nineteenth-century British newspapers and public opinion has been the subject of debate since the period itself, when J. A. Hobson named the press as a 'most potent engine' for promoting imperialist attitudes among the masses during the South African War.[3] The abolition of the 'taxes on knowledge' across the 1850s had led to a publishing boom in more affordable newspapers. In the same period, the Crimean War and the pioneering war correspondence of figures like William Howard Russell revealed a keen appetite among this new reading public for journalism which vividly brought home to them the experiences of modern warfare, and which allowed them to participate vicariously through the medium of letters and subscription funds.[4] This new sense of enthusiastic involvement was satirised in a famous *Punch* cartoon, which saw an excited Victorian father wielding a poker like a sabre as he read the newspaper report of the charge of the Light Brigade out to his family.[5] Coinciding with a period of widening franchise and education reforms which vastly increased the size of the reading public, the power of the press was alternately feared and celebrated by commentators across the political spectrum for its potential influence over new voters. To what extent were these anticipations rooted in reality? Modern efforts to recover past public opinion from newspaper evidence have been dogged by doubts and debate over their representativeness or sensationalism.[6] The issue has been put neatly by James Thompson: did nineteenth-century newspapers mirror or mould the opinions of their readers?[7] It is a question which intersects with another long-running debate in imperial cultural history over the level of enthusiasm and awareness surrounding imperial issues among the metropolitan British public.

The contemporary press discourses around imperial sieges can help us to shed light on these related issues. With its life-or-death stakes, the siege's spectacle of outnumbered Britons surrounded by enemies was inherently dramatic for contemporaries, and it became an increasingly common story in an expanding but frequently undermanned empire. These defences made

---

3   J. A. Hobson, *Imperialism: A Study* (London: James Nisbet & Co., 1902), p. 228.
4   See Stefanie Markovits, 'Rushing into Print: "Participatory Journalism" during the Crimean War', *Victorian Studies*, 50 (Summer 2008), pp. 560–2.
5   John Leech, 'Enthusiasm of Paterfamilias', *Punch*, 25 November 1854.
6   See Richard Price, *An Imperial War and the British Working Class* (London: Routledge and Kegan Paul 1972), p. 140.
7   James Thompson, *British Political Culture and the Idea of 'Public Opinion', 1867–1914* (Cambridge: Cambridge University Press, 2013).

for excellent copy in contemporary journalism. Unlike the general run of imperial warfare in which battles were reported after the fact, they were often months-long events, encouraging a sense of ongoing emotional engagement. This engagement in turn short-circuited any debate on the propriety of imperial policy—immediate sympathy, support, and relief were the only acceptable responses within the shared cultural common sense expressed in the press through its coverage, editorial declarations, and letters pages. One key factor in the moulding of this common sense was the fact that such siege stories held special resonances for an island nation with a traditionally insular, defensive self-image. Besieged garrisons were repeatedly represented as microcosms of their island homeland, islands of British virtue which must be defended as resolutely as Britain itself. By conflating home and imperial defence, the press discourses around sieges helped to justify and popularise imperial conflicts which could often be controversial.

This chapter will focus on three episodes in which this mythic image of the colonial siege was generated, propagated, and interrogated in the contemporary press. In 1857, the initially critical metropolitan response to the Indian Rebellion was shifted decisively by the long-running spectacle of besieged British garrisons falling to rebels or enduring against their attacks. The mission of General Charles Gordon to Khartoum in 1884–5 became a media battleground in which the support of 'public opinion' for sending a relief force to save him was whipped up by his press advocates using Gordon's dispatches from the besieged city. Finally, the South African War witnessed a profound rupture between the expectations of war correspondents who found themselves in besieged towns and the squalid realities which they attempted to express in correspondence and in locally-printed 'siege newspapers'. The story of these sieges and their receptions on the home front is entangled with the development of the nineteenth-century British press, from the birth of war correspondence in the Crimea, to the campaigning journalism of figures like W. T. Stead, and the emergence of populist mass-market newspapers like the *Daily Mail* in the 1890s. Tracing the impact and reception of imperial sieges through the press can help us to address the question of newspapers as mirrors or moulders of public opinion, and can help us to understand how popular metropolitan imperialism could often be expressed not as a strict creed, but as a reflex touched off by external events.

1 Details and the Myth: Reporting on the Indian Rebellion Sieges

In John Ritchie's 1858 crowd painting 'A Summer Day in Hyde Park', something of a shadow is cast on the bright scene by the leftmost figure, a gentleman with

FIGURE 13.1 John Ritchie, 'A Summer Day in Hyde Park' (detail) (oil on canvas, 1858), Museum of London Collections, MOL 5636
© MUSEUM OF LONDON / BRIDGEMAN IMAGES

his back turned to the scenes of holiday gaiety as he intently peruses a newspaper report on the Indian Rebellion (Figure 13.1). Following the news from India through the columns of the daily press formed a resonant generational memory for contemporaries, with the ongoing perils of besieged Indian garrisons represented as being unavoidably present even amid the leisurely scenes of the imperial capital.[8] With news taking up to six weeks to reach Britain, *The Times* was the only paper to maintain Indian correspondents prior to 1857, and formed the wellspring from which early reports and opinions were diffused throughout the British press.[9] Attempting to decipher news from India could present a bewildering picture. Brief, often cryptic telegraphic news summaries were printed alongside full reports which took longer to arrive, as well as official dispatches, general orders, personal correspondence, and editorial speculation. In early summer the serious extent of the Rebellion was yet to emerge clearly from this confusion, and much of the coverage had a critical tone. Few outlets went quite as far as the radical *Reynolds's Newspaper*, which declared the sepoys to be fighting in a righteous national struggle like the Poles

---

8 John Ritchie, 'A Summer Day in Hyde Park' (oil on canvas, 1858), Museum of London Collections.

9 Chandrika Kaul, *Reporting the Raj: The British Press and India, c. 1880–1922* (Manchester: Manchester University Press, 2003), p. 59.

or Italians, but there was widespread criticism directed against the greedy, inept East India Company. The 'mal-administration and incapacity' of the Company's government was blamed for provoking a crisis which had imperilled Britain's international standing and would now need to be quashed at the taxpayers' expense.[10]

Towards the end of August, however, the tone of this coverage changed rapidly due to successive stories about besieged British garrisons which revealed the life-or-death stakes of such conflicts and generated intense public sympathy. All the dispatches received from the Ganges river military station of Cawnpore (now Kanpur) had been mildly positive, with the commander declaring his confidence that the garrison could hold out until the rebels tired of assaulting them. Late on 21 August, however, *The Times* received a 'meagre and confused' telegraphic message reporting 'the taking of Cawnpore by the rebels and the massacre of the Europeans there'.[11] A week of uncertainty and speculation followed before, on 28 August, *The Times* confirmed: 'The garrison, pressed by famine, surrendered the place to Nana Sahib, by whom, in violation of his solemn promises, all were massacred'. A letter from Bombay the following day heightened the horror by relaying the rumour that Cawnpore's women had been sold to rebels in the bazaar, while further fabricated atrocity stories would circulate of children tortured in front of their parents, and women stripped naked and crucified.[12]

Throughout September, the publication of accounts of the massacre's aftermath kept public anger at a high pitch.[13] Nana Sahib became the arch-villain of the conflict, damned in countless editorials and burned in effigy on Guy Fawkes Night.[14] Newspaper letters pages formed a key site in which this vengeful mood could be shared—in the *Liverpool Mercury* one reader suggested that, once caught and executed, Nana's body should be put on display 'in the British Museum, or in the Tower, or in the Crystal Palace'.[15] In his correspondence, Thomas Macaulay expressed concerns about the brutalising effects of this new vengeful consensus. Even the radical anti-war Liberal

---

10 *Bury and Norwich Post*, 8 September 1857. See Heather Streets, *Martial Races: The Military, Race and Masculinity in British Imperial Culture, 1857–1914* (Manchester: Manchester University Press, 2004), p. 38; Salahuddin Malik, *1857: War of Independence or clash of civilizations? British public reactions* (Oxford: Oxford University Press, 2008).
11 *The Times*, 22 August 1857.
12 *The Times*, 28 & 29 August 1857, 27 November 1857.
13 *The Times*, 19 September 1857.
14 Brian Wallace, 'Nana Sahib in British Culture and Memory', *Historical Journal*, 58/2 (June 2015), pp. 589–613.
15 *Liverpool Mercury*, 28 October 1857.

John Bright was calling for 'vigorous suppression', he noted, while newspaper accounts of sepoys being blown from cannons had been 'read with delight by people who three weeks ago were against all capital punishment'.[16] It was a bloodthirsty mood which would become uncomfortable to recall for later generations. Researching 1857 for her novels decades later, Flora Annie Steel found herself shocked by the vitriol which she discovered: 'Nothing is more remarkable, nothing more sad, than to look through the newspapers of that time and note the bloodthirsty tone of the letters to the editor, especially those of many Christian clergymen'.[17]

The hopes, fears, and speculation of a fast-moving public discourse with column inches to fill helped to shape the memory of the conflict long before the facts could be determined. In early September, an extract from a letter appeared in *The Times* telling how Jhansi Fort had been overrun by rebels in June, forcing the British superintendent Captain Alexander Skene to barricade himself in a small tower with his wife Margaret. With ladders being brought against the tower, the letter tersely concluded, 'Skene then saw it was of no use going on any more; so he kissed his wife, shot her, and then himself'.[18] Appearing shortly after the news of Cawnpore, this report of a miniature siege with its tragic-heroic denouement was seized upon by the press, being reprinted and commented upon over several weeks. The *Glasgow Herald* offered its judgement with the story's headline, 'Roman Heroism and Devotion', while in the *Hull Packet*, similarly, the tale was presented as evidence that 'truly, the heroic age is not past'.[19] Not all were convinced, of course. In a private letter, the Conservative MP Benjamin Disraeli expressed cynicism about the story, speculating about the extent to which it had 'stimulated subscriptions, as it certainly has the warlike passions of the people'. 'The details of all these stories is suspicious', he added. 'Details are a feature of the Myth ... Who can have seen these things? Who heard them?'.[20]

Disraeli's doubts were understandable; the Rebellion inspired an outpouring of journalism in which the lack of more reliable correspondence, the remoteness and exoticism of the locale, and the high sales guaranteed by such

---

16 Thomas Babington Macaulay, G.O. Trevelyan (ed.), *The Life and Letters of Lord Macaulay* (2 vols., London, Harper & Bros, 1876), v. II, p. 434.
17 Flora Annie Steel, *The Garden of Fidelity: Being the autobiography of Flora Annie Steel, 1847–1929* (London: Macmillan & Co., 1929), p. 15.
18 *The Times*, 2 September 1857.
19 *Glasgow Herald*, 7 September. *Hull Packet*, 4 September 1857.
20 Letter to Lady Londonderry, Hughenden, 16 September 1875, Benjamin Disraeli, M.G. Wiebe, Mary S. Millar, Anne P. Robson, Ellen Hawman (eds.), *Benjamin Disraeli: Letters* (9 vols., Toronto: University of Toronto Press, 1982–), v. 7, p. 68.

lurid tales, saw many stories of dubious provenance reported as fact in the metropolitan press.[21] This first draft of history could prove enduring. Barely a week after the original report, a more accurate account had arrived revealing that Skene and his companions had actually been killed after an attempt at a surrender.[22] This less satisfying account never truly supplanted the earlier report in the public memory, however. In his contemporary 'Mutiny' chronicle pieced together from journalism, letters, and official reports, Charles Ball simply included both versions of the fall of Jhansi while noting that the original letter 'varie[d] in some important particulars' from other accounts.[23] A similar dynamic would be seen in the dramatic story of Jessie Brown, a Scottish woman who had purportedly been the first to hear the bagpipes of Havelock's Highlanders approaching to relieve Lucknow. To an even greater extent than the Skenes, Jessie became what Projit Bihari Mukharji has dubbed a 'commoditized legend', inspiring theatre, poetry, art, and fiction, despite the swift debunking of the story.[24] In his 1859 exposé of the false stories which had proliferated during the Rebellion, the journalist Edward Leckey despaired at how many had already been fixed in the public memory by a sensation-hungry media. Many people would 'refuse to disbelieve a story which they have once seen in print', he wrote, with the difficulties of convincing them increased a hundredfold if this story had been accompanied by a picture.[25]

The 'never-to-be-forgotten horrors' of the past weeks had induced a national unity and 'craving for useful activity' surpassing even the Crimean War, according to the *Manchester Guardian*, and this impulse manifested itself in the organisation of local relief funds and in an army recruitment drive.[26] They had also led to an intense public anxiety over the status of the Lucknow garrison. Civilian militias were vital in the defence, and the stories of clerks, merchants, and schoolboys manning the barricades while ladies took on nursing duties made Lucknow an especially relatable site of imperial warfare for the home public. One *Times* editorial identified a general mood of popular volunteer

---

21 See Rebecca Merritt, 'Public Perceptions of 1857: An overview of British press responses to the Indian Uprising', in Crispin Bates and Andrea Major (eds.), *Mutiny at the Margins vol 2: Britain and the Indian Uprising* (London: Sage, 2013).
22 *The Times*, 11 September 1857.
23 Charles Ball, *The History of the Indian Mutiny* (2 vols., London: The London Printing and Publishing Company, 1858), v. 1, p. 274. See Christopher Herbert, *War of No Pity: The Indian Mutiny and Victorian Trauma* (Princeton: Princeton University Press, 2008), p. 150.
24 Projit Bihari Mukharji, 'Jessie's Dream at Lucknow: Popular Memorializations of Dissent, Ambiguity and Class in the Heart of Empire', *Studies in History*, 24/1 (2008), pp. 77–113.
25 Edward Leckey, *Fictions Connected With the Indian Outbreak of 1857 Exposed* (Bombay: Chesson & Woodhall, 1859), p. 137.
26 *Manchester Guardian*, 21 September 1857.

militarism: 'we should all like a little fighting, and we long to be there, and fancy to ourselves how we should do it ...'.[27] Lucknow's commander Henry Lawrence was a civilian administrator rather than a soldier and became one of the earliest victims of the siege, issuing the final order of 'no surrender' before succumbing to mortal wounds. Contradictory reports only added to the tension—on one occasion, despatches from two ships which had arrived at Suez within a day of each other were published in adjoining columns, and respectively declared the garrison to be safe, or running desperately low on provisions.[28] Filling this void of uncertainty, each Indian mail was closely perused for details of the halting advances of General Henry Havelock's relief force, which were reported with all the drama, detail, and analysis of a race meeting.[29] Finally, on 11 November, news arrived of Havelock's 25 September arrival at the garrison 'just as it was mined, and ready to be blown up by its besiegers', appearing in evening editions as well as being telegraphed across the country and pasted up in the windows of newspaper offices for the edification of the crowds awaiting the latest despatches, among whom 'the greatest enthusiasm prevailed'.[30] Accounts of the celebrations which greeted the news became news stories in themselves, reinforcing the consensus that this was a truly national occasion. *The Times* declared that the existential threat of colonial warfare, and the traditional national virtues opposed to it—'endurance, intrepidity, and determination'—made the Rebellion and its sieges a conflict in which Britons across the class and political spectrum could enthusiastically participate.[31] The siege was elevated in this patriotic discourse to an explicit test of national character, with the garrison as a microcosm of the frequently-embattled island nation.

Havelock had only succeeded in reinforcing the garrison, however, with insufficient numbers to break out of the rebel encirclement—the final relief would be left to the force now advancing under Sir Colin Campbell. In the six-week 'blockade' period which followed, the conflation of home and imperial defence was elaborated upon in *The Times*, which declared that Britons had not felt such an atmosphere of immediate danger since the invasion scares of the Napoleonic Wars.[32] The long suspense was ended on 23 December when a telegram arrived detailing Campbell's fight through the city and relief of the Residency.[33] To hear the press tell it, this was a feat by which he had saved not

---

27 *The Times*, 3 October 1857.
28 *The Times*, 29 September 1857.
29 *Homeward Mail*, 1 October 1857.
30 *Morning Post*, 11 November 1857; *Lancaster Gazette*, 14 November 1857.
31 *The Times*, 13 November 1857.
32 *The Times*, 12 December 1857.
33 *Liverpool Mercury*, 23 December 1857.

only the garrison, but Christmas itself. '"Thank GOD for that", is the word that will ring from end to end of England,' the *Daily News* declared. 'The spectre is chased from our Christmas revelries'.[34] One correspondent offered a vivid description of the celebratory mood in London:

> The joy manifested on Wednesday, as the relief of Lucknow circulated along the streets, in the clubs, divans, and all places whither Londoners resort, was intense. It beamed on every countenance ... In the Courts of Justice—in all places where meetings were being held—the proceedings were interrupted, and the telegram read.[35]

The ferment of national unity stirred up by Lucknow even overcame political antagonisms, however briefly. The radical *Reynolds's Newspaper*, which had regularly proclaimed the 'right and justice' of the rebel cause, was compelled to profess a 'profound satisfaction at the rescue of the helpless, innocent, and unoffending women and children'.[36] This ambivalence may reflect what Thompson identified as the limitations which were seen as being placed upon newspapers' abilities to 'mould' opinion; ultimately, they needed to remain in proximity to the views of their readers rather than strike out upon a radically different course.[37] The civilian element of Lucknow had combined with its protracted, anxiety-inducing length and the identification of the garrison as a microcosm of Britain to render the siege an event apparently elevated beyond the rout of partisan debate. The beginning of the conflict had been marked by divisions and recriminations, but following the twin sieges of Cawnpore and Lucknow through the columns of the daily press had helped to foster a popular vision of imperial sieges as sites of national unity across political, class, and national boundaries. It was a vision which would be repeatedly revived across the coming decades.

2 'We Are a Wonderful People': General Gordon and the Battle for Public Opinion

The most popular Victorian images of General Charles Gordon almost invariably presented him as an isolated figure, set apart from others by his sense of duty and heroic willingness to expose himself to danger. These images

---

34 *Daily News*, 24 December 1857.
35 *Hampshire Advertiser*, 26 December 1857.
36 *Reynolds's Newspaper*, 27 December 1857.
37 Thompson, *Public Opinion*, p. 96.

encompassed episodes from his early career commanding Chinese troops or battling slavers in the Sudan, but were most famously drawn from his final days defending the Sudanese capital Khartoum from Mahdist rebels and waiting in vain for a British relief force to arrive. One early hagiographer was Winston Churchill, who gave a vivid expression to this narrative in *The River War*: 'From the flat roof of his palace his telescope commanded a view of the forts and lines. Here he would spend the greater part of each day, scrutinizing the defences and the surrounding country with his powerful glass'.[38] The most iconic example, however, was the widely-circulated account of his death when the city fell on 26 January 1885, with Gordon said to have confronted the attackers before being cut down.[39] George William Joy's painting of this lonely martyrdom was a fixture in British schoolrooms for generations, and for contemporaries as well as imperial nostalgists inspired by these images, Gordon was always imagined as having been alone at Khartoum.[40] This unworldly image can obscure the fact that Gordon was also an adroit media figure who proved surprisingly adept at self-promotion and speculated repeatedly in his siege journals on the degree to which his newspaper allies could sway public opinion in his favour. Historical as well as moral imperatives were presented as arguments for sending a relief force to save Khartoum, as Gordon and his allies weaponised the siege narratives which emerged from 1857 in order to mobilise public opinion and direct pressure on the government. This section will trace how this battle for public opinion was played out from the journals kept by Gordon in Khartoum and intended for public consumption, to the journalism which championed his cause back in Britain.

Gordon's part in the crisis had been something of a media campaign from the outset. When the religious revolt led by Muhammad Ahmed, the Mahdi, rendered the Sudan impossible to hold for the impoverished Cairo government, Gladstone's government demanded that Egypt withdraw its garrisons. A faction within the War Office was opposed to this retreat, viewing Gladstone as soft on imperial commitments after the unpopular concessions to the South African Boer states in 1882. These concerns were shared by the Liberal Imperialist fixer Reginald Brett, later Viscount Esher, who had made a practice of exerting covert pressure on the government through press campaigns, and who was an old

---

38 Winston Spencer Churchill, *The River War: An historical account of the reconquest of the Sudan* (2 vols., London: Longmans, Green & Co., 1899), v. I, pp. 87–8.

39 See Douglas H. Johnson, 'The Death of Gordon: A Victorian myth', *Journal of Imperial and Commonwealth History* 10/3 (1982), pp. 285–310.

40 A.N. Wilson, *The Victorians* (London: Hutchinson, 2002), pp. 470–1.

acquaintance of Gordon.[41] His chief ally was W. T. Stead, the crusading editor of the *Pall Mall Gazette* whose recent journalism on urban slums had helped to raise a public outcry on the subject.[42] Brett presented the Sudan crisis to Stead as a new moral crusade, along with a ready-made hero in the form of the famous officer 'Chinese' Gordon.[43] This expertise was highlighted in a format new to British journalism—an in-depth interview with Gordon published in the *Pall Mall Gazette* on 9 January 1884, in which Gordon offered his opinion on what should be done to retrieve the situation. This implicit appeal to Gordon as the solution was made explicit in the editorial which accompanied the article, demanding 'Chinese Gordon for the Sudan'.[44] The cry was taken up throughout the press, and within a few weeks, the Gladstone government had bowed to this pressure, sending Gordon out with vague orders to supervise the evacuation. With his long career of commanding native troops alongside a reputation as a devout Christian warrior, Gordon was an easy hero to promote in the press as the right man for this job. However, he was also eccentrically religious, fatalistic, and impulsive—as it turned out, a poor choice to enact the evacuation policy which he would later derisively term 'the skedaddle programme'.[45] Shortly after arriving in Khartoum in February 1884, he decided that his orders required him not only to evacuate the Sudan, but to leave behind a stable successor regime—a task which would require sending in British troops to defeat the Mahdi. Gladstone was appalled and refused to send relief, while Gordon refused to leave Khartoum without it, insisting that he would rather die than leave his post.

The public agitation which mounted over the following months included heated debates in Parliament, mass indignation meetings, and even the brief existence of a subscription fund intended to hire a private army.[46] The government line on Gordon was that he should simply be arranging to evacuate the garrisons before taking a steamer back up the Nile to safety, rather than striking Christ-like poses on the battlements of Khartoum. Briefing against him in the Commons lobby, one anonymous Liberal MP was reported as declaring it

---

41   See J.O. Baylen, 'Politics and the "New Journalism": Lord Esher's Use of the *Pall Mall Gazette*', *Victorian Periodicals Review*, 20/4 (Winter 1987), pp. 126–141.
42   Anthony S. Wohl, 'The Bitter Cry of Outcast London', *International Review of Social History*, 13 (August 1968), pp. 209–11.
43   Baylen, 'Politics', p. 127.
44   *Pall Mall Gazette*, 9 January 1884.
45   Charles George Gordon & A. Egmont Hake (eds.), *The Journals of Major-Gen. C.G. Gordon, C.B., at Kartoum: Printed from the original MSS* (London:,Kegan, Paul, Trench & Co. 1885), 3 October 1884, p. 138.
46   *York Herald*, 20 May 1884; *Reynolds's Newspaper*, 18 May 1884.

'absurd' for one man 'with nothing but a walking stick and a change of linen ... to fancy that his hazy fanaticism could settle one of the biggest problems in Eastern history'.[47] This dismissive judgment of Gordon as a fanatical loner missed the degree to which his presence in Khartoum was achieving precisely what he and his imperialist allies had set out to do: generating a public outcry in favour of retaining the Sudan through emotive appeals in the press which invoked the siege narratives familiar since 1857. One of Gordon's first acts on reaching Khartoum was befriending and bedazzling the *Times* correspondent Frank Power, and Gladstone despaired at his 'too free communications' with journalists.[48] Even as he bombarded British officials with demands for relief against the encroaching Mahdist forces, Gordon was also calculating precisely when his letters ought to reach the London papers. One such letter warned that the government risked 'indelible disgrace' if it failed to send relief. In his revisionist account, Lytton Strachey offered what he claimed was an eyewitness account of the moment that this barb reached Gladstone:

> 'He took up the paper, his eye instantly fell on the telegram, and he read it through. As he read, his face hardened and whitened, the eyes burned as I have seen them once or twice in the House of Commons when he was angered—burned with a deep fire ...'.[49]

With messages such as these, Gordon was bypassing his nominal superiors in order to make direct appeals to British public opinion through the medium of the press. His posthumously-published journals made clear that this was a deliberate strategy, with his eclectic musings including repeated populist appeals to the character of the British people. On 13 October, he wrote: 'We are a wonderful people; it was never our Government which made us a great nation ...'. The entry was accompanied by a cartoon in which Gordon imagined how this national virtue would be channelled, sketching a protesting Gladstone being pushed reluctantly towards the Sudan by figures representing the 'British Public Press' (or 'Pressure'?)—the *Daily News*, *Times*, *Standard*, and *Pall Mall Gazette* (Figure 13.2).[50]

He was not alone in his belief that public pressure would demand a relief force—as early as April 1884, General Garnet Wolseley had warned the

---

47 *Sheffield & Rotherham Independent*, 10 May 1884.
48 Edward Berenson, *Heroes of Empire: Five charismatic men and the conquest of Africa* (Berkeley: University of California Press, 2011), p. 107.
49 Lytton Strachey, *Eminent Victorians* (London: Chatto & Windus, 1918), p. 268.
50 Gordon, *Journals*, 13 October 1884, pp. 191–2.

FIGURE 13.2   Charles Gordon, *Journals*, 13 October 1884, p. 191

government in a private letter: 'The English people will force you to do this, whether you like it or not'.[51] Both Gordon himself and the metropolitan newspapers advocating on his behalf repeatedly invoked the consensus siege narratives of 1857 as precedents for the supposed unity of public opinion regarding the siege of Khartoum. During the agitation for relief, the *Leeds Mercury* declared the nation's emotional investment in Gordon unsurpassed 'since the days when Havelock was making his immortal march upon Cawnpore and Lucknow'.[52] The *Pall Mall Gazette* greeted one of the rare Khartoum telegrams with an extended discussion of Lucknow, a comparison also made independently over the following days in the *Birmingham Daily Post* and the *Leicester Chronicle*.[53] The latter described the siege explicitly as 'An Egyptian Lucknow', with Gordon as its composite 'Lawrence-Havelock'.[54] Perhaps most famously, Gordon concluded his final letter to his sister with a postscript invoking the epitaph of Lawrence: 'I am quite happy, thank God, & like Lawrence, I have "*tried* to do my duty"'.[55]

When Gladstone finally conceded and a relief column was dispatched up the Nile, it was accompanied by swarms of special correspondents and war artists feeding the public appetite for a new relief of Lucknow. But unlike Lucknow, this relief column arrived too late, and when rumours of the fall of Khartoum and the death of Gordon began to reach Britain around 5 February 1885, they

---

51   Charles Chenevix Trench, *The Road to Khartoum: A life of General Charles Gordon* (New York: W. W. Norton, 1978), p. 250.
52   *Leeds Mercury*, 21 April 1884.
53   *Pall Mall Gazette*, 29 September 1884.
54   *Birmingham Daily Post*, 30 September 1884. *Leicester Chronicle*, 11 October 1884.
55   Charles Gordon, *Letters of General C.G. Gordon to his sister* (London: Macmillan & Co., 1888), p. 290.

prompted intense shock and anger. As in 1857, the failed defence was described by commentators as an occasion of national unity across classes. One London correspondent noted that the agitated crowds gathered around the newspaper placards included many of 'the class of persons who on ordinary occasions would not have concerned themselves with public news, more especially in foreign parts'.[56] In the *Pall Mall Gazette*, Gordon's martyrdom was offered as evidence that, despite official 'short-sighted selfishness', the spirit of Arthur, Alfred, and Cromwell still animated the British race.[57] This traditional, purportedly apolitical vision of Gordon's heroism encouraged some Conservatives to use Khartoum as a vehicle through which to encourage more partisan and imperialist attitudes in the masses. In his introduction to Gordon's *Journals*, their editor A. Egmont Hake declared his hope that they would 'be read eagerly by the working classes'.[58] As Fergus Nicoll has traced, Hake was himself a Conservative activist, and lost no opportunity to damn the Gladstone government in pungent footnotes. On a nationwide lecture tour after the publication, he condemned the Liberals even as he stressed Gordon's nonpartisan credentials as a man motivated by 'English interests, English honour, and English reputation (cheers)'.[59]

In all of this, it is possible to discern the hope that Khartoum could prove an imperialist education for a working-class population which might win them away from Gladstone's creed of foreign non-intervention. The national unity narrative typical of imperial sieges was here sharpened into a partisan weapon, and the patriotic audiences and readers who imagined themselves standing next to Gordon on the palace roof in Khartoum were encouraged to see not just the Mahdi through their telescope, but the detested Gladstone and his 'Anti-National' followers. A past master of electioneering, Gladstone had himself written extensively on the role of public opinion as expressed and guided from the platform. Now, it appeared, the press was increasingly contesting this role, or asserting the latent power it had always possessed as the medium through which the words of the platform reached beyond their immediate audience.[60] In any case, the statesman knew his public too well to protest fruitlessly against Gordon's canonisation. Writing to a former colleague in 1890, Gladstone conceded that Gordon had been 'a hero, and a hero of heroes', only adding that it was 'unfortunate that he should claim the hero's privilege

56 *Berrow's Worcester Journal*, 14 February 1885.
57 *Pall Mall Gazette*, 11 February 1885.
58 Hake, 'Introduction', *Journals*, xxxii.
59 Fergus Nicoll, '"Truest History, Struck Off at White Heat": The Politics of Editing Gordon's Khartoum Journals', *Journal of Imperial and Commonwealth History*, 38 (2001), p. 37.
60 Thompson, *Public Opinion*, pp. 59–60, p. 87.

by turning upside down and inside out every idea and intention with which he had left England'. As for himself, he must continue to 'suffer in silence' where Khartoum was concerned.[61]

3   'Veiled Hints and Growlings Cannot be Permitted': Newspapers under Siege in South Africa

If Gordon's desperate letters from Khartoum had been intended to arouse the conscience of the nation, a striking contrast was offered by the most famous dispatch to emerge from the besieged South African village of Mafeking during its seven-month siege in 1899–1900: 'October 21st. All well. Four hours' bombardment. One dog killed'.[62]

The colonial siege had taken its place among the defining narratives of British imperialism by the end of the century, and reached something of an apotheosis in the defences of the South African War. In the war against the Boers, the beleaguered towns of Ladysmith, Kimberley, and Mafeking stood as reassuring bulwarks amid the upsets of the early conflict—familiar, traditional stories of Britons behaving well under siege. As a distillation of this gratifying narrative, the exaggeratedly laconic telegram from Mafeking became a sensation in the home press, reprinted, celebrated, and inspiring editorials and topical poetry. It also helped to establish the metropolitan celebrity of its author, Colonel Robert Baden-Powell, who, amid a troubling wider picture of reverses and official incompetence, offered a cheerful and optimistic account of events which resonated with a grateful reading public. Baden-Powell's tone may have differed significantly from Gordon's but, like the defender of Khartoum before him, his outsized character and long endurance made him a popular figure even among many who opposed the controversial war in which he was playing a leading part. One writer recalled: 'When men opened their newspapers in the railway carriage it was with the remark, "How's old B.-P. getting along?"'.[63]

These commuters were more than likely to have been skimming over daily newspapers representing what the cultural critic Matthew Arnold had in 1887 christened the 'New Journalism'. It was a form pioneered in Stead's *Pall Mall Gazette* which was more vivid, novel, and adventurous in its presentation

---

61   John Morley, *The Life of William Ewart Gladstone* (2 vols., London: Macmillan Co., 1903), v. III, pp. 168–9.
62   *Daily Mail*, 30 October 1899.
63   Harold Begbie, *The Story of Baden-Powell* (London: Grant Richards, 1900), p. 195. See also Robert H. MacDonald, *Sons of the Empire: The Frontier and the Boy Scout Movement, 1890–1918* (Toronto: University of Toronto Press, 1993), pp. 101–3.

than the old established broadsheets—but also more 'feather-brained', Arnold lamented, guided by emotion and prone to false statements and opinionated wishful thinking.[64] Historians have disputed the usefulness of this definition born from elite distaste for popular mass media, while generally acknowledging that the term does necessary work in delineating the recognisably modern newspaper market which had emerged across the 1880s and 1890s as the culmination of economic and social forces which had been building since the 'taxes on knowledge' were repealed in the 1850s.[65] Alfred Harmsworth's new *Daily Mail* had found great success in bellicose jingoism, celebrating the small wars of empire and their soldier-celebrities like the 'Avenger of Gordon' Lord Kitchener, a formula which was attracting almost a million readers by 1900.[66]

With the Uitlander crisis deepening in South Africa across 1899, British newspapers dispatched boatloads of correspondents, war artists, and photographers to the likely theatre of war. Many deliberately headed for the garrisons bordering Boer territory which were expected to come under siege, anticipating a frontline view of the next Lucknow.[67] The *Morning Post* correspondent Winston Churchill was captured by the Boers while hurrying towards Ladysmith, but each of the garrisons ended up with such a healthy complement of correspondents that locally-printed siege newspapers were established to make use of their talents when Boer forces crossed the border in October 1899 and encircled the towns.[68] The *Ladysmith Bombshell*, *Ladysmith Lyre*, and *Mafeking Mail* were intended as public services through which the journalists would keep spirits up and convey updates from the military authorities.[69] However, as the sieges dragged on without the anticipated swift relief, the siege newspapers of both towns also became sites of tension and censorship in which Lucknow-inspired visions of besieged social cohesion came into conflict with the squalid and dispiriting reality.

Competition between rival correspondents combined with official censorship and the difficulties of comprehending long-range modern warfare led to a

---

64   Matthew Arnold, 'Up to Easter', *Nineteenth Century* (May 1887), pp. 638–9.
65   See Mark Hampton, 'Review: Rethinking the "New Journalism," 1850s–1930s', *Journal of British Studies*, 43 (April 2004), pp. 278–90.
66   M.D. Blanch, 'British Society and the War', in Peter Warwick and S.B. Spies (eds.), *The South African War: The Anglo-Boer War 1899–1902* (London: Longman, 1980), p. 216.
67   Henry Nevinson, *Ladysmith: The diary of a siege* (London: Methuen, 1900), p. 9.
68   Winston Churchill, *London to Ladysmith via Pretoria* (London: Longmans & Co., 1900), p. 28, p. 38.
69   Matters were notably different in the besieged mining town of Kimberley, where from the outset De Beers tycoon Cecil Rhodes used his established *Diamond Fields Advertiser* newspaper to promote his own authority and criticise military officials. See Thomas Pakenham, *The Boer War* (London, 1979), 322.

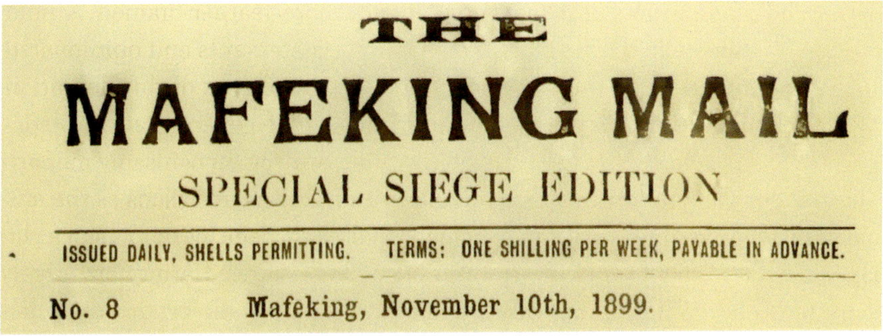
THE

MAFEKING MAIL

SPECIAL SIEGE EDITION

ISSUED DAILY, SHELLS PERMITTING. TERMS: ONE SHILLING PER WEEK, PAYABLE IN ADVANCE.

No. 8 Mafeking, November 10th, 1899.

FIGURE 13.3 *The Mafeking Mail* siege newspaper masthead, 10 November 1899

great deal of distorted, chauvinistic journalism in South Africa. Confronted by unglamorous modern war, the Australian correspondent Donald MacDonald admitted that 'the war artist had to presuppose, the war correspondent to imagine, much'.[70] In the early editions of the siege newspapers, this imagination manifested in patriotic depictions of endurance and *sangfroid*. Like their metropolitan counterparts, the siege newspapers both mirrored and attempted to guide public opinion. Their contents were a mix of official reports, jokes, ads, patriotic verse, and cartoons, intended to boost morale and stave off information starvation. A typical early *Lyre* cartoon depicted two officers standing casually under artillery fire, with the caption: 'We'd better take umbrellas, old chap—I fancy it's going to shell'.[71] The news of their relief force's defeat at Colenso on 15 December saw Ladysmith's press corps instructed that their mission to 'keep the town cheerful' was now more important than ever, and the next *Bombshell* accordingly opened with the apologetic but comic headline 'SANTA CLAUS DELAYED'.[72] Baden-Powell himself served as editor of the *Mafeking Mail*, publicising the sports days and amateur theatricals with which he set out to distract and entertain the garrison (Figure 13.3).

In both towns, however, this humorous façade of plucky solidarity gradually developed cracks which reflected the civilian populations' growing disillusionment with the military authorities. Some content in Ladysmith's papers become strikingly bitter as the months wore on, so that by 8 January, 'The Civilian's Complaint' poem could demand:

70 Donald MacDonald, *How We Kept the Flag Flying: The story of the siege of Ladysmith* (London: Ward, Lock & Co., 1900), p. 149.

71 *Ladysmith Lyre*, 13 December 1899.

72 Nevinson, *Ladysmith*, 177. *Ladysmith Bombshell*, 23 December 1899.

> Who made a mess of this ere war?
> Who dilly-dallied from afar ...?
> Who told us when this siege begun
> Our enemies right soon should run?[73]

The slender daily rations were served out in Ladysmith amid barbed wire and barriers, leading MacDonald to speculate that the military feared their civilian charges would eventually riot.[74] Plucky, high-spirited Mafeking largely acquired this reputation because Baden-Powell personally censored all correspondence. The *Mafeking Mail* writers found innocuous items like 'a mild grumble at the dearth of news' or a satire on the soup kitchen both 'ruthlessly cut out'.[75] More seriously, stories about Baden-Powell's rationing policy of driving starving black locals out of town were written by *The Times* correspondent Ian Hamilton and *Pall Mall Gazette* correspondent J. Emerson Neilly, but only made public in their book-length accounts after the siege was over.[76] The reality behind Mafeking's jolly comic-opera image was one of doubts and fluctuating morale, which reached such an extent that Baden-Powell issued an editorial condemnation of 'wiseacres' and 'grumblers' on 29 March. 'Veiled hints and growlings cannot be permitted', he warned. 'At such times as these they are apt to put people "on edge" and to alarm the ladies'.[77]

Only the censored picture reached the home public at the time, then, and the upbeat, patriotic reports from Mafeking were especially welcome in the 'Black Week' of December 1899, when news of successive defeats dealt a serious blow to morale. For the first time since 1857, large civilian populations were besieged alongside soldiers, and coverage of the sieges often enlisted metropolitan sympathy by focusing on elements like Ladysmith's civilian Town Guard, or the Mafeking Cadet Corps of uniformed bicycle messengers who would form the genesis for the Boy Scouts. *The Times* declared that 'at Mafeking we have the common man of the Empire ... with his back to the wall', proving 'the fundamental grit of the breed'.[78] Several factors made this theme more pressing than ever. As Brad Beaven has examined, this was the first contemporary conflict in which metropolitan 'citizen soldiers' were raised and deployed en

---

73   *Ladysmith Bombshell*, 8 January 1900.
74   MacDonald, *Flag*, 235.
75   Philip Knightley, *The First Casualty: The war correspondent as hero and myth-maker from the Crimea to Kosovo* (London: Deutsch, 1975), p. 73. 'Preface', in *The Mafeking Mail* (Mafeking, 1899–1900).
76   Knightley, *Casualty*, pp. 72–4.
77   *Mafeking Mail*, 29 March 1900.
78   *The Times*, 20 May 1900.

masse.[79] The beleaguered civilians in South Africa could be invoked as inspirations and spurs to action for these new soldiers, with the war capable of being presented as a rescue mission on behalf of people much like themselves. One contemporary recalled how Mafeking's 'special appeal to the imagination' lay in its being 'almost an impromptu civilian defence'.[80]

With this imaginative engagement built up over months of tension and delays, the eventual reliefs of the garrisons were moments of an insistent national unity both generated and amplified by the press. 'While the Queen congratulated her soldiers, the slum hung out its little Union Jacks', the *Pall Mall Gazette* enthused of Ladysmith Day.[81] After the relief of Kimberley on 15 February 1900 and the Ladysmith Day celebrations on 1 March, the relief of Mafeking was widely anticipated. When the news arrived in Fleet Street via a Reuter's telegram just before 10pm on 18 May 1900, telegrams to local newspapers around the country quickly spread the tidings.[82] Factory sirens and church bells announced the news and crowds thronged into the streets of cities and towns across Britain in a patriotic bacchanalia of dancing, singing, and speechifying. Imperial and home defence were once again conflated in editorial discourses, with the *Birmingham Daily Post* stating that the South African garrisons' endurance had been mirrored by the 'moral courage which this nation showed by passive endurance at home'.[83] The cross-class, bipartisan enthusiasm of the relief was the subject for much comment, with even the resolutely anti-war Liberal John Morley momentarily setting aside his political views to praise Baden-Powell in a speech gleefully reported by the pro-war press.[84] 'Differ about the policy of the war and the results of the war as they might', Morley declared, every Englishman could safely admire the 'physical and moral pluck' of Mafeking.[85] Coming from this unlikely source, the *Observer*'s leader-writer mused, these sentiments neatly demonstrated 'how universal is that emotion of mingled joy and pride with the expression

---

79 Brad Beaven, 'The Provincial Press, Civic Ceremony and the Citizen-Soldier During the Boer War, 1899–1902: A Study of Local Patriotism', *Journal of Imperial and Commonwealth Studies*, 37 (2009), p. 208.
80 R. H. Gretton, *A Modern History of the English People* (2 vols., London: Grant Richards, 1913), v, II, p. 93.
81 *Pall Mall Gazette*, 2 March 1900.
82 *Northern Echo*, 19 May 1900.
83 *Morning Post*, 21 May 1900; *Birmingham Daily Post*, 21 May 1900.
84 H. C. G. Matthew, *The Liberal Imperialists: The ideas and politics of a post-Gladstonian élite* (Oxford: Oxford University Press, 1973), pp. 43–5.
85 *Birmingham Daily Post*, 21 May 1900.

of which the whole air of England seems still to be vibrating'—whatever one thought of the wider war, there could be 'no two opinions' about Mafeking.[86]

With a little more distance, however, the fervour of these scenes began to seem regrettable and even un-English to some commentators. Comparisons to Lucknow had been rife in the coverage of Mafeking's relief—but as one concerned writer noted, a more sober mid-Victorian generation had managed to celebrate that arguably more momentous relief without swinging from lampposts.[87] In June, a writer in the *Anglo-Saxon Review* mournfully declared such scenes to be more expected of 'Frenchmen, or Irishmen, or Italians' than the supposedly-phlegmatic British. The responsibility, they declared, lay with the ability of the relentless modern press to 'get upon the nerves' of the home public 'who stay at home and read the newspapers four times a day'.[88]

This chapter has traced how the long communal experience of following imperial sieges through the daily press not only got on the nerves of the home public, but conditioned its reflexes to provoke certain reactions and expectations around imperial warfare. Through emotive coverage which encouraged an intense sympathy and identification with besieged garrisons, newspapers helped to fashion a cultural common sense in which aggressive imperial expansion could be reimagined as simply holding the fort, and critiques of imperial policy could be damned as betrayals of these far-flung garrisons. Editors and journalists may have struggled to deliberately mould public opinion, but the serialised newspaper medium through which the public experienced sieges nevertheless formed the channels through which public opinion would most easily flow. Sieges became the sites for a reflexive imperialism, defensive and purportedly apolitical, arousing in public opinion the same emotional responses as the defence of Britain itself. The solidarity invoked on these occasions was always exaggerated and limited, of course—private soldiers died of malnutrition in Lucknow while their superiors hoarded food, and Irish Nationalists offered up cheers for the 'bowld sepoys', the Mahdi, and the Boers in turn. On a broader scale, though, their defensive nature made these imperial sieges a uniquely morally palatable form of imperial warfare for contemporaries who might have been uneasy over the merits of imperial expansion. If the newspaper medium changed dramatically from the six-week wait for dispatches in 1857 to the hourly telegrams and special correspondents of 1899, this fundamental, gratifying message at least remained consistent.

---

86   *Observer*, 20 May 1900.
87   *Outlook*, 26 May 1900.
88   *Anglo-Saxon Review* (June 1900), p. 240.

CHAPTER 14

The Czechoslovak Media Landscape in 1938
A Lack of Media-Induced Anxiety, and the Origins of the 'Munich Betrayal'

Johana Kłusek

The Munich Agreement, signed on 30 September 1938 by Adolf Hitler, Édouard Daladier, Neville Chamberlain and Benito Mussolini, turned the Czechoslovak borderland—mainly inhabited by Sudeten Germans—over to Nazi Germany.*
It became one of the most exciting news events of that year, next to the Anschluss of Austria in March and Kristallnacht later in November. The immediate impact of the Agreement was limited geographically, but in the longer-term, it represented one of the turning points in the descent towards war. The British military attaché in Prague, Humphrey Stronge, observing the crisis first-hand, concluded that:

> The loss of Czechoslovakia, as a future ally with its strong military and weapons arsenal, combined with its economic wealth, was the biggest step back in Europe since Hitler got to power ... this event—much more than any other—determined the course of world history in subsequent years.[1]

Even greater was the influence of the Munich Agreement on the geopolitics of Central Europe. It marked the beginning of the Western powers' general withdrawal from the region. This process, initiated in the late 1930s, was to last for a decade more when a series of coup d'états plunged the region into the iron embrace of the Soviet Union.

If for most Europeans this event remains important symbolically, for the Czech people it has triggered a far more complex response. Jan Tesař, for instance, considers deliberations about the 'Munich Betrayal' and whether 'we were supposed to defend ourselves or not' to be one of the core identifying characteristics of Czechness.[2] All post-war regimes were forced to confront

---

* This publication was supported by the svv project of the Institute of International Studies, FSV UK n. 260594.
1 'Personal Memorandum relating to the state of morale and general readiness fro war of the army of the Czechoslovak Republic at the time of the Munich crisis in September 1938 and the period immediately preceding it' cited in Robert Kvaček, Aleš Chalupa, Miloš Heyduk, *Československý rok 1938* (Praha: Panorama, 1988), pp. 226–227.
2 Jan Tesař, *Mnichovský komplex: Jeho příčiny a důsledky* (Praha: Prostor, 2014), p. 11.

and negotiate this issue. They used it to shape their own political agendas, and in the process influenced the way that Czechs thought about themselves. General sentiment held the assumption that if the Western powers betrayed Czechoslovakia once, then they could do it again. The post-1948 interpretation worked within the same paradigm. Communists often referred to the First Czechoslovak Republic as the 'Pre-Munich republic'. This description drew attention to the way the state ceased to exist and therefore to the failure of a foreign policy wrongly orientated towards the West.[3] The Soviet Union emerged as the only ally of the Republic not tarnished by betrayal.

Before 1989, the standard communist interpretation of this period sought to emphasise the role of the bourgeois establishment and of capitalist Western powers. After 1989, in a new world where Western powers came to be trusted, discourse on the Munich Agreement moved towards assigning responsibility for the growth of Nazism to Communism, and to discussion of the failure of the Czech state to provide sufficient rights to national minorities.[4] These twin rhetorical thrusts reflected shifting attitudes, and a shifting international relations ecology.

Much has been written on how the Munich Agreement should be interpreted, as well as on the ideology-focused debates which spoke in terms of victims and culprits.[5] This study will move away from this, and instead explore the roots of the feeling of betrayal as it was expressed in the media discourse of 1938. It will show that a lack of a healthy media-induced anxiety can lead to a toxic anxiety-induced discursive space, dangerous in its effects. A lack of critical thinking on the side of the discourse producers as well as discourse audience lies in the spotlight. This study argues that Czech society was not prepared for the blow of Munich; even the leading intellectuals of the time failed to understand or contextualise the international events which preceded the September accords. The West's inaction regarding the Anschluss of Austria or Franco's advancement in the Spanish Civil War, ought to have boosted vigilance regarding the safety guarantees of Czechoslovakia. This did not happen, and when it did in the very last days before the meeting in Munich, it was already too late. The only voice on the media scene which defied the wishful thinking of liberal circles was systematically undermined for its presumed ideological bias. The official daily of the Czechoslovak Communist Party *Rudé právo* (Red

---

3 Stanislav Holubec, *Ještě nejsme za vodou: Obrazy druhých a historická paměť v období postkomunistické transformace* (Praha: Scriptorium, 2015), p. 39.
4 Ibid., p. 106.
5 See the complex analysis of the topic by Beata Kubok, Czeska koncepcja zdrady jako element mitu monachijskiego', *Adeptus* 12 (2018), 1–17.

Justice) was, indeed, ideologically biased. However, the authenticity of its independent and often highly prophetic analyses cannot be denied. Its suppression did not serve useful ends. Therefore, this chapter will argue that the lack of media-induced anxiety, which would normally represent a sign of sensible and prudent journalism, would in fact have disastrous ramifications for interwar Czechoslovakia. The notion of 'Munich Betrayal' was later spread and strengthened by a newly awakened anxiety-inducing media, and the intellectuals who had failed to foresee what was coming.

This chapter is divided into three sections. In the first, we will look at the normative role of intellectuals and in the particular at Czech public intellectuals. It was these very intellectuals who helped grow the disappointment over Munich, and transform it into a form of almost pathological scepticism towards the West. The general role of the press in 1938 is at this point also briefly discussed. Secondly, we will examine two exciting news stories of 1938—the Anschluss of Austria and the Runciman Mission—and how these events were commented on and analysed by two representative dailies: the liberal pro-government *Lidové noviny* (People's News) and the communist *Rudé právo*. Lastly, we will look closely at the post-September bitterness and anxiety that the liberal press helped shape, spread and finally anchor within the Czech cultural and historical memory.

1 Czech Intellectuals and Their Role in Society

According to Hannah Arendt

> in contrast to the ancient philosopher, whose existential stance was to remove himself from public engagement to the position of an insightful theorist, the modern intellectual believes in the public use of reason, which destroys prejudice and opens up narrow horizons.[6]

Czech intellectuals in the first half of the twentieth century were no exception from the general European trend. Yet, their influence on public affairs has been particularly strong given that the borders between political and cultural activity have remained historically blurred in Czech lands. The roots of the arrangement can be traced to the seventeenth century, when the ruling elite in both secular and religious life came to be perceived as ethnically and religiously

---

6 Cited in Bedřich Loewenstein, *My a ti druzí: Dějiny, psychologie, antropologie* (Brno: Doplněk, 1997), p. 18.

foreign. After the Battle of White Mountain in 1620, the country was subdued by the Habsburgs and underwent a rigorous process of Catholic Reformation. Approximately five-sixths of the Czech Protestant nobility fled into exile. Therefore, it was intelligentsia recruited from the Czech-speaking bourgeoisie that in the subsequent decades influenced statehood and national identity. Two centuries later, there was a national revival, with writers, linguists and scholars filling the space which in other countries such as Poland was occupied by the aristocracy.[7] The cultural elite slowly transformed into political elite at the turn of the twentieth century and strongly affected the institutional character of the First Republic formed after the First World War. The system relied heavily on the authority of its founding father Tomáš Garrigue Masaryk—a philosopher, sociologist and scholar.

Even though Masaryk's interwar Czechoslovakia is known rightfully as the only Central European democracy which lasted until the Second World War, it had its limits. Two extra-constitutional power centres influenced the political life of the First Republic. There was the so-called *Pětka* (The Five), which comprised the leaders of the five strongest political parties. With the exception of three years, the *Pětka* ruled the country as a coalition for twenty years. There was also the *Hrad* (the Castle—the seat of Czech kings and later presidents) centred around Masaryk and Edvard Beneš, who served as Minister of Foreign Affairs before becoming President. The *Hrad* controlled the country's foreign policy, which was orientated largely towards the Western powers. Both extra-constitutional power centres diminished opportunities for the emergence of viable political alternatives. For example the Communist Party was not abolished unlike in other Central European countries; however, its reputation was undermined constantly.

The Republic's liberal elites were lured by Masaryk's charisma and intellectual capacity. He himself took part in meetings of the *Páteční* (Friday Men), a group of writers and journalists organized by the writer Karel Čapek. The connection between the President and the leading liberal intellectuals of the time was, therefore, not only theoretical, but direct. The demand Max Weber placed on an ideal intellectual—'to stand in a tradition of prophetic tribunal above the world and to stay above political power'—could not be met.[8] The Republic's strong political as well as cultural affiliation to the West (especially France and then Britain) was, as will be shown, leaking constantly into the dominant media discourses. Voices calling for caution in reliance on France

---

7   Bradley F. Abrams, *The Struggle for the Soul of the Nation: Czech Culture and the Rise of Communism* (Oxford: Rowman and Littlefield Publishers), p. 40.
8   Bedřich Loewenstein, *My a ti druzí: Dějiny, psychologie, antropologie* (Brno: Doplněk, 1997), pp. 16–17.

and Britain or calling for an alternative alignment were blunted by the halo surrounding the 'guardians' of *Hrad*.

Yet, liberal thinkers were not the only group that had a problem living up to the theoretical ideal of a public intellectual. For Bedřich Loewenstein, intellectuals should exhibit material and spiritual independence, the ability to problematize the nature of a given situation, and the ability to establish the wider context in which it should be understood.[9] The liberals of the First Republic would have trouble with each of these. Yet, the leftist intellectuals of the time, who would criticize the domestic and foreign policies of the *Pětka*, struggled with other features of what an ideal public intellectual should be as defined by Loewenstein. Most importantly, they had a strong tendency to oppose the existing reality with 'undesirable utopian visions of a world where everything was better and where all problems were solved by a magic wand'.[10] Bold and often just criticism of the capitalist West was rarely met with an objective assessment of the socialist alternative.

2 Media in Interwar Czechoslovakia

Even though media in interwar Czechoslovakia were theoretically divided into two groups—the official periodicals of political parties, and independent periodicals—political leanings were detectable in all of them. This chapter focuses on two titles—*Rudé právo* that, as the official periodical of the Communist Party, falls into the first group, and *Lidové noviny*, which falls into the second.

Andrea Orzoff called *Lidové noviny* the flagship paper of the First Republic and Prague's *Le Monde*.[11] Their chief commentators were Masaryk's adherents and they continued to be loyal to the *Hrad's* political line, even after his death. The well-known connection between the President 'liberator', as Masaryk was nicknamed, and intellectuals publishing in *Lidové noviny* such as Ferdinand Peroutka, Hubert Ripka, Karel Čapek and Ivo Ducháček, bestowed on them the authority of their mentor. The daily circulation of the paper oscillated around 90,000 copies in the late 1930s.[12]

---

9   Ibid., p. 16.
10 Ibid.
11 Andrea Orzoff, *Battle for the Castle: The Myth of Czechoslovakia in Europe, 1914–1948* (Oxford: University Press, 2009), p. 79.
12 Jakub Končelík, Pavel Večeřa, Petr Orság, *Dějiny českých médií 20. století* (Praha: Portál, 2010), p. 39.

The official paper of the Communist Party *Rudé právo* had a comparable number of daily copies at the time, around 80,000.[13] Robert Kvaček points out that the daily's production offered ideological commentary not only within its political sections but across all types of articles.[14]

As far as the censorship is concerned, press freedom was guaranteed by the Czechoslovak Constitution of 1920. Press legislation descended directly from the Austro-Hungarian legislation, with the exception that it was supplemented by special provisions in the 1930s, responding primarily to the increasing threat to the Republic by Nazi Germany. Three acts gradually came into force: the Act for the Protection of the Republic; the so-called Small Press Acts of 1933 and 1934; and the Act on Extraordinary Measures, which was adopted on 23 September 1938 on the day of general mobilization of the army. Until then, censorship only really affected media expressing ideological reservations about the character of the First Republic.[15] Nevertheless, until mid-1938, censorship interventions can be described as relatively limited. Another factor shaping censorship practice was a generally tolerant social atmosphere. However, after Munich, the press and censorship acquired a new character. The adoption of the Act on Extraordinary Measures meant in practice a suspension of constitutional guarantees, including freedom of the press. On 26 September, the Central Censorship Commission was established to implement so-called preliminary censorship.[16]

3   Exciting News: the Anschluss of Austria

The annexation of Austria by Germany on 13 March 1938 caused uproar around the world. For Czechoslovakia, it meant that it became much more vulnerable. Now, Germany encircled Bohemia and Moravia. Moreover, the lack of reaction from the international community, particularly the League of Nations, was profoundly worrisome, signalling a general reluctance to oppose Germany's overt expansionist agenda.

---

13 Milena Beránková, 'Československá žurnalistiky v letech 1918–1938', in *Dějiny československé žurnalistiky III. díl—Český a slovenský tisk v letech 1918–1944* (Praha: Novinář, 1988), p. 59.

14 Robert Kvaček, Aleš Chalupa, Miloš Heyduk, *Československý rok 1938*, p. 38.

15 Jakub Končelík, Pavel Večeřa, Petr Orság, *Dějiny českých médií 20. století*, pp. 32–35.

16 Milena Beránková, Alena Křivánková, Fraňo Ruttkay, *Dějiny československé žurnalistiky III. díl—Český a slovenský tisk v letech 1918–1944* (Praha: Vydavatelství a nakladatelství Novinář, 1988), pp. 206–208.

Czech newspapers focused primarily on the reactions of France and Britain, as France was bound to Czechoslovakia by the Treaty of Alliance and Friendship of 1924 and the military pact of 1925. Britain too was key; without its consent, France would not intervene. Hence, a careful condemnation of Anschluss by the British Secretary of State Edward Halifax became a springboard for the analysis of the event in Czechoslovakia. If there was initial mild optimism at these remarks, commentators soon had to contend with the words of the Parliamentary Secretary to the Ministry of Labour Alan Lennox-Boyd, who publicly proclaimed that he could imagine 'nothing more ridiculous than a guarantee that the frontiers of Czechoslovakia should not be violated'.[17] This remark was in step with the statement Chamberlain made a month earlier on the floor of Parliament when he urged the importance of deceiving small nations into believing that the League of Nations would protect them from attack.[18] Even though Chamberlain immediately denied that his government shared the views of Lennox-Boyd, the affair provoked debate.

On 16 March, Jan Münzer wrote in a reaction that 'England will never give us a guarantee of friendship, but we already have something far more binding: an awareness of its interest in us'.[19] Three days later, Czechs could read in the same paper that:

> Not only in France, but also in the Anglo-Saxon world they understand that just as they could not allow the destruction of Serbia or Belgium, they cannot afford losing such an important position of their own as Czechoslovakia ... In the last few days, we have been admitted by Great Britain into its company, to its great, peaceful and democratic club with a long, beautiful tradition. They are used to good manners there.[20]

Ferdinand Peroutka, one of the most respected intellectuals of the time, went further. He commented on Chamberlain's speech of 24 February 1938, in which the chief proponent of appeasement repeated that Britain's main interest was to preserve peace but was ready to stick by its commitments. The self-confidence and the impression of infallibility of Peroutka's editorial is typical of the tone on foreign affairs adopted by *Lidové noviny* at the time.

---

17   Cited in 'Prudká debata o Československu', *Lidové noviny*, 22 March 1938; see HC Deb (21 March 1938). vol. 333, col. 951–966, Available at the official report of all Parliamentary debates (hansard.parliament.uk).
18   HC Deb (7 March 1938). vol. 332, col. 1565, available at the official report of all Parliamentary debates (hansard.parliament.uk).
19   Jan Münzer, 'Přátelství protokolární', *Lidové noviny*, 16 March 1938.
20   'Vracejí se časy starých soupeřů', *Lidové noviny*, 19 March 1938.

Laymen are unable to judge the meaning of Chamberlain's words, nor are all those that a foolish publisher chose to run in a newspaper. Their meaning can be judged only by those who have studied the methods of British foreign policy at least a little bit. The world of our homeland is unable to understand that the quiet voice of a British prime minister, even his whisper, has far greater influence than loud cries in the papers.[21]

Kamil Krofta, the Czech Minister for Foreign Affairs took a similar stance to the general mood in Czechoslovakia in March when, a few months earlier, he disagreed resolutely with the assessments of a meeting between Hitler and Halifax in Berchtesgaden that claimed it would have negative consequences for Czechoslovakia.[22] When asked about the meeting at the Senate's Committee of Foreign Affairs he refuted the suggestion that Britain would leave Germany a free hand in Central Europe.[23] The truth, though—as we now know—was that Halifax at that occasion assured Hitler about Britain's lack of interest in Austria, Danzig and Czechoslovakia.[24]

Lidové noviny followed the official governmental line faithfully. However, the language used by the politicians was supplemented in reports with Anglophilic stereotypes and somewhat fanciful notions, such as that which compared the importance of Czechoslovakia to the importance of Belgium.[25] These geopolitical fantasies were hardly rare on the pages of the paper. In May, the daily assured its readers that the borders of British interests were no longer on the Rhine, as in the past, but now on the Danube.[26] Typically, no references were used to evidence such bold statements. Instead of encouraging the readership to be vigilant of the evolving situation, the newspapers instead tried to maintain an atmosphere of security and calm.

In contrast, the Communist daily *Rudé právo* evaluated Lennox-Boyd's utterance in a far more balanced way. On 24 March, the daily wrote that Lennox-Boyd 'only interpreted, in a drastic and undiplomatic way, the stance of a group of Hitler-sympathizing lords, who influence Chamberlain's government'.[27] On the account of Chamberlain's speech, *Rudé právo* wrote:

---

21   Ferdinand Peroutka, 'Jedna řeč—a její posluchači', *Lidové noviny*, 27 March 1938.
22   For details about the meeting between the British Foreign Secretary the Earl of Halifax and Adolf Hitler in Berchtesgaden in November 1937 see the chapter entitled 'Hitler Sees His Chance' in David Faber, *Munich 1938. Appeasement and World War II* (New York: Simon and Schuster, 2008), pp. 14–48.
23   Robert Kvaček, Aleš Chalupa, Miloš Heyduk, *Československý rok 1938*, p. 25.
24   David Faber, *Munich 1938. Appeasement and World War II*, p. 40.
25   'Vracejí se časy starých soupeřů', *Lidové noviny*, 19 March 1938.
26   Ivo Ducháček, 'Otěže do rukou Anglie', *Lidové noviny*, 4 May 1938.
27   'Kam žene Evropu Chamberlain', *Rudé právo*, 24 March 1938.

If Mr. Chamberlain does not mind the terrible destruction and slaughter of Spanish cities when he makes 'gentlemanly agreements' with those whose planes do the destruction, then Europe will be always in danger of new aggression and violence and there will be no real peace for us or for anybody else in Europe.[28]

The general scepticism regarding the preparedness of Western powers to intervene in favour of Czechoslovakia was, however, often wrongly countered with an emphasis on public opinion amongst British workers, which communist intellectuals assumed to be on the side of intervention:

> England is no tea society ... England is also, and above all, the millions of workers, the millions of hands that spin the wheels of factories and ships. England is also the millions of heads whose opinion every government that wants to stay in power in Britain must take into account.[29]

Therefore, even though the line taken by the paper opposed the liberal position by warning systematically of the fading loyalty of the Western powers, it offered instead the hollow prospect of some form of socialist internationalism.

4 Exciting News: Runciman Mission

Tension grew in the months that followed the Anschluss of Austria. In mid-May, leftist intellectuals published a manifesto called *Věrni zůstaneme* (Faithfull we will stay) which called for the protection of the integrity and inviolable sovereignty of the Republic. In three months, a million people had signed it. The major sports event of the year—the Tenth All Sokols Slet did not remain apolitical. It boasted almost three hundred and fifty-thousand participating gymnasts, and more than two million spectators and the accompanying parade through Prague became one of the biggest national demonstrations against Nazism of 1938.[30] Surprisingly, fear of Germany, and anxiety arising from the fact that Czechoslovakia represented a logical next step in Hitler's *Drang nach Osten* was not accompanied by any recalibration in the Czech public's understanding of the attitudes of the increasingly reluctant France and Britain.

The second exciting news story of 1938 concerned the Czechoslovak government's escalating conflict with the pro-Nazi Sudeten Germans led by Konrad

---

28   'Anglie není žádná čajová společnost', *Rudé právo*, 27 March 1938.
29   Ibid.
30   'Poprvé na Strahově', *Československý sport*, 4 June 1985, p. 3.

Henlein. In June, the government approved a revised version of the *Národnostní statut* (National statute), which anticipated home rule for border regions in which Sudeten Germans were in the majority. There was a profound danger that the conflict could further escalate. Henlein, acting in direct cooperation with Hitler, increased his demands repeatedly; negotiations soon approached stalemate. In response, the Czechoslovak government accepted the offer of what they had assumed would have been impartial mediation from Britain. The mission of the special envoy Lord Walter Runciman arrived in Prague on 3 August 1938. He was accompanied by officers of the Foreign Office, some of whom made no secret of their sympathies towards the idea of the disputed territories' cession to Germany. Before Runciman left London, he was warned by Edward Halifax that he must not

> take any action that would have the effect of committing this country further than it is already committed, to take action in the event of Germany taking military action.[31]

Despite the fact that none of this information was revealed publicly at the time, Czech liberal media discourse on the Runciman mission was again characterized by an extreme lack of objectivity and critique.

The interpretation of this event by the Communist daily was, as was the case with the Anschluss, different. *Rudé právo* was highly critical. The paper promptly described the mission as an unacceptable intervention in the domestic affairs of Czechoslovakia and warned that it was most probably initiated by Hitler himself.[32] The communist politician Vlado Clementis even made public what he had learned from talks with British politicians in May, and what we today know was a rather accurate description of the situation:

> I happened to be staying in London at that time ... and I spoke with English politicians of all parties. With few exceptions, almost everyone described Chamberlain's political conception of Czechoslovakia to me as follows: Czechoslovakia is seen as another Austria that cannot be helped. And the 'peaceful' subjugation of Czechoslovakia by Germany is not so much against his wishes.[33]

---

31 Cited in David Faber, *Munich 1938. Appeasement and World War II*, p. 206.
32 'Kdo to dovolil', *Rudé právo*, 29 July 1938; 'Lord Runciman přijíždí do Prahy', *Rudé právo*, 2 August 1938.
33 Vlado Clementis, 'v jakých rukou je světový mír', *Rudé právo*, 3 August 1938.

Rudé právo again, though, placed a rather unfortunate emphasis on the socialist solidarity that would supposedly have made a difference:

> Even the English lords cannot leave without paying the innkeeper—the English public put a stop to the special deals they hoped to get from Mussolini. The secret deals they are making with Hitler's adjutants will not be recognized by those who are supposed to pay for them. The English public is on guard, and the patience of the French people has its limits as well.[34]

However, the level of criticism that the paper could publish was already then limited by censorship.[35] *Rudé právo* was abolished three weeks after the Munich Agreement was signed.

On the contrary, liberal intellectuals' trust in the best intentions of Runciman was high from the very beginning and it was not disrupted even by the weekends that Runciman spent in the company of aristocrats sympathizing with Henlein and the Nazi cause. *Lidové noviny* welcomed 'the courier of British liberal democracy'.[36] It emphasised in particular Runciman's objectivity and democratic conviction. Respected writer Jan Drda relied on comparisons between Woodrow Wilson and Runciman, and made the readership aware that the 'old gentleman of the noble features is aware of his mission's gravity'.[37] This highly idealistic prism was complemented by a further parade of Anglophilic stereotypes. Runciman was even praised for his choice of transport—his train represented 'safe advancement', a typical British approach.[38] His 'seriousness was tinged by the usual British humour'.[39] Drda finished his commentary proclaiming pathetically that: 'when we see his grey head and his most beautiful eyes which have remained sparkling with brilliance and decisiveness for over 60 years, we believe'.[40] Typically, the writer did not explain what 'we' were supposed to believe. It is hard to imagine that readers of *Lidové noviny* could have anticipated how things would evolve only two months later as they were continuously presented with the rosiest of pictures of international, and now also domestic events.

---

34   'Rada Runcimanovi', *Rudé právo*, 30 July 1938.
35   Eduard Urx, 'Lord a lid', 7 August 1938.
36   Hubert Ripka, 'Těžký úkol Runcimanův', *Lidové noviny*, 3 August 1938.
37   Jan Drda, 'Vyslanec demokracie', *Lidové noviny*, 4 August 1938.
38   'Runciman odjel do Prahy', *Lidové noviny*, 3 August 1938.
39   'První rozhovor s novináři v Praze', *Lidové noviny*, 4 August 1938.
40   Jan Drda, 'Vyslanec demokracie'.

The extent of the enthusiasm of liberal commentators is particularly surprising in the context of memories of prominent politicians and diplomats who were part of the same liberal intellectual circle. For example, Jan Masaryk, Czechoslovak ambassador in London and son of Tomáš Garrigue Masaryk, wrote in 1938:

> The English feel an intense dislike towards us. We are nothing but a burden for them and they curse the day our country was founded. We have negative value for England … It is very difficult to talk to Chamberlain—he is hard-headed, and his ignorance is tremendous.[41]

Edvard Beneš' Chief of Staff Jaromír Smutný recalled the arrival of Runciman differently to the *Lidové noviny*:

> The old man looks more like a grandpa … I can't imagine that he would be the type of person able to grasp the problem that he came here to help us solve.[42]

Runciman also made a different impression on foreign journalists who reported on the mission to the Western press. American journalist and later historian Willian L. Shirer reflected mercilessly on Runciman's appearance, describing him as 'a taciturn, thin-lipped little man with a bald head so round it looks like a mis-shapen egg'.[43] Other reporters paid attention to Runciman's wife; John Wheeler Bennett described her as a 'lady with the consciously superior air of Britons on foreign soil'.[44]

Runciman stayed in Czechoslovakia for almost two months. No mention was made of Runciman's meeting with Konrad Henlein at Červený Hrádek on 18 August, nor were there any reports marking the end of his mission in September. The fact that news of Runciman's departure was left unreported in a once highly supportive newspaper suggests that the cognitive dissonance of the liberal intellectuals was reaching its limits.

It is possible that the *Hrad* circle through its mouthpiece the *Lidové noviny* needed to show to the British and indeed to the international community as a

---

41 Cited in Robert Kvaček, Aleš Chalupa, Miloš Heyduk, *Československý rok 1938*, p. 116.
42 Ibid., p. 139.
43 William L. Shirer, *Berlin Diary: The Journal of a Foreign Correspondent 1934–1941* (New York: Alfred A. Knopf, 1942), p. 121.
44 John W. Wheeler Bennett, *Munich: Prologue to Tragedy* (London: Macmillan, 1948), p. 77.

whole, that they were approachable and willing to cooperate. The enthusiastic way in which Runciman was welcomed may, therefore, have been deliberately exaggerated. Yet, more likely, what is revealed in the stance taken by the paper was the naivety of the liberal elites, and their entirely erroneous evaluation of the international political landscape. The deeply held affection of the country's elites towards French and British cultures prevented the Czechs from seeing the brutal reality of interwar politics. For France and Britain, there was definitely no appetite to shift their sphere of interest away from the Rhine to the Danube.

5   The Post-Munich Anxiety

By late September, articles which had been overflowing with optimism were slowly replaced with those anticipating catastrophe. From this date, the prevailing emotion was not anger but sadness and resignation. A week before the Munich Agreement was signed, *Lidové noviny* ran a piece in the form of an open letter nominally addressed to English teachers and professors. The paper begged these educators to explain to British children what was happening in Czechoslovakia based on the example of the Battle of Hastings. The hope was to establish a common cause and make what was happening so far from Britain's shores seem less distant. Despite the usage of the second-person narrative, the article was of course intended for a domestic Czech audience.

> Summon your students and have them sing the old carol about the Good King Wenceslas, which they are so happy to sing at Christmas. ... Tell them that Good King Wenceslas, a king from more than a thousand years ago, ruled the very borders, which are now to be torn apart by an external decision for the first time ... Tell those young boys that shortly before the Anglo-Saxon nation was forced under the yoke of the Norman conquerors by the lost battle of Hastings, our Czech Duke Břetislav was already chasing the armies of the German Emperor Henry out from this country, as was the case before and after. I don't know what is being taught in English schools about the two hundred years of English subjugation that followed the Battle of Hastings. We have learned in our schools that this is a great example of how a strong nation cannot be destroyed and defeated. ... We are also not afraid of any oppression. ... But if you tell your boys about us, tell them what is the main difference between that Anglo-Saxon fate then and that of Czechoslovakia now: Anglo-Saxon

freedom was lost in battle. I think the difference will be understood in Kipling's home country.[45]

Now, clearly, the former confidence that had so characterised the media discourse had dissipated, and been overtaken by self-pity. Also, a tangible reproach emerges in the discourse for the first time. The author presents the Czechs as equal to the British but is suddenly aware that this might not be the natural understanding of the British. He has to explain why the Czechs and the British should fight side by side against the Germans using an historical event a thousand years in the past; he can hardly evoke examples from current affairs to do so.

On the morning of 30 September 1938, there was an utter collapse of the logic of the multi-layered construction worldview Czechs were taught to believe in during the twenty years of the First Republic. It was decided that the country would accept the decision of the Western powers and renounce the border territories without a fight. The liberal media immediately put the blame on the 'treacherous' allies. Any sense of self-criticism that would take into account the country's own foreign policy failures would be entirely absent. The foundation for the 'Munich Betrayal' myth was laid.

Most of the articles published in the *Lidové noviny* during the first weeks after the Munich Agreement were dominated by grief imbued by pathos. However, there were also ironic and sarcastic comments on show. A mere week after Munich, Edmund Konrád wrote for *Lidové noviny* an account of the British as 'ex-friends':

> Their songs, pictures and books seem a tad too selfish to us now; their thoughts seem dishonest and false. Their words taste bitter in our mouths.[46]

According to Konrád, Czechs needed a break from the British; he advised them instead to focus on themselves. There was also a growing number of nationalist calls for the removal of shop signs in foreign languages, specifically signs in French and English:

> 'Coiffeurs' and 'tailors' should disappear, because they give foreigners a false impression that the coiffeur is some Mr. Dupont with whom they can speak French, and the tailor is some Mr. Brown with whom they

---

45 'Prosba do Anglie', *Lidové noviny*, 21 September 1938.
46 Edmund Konrád, 'Křižovatka kulturní', *Lidové noviny*, 7 October 1938.

could 'how-do-you-do …'. We understand, of course, that a distinguished Englishmen, who knows nothing about the country he graced with his presence, cannot be bothered with such a simple task, like a simple Czech servant.[47]

The article suggested that Czechs should not make it easy for foreigners; after all they themselves hardly had it easy abroad. The Municipality of Prague proclaimed that 'it is necessary that the capital city of Prague, as a representative of our state, be completely Czech in terms of language and that it be free of all unnecessary, indecent and burdensome foreign signs'.[48]

In only a few days, Britain and France went from being admired social and cultural role models into enemies. What was interpreted as a political betrayal immediately changed attitudes that would have seemed unshakeable before. The higher classes, previously respected and admired in numerous articles, now became targets of scorching critique. Attention became focused on the ordinary population, a group respected only by the left before. On 8 October, Otto Rádl wrote in *Lidové noviny*:

> I've talked to people on buses, at train stations, in garages, in tea rooms, in meetings, in reading rooms, on the streets … It's strange that nobody rejoices in that peace, nobody trusts it. Those little people of unknown names have something inside them that politicians don't have: conscience, a wonderfully alive and sincere conscience that feels shame—a burning shame of betrayal.[49]

This socially conscious approach mirrored general political developments in 1940s Europe. However, while in Western Europe this would translate into support of the democratic left, Czechs were forced to contend with a left which would only pretend to be democratic. While the grudge against the Western elites was moderated at least in public during the war, it would re-emerge quickly after 1945 and help the Communist party to win the parliamentary election in 1946, and later to align the nation within the orbit of the Soviet Union. The independence that Karel Čapek wished for the Czechs when he wrote two days after Munich that 'only when we lean on one another can we

---

47 Karel Blažek, 'Coiffeur a tailor', *Lidové noviny*, 19 November 1938.
48 The ruling of the Prague City Council from 1 October 1938 as cited in Robert Kvaček, Aleš Chalupa, Miloš Heyduk, *Československý rok 1938*, pp. 248–249.
49 Otto Rádl, 'Svědomí', *Lidové noviny*, 8 October 1938.

keep our national strength and cool composure', would remain only as a one further expression of wishful thinking.⁵⁰

The example of the Czech media landscape in 1938 proves that words do not really have objective meanings of their own. Meanings are ascribed by those who interpret them. Czech liberal intellectuals filled the meanings of the words uttered by Western statesmen as well as the portraits of the Western powers with those imagined constructions they needed to rationalize their own life—inherently linked to the existence of First Czechoslovak Republic. Communist intellectuals subjected the words of British and French politicians to a thorough critique. However, they were unable to draw conclusions independent of the assertions dictated by the general internationalist discourse of the time. As a result, both groups contributed to embedding of the 'Munich Trauma' that would later have such a substantial impact on the cultural memory of the Czech people.

The story of the deceptive Czech media of 1938 confirms also general reflections about the way in which intellectuals interact with public discourse. According to Bedřich Loewenstein, intellectuals often fail to recognize their instrumentalization and the fact that they can become false prophets. The desire to play a seemingly important advisory role prevents them from seeing reality without distortion. Loewenstein finished his reflection by saying that 'the result of their (intellectuals) attempts to shape reality has always been not that reality succumbed to the ideologues, but rather that it has been lost'.⁵¹ That is also the case of the Czechoslovak interwar love affair with the West. It was lost due to the lack of prudent interpretation of world affairs before Munich and subsequent popularization of the notion of 'betrayal'. As a result, there was no chance to reform the unhealthy relationship between Czech society, the West and the East, and to build it upon more stable and pragmatic foundations. Instead, public intellectuals kept switching their affection between West and East and thus prevented the Czechs from leaning on themselves.

---

50   Cited in Petr Hlaváček (ed.), *Západ, nebo Východ? České reflexe Evropy 1918–1948* (Praha: Academia, 2016), p. 509.
51   Bedřich Loewenstein, *My a ti druzí: Dějiny, psychologie, antropologie*, pp. 23–25.

CHAPTER 15

All Quiet on the Domestic Front?

Dealing with Anxiety in Late Socialist Czechoslovak Media

Ondřej Daniel and Jakub Machek

This chapter will explore how anxiety was managed and expressed in late-socialist Czechoslovak media.[1] We will look for evidence of anxiety as it was conveyed through media reports on everyday accidents and violent crime, as well as in the themes dealt with in some of the most popular television series. In general terms, we argue that anxiety-related information as broadcast in the media followed two distinct phases. During the 1970s, anything threatening or unsettling to the viewer was generally avoided; when disquieting information was communicated, it chiefly related to foreign news, or domestic social groups perceived as problematic to the state. There was a shift in the 1980s, when more challenging narratives came to the fore and included domestic news topics. More attention was afforded to perceived problems within socialist society, with the aim of encouraging renewal from within. Nevertheless, the layer of anxiety-free media production which characterised the 1970s continued in the 1980s and functioned in parallel with this new more critical and reflective agenda.

This chapter seeks to explore these layers, and in turn understand how anxiety was communicated in the media of the Czechoslovak Socialist Republic. It will seek first to offer some context for the policy pursued in the 1970s and 1980s which aimed to normalise the communist perspective of the Republic and maintain public calm and order, before analysing one specific case study—news coverage of a mass murder which occurred in 1973. We will then turn our attention to television series which sought to support the normalisation of communist rule across society, as well as musical films, a genre targeted specifically at younger generations. With a generational turn and growing fatigue at anxiety-free production, by the 1980s, especially the second half of

---

1   This research was supported in part by the Cooperatio Program (research area History) provided by Charles University and implemented at the Faculty of Arts of Charles University, and in part by research project no. 74–01 of the Metropolitan University of Prague, 'Political Science, Culture, Media and Language', which was undertaken in 2020 based on a grant from the Institutional Fund for the Long-Term Strategic Development of Research Organisations.

the decade, there was a more socially-aware media production inspired by 'perestroika'. This, we will investigate by way of a further case study, the depiction of football-related violence.

The authors of this chapter are themselves part of the generational cohort of middle-aged 'Husák's children' (*Husákovy děti*), so-called after the last socialist president. Some of the media strategies and depicted phenomena may well have had a strong impact on us due to the fact that we were in our formative years when first seeing them. We have witnessed these periods in the history of the state first hand. Our methodology, however, does not follow memory studies, but rather we have pursued a cultural historical approach to media history. We have worked in several media archives, including *Kramerius* (The Library of the Digitised Press), *Národní filmový archiv* (The National Film Archive), YouTube and the general film sharing platform *Ulož.to*. In addition, we have explored newspaper coverage from a range of titles conserved in the *Národní knihovna České republiky*, the National Library of the Czech Republic.

1   Maintaining Calm and Order: Czechoslovak Media in the 1970s and 1980s

Avoiding public anxiety by careful selection of what was permitted to be reported in the media was a strategy intimately connected to the power structure which followed the Warsaw Pact invasion of Czechoslovakia. Following the suppression of the Prague Spring in August 1968, the newly installed authorities called for a restoration of order and a reversal of the previous liberalisation of political, social and cultural life. The limited restoration of civic society during the Prague Spring was viewed after its suppression with profound suspicion as a period of chaos, disorder and irresponsibility. The Spring movement had provoked irrational and dangerous thinking and had incited the overthrow of orderly government and the destruction of socialism.[2]

It is no coincidence that one of the propagandistic representations of the events of the Prague Spring, the allegorical film *Hroch* (*Hippo*, 1973, dir. K. Steklý), portrayed this period as a collective frenzy caused by tabloid coverage and the return of religious and esoteric elements—all driven, of course, by the desire of anti-socialist forces to seize power with the help of a deluded crowd. Any public excitement was perceived as dangerous. It was rejected both for ideological reasons elaborated in the official explanation of the events

---

[2]   Jakub Rákosník, Matěj Spurný and Jiří Štaif, *Milníky moderních českých dějin: krize konsenzu a legitimity v letech 1848–1989* (Praha: Argo, 2018), p. 247.

associated with 1968 in the document entitled *Poučení z krizového vývoje* (*Lessons from the Crisis*, 1970) as well as for practical reasons—the fear of any large gathering not under the full control of the authorities.

Official ideology still followed the Marxism-Leninism taught in schools, and repeated in public speeches and statements, but pragmatism dominated the approach of the authorities, and this was based on attempts to find consensus within a largely disillusioned society. Energetic attempts to mobilise people in the building of a socialist society was instead replaced by the offer of a quiet, peaceful, undisturbed and secure life under the socialist dictatorship.[3] Indeed, the phrase 'quiet life' appeared with great frequency in the official speeches in the early 1970s. Gustáv Husák, who became head of the Communist Party of Czechoslovakia in 1969 and remained in office until the end of the 1980s (he was also President of Czechoslovakia from 1975), explained:

> A normal person wants to live quietly, without certain groups turning us into a jungle, and therefore we must appeal to people so that they condemn this. This party wants to safeguard the quiet life.[4]

In the same way, Husák summarised the first four years of governance of the post-invasion authorities:

> Our party during four short years, supported by millions of workers, has led society to the present quiet, and I should say, sunny days, in which we can think about current problems, without danger or worries about tomorrow or next week.[5]

---

3   Paulina Bren, 'Weekend Getaways: The Chata, the Tramp, and the Politics of Private Life in Post-1968 Czechoslovakia', in D. Crowley et al. (eds.), *Socialist Spaces. Sites of Everyday Life in Eastern Bloc* (Oxford, New York: Berg, 2002), p. 125, 126; Pavel Kolář, Michal Pullmann, 'Násilí a klid na práci', in Pavel Kolář etc. (eds.), *Co byla normalizace?: studie o pozdním socialismu* (Praha: NLN, 2016), p. 64.
4   Bren, 'Weekend Getaways', p. 123.
5   Gustáv Husák, 'Jsme hrdi na úspěchy, kterých jsem dosáhli', *Rudé právo*, 53 (16 April 1973), p. 3. This formulation appeared twice in *Rudé pravo* in 1973, the first time in a printed speech by Gustáv Husák at the party conference of the 1st district in Bratislava, the second in a slightly modified version in an anonymous editorial on 18 August (p. 1). The praxis of taking ideological phrases over from text to text is analysed by Petr Fidelius, *Řeč komunistické moci* (Praha: Triáda, 1998) and the meaning of these operations is also explained by Alexei Yurchak, *Everything Was Forever, Until It Was No More: The Last Soviet Generation* (Princeton, N.J.: Princeton University Press, 2005).

Peace of mind at work and a safe life became a fundamental offer of the new authorities to citizens. In addition to the promise of satisfying basic material needs and an improved standard of living, the regime's offer included the provision of basic security: defence, employment, and low crime—all contrasted with a wholly negative depiction of life on the other side of the Iron Curtain. According to Czechoslovak media coverage of the West, everyday life involved dealing with a number of threats, not least street violence, drugs and terrorism.

After the brief relaxation of freedom of speech and the boom of media commenting on politics in 1968, censorship was reintroduced, and the media came under strict control once again. In order to present the state's ideological offer to the public, the propagandistic effort was shifted to popular culture. This would represent a very clear departure from the socialist realism approach which characterised the 1950s.[6] In the 1970s and 1980s, popular media items were carefully framed in accordance with prevailing ideological needs, and conscientiously controlled by authorities during the full production process.[7] Unlike in the 1950s, a substantial portion of magazines, books, television programmes and, above all, film-making were popular enough to be profitable and were frequented by audiences as a source of entertainment and information. This way, the popular media was used as a suitable vehicle for less conspicuous ideological messages, directed more towards lifestyles, everyday attitudes and the basic idea of a life in the socialist society. This life was depicted as more peaceful and secure than its capitalist counterparts, even if the Czechoslovak population recognised the West as more affluent economically. In keeping with the pragmatic ideology of maintaining a quiet and secure life, there was one important request on all media, and that was to avoid topics related to anything threatening or unsettling to the audience when concerning domestic issues. However, the depiction of the non-socialist world could and should include all prevalent dangers. In the following section, we will show a few examples of how this avoidance of everything uncertain, threatening and exciting was pursued.

---

6 Socialist realism was introduced in the Soviet Union in the 1930s as the only required official artistic style. The basis was the idea of a new, classless art that would be both artistic, acceptable to the masses and ideologically educational. As a result, avant-garde breakthroughs and popular genres were rejected as bourgeois, reflecting the inequalities of capitalist society. New works, especially in Czechoslovakia in the 1950s, were formalist, lifeless and quickly abandoned and forgotten with the end of Stalinism.

7 Jarmila Cysařová, *Televize a totalitní moc 1969–1975* (Praha: Ústav pro soudobé dějiny), p. 86.

2   News—the Case of Olga Hepnarová

The daily news coverage during the normalisation period of the 1970s and 1980s fully met propaganda needs, showing the socialist bloc positively with only minor imperfections and focusing more on the problems experienced by the Western capitalist states and the Third World, depicted as a victim of the former. In the news, there were only limited and brief reports about domestic accidents, disasters and violent crimes. Events, though, that might have disturbed the image of a peaceful life in Czechoslovakia, but at the same time could not be entirely ignored, did present a problem. This can be illustrated by the case of Olga Hepnarová, the last woman sentenced to death in Czechoslovakia. Hepnarová, apparently as a consequence of psychological disturbance, drove a truck into a group of people waiting at a tram stop in Prague in 1973, killing eight. The largest mass murder in Czechoslovak territory since the end of the Second World War, which took place close to the centre of the capital, could not be concealed, or at least not completely. The case captivated the public's attention and provoked a broad social response. It did so, however, in spite of highly limited and restricted coverage in the media. References in the media were limited to very brief and neutral comments, and followed closely official statements issued by the state news agency.[8]

Soon after the event, the media, controlled by the authorities, offered only a brief agency report, which was then picked up by the newspapers with only minor modifications; the most widely read was *Rudé právo* (*Red Justice*), a newspaper published by the Communist Party of Czechoslovakia, initially reported a smaller number of victims than even the official line from the state agency. The first two-paragraph report appeared on the second page under the headline 'Tragic consequences of a road accident':

> Tuesday afternoon, a female driver was unable to control a lorry [...] and drove into pedestrians waiting for a tram. [...] The aftermath of the accident is tragic, leaving three dead at the scene. [...] The causes of the accident are being investigated.[9]

A day later, additional clarification was issued on the second page, with the headline 'More to the tragic road accident', which included further details such

---

8 There exist familiar simple rhymes which testify, among other things, to the unknowingness of the details of the accident in the collective memory: 'Na přechodu pro chodce, drtí Tatra důchodce' (At a pedestrian crossing, a Tatra lorry crushes a pensioner).
9 *Rudé právo*, 53 (11 July 1973), p. 2.

as the age of the driver and that no alcohol or drugs were involved.[10] Such short notices consciously avoided offering any reason for the accident, despite the fact that journalists must surely have been aware of Hepnarová's statements to those who had helped pull her from the wreckage that this was a deliberate act. Some newspapers had even received a letter from Hepnarová herself making the same claims. *Rudé právo* also continued to report a lower number of dead and injured. Other dailies reported similarly in one or two reports, but with a more precise number of victims.[11]

While the details of the incident were spread amongst the population by word of mouth, further newspaper reports of the event were not published until a year later, with the reporting of the outcome of the trial in April 1974 and details of the unsuccessful appeal in June. Reports on the appeal were brief, but more attention was given to the outcome of the trial, with the headline 'Verdict delivered'.[12] For the first time, Hepnarová's full name was given, not just her initials or first name as in the previous year. The article did not follow a simple agency report but was introduced by the journalist's initials. In addition to summarising the events, it focused on explaining and defending capital punishment: 'the only punishment society can use to protect itself from such an individual', emphasising the impossibility of reform, echoing Hepnarová's words that she regretted not killing more people, and listing the other methods of mass murder she had considered. Finally, the journalist emphasised just how many people tried to help Hepnarová during her lifetime, 'many times offering her a helping hand, giving her great opportunities to participate in society at large'. However, Hepnarová 'did not recognize any authority, the slightest obligation, did not feel the need to obey the laws of society'. The article thus highlights the deliberate disturbance of social peace and security by an individual who, despite all-encompassing social care, was unwilling to listen to authority, duty and 'the laws of society'. The article concluded with an unusually expressive passage that was more reminiscent of reports on capitalist countries, or of the Stalinist 1950's, with the statement that Hepnarová 'increasingly fermented her hatred, anger and bloodthirsty plans'.[13] The use of the death penalty after the end of the Stalin era was limited to mass and sexually motivated murders. Those punished were no longer political enemies, but they were depicted as monsters threatening the healthy development of society.[14]

10 *Rudé právo*, 53 (22 June 1973), p. 2; (25 June 1973), p. 4.
11 Ditta Kotoučová, *Kauza Olgy Hepnarové v českém filmu*, Master thesis, (Praha: FSV UK, 2018), pp. 56–57.
12 *Rudé právo*, 54 (8 April 1974), p. 2.
13 fř, *Rozsudek vynesen*, *Rudé právo*, 54 (8 April 1974), p. 2.
14 Kolář, Pullmann, 'Násilí a klid na práci', p. 65.

All three articles from this year which reported on the crash appeared inconspicuously in the middle of the paper, on a page devoted to brief crime, courtroom, and telephone reports, to television and radio programmes, and to crossword puzzles. The execution, carried out the following year, was not mentioned at all, at least not in *Rudé právo*.[15] The only other mention of the case that we have been able to trace so far in the press came in 1979, five years after the crash, and appeared in the youth lifestyle magazine *Mladý svět* (*Young World*), a periodical fairly adept at avoiding censorship interference. There was a report on the trial of a group of bank robbers which included a passing reference to the fact that Hepnarová had previously been sentenced to death in the same courtroom.[16]

3   The Broadcast Media: From Crime TV to Musicals

It was not only the news media that served the authorities' efforts to portray calm and avoid anxiety. Fictional television programmes and films were framed to the same ends, as were western productions selected for broadcast—all designed to contrast domestic serenity with the dangers of life in the West. Crime films and series were seen as a useful tool in this effort. Most Western productions did not reach Czechoslovak cinemas and television screens. Action genres such as those in the James Bond franchise were perceived as too bloody and politically problematic. Yet, crime investigation dramas were acceptable, and did become an accessible window into the Western world for Czechoslovak viewers. In the 1970s and 1980s, some series became very popular indeed, including the British series *The Professionals* (1977–83), with the omission of some ideologically problematic episodes, and the Italian *La piovra* (*The Octopus*, 1984–92) which centred on the investigation of mafia crimes. Broadcasting series which depicted serious crimes was clearly meant to serve as a counterpoint to the tranquillity of Czechoslovak life. There was a very successful home-grown crime series, repeated throughout the 1970s, *Hříšní lidé města pražského* (*The Sinful People of Prague*, 1969), but notably this was not set in contemporary Czechoslovakia but rather in the capitalist interwar period. Investigation crimes in the past scarcely provoked feelings of danger and anxiety.

---

15   Unfortunately, only *Rudé právo* appears among the Czech dailies for the years examined, but it can be assumed that other newspapers published similarly limited information.
16   *Mladý svět*, 21/6 (1979), p. 20.

Another interesting example is that of the TV series *Třicet případů majora Zemana* (*Thirty Cases of Major Zeman*, 1974–9), directed again by Jiří Sequens as the previous series, commissioned by the authorities to celebrate the achievements of the socialist police. The cases selected for dramatization were inspired by real events, showing crimes arising by those out with the boundaries of the true socialist society. The crimes depicted were committed predominantly by groups such as: emigrants, former capitalists, church officials, and western spies. The danger thus came either from outside of the socialist world, or from an internal enemy influenced by external ideological propaganda or be greed or other motives anathema to the socialist community. Emphasis was placed on the ability of the police to solve cases and to restore order. In contemporary cases, the criminals became dissidents with a dangerous influence on the youth—a warning of the disruption and disorder associated with events in 1968. These episodes again highlighted the desire for peace among the majority of the population. It was not until the second half of the 1980s that the subject of everyday domestic crime was brought to a television series.

The most popular prime time TV series combined the melodrama of soap operas with the depiction of the everyday life of a variety of occupations, from farmers to salesmen and engineers to local authorities. They were watched sometimes by ninety per cent of the TV audience. The series *Okres na severu* (*The District in the North*, 1981) focused on the work and life of a regional communist leader. The main storyline narrated the search for a solution to quickly restore operations at a chemical plant following an explosion. The explosion itself was not depicted nor were its victims, so the story revolved around management, and in particular the division of responsibilities between corporate and party management. The emphasis was placed on finding rational solutions to problems and depicted the selfless involvement of the workers. This was similar to the TV series *Sanitka* (*The Ambulance*, 1984), which depicted the work and lives of paramedics. Its final episode dramatised the Yugoslav plane crash near Prague in 1975, a real event. It focused not on the crash itself, but on the capabilities and the commitment of the rescue workers, and the organised way in which they came together. The core message of these series was to reassure the audience that if an unfortunate accident were to occur, the relevant forces stood ready to solve even the most dangerous problems quickly and rationally; people would be safe, and peace would be restored.

A further example of the media's portrayal of Czechoslovakia in the 1970s and first half of the 1980s as a society without anxiety can be found in the musical film *Romance za korunu* (*Romance for a Crown*, 1975). It is the type of period production that Štěpán Hulík has referred to as bland and schematic, often centered on the lives of young factory workers, and which was intended to address serious social and ethical problems. Such productions were usually only of minor interest to the audience, especially if combined with explicit propaganda intent, filmed purely to order, with no assumption of any popularity with the public.[17] But *Romance for a Crown*, thanks to the involvement of some of the most popular pop stars of the period became a successful film.

The film narrated a night out for Prague's working-class apprentices. The film attempted to show that there was no generational gap in Czechoslovak society; there was no conflict, no tension and no difference in values between generational cohorts. It showed that the older generation fully understood the problems of the youth and enthusiastically helped them with those problems. The film was prepared during the initial phase of post-occupation cinema, when a way was sought to balance popular and propaganda components. It depicted an ideal conflict-free society; at its core was a society, of all generations, living a quiet and happy life, with the certainty of a livelihood. There was also an emphasis on material values with numerous references to cheap but quality goods.

4 Growing Critique of Socialist Problems

Consumers of Czechoslovak media were not spared completely from shocking news. Most commonly, where such news stories were published or broadcast, they brought to light information about negative aspects of life in the 'rotten West'. From the late 1970s, however, viewers were confronted with a new and more critical domestic artistic production focusing on darker sides of late socialist modernity. One of the turning points was a film called *Panelstory aneb jak se rodí sídliště*, (*Story from a Housing Estate*, 1979) which dealt with the social isolation felt at the newly built suburbs of Prague. It was directed by Věra Chytilová, probably the most important female film maker in the history of Czechoslovak cinema.[18] Screening of the movie combining a documentary with fictional film, though, confined to only very carefully chosen cinemas. Its participation at international film festivals was only possible because of the tenacity of its director. The personality and strong involvement of Chytilová also enabled her to negotiate all necessary permissions before shooting started. The director was helped by the fact that production coincided

---

17 Štěpán Hulík, *Kinematografie zapomnění: počátky normalizace ve Filmovém studiu Barrandov* (Praha: Academia 2011), pp. 289–294.
18 S. Přádná, 'Balancování na hraně možného. Tvorba Věry Chytilové v období normalizace', in P. Kopal (ed.), *Film a dějiny 4. Normalizace* (Praha: Casablanca, ÚSTR 2014), pp. 41–71.

with an important shift in the culture of Czechoslovak cinema, linked to the end of Ludvík Toman's tenure as chief commissioning editor of Barrandov Studios; Toman had dutifully blocked any deviation from the set ideological line throughout the 1970s.[19] Now entering the 1980s, there was something of a relaxation in control.

Following Chytilová's pioneering movie, several other journalistic accounts followed in the 1980s which would question socialist modernity in a critical fashion. Most such reports focused on different aspects of drug abuse in Czechoslovakia. The abuse of opioids, methamphetamine and prescription drugs came to be linked with topics such as boredom and isolation resulting from socialist consumer-oriented lifestyles. The Czechoslovak state socialist regime of the 1970s and 1980s put the topics of 'calm for work' into the fore and secured basic nutritional as well as cultural satisfaction to its citizens. This has resulted in their turning into private and privatized spaces. The Czechoslovak interest in drugs surely also resulted from the cultural transfer of global countercultures and from the particularly medicalized local context with strong pharmaceutical production. One of the first to tackle this important and widespread social phenomenon was the account of Josef Klíma in *Náruživost* (*Heavy Use*, 1983).[20] A particularly important book dealing with the same matter was *Memento* by Radek John (1986).[21] *Memento*, with its combination of fiction and contemporary commentary, became a highly important reference point for the non-conformist Czechoslovak youth discovering a path to altered states of minds.

Memento was a product typical of 'perestroika', a period from 1985 which saw profound changes in economic, social and cultural spheres. Policies in the Soviet Union served as an example for the rest of the Soviet bloc with their aims of overall modernisation in order to catch up with the West. However, several countries which formed part of the Soviet bloc, including Czechoslovakia, were reluctant to embrace this model. Internal tensions dogged the remaining years of the Communist party of Czechoslovakia dictatorship until the winter of 1989–1990.[22] These tensions also manifested themselves in the media sphere with the simultaneous existence of two models, an anxiety-free 'normalisation' model, and a 'perestroika' model, which sought to re-envision society along socialist lines but by paying careful attention to its problems.

---

19   Hulík, *Kinematografie zapomnění*, pp. 157, 170–176.
20   Josef Klíma, *Náruživost* (Praha: Práce, 1983).
21   Radek John, *Memento* (Praha: Československý spisovatel, 1986).
22   Michal Pullmann, *Konec experimentu: Přestavba a pád komunismu v Československu* (Praha: Skriptorium 2011).

5 Working Class Youth Going Wild

An important feature of the media production of the 'perestroika' stage of late-state socialism was a fixation on juvenile delinquency and issues linked with different subcultures. One article offers a particularly instructive example—Gerhard Kromschröder's article '*100+1 zahraničních zajímavostí*' (*Hundred and one of foreign curiosities*) which was originally published in the West German magazine *Spiegel* and then translated into Czech in 1986 and published in issue 18 of the popular review of foreign press.[23] This Kromschröder's article contained shocking information about gangs of racist skinheads cruising Western European cities at night in search of defenceless immigrant victims, fuelled by alcohol and masculine camaraderie. Some sections of Czechoslovak society might have been frightened by such depictions, especially those content to pursue 'peace of mind' and 'socialist legality'. For others, usually young male Czechoslovaks, the aestheticized violence depicted in the article served as an impulse to adapt the skinhead style. Skinheads in late 1980's Czechoslovakia came to follow the heavily far-right politicised version depicted in '*100+1 zahraničních zajímavostí*' without any reflection of the historical development of the skinhead style, a fact which would have important consequences to the subcultural racist violence of the 1990s.

An important feature of the 'perestroika' critique was that the Socialist authorities, and that category included teachers, would be portrayed as inexperienced and unprepared for the changing nature of work with the youth. There was a certain number of expert commentaries printed in the magazine *Tvorba* (*Creation*) dedicated to such issues. The media also came to pay greater attention to the class backgrounds of those involved in delinquency. Explaining acts of vandalism at heavy metal concerts, violence at the newly built suburbs of large cities or at rural dance parties, a pattern of demonisation can be traced, where trainee labourers were targeted as the principal perpetrators.[24] This special attention to apprentices, and linking the working class youth with perpetrators, was a consequence not only of the place such groups played in Marxist-Leninist ideology as the vanguard of the proletarian state. It may also have resulted from a new policy of class bashing by the late state socialist, with technocrats trying to secure their hegemony during the

---

23 Gerhard Kromschröder, Gewalt ohne Grenzen, *Stern*, 25 (12 June 1986); Czech translation Holohlavci, to jsou pane chlapci, *100+1 zahraničních zajímavostí*, 18 (1 September 1986), pp. 9–12.
24 Authors such as Růžena Luňáková, Jan Votruba and Miloslav Šmídmajer, dedicated increased attention to the topics of juvenile delinquency and subcultures in *Tvorba* throughout 1987.

uncertain times of 'perestroika' by portraying the working class and its youth as violent, irresponsible, and dangerous.

These issues would be crucial for the production and reception of the Czechoslovak film *Proč?* (*Why?*, 1987) directed by Karel Smyczek and based on real-life events. The film reconstructed one night in June 1985 when hooligans associated with the football team Sparta Prague targeted an express train, vandalising several of its carriages and harassing its passengers. With its sociologically-informed interest in its hooligan protagonists and its scenes inspired by exploitation cinema, *Proč?* remained one of the most striking records of its era for contemporary critics. The hooligans' attack prompted a moral panic that continued around the film's premiere in October 1987 and is recorded in diverse media outlets.

In reply to the central question of the film, why such a senseless act of violence occurred, the film not only linked the explanation to the mimetic ecstasy inspired by the situation at and around British stadiums in the 1980s, but also related football violence with a broader social and existential critique. The overall explanation of this outbreak of generational nihilism was explained not only through boredom, alcohol and group behaviour but also by pointing to the dysfunction with many Czechoslovak families, their lack of informed perspective, feelings of cultural isolation, and limited possibilities available to them to satisfy their consumer tastes. Some of these points would be of a more general nature but several reflected particular experiences of life in the socialist Czechoslovakia state. As a consequence, the anxiety induced by Smyczek's film about frenzied ecstatic violence also came to have a mobilising effect. More than three decades from its premiere, it has remained so legendary among local hooligans and their sympathisers that many of the dialogues from the film continue to be exchanged in the real world, while chants from *Proč?* continue to reverberate around football stadia, and on the trains that carry fans to and from matches.

The dual regimes of anxiety-free and anxiety-fuelled media production existed in parallel within the 1970s and 1980s' Czechoslovak mediascape. Where the media was focused on the domestic Czechoslovak situation, there was little to no level of anxiety in evidence, reflecting the state-controlled media aims of silencing violence within the public sphere after the 1968 occupation. Where anxiety within the media was evident, it was used to denigrate the image of the West, or later, as part of determined efforts to reflect and help rebuild the structures of socialist society. These regimes can be understood as parallel and simultaneous regimes of anxiety and calm. Their explanation may in part point to the rather marginal place violence had in Czech culture and history. The violence had thus a shocking and mobilizing potential particular to the Czech society. This idea may be best illustrated in the issues of non-violence in the November 1989 'Velvet Revolution'. The mobilising slogan then read along the lines 'They beat our children!' with shocking information about violent repression of the pacific student demonstration. However, the violence that reappeared in the second half of the 1980s focusing on delinquency, accelerated in early spring of 1990. Emblematic events related to street racism against Roma, Vietnamese and Africans as well as a prison mutiny in the Slovak town of Leopoldov in the early spring of 1990 provided a brand new aesthetic of media messages with levels of violence unseen before. During the post-socialist decades that followed, both symbolic and physical violence as well as particular capacities inherent in the Czech culture to evade the open conflict, can be documented in media messages.

We have also aimed in this chapter to analyse the unintended consequences of panicked news items and films, pointing to losses in translation during the processes of encoding and decoding. Oppositional readings of the article about skinheads and the film about football hooligans established an iconic model that is still imitated. These examples of the Czechoslovak media in the two decades in question point to the necessity of underlining the public as an agent, even in the contexts of state-controlled media.

CHAPTER 16

The Media Portrayal of Radical Irish Republicans
An Anthropological Perspective

Aodhán (Maria-Valeria) Morris

This chapter will evaluate media portrayals of contemporary physical force Irish Republicans in both news media and popular culture. It will also adopt an anthropological perspective, focusing on the stigma conveyed in portrayals of Irish Republicans and the resulting re-actualisation of symbolic resistance practices within the Republican community.

A range of primary source materials were analysed in preparing this chapter, including media narratives, as well as popular books and comics featuring anti-Good Friday Agreement (hereafter GFA) Republicans. Fieldwork was also possible, though the COVID-19 pandemic necessitated digital ethnography rather than face to face interviews. A number of phone and email interviews were conducted with members of the anti-GFA Republican community engaging in peaceful campaigning and social work. Contact was also established via the Telegram messaging service with an anonymous member of the wider Republican movement, who kindly agreed to distribute questionnaires among persons presumably involved in armed struggle.

Given the sensitive nature of respondents' presumed activities and the risk of prosecution if identified, extra care was taken to protect the anonymity of sources. The questionnaires were designed in a way that would exclude disclosure of any presumed illegal actions or personal details, such as the age range, gender, education, professional occupation, or location of respondents. The written responses were photographed and sent via a secure Telegram channel; after keying in the responses into an Excel file, the source photos were deleted. Two questionnaires were issued; the first concerned rebel music within the contemporary radical Republican community, while the second focused on the impact of anti-Republican imagery in the media on the respondents' daily lives. The first set of questions was as follows:

a) Whether the respondent identifies themselves as a Republican.
b) What function, significance and role, in their experience and opinion, does rebel music have in Republican community and Republican activism?

c) What would they consider exactly to constitute rebel music, and what would be the typical situations/practices in the community in regard to playing rebel music / listening to it?
d) What was their opinion on artists exploiting paramilitary Republican imagery, and whether there would be any intersection between rebel music scene and socialist and anarchist punk scene and vice versa?

In total, ten anonymous handwritten answers to this questionnaire were received, along with one non-anonymous communication.[1]

All respondents, both militant and nonviolent, were either aligned with or sympathetic to Republican Sinn Féin (hereafter RSF). This is important in the context of the extremely fragmented nature of the anti-GFA Republican movement; each organization within this political landscape exhibits different identities of nationalism and socialism, the two founding pillars of the Republican creed.[2] The wider RSF movement enjoys far less media attention than Saoradh or the New IRA, and rarely makes the headlines. Since the wider RSF movement distinguishes itself from other militant Republican organisations and sees itself as a distinct force with a unique continuity from the First Dáil Éireann onwards, it is important to emphasise that the research which follows in this chapter is based solely on the data obtained on this specific alignment within the Republican movement. This particular group is itself notably pluralistic in its attitudes. For example, while some of the 'underground' respondents to the questionnaires placed more emphasis on cultural nationalism and expressed some conservative views, others were clearly of a Marxist persuasion.

1 Radical Republicanism in Post-Troubles Fiction

The phenomenon of the 'Troubles thriller' has been well researched, with its familiar and consistent tropes clearly delineated. The irrational, animalistic, sexual predator, and more often than not physically deformed IRA gunman, forms one of the genre's key elements.[3] In the later years of the genre, by the 1980s and into the 1990s, the typical antagonists of this genre of fiction began

---

[1] A more detailed examination of the data can be found in: Maria-Valeria Morris, '"That's what they won't take from you": Irish rebel music as a resistance practice in contemporary radical Republican community', *Urban Folklore & Anthropology*, III:3/ 4 (2021), pp. 122–139.
[2] Marisa McGlinchey, *Unfinished business: The politics of 'dissident' Irish republicanism* (Manchester: Manchester University Press, 2019), pp. 69–70.
[3] Laura Pelaschiar, 'Terrorists and freedom fighters in Northern Irish fiction', *The Irish Review (1986–)*, 40/41 (2009), pp. 56–57.

to include British operatives and undercover agents who adopted brutal and questionable methods of achieving their goals.[4] Yet, the very unflattering portrayal of the Republican paramilitary remained constant, if developed, perhaps, with dark irony which literary scholars such as Rafferty and Pelaschiar have interpreted as a way of confronting the trauma of the Troubles for both the writers and the readership in the North of Ireland.

Very occasionally, a Republican paramilitary character from the pre-1998 campaign was represented as someone other than a generic bloodthirsty thug. These rare cases tend to be categorized as 'real' highbrow literature as opposed to genre fiction. A fine example of this is Mark Mulholland's *A Mad and Wonderful Thing*, which has been analysed so well by Fiona McCann.[5] Johnny Donnelly, the protagonist, is portrayed in a far more nuanced and complex fashion than might have been expected. Unlike his mindlessly violent counterpart from the paperback thriller genre, Johnny is kind, cordial, intelligent and charming—except when he is not. Nevertheless, Johnny's humanity and complexity as a character is only possible because he is destined to repent; he dies while trying to prevent a bombing organized by his own comrades who, unlike Johnny, remain firmly opposed to the upcoming IRA ceasefire.

The critical and popular acclaim enjoyed by Mulholland's novel stands in stark contrast to the reception of Edna O'Brien's *House of Splendid Isolation*.[6] O'Brien's nuanced and psychologically driven portrayal of her paramilitary character McGreevy was met with harsh criticism and considered far-fetched.[7] Such criticism seems unfair, given the thoroughness of O'Brien's research; she interviewed Republican prisoners, including Dominic McGlinchey, who the McGreevy character is at least partly based on. Despite the position of the critics, O'Brien's portrayal of a Republican paramilitary character is probably among the most realistic ever. Arguably, of course, the difference in the way that Mulholland's Donnelly and O'Brien's McGreevy characters were received by both critics and the reading public alike, lies less in the realism of their portrayal, and more with the qualities they exhibit and represent. In post-Troubles fiction, a penitent sinner is allowed in the rank and file of the Provisional

---

4 Pauline Rafferty, 'Identifying diachronic transformations in popular culture genres: a cultural-materialist approach to the history of popular literature publishing', *Library History*, 24/4 (2008), pp. 268–270.
5 Mark Mulholland, *A mad and wonderful thing* (London: Scribe Publications, 2014); Fiona McCann, 'Northern Irish fiction after the Troubles', in L. Harte (ed.), *The Oxford handbook of modern Irish fiction* (Oxford: Oxford University Press, 2020), pp. 559–563.
6 Edna O'Brien, *House of Splendid Isolation* (London: Weidenfeld & Nicolson, 1994).
7 See, for example, Richard Bradford, *The novel now: contemporary British fiction* (Oxford: Blackwell Publishing Ltd, 2007), p. 234.

Irish Republican Army (hereafter PIRA). The generic bloodthirsty thug is now the dissident. Unlike McGreevy, Donnelly repents and thus earns himself a peaceful afterlife; his final purgatorial battle is waged against his unrepentant comrades.

Stuart Neville's debut novel *The Ghosts of Belfast*, also published as *The Twelve*, serves as a fine example here.[8] The protagonist, Gerry Fegan, used to be an effective and unflinching PIRA gunman. Now, though, he is a mentally unstable recluse with a drinking problem, haunted by the twelve people he had killed during his days of active insurgency—from civilians killed by a bomb which had exploded prematurely to the execution of Loyalist paramilitaries. To make peace with his conscience and get rid of the ghosts tormenting him day and night, Gerry embarked on a crusade of redemption, executing those who had been giving him the orders to kill. Gerry's ex-comrades, who he is hunting down, are now well-established Republican politicians and known advocates in favour of the peace process. These figures are, of course, pure evil, and exploit the peace process to line their own pockets and garner power, while dabbling in drug dealing and human trafficking after hours. While evil, these men are at least portrayed as capable, and as such constitute worthy adversaries for Gerry. Another character who Gerry is pitted against is a British undercover agent who is portrayed in a marginally sympathetic light; he does not deal drugs nor purchase underage sex slaves or kick dogs, which former paramilitaries in the novel do aplenty. There is whole group of Republican characters, however, who exist in the novel for the sole purpose to serve as a bleak background to the genuine threat presented by others, that is a 'dissident' anti-ceasefire splinter group.

This group is portrayed specifically as being outdated and inadequate in their assessment of themselves, even in their appearance. While 'mainstream' Republicans wear either expensive tailored suits or regular unremarkable garb, the members of the 'dissident' group are depicted as overweight middle-aged men trying to squeeze pathetically into trendy skinny jeans. They are, of course, all alcoholics who start drinking in the early morning and pass out by night with a can of beer in hand. The most daring exploit carried out by them is a robbery of a village post office, and even that they manage to botch. The undercover agent who monitors the group on the orders both from 'mainstream' Republicans and from his actual commanding officers, begs to be freed from this extremely boring duty. To cut a long story short, the novel suggests, in full compliance with the Troubles thriller canon, that while all unapologetic

---

8 Stuart Neville, *The Ghosts of Belfast* (New York: Soho Press, 2009). Also published as: Stuart Neville, *The Twelve* (New York: Vintage, 2010).

IRA men are evil, those of them who choose to continue the armed campaign are both evil and hopelessly stupid.

2   Comic Books

A similar narrative persists in comic book writing. Among the most colourful examples are the works of Garth Ennis, who has addressed the Troubles from the very beginning of his career. Apart from darkly comedic irreverent follow-ups to his debut work *Troubled Souls*, Ennis revisits the Troubles in *Punisher: Business as Usual* (2003), where the protagonist Frank Castle, a hardened vigilante, visits the North of Ireland to lend a helping hand to an old friend, a British ex-military man.[9] Meeting Frank ends badly both for a Provisional IRA (Provo) and a Loyalist. Frank kneecaps them both and leaves them to bleed to death next to a discharged gun with which they still try to kill each other. But Ennis's views on anti-ceasefire Republicans are even harder. In *Punisher MAX: Kitchen Irish* Frank deals with an Irish gang consisting of 'dissident' Republicans who prove to be mere bandits, sadistic and spiteful towards their sole support base—the naïve 'Plastic Paddies' who praise them as unflinching heroes.[10] To highlight the naïveté, the leading 'dissident', a merciless gang boss horribly disfigured by his own bomb (yet again in full compliance with the 'Troubles thriller' tropes), hardly waits two minutes after being praised as a hero before using the most vocal of his admirers as a human shield.

Nevertheless, these 'dissident' villains are at least capable of giving Frank a good run for his money. Unlike them, the young 'dissident' Republicans of *James Bond: M* (2018) by Declan Shalvey and P. J. Holden are on par with their older comrades from *The Ghosts of Belfast*.[11] While James Bond's future handler, a veteran of the Troubles on the British side, roams the streets of Belfast to settle old scores with his former sergeant, now a Loyalist paramilitary, he also encounters both ex-Provos and young rebels. The former end up in his command. The latter are portrayed as a clueless, incapable posse of socially-disadvantaged children, who are quick to anger but quicker to cowardice, and end up in M's command as well.

---

9   Garth Ennis, John McCrea, *Troubled souls* (London: Fleetway Publications, 1990); Garth Ennis, Steve Dillon, Darick Robertson, *The punisher vol. 3: business as usual* (New York: Marvel Comics, 2003).

10 Garth Ennis, Leandro Fernandez, *Punisher MAX: Kitchen Irish* (New York: Marvel Comics, 2005).

11 Declan Shalvey, P. J. Holden, Dearbhla Kelly, *James Bond: M* (Mount Laurel: Dynamite Entertainment, 2018).

We can compare and contrast this to the young gunman Barr in *The Last Crossing* by Brian McGilloway.[12] He has the looks and mannerisms of a typical naïve youth, entranced by the romantic notion of a war he is too young to have seen. This, though, is a ruse which is upended in the novel's final plot twist; Barr's unflinching loyalty to his ex-Provo uncle, now a politician enjoying the spoils of the peace process, goes far beyond condoning his uncle's actions during the war. After Barr's true colours are established, the author starts portraying him as a creepy and ruthless killer who, in a very calm and calculated manner, disposes of the most rebellious of his uncle's ex-comrades. That character, Hugh Duggan, is not an active 'dissident', but he is the most vocal in criticising the ceasefire. Naturally, he is portrayed as an alcoholic who hates paying child support and has a history of condoning drug dealing.

These types of 'dissident' Republican portrayals: the bloodthirsty career criminal capable of any evil; the fool living in the past; and any combination of the two, are very similar to the resident Provo types of the old school 'Troubles thriller', before the penitent sinner was allowed on stage. They are so prominent, in fact, that they have even made their way into non-western mass culture as popular villains of the week, for instance *Major Grom: The Children of St. Patrick* published by Bubble Comics in Russia.[13] The traits that these 'dissident' characters have in common across the many narrative forms are:
- Nostalgia of the turbulent past and incapability to accept the radically altered political and social landscape.
- Career criminality.
- Irrational appetite for violence and/or sexual predatoriness/promiscuity.
- Drinking problems and overall mental instability.

One could probably say that the reason behind copying and pasting this character of an absurdly unsophisticated, unhinged thug from book to book, from comic to comic is as simple as it is practical; the lowbrow thriller needs a trustworthy set of easy-to-hate villains that would give the reader the eponymous thrills; the evil dissident always delivers. As we will see, however, these very same tropes exist within news media too, despite news supposedly seeking to convey analysis which was factually rather than emotionally driven.

---

12 Brian McGilloway, *The last crossing* (Boston: Little, Brown Book Group, 2021).
13 Artem Gabrelyanov, Ivan Skorokhodov, Anastasia Kim, *Major Grom: the children of St. Patrick* (Moscow: Bubble Comics, 2015).

3 News Media Language on 'Dissident' Republicans

According to Sophie A. Whiting, the key 'Provisional'—as in pro-peace, 'mainstream' Republican—media concepts that 'underground' Republican media strives to counter are the following:
- Senseless obsession with violence.
- Equally senseless determination to drag the community into the violent past.
- Irrational psychotic evilness.
- 'Dissent' as treason and/or voluntary self-alienation from the 'normal' community.[14]

These representations are specifically designed to alienate their subject further from the reader. Whiting explores the political benefits of constructing such an image of dissident 'them' to oppose the law-abiding, pro-peace 'us': simplification of the discourse—'good' vs 'evil', 'us' vs 'them', instead of multiple individuals and groups with their own reasonings and complex motivations; depoliticising anti-GFA Republicanism, a mindless evil is certainly not a force with solutions to prevailing social and economic problems; and reification of the image of the former Provisionals as the only genuine Irish Republicans and, therefore, the ultimate gatekeepers of what Republicanism is and what it is not.[15]

Kevin Hearty has also explored contemporary Provisional discourses on 'dissident' Republicanism and finds that they are, to a very large extent, similar to decades-old narrative templates used to describe previous incarnations of Irish Republican armed struggle. These narrative templates are those of: irrationality (militant purity vs pro-peace pragmatism); criminality—particularly hurtful for traditional anti-GFA Republicans due to their vigilante activities; treason against their own community; and lack of popular support—'dissident' groups are portrayed as micro groups, unsupported and ostracised by the civilian population.[16] The resulting image of an irrational, thuggish remnant of the past trying to drag the unwilling civilian population back into decades of violence and carnage, is very close to that portrayed in the Provisional press.

There is a good deal of bad blood between the Provisionals and their former comrades. One wonders if unaffiliated news media would paint another

---

14   Sophie A. Whiting, 'The discourse of defence: 'dissident' Irish Republican newspapers and the 'propaganda war'', *Terrorism and Political Violence*, 24/3 (2012), pp. 485–488.
15   Whiting, 'The discourse of defence', p. 488.
16   Kevin Hearty, 'From "former comrades" to "near enemy": the narrative template of "armed struggle" and conflicting discourses on Violent Dissident Irish Republican activity (VDR)', *Critical Studies on Terrorism*, 9 (2016), pp. 269–291.

picture. To find that out, text analysis was run on a corpus of random news and opinion pieces from several Irish and British news media that mentioned 'dissident' Republicanism or any of the post-GFA IRAs in particular—namely the BBC, *The Belfast Telegraph, Derry Now, The Guardian, The Irish Independent, The Irish News, The Irish Times,* RTÉ, *TheJournal.ie,* and *The Times*). 50 sample texts were selected, while trying to reasonably limit inclusion of police reports due to their stylistic homogeneity. While by no means exhaustive, this analysis proved intriguing. The original hypothesis was that 'civilian' news media narratives would replicate, to an extent, the narrative patterns characteristic of the Provisional press as discussed above. To test this, five thematic categories were explored: namely, 'Belonging/clinging to the past', 'Being inadequate/minor', 'Criminality', 'Innate evilness/madness', and 'Being enemies of their own community'. Instances where these categories appeared within news narratives were counted. The results of this analysis are presented in Table 16.1.

An active presence of 'past vs. now' narratives and of narratives mocking and diminishing the opponent was quite expected, both within the dominant 'The Troubles are over for good' narrative, and with regard to the fact that mocking and/or ridiculing the opponent is one of the most widespread defence mechanisms. But beyond this, one category clearly stands out in terms of general frequency with respect of its intensity, where an author reiterates their point continuously throughout the same piece. Contrary to what was originally supposed, that 'criminality' and 'enemies of their own community'

TABLE 16.1   Frequency of 'Provisional' tropes encountered in news narratives about radical Republicans, from a selection of 50 articles

	Belonging or clinging to the past	Being inadequate and/or minor	Criminality	Innate evilness and/or madness	Being enemies of their own community
Counts (at least 1 mention per text)	26/50	26/50	18/50	28/50	20/50
Counts (total, including multiple mentions in one text)	37	42	33	61	45

narratives would be prevalent due to their relation to the wider 'public good' discourse, the primary line of 'dissident' portrayal in the media was in fact that of irrational evil madmen.

This representation, seemingly taken straight out of a paperback Troubles thriller, is, of course, factually inaccurate. Robert W. White notes that indiscriminately labelling political groups that engage in armed struggle against the state as 'terrorists' does nothing for actual understanding of the complex issues that lead people to taking up arms and risking their well-being, freedom and their very lives for a political goal.[17] Upon seeing beyond the 'terrorist' label, however, one discovers that the anti-GFA Republican movement, including organizations voicing support for or directly engaging in armed struggle, is not, in fact, centred around armed resistance. Rather, armed resistance is one of the many parts in a complex set of activities, mostly nonviolent. The reasons that led people to pursue military activism are the same that led them to taking up nonviolent activism, and do not, in either case, include either the 'irrational thirst for violence' or 'grooming of the young' so commonly attributed to anti-GFA Republicans by the media. White engaged in participant observation of Republican colour parties—demonstrations and marches accompanied by Republicans in military garb carrying Republican flags and banners—and commemorative events performed by the RSF movement for several years, and has concluded that all of these events, often interpreted as 'shows of strength' by the press and the public, were peaceful, and that confrontations, wherever they happened, were initiated by the police, with Republicans trying to defuse tensions whenever possible.[18] These events were also intended to provide a sense of belonging and of mutual support to a small marginalised community, and did not involve any 'grooming' or 'indoctrinating', with Republican family upbringing and/or attendance of Republican events not necessarily resulting in a participant developing interest in the movement.

Another matter that deserves mention here is Republican anti-drug vigilantism, which is condemned by the media and lends a fair share of emotionally charged words to the corpus analysed above. On a more thorough examination, though, it proves to have quite a lot in common with White's assessment of nonviolent assemblies. According to field data and analysis by McGlinchey, Republican anti-drug and anti-crime vigilantism is filling a painful vacuum in effective policing that was left after the Good Friday Agreement both by the disbandment of the PIRA and the historically embedded distrust towards

---

17   Robert W. White, 'Why "dissident" Irish Republicans haven't gone away: a visual study of the persistence of 'terrorism', *Contention*, 9/1 (2021), p. 64.
18   White, 'Why "dissident" Irish Republicans haven't gone away', pp. 76–91.

the police. While not everyone within anti-GFA Republican circles supports it, those who do see it not as a method of 'control' but as an unfortunate but necessary form of community protection. It should also be pointed out that, just like with violent and nonviolent activities in the Republican movement in general, these measures do not exist in some 'ghetto' of violence but are, in fact, executed simultaneously with many non-violent forms of Republican community support and social work aimed at deterring vulnerable people from criminality and drug use.[19] For example, Dieter Reinisch provides transcripts of in-depth interviews with young Na Fianna members who name Republican organisations and Republican social initiatives as key factors that helped them steer clear of anti-social behaviour and addiction.[20]

Assessing these phenomena in full detail is not possible here. Importantly, however, the angry 'dissident' savage with an irrational thirst for violence, who inhabits mass culture and mass media, has nothing in common with actual radical Republicans and their motivations, and, if anything, this imagery only clouds public and scholarly judgement. But, from an anthropological perspective, there is a reason it persists.

Eda Kalmre writes, following Diarmuid Ó Giolláin, Patricia A. Turner, and Carlo Ginzburg among others, that a divided and traumatised society will inevitably seek unity, and that unity is best and easiest found against an adversary.[21] Labelling a certain category of individuals as the 'Enemy Other', excluding them from the 'normal' community, is the position of power. The more bestial this designated enemy, this dragon to kill, the better. Narratives of extreme, phantasmagorical violence and barbarity serve to dehumanise their subjects, so that consolidation against them and using them as a designated outlet for social tensions and animosity is made more seamless and more plausible.[22] The imagining of an 'Enemy Other' who partakes in unspeakable atrocities, from black magic and cannibalism to their modern counterpart, waging war for the sake of war, allows the divided public to consolidate against imaginary evil and makes navigating times of uncertainty easier.

---

19 McGlinchey, *Unfinished business*, pp. 186–192.
20 Dieter Reinisch, 'Teenagers and young adults in dissident Irish republicanism: a case study of Na Fianna Éireann in Dublin', *Critical Studies on Terrorism*, 13/4 (2020), p. 712.
21 Diarmuid Ó Giolláin, 'Myth and history: exotic foreigners in folk-belief', *Temenos*, 23 (1987), pp. 59–80; Patricia A. Turner, *I heard it through the grapevine: rumor in African-American culture* (Berkeley, Los Angeles & London: University of Californian Press, 1993); Carlo Ginzburg, *Ecstasies* (Chicago: The University of Chicago Press, 1991).
22 Eda Kalmre, *The human sausage factory. A study of post-war rumour in Tartu* (Amsterdam & New York: Rodopi B.V., 2013), pp. 67–69.

The bitter reality, though, is that on the receiving end of this ancient coping mechanism there are actual human beings portrayed as the ultimate monster, members of the very same communities that shun and exclude them. The narrative of the 'mad evil dissident', seeping from screens and headlines into everyday interactions, has very real power to damage and ruin personal and professional lives.

4   Anti-Republican Stigma and Its Consequences

White mentions how one of his respondents, as a child, was told by a well-known senior Republican not to be afraid to tell people that she is a Republican.[23] One might ask, why would someone be afraid to mention their political beliefs to people? While undertaking research for another article, on contemporary Irish rebel music, respondents to a questionnaire often mentioned how anti-Republican imagery negatively affected their personal and professional lives. One interviewee explained:

> And the state propaganda mentioned earlier does have an effect, I have been shunned by people once they know of my political beliefs and sadly it did effect [sic] my relationship with my mother once she became aware of my involvement.[24]

In a second questionnaire, the following questions were posed to both militant and nonviolent anti-GFA supporters:
1. Have you ever experienced prejudice / stigma on a personal level (interpersonal relationships, professional relationships, etc.) because of being an anti-GFA republican?
2. Do you think that the mass media portrayal of contemporary Irish republican movement can fuel and encourage such stigma?

The (overall five) replies to these questions included repercussions people faced at work, including those who were not directly involved in the Republican movement in any manner, but who just said something positive about Republican political parties:

---

23   White, 'Why "dissident" Irish Republicans haven't gone away', p. 76.
24   E-mail interview 1.

> Yes, a few moments at work. There was a guy who talked about RSF good, so he was shunned.[25]

> Plenty at work and in life ... Was arrested a few times ... Was fired (same reason) from prev. work.[26]

Respondents felt the necessity to keep their politics a secret, both within the work environment and with friends and family members:

> You always need to keep your mouth shut, otherwise guards will come, friend or co-worker will rat.[27]

> [Distant family members—M.M.] made lots of comments too. All negative ... But my family's not ... Still they don't know half of it.[28]

> Yes, but I mostly hear of it than experience. Keeping my head out of showing, so people don't know. That is for a reason of course. Even my family doesn't know. Safer that way.[29]

When the respondents did express their political opinions, reaction was far from pleasant:

> Another thing is that constant freak/suspicion: 'You said that /something pro-RA/, are you a dissident?' Voice like 'Ya have AIDS and/or eat children?'[30]

> Plenty at work and in life. Ranting on the evil of evil terrorists, telling bullshit stories of drug wars and such, that's daily on.[31]

Sometimes revealing the respondent's political beliefs led to a deterioration and eventual severing of family ties:

---

25 Questionnaires pack 2, handout 1.
26 Questionnaires pack 2, handout 4.
27 Questionnaires pack 2, handout 2.
28 Questionnaires pack 2, handout 1.
29 Questionnaires pack 2, handout 3.
30 Questionnaires pack 2, handout 1.
31 Questionnaires pack 2, handout 4.

> Family conflicts. Dad is a big FS supporter. So get to hear lots of bullshite over the years. Haven't spoken to him for a decade or so now. Guess that counts.[32]

> Yes, I have suffered stigma, and the mass media plays a huge part in this and I would argue they are an integral tool in the portrayal of Republicans as some form of demons. Case in point; the mass media will portray Irish Republicans as warmongers, criminals and all-round degenerates, this suits the state and their hopes to maintain their grip on power. I have had one girlfriend walk out of my life once she realised I was a Republican and even my own mother disowned me over my involvement in Republicanism and the belief we were/are just criminals.[33]

The questions posed in these questionnaires did not concern, or imply, anything related to militant actions, and the animosity experienced by interviewees was directed at them for simply voicing their lack of support for the Good Friday Agreement. Where opinions were voiced and actual confrontations occurred, the way the interviewees were perceived by their opponent(s) was strikingly reminiscent of the imagery prominent in media narratives ('evil of evil terrorists', 'drug wars'), with the dominant reaction being one of fear rather engagement in rational political debate. As another interviewee expressed it, 'people are scared of ghosts, the ones they imagine'.[34]

5   Rebellion Once Again

Such an atmosphere of suspicion, fear and disgust which permeated all spheres of life, from family home to workplace, provided the impetus and space for the development of a counter narrative. Practices of resistance helped individuals cope with pressure and trauma. One such practice of resistance involved a renewed emphasis on original meanings within Irish rebel music.

Irish rebel music holds an ambiguous position in media narratives. On the one hand, classic rebel songs can occasionally make it to prime-time television. Bands such as The Wolfe Tones, who penned some iconic rebel ballads, are well-loved and celebrated in Ireland. On the other hand, the very same songs can often be met with outcry and labelled as sectarian material. For example,

---

32   Questionnaires pack 2, handout 5.
33   E-mail interview 2.
34   Questionnaires pack 2, handout 2.

'Come Out Ye Black and Tans' was considered mostly appropriate to be aired on the BBC, but it caused an outrage when a Sinn Féin TD sang it to celebrate his victory in the elections.[35] The key difference between these cases is not the song material itself, but the communicative situation in which the songs were performed. According to the latter, the same text can be framed either as history and heritage, a safely defused remnant of a finite past, or an incendiary commentary on current events.

The concept of continuity, so important in traditional Republican discourse as the source of legitimacy over quantitative mandates of popular support, is obviously at play here as well. Wherever the continuity between the 'Old' IRA, PIRA and current traditional Republicans is unbroken, this challenges the 'mainstream' Republicans' right to serve as Republicanism's only gatekeeper. This is where the border between the past and the present becomes fragile, where the inevitability of the uneasy peace is called into question, and where decades-old songs begin to reassume their original rebellious tenor. Of course, the singer and the audience both constitute an integral part of the communicative circuit that helps highlight or downplay this continuity.

Stephen R. Millar has written of how the same song can be seen as a commentary on the past in pro-GFA venues and as a contemporary rebel song if sung in a venue associated with anti-GFA circles.[36] The environment and the known alignments of the singers and the audience help frame the lyrics either as an act of cultural memory, or of symbolic resistance.[37] Naturally, both audiences, the 'memorial' and the 'rebel' guard their borders fervently. When a rebel song is sung beyond an 'official' memorial safe space or the rebel 'ghetto', be it blaring from an election van, chanted by football fans or teenagers at a music festival, the 'non-rebel' spectators see it as dangerous, and are often quick to condemn it as sectarian hate speech. On the other hand, when 'rebel' audiences hear rebel material sung as part of tourist entertainment, they can feel hurt. One of my respondents described those singing rebel songs recreationally as 'empty-headed idiots singing Roll of Honour for fun'.[38]

Commemorative events and colour parties can also act as an opportunity to form and sustain a collective identity, which, in turn, can help sustain the

---

35 For a detailed analysis of these and other cases, see Maria-Valeria Morris, '"That's what they won't take from you": Irish rebel music as a resistance practice in contemporary radical Republican community', *Urban Folklore & Anthropology*, III:3/4 (2021), p. 126.
36 Stephen R. Millar, *Sounding dissent: rebel songs, resistance, and Irish Republicanism* (Ann Arbor: University of Michigan Press, 2020), pp. 196–197.
37 These terms were coined by James C. Scott, *Domination and the arts of resistance: hidden transcripts* (New Haven and London: Yale University Press, 1990).
38 Questionnaires pack 1, handout 8.

culture of resistance.[39] Rebel music functions within the community in a similar way, and is intrinsically intertwined with the very notions of Republicanism, Irishness, resistance and martyrdom:

> Music for me is a part of Irish identity and always was such. Republican identity is for me another word for Irish identity or should be. So music and Republican identity are intertwined. Like in the past it was that poets were the leaders of rebellions against English, likes of Padraig Pearse or James Mangan or Bobby Sands. Basically for me it seems natural in our spirit and maybe rebel spirit in general.[40]

> No Irish Republic without Irish people. No Irish people without Irish history, language, music, sport. It is a part of who we are and who should we be.[41]

> For Irish people, in Irish culture, music was always something more. Without music and without history there won't be a nation.[42]

> Irish republicanism was always more than just a political movement and/or military struggle against the foreign occupation. It was always intertwined with the Irish culture, language, traditions. That's why rebel music is so important in Republican movement and that's also why there's no such thing as "unionist music", for while the Republicans represent the nation, loyalists represent the state, the empire.[43]

> In my opinion, the rebel music first and foremost inspires, it keeps the fire alive so we remember the sacrifices that were made and don't turn the blind eye to the injustices, everyday injustices. Here if you hear of it, if you've listened, if you've learned something—it is a victory already. In my opinion when we listen or sing our songs we show the respect to our great heroes and follow their footsteps. It is up to us to finish what they began, so it is an inspiration and also a way to always remember who we are.[44]

---

39   White, 'Why 'dissident' Irish Republicans haven't gone away', pp. 88–89.
40   Questionnaires pack 1, handout 2.
41   Questionnaires pack 1, handout 5.
42   Questionnaires pack 1, handout 6.
43   Questionnaires pack 1, handout 10.
44   Questionnaires pack 1, handout 7.

Other than that, song of struggle, of rebellion will keep you alive, will keep your spirits high. Just another reminder of what we [are] fighting for.[45]

Playing a song, then, in a specific marked location can alter its perception; the same song played in a 'mainstream' and in a 'hard-line' Republican venue would be, anthropologically speaking, two different songs. Attending such specific locations and/or events means creating a communicative situation that reverts a 'tamed' text into its original rebellious self. But this act of symbolic rebellion was not aimed at outside audiences as some 'show of strength'. An outsider would not likely see through the well-known folk tunes into the actual context. The 'rebel' rebel songs were and are, first and foremost, intended to inspire and support the members of the community themselves, to inspire and 'keep spirits high'. As one of my respondents puts it,

I think it's hard not to sing, like when it's a hunger or a war, or a rebellion, or poverty, or you're homeless; that's something you will not lose. That's what they won't take from you in prison camp or block cell. That's why it is still there and will always be.[46]

The language of the mass media, whether in fiction or cartoons, or in the news media, has tended to transmit a very one-dimensional and grim image of radical Republicans as intrinsically villainous, bloodthirsty thugs. This image is factually inaccurate, and fuels a stigma that, in turn, can have a very negative influence on people's everyday lives by creating an unhealthy climate of suspicion and alienation. As we have seen here, the challenge of coping with this pressure has led to the emergence of open and more subtle resistance strategies, such as public commemorative events or recapturing the revolutionary essence of traditional Irish rebel music—moving it from the realm of cultural memory back into the realm of current political affairs. These acts are often interpreted as a threat or as a 'show of strength' and can certainly provoke yet further media and public anger and suspicion. In truth, though, such practices are mostly ingroup and designed to help sustain a persecuted and ostracized identity.

---

45 Questionnaires pack 1, handout 9.
46 Questionnaires pack 1, handout 4.

SECTION 6

Trouble in the Headlines

CHAPTER 17

Hyde and the Media—Friend or Foe?

Máire Nic an Bhaird

Douglas Hyde, *Dubhghlas de hÍde*, was born in Castlerea, County Roscommon on 17 January 1860 and died on 12 July 1949. Also known as *An Craoibhín Aoibhinn* (literally 'the pleasant little branch'), Hyde was an academic, linguist, scholar of the Irish language, and statesman who served as the first President of Ireland from June 1938 to June 1945. He was a leading figure in the Gaelic revival, and was co-founder and first President of the Gaelic League which was established in 1893, and which became one of the most influential cultural organisations in Ireland at the time. It was through Hyde's force of personality and the relatively favourable temper of his time, that he was able to bring his concern for the future of the Irish language and its culture to centre stage in the public sphere at the beginning of the twentieth century.[1]

It was not unusual for Irish public figures in the latter part of the nineteenth century and the opening decades of the twentieth, to embark upon a lecture tour of North America because they understood that the Irish in America represented moral and financial support for Irish nationalist movements. W. B. Yeats embarked upon his first lecture tour in 1903–1904 and Oscar Wilde's first tour took place in 1882.[2] Douglas Hyde, as president of the Gaelic League, conducted his fundraising lecture tour of North America in 1905–1906. Unlike most Irish visitors, Hyde published a detailed account of his lecture tour in his autobiographical book *Mo Thurus go hAmerice* which provides a picture of Irish America at the start of the twentieth century.[3] Hyde attracted considerable media attention wherever he went during his tour. Douglas Hyde was a life-long generator, collector and recorder of ego-documents and ephemera—letters,

---

1 For biographical information on Douglas Hyde's life, see Janet Dunleavy, Gareth Dunleavy, *Douglas Hyde, A Maker of Modern Ireland* (Oxford: University of California Press, 1991).
2 Nick Frigo, 'Posing and posters: Oscar Wilde in America—1882', *The Wildean*, 30 (2007), pp. 73–85; Robert Mahony, 'Yeats and the Irish language revival: An unpublished lecture', *Irish University Review*, 19 (1989), pp. 220–226.
3 Máire Nic an Bhaird, 'Mo thurus go hAmerica: tionchar na féinchinsireachta', in Attracta Halpin, Áine Mannion (eds.), *Douglas Hyde: the Professor of Irish who became President of Ireland* (Dublin: National University of Ireland, 2016), pp. 46–47.

diaries, drafts of speeches, newspaper cuttings and photographs.[4] Hyde, a cultural activist, had an astute appreciation of the importance of publicity and public relations, as did John Quinn, The Irish-American New York lawyer, and Father Peter Yorke, the Irish-born Catholic priest in San Francisco, who were the principal organisers of Hyde's 1905–1906 fund-raising tour of America for the Gaelic League. It is this clever strategic use of the media that will be examined in this chapter.

1 The Morrisroe-Connolly Collection, G 37 at the James Hardiman Library

The James Hardiman Library at the National University of Ireland Galway, contains an album of press cuttings from Hyde's American tour, from February to June 1906, mainly from American newspapers, and others dealing with Hyde's triumphant return to Ireland.[5] This volume, named Volume 2, was prepared by Úna Ní Ógáin, a Gaelic League colleague of Hyde and highlights the vital use of the newspapers for promoting this lecture tour and how the media helped to propel Hyde to the forefront of Irish international relations, thus carving out his future career as a statesman. It is assumed that the first volume is either lost or missing. The National Library of Ireland acquired a similar, if less elaborate, scrapbook for 1903–1904, compiled by Hyde himself.[6] It would appear, therefore, that Hyde compiled scrapbooks of his own and of the Gaelic League's activities over the years. The Galway volume is a testimony to the international public recognition accorded to Hyde as the pioneering leader of the Gaelic Revival and its campaign of cultural disruption.

The Protestant nationalist Úna Ní Ógáin (Jane Agnes Emily Young) was born in 1868. She lived in a beautiful house in Brockley Park, County Laois. Úna began collecting religious poems around 1915.[7] In 1928, C. S. Ó Fallamhain published *Dánta Dé idir Sean agus Nua*. Úna collected the words and the airs and edited the book which she then dedicated to Douglas Hyde. He was her inspiration in regard to the Irish language. However, Úna died in 1927, therefore

---

4 Máire Nic an Bhaird, 'Reading between the lines: Hyde's writings, 1916', *Éire-Ireland*, 53 (2018), p. 48.
5 This volume can be viewed in The Morrisroe Connolly Collection, MS G 37 at the James Hardiman Library, National University of Ireland, Galway (hereafter NUI Galway).
6 National Library Ireland, MS 42,685.
7 See www.ainm.ie for more biographical information on Úna Ní Ógain. https://www.ainm.ie/Bio.aspx?ID=209.

it was Hyde who ensured that this collection was published. Here is an extract from the letter Hyde wrote to Dr Lawlor in 1928 about Úna's publication.

> My Dear Dr Lawlor. I am sending you a translation of the Irish hymns and music that Miss Young collected. When she died, a year ago, I took over the work of seeing it through the press, with more trouble than any two of my own books ever did. I only wish Miss Young had lived to see her book in print. Yours very truly Douglas Hyde.[8]

Perhaps Úna Ní Ógáin collated Volume 2 by way of a Christmas gift for Hyde in 1906. As you can see in Figure 17.1, the following is written; 'An Craoibhín Aoibhinn from his friend Ú Ní Ó Nodhlaig 1906'.

The Galway volume is a testimony to the international public recognition accorded to Hyde as the pioneering leader of the Gaelic Revival and its campaign of cultural disruption. Hyde's ability and skill in understanding his audience and adapting accordingly, abstaining from controversy, dealing with the press and rousing audiences with his speech delivery were honed during this trip. Hyde's American Journey was the beginning of a new stage in Hyde's public role in Irish affairs.

2 John Quinn and Father Peter Yorke, the Public Relations Duo

The newspapers provided a platform for the dissemination of nationalist and revivalist ideals so their importance as an instrument of change must not be overlooked. In the early 1900s, the news reached the public in print and newspapers were at the height of their power and influence in North America.[9] They were inexpensive and ubiquitous. The publishers and editors of the largest daily newspapers of that time had enormous political and social influence.[10] Newspapers carry the news of the world and it is fascinating to look at the press cuttings in Úna Ní Ógáin's volume because they allow us understand how Hyde used the media to promote his tour. Hyde had an astute appreciation of the importance of publicity and public relations, as did John Quinn and

---

8   Representative Church Body Library, Dublin, 38/3/429.
9   Aoife Whelan,'Irish Independent coverage of Douglas Hyde's vision for a De-Anglicised Ireland', in Liam Mac Mathúna Máire Nic an Bhaird (eds.), *Douglas Hyde: Irish ideology and International Impact* (Dublin: The National University Ireland, 2022).
10 Úna Ní Bhroiméil, *Building Irish identity in America* (Dublin: Four Courts Press, 2003).

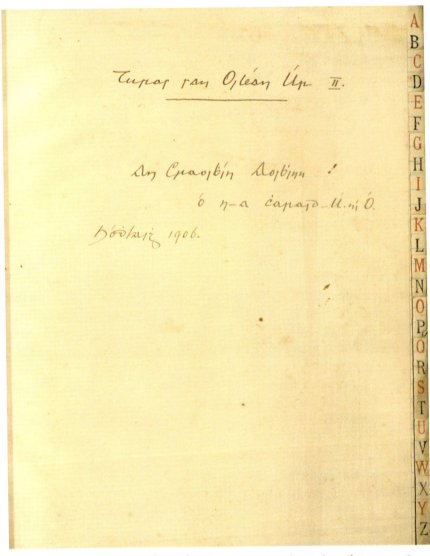

FIGURE 17.1 Inside cover of Úna Ní Ógáin's album presented to Hyde at Christmas 1906
IMAGE COURTESY OF THE JAMES HARDIMAN LIBRARY, MORRISROE-CONNOLLY COLLECTION, AT NUI GALWAY, G37, HYDE SCRAPBOOK

Father Peter Yorke. John Quinn was born in Ohio in 1870, and he was the eldest son of Irish immigrants. His mother was from County Cork and his father from County Limerick. He studied at Georgetown University and Harvard and then moved to New York where he quickly established himself as an accomplished and affluent lawyer.¹¹ John Quinn was fascinated by literature and the Irish culture, and as such became a patron of the arts and a champion of the Revival Period. Quinn visited Ireland and spent time in Lady Gregory's Coole Park in 1902 where he met Douglas Hyde for the first time. *Mo Thuras go hAmerice (My American Journey)* is dedicated to John Quinn which highlights how Hyde wished to bestow a very high honour on John Quinn and to praise him for his work as chief organiser of the tour. This also highlights the importance of John Quinn to the whole operation.

> I first encountered John Quinn, an American lawyer from New York, in August 1902. I clearly remember the first occasion I saw him. Lady Gregory, Edward Martin from Tulira, and a large crowd had gathered in Killeeneen Cemetery, where a fine inscribed stone memorial has been erected, inscribed with gold letters, in memory of the poet Raftery ... I conversed with the American and he enquired about the Irish language in Ireland. He apparently heeded my answers, as I received one or two letters from him once he returned to New York, stating that, if possible, I should come to America where I would receive assistance from him, and others ... I became very friendly with him ... The Gaelic considered the possibility of sending someone to fundraise in America, I alone was available, and, as I was president of the League since its establishment, there was, in their opinion, no one more suitable than me.¹²

Father Peter Yorke was born in Galway (1864–1925); he was an Irish-American Catholic priest and a cultural activist. He attended St Patrick's College, Maynooth where he studied for four years before moving to the Archdiocese of San Francisco, where he became the editor of *The Monitor*, the official newspaper of the archdiocese. In 1902, he founded and edited a local San Francisco newspaper titled *The Leader*. He also founded the Californian branch of the Gaelic League.¹³

John Quinn was chief organiser of the overall tour, whilst Father Peter Yorke worked heavily on promoting and organising the San Francisco leg. Both aimed

---

11 B.L.Reid, *The Man from New York John Quinn and his Friends* (New York: Oxford University Press, 1968), p. 3.
12 Douglas Hyde, *My American Journey*, Liam Mac Mathuna, Brian Ó Conchubhair, Niall Comer, Cuan Ó Seireadáin, Máire Nic an Bhaird (eds.) (Dublin: University College Dublin Press, 2019), pp. 3–4.
13 James P. Walsh, Timothy Foley, 'Father Peter C. Yorke Irish-American leader', *Studia Hibernica*, 14 (1974), pp. 90–103.

to increase Hyde's overall reputation in America. The public relations plan that Quinn and Yorke created and implemented was a strategic communication process that contributed significantly to the success of Hyde's tour. Understanding the target audience is the most important part of any successful public relations strategy and Quinn, Yorke and Hyde knew their audiences. The publicity that Hyde achieved through newspapers at the time helped to heighten the public awareness of Hyde, his lecture tour and his fundraising mission. Hyde understood that 'newspapers, periodicals and journals played a pivotal role in developing this nationalist culture in line with the 'Irish-Ireland' ideology'.[14] This was a highly successful marketing campaign. Publicity through the newspapers helped Hyde to get his story out there, helped others to become aware of him and his organisation. Media played a very significant role in keeping everyone updated about his tour schedule and the successes. The most important function of the media is to disseminate news to the masses concerning vital occurrences or important information. The American newspapers did exactly this, as can be seen through Úna Ní Ógáin's album where she kept newspaper reports and lecture pamphlets which help showcase this strategic marketing machine that aided the successful tour of America.

The media aimed to inform, educate and entertain. The same may be said of the Conradh na Gaeilge (Gaelic League) in its early years.[15] What set the League apart from earlier language organisations, such as the Society for the Preservation of the Irish Language and the Gaelic Union was its success at a grassroots level.[16] The network of branches filtered down from national and regional committees to local groups, along the same lines as the Gaelic Athletic Association (GAA) club structure. Contemporary accounts of branch meetings tell us that literature was discussed, poetry was read, songs were sung in Irish, and that lectures were given on various topics relevant to the movement. An article published in the Gaelic League's newspaper *An Claidheamh Soluis* in December 1899 informs readers that the 'interesting piece in Irish in [the] *Irish Daily Independent* was read and listened to with great attention at a recent Gaelic League class'.[17] This highlights the important role of the media

---

14   Whelan, 'Irish Independent coverage of Douglas Hyde's vision for a De-Anglicised Ireland', p. 70.
15   For a history of Conradh na Gaeilge, see Pádraig Ó Fearaíl, *The Story of Conradh na Gaeilge: A History of the Gaelic League* (Dublin: Conradh na Gaeilge, 1975).
16   The Society for the Preservation of the Irish Language was founded in 1876. The Gaelic Union was founded in 1880.
17   Regina Uí Chollatáin, 'Literature reviews in An Claidheamh Soluis: A journalistic insight to Irish literary reviews in the Revival Period 1899–1932', *Proceedings of the Harvard Celtic Colloquium*, 23 (2003), pp. 284–298.

both in reporting the League's activities and in providing reading material for their classes.[18]

The newspapers at the time not only reported on Hyde's lectures but they also informed the public about when and where they would be held. For example, *The Washington Times, Washington Post* and the *Sunday Star* publicised his Washington lecture on 20 May 1906. Language such as 'One of Ireland's great men to Lecture in this City', 'Leader of his people', 'He is regarded as one of the greatest men in Ireland' was used.[19] Large font headlines were deployed which would have helped increase publicity; indeed the use of attention-grabbing headlines is prominent throughout this volume.

3   Hyde's American Tour 1905–1906 as Reported Through Press Cuttings

Douglas Hyde left his home in Ratra in County Roscommon, Ireland on 6 November 1905, as he and his wife Lucy Cometina Kurtz set off on his lecture trip to America to promote the Gaelic League. Hyde was 46 years of age. Hyde and Lucy said farewell to their two young children, Nuala and Úna as they left their home in Ratra. He went to the Gresham Hotel on Sackville Street Dublin. At 7.15 p.m. that evening a giant torchlight procession bid farewell to Hyde and brought him to Knightsbridge station.[20] On 8 November, he boarded the SS Majestic in Queenstown.[21] Hyde landed on Wednesday 15 November 1905 in New York. He returned to Ireland on 24 June 1906 with many stories and memories from his trip. His journey spread right across the States from the eastern to the western seaboard and made its way home to Ireland too. Hyde's 1904–1907 diary which is housed in the National Library Ireland in Dublin and is digitised, includes Hyde's diary entries from the day he left Ratra on 6 November 1905 until 1 January 1906. He stopped mid-sentence on 1 January and did not pick up this diary until after he returns to Ireland in August 1906.[22] The cover of this

---

18   Regina Uí Chollatain, *An Claidheamh Soluis agus Fáinne an Lae 1899–1932* (Dublin: Cois Life, 2004).
19   G37, Hyde Scrapbook, Morrisroe-Connolly Collection, James Hardiman Library, NUI Galway.
20   Nuala Eibhlín Hyde was born in 1894, Úna Mary Hyde was born in 1896. Sackville Street, Dublin is now known as O' Connell Street. Knightsbridge Station is now known as Heuston Station.
21   Queenstown, Cork is now known as Cobh. For a more detailed account from Hyde's own pen, see 6–8 November in Hyde's 1904–1907 diary, available in The National Library Ireland, LS G 1047.
22   National Library Ireland, LS G 1047.

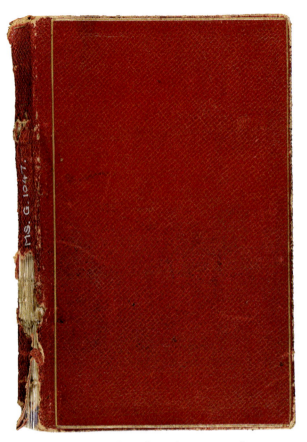

FIGURE 17.2   Cover of Douglas Hyde's 1904–1907 diary
COURTESY OF THE NATIONAL LIBRARY
IRELAND, LS G 1047

diary can be seen in Figure 17.2. This trip was about fundraising and highlighting the Irish revival. For example, in his diary on 28 November 1905 when he is in Hartford Connecticut, Hyde writes that he went into the big city and asked the wealthy people for money. He was promised 200 dollars from one man. He concludes that day as he did many a diary entry with reference to the weather, 'D'iarr mé airgead ó na daoinibh saidhbhre … lá an fhliuch san trathnóna', 'I asked for money from the rich people … a very wet day in the evening'.[23]

John Quinn organised a very tight schedule for Hyde as can be seen from Figure 17.3 which shows a page from his American tour schedule from 20 November to 12 December 1905. Hyde worked extremely hard on his lecture tour, though John Quinn ensured that he was well looked after. This is evident

---

23   National Library Ireland, LS G 1047.

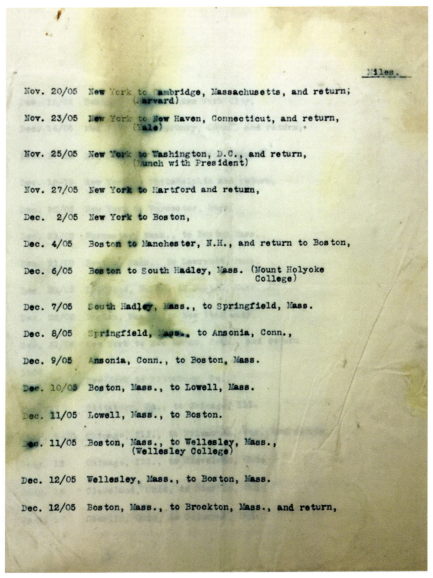

FIGURE 17.3 Hyde's American tour schedule
IMAGE COURTESY OF THE NATIONAL LIBRARY IRELAND, NLI LS 18 253

in Hyde's diary entry of 29 November 1905 where he says that he had a cold and hoarseness, so John Quinn would not let him out and brought his dinner to him, '29 November: Slaighdeán beag orm agus pitheachán … Ní leigfi mac Uí Cuinn amach mé'.[24]

---

24 National Library Ireland LS G 1047.

The album is not in chronological order of the American tour, though the places he visited on his lecture tour are arranged alphabetically. There is not only written text visible throughout this album, but also sketches of Hyde, as well as photographs from the newspaper articles. These images are incredibly important, as they allow us to understand more about Hyde's speeches, and in particular grasp a sense of his charisma, and how he used the media to increase his notoriety and ensure the success of his lecture tour.[25] For the readers of these newspapers, such pictures would have had a huge visual impact, communicating Hyde's importance; he was a man that ought be listened to and heeded. This visual content was an incredibly effective medium to help encourage the support of this lecture tour via the media. The importance of the visual is seen in an image of Hyde, collected by Úna Ní Ógáin, called 'Dr Douglas Hyde a distinguished Irish orator. Addressed a large audience in the Massey Hall last night, on the objects of the Gaelic League' which was taken from *The News*, Toronto on Friday 18 May 1906. As is seen in Figure 17.4, Douglas Hyde is standing tall, looking powerful; his moustache is the most striking physical feature, enhancing his already enigmatic character. The following sentence appears around his figure, 'None of the good old Irish songs were forgotten'. Hyde's non-partisan attitude which he publicly held, and which allowed him to be a very suitable statesman as Ireland's first President is seen in this article about his speech in Massey Hall, Toronto—'Irish orator sings the

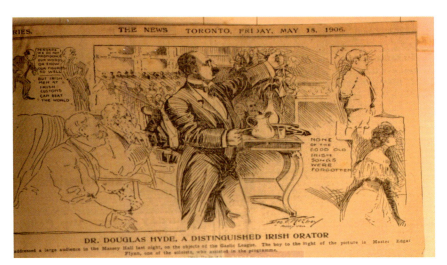

FIGURE 17.4   Dr. Douglas Hyde, A Distinguished Irish Orator addressing a large audience in the Massey Hall, Toronto (*The News*, Toronto, 18 May 1906)

---

25   National Library Ireland NLI LS 18, 259.

praises of the emerald isle of the sea and held the sons of Ireland in a trance of enthusiasm—the Gaelic League is a dove of peace, presenting neither clique, faction nor party'.[26]

4 Newspaper Cuttings of Hyde's Californian Tour Feb/March 1906

Úna Ní Ógáin's press cuttings offer insight into the Californian leg of Hyde's lecture tour which took place during February and March 1906, and of the vital role played by newspapers in supporting and marketing it. The news reports also highlight the role played by Father Yorke throughout, but especially in aiding the San Francisco fundraising campaign.[27] The article 'Gaelic Scholar Addresses Audience at University on Entertaining Subject' in the *San Francisco Call* published on 4 March 1906 offers information on Hyde's lecture in Berkeley University the previous day.[28] It is noted that Father Yorke introduced Hyde's lecture on the history of folktales, and that he played a key role in the organisation of a lavish banquet at the Palace Hotel in San Francisco.[29] Table 17.1 offers an overview of the locations in California in which Hyde delivered lectures in this period.

TABLE 17.1   Hyde's lecture locations in California from 21 February 1906 to 22 March 1906. Taken from National Library Ireland MS 18 253

Date	Location
21 February 1906	The Palace Hotel, San Francisco
23 February 1906	Coláiste Iognáid Naomhtha
26 February 1906	San Jose
1 March 1906	Oakland
2 March 1906	Tivoli Opera House, San Francisco

26 G37, Hyde Scrapbook, Morrisroe-Connolly Collection, James Hardiman Library, NUI Galway.
27 'Father Yorke was the head and front, the life and soul of the work done for Douglas Hyde on the Pacific Coast and his paper the *San Francisco Leader*, was its organ and mouthpiece'. *Gaelic American*, 5 May 1906. G37, Hyde Scrapbook, Morrisroe-Connolly Collection, James Hardiman Library, NUI Galway.
28 G37, Hyde Scrapbook, Morrisroe-Connolly Collection, James Hardiman Library, NUI Galway.
29 See Hyde, *My American Journey*, pp. 103–106 for a detailed account of Father Peter Yorke's involvement with Douglas Hyde on his lecture tour.

TABLE 17.1 Hyde's lecture locations in California (*cont.*)

Date	Location
3 March 1906	Berkeley University
4 March 1906	Eaglais an Dochtúra Clampett
6 March 1906	Sacramento in California
7 March 1906	Coláiste na mBráthar gCríostamhail, Coláiste na mBráithre Chroidhe Naomhtha
8 March 1906	Santa Barbara
10 March 1906	Los Angeles
12 March 1906	Los Angeles
13 March 1906	Coláiste San Vincent
15 March 1906	San Francisco
16 March 1906	San José—Coláiste Chumainn Íosa, Santa Clara
17 March 1906	San Francisco
21 March 1906	Comhdháil Bhliadhantamhail Chonnartha na Gaedhilge in California
22 March 1906	Halla Naomh Peadair

Úna Ní Ógáin collected the Douglas Hyde St Patrick's Day edition of the *San Francisco Leader* for her album.[30] This newspaper was founded by Father Peter Yorke in 1902. On the front cover there was a picture of Douglas Hyde, Lucy Hyde, Glendalough and Frank J. Sullivan. The title of the edition was 'The Leader—Dr Douglas Hyde Edition—Glowing Tribute to Hyde'. There was a discussion about the banquet given to Hyde in the Palace Hotel on Friday 21 February 1906, which noted that the 'banquet given to Dr. Douglas Hyde at the Palace Hotel, was the most brilliant social gathering ever held in San Francisco'.[31] *The Leader* described the success of Hyde's visit to the Tivoli Theatre in the article: 'Dr Douglas Hyde's Big Reception—The Grand Welcome given to the Craiobhín at the Tivoli Opera House on Sunday Afternoon, February 17th, Multitudes in Attendance':

---

30   St Patrick's Day edition dated 17 March 1906, G37, Hyde Scrapbook, Morrisroe-Connolly Collection, James Hardiman Library, NUI Galway.

31   *San Francisco Leader*, 17 March 1906, G37, Hyde Scrapbook, Morrisroe-Connolly Collection, James Hardiman Library, NUI Galway.

Never did San Francisco give a heartier greeting to an honored visitor than was extended to Dr Douglas Hyde at the Tivoli Theatre. Thousands attended the reception despite the stormy nature of the day. And what an enthusiastic gathering it was! The majority of those in attendance belonged to the Irish race, either by birth or decent, there were others present from motives of pure admiration for the foremost Irishman of the day and the noble movement of which he is the leader.

Frank J. Sullivan was the chairman of the event and we can see his admiration of Hyde in a letter he wrote to him after his visit.[32] The numerous letters housed in the National Library Ireland show the positive response and near celebrity status conferred upon Hyde during his tour. For example, Hyde received this letter from Frank J. Sullivan on the 9 August 1906:

My dear friend, I had hoped to meet you once more before you sailed for home but circumstances did not permit my leaving the city. Since we met here I have followed closely every line published about your great success in this broad big-hearted country and rest assured that the greater your success the more joy it gave me.[33]

The poem printed on the front of *The Collegian*—a newspaper of Oakland City University established in 1885—was delivered to Hyde during his lecture to hundreds at the Maedonough Theatre in Oakland on 1 March 1906. There was a lot of thought and effort put into the welcoming of Hyde, including songs and poetry written about him or dedicated to him. The poem *Welcome to Dr Douglas Hyde* focused on news and the importance of news from Ireland. It is poignant that this poem, which emphasised the importance of news from Ireland for the wellbeing of the Irish immigrants, was printed in a newspaper which reached not just the public present at Hyde's lecture, but also the readers of *The Collegian*.

Welcome to Dr Douglas Hyde
You bring glad news from our old Ireland
News to cheer the exiles soul
You bring glad news from holy Ireland

---

32   See The Noel Sullivan Papers, BANC MSS C-B 801, The Bancroft Library, University of California, Berkeley for information on his relationship with his father Frank J. Sullivan whose family had immigrated to America in 1844.
33   National Library Ireland, LS 18, 253.

> Where green hills rise and clear stream toll
> You come to preach that Land a nation
> Land the fairest every sung
> You come to preach the restoration
> Of our grand old Keltic tongue.
> From your mission, home returning
> Radiant at your great success
> Take this message brightly burning
> To our kindred in distress
> Tell them, make them tell each other
> Let them plainly understand
> That every exiled banished brother
> Loves till death his native land
> Welcome here! An Irish greeting!
> Céad Mile Failte! Thrice happy meeting!
> Welcome, welcome to our coast![34]

In the *San Francisco Call* newspaper, where Mark Twain had once worked as a writer from 1863 to 1864, the following appeared on 2 March 1906 in relation to Hyde's Oakland lecture: 'By his own unaided efforts, Hyde has done more to bring together and nationalise the Irish people than any other man of his generation'.[35] Father Yorke escorted Hyde to the city, and introduced him to the Oakland crowd as the 'ambassador of Irish Ireland'. On 3 March 1906, the *San Francisco Examiner* described his lecture thus:

> The Tivoli opera house was crowded to its utmost capacity yesterday afternoon with boys and girls from the city's public schools and their teachers all eager to hear the famous Gaelic educator Dr Douglas Hyde ... Folklore is in danger of extinction. It is the unwritten literature, so easily lost.[36]

---

[34] G37, Hyde Scrapbook, Morrisroe-Connolly Collection, James Hardiman Library, NUI Galway.

[35] G37, Hyde Scrapbook, Morrisroe-Connolly Collection, James Hardiman Library, NUI Galway.

[36] G37, Hyde Scrapbook, Morrisroe-Connolly Collection, James Hardiman Library, NUI Galway.

Hyde understood the importance of preserving the Irish language, literature and culture, and it is noteworthy that he delivered this speech to children in San Francisco in the Tivoli Theatre.[37]

Douglas Hyde and his promoters Father Yorke and John Quinn used the media to advertise his cultural events and lectures when in San Francisco. In the *San Francisco Call* the following was written in the morning paper on 5 March 1906:

> Famous Irishman to be guest of honour at recreation park this afternoon. Dr Douglas Hyde will be the guest of honour at the athletic games in recreation park eight and Harrison street this afternoon at 2 o clock. The admission fee will be 25 cents. There will be hurling and football.[38]

On 6 March 1906, the same paper reported the great success of this event, held at an amateur practice field, where practices were held prior to professional games.

> At recreation park yesterday several thousands gathered to witness the sons of Erin take part in their favourite games hurling and Gaelic football. Dr Douglas Hyde was the most conspicuous personage in the grand stand.[39]

The publication *The Tidings* was founded in 1895, and remains the oldest continuously published Catholic periodical on the west coast of the United States. It is also the oldest weekly periodical in the Los Angeles market. The last issue of *The Tidings* was published in June 2016; a month later, in July 2016, it was transformed into the multimedia news platform *Angelus*.[40] In *The Tidings* there is an article about Douglas Hyde from March 1906 with the almost biblical title : 'Prepare for the coming of Dr Hyde'. The headline is engaging and encourages the readers to read more about the man in the photo, illuminated by the light shining on his face. The article itself highlights to the reader his

---

37 The importance of school children in preserving the oral and folkloric tradition of Ireland would be demonstrated even more dramatically during the 1930s as part of The Schools' Scheme. On the history of this Scéim na Scol, see https://www.duchas.ie/download/schools-scheme-ocathain.pdf.
38 *San Francisco Call*, 5 March 1906, James Hardiman Library, G37, NUI Galway.
39 G37, Hyde Scrapbook, Morrisroe-Connolly Collection, James Hardiman Library, NUI Galway.
40 For more information, see https://angelusnews.com/about/.

importance and the vast knowledge that he holds and will share at this meeting in Los Angeles on 12 March 1906:

> The Dr Hyde executive committee has been doing quiet but effective work within the past two weeks and arrangements are now almost completed for the reception to the distinguished Irish leader ... Dr Hyde has given his full consent to the program as outlined and the arrangements of the executive committee provide for each detail to be carried out without any hitch whatever. Dr Hyde will arrive here next Thursday on the owl train.[41]

Hyde stayed in Hotel Alexandria which was constructed as a luxury hotel at the beginning of the twentieth century in what was then the heart of downtown Los Angeles.[42] The article shared with the public the detail, planning and depth of work needed for Hyde's visits. It continued to urge those who wish to do so to get their tickets. Clearly, newspapers were a powerful marketing vehicle and dissemination tool for this lecture tour.

> Those desirous of securing seats for the mass meeting on 12th March, are urgently advised by the executive committee to procure their seats at once, as the committee expects that the demand will exceed supply and standing room under the city ordinances cannot be allowed and no admission can be accorded to any person for whom a set is not provided under penalty of subjecting the management to arrest for misdemeanour.[43]

The Irish World and American Industrial Liberator newspaper was founded by Patrick Ford in New York City in 1870.[44] *The Irish World* became the principal newspaper of Irish America as it promised more reading material than any other paper in America and outsold John Boyle O'Reilly's *Boston Pilot*.[45] On 10 March 1906, during his time in California, Douglas Hyde was presented in *The Irish World* as a man of strength and as a leader who oozes charisma. He is pictured in the newspaper in various standing positions when orating during

---

41   G37, Hyde Scrapbook, Morrisroe-Connolly Collection, James Hardiman Library, NUI Galway.
42   Hyde, *My American Journey*, p. 331.
43   G37, Hyde Scrapbook, Morrisroe-Connolly Collection, James Hardiman Library, NUI Galway.
44   See https://nyshistoricnewspapers.org/lccn/sn83030537/1887-11-12/ed-1/ for digital access to publications from the Irish World (1878–1951).
45   See Anthony G. Evans, *Fanatic heart: A life of John Boyle O'Reilly* (Boston: Northeastern University Press, 1997).

his tour. Even the use of the phrase 'Addressing Great Audiences in California' highlights the impact of his tour and the eagerness of newspapers to help the marketing machine in order to raise funds for an Irish Ireland. Surrounding the figures of Hyde in this newspaper are words from his speeches such as: 'The greatest misfortune that ever befell Ireland was the loss of its language', and 'I am here to explain to you the life and death struggle upon which we are now engaged in Ireland'. Hyde regularly used the phrase 'life and death struggle' when lecturing, and this conscious phraseology was designed to encourage people to donate generously. He was a clever orator and chose his words carefully to ensure an emotive response from the audience, and also to ensure drama in the newspapers, which would in turn encourage greater interest in his lecture tour. There is an example of Hyde's lecture tour speech which can be found in the National Library Ireland and which he gave to the crowds when in Chicago. He used emotive language and the imagery of the 'life and death struggle' is again employed in this speech. His natural acting abilities helped him in his endeavour to move the masses towards the Gaelic League and to promote its importance. This speech highlights the phrase which the newspaper used again and again as was seen in *The Irish World and American Industrial*, 'life and death struggle'.

> I am not exaggerating when I say that I look upon the moral support of the Irish in America to be the most valuable asset that the Gaelic League at home could have ... I am here to-day to explain to you the life and death struggle upon which we are engaged in Ireland. I see that the papers say that this is the last grand struggle of the Irish race to preserve their language. Oh, Ladies and Gentlemen: it is ten times, it is a hundred times, it is a thousand times more far-reaching than that; it is the last possible life and death struggle of the Irish race to preserve not only their own language but their national identity.[46]

Douglas Hyde was astute in keeping the media on side and wrote to the *Telegram* on Wednesday 20 March 1906 to thank the staff for spreading his word via their newspapers. The title of the piece was 'Greeting by Dr Douglas Hyde in Gaelic, written for the Telegram this morning':

> A chairde agus a chlanna Gaedheal,
> Thainig mé in bhur measg mar theachtaire ó Éirinn, le h-innsant daoibh cad tá ar siubhal againn i n-Eirinn agus mar tá an Gaedheal ag dul i n-uchtar agus an gall ag dul i n-íochtar i nEirinn indiu. Tá mé

---

[46] National Library Ireland NLI 18, 253.

buidheach daoibh go léir agus de phaipearaibh na tíre seo uile, agus go mhór-mór de thelegram—an-trathnóna, ar son chomh tapa agus chomh géar—inntinneach do innigeadas mo scéal. Beannacht Dé orraibh,
Mise,
An Craoibhín.
Dear friends and Irish family,
I came in your presence as a messenger from Ireland, to tell you what is happening in Ireland and how the Irishman is gaining strength and the Englishman is weaking in Ireland today. I am thankful to you all and to the newspapers of this whole country, and especially the Evening Telegram for telling my story so quickly and so astutely. May God bless you,
Yours truly, An Craoibhín.[47]

5 The Great Earthquake and Fire of San Francisco, 1906

The newspaper *The San Francisco Examiner* is a newspaper distributed in and around San Francisco, California and has been published since 1863. Less than a month after the *San Francisco Examiner* highlighted Douglas Hyde's tour of the city, its offices would be destroyed by the great earthquake and fire of 18 April 1906. High intensity shaking and devastating fires broke out in the city and lasted for several days. Thousands of homes were destroyed and up to 3,000 people died.[48] The death toll remains the greatest loss of life from a natural disaster in California's history. Though Hyde and Lucy had left San Francisco on 26 March 1906, after spending nearly 6 weeks there, the impact of the earthquake would have a great effect upon him. Hyde wrote in *Mo Thurus go hAmerice*:

> When it was getting dark and I was on the train I read a notice in the paper that San Francisco was on fire. The story scared me and I waited impatiently until I heard more. It hit my core when I thought about the loyal peoples and the great friends I had left behind me there.[49]

---

47   Translation by author. G37, Hyde Scrapbook, Morrisroe-Connolly Collection, James Hardiman Library, NUI Galway.
48   Mary McD. Gordon & Cameron King, 'Earthquake and fire in San Francisco', Huntington Library Quarterly, 48 (1985) pp. 69–79.
49   Hyde, *My American Journey*, p. 140.

When Leo Varadkar visited San Fran on his first official visit as Irish Taoiseach in 2017, he gave the following speech at the City Hall in San Francisco:

> In 1906, the founder of the Gaelic League, and our future President, Douglas Hyde, visited San Francisco, and his biographers record that the city 'captured his heart'. The story of his visit made the front page of the *San Francisco Examiner* and it was noted that all of San Francisco seemed to want to embrace him. He raised significant funds in support of Irish culture and the Irish language. However a couple of months later, when the devastating earthquake hit this city, he returned all the money and donated it to crisis relief. It was an act which showed the genuine bond of affection between our people, a bond which has been strengthened by more recent tragedies. Hyde found in San Francisco a strong and vibrant Irish community.[50]

Hyde's understanding of keeping memories, documenting personal data, collecting folklore, the importance of posterity and social historical documents is seen in his eagerness to keep accurate accounts of his life through ego-documents.[51] Douglas Hyde's personal writings can be classified as ego-documents: where '… the 'I', the writer, is continuously present in the text as the writing and describing subject'.[52] If we now have social media and mobile phones to record our memories and help us to efficiently share our adventures with others, Hyde used postcards to share his exciting news with his friends and children. The images on the postcards had a real quality to them and his children may well have felt more connected with their father when they received them.[53] They were in a way seeing what had been in front of their parents' eyes. Postcards were not expensive and it was a real pastime of the Victorian and Edwardian eras, and helped Hyde keep in contact with his

---

50 https://merrionstreet.ie/en/category-index/international/united-states/speech_by_an_taoiseach_leo_varadkar_t_d_at_irish_community_reception_thursday_2_november_city_hall_san_francisco.131538.shortcut.html..

51 Máire Nic an Bhaird & Liam Mac Mathúna 'Douglas Hyde (1860–1949)—First Steps in the creation of a linguist', in Rebecca Barr, Sarah-Anne Buckley & Muireann O'Cinneide (eds.), *Literacies and the Irish in the Nineteenth Century* (Liverpool: Liverpool University Press, 2018), pp. 28–50.

52 Rudolf Dekker, *Egodocuments and history : autobiographical writing in its social context since the Middle Ages* (Netherlands: Uitgeverij Verlroren 2002) p. 1.

53 See Aidan Heavey Library, Athlone for the Aidan Heavey Douglas Hyde Collection, where there are numerous postcards that Douglas Hyde and Lucy Hyde posted to their children Úna and Nuala Hyde during their American trip.

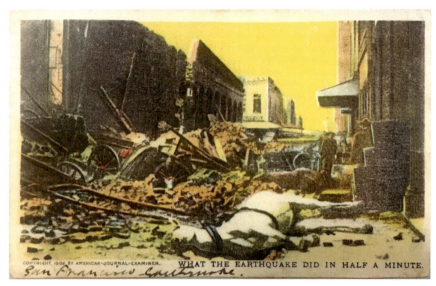

FIGURE 17.5   Postcard sent by Douglas Hyde entitled *What the Earthquake did in Half a Minute*. It depicts a scene from the stark aftermath of the 1906 San Francisco earthquake and fire
IMAGE COURTESY OF AIDAN HEAVEY COLLECTION, ATHLONE, CO. WESTMEATH, IRELAND, DPC-AT-045

girls when away for the 8 month period.[54] One postcard, 'What the Earthquake did in half a minute', was sent from Douglas Hyde to his daughter Nuala on 7 May 1906 and, as seen in Figure 17.5, shows the destruction which devastated San Francisco.[55] Lucy also sent the San Francisco news home to the girls in postcard format, including one to Úna dated 26 April 1906 which must have been hard for her to read and then share with her sister Nuala.

> The recent earthquake and fire have swallowed up these five idols. We just escaped in time. You never would have seen us again if we had remained on. Everything was burnt up. Our grand hotel and all Chinese town all burnt and lots of Chinese too. Save all postcards. All very valuable now. LH.[56]

---

54   Séamus Kearns, 'Picture postcards as a source for social historians', *Saothar*, 22 (1997) pp. 128–33.
55   Aidan Heavey Collection, Westmeath Libraries.
56   Aidan Heavey Collection, Westmeath Libraries.

The language used in a newspaper article from *The World* called 'Big Meeting to Aid San Francisco' on 3 May 1906 is powerful. This emotive language would encourage empathy and generous donations.

> Dr Douglas Hyde, The Foremost Celt now living will preside … Dr Hyde knew that Father Yorke was doing a giant's work in caring for the many poor and helped persons who had left San Francisco and had flocked to Oakland. He said … that whatever he could contribute out of the Gaelic money raised in this country should be sent to Father Yorke … he felt he was doing the best for the needy by giving in to the hands of this good priest the 5,000 dollars which he at once determinds to send them … The 5,000 dollars which he has given to the San Francisco fund represents literally the work of his own hands and the sweat of his brow. To use the Doctor's own impressive words: 'My heart has been broken and the great pleasure of any visit to this great country has been spoiled by the appalling calamity that has overtaken the people of San Francisco and my first thought was to give what I felt I could to the relief of their suffering. My second thought was to arrange for the telegraphing of the money. It went on Monday by telegraph'.

This may be construed as an extremely clever publicity stunt to ensure that the newspapers were able to share the news that Douglas Hyde was giving his money back to aid the people of San Francisco. However, from reading his personal diaries and from his book *My American Journey*, it is certain that this natural disaster had a profound effect on Hyde. Hyde felt very close to the people of San Francisco and was indeed very much loved by them.

> As night fell, while aboard the train, I saw a newspaper notice that San Francisco was burning. The news greatly disturbed me and I waited anxiously for more information. It worried my heart to think of those loyal people and good friends I had left behind there. No further information, however, was to be had that night nor any accurate information for several days … the 19th day of April. First thing in the morning, I bought every newspaper and read all the incredible news about San Francisco, how the Cliff House had fallen into the sea etc., etc., things that were all false. I sent one or two telegrams to San Francisco but they were never delivered, it seems.[57]

---

57   Hyde, *My American Journey*, p. 128.

However, one of Hyde's telegrams did deliver, and a copy is housed in the National Library of Ireland. Hyde wrote to Frank J. Sullivan on 24 April 1906 that he was 'overwhelmed with sorrow at the great calamity. Hope and trust you all have escaped any personal injury. Douglas Hyde'.[58] Before leaving San Francisco on 26 March 1906, an Irish poem 'Dán don Chraoibhín', written by William G. Egan, was presented to Dr Douglas Hyde and was published in *The Irish World*.[59] It is obvious that the people of San Francisco held him in high esteem as is illustrated by the use of the words mannerly, wise man and majestic.

> Buadh is Beannacht leat a Shaoi
> A Chraoibhin Aoibhinn mhodhamhuil mhordha
> Failte is Failte le gradh ár gcroidhe
> Annso anocht san iarthar ordha.

> Best wishes to you wise man
> Dear mannerly and majestic Craoibhin Aoibhinn
> A huge welcome with the love of our hearts
> Here tonight in the golden West.[60]

Hyde's generosity and heroic nature were publicised in numerous newspapers as can be seen from the press cuttings in the Galway volume. In the *Gaelic American*, printed on 5 May 1906, Hyde is described as a man of integrity, self-awareness, gratitude, influence, empathy, and excellent communication skills. These are characteristics of a great leader, of a man who would be an ideal candidate for the position of Ireland's first President:

> Dr Douglas Hyde has returned from his triumphant tour of the United States. On Saturday night next he will preside at a great mass-meeting in the Grand Central Palace, which has been called by the Irish volunteers to aid the fund for the San Francisco sufferers. It has been the source of great delight to the many hundreds of friends which Dr Hyde has made in this country during his visit of the past five months to know that immediately on his return from Memphis and Baltimore his first thought was the generous one of aiding the stricken people of San Francisco. Dr Hyde left

---

58 Hyde, *My American Journey*, p. 130.
59 G37, Hyde Scrapbook, Morrisroe-Connolly Collection, James Hardiman Library, NUI Galway.
60 Translation by Máire Nic an Bhaird.

San Francisco some two weeks before the earthquake. Perhaps no man in his day and generation had received a more generous and courteous reception than Dr Hyde received on the Pacific Coast. He was charmed with the people with the type of Irishmen he met there. He succeeded there and throughout the country in a wonderful way in bringing together Irishmen of all creeds and denominations and classes.[61]

6   Hyde's Return Home

The news made its way home to Ireland, and the image of Hyde returning from America in *The Irish Independent* is a scene of jubilation and success.[62] *The Irish Independent* published this picture 'Filleadh an Chraoibhín' as seen in Figure 17.6 on 25 June 1906, 'Arrival of Dr Douglas Hyde at Kingsbridge Station yesterday evening 'Filleadh An Chraoibhin'. The hats are raised and Hyde's moustache makes him stand out from the crowd. There are no women to be seen, and Hyde is taller and dominant. Even the language used to describe the American Tour has spiritual connotations—'An Craoibhín's Mission'. The tour itself was publicised as a huge success in papers in Ireland and abroad, with Hyde described as a 'hero'. Hyde was indeed feted as an idol and superstar upon his return, and it was the newspapers that helped ensure his celebratory status.

When we consider media coverage of Hyde's visit, the impact of the American newspapers was twofold. Firstly, this coverage rallied audiences who turned out to hear Hyde speak. Secondly, that portion of the public unable to attend, could read reports in the newspapers of those lectures and speeches. This made Hyde's words available not just to the Irish or Irish supporters in the local area but also to the newspapers back home. These newspaper reports impacted and inspired revivalists back in Ireland. Hyde's dramatic personality and ease as an orator made him a force to be reckoned with, and his tour of America beginning in Boston in 1905 and ending in New York seven months later, raised more than 64,000 dollars for the Gaelic League. This American adventure helped prepare Hyde for his academic career as the first Professor of Modern Irish in University College Dublin (1909–1932), and also as the first President of Ireland (1938–1945). His skills in understanding his audience,

---

61   G37, Hyde Scrapbook, Morrisroe-Connolly Collection, James Hardiman Library, NUI Galway.
62   Aoife Whelan, 'Language revival and conflicting identities in *The Irish Independent*, 1905–1922', *Irish Studies Review*, 22 (2014).

FIGURE 17.6   Filleadh an Chraoibhín—Hyde's return from America (June 1906)

adapting where necessary, abstaining from controversy, dealing with the press, and rousing audiences, were honed during this trip. The American tour would mark the beginning of a new stage in Hyde's public role in Irish affairs.

CHAPTER 18

The German Air Campaign against Britain, 1915–18, and British Cartoon Responses

Chris Williams

Germany's Great War aerial campaign against Britain began in earnest on 19 January 1915 when Zeppelin *L3* dropped bombs on Great Yarmouth.[1] A few days earlier Kaiser Wilhelm II had given his approval for air raids on Britain. In carrying out these raids the German army and navy initially made use of their respective fleets of Zeppelin airships.[2]

By the outbreak of war, Count Ferdinand von Zeppelin had spent over three decades developing the rigid airship or dirigible that became known by his family name. His was not the first, nor the only invention of this type, not even in Germany, but in 1907–1908 his craft completed long-distance trips lasting eight and twelve hours respectively, and thus caught the imagination of the German public and military establishment.[3] The Kaiser hailed the Count as 'the greatest German of the twentieth century', and speculation began as to the airship's military possibilities. H. G. Wells's dystopian novel, *The War in the Air* (1908), imagined a German Zeppelin fleet reducing New York to rubble.[4] Although the first trans-Atlantic airship crossing was at this point more than a decade away (achieved by the British *R34* in July 1919) it was not stretching credulity very far to imagine the impact Zeppelin raids might have on Britain. Such a prospect was captured in a variety of media almost immediately, including 'Zeppelins Schatten' ('The Shadow of the Zeppelin'), Heinrich Kley's full-page cartoon for the German magazine *Simplicissimus* (16 November 1908). The

---

1 The support of the Heritage Lottery Fund, of Swansea University, Cardiff University, and of University College Cork made possible the research that underpins this chapter.
2 The army and navy had separate fleets, the former originally intended for bombing of military and strategic targets and the latter for naval reconnaissance. Both were utilised for bombing missions against Britain.
3 The first dirigible was built in 1884, the first military airship in 1906, both in France. German company Luftschiffbau Schütte-Lanz GmbH began airship production in 1911.
4 Robert Wohl, *A Passion for Wings: Aviation and the Western Imagination, 1908–1918* (New Haven: Yale University Press, 1994), pp. 71–74.

British press speculated that Zeppelins might facilitate a German invasion, generating an 'airship scare' in 1909.[5]

The development of the airship and aeroplane raised difficult questions about the ramifications of technological advances for international law, particularly in wartime. The Hague Peace Conference of 1907 had reached tentative agreement that undefended towns and villages should not be bombed. However, this left room for interpretation as to what was 'defended' and 'undefended'. Nor did it clarify the status of facilities such as dockyards or factories which might be thought legitimate targets (in that they enabled a country's war effort) but the bombing of which—even if precise—would inevitably risk civilian lives. The indiscriminate strategic bombing of Allied towns and cities by Germany in the early stages of the Great War clearly constituted, as John H. Morrow has noted, 'a major transgression of the accepted norms and provisions of international law'.[6]

Before 1914 was over Zeppelins had launched attacks on a number of French and Belgian cities, including Liège, Antwerp, Ostend, Zeebrugge, Dunkirk, Calais and Lille.[7] From January 1915 Britain was the major target for German airships, with raids by Zeppelins peaking in 1916, after which they were increasingly superseded by those undertaken by Gotha-IV and R-Giant bombers. Over 100 air raids were launched against Britain during the war, involving the dropping of over 270 tons of bombs, and the killing of at least 1,239 people, mostly civilians, and including 366 women and 252 children.[8] Compared with the bombing campaigns of later wars these statistics appear paltry indeed. The bombing of Coventry on 14 November 1940 alone involved the dropping of 500 tons of bombs and the death of over 500 people, that of Dresden in February 1945 amounted to nearly 4,000 tons of bombs and between 22,000 and 25,000 fatalities. Yet, at the time, the prospect of death raining down from the air (even if it was, in historical terms, a light drizzle rather than a deluge) was entirely novel and potentially terrifying. This chapter uses the evidence of newspaper and magazine cartoons to assess the novelty, the terror, and other

---

5 See Jay Winter, 'Introduction', to H. G. Wells, *The War in the Air* (London: Penguin, 2005); John H. Morrow, *The Great War in the Air: Military Aviation from 1909 to 1921* (Washington: Smithsonian Institution Press, 1993), pp. 2–3.
6 John H. Morrow, 'The War in the Air', in John Horne (ed.), *A Companion to World War I* (Oxford: Wiley-Blackwell, 2010), p. 167.
7 Morrow, *Great War in the Air*, p. 68.
8 Richard Overy, *The Bombing War: Europe 1939–1945* (London: Penguin, 2013), pp. 20–22. H. A. Jones, *The War in the Air: Being the Story of the part played in the Great War by the Royal Air Force* (London: Imperial War Museum, 1935), vol 5, p. 153, suggests 1,414.

reactions of the British public to the unprecedented German aerial bombing of Britain during the Great War.

1   The Nature of Contemporary Cartoon Evidence

Cartoons were to be found in many British newspapers and magazines by the second decade of the twentieth century. *Punch*, the primary satirical journal, had seen off its Victorian competitors (*Judy* and *Fun*) but was still competing for readers with magazines that combined cartoons with photographs, such as *Sketch*, *Bystander*, *London Opinion* and the *Illustrated Sporting and Dramatic News*. *The Times* did not carry cartoons, but other papers did, including the *Daily Mirror*, *Daily Herald*, *Daily Graphic* and *Evening News* as well as a variety of provincial publications. Almost all professional newspaper cartoonists were male; many were based in London and contributed to a variety of outlets. Their work clearly tells us something about their own personal understanding and interpretation of the war, and may also reveal elements of the wider public response to its vicissitudes. Cartoons necessarily aim to strike a chord with the readers of the newspapers and magazines in which they are published, either resonating in harmony with existing views or (less frequently) challenging commonly-held notions by their dissonance. They are a necessarily imperfect window onto public opinion.

One particular quality of the work of cartoonists is its immediacy. In producing for daily or weekly publications, cartoonists had to respond to what they understood to be the rapidly-changing nature of the events under scrutiny, with all the limitations in terms of information and perspective that involved. Such responses, and the reactions of their readers, were very much of the moment. They were unmediated by hindsight, ignorant of how things would turn out, and prioritised what appeared at the time to be the most urgent questions of the day, as opposed to those identified as such by later historians. In the context of the Great War this is a quality which distinguishes them from many other forms of creative testimony (such as memoirs, novels, plays, films and works of art). The regularity and instantaneity of the cartoon gave it something of the quality of a contemporary diary, albeit one written for urgent public consumption. Furthermore, cartoons being an essentially visual medium, they were particularly appropriate for vividly capturing a range of emotional reactions to the war's key moments. Outrage, apprehension, empathy, anxiety, even amusement and irony, are all sentiments that may be expressed in newspaper editorials, but they were conveyed often more directly and powerfully in graphic form.

That said, cartoons demand respectful handling as multi-layered primary sources. Cartoonists might look to deliver a clear message, but irrespective of design their art was often capable of divergent and contradictory interpretations. Once a cartoon was published then the artist lost any control over how the image might be read by his audience. Evidence of such interpretations is usually elusive, but by reading oneself back into the very specific context of the cartoon one may be able to suggest at least some of the possible responses to the artist's work, as well as speculating as to the artist's conscious and unconscious intentions. Cartoons need to be understood as much more than visual illustrations of broader historical trends or opinions (though they may be both), or as offering only a unilinear interpretation to their readers. Anachronistic readings, as well as assumptions made about meanings founded on anything less than a full appreciation of the historical context, must be avoided.[9]

An example of how a single image could generate different interpretations is provided by Figure 18.1, a cartoon by Louis Raemaekers, originally titled 'Culture from the Sky' when it was published in *De Telegraaf* of Amsterdam on 8 January 1915, and subsequently republished in the Raemaekers collection *Het Toppunt der Beschaving*.[10] The image shows a woman's body being taken away by what appear to be French gendarmes, whilst the casualty's father or husband gestures angrily at the German airmen responsible for his loss. The cartoon was reissued by the London magazine *Land and Water* (as 'The Wonders of Culture') in June 1916, with a commentary by the novelist and journalist Clive Holland. Holland argued that this form of 'Kultur' was 'at one and the same time the most insensate and damnable'. It would not accomplish 'the subjugation by terror of the people for which the Germans seem to hope', for '[i]n reality it inflicts misery and death upon a mere handful of people'. Yet when (as 'Culture Has Passed By') the same image appeared in the 1916 volume *The Great War: A Neutral's Indictment*, it was accompanied by a different commentary by editor and writer Edward Garnett, who noted that Germany deflected complaints of the 'frightfulness' of Zeppelin bombing by pleading their military necessity, and concluded alarmingly that '[e]xperts predict that aerial invasions of England by super-Zeppelins armed with "aerial torpedoes of

---

9   See Richard Scully and Marian Quartly 'Using Cartoons as Historical Evidence', in Scully and Quartly (eds.), *Drawing the Line: Using Cartoons as Historical Evidence* (Monash: Monash University Press, 2009).

10 For Raemaekers see Ariane de Ranitz, *Louis Raemaekers—'Armed with Pen and Pencil'— How a Dutch cartoonist became world famous during the First World War* (Roermond: Louis Raemaekers Foundation, 2014).

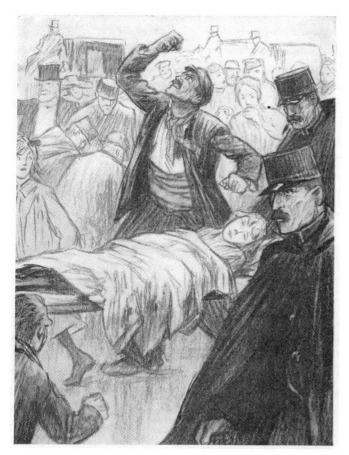

FIGURE 18.1   Louis Raemaekers, 'The Wonders of Culture', *'Land and Water' Edition of Raemaekers Cartoons* (London: Land and Water, 1916), Part 8

tremendous force" will be a thing of the near future'.[11] The necessarily brief (and anonymous) commentary that accompanied the Black Cat cigarette card version of the same image was more conventional, arguing that it 'shows the value of the German claim to the possession of "Kultur" and civilising influence'.[12]

It is contended that cartoons, along with other forms of media communication, were central to how the German aerial threat (both real and imagined) was experienced on a daily and weekly basis by the British reading public.

---

11   *The Great War: A Neutral's Indictment. One Hundred Cartoons by Louis Raemaekers* (London: The Fine Art Society, 1916), plate 42.
12   The cigarette card series was issued from 1916 to 1918.

Cartoons offer evidence of both the visual representation, and the management, of public anxiety, anger, and amusement related to civilian vulnerability to air attack, and the political and strategic lessons to be drawn from the same. The cartoonist could be both an active agent in the construction of public understanding, and offer unwitting testimony to widely-held fears and assumptions.

To date there has been no consideration in any depth of the cartoon evidence for British reactions to German air raids during the Great War. Susan Grayzel, in her monograph *At Home and Under Fire* does refer to two cartoons from *Punch*, but neither is reproduced, and both appear to have been encountered not in the pages of the magazine itself, but in the 1920 retrospective publication *Mr Punch's History of the Great War*.[13] The extent to which these images are representative of *Punch*'s responses to bombing is doubtful, given that neither is a full page 'cartoon' or 'big cut', so important a feature of the magazine.[14]

For this study of reactions to Germany's wartime air campaign against Britain, more than two hundred cartoons drawn by over forty artists spread over more than twenty publications have been consulted (see Table 18.1). The survey included the entirety (for the war years) of *Punch*, the mass-market Sunday paper the *News of the World* and the popular Cardiff daily the *Western Mail*, as well as all of the *Land and Water* Raemaekers series (and much more besides by this artist). Stand-alone collections appearing in wartime such as those by Will Dyson, William Heath Robinson and Jack Walker were also assessed, as were individual cartoons reproduced in a range of other works. Most cartoonists were British-born, but there were those who had come to Britain to work from Australia, Ireland, the Netherlands, New Zealand and even Turkey. All were male, and they ranged in age (at the outbreak of war) from 28 to 54, with the average age being 42 (above that at which the British Army accepted recruits). Politically it is fair to say that all were committed to winning the war, and that relatively few could have been identified as 'left-wing'. Some saw service in uniform, be that in combat roles overseas (examples include Beuttler,

---

13   Susan R. Grayzel, *At Home and Under Fire: Air Raids and Culture in Britain from the Great War to the Blitz* (Cambridge: Cambridge University Press, 2012). Scully and Quartly, *Drawing the Line: Using Cartoons as Historical Evidence* note the problem of relying on cartoon anthologies, singling out *Mr Punch's History of the Great War* in particular. Lesley Milne, *Laughter and War: Humorous-Satirical Magazines in Britain, France, Germany and Russia 1914–1918* (Newcastle upon Tyne: Cambridge Scholars Publishing, 2017), pp. 92–95, makes passing reference to *Punch*'s response to aerial bombing.

14   The sketches, by Lewis Baumer and George Belcher, appeared on 30 August 1916 and 31 October 1917.

Grave, Mills, Pears, Rountree and Shepard) or as a special constable at home, as was the case for Frank Townsend for instance. This survey still falls short of being comprehensive, given the increasing frequency with which provincial daily and weekly newspapers were beginning to carry cartoons, but it is more extensive than anything previously attempted and offers preliminary suggestions about the way the German aerial bombing of Britain was represented and interpreted by a range of topical and satirical visual artists.

TABLE 18.1 Cartoons and publications assessed

Cartoonist	Year of birth	Published in	Wartime collections
Armour, G. D.	Not known	*Punch*	
Baumer, Lewis	1870	*Punch*	
Belcher, George	1875	*Punch*	
Beuttler, Edward	1880	*Bystander*	
Bird, W. (Yeats, Jack Butler)	1871	*Punch*	
Brock, Henry M.	1875	*Punch*	
Brook, Ricardo	Not known	*Punch*	
Dowd, J. H.	Not known	*Bystander*	
Dyson, Will	1880	*Daily Herald, Daily Mail*	*Kultur Cartoons* (1915)
Fearon, Percy Hutton	1874	*Evening News*	*Poy's War Cartoons* (1915)
Grave, Charles	1886	*Punch*	
Harrison, Charles	1860	*Punch*	
Hart, Frank	1878	*Punch*	
Haselden, W. K.	1872	*Punch, Daily Mirror*	
Hickling, P. B.	Not known	*Punch*	
Jennis, Gurnell Charles	1874	*Punch*	
Lewin, Frederick George	1861	*Punch*	
Low, Harry	Not known	*Punch*	
Mills, A. Wallis	1878	*Punch, Sketch*	
Morrow, George	1869	*Punch*	
Partridge, Bernard	1861	*Punch*	
Patten, L.	Not known	*Punch*	
Pears, Charles	1873	*Punch*	
Pegram, Fred	1870	*Punch*	

TABLE 18.1   Cartoons and publications assessed *(cont.)*

Cartoonist	Year of birth	Published in	Wartime collections
Raemaekers, Louis	1869	*Land and Water*	Various collections published in English
Raven-Hill, Leonard	1867	*Punch*	
Reynolds, Frank	1876	*Punch*	
Robinson, William Heath	1872	*Illustrated Sporting and Dramatic News, London Opinion, Pearson's, Sketch, Strand, To-day*	*Some Frightful War Pictures* (1915) *Hunlikely!* (1916) *The Saintly Hun* (1917)
Rountree, Harry	1878	*Bystander, Punch*	
Shepard, Ernest H.	1879	*Punch*	
Shepperson, Claude Allin	1867	*Punch*	
Stampa, Giorgio Loraine	1878	*Punch*	
Staniforth, Joseph Morewood	1863	*News of the World, Western Mail* (Cardiff)	*Cartoons of the War by 'J.M.S.'* (1914–15)
Sullivan, Edmund Joseph	1869		*The Kaiser's Garland* (1915)
Townsend, Frank	1868	*Punch*	
Walker, Jack	Not known	*Daily Graphic*	*Daily Graphic Special War Cartoons* (1914–15)
Wilson, David	1873	*Punch*	

There are significant variations in the kinds of cartoons surveyed. Some, such as those appearing in conventional newspapers, tended to be 'political' or 'editorial' cartoons, taking the form of a serious visual commentary on matters of national and international importance. The cartoons of J. M. Staniforth, for example, fall clearly into this category, as do those of Will Dyson, E. J. Sullivan and Jack Walker. They might poke fun (particularly at Britain's enemies), and they sometimes used irony or sarcasm, but they were not primarily attempting to evoke laughter from their readers. The art of Louis Raemaekers was equally serious, but entirely devoid of any humorous intent. For British audiences, Raemaekers's work was invariably accompanied by a stern commentary provided by a literary or intellectual figure. At the other extreme were the fantastical speculations of William Heath Robinson, who found limitless imaginative possibilities in the novel technologies of the conflict, and whose name has been given to an entire genre of elaborate and ingenious impossible inventions. *Punch*, which as a weekly and heavily illustrated satirical magazine generated a large number of images relating to aerial bombing, included a range of types of cartoon. At one end of the spectrum were the full-page 'big cuts', drawn during the war years by Bernard Partridge, Leonard Raven-Hill or Frank Townsend. These were approximations of 'editorial' cartoons, serious in orientation, if sometimes playful in image. At the other end were the plentiful 'sketches', humorous cartoons designed to amuse. These have often been disregarded by historians, but the butts of their jokes could be revealing, and it may be argued that what they chose to satirise and how they did it can tell us much about prevalent attitudes, at least amongst the urban middle-class males who are considered to have comprised the bulk of the magazine's readership. Some of *Punch*'s artists concentrated entirely on humour, whilst others—Frank Townsend is the best example from this period—worked across the spectrum from 'joke' to 'editorial' cartoons.

Cartoons produced on a daily and/or weekly basis had the characteristic of instantaneity. Yet *Punch* cartoons were also bound into half-yearly volumes which could be purchased for longer-term reflection. Some other cartoonists—such as Dyson, 'Poy', Heath Robinson, Staniforth and Walker—had their work published in stand-alone volumes, while Raemaekers had his original compositions reissued as fortnightly *Land and Water* publications, and bound into various compendium volumes. A cartoon that might have had one dominant meaning at the time of initial publication could easily find itself floating free of its original contextual moorings by the time of its reissue.[15]

In terms of subject matter, British cartoons responding to the German bombing campaign may be placed (inevitably somewhat approximately) in one of four categories. These were: images expressing moral outrage over Germany's use of aerial bombing of civilian targets; those calling for reprisals against German towns and cities either as a deterrent to further German raids and/or as acts of revenge, particularly in the light of the inability of the British authorities to offer effective protection against assault from the skies; artwork

---

15 Nicholas Hiley, '"A New and Vital Moral Factor": Cartoon Book Publishing in Britain during the First World War', in Mary Hammond and Shafquat Towheed (eds.), *Publishing in the First World War: Essays in Book History* (Houndmills: Palgrave, 2007), pp. 148–177.

celebrating the shooting down of Zeppelins and the thwarting of German strategic bombing; and cartoons conveying and constructing cheery stoicism or even playful insouciance on the part of the general public in the face of airborne terror. In the remainder of this chapter these categories will be discussed and illustrated with a limited number of examples.

2 Moral Outrage

British moral outrage over Zeppelin raids was part of a wider revulsion at German methods of conducting the war, which embraced the German shelling in 1914 of Hartlepool and Scarborough, the German U-boat campaign against merchant shipping and passenger liners, and the German treatment of Belgian civilians and the destruction of Belgian cultural heritage. Aerial bombing was in some respects even worse than either the submarine sinkings whose potential victims were civilians who worked at sea or who elected to travel by sea, or the treatment of Belgian civilians (in the way of the German advance in 1914). Those on the receiving end of air raids were ordinary civilians who might be subject to bombing in their place of work or in their own homes. In launching such attacks Germany could be presented as barbaric, immoral, uncivilised, and as committing atrocities.

Cartoons condemning German bombing pre-dated the assault on Britain. Figure 18.2—Will Dyson's 'Wonders of Science!'—published in the *Daily Mail* on 1 January 1915 and in Dyson's publication *Kultur Cartoons*, showed two Pickelhaube-wearing apes dropping bombs from an aeroplane on a generic but undefended city, presumably prompted by German bombing of France and Belgium.[16] Dyson was the left-wing *Daily Herald*'s staff cartoonist, and someone of strong socialist views, but *Kultur Cartoons* took a strongly anti-German stance. Adrian Gregory has suggested that 'Wonders of Science!' 'opened the possibility that the Germans as a people were intrinsically flawed, probably depraved, and possibly evil'.[17] In these early stages of the war the very concept of German 'Kultur' was being constructed by British commentators as the antithesis of 'Civilisation', and the onset of Zeppelin raids in 1915 only sharpened such a perspective.

---

16   Will Dyson, *Kultur Cartoons* (London: Stanley Paul, 1915).
17   Adrian Gregory, 'A Clash of Cultures: The British Press and the Opening of the Great War', in Troy R. E. Paddock (ed.), *A Call to Arms: Propaganda, Public Opinion, and Newspapers in the Great War* (Westport, Connecticut: Praeger, 2004), p. 38.

FIGURE 18.2 Will Dyson, 'Wonders of Science!', *Kultur Cartoons* (London: Stanley Paul, 1915)

Dyson's cartoon output did not dwell long on German air strategy, as in 1915 he mobilised his artistic skills to oppose the policy of conscription and, in 1916, left Fleet Street to take up a position as an official war artist with the Australian Imperial Force. The visceral anti-German tenor of Dyson's cartoons was then, if anything, exceeded in British print media by those of the Dutch artist Louis Raemaekers. Raemaekers's works first appeared in the Amsterdam newspaper *De Telegraaf*, and were republished in the Netherlands in collections titled *Het Toppunt der Beschaving* (*The Pinnacle of Civilisation*). By December 1915 his work was being exhibited in London, and it was decided by the magazine *Land and Water* to republish a total of 312 Raemaekers' cartoons in fortnightly instalments, running from February 1916 to February 1917. Each cartoon was accompanied by a commentary, penned by various intellectuals and public figures including Hilaire Belloc, John Buchan and G. K. Chesterton. The titles given to the republished cartoons were not necessarily translations of the originals, but could be adjusted to align with the commentator's interpretation. Such interpretations were very much the authors' own responses to the cartoons as they were being viewed at the time, some months, if not years, after they had first been published.

To give an example, Figure 18.3—'The Zeppelin Triumph'—had appeared in *Het Toppunt der Beschaving* (with the title 'Zeppelin-Triomf') in July 1915, but was issued in the *Land and Water* series in March 1916. It seems probable that Raemaekers here was responding either to the early raids on London of May/June 1915, or, perhaps more likely given that at this time he was still working in the Netherlands, to raids on French or Belgian cities. But by March 1916 the German bombing of Britain had intensified significantly, and the cartoon would have been viewed in a different light. The changed reading context would have been reinforced by the *Land and Water* commentary supplied by the Oxford philosopher turned *Daily Telegraph* journalist and editor of the *Fortnightly Review* W. L. Courtney, who referred specifically to the experience of 'the last few months', 'the history of the last few Zeppelin raids in England', 'the last raid over the Midlands' (which would have been that of 31 January / 1 February 1916) and the fact that 'some of the points of attack are theatres' (a reference to the bombing of the Lyceum Theatre in Exeter Street, London, on 13/14 October 1915.

Whatever the contextual translation, Raemaekers's cartoon clearly identified the killing of a female civilian, wife and mother as a 'triumphant' outcome of a Zeppelin raid. For Courtney, the moral lesson was clear:

> When the future historian gives to another age his account of all that is included in German 'frightfulness', there is no feature upon which he will dilate more emphatically than the extraordinary use made by the enemy of their Zeppelin fleet. ...
>
> In that reckless crusade which the Central Powers are waging against all the higher laws of morality and civilisation, some of the heaviest blows fall on the defenceless. It is this appalling inhumanity, this godless desire to maim and wound and kill, which nerves the arms of the Allies, who know that in a case like this they are fighting for freedom and for the Divine laws of mercy and loving-kindness.

A more violent image—'The Zeppelin War'—depicting an explosion detonating amongst civilians, appeared in Part 20 of the *Land and Water* series in

FIGURE 18.3　Louis Raemaekers, 'The Zeppelin Triumph', *'Land and Water' Edition*, Part 3. 'But Mother had done nothing wrong, had she, Daddy?'

November 1916. The journalist and novelist Charles Vivian there saw in aerial bombing a 'manifestation of the German spirit': 'Germany alone among the nations has built Zeppelins ... Germany alone has pinned faith to terrorism and murder'.

Blame for what were understood as German war crimes was routinely laid at the feet of Kaiser Wilhelm, and it was easy for cartoonists to depict him in unflattering guises. Figure 18.4—Raemaekers's 'The Zeppelin Raider'—had first been published in *De Telegraaf* on 30 March 1916 under the title (translated) 'The Intensified Submarine War', but was retitled for the *Land and Water* issue. The Kaiser is portrayed as a child murderer, responsible for slitting the

FIGURE 18.4   Louis Raemaekers, 'The Zeppelin Raider', *'Land and Water' Edition*, Part 14

throats of four sleeping infants. The cartoon was accompanied by the commentary of the novelist Henry de Vere Stacpoole, at this time living in the Essex village of Castle Hedingham, very much on the regular Zeppelin flight path into London. Stacpoole pointed out that what was an explicit and violent cartoon by British standards was 'far less terrible than the reality … children torn to pieces by high explosives are far more horrible to look at than children with their throats cut'. By chance this cartoon would have reached its British readership at around the time that a sixth Zeppelin raid was made on London, when on 25 August *L31* dropped 44 bombs on the Isle of Dogs, Deptford, Greenwich, Blackheath, Eltham and Plumstead, killing twenty-two people, including eleven-year-old Gladys Allen. 'The Zeppelin Bag', a similar image suggesting

FIGURE 18.5   J. M. Staniforth, 'Gott Mit Uns', *Western Mail*, 27 December 1917.
'The year 1917, with its great battles, has proved that the German people has in the Lord of Creation above an unconditional and avowed ally, on Whom it can absolutely rely. Without Him all would have been in vain ... You have seen how in this last four years of war God's hand has visibly prevailed, punished treachery, and rewarded heroic perseverance'—Kaiser's address to his troops.

the Kaiser's culpability for the death of innocent children, appeared in *Land and Water* in November 1916.

Figure 18.5—J. M. Staniforth's 'Gott Mit Uns'—also attributed blame to the Kaiser for the slaughter of innocents. Appearing in the Cardiff daily the *Western Mail* on 27 December 1917 it was likely inspired by the German bomber raid on London of 18 December 1917, which had left thirteen dead and seventy-nine injured in the most effective attack since that by Zeppelins on 8/9 September 1915. 'Gott Mit Uns', unlike 'The Zeppelin Raider', eschews allegory, but exhibits some restraint in that whilst buildings are devastated, the bodies of the dead children are left intact. The image was accompanied by an extract from the Kaiser's address of 22 December 1917 (which had been reported in the British press) and the title—'God With Us'—is clearly sarcastic.

3 Reprisals and Frustration

It was one thing to be outraged by Zeppelin or bomber attacks, but quite another to do something about them, and the reality was that the primitive nature of air defences, especially in the early phases of the war, meant that air raids could not easily be prevented. As a consequence, by June 1915 there were strident, even hysterical calls for reprisals on German manufacturing towns in order to deter future raids.[18] Isolated British attacks did take place, such as those on Karlsruhe in 1915 (celebrated by Leonard Raven-Hill's 'Injured Innocence', *Punch*, 23 June 1915), but it was not until late 1917 that there was official approval for a planned campaign of British strategic bombing of German towns and cities. In the last year of the conflict many British raids were launched, hitting cities including Düsseldorf, Cologne, Stuttgart, Koblenz, Heidelberg, Strasbourg and Metz.

Figure 18.6—Frank Townsend's 'Funk Holes for Ministers' (*Punch*, 29 March 1916)—reflected the pressure the government came under over the reprisals question in the spring of 1916, provoked by the Zeppelin raid of 31 January / 1 February. This had set out with the intention of attacking Liverpool but, owing to poor weather and navigational challenges, led instead to the bombing of a number of sites in the Midlands and the killing of seventy people. As the official history records, 'The defence during the attack was negligible', with no hits on Zeppelins by anti-aircraft guns and no sightings of the airships by the British pilots who took off to intercept them.[19] The raid prompted an urgent discussion in the press and in Parliament about the need to extend air defence measures, as well as raising the question of reprisals. The cartoon shows the front bench of the House of Commons, with Arthur Balfour, then First Lord

---

18   Morrow, *Great War in the Air*, pp. 120–121.
19   H. A. Jones, *The War in the Air: Being the Story of the part played in the Great War by the Royal Air Force*, (London: Imperial War Museum, 1931), vol 3., pp. 135–144.

FIGURE 18.6   Frank Townsend, 'Essence of Parliament: Funk-Holes for Ministers—designed for protection against raids by our air-experts', *Punch*, 29 March 1916

of the Admiralty (the Navy had been, until some weeks earlier, responsible for the aerial defence of London), and Harold 'Jack' Tennant, Under-Secretary of State for War, sheltering beneath a shelter of sandbags whilst the Foreign Secretary Sir Edward Grey, Prime Minister Asquith and Minister of Munitions Lloyd George adopt more relaxed poses.

Eighteenth months later and Staniforth's *Western Mail* cartoon of 27 September 1917 (Figure 18.7) was unambiguous as to the need for reprisals, stating in its title that they were 'The Only Way To Stop It', and specifically identifying the German city of Essen as a target. This was a response to the intensive German bombing campaign that had begun on 24 September 1917, with a mixture of Gothas and Zeppelins attacking targets in Yorkshire, Lincolnshire, London, Kent and Essex. As the official history put it, these attacks 'remained more vividly than any others in the memory of most of those who lived through the air raids on England', and are here contrasted with a British attack on the Jabbeke Aerodrome at Varssenaere / Varsenare, behind German lines in Belgium. Brief details of that raid were carried in newspapers on 26 September 1917, indicating that 'a large number of bombs were dropped, mostly falling amongst the sheds and hangars and also among the aeroplanes lined upon the aerodrome'.[20] This report allowed Staniforth to suggest in one placard 'amount of damage

---

20   Jones, *War in the Air*, 5, p. 78; *Daily Mirror*, 26 September 1917.

FIGURE 18.7 J. M. Staniforth, 'The Only Way To Stop It', *Western Mail*, 27 September 1917. John Bull: 'H'm! I shall be better satisfied when I read of my air-men taking reprisals on Essen and other German towns. Until then I must expect those raids on London to continue'.

unknown', by contrast with the 'many casualties and considerable damage done' by the German raid in civilian districts. The placard in the background reminds the reader of the moral turpitude of the enemy, in that they express 'great German joy' at the news of London's bombing, thus suggesting that they fully deserve to be the target of reciprocal treatment.

FIGURE 18.8   Frank Townsend, 'The Letter and the Spirit', Punch, 10 October 1917.
Prime Minister: 'You young rascal! I never said that'. Newsboy: 'Well, I'll lay yer meant it.'

Whether or not one supported reprisal raids as a deterrent to continued German bombing, there were many who believed that the British authorities were to blame for their failure to protect civilians from air attack. In this regard, air raids were a double-edged sword politically. As the official historian noted, they were 'often used by the Government to stimulate recruiting ... but there were times also ... when the attacks acted on public opinion until the

Government were compelled to vitalize their air policy'.[21] Frank Townsend's 'The Letter and the Spirit' (*Punch*, 10 October 1917) (Figure 18.8) implicitly accused Prime Minister Lloyd George of meaning one thing if saying another. A week earlier newspapers had reported Lloyd George visiting bombed districts of London after the best part of a week of sustained air raids, and after a particularly heavy raid on west London on the night of 1/2 October.

> A man shouted 'Reprisals, Mr Lloyd George, on German towns'. The cry was received with a shout of approval, and the Prime Minister was heard by those near him to say: 'We shall do that'.[22]

In some newspapers this was elaborated further, with Lloyd George apparently saying 'We'll give it them all back. We'll give them hell. And we'll give it them soon. We shall bomb Germany with compound interest'.[23] Yet simultaneously reports emerged stating that the Premier was 'greatly surprised by the vigour of the language attributed to him' and that he had 'no recollection of using such language'.[24] As long-range bombing operations from an aerodrome near Nancy were authorised the *Yorkshire Post* reflected 'probably most people would like to be assured that the British Prime Minister did not announce in these terms the policy his Government have been reluctantly driven to adopt'.[25] Townsend clearly took this episode as inspiration for his cartoon.

4 Celebration

Although the early stages of the war saw Britain apparently unable to thwart Zeppelin raids, gradually the calibre of anti-aircraft defences and of fighter pilots prepared and able to engage airships tipped the balance towards the defence. Increasingly, Zeppelins were revealed as vulnerable, and German losses were celebrated with enthusiasm by cartoonists.

The destruction of *LZ37* by Flight Sub-Lieutenant R. A. J. Warneford of the Royal Naval Air Service on 7 June 1915—the first Zeppelin to be destroyed in combat—was an important milestone. Four airships had set out on the evening of 6 June to attack London or other suitable targets, but only *L9* had

---

21 Jones, *War in the Air*, 5, p. 153.
22 *Evening Mail*, 3 October 1917.
23 *Aberdeen Evening Express*, 4 October 1917.
24 *Hull Daily Mail*, 4 October 1917.
25 *Yorkshire Post and Leeds Intelligencer*, 10 October 1917.

FIGURE 18.9 'Poy', 'Sausage for Tea', *Poy's War Cartoons from 'The Evening News'* (London: Simpkin, Marshall, Hamilton, Kent & Co., 1915). A cartoon on the great feat of the late Lieut. Warneford, V.C.

reached Britain, bombing Hull and killing twenty-four people. *LZ37* encountered fog and abandoned the raid, but had been spotted, bombed from above by Warneford, and crashed near Ghent with only one crew member surviving. 'Poy' celebrated the occasion with 'Sausage for Tea' (Figure 18.9). Warneford himself had been killed in a crash less than a fortnight after his Victoria Cross-winning exploit.

Warneford's success was isolated, and it was not until the following year that Zeppelin losses began to mount. A raid launched on 23/24 September 1916 saw two airships, *L32* and *L33*, shot down, some three weeks after *SL11* had become the first airship to be brought down on British soil. The demise of *L32* in particular caught the popular imagination, it catching fire in the air and plunging to the ground near Billericay in Essex. Raemaekers's 'The Seventh Zeppelin', showing two flaming skeletons falling from the sky may have been inspired by this episode, and was certainly connected to it by a lengthy report from the *Evening Standard* of 25 September 1916 when it appeared in the compilation volume *The Great War in 1916*. According to the newspaper '[o]f the crew all but one were no more than grim semblances of humanity, of trunk and limbs not only broken but also desiccated'.[26] A similar image, 'The Fall of the Child-Slayer', showing the Kaiser in the form of a human torch plummeting

---

26 *The Great War in 1916: A Neutral's Indictment. Sixty Cartoons by Louis Raemaekers* (London: Fine Art Society, 1917), plate 22.

FIGURE 18.10   Frank Townsend, 'A Wasted Life', *Punch*, 27 September 1916.
Kaiser (to Count Zeppelin): 'Tell me, Count, why didn't you invent something useful, like the "tanks"?'

to earth, appeared in Part 23 of the *Land and Water* series (December 1916), whilst 'And Such a Brave Zepp He Was' (*Land and Water*, Part 17, October 1916) depicted the tearful German Emperor mourning the loss of another airship.

Frank Townsend celebrated what the official history titled 'The Defeat of the Zeppelin' in lighter vein in—his 'A Wasted Life' (*Punch*, 27 September 1916) (Figure 18.10) showing the Kaiser upbraiding Count Zeppelin for not having invented 'something useful, like the "tanks"'—a reference to the first deployment of the tank by the British at Flers-Courcelette on the Somme on 15 September 1916.[27]

---

27   Jones, *War in the Air*, 3, p. 222.

FIGURE 18.11   J. M. Staniforth, 'To The Vile Dust', *Western Mail*, 19 June 1917. 'To the vile dust from whence they sprung, Unwept, unhonour'd, and unsung.'

Figure 18.11—J. M. Staniforth's 'To the Vile Dust' (*Western Mail*, 19 June 1917)—also celebrated the demise of a Zeppelin, after *L48* was shot down near Therberton, Suffolk, on 17 June, with the loss of sixteen of her crew of nineteen. The title and caption were taken from Walter Scott's 'Lay of the Last Minstrel' (1805). The cartoonist evinces no sympathy for the enemy, their burning skeletons and dismembered corpses gruesomely depicted in the foreground, whilst the wrecked structure of the airship smoulders behind. By contrast, the Royal Flying Corps in marking the grave of the crew of *L48* used the text 'Who art thou that judgest another man's servant. To his own master he standeth or falleth'.[28]

---

28   Jones, *War in the Air*, 5, p. 34.

5 Cheery Stoicism

By far the largest number of cartoon images relating to the air war fall into the category of 'humorous' sketches, a majority of them, inevitably, being found in the pages of *Punch*. Because they were usually the least didactic in intent, such cartoons can be very revealing of the climate of public opinion. Susan Grayzel summarises the message of the aforementioned anthologised *Punch* cartoons by Lewis Baumer and George Belcher as, in the first instance, making light of the Zeppelins, which simply become a matter for public interest, and as suggesting 'that fundamentally Britons of all sexes and classes would not be intimidated by air raids'.[29]

By considering more than a hundred humorous cartoons one can take the analysis further. The advent of the Zeppelin threat provided an opportunity for cartoonists to poke fun at a variety of familiar targets, including children, country dwellers, servants and women in general, who were now struggling to come to terms with the technological novelty of the airship and its death-dealing properties (including being able to pronounce 'Zeppelin', as opposed to 'Zellerpins' or 'Zeppelines'). Figure 18.12—Frank Townsend's sketch of 3 November 1915—appeared only a few weeks after the fifth Zeppelin raid on London (the 'Theatreland' raid of 13/14 October 1915) had inflicted the highest casualties (71 dead) in a single raid on the capital, also causing extensive damage to districts of central London. Picking up on the fact that there was a tendency for interested civilians to come out into the streets to watch the novel if chilling spectacle of airships floating high above and dropping bombs, Townsend shows a clearly wealthy couple both fascinated and gripped by the prospect of death from the sky. Despite the threat, the cartoonist emphasises the humour to be found in the situation, especially in the foolish (but admirable?) sang-froid of husband and wife.

Cartoons could also be revelatory of the impact of the aerial threat on public assumptions. In Figure 18.13, 'Echoes of the Air-Raids', from *Punch*, 17 October 1917, Frank Townsend shows two young working-class 'souvenir hunters', scouring the streets of London in vain for items of interest. Frustrated on this occasion, they take comfort in the knowledge that another raid will follow as sure as night follows day: the air raid is now a regular feature of their lives.

---

29 Grayzel, *At Home and Under Fire*, pp. 60, 83.

THE GERMAN AIR CAMPAIGN AGAINST BRITAIN 377

FIGURE 18.12   Frank Townsend, *Punch*, 3 November 1915. 'By Jove! Isn't it low? I believe I could hit it with my gun!' 'Oh, please, dear, don't do anything to irritate it!'

FIGURE 18.13   Frank Townsend, 'Echoes of the Air-Raids', *Punch*, 17 October 1917; 'First Souvenir-Hunter: 'Found anyfink, 'Erb?' Second ditto: 'No; but that'll be all right. They're sure to come again termorrer night.'

Even when on the receiving end of a bomb blast, cartoonists depicted stoical resolve. Lewis Baumer, in 'Zepp! Zepp! Hurray' (*The Sketch*, 31 May 1916) showed a bourgeois family contemplating the up-side of having a bomb crater in their garden. Although all the glass panes of their door and windows have been shattered by the blast, and their lawn has disappeared, the man of the house nonchalantly puffs away at his pipe, his hands in his pockets, while his wife, hitching up her dress to avoid getting it dirty, finds the silver lining in this particular cloud: 'Well, you always wanted a rock garden, didn't you, dear?' The stability of the family unit is undisturbed, despite the devastation hurled from above by the German barbarians. And G. L. Stampa, in 'Grit' (*Punch*, 22 September 1915) showed grocer 'John Smith' carrying on with 'business as usual', despite the destruction of his shop in a Zeppelin raid.

Yet although most cartoons were upbeat and resolute, there were some which communicated something less than the cohesion and shared purpose of a society at war. *Punch* carried a number utilising the stereotype of the money-grabbing or self-interested Jew, such as the cinema proprietor whose business was being ruined by the Germans giving a 'free show' of their own (G. D. Armour, 'The Morning After An Air Raid', *Punch*, 29 September 1915), or the 'indignant Alien' who had decamped to Maidenhead during the period of the full moon to avoid the bombing only for the Germans to cease their campaign (Lewis Baumer, 'Our Maidenhead Bomb-Dodgers', *Punch*, 17 April 1918). P. B. Hickling's 'During a Zeppelin Raid' (*Punch*, 17 November 1915) showed an 'unstarred man' (someone eligible for military service) taking refuge in the nearest building, only unhappily to find it an army recruiting office, while Harry Low's 'Munition Worker' (*Punch*, 20 October 1915) realises the unexploded anti-aircraft shell that has destroyed his potted plants is one he made himself.

Despite these discordant notes, in the humorous cartoon responses to aerial bombing we generally see displays of playful indifference, insouciance, stoicism, fortitude, doggedness and phlegm. Susan Grayzel argues that humour played a part in minimizing the 'fear' and 'anxiety' caused by bombing.[30] Yet a reasonable objection to the suggestion that public stoicism and cheerfulness in the face of adversity is evidenced by contemporary cartoons would be that such stoicism and cheerfulness was 'performed' or, as Grayzel has suggested,

---

30 Ibid., p. 92.

was 'retroactive'.³¹ It is certainly true that cartoons could only ever present a partial representation of the public mood. Cartoonists self-censored, and were unlikely to seek to have published images which might undermine morale or be seen as defeatist. They would be wary of commenting on the fright that appears to have gripped the British civilian population under aerial bombardment at various points during the war. There were occasional scares: on 10 February 1916 rumours of an approaching massive Zeppelin raid caused widespread consternation in places as far apart as Bath and Barnsley and, in September 1917, a week of continuous bombing, according to Martin Gilbert, 'reduced many in the East End of London to panic', with up to 300,000 people seeking shelter in the London underground.³² Some inhabitants of Hull were known to decamp from the city when anticipating aerial attacks (usually around the time of the full moon) and spend the night in the surrounding countryside.³³ Little of such reactions appears in the cartoons; they were, on balance, relatively muted and contained. Frank Reynolds's 'Conjurer (unconscious of the approach of hostile aircraft)' (*Punch*, 5 July 1916) depicts a crowd fleeing for their lives. Bernard Partridge's 'big cut' 'The Business of the Moment' (*Punch*, 18 July 1917) had a rather alarmed John Bull promising the German bomber aircraft that 'I've learned how to deal with your Zepp brother, and now I'm going to attend to you', suggesting that the threat had yet to be contained. George Morrow's 'The Air-Raid Season' (*Punch*, 31 October 1917) shows an enormous queue of applicants—most of respectable and wealthy appearance—for an advertised post of 'cellarman', suggesting (seriously or whimsically it is difficult to know) a level of public anxiety not commonly revealed. Overall, however, cartoons drawn in response to German bombing raids on Britain during the Great War would appear to support both H. A. Jones's suggestion that air attacks on cities 'led for the most part to a stiffening of the national temper', and John H. Morrow's argument that there was 'little evidence of civilian collapse under aerial bombardment beyond some panic in London during early air attacks'.³⁴

This chapter has argued that cartoons, both 'editorial' and 'humorous', merit serious consideration as a significant source of evidence for popular

---

31 Ibid., p. 91.
32 Jones, *War in the Air*, 3, p. 146, 5, pp. 89–90; Gilbert, *The Routledge Atlas of the First World War: The Complete History* (London: Routledge, 1994), pp. 69–70.
33 Morrow, *Great War in the Air*, p. 21.
34 Jones, *War in the Air*, 5, p. 153; Morrow, 'The War in the Air', in Hew Strachan (ed.), *The Oxford Illustrated History of the First World War* (Oxford: Oxford University Press, 1998), p. 277.

attitudes and reactions to the novelty of death and danger from the air. They may be considered at least as important as the evidence to be found in newspaper editorial columns or letters to the press, and are less obviously one-dimensional than propaganda posters. Spanning a range of emotions from outrage to self-mockery, they convey something of the perspectives of the moment, and allow glimpses of the essential resilience of British society during its first total war.

CHAPTER 19

'Every Night You Take Up the Paper You Find Someone Has Either Been Killed or Severely Injured'

The Irish Press's Portrayal of Road Traffic Accidents in the Early Motoring Era

Leanne Blaney

The motorcar's arrival changed Ireland. First imported in 1896, few could have fathomed that this new form of locomotion would be a catalyst of disruption to the traditional social order of the road, causing the transformation of established social practices and the permanent alteration of urban and rural planning. The motorcar would also have an irreversible negative impact upon road safety, with the number of fatal road traffic accidents steadily rising for much of the early motoring era.[1]

Ireland was not unique in this regard. Studies by Paul Barrett, Steffen Bohm, Cotton Saeiler, Clay McShane, Peter D. Norton, John Urry, Steven Parissien and most recently Éamon Ó Cofaigh have examined the role of the motorcar upon various countries following its introduction and popularisation during the late nineteenth and early twentieth centuries.[2] Their work demonstrates that certain trends were evident across a range of countries, such as the United States of America (hereafter USA), France, Germany, Australia and Sweden. One of these shared trends was the close relationship enjoyed between the motor industry and the press. From the beginning the press 'devoted much space to the [motorcar] in an attempt to attract readers and also to promote

---

1 1959 is generally considered by cultural and motoring historians as the year in which the 'Golden Age' of the motorcar was reached. As such, we tend to refer to 1959 as the end of the early motoring era. For further details see Steven Parissien, *The Life Of The Automobile: A New History Of The Motor Car* (London: Atlantic Books, 2013).

2 Recommended works include: Peter Thorold, *The Motoring Age: The Automobile and Britain 1896–1939* (London: Thistle Publishing 2003); Cotton Seiler, *Republic of Drivers: A Cultural History of Automobility in America* (Chicago: University of Chicago Press, 2008); L.J.K. Setright, *Drive On! A Social History of the Motor Car* (London: Granta Books, 2002); Steffen Bohm et al. (eds.), *Against Automobility* (Oxford: Blackwell Publishing, 2006); Douglas Brinkley, *Wheels for the World* (London: Penguin Random House, 2004), and James J. Flink, *The Automobile Age* (London: Massachusetts Institute of Technology Press, 1990).

the car itself'.[3] Subsequently, as mass motoring advanced, the press continued to encourage the public to recognise 'the steady technological progress being made' and 'how this could benefit [their] country'.[4] Norton and Ó Cofaigh have addressed the press's potentially vested interest in advancing the case for growing automobility. They note the abundant advertisements placed by motor agents, motor manufacturers and subsidiary motor industries (including oil companies), which frequently dominated space on the advertisement pages of periodicals. Such economic contributions could arguably have swayed these periodicals' coverage of the role of motorcars and motorists in causing or being involved in mounting road traffic accidents and fatalities.

This chapter will assess how Irish local and national newspapers and periodicals reported road traffic accidents and fatalities during the early motoring era, highlighting any variance in coverage offered by periodicals that were sympathetic to motorists and the motor industry and those that were not. It will also consider whether the type of coverage in Irish media changed, as motoring became more commonplace and less associated with particular social classes and geographical areas.

Peter D. Norton's 'Four Paradigms', which chart the evolution of traffic safety in twentieth century streets and urban landscapes across the USA provide an analytical framework for this chapter; these paradigms are: 'Safety First, Control, Crashworthiness and Responsibility'.[5] Though they are generally considered sequential, Norton intended that when applied to other countries, historians 'borrow, modify or replace them' as appropriate.[6] This will be the case in what follows.

It should be acknowledged that in many ways Ireland's experience of motoring was unique within the wider Western world. Unlike Britain—where private railway companies enjoyed a monopoly on the country's transport network and thus had a vested interest in maintaining the status quo—Ireland was keen to embrace the motorcar. Irish politicians, such as Viscount Thomas Clifden recognised the opportunity that motorcars could offer to farmers, assisting in 'the transit of farm produce from farm to the market town'.[7] And Frederick W. Crossley (founder of the Irish Tourist Development Association

---

3 Eamon Ó Cofaigh, *A Vehicle for Change: Popular Representations of the Automobile in 20th Century France* (Liverpool: Liverpool University Press, 2022), p. 8.
4 Ibid.
5 For more detail, see: Peter Norton, 'Four Paradigms: Traffic Safety in the Twentieth-Century United Sates', *Technology and Culture*, Vol. 56, No. 2 SPECIAL ISSUE: (Auto) Mobility, Accidents and Danger (April 2015), pp. 319–334.
6 Norton, 'Four Paradigms', p. 319.
7 H.L. Debate, Vol. 39: 1490–5, 23 April 1896.

in 1891 and later the Irish Tourist Association in 1895) recognised the potential boon to Irish tourism if motoring holidays became popular across the island.[8]

Such foresight was impressive, in a country where there 'was no more than between fifty and one hundred cars' by 1900 and a substantial proportion of the national economy was centred around the equine industry.[9] Progress was initially slow: by 1913 there were 6,549 motorcars registered in Ireland, a number exceeded by the city boroughs of Paris in 1897, when over 7,000 cars were registered with their authorities.[10] As such, Ireland did not experience the same levels of mass motoring as their European contemporaries—and therefore less exposure to the negative aspects of motoring. By the beginning of the twentieth century, for example, the Bois de Boulogne was already being described as 'particularly hazardous' on account of the frequency of road traffic accidents, and there existed a hostile attitude between French motorists and pedestrians. This growing hostility was evidenced in the motoring magazine *La Locomotion Automobile*, which suggested that if pedestrians intended to carry revolvers (in order to protect themselves from reckless motorists), motorists would begin to arm themselves with machine guns.[11]

It could also be argued that the Irish were unable to devote the same level of attention to road safety in the early decades of the twentieth century. After all, between 1914 and 1923, Ireland bore witness to: the First World War; a global health pandemic; the War of Independence; the partition of the island and the formation of two new states; and the subsequent Civil War. Therefore, the press coverage devoted to road traffic accidents during the course of the early twentieth century, while still notable, was not as prolific as it could have been in times of peace.

The Irish press still maintained a significant role in advancing automobility and influencing the public's attitude towards motorcars, motorists and road traffic accidents. Indeed, the influence of two leading Irish pressmen Richard J. Mecredy, editor of the *Irish Wheelman*, and Alfred Harmsworth, more frequently known as Lord Northcliffe, founder of the *Daily Mail*, had helped ensure a generally positive Irish welcome for the first motorcars to

---

8   Irene Furlong, *Irish Tourism, 1880–1980* (Dublin: Irish Academic Press, 2009), pp. 19–21.
9   Cornelius F. Smith, *The History Of The Royal Irish Automobile Club, 1901–1991* (Dublin: Royal Irish Automobile Club, 1994), p. 32 and Caitriona Clear, *Social Change and Everyday Life in Ireland, 1850–1922* (Manchester: Manchester University Press, 2007), p. 7. Over 630,000 horses were recorded in Ireland in 1895. By 1901, over half a million horses were described as 'working', either in agriculture or industry.
10 Michael Flower and Raymond Jones, *100 Years of Motoring: An RAC Social History of the Car* (London: The Royal Automobile Association, 1981), p. 37.
11 Ibid.

arrive in the country.[12] Mecredy, a successful competitive cyclist in his youth, typified the evolution of ardent Irish cyclists into pioneering motorists. He had been wholly against what he termed 'oil pots' until his friend, the Australian cyclist Selwyn Edge, had convinced him to take a spin in Edge's new motorcar. By the end of this auspicious journey, Mecredy was a convert—so much so, that by 1900, he had founded *The Motor News*, Ireland's first motoring journal, which was aimed at encouraging and educating Ireland's early motorists.[13]

From the outset, coverage of road traffic accidents involving motorists, both local and international, were provided in this publication, with Mecredy eager to offer a true representation of what life was really like for the intrepid Irish motorist. As this example shows, the tone during the first years of the periodical tended to be sympathetic to the motorist:

> Colonel Magrath, of Wexford, has had cruel luck with the new car just built for him … All went well until he had passed under the embankment for the new railway near Lucy Rock, where suddenly the car became uncontrollable and ran into a telegraph post. On investigation it was found that the accident had been caused [because] some twenty or thirty yards of telephone wire [had been] left across the road.[14]

A tendency to portray many of these early accidents as the result of motorcars being forced to share roads with other road users, who were generally ignorant of motorcars and what motoring entailed, was also evident.

Public roads had long been considered places of danger, 'whether from horse and cart, steam wagon, tram or bicycle'.[15] People used roads and streets for a multitude of purposes, and this meant that accidents did occur. Reports

---

12 For more detail on Harmsworth, see Richard Bourne, *Lords of Fleet Street: The Harmsworth Dynasty* (London: Unwin Hyman, 2015); Andrew Roberts, *The Chief: The Life of Lord Northcliffe Britain's Greatest Press Baron* (London: Simon & Schuster Ltd., 2022); and S. J. Taylor, *The Great Outsiders: Northcliffe, Rothermere and the 'Daily Mail'* (London: W & N, 1996).

13 For more detail on R. J Mecredy, see Nicholas Allen and Bob Montgomery, 'Mecredy, Richard James Patrick', in James McGuire and James Quinn (eds.), *Dictionary of Irish Biography* (Cambridge: Cambridge University Press, 2009), and Bob Montgomery, *R J Mecredy: The Father of Irish Motoring* (Meath: Dreoilín Press, 2003).

14 *The Motor News*, March 1900.

15 Gijs Mom, 'Civilized Adventure as a Remedy for Nervous Times: Early Automobilism and Fin-de-siècle Culture', *History of Technology*, vol. 23, (2011), pp. 157–190, and Bill Luckin, 'Drunk Driving: Britain 1800–1920', in Tom Crook and Mike Esbester (eds.), *Governing Risks in Modern Britain: Danger, Safety and Accidents, c.1800–2000* (London: Palgrave Macmillan, 2016), pp. 171–194.

of these accidents and the inquests that followed were frequently produced in contemporary periodicals and papers. Indeed, the eighteenth-century Irish newspaper *Pue's Occurrence* frequently contained brief synopses of recent road accidents, including a report of an incident in August 1789: 'Thursday laft a Man was jamm'd between two Carts on Milltown Road, by which accident his Coller [sic] Bone was broke and otherwifth greatly hurt'.[16] By the nineteenth century, the prevalence of the popular press and local journalism meant that it was possible for local provincial papers such as the *Derry Journal* to have a court reporter present at the inquest into deaths resulting from road accidents. This was true of the inquest into the death of Margaret McKay, who was killed travelling home from market when the cart she was travelling in was upturned by an uneven pothole. A report in the *Derry Journal* includes a direct quotation from the Coroner, Dr Tyrell who noted: 'This is the *fifty-seventh* inquest [held] in the Southern division ... since the presenting term at the last Summer Assizes; and ... about one-fifth of these casualties have occurred from ... culpable negligence on the public roads'.[17]

Norton suggests that his 'Safety First' paradigm, coined appropriately because it was the most common safety slogan during the era, be ascribed to the years 1900–1920 in the USA.[18] During this period, motorcars were perceived as dangerous newcomers and both cars and their drivers were considered less legitimate users of the streets and road than pedestrians. Norton argues that the association between cars and speed (and speed equated to danger) meant that cars were frequently considered 'inherently dangerous instrumentally'. As operators of these vehicles, motorists bore the sole responsibility for protecting others.[19] He notes that when an accident did occur, especially when it involved an infant, the prescribed presumption, including in press coverage, was that the motorist was guilty and the pedestrian innocent.

A consideration of the coverage of motoring accidents in Irish newspapers and periodicals published during the same period suggests that the Irish did not ascribe to this paradigm. Instead, coverage of motor accidents tended to be nuanced, especially when expressing judgement against the motorist. It could be argued that, in an effort to continue to popularise pro-motoring ideology among a wider Irish readership, journalists were keen to focus on the positives that motoring offered society. Certainly, tales of motoring accidents could be presented in a light-hearted manner, especially in publications sympathetic to

---

16   *Pue's Occurrence*, 19 August 1749.
17   *Derry Journal*, 14 November 1837.
18   Norton, 'Four Paradigms', p. 325.
19   Ibid.

motoring values. A May 1914 edition of *The Motor News* included coverage of how a party of Belfast motorists came upon 'a rather extraordinary accident at Julianstown' where: '... they saw a motor car stopped, but with the engine still running. The lefthand front mudguard was badly broken and close by was a horse attached to a car and trap, steady on three legs, the fourth leg being completely severed below the knee'.[20] The article contained no reference to the reaction of the motorist or the owner of the horse. Readers were not offered any resolution to the incident, nor were they given any details of any reparations made in the aftermath of the accident. Commonly during this period—when motor insurance was in its infancy and few motorists possessed it—the expectation was that the motorist (usually a wealthy individual of a higher social status than their pedestrian counterpart) would make a monetary donation to the affected road user, to cover the costs incurred by the accident. Therefore, it is likely that the owner of the horse was compensated for the injuries the unfortunate animal had sustained. Reportage of the incident underlined the attitude of commodity that characterised the relationship between man and equine at this time. In fact, one of the most frequently cited benefits of motoring over more traditional forms of transit was that motorcars were considered safer than the 'friend of man', who—according to a national health and safety report published in 1904—was responsible for causing on average one human fatality per day.[21]

Press coverage of motor accidents during this era may well have been influenced in their reporting by the fact that many of the newspaper editors were keen, or aspiring, motorists themselves. As such, they would have socialised with the relatively small and select group of Irish motorists in the country at the time. Analysis of contemporary membership records of Ireland's only motoring association, the Irish Automobile Club, illustrates this effectively.[22] It is possible to detect an obvious bias towards the motorist in contemporary publications, particularly in reports on accidents that involved motorists known to the journalists and editors. A Christmas edition of *The Motor News*, for instance, reported 'a sad motor accident in Dublin whereby Miss Perry of Foxrock was the innocent cause of death of an old woman named Mary Bolger'. The article stated how 'numerous witnesses' could testify that Miss Perry, described as 'an extraordinarily cautious and considerate driver', had been driving at a very slow pace when the victim, described as an 'old

---

20   *The Motor News*, 29 May 1914.
21   *The Motor News*, 24 December 1904.
22   *Irish Motor Directory, 1906*; *The Irish Motorists' Handbook 1912–13*; *Tempest's Irish Motor Directory, 1909*, and *Tempest's Irish Motor Directory, 1911–12*.

woman ... over 80 years of age, who was blind in one eye and [had] a cataract in the other', crossed the road despite a nearby tram sounding a warning that it was not safe to do so. Miss Perry apparently jammed on her brakes but owing to wet conditions failed to stop the car and knocked over the old woman. While the description of the victim's death was prosaic: 'one of the [car] wheels went over [the deceased's] chest, breaking her ribs and killing her instantly', more emotive language was employed to explain how, in the aftermath of the accident, the motorist was 'prostrated with grief'. The article concluded by observing that neither the jury involved in the corresponding court case, nor any of *The Motor News'* readership would expect that the female motorist to have 'any grounds for self-reproach'.[23] No such sympathy, though, was apparent for the victim.

Publications intended for an audience greater than simply the Irish motoring fraternity preferred to focus on what they believed would be of greater interest to the readership—such as the legalities of the court cases—rather than attempting to evaluate or pass commentary on the responsibility or victimhood of the motorists and pedestrians involved in road accidents. Again, this is demonstrative of a lack of alignment with Norton's 'Safety First' paradigm.

The *Irish Times*, in their coverage of the 1913 'Spire v. Carew' case in 1913, focused on reporting the key legal characters of the case, including 'Mr Justice Dodd' and the legal representatives on both sides, rather than identifying the child 'injured' by 'being run over by a car the property of the defendant on the 14th October 1912'.[24] There was also no evidence of the accident being reported in any of the local or national press after it occurred in 1912. The Spire v. Carew case reflects how, similarly to many other countries during this period, children formed the majority of victims who were reported injured or killed in motor accidents in Ireland.

However, attitudes expressed in Irish courts and newspapers differed from those prevalent in American society. In the USA, Norton notes how the rising number of children killed in road traffic accidents prompted city councils to embark proactively on blunt advertising campaigns aimed specifically at motorists.[25] The Safety Commission of Oak Park, Illinois posted fifty large signs around the city in 1922 warning motorists 'DON'T KILL A CHILD', while their Memphis counterparts devised a poster depicting an unidentified man, either the father or the motorist, clasping the 'tiny, limp body of a struck down

---

23 *The Motor News*, 24 December 1904.
24 *Irish Times*, 28 October 1913.
25 Peter D. Norton, *Fighting Traffic: The Dawn Of The Motor Age In The American City*, (Massachusetts: Massachusetts Institute of Technology, 2011), p. 39.

girl'.[26] Keen to appeal to motorists' conscience by prompting a strong emotive reaction, and influenced by the public displays of grief and memorial which followed in the years after Armistice Day in 1918, USA city traffic safety campaigns heavily emphasised memorials for the 'innocent' dead. Baltimore, for example, erected a '25-foot wood and plaster obelisk ... carefully built to resemble a permanent stone memorial'. It was intended to memorialise the '130 children killed in road traffic accidents across the city' during the previous year, and at the public declaration, the mayor was accompanied by several hundred school children, Girl Scouts and Boy Scouts, as well as a delegation from the Women's Civic League.[27] For these sections of society, there was no question that the responsibility for Norton's paradigms of 'Control' and 'Ownership' rested squarely on the shoulders of motorists and the motoring community.

In Ireland, disparity existed. Examination of court case transcripts and press coverage indicate that motorcars were regularly recognised as accessories responsible for causing the fatal injuries leading to a child's death. Yet, the prevailing attitude, held by the courts and journalists alike, was that 'ownership' of many accidents lay with the child and their actions, as opposed to the motorist involved. Owing to this, inquests frequently concluded with recommendations that motorists should take more care when driving, but the reason for the death of the deceased was officially recorded as an accident. This was in evidence at the inquests into the deaths of Catherine Mullane and Daniel O'Donnell McFall, both of which were initially reported in the local press and then subsequently in the *Irish Times*.

Catherine Mullane's death occurred in Cork when the little girl was knocked down and killed by a motorcar, driven by Miss Frances Gertrude Hughes of Dunkettle, on the evening prior to the inquest. Evidence presented found that the motor car was travelling at 'no more than ten miles per hour' and that Mullane had run from behind a pump on the roadside, therefore out of the motorist's sight, and had been struck by the car and killed outright.[28] The jury agreed unanimously that the fatal collision was an unavoidable accident, brought about by the child's naivety and rash action. One juror, though, did insist upon adding a rider, 'condemning the reckless driving of motor cars through villages, and the absolute disregard for human life on the part of owners and chauffeurs'. The coroner agreed as 'to the reckless manner in which

---

26　Norton, *Fighting Traffic*, p. 39.
27　Norton, *Fighting Traffic*, p. 41.
28　*Irish Times*, 13 June 1910.

motors were driven through villages and towns' and advised that should 'any owners or driver come before him, he would certainly not spare them'.²⁹

The coroner's admonishment was not unusual; robust warnings were frequently provided by magistrates, judges and members of the Royal Irish Constabulary, but the punishment imposed on the motorist under examination, if there was one, could be rather less severe. The fact that the motorist in this case, was a 42-year old widow, may well explain why she was 'spared' a more severe punishment. A middle-aged female widow hailing from a local provincial town did not fit the image of the evil motorist or reckless driver, usually depicted as male.³⁰

Even when the motorist involved was male, they could be spared if they demonstrated care and consideration in the aftermath of the accident. This was in evidence at the inquest of five-year old Daniel O'Donnell McFall, who was struck by a motorcar in Belfast in May 1913. The jury 'exonerated the driver from any blame' after hearing how the child had let go of his guardian's hand and ran across a tram in front of the motorcar. The boy had received immediate assistance from both the tram conductor and the motorist in question, who brought him straight to the Royal Victoria Hospital, where he subsequently passed away. The only recommendation to emerge out of the inquest was directed towards the Police Committee of the City Corporation that a 'by-law [be introduced] regulating the speed of motor cars when passing tramcars standing at a "Stop" pole'.³¹

When considering the reasons why the Irish response to the death of children was comparatively more muted than their US counterparts, there were clearly differences in culture and the way grief was demonstrated. Yet, it must be acknowledged that at the time Ireland's infant mortality rate continued to hover around 94.6 per 1,000 registered live births, 123.1 per 1,000 for towns over 10,000 people, and 75.5 per 1,000 in the remaining areas.³² The reality was that the death of a child was an unfortunate but relatively common occurrence in Irish society. Arguably, there existed a recognition that the untimely death of a child resulting from a motor accident was a tragedy, yet there was no certainty that the child would avoid fatal illnesses, such as typhoid, tuberculosis or appendicitis, and survive to adulthood.

---

29 *Irish Times*, 13 June 1910.
30 Norton, *Fighting Traffic*, p. 29.
31 *Irish Times*, 17 May 1916.
32 Ciara Breathnach and Brian Gurrin, 'A tale of two cities—infant mortality and cause of infant death, Dublin 1864–1910', *Urban History*, volume 44, issue 4, (November 2017), pp. 647–677.

Ultimately, attitudes would change. After the Partition of Ireland in 1921, the success of both Northern Ireland and the Free State depended heavily upon embracing and using motorcars, as the two new states tried to rebuild and forge ahead into uncertain futures. Writing in 1923, Mecredy summarised this belief stating:

> If Ireland is to progress, and out of the chaos of recent years to build up a strong and prosperous nation, the motor car will be one of her greatest assets; one of the most valuable instruments with which her prosperity will be fashioned. Every trade, every business, every industry will be our customers. There is not a single enterprise in the commercial world which can do without our motor cars and once we can stop squabbling and set about the task of building up the nation we shall want all the motors we can get.[33]

Greater automobility meant greater frequency of road accidents and fatalities, as evidenced in contemporary press coverage. Except for the introduction of road signs in 1926, both Irish states failed to invest or introduce proactive measures intended to educate the general public about road safety. Instead, in the face of the emergence of a public attitude, which aligned with the four paradigms identified by Norton, it fell to private companies involved in the international motor industry to try and educate the public on road safety. For example, Pratt's—the subsidiary company of Irish American Oil—sought to incorporate valuable road safety knowledge into their advertising.[34] While commendable, this had a limited impact, because advertisements were placed chiefly in motoring journals or the dedicated motoring pages of newspaper, which were usually not of interest to the intended audience which was primarily young children and the elderly. This high level of ignorance among pedestrians proved fatal. Statistics relating to motor accidents and fatalities demonstrate how, of the 1,582 motor accidents recorded in Northern Ireland in 1931, forty-four per cent were found to have been caused by pedestrians.[35]

In contrast, only seventeen per cent of accidents were attributed to negligent driving.[36] However, it is apparent in coverage of road accidents from this period that the motorists involved now faced more severe punishments. In 1926, Michael Tracey, a chauffeur for Senator Michael Fanning, was arrested

---

33   *The Motor News*, 6 January 1923.
34   *The Motor News*, 9 January 1926.
35   *Ulster Year Book*, 1932.
36   *Ulster Year Book*, 1932.

and charged after the vehicle he was driving fatally struck John Kavanagh, aged 53, who had been walking home from devotions on a road near Newbridge, Co. Kildare. The *Leinster Leader* noted that Tracey had complied fully with the legal authorities and had stopped immediately following the collision to offer assistance to Kavanagh. Unfortunately, his efforts were futile, as Kavanagh had been killed outright. Despite the jury at the initial inquest reaching the conclusion that the fatality had been unavoidable as the accident had occurred at night, when the car lights would have blinded both the pedestrian and the motorist, Tracey was still forced to stand trial.[37]

Similarly, in 1929, the death of auctioneer Daniel Irwin Higgins in a collision between a motor car and an Irish Omnibus Company bus (hereafter IOC), resulted in the bus driver being charged with murder. This demonstrated the severity with which the authorities now treated those they believed to be 'offending' motorists. However, at the resulting court trial, following reviews of the collected witness statements and evidence relating to the accident, the judge determined that there was not enough evidence to charge the defendant with either murder or manslaughter.[38] Local papers placed a greater value on providing the personal particulars of the victims of motor accidents, which was in stark contrast to the dry and impersonal details preferred by the national press. The *Western People*, for example, dedicated a significant portion of their report on Higgins' death to details of his character. Describing him as a 'progressive and thrifty' man, possessing 'a quiet and inoffensive disposition', the paper recalled how he had previously been a 'first prize winner under the Co. Kildare Agricultural Committee's Cottage Scheme'.[39]

At the same time, there were some local reporters who continued to focus on the more pragmatic impact of road accidents and fatalities. A *Kerry News* columnist writing in 1933 acknowledged that 'motor accidents, the whole world over, are reaching alarming proportions in recent years' and that 'Irish motor fatalities are likewise on the steady increase. This might only be expected with the increase in motor traffic, the narrowness of most of our highways and many people, not fully realising the danger of keeping to the wrong side of the road'. The columnist further observed that 'even where the greatest care is exercised and the most drastic traffic laws are in operation, accidents will inevitably happen', and reasoned that that, in order 'to protect the dependents of victims of motor accidents, we think third party insurance should be made compulsory in this country'. The report further noted that 'At present, families may be

---

37   *Leinster Leader*, 9 October 1926.
38   *Western People*, 10 August 1929.
39   *Western People*, 10 August 1929.

deprived of their breadwinner through accident, and the person responsible may be a man of straw, leaving the victims' dependents in destitution'. In order, therefore 'to safeguard the innocent and to prevent unnecessary suffering to people who have already supped to excess of bitter sorrow, compulsory insurance should be resorted to'. Highlighting that 'such a clause is foreshadowed in the [upcoming] Transport Bill", the lengthy article concluded with the assurance that '... no more necessary legislation could pass through the Dáil'.[40]

Though impassioned, this article illustrates how perception as opposed to reality could easily tip the public's view on a contentious issue. Journalists often did not have the time, nor—in the case of the journalists writing for regional local papers—the resources, to undertake substantial research into the subjects on which they based their articles; instead, they tended to rely on popular opinion and allowed their own prejudices and bias to influence their reporting. While the columnist for the *Kerry News* decried the disproportionate loss of working men, statistics clearly indicate that male breadwinners did not comprise the majority of victims of road traffic accidents. Whether deliberately seeking to provoke a reaction or prompt controversy, the Irish press were willing to peddle what had become accepted tropes of motoring life. This included misogyny against female motorists, who were regularly depicted as being careless and likely to disregard the safety of others when it suited them to do so. The *Irish Times* contributed to this prejudice in October 1934, in their coverage of a German manslaughter case. The defendant, the eighteen-year-old daughter of a leading figure in Hitler's Sturmabteilung (SA), was acquitted, despite witnesses having watched her knock down and kill a sixty-five year old man and severely injure his wife and daughter at a pedestrian crossing. The press reported that the motorist's defence rested on her claim that she was 'rather in a hurry and that the traffic light was green'.[41] Attributing this callous comment to the defendant did little to counteract the long-held prejudices against female motorists, nor did it diminish any implication that her father's position may have influenced the outcome of the trial.

Journalists were not unique in promoting the idea of motorists being reckless speed merchants for entertainment. Since the invention of the motorcar, many authors, creatives and directors involved in the global media industries employed this classic trope to entertain and shock their audiences. Indeed, in his 1900 movie *Explosion of a Motor Car*, the English film pioneer, Cecil Hepworth, included dramatic scenes of a motorcar exploding, sending the

---

40   *Kerry News*, 12 July 1933.
41   *Irish Times*, October 1934.

body parts of the vehicle's passenger into the sky, before they showered an unfortunate policeman.[42]

In the case of Ireland, no motoring issue would prove more contentious within the public discourse than the matter of drink driving. Aligning with the growing national recognition that alcohol abuse was prevalent across all sections of Irish society, many papers and periodicals began a steady campaign against intoxicated motorists who got behind the wheel of a car. These individuals were portrayed as an inherent danger and risk to the lives of the general public. However, there exists a discrepancy between the perception and reality of the levels of drink driving on Irish roads for much of the twentieth century. Anecdotally, there can be no question that driving under the influence of alcohol was and continued to be a very real risk to all Irish road users. Despite this, official records naming drink driving as the cause of motor accidents tend to be comparatively few, especially during the early motoring period; this is because it was often difficult to satisfy the legal necessity of obtaining a professional medical diagnosis of intoxication over the legal limit. Officially, the rates of accidents attributed to excessive speed and improperly overtaking, as well as pedestrians being at fault, were often greater than the number of accidents attributed to drink driving.

Yet, an overview of press coverage during this period would indicate that this discrepancy did not exist. Instead, there is blatant derision exhibited both in articles and editorials towards motorists guilty of such action. In particular, the *Irish Times* regularly adopted a tone of disapproval when reporting on such incidents. In 1938, under the headline 'Driver Did Not Remember', a Dublin District court reporter went to considerable effort to detail how the defendant, one 'William John Henderson', had got behind the wheel of his motorcar having enjoyed a 'black velvet' with friends at lunch. The 'black velvet', it transpired, was made up of 'two bottles of stout and a bottle of champagne'. He had driven through Rathmines and had been in the process of overtaking a van when his memory went blank. His next confirmed recollection was awaking the following morning to find his face covered in cuts and with sore knees. Subsequently, he learned that he had acquired a concussion, a broken rib and severe bruising to his knees. He also learned that he had been arrested for causing an accident by driving into pedestrian Mrs Annie Werner, who had been badly injured as a result.[43]

---

42 Dorit Muller, 'Transfers between Media and Mobility: Automobilism, Early Cinema and Literature, 1900–1920', *Transfers*, vol. 1, no. 1 (Spring 2011), p. 54.
43 *Irish Times*, 2 March 1938.

During the 1930s, with censorship rife following the enactment of the Censorship of Publication Act in 1929, Irish newspapers and periodicals were forced to focus on 'appropriate' domestic issues.[44] Road safety was a popular choice because it was largely devoid of any political or religious rhetoric. Thus, throughout the 1930s, newspapers frequently collaborated with civilian action groups such as the: Traffic & Safety First Association of Ireland; the Association for the Prevention of Intemperance; and The "Safety First" Association of Ireland, to campaign for tougher custodial sentences for motorists found guilty of drink-driving. The prolific coverage of road traffic accidents throughout the 1930s, combined with the increased ownership and use of motorcars across Ireland (and therefore a substantial rise in the frequency of road traffic accidents), prompted the Irish public to embrace Norton's 'Ownership' paradigm on the eve of The Emergency. In one telling letter, written to the editor of the *Evening Herald* in 1938, the author warned 'it is about time that somebody took notice of motor accidents ... Every night you take up the paper you find someone has either been killed or severely injured. ... Wake up Dublin, before we have a city of cripples'.[45]

When normal reporting resumed at the end of the Emergency (or World War II for the newspapers and journalists based in Northern Ireland), the press continued to report regularly on motor traffic accidents, especially in local publications. Eager to bolster news reporting in small rural villages and towns—then being decimated by increased levels of emigration and migration to the ever-expanding cities in search of better employment opportunities—local journalists found themselves reporting on 'narrowly avoided' road accidents or collisions in which 'everyone escaped injury'. They also continued to focus on publishing poignant accounts of fatal accidents, including detailed descriptions of victims and the impact of their death upon those left behind. To maximise impact, the local and regional press reports became lengthier and more emotive.

A September 1953 edition of the *Ballina Herald* detailed the tragic death of Reverend Noel Rowland using the following format. Under the headline 'Ballylahan Motor Accident has fatal result' and a corresponding subtitle 'Sad Death of Clerical Student', the local paper described in detail how 'an unusual type of motoring accident [occurred] at Ballylahan bridge'. The deceased, referred to by name, was a young clerical student on leave who set out in a motor van accompanied by some neighbours to visit the holy shrine at Knock.

---

44 John Horgan, 'Saving us from ourselves: contraception, censorship and the 'evil literature' controversy of 1926', *Irish Communications Review*, vol. 5 (1995), p. 61.

45 NAI, JUS/90/105/63, Road Traffic Act, 1933: Road Traffic Statistics.

Evidently conscious that readers would have been familiar with the locality, the article detailed how the van passed 'under the plantation at Mr Farrs, on the Foxford side of the bridge'. Explaining how the accident was the result of a recent storm which 'dislodged a heavy branch of a tree [that] fell directly on the [passing] vehicle', the report also provided an eyewitness account from one of the surviving passengers, 'Mrs Ellen Byron', who spotted the deceased bearing a serious head injury. Poignantly, the article concluded with a brief description provided by the deceased's brother, noting that he would have been '25 years [old] in December' and that the last time he had seen his brother alive was on the morning of the accident 'then in his usual good health'.[46]

Whether intended as sensitive reporting or constructed to prompt an emotive response from the readership, there can be no question that by the end of the early motoring era, press coverage of road traffic accidents primarily focused on the victims, as opposed to the mechanics of the vehicle, the accident, or the subsequent legal resolution to the incident. The commonality of motoring and motor accidents in 1950s Ireland meant that the public no longer needed the logistics of the accident explained to them. Now, the focus was mainly on prompting readers to recognise the humanity of the victims who lay behind every headline and statistic about road accidents and fatalities. Reports were designed to remind their readers that, somewhere in Ireland, there lived a family to whom a loved one who would not be returning home.

---

46   *Ballina Herald*, 12 September 1953.

CHAPTER 20

Making a Splash

A Brief History of Headlines

Daniel Carey

In James Joyce's *Ulysses*, Leopold Bloom works as an advertising canvasser for *The Freeman's Journal and National Press*, a daily newspaper published in Dublin. His visit to the newspaper's offices is depicted in the Aeolus episode (Episode 7) of *Ulysses*, a section of the book where—with form mirroring content—a series of newspaper-style headlines are dotted throughout the text. These headlines were a late addition to the episode, 'appended as the novel went to press'.[1] They have been described in various ways—as headlines, captions, or subheads. Terence Killeen points out that strictly speaking, they are crossheads, 'lesser headlines that break up a long slap of text', which are 'no longer much used' in journalism.[2] A few of these 'lesser headlines' read almost like stage directions: 'WE SEE THE CANVASSER AT WORK' or 'EXIT BLOOM'.[3] Some could work as headlines even in the twenty-first century: 'NOTED CHURCHMAN AN OCCASIONAL CONTRIBUTOR', 'MEMORABLE BATTLES RECALLED', 'THE GRANDEUR THAT WAS ROME', 'DEAR DIRTY DUBLIN'.[4] Others are clearly meant as parody, such as the highly formal 'WITH UNFEIGNED REGRET IT IS WE ANNOUNCE THE DISSOLUTION OF A MOST RESPECTED DUBLIN BURGESS'.[5] The alliteration at the beginning of the final headline—'DIMINISHED DIGITS PROVE TOO TITILLATING FOR FRISKY FRUMPS'—would not be out of place in today's tabloids, over a century after *Ulysses* was first published.[6]

This chapter—examining Irish newspaper headlines and the stories behind them—draws on interviews conducted for a research project examining the

---

1   Archie K. Loss, 'Joyce's Use of Collage in "Aeolus"', *Journal of Modern Literature*, 9/2 (1982), pp. 175–182, (p. 175).
2   Terence Killeen, 'From the *"Freeman's General"* to the "dully expressed": James Joyce and journalism', in Kevin Rafter (ed.), *Irish journalism before independence: More a disease than a profession* (Manchester: Manchester University Press, 2011), p. 207.
3   James Joyce, *Ulysses* (Oxford: Oxford University Press, 1993 [1922]), pp. 115, 124.
4   Joyce, *Ulysses*, pp. 117, 122, 126, 139.
5   Joyce, *Ulysses*, p. 114.
6   Joyce, *Ulysses*, p. 143.

working lives of former journalists and editors in Ireland between 1950 and 2020. Based on extensive oral history interviews with various Irish print journalists, it surveys the changing technology behind headline-writing, the role of the sub-editors who traditionally devised headlines, the restrictions imposed by space and early deadlines, and the impact of format (broadsheet or tabloid) on headlines. Though the focus is predominantly on Ireland, the chapter begins with a short history of headlines in an international context.

1   Early Days

Andrew Pettegree points out that as well as being 'not much fun to read', the newspapers which emerged in Europe in the early seventeenth century offered 'very little help' to readers: there was no explanation, comment or commentary; the most important story was seldom placed first; there were no headlines, and no illustrations.[7] Until the end of the eighteenth century, Pettegree notes, many newspapers were essentially produced single-handed, which makes them in some ways marvels of creation but strikingly devoid of 'design innovation'. Again, virtually 'no use [was] made of headlines, or of illustration'.[8]

There were occasional exceptions, including *Nieuwe Tijdinghen* 'New Tidings', a seventeenth-century Antwerp publication produced by Abraham Verhoeven, where the title picked out 'the story most likely to interest readers'. In this Pettegree identifies 'the origins of the headline', but he also explains that the incident thus highlighted 'would not necessarily be the first report in the text, nor ... the story that occupied most space'. An example he gives from 1621 headlined the burial of a general, where the relevant story appeared 'only as a small report on page seven'.[9] One hundred and sixty years later, the *Boston Gazette* greeted the surrender of the British army commander at the siege of Yorktown in 1781 with the words 'Cornwallis TAKEN!' in large type. In 1865, *The New-York Times* (which retained the hyphen in its name until 1896) carried the front-page heading 'Steamer Sunk at Sea'. These examples have, as Robert E. Garst and Theodore M. Bernstein acknowledge, 'the ring of a modern headline', but they were exceptional for their respective times.[10]

---

[7] Andrew Pettegree, *The Invention of News: How the world came to know about itself* (New Haven, Connecticut: Yale University Press, 2014), pp. 8–9.
[8] Pettegree, *The Invention of News*, p. 313.
[9] Pettegree, *The Invention of News*, p. 192.
[10] Robert E. Garst and Theodore M. Bernstein, *Headlines and Deadlines: A Manual for Copy Editors* (4th ed.) (New York: Columbia University Press, 1982), p. 95.

Garst and Bernstein, who consider the headline 'almost exclusively an American development', identify the late nineteenth century as a crucial period in its development. Specifically, they regard the Spanish-American War as a key turning point. From 'earliest times' up to that 1898 conflict, they say, 'the accepted headline' was 'the label' or caption—a generic description of the subject below, like 'foreign affairs' or 'the presidential campaign'. While reluctant to identify a specific 'line of demarcation', they suggest that 'in a general way', the Spanish-American War—a period of intense competition between newspapers—helped usher in 'the headline that said something'. The label or caption was 'imprisoned within the rules of a single column'. By contrast, the sinking of the USS Maine in April 1898 received headlines in the *New York World* and *New York Journal*, owned by Joseph Pulitzer and William Randolph Hearst respectively, which ran 'the full width of the page'.[11]

Yet—without the impetus of a war—similar moves were also afoot in the late nineteenth century on the other side of the Atlantic Ocean. In Britain, the rise of the so-called 'new journalism' was initially associated with W. T. Stead, editor of *The Pall Mall Gazette*, and T. P. O'Connor, editor of *The Star*. The elements of this 'new journalism' included changes to content—condensed reportage, interviews, human-interest stories, personalised reporting, serials, and a focus on scandal and crime news—but also layout. As media historian Mark O'Brien notes, 'the paragraph replaced the lengthy column while headlines and crossheads were introduced to break up the masses of text on each page'.[12] Under Sir Alfred Harmsworth (later Lord Northcliffe), the new *Daily Mail*—launched in 1896—adopted elements of the 'new journalism' to produce a mass-circulation newspaper which cost a halfpenny. Harmsworth, a native of Dublin, advised *Irish Independent* owner William Martin Murphy to transform his publication 'into a modern newspaper' along similar lines, and by September 1914, sales of the *Irish Independent* had reached almost 107,000.[13]

---

11   Garst and Bernstein, *Headlines and Deadlines*, pp. 93–97.
12   Mark O'Brien, 'Journalism in Ireland: the evolution of a profession', in Kevin Rafter (ed.), *Irish journalism before independence: More a disease than a profession* (Manchester: Manchester University Press, 2011), p. 20.
13   Pádraig Yeates, 'The life and career of William Martin Murphy', in Mark O'Brien and Kevin Rafter (eds.), *Independent Newspapers: A History* (Dublin: Four Courts Press, 2012), pp. 13–14.

2   Banner Headlines

Advances in headlines became possible with the invention in 1906 of the Ludlow machine—'relatively inexpensive' and 'easy to operate', it cast 'solid line slugs' from hand-set matrices used primarily for newspaper and advertising headlines.[14] Tony Gray notes that in the thirty-five years during which RM ('Bertie') Smyllie worked for the *Irish Times* (until his death in 1954), the arrival of a Ludlow machine was the only 'major technological breakthrough in the printing industry'.[15] At the beginning of Smyllie's journalistic career, headlines were still set by hand, and it was 'often very difficult for a compositor to find undamaged letters'.[16]

The *Irish Press* was the first Irish daily newspaper to put news stories (and headlines) on its front page. Its first issue, published in 1931, carried a banner headline which ran the full seven columns of its front page, announcing—entirely in capital letters—'Emergency measures to aid flood sufferers'. The story below, about flooding in 'Dublin and district', was confined to the two left-hand columns. But the four cross-heads—'Convent thrown open to succour homeless', 'Trail of destruction in wake of rainstorm', 'Large area still submerged' and 'Relief fund opened'—provided enough detail to give a summary of the story's highlights.[17] The *Irish Independent* of the same day also ran a headline related to the flooding across the full width of a page—strikingly titled '500 persons homeless in Little Bray'—though readers had to go to page nine to find it.[18] The front page of the *Irish Independent* was, like many newspapers in that era, devoted to advertising and displaying a list of births, marriages and deaths. It did not put news (and headlines) on the front page until 1961, a full twenty years after the *Irish Times*, though its sister paper the *Sunday Independent* had done so since its inception in 1905.

As the example of the USS Maine shows, big stories can sometimes lead to innovation in headlines. A fatal fire at a cinema in the town of Drumcollogher in 1926 similarly prompted the *Limerick Leader* to run a banner headline. 'Between 50 & 60 Presumed Dead in Limerick Fire' it announced across the top of page three, as page one was still devoted to advertising.[19] Historian Mainchin Seoighe believes it was the first time a *Leader* headline had run 'the

---

14   Lorraine Ferguson and Douglass Scott, 'A Time Line of American Typography', *Design Quarterly*, 148 (1990), p. 39.
15   Tony Gray, *Mr Smyllie, Sir* (Dublin: Gill and Macmillan, 1991), p. 80.
16   Gray, *Mr Smyllie, Sir*, p. 83.
17   *Irish Press*, 5 September 1931.
18   *Irish Independent*, 5 September 1931.
19   *Limerick Leader*, 6 September 1926.

full width of the page'.[20] Keith Baker, later head of news and current affairs at BBC Northern Ireland, joined the *Belfast Telegraph* in 1969 just as the Northern Ireland Troubles were beginning. 'It was a hell of a time to be working in any form of media', he told Ivor Kenny decades later. 'We were seeing the place change before our eyes and the headline type just kept getting bigger'.[21]

Headlines—used and unused—can offer insight into the societal norms of an era. A report presented in 1964 to John Charles McQuaid, Catholic Archbishop of Dublin, observed that 'a favourite occupation in every newsroom is the writing of imaginary headlines for religious news, headlines which, of course, could never be printed'.[22] Meanwhile, in the real world, the *Limerick Leader* ran a lead story based on the Bishop of Limerick's pastoral letter every year between 1952 and 1960 with the exception of 1956, when a story devoted to a parade organised by the Pioneer Association took pride of place.[23] Some of the headlines that appeared over those stories—'Material Progress But No Corresponding Advance In The Moral Order'; 'Individual Prior To The State And Not Its Mere Instrument'; 'Contrast Between God's Way And The Vain Wisdom Of The World'; 'Inestimable Value Of The Mass'—could have appeared in church newsletters and been written by clergymen.[24]

In the twenty-first century, headlines can be created and placed in seconds. Historically, however, it was a much more laborious process. Seán Rice joined the *Connaught Telegraph* in County Mayo in 1965 and was sometimes given the job of putting headlines on stories which appeared on the front and back pages. In the pre-digital age, this was not always straightforward. 'The letters [used in headlines] were on a little wooden block ... and each letter was done separately. You had to pick them and put them in', Rice explained. Sometimes he would write out a proposed headline for the story only to learn that it was not possible to reproduce it for the paper due to a shortage of letters—being told, for instance: 'We cannot do that headline ... because there are four Es in that headline and we have only three!'.[25] It was not uncommon that a shortage of certain letters required that the headline be rewritten multiple times. By 1980, when Claire Grady worked at the *Mayo News* in her native town of

---

20   Hugh Oram, *The Newspaper Book: A History of Newspapers in Ireland, 1649–1983* (Dublin: MO Books, 1983), p. 162.
21   Ivor Kenny, *Talking to Ourselves: Conversations with Editors of the Irish News Media* (Galway: Kenny's Book Shop and Art Gallery, 1994), p. 84.
22   Dublin Diocesan Archives, XXVI/e/78 (Public Image Committee), 'The Journalist and the Church'.
23   *Limerick Leader*, 13 February 1956.
24   *Limerick Leader*, 16 February 1953; 4 March 1957; 17 February 1958; 9 February 1959.
25   Author interview with Seán Rice, 10 January 2019.

Westport, newspapers were still 'industrial' workplaces, and headlines were a sufficiently pain-staking operation that they would not be altered without very good reason. 'Just because you fancied a different headline on [a story], you wouldn't go [changing it] willy-nilly', she said. At the *Tallaght Echo*, a local newspaper in Dublin where Grady worked from 1983 to 1985, a lay-out specialist physically cut out headlines with a knife and fitted them onto pages.[26]

3   The Sub-editor's Job

When John Brophy joined the *Irish Press* as a copy-boy in 1967, he was asked by news editor Bill Redmond if he wanted to 'chase ambulances' or 'sit writing headlines'. Brophy, a philosophy graduate whose father had contributed to the *American Catholic Press*, had run school magazines, and had some experience writing headlines. After a few months of running errands and making tea, he got a call to sit at the sub-editors' desk.[27] What did that job involve? The poet, biographer, political propagandist and *Irish Press* writer Aodh de Blacam described a sub-editor as 'someone who crossed out other men's words and went home in the dark'.[28] A more technical definition comes from K.M. Shrivastava, who said that sub-editing involves making material 'fit to print', a process which includes 'collecting, arranging, reducing, translating and adapting' it for publication.[29]

Brophy recalls that the tools of the sub-editor's trade in the 1960s included carbon paper, pens, copy paper and rulers—though he was not sure what the latter was used for. The *Irish Press* sub-editors' desk was in the shape of a double L. The group which sat there included 'a lot of older people'. George Crilly had covered the early days of Dáil Éireann (the initially illegal Irish parliament in Dublin during the Anglo-Irish War of 1919–1921). Leo Walsh had been the last editor of the *Evening Mail* before it folded in 1962. Seamus de Faoite, who was also the *Irish Press* film critic, was a well-known short story writer. 'If anybody had a query', Brophy explains, 'you merely had to call it out … call out loud, and you got the collective wisdom of the people there, which was extensive'.[30]

Joe Breen joined the *Irish Times* in 1973 as a nineteen-year-old copy-sorter. He was introduced to chief sub-editor Noel Fee, whom he describes as 'an

---

26   Author interview with Claire Grady, 12 February 2020.
27   Author interview with John Brophy, 31 July 2018.
28   Tim Pat Coogan, *A Memoir* (London: Weidenfeld & Nicolson, 2008), p. 85.
29   K. M. Shrivastava, *News Reporting and Editing* (New Delhi: Sterling Publishers, 1987), p. 7.
30   Author interview with John Brophy, op. cit.

amazing man' and a 'brilliant' and 'exacting' teacher, 'who sub-edited conversation'. Careless terminology was not tolerated—'You didn't get away with anything'. Eighteen months after joining the *Irish Times*, Breen became a junior sub-editor, and was given a short item (of perhaps sixty words) by Fee to examine. Over a two-hour period, he kept 'going back' to Fee 'with a new headline', and the chief sub-editor 'kept throwing it back at him'. Decades on, he can 'still remember' some of the early lessons in newspaper language he learned from Fee, whose pithy corrections included 'fish are gutted, houses are destroyed'.[31]

The sub-editor's job had its own specifications and even its own language, which was often impenetrable to those hearing it for the first time. Pat Brennan worked as a reporter and editor in the current-affairs magazine *Magill* and the short-lived women's magazine *Status*. But sub-editing was completely new to her when, in 1983, she took a shift in the *Irish Press*. She has a particular vivid memory of one task she was set early in her new role:

> I really just talked my way in. And I had *no* idea what I was doing. I'd never worked in hot metal; I'd never worked in subbing ... And John Banville was the chief sub, and I remember somebody I worked with—it probably was [John] Banville—handing me a piece of copy [text] and saying: 'Edit two of twenty with a two-point hood'. And I thought: yeah, two of twenty with a two-point hood![32]

Brennan had no idea of the meaning of the instruction from Banville, who later became a well-known author. Her immediate priority was 'to find somebody ... decent', a helpful colleague, and secure 'the most information' possible from them while 'asking the fewest questions' which might expose her ignorance. Translating the instruction more than thirty years later, she said: 'It was a single-column story, and two of twenty was two decks of twenty-point headline, and the two-point hood [meant] it had to be indented for ... a little line to go around it'.[33] Brennan eventually became a full-time feature writer with the *Irish Press*, where she edited the women's page for a period. Like Frank McDonald, who recalls printers and journalists facing each other 'over the frame of a page as columns were filled with cooling hot metal and headlines formed from a matrix of steel letters', Brennan became used to reading headlines upside down and back to front.[34] To this day, she says: 'If I hit a transpar-

---

31 Author interview with Joe Breen, 2 July 2018.
32 Author interview with Pat Brennan, 28 February 2019.
33 Author interview with Pat Brennan, op. cit.
34 Frank McDonald, *Truly Frank: A Dublin Memoir* (Dublin: Penguin, 2018), p. 77.

ent door that has "Pull" and "Push" this way and that way, I'm not sure which one to read!'.[35]

Traditionally, headlines in most newspapers were written not by journalists, but by sub-editors. This is not a distinction that is widely understood by the general public or, indeed, by all budding journalists. In 1981, Lara Marlowe picked up a copy of the Paris-based *International Herald Tribune* and turned to the back page:

> There was a photograph of Alain Robbe-Grillet, the 'father of the *nouveau roman*', whom I had just interviewed. I didn't know then that sub-editors, not reporters, write headlines. The title on the article was different from the one I had thought up before posting my copy ... *The bastards*, I thought; *they ran an article by somebody else*. Then my eyes fell to the byline, where I read for the first time ever in a daily newspaper: 'by Lara Marlowe'. I yelped for joy, leapt in the air and ran around in circles. My life as a journalist had started.[36]

Sub-editing was traditionally a task performed 'in house', by people based in the newspaper office. But in 2007, Independent News and Media (INM) began outsourcing their 'down-table' sub-editing.[37] Claire Grady, who later became editor of two newspapers published by INM (the *Evening Herald* and *Irish Independent*), explains that it 'took a while' for the external sub-editors (initially based in in Dublin, and later in France) to understand the specifics of 'tone' and 'language' employed by the papers. 'Most newspapers have their own voice', she elaborated. 'There's words they use in a headline; there's words [they] *don't* use in a headline. When you're subbing stuff ... there's important details to leave in'.[38] The changeover, she notes, 'saved the company money' and involved 'very generous redundancies', but it was never 'really fully resolved ... how effective' the outsourcing was. Sub-editing was subsequently brought back under the Independent News and Media umbrella. Brendan Morley, who

---

35   Author interview with Pat Brennan, op. cit.
36   Lara Marlowe, *The Things I've Seen: Nine Lives of a Foreign Correspondent* (Dublin: Liberties Press, 2010), p. 13.
37   'Down-table subbing' is explained as follows in Andy Bull's e-book *The NCTJ Essential Guide To Careers In Journalism* (London: Sage Publications, 2007), p. 267: 'On a sub-editor's desk, there has traditionally been one end where the chief sub and his or her deputy sits. Close to them sit the senior subs. More junior sub and freelances will sit at the far end. Today the rigid seating structure is often not maintained, but the distinction between up and down table subs is. Every young sub's ambition is to move up the table'.
38   Author interview with Claire Grady, op. cit.

worked for both the external company and for INM, thinks the idea behind their integration was 'to effectively eradicate the layer of sub-editors', by getting journalists 'writing to fit shapes on the page'.[39] Grady endorses Morley's view, saying that the introduction of 'write-to-fit' for journalists was designed to 'theoretically' remove the 'need for subbing' of any kind; even headlines would be written by the journalist. But she adds that this plan 'hadn't really come to fruition' by the time she left the company in 2014.[40]

4   Restrictions

According to Dick O'Riordan, the last editor of the *Evening Press* before its closure in 1995, there was traditionally not enough space in some newspapers to allow sub-editors to put accurate headlines above stories. He reflected on the difficulties of getting the necessary detail into headlines in the period when newspaper pages were made up by hand and headlines had to fit in 'three lines of ten letters'.[41] O'Riordan worked for the Irish Press Group for over three decades from 1961 onwards. He indicates that before the advent of computer technology, sub-editors 'had a very tricky time, particularly on single-column stories' in devising suitable headlines for small spaces. This restriction meant, according to O'Riordan, that 'you could go through papers and see … the same sort of headline on about five different stories'; fatal road accidents would, he remembers, invariably be titled 'Man dies in crash'. The extra space available now is, he concludes, 'all for the better'.[42]

Early deadlines can also pose problems for newspapers. During Pat Brennan's time at the *Sunday Tribune*, where she worked as news editor, a lifestyle and features magazine was wrapped around the broadsheet newspaper to give the publication a full-colour front page. This 'wraparound', she indicates, gave it 'a standout presence on the news-stands', and its magazine-style headlines played to the strengths of editor Vincent Browne. But the colour wraparound was printed on Friday. This meant, Brennan explained, 'that you had to make a decision early in the week to do a story that was strong enough to put on the cover' and 'from Thursday night onwards, you were just hoping that something huge didn't break'.[43] Big news events that happened on Friday or Saturday did not end up on the front page of the *Sunday Tribune*. One such example

---

39   Author interview with Brendan Morley, 17 July 2018.
40   Author interview with Claire Grady, op. cit.
41   Author interview with Dick O'Riordan, 13 May 2019.
42   Author interview with Dick O'Riordan, op. cit.
43   Author interview with Pat Brennan, op. cit.

occurred after photographer John Carlos got what Brennan calls 'fantastic pictures' of a Garda (policeman) discharging his firearm in central Dublin after the release of IRA suspect Evelyn Glenholmes.⁴⁴ They were, says, Brennan, 'the best pictures of a breaking story' but because the event happened on a Saturday, the photographs could only appear 'inside' the paper'.⁴⁵ That week's cover featured a picture of actor Clint Eastwood, who was running for mayor of Carmel, California, an election he went on to win.⁴⁶

One workaround the *Sunday Tribune* could occasionally avail of was if a big event scheduled for a Saturday was in some way predictable. Brennan cites the example of the Republic of Ireland football team losing (on a Saturday) to Italy in the 1990 World Cup quarter-final. The following day, the *Sunday Tribune*'s front page was dominated by a photograph of a penalty save by Ireland goalkeeper Packie Bonner from an earlier game against Romania. It also included an inset team photograph and the headline 'They've done us proud' which the *Tribune* editorial team knew would work regardless of the result of the Italy game.⁴⁷ 'You can do big stories well in a magazine format, but there is a price to pay for that', Brennan concludes.⁴⁸

5   Tabloid Influence

Some headlines have become the stuff of journalistic legend, and many of the most memorable have appeared in tabloid newspapers. Examples include the *New York Post*'s 'Headless body in topless bar', depicting a grisly crime from 1983, and *The Sun*'s 1986 effort 'Freddie Starr ate my hamster'.⁴⁹ The *Irish Daily Star* got lots of attention for a headline it produced after the extension of the COVID-19 'lockdown', or stay-at-home order, in April 2020. Noting that those planning to holiday abroad might find themselves turned back at police checkpoints near Dublin Airport, its headline advised readers to 'Go out your back and tan', a play on the Irish rebel song 'Come out, ye Black and Tans'.⁵⁰

---

44   *Sunday Tribune*, 23 March 1986.
45   Author interview with Pat Brennan, op. cit.
46   See also Pat Brennan and Brian Trench, 'The Tribune's turbulent times', in Joe Breen and Mark O'Brien (eds.), *The Sunday Papers: A history of Ireland's weekly press* (Dublin: Four Courts Press, 2018), pp. 161–182.
47   *Sunday Tribune*, 1 July 1990.
48   Author interview with Pat Brennan, op. cit.
49   *New York Post*, 15 April 1983; *The Sun*, 13 March 1986.
50   *Irish Daily Star*, 8 April 2020. The name 'Black and Tans' referred to the British ex-servicemen who were recruited by the British government in 1920–1, during the Irish War of Independence, to reinforce the Royal Irish Constabulary. Their nickname came from the colour of their uniforms, a mix of dark police green and military khaki. See D. M. Leeson,

Some of the *Irish Daily Star*'s front pages during the economic crisis of the early twenty-first century provoked controversy at a time when intense public anger was directed at politicians and bankers. In March 2010, the headline 'They deserve to be shot' appeared on its front page alongside photographs of bankers Seán FitzPatrick and Michael Fingleton above the sub-heading 'These two bastards have cost us 25 billion euro'.[51] FitzPatrick, the former chairman of Anglo Irish Bank, became 'Ireland's most famous hero turned villain' after the economic crash. He resigned in December 2008 after admitting that the bank had for years transferred personal loans it had made to him (worth more than €80 million at their peak) to the balance sheet of Irish Nationwide Building Society in order to keep the loans a secret. That 'warehousing' revelation had also forced the resignation of Fingleton, the 'charismatic' chief executive of Irish Nationwide.[52] The *Irish Daily Star* 'later appealed to its readers not to take its suggestion literally', Dearbhail McDonald writes in her book *Bust*, 'but others joined the fray, pursuing FitzPatrick when he flew to Marbella', where he was dubbed the 'pariah on the playa' by the Irish edition of the *Daily Mirror*.[53]

There was also controversy after the death in 1997 of Brendan O'Donnell, who was serving a life sentence for the 1994 murders of Imelda Riney, her three-year-old son Liam, and a Catholic priest, Father Joe Walsh. 'May he rot in hell', read the headline on the front page of the *Irish Mirror*, with the sub-title: 'Delight at triple murderer's death'.[54] Michael Coady, a columnist with County Tipperary newspaper *The Nationalist*, accused the tabloid newspapers of 'luridly having a field day' over O'Donnell's death.[55] In his autobiography, John Kierans—who later became editor of the *Irish Mirror*—wrote that the headline 'upset some of our politically correct friends in RTÉ' (the State broadcaster). But having witnessed the gunfight which preceded O'Donnell's arrest, Kierans remained unapologetic, saying that those criticising the tabloid coverage 'never saw the madness in Brendan O'Donnell's eyes like I did'.[56]

Gerald Flynn worked as a sub-editor for *The Star* after its entry into the Irish market in 1987 as a joint venture between the Independent and Express

---

The Black and Tans: British Police and Auxiliaries in the Irish War of Independence, 1920–1921 (Oxford: Oxford University Press, 2011), p. ix.

51 *Irish Daily Star*, 31 March 2010.
52 Dearbhail McDonald, *Bust: How the Courts Have Exposed the Rotten Heart of the Irish Economy* (Dublin: Penguin Ireland, 2010), pp. 127–8, 136, 219.
53 McDonald, *Bust*, p. 220.
54 *Irish Mirror*, 25 July 1997.
55 *The Nationalist*, 2 August 1997.
56 John Kierans, *Stop The Press! An Inside Story of the Tabloids in Ireland* (Dublin: Merlin Publishing, 2008), p. 152.

groups. Sold 'at a lower price than indigenous titles' and 'hugely successful in attracting readers', the headlines in its different editions sometimes 'revealed sensitive localisation', O'Brien notes.[57] Using a scalpel, one of Flynn's jobs was to physically cut out British material deemed unsuitable for an Irish audience, such as stories about 'our beloved Queen Mum visiting a flower show'.[58] Such material was replaced by free adverts for the Society of St Vincent de Paul, a Christian voluntary organisation involved in charitable work. On a more serious note, Flynn remembers the differing reactions to IRA activities in *The Star*'s British and Irish editions. When the SAS shot and killed three IRA members in Gibraltar in 1988, the headline in the British edition was 'SAS rub out IRA rats', whereas the Irish edition's headline was 'SAS shoot dead three IRA men'.[59]

Interviewees differed on the merits of tabloid newspapers, though many believe that the rise of tabloids has impacted on various aspects of journalism, including headline-writing. Dick O'Riordan regards the tabloid as one of the great innovations of twentieth-century newspapers, and respects their 'very crisp, very stark' stories. He is an admirer of what he calls 'conservative tabloids' like *El País* (Spain) and *la Repubblica* (Italy). However, he feels that some tabloid newspapers have been reduced to 'look like comic cuts' and produce 'a total excess' of what he calls 'headline extravaganzas' where 'there seems to have to be a pun [in] *every* headline'.[60] Puns were not the exclusive preserve of tabloids, however. John Cunningham, former editor of the Galway-based *Connacht Tribune*, had fond memories of Johnny McMahon, who 'produced headings that nobody else could think of' for the *Galway Observer*. 'A former county manager, CI O'Flynn, was involved in a row with CIE [Córas Iompair Éireann, the State transport company] and Johnny did a heading, "CI Doesn't See Eye to Eye With CIE"', Cunningham told Ivor Kenny.[61]

Gerald Flynn suggested that when he was starting out in journalism, 'there seemed to be a certain rule that you *never* put a question mark in a headline'. Yet, he noted, 'the British papers and the tabloids seemed to do it all the time'.[62] In its first ever tabloid edition in 1988, the *Irish Press* put a question mark at the end of the headline on its lead story about the hijacking of a

---

57   Mark O'Brien, 'The metropolitan press: connections and competition between Britain and Ireland', in Mark Conboy, and Adrian Bingham, *Edinburgh History of the British and Irish Press, Vol. 3: Competition and Disruption, 1900–2017* (Edinburgh: Edinburgh University Press, 2020), p. 637.
58   Author interview with Gerald Flynn, 17 September 2018.
59   *Irish Times*, 3 September 1988.
60   Author interview with Dick O'Riordan, op. cit.
61   Kenny, *Talking to Ourselves*, p. 375.
62   Author interview with Gerald Flynn, op. cit.

Kuwaiti jumbo jet, asking 'Yasser to the rescue?' beside a picture of Palestinian Liberation Organisation chairman Yasser Arafat.[63] Unimpressed, *Irish Press* reporter Chris Dooley commented upon seeing it: 'I thought people bought newspapers for answers, not questions'.[64]

6 Broadsheets and Headlines

The *Irish Press* was not the only Irish newspaper to change formats. In 2004, the *Irish Independent*—which had traditionally been available only as a broadsheet—also began producing a 'compact' or tabloid-sized edition. By December 2012, eight out of ten copies sold were in compact format, and the broadsheet version was phased out.[65] Joe Breen recalls that when the *Irish Times* investigated the possibility of launching a Sunday edition in the late 1990s, mock-ups were designed by Stephen Ryan, a 'brilliant' designer who had worked for the *Sunday Business Post* and *Sunday Tribune*. The proposed publication—which never saw the light of day—was entitled *The Irish Times on Sunday*, and it had 'lots of big blurbs, big lead stories' and 'very large headlines'. Breen subsequently worked on redesigns of the *Irish Times* in 2003 and 2008 and experimented with what the newspaper would look like as a tabloid. Examining the patterns in commuting, and the large number of people travelling in crowded buses and trains, where there was 'just no room' for people to unfurl a broadsheet, Breen felt that changing the size of the newspaper was an idea worth exploring. He had hoped that the decision of the high-brow London *Independent* to adopt the 'compact' format would allow the *Irish Times* to follow suit, but he found that the idea 'caused real angst' within the organisation, and the response from some colleagues was 'verging on ... really hostile'. The idea of a tabloid *Irish Times* was, he says, 'just beyond' what many of them could comprehend, adding: 'It would have been like taking away their underpants!'[66] The proposal was ultimately dropped.

Headlines in broadsheet newspapers are often less memorable than their tabloid counterparts, but sometimes a straightforward factual headline can tell a story in very stark terms. This was the case with one which appeared above

---

63 'Yasser to the rescue?', *Irish Press*, 11 April 1988.
64 Ray Burke, *Press Delete: The Decline and Fall of the Irish Press* (Dublin: Currach Press, 2005), p. 68.
65 'A message from the editor to you, our reader', *Irish Independent*, 21 December 2012. Available online: https://www.independent.ie/irish-news/a-message-from-the-editor-to-you-our-reader-28950248.html (accessed 2 October 2021).
66 Author interview with Joe Breen, op. cit.

a story written by Emily O'Reilly on the front page of the *Sunday Tribune* in 1984. Headlined 'Girl, 15, dies after giving birth in field', it included details of the death of teenager Ann Lovett and her stillborn baby in Granard, County Longford. The story had been assigned to O'Reilly by the *Sunday Tribune* news editor Brian Trench, who had received an anonymous call about the incident from an informant who mentioned the name of the town and of the girl. She found a death notice in the *Irish Independent* of the previous Thursday, which contained details of Ann Lovett's funeral arrangements, and described her death as having taken place 'suddenly'. There was no reference to a baby.[67] O'Reilly confirmed the veracity of the story with the Garda Síochána (police) and the nuns who had taught Ann Lovett at the local convent school. The story, which ran to ten paragraphs and appeared two days after her burial, identified the teenager by name and said she had apparently concealed her pregnancy and had attended school in the local convent until the day of her death'.[68] The decision on whether or not to use her name was debated in the *Sunday Tribune* newsroom. Journalist Maggie O'Kane predicted that no one would remember an anonymous child, but that everyone would remember the name Ann Lovett.[69] O'Reilly travelled to Granard that following week, a journalistic assignment she described as 'difficult':

> The town felt they were being scandalised and they were being blamed, and [were] very hostile to journalists—I could understand that. So we sort of crept around the place trying to get people to talk to us, and obviously didn't get that much information.[70]

A week after the initial story ran, the *Sunday Tribune* devoted two pages to Ann Lovett and related stories, including personal experiences of religious-run mother and baby homes.[71] The following July, Emily O'Reilly wrote of four other deaths of babies 'in unexplained circumstances'.[72] Amid much public disquiet, broadcaster Gay Byrne received numerous letters from women who, sometimes decades earlier, had hidden a pregnancy, given birth in secret, or committed infanticide. On 23 February 1984, a selection of these letters were read out on The Gay Byrne Show, and the result, O'Reilly recalled, was 'powerful'

---

67 *Irish Independent*, 2 February 1984, p. 19.
68 *Sunday Tribune*, 5 February 1984.
69 *Irish Times*, 31 January 2004.
70 Author interview with Emily O'Reilly, 19 September 2018.
71 *Sunday Tribune*, 12 February 1984.
72 *Sunday Tribune*, 1 July 1984.

radio as 'a whole layer of past Ireland came out'.[73] The letters contained stories 'that had been told to no-one; stories that had been bottled up and swallowed down' and constituted, according to *Irish Times* columnist Fintan O'Toole, 'the most devastating piece of broadcasting' in Irish history.[74]

7 Changing Times

The function of the headline has changed in recent decades, a point explored in a 2017 article jointly written by Jeffrey Kuiken, Anne Schuth, Martijn Spitters and Maarten Marx. The sub-title of the conference which inspired this present volume—'Event, Narration and Impact from Past to Present'—is the kind of headline one traditionally expected to see in a physical newspaper, something which aimed 'to give the reader … a clear understanding of what the article' below it was about. The main conference title—'EXCITING NEWS!', with capital letters and an exclamation mark—is more typical of modern headlines, where the intention is to lure the online reader 'into opening [a] link'.[75]

Claire Grady spent much of her career at the *Evening Herald*, which until 1995 was in direct competition with the *Evening Press*. While both papers had their loyal readers, Grady and other reporters were always looking for eye-catching front-page stories, in the knowledge that 'if you got the headline, you're going to pick up sales'. Before the arrival of the internet, she notes, many people first learned 'the news of the day' by picking up an evening newspaper. Grady believes that the public perception of journalists became more negative during her career, and she thinks the increasingly desk-bound nature of the job is partly responsible for this antipathy. Headlines, traditionally a way to connect with readers, became in the twenty-first century a term of abuse among certain members of the public, who would say 'Oh … you're all the same, journalists, looking for tabloid headlines'.[76]

---

73 Author interview with Emily O'Reilly, op. cit.
74 *Irish Times*, 9 September 1989.
75 Jeffrey Kuiken, Anne Schuth, Martijn Spitters and Maarten Marx, 'Effective Headlines of Newspaper Articles in a Digital Environment', *Digital Journalism*, 5/10 (2017), p. 1300. DOI: 10.1080/21670811.2017.1279978. See also Teun A. van Dijk, *News as Discourse* (Hillsdale: Lawrence Erlbaum Associates, 1988) and Yimin Chen, Niall J Conroy and Victoria L Rubin, 'News in an Online World: The Need for an Automatic Crap Detector', in *Proceedings of the 78th ASIS&T Annual Meeting: Information Science with Impact: Research in and for the Community*, 81, American Society for Information Science, (2015), pp. 1–4.
76 Author interview with Claire Grady, op. cit.

Joe Breen, who had a keen interest in the internet from the beginning, recalls the early days of newspapers going online. In many cases, papers were just posting 'white type on green screens', but he remembers a visit to the *San Jose Mercury News* as a game-changer. An editor at the Silicon Valley publication was creating web pages using HTML, with a recognisably hierarchical structure. 'It was still pretty basic', he says. 'But there was a headline. There was a by-line. There was an introduction ... [It was more than] just a mass of text'. The *Irish Times* was, he estimates, among 'the first twenty' newspapers in the world to have a web presence when they went live in September 1994. Breen, who headed up the initial incarnation of *The Irish Times* on the Web, is interested in 'visual change', and reminds us that the way both websites and newspaper look now was not pre-ordained.

> People tend to think of newspapers arriving almost like fully-formed: headlines, pictures, stories, broken down into ... some kind of seamless layout. [But] this is all part of a thing that happens over a hundred years. A lot of it is driven, ironically, by advertising. They're the ones who bring all of the graphical elements into it. And then it's adapted by journalists to tell stories ... I think in visual terms ... web pages still operate on the idea of the interaction between the picture, the text and the headline.[77]

Dick O'Riordan judges that 'if you have a good headline ... a good sub-head ... a good caption, and ... a good quote, you shouldn't really have to *read* the story!'.[78] O'Riordan believes that readers will know from the information in those four elements whether the story is of interest to them. John Kierans insists that a 'golden rule' of tabloid journalism is that any story without 'a decent page one headline' could not go on the front page, reasoning that 'a boring headline meant a boring story'.[79]

Seán Rice worries that changing consumption patterns—where people are increasingly 'getting the news headlines on [their] phones, and they're not bothering' to read 'the *background* to the story'—means the public understanding of events is being reduced.[80] The issue of readers focusing on headlines to the exclusion of everything else informed a decision taken by the Italian edition of *Wired* magazine in June 2021 to remove the titles from all its articles for a twenty-four-hour period. Instead, every article appeared under the same

---

77 Author interview with Joe Breen, op. cit.
78 Author interview with Dick O'Riordan, op. cit.
79 Kierans, *Stop The Press*, p. 266.
80 Author interview with Seán Rice, op. cit.

headline: '*Questo articolo non ha titolo*', or 'This article has no title'. The aim of the initiative was to highlight the importance of reading beyond the headlines, which—according to *Wired Italia* editor-in-chief Federico Ferrazza—'often summarise and oversimplify'. Referring to the experiment as 'a provocation', Ferrazza called it 'a way to invite our readers not to remain only on the surface of a title, but to delve into it in more depth'.[81] While its popularity in print may have waned, the headline has become even more powerful—and problematic—in the digital age.

---

81 'Questo articolo non ha titolo' ['This article has no title'], *Varese News*, 30 June 2021. Available online: https://www.varesenews.it/2021/06/articolo-non-titolo/1356051/ (accessed 2 October 2021). Author's translation from Italian, with assistance from Fabrizio Leonardo Cuccu, Denise Ripamonti and Georgina Carey.

PART 4

Beyond the News

∴

CHAPTER 21

Challenges beyond the News

Events, Neglected Voices and Collective Consciousness

Jane L. Chapman

Lesser-known late nineteenth and early twentieth century illustrative and textual sources in newspaper print from the UK, New Zealand, Germany, and Japan can help build an argument that the study of events needs to be combined with analysis of collective consciousness. This offers the potential to both rearticulate structures and transform culture. Significantly, events are defined as not only spatial, that is confined to a country or countries, or places, or towns, or cities, but also as being emotional, and temporal. For the scholar, they amount to more than purely narrative. Most importantly, events can interact, or overlap, with themes.

1 Neglected Voices

The study of newspapers should extend beyond main events to embrace themes, undercurrents, sub-cultures and neglected voices. For the researcher 'neglected voices' in newspaper archives constitute sources that may be unpredictable and obscure yet still provide a narrative. The written texts and illustrative records associated with neglected voices that this chapter presents have been hitherto under-emphasised by scholars. This may be the voice of individuals, but more frequently of organisations involved with specific issues, topics or themes. What they have to say collectively may be found in special interest newspapers, and either covering events such as riots, or even rumours, and contemporary opinions. The researcher can cast a wider net by consulting a range of sources including songs, posters, graffiti, and drawings. This method of working requires patience and can be slow, for even small acts of contemporary recording contribute to collective consciousness.

A shared perception of belonging that may emerge in the printed word helps to crystallise perceptions of events, especially when contexts are fully appreciated, for these too will help to define an event. Such evidence will offer the potential for scholars to reaffirm the scope and previous significance of expression that uses the printed word, beyond the mere analysis of news events as a headline. The examples that are referred to in this chapter are sometimes neglected in a range of different ways: they may be produced and communicated using a format that scholarship sometimes overlooks, such as cartoons, poster format, or comic strips. They may also articulate the standpoint at the time of writing of a neglected minority, exemplified here by black people or disenfranchised working-class women in Britain. Except for one important nineteenth century example, other examples mainly derive from the aftermath of the First World War—a period when, according to Hannah Arendt, 'Hatred, certainly not lacking in the pre-war world, began to play a central role in public affairs everywhere'.[1] This epoch was punctuated internationally by race riots and social unrest.[2] In the case both of the black diaspora and working women's equality (see below), the window of opportunity for progress presented by the aftermaths of war, before the onset of the Great Depression, was short (although, of course, it reopened later in the twentieth century).

In terms of the involvement of women in politics, for example female participation in Britain's Labour Party, as articulated in their own newspaper, the influence of one major event—the First World War—is clear. During the conflict, 1,200,000 women in Britain worked for the first time in their lives, and 750,000 of them joined trades unions, but the end of war saw a dramatic about-turn in social attitudes, with public campaigns demonising female workers only months after they had previously been hailed as wartime heroines.

Events changed rapidly: mass dismissals of women, with the intention of ceding much needed jobs to returning male veterans during a post-war recession, soon became the order of the day. Yet as women in Britain over the age of 30 were given the vote for the first time, this aftermaths period also witnessed an unprecedented phenomenon in the then pioneering Labour Party. During the interwar period, Labour replaced the Liberal party in Britain as the second party of government—an event in itself—but one that can be more accurately described as a political trend. A surge in female membership introduced new participants into public life, and these voices were given confidence by their

---

1 Hannah Arendt, *The Origins of Totalitarianism* (New York: Schocken Books, 1951), p. 26.
2 For more on these aspects, see inter alia: Jacqueline Jenkinson, *Black 1919: Riots, Racism and Resistance in Imperial Britain* (Liverpool: Liverpool University Press, 2009); Robert Gerwarth & John Horne (eds.), *War in Peace: Paramilitary Violence in Europe After the Great War* (Oxford: Oxford University Press, 2012); Robert Gerwarth & Erez Manela (eds.), *Empires at War, 1911–1923* (Oxford, Oxford University Press, 2015); Hakim Adi, *Pan-Africanism and Communism: The Communist International, Africa and Diaspora, 1919–1939* (Trenton: Africa World Press, 2013); Tina Campt, *Other German: Black Germans and the Politics of Race, Gender and Memory in the Third Reich* (Michigan: University of Michigan Press, 2004); Stephen Castles & Godula Kosack, *Immigrants Workers and Class Structure in Western Europe* (Oxford: Oxford University Press, 2004).

own newspaper, *Labour Woman*.³ This large increase in newspaper readership, according to Tusan, was reflected more generally by communities of women inspired to 'affect social change by creating a new gender based political culture that commandeered public space'.⁴ In fact, she estimates that there were some one hundred and fifty different examples of female run newspapers and periodicals over a longer period. It is important at this stage to clearly differentiate between the significance of the message and the position in society of the writers. The apparent or superficial obscurity of minority status that is often a defining characteristic of neglected voices should not mask the originality of people's expression, often articulated in contexts that are dangerous or hostile to the interests of the protagonists featured. William H. Sewell Junior reflects on this point when he argues that events change structures, and they do this as acts of collective creativity.⁵ In other words, events are more than purely narrative or even purely impact—they have a content value that resonates from an event.

These contentions have earlier intellectual roots, of course, to be found in the cultural theories of New Cultural History, for instance, as well as in the work of E. H. Carr and R. G. Collingwood, and that of Derrida.⁶ New Cultural History reached its peak in the 1980s, and since then it has led to a democratization of history in two ways: as an extension of the range of sources used in research, and at the same time a democratization in the categories of people and subject matter studied. Derrida's theory of traces is particularly important, for it supports the proposition that the researcher can find traces of neglected voices in records and that these can contribute to the making of history. Some sources may be incomplete—an impediment that was effectively recognized

---

3 Jane L. Chapman, 'The Struggles and Economic Hardship of Women Working Class Activists, 1918–1923', in Allison Cavanagh and John Steel (eds.), *Letters to the Editor; Comparative and Historical Perspectives* (Basingstoke: Palgrave Macmillan, 2019), p. 109. *Labour Woman* monthly editions 1918–1923, The Women's Library, London School of Economics and Political Science (hereafter LSE), LSE DS/329.

4 Michelle Tusan, *Women Making News: Gender and Journalism in Modern Britain* (Urbana: University of Illinois Press, 2005), p. 4.

5 William H. Sewell, *Logics of History: Social Theory and Social Transformation* (Chicago: University of Chicago Press, 2005).

6 E.H. Carr, *What is History?* (London: Penguin, 1964); R.G. Collingwood, *The Historical Imagination: An Inaugural Lecture Delivered before the University of Oxford on 28 October 1935* (Oxford: Oxford University Press, 1935); Jacques Derrida, *Margins of Philosophy*, trans. A Bass (Chicago: University of Chicago Press, 1982); Jacques Derrida, *Acts of Literature* (New York: Routledge, 1992); Jacques Derrida, 'The Poetics and Politics of Witnessing', in Thomas Dutoit & Outi Pasanen (eds.), *Sovereignties in Question: the Poetics of Paul Celan* (New York: Fordham University Press, 2005), pp. 65–96.

by Stuart Hall when he tackled the theme that for some groups in society history often appears a minority event (for example, black history), the speaking which previously had no language.[7]

In a 2020 essay in the American Historical Association Magazine *Perspectives*, Robert Darnton discusses collective consciousness as an historical force, but what he does not elaborate on is the fact that sometimes the absorption of events into collective consciousness can be very slow and very difficult.[8] The process is not an easy one. In the relationships between events and collective consciousness, what is the role of events as they become absorbed in a collective worldview?

The study of neglected voices can represent a piece of the collective consciousness in the jigsaw of the past, providing a path along the road to more general acceptance within the scholarly body of knowledge. John Harris, a survivor of the First World War who belonged to the volunteer regiment the 'Sheffield Pals' recognised this fragility when he summed up his experience of the battle of the Somme: 'It was two years in the making, but it was 10 minutes in the destroying, that was our history'.[9]

Similarly, black soldiers had to fight after the First World War to be remembered for their contribution to the conflict.[10] This process emerges in letters of complaint by black people and ethnic minorities. Many of these people had travelled to Britain for wartime employment, in the shipping industry for instance, but were faced with compulsory repatriation at the end of hostilities because returning British troops tended to be considered the top priority for peacetime employment.[11]

---

7   Stuart Hall, *Questions of Cultural Identity* (London: Sage, 1996).
8   Robert Darnton, 'A New View of Event History', *Perspectives on History,* American Historical Association, September (2020), https://www.historians.org/publications-and-directories/perspectives-on-history/october-2020/a-new-view-of-event-history-collective-consciousness-as-a-historical-force (accessed 30.11.2021).
9   http://shefflibraries.blogspot.com/2020/04/the-sheffield-pals.html, (accessed 30.11.2021).
10 For more on black soldiers and the conflict, see Peter Fryer, *Staying Power: The History of Black People in Britain* (London: Pluto Press, 1984); Ray Costello, *Black Tommies: British Soldiers of African Descent in the First World War* (Liverpool: Liverpool University, 2015); David Olusoga, *The World's War: Forgotten Soldiers of Empire* (London: Head of Zeus, 2014); Richard Smith, 'The Impact of the First World War on Pan Africanism', in Debra R. Cohen and Douglas Higbee (eds.), *Options for Teaching Representations of the First World War* (New York: Modern Languages Association, 2015); Richard Smith, 'Colonial Soldiers: Race, Military Service and Masculinity During and Beyond World Wars I and II', in Karen Hagemann, Stefan Dudink and Sonya Rose (eds.), *Oxford Handbook of Gender, War, and the Western World since 1600* (New York: Oxford University Press, 2020).
11 Jane L. Chapman, *African and Afro-Caribbean Repatriation, 1919–1922: Black Voices* (Basingstoke: Palgrave Macmillan, 2018).

Sometimes events throw up messages that appear to have been neglected in the process of incorporation into collective consciousness, such as compulsory repatriation. Unpopular messages are often squeezed out in later descriptions of events, as Halls quote suggests. If it is so problematic to extend a definition of events into something more complex, why bother? The reason is simple: because otherwise elements that contribute to the very complexity of history and add significance to the event become forgotten history.

2   Newspapers as Historical Sources

There are vast arrays of newspaper sources that can aid the mission to focus on neglected voices that can contribute to the reconstruction of a more inclusive history that focuses on the effect of an event. Yet in cases where the newspaper is not specifically produced by a pressure group, social movement, or other organisation as a direct product of their own (neglected) collective consciousness, there is often a lack of direct voices. In this case the researcher is more reliant on third party views about those people who were silent and did not write themselves, for whatever reason—sometimes illiteracy, or lack of time, or lack of access, or lack of social recognition, or lack of enfranchisement in various ways such as the vote or property ownership.

However, when it comes to minority voices influenced by an event, third party views can often be not only disapproving, but outright offensive by today's standards, and that is particularly true of research into compulsory repatriation, where some of the civil service and army records about people who are being repatriated from and after the First World War, are blatantly racist by our modern standards. So, for instance, *The Times* referred to the neighbourhood of the black community in Cardiff as 'Nigger Town'. Government reports also used disapproving forms of expression.[12]

3   Events or Themes?

Very often events tend to interact with themes or phenomena with longer term impact, such as the Treaty of Versailles. The themes can be ongoing and longer term, but evidence, even visual examples, can present conflicting interpretations of the same event. When the Treaty of Versailles specified Allied occupation of Germany (aimed at preventing the First World War happening

---

12   The National Archives, C.O. 323/816; *The Times* 13 June 1919, p. 9.

again, so it was thought) French Senegalese troops who had been so brave in the First World War were posted as part of the allied contribution. Use of black troops and in particular use of African regiments in the post-war occupation of German territories provoked widespread debate internationally about race and national identity, including protests in New York. The event became inseparable from the attitudes and debates that characterized it. This was demonstrated by the retrospective label of the 'Black Shame'.[13] In 1923, *Kladderadatsch*, a satirical German language magazine, published what appears today to be a shocking cartoon as a full front page, depicting an enormous black gorilla with a human face and French 'kepi' military hat. The monster is abducting a pure white, virginal maiden as his victim, secured tightly under his arm. This graphic representation of race makes for quite uncomfortable consumption from a twenty-first century perspective.[14]

In contrast, black people's reactions at the time have been recorded and are well summarized by another illustrative visual, which served as a front page for the *African Telegraph*. This short-lived newspaper (1918–1919) served the black diaspora in Britain and elsewhere.[15] In the image, the black man points to the Treaty of Versailles and the call for peace. According to traditional illustrative style, peace is personified here as a pure white, angelic looking female, but next to her the African male—who is represented as assertive, and intelligent—is saying, 'Where are the Africans? Where are we?' In his hands he is holding ribbons that he would like to have put on the wreath of peace that the female is carrying. The ribbons each list aspects of the specifically black experience, and these are offered up as representing the discrimination that black people faced at the time: intellectual slavery, criminal codes with black prejudice, pass laws, colour bars, and riots against black people. As Darnton says, 'Events come clothed in attitudes, values, frames of mind, recollections of the past, and projections into the future, full of passion, hope, and fear'.[16]

Certainly, the Great War was one such event. Racial issues with gender, class, and sexual overtones, as a relatively new theme for contemporary media comment, contributed to a largely unacknowledged (to date) revival in the fortunes of newspapers and periodicals in the aftermaths of the Great War.[17]

---

13 Dick van Galen Last with Ralf Futselaar, *Black Shame: African Soldiers in Europe, 1914–1922*, trans. Marjolijn de Jager (London: Bloomsbury, 2015).
14 *Kladderadatsch* https://www.ub.uniheidelberg.de/Englisch/helios/digi/kladderadatsch.html (accessed 30.11.2021).
15 Jane L. Chapman, *Early Black Media, 1918–1924: Print Pioneers in Britain* (Basingstoke: Palgrave Macmillan, 2018), pp. 48–52.
16 Darnton, 'A New View of Event History', p. 9.
17 Ibid., p. 42.

The impact of this event in terms of newspaper history deserves greater scholarly attention. However, there is a caveat. Irrespective of the period or example from the past, there is obviously baggage to consider when analysing events, and it is not just created by the event by itself. There is a tension between events and ongoing issues, even in a cartoon. That tension is evidenced by, and is evidenced in, newspapers as an aspect of discursive writing. For media and literary researchers, this tension is manna: it needs to be found, analysed, highlighted, and even celebrated.

What, precisely, is the tension that is embedded in events? When it comes to the role of the press we often point to a tension between various newspapers—for instance, between tabloid newspapers in the modern age and a broadsheet, or between left-wing and right-wing newspapers. This tends to be irrespective of country. In addition, tension can be located within the newspaper itself, and it may well be a tension between events and the ongoing issue.

A notable newspaper event from 1888 illustrates the nature of tension. During that year, *The Telegraph* in Britain published 27,000 readers' letters that were prompted by one article only.[18] This shows the power of the press for discussion and discourse, and the power of news. Feminist Mona Caird wrote in the *Westminster Review* and the *Fortnightly Review* that marriage was a vexatious failure. Her 1888 essay 'Marriage' analysed the history of the abuse of women under the system of marriage and provoked a series in *The Daily Telegraph* called Is Marriage a Failure?[19] As stated, this elicited 27,000 readers' letters in response. Clearly, this was highly topical as a theme—not an event—and Caird's words resonated widely: 'To place the sexes in the relationship of possessor and possessed, patron and dependent, is almost equivalent to saying in so many words, to the male half of humanity: "Here is your legitimate prey, pursue it"'.[20] Maybe *the perception* of events is as important as the events themselves, particularly if it excites so much interest. It is possible to argue that the topic of news is in fact an ongoing theme as much as an event to analyse.

4   Special Interest Newspapers and Periodicals

The potential of specialist newspapers as a source for media historians is sometimes overlooked, especially for the study of both impact and narrative of

---

18   https://www.bl.uk/collection-items/the-morality-of-marriage (accessed 30.11.2021).
19   Alice Mona Caird, *The morality of marriage and other essays on the status and destiny of women* (London: George Redway, 1897), p. 215.
20   Ibid.

events. As a trench newspaper The *Chronicles of the New Zealand Expeditionary Force*, from the First World War is a good example.[21] Soldiers more generally felt that the conflict represented an event in the experiences of military recruits that should be recorded in and through their own newspaper, if only to entertain their fellow readers.[22] For most volunteers, this was their first experience of the armed forces. In fact, a circulation of around 25,000 suggests interested readership to be much broader, extending to other Anzacs and to people in Britain.[23]

Events within the daily life of a soldier during the war provided regular opportunities to comment on initial reactions to men's military experience. Before they were sent to the front, many volunteers were sent to undergo training on Salisbury Plain in England. A route march whilst carrying heavy kit was frequently organized as an initial test of fitness—which in most cases needed to be improved upon prior to exposure to the harsh realities of the fronts. A multi-panelled illustrative narrative composed by one New Zealander recruit tells the story, and in the process provides an insight into collective consciousness. In this one-off mini comic strip, the everyday hero sets off with gusto for a route march.[24] After ten miles, he is beginning to flag, and his rucksack is beginning to look more prominent on his back. By the time that he has only two and a half miles left of the ordeal remaining, his rucksack has become enormous, his boots have become completely oversized, and he is sweating streams. When he finally returns to Sling camp as the end destination, his rucksack appears to be totally squashing him, and so do his monstrous boots. This is a salutary story about how to carry military kit, and it raises the question—how should the event be defined? Was it the Great War itself, or the route march on Salisbury Plain? Perhaps more importantly does the event matter, or is it the articulation of what New Cultural History calls 'mentalities', in this case the feelings amongst the lower ranks. The short answer, of course, is that this will depend on the scholar's research question.

---

21 https://nla.gov.au/nla.obj-6839072 (accessed 30.11.2021).
22 For more on textual approaches to trench publications, see J.G. Fuller, *Troop Morale and Popular Culture in the British and Dominion Armies 1914–1918* (Oxford: Oxford University Press, 1990).; see also Jane Chapman and Daniel Ellin, 'Multi-Panel Comic Narratives as Citizen's Journalism', *Australian Journal of Communication*, 39/3 (2012), pp. 1–22.
23 For more on how the men's cartoons were featured as self-deprecating humour, see Jane Chapman & Daniel Ellin, 'Dominion cartoon satire as trench culture narratives: complaints, endurance and stoicism', *The Round Table: The Commonwealth Journal of International Affairs*, 103/2 (2014), pp. 175–192.
24 On comic strips as a source, see Jane L. Chapman, Anna Hoyles, Andrew Kerr & Adam Sherif, *Comics and the World Wars. A Cultural Record* (Basingstoke: Palgrave Macmillan, 2015).

5 Collective Consciousness

The humour of this illustrative source is cynical but harmlessly affectionate, summed up by a final caption 'in loving memory of the march to Sling in 1917'. It is worth noting that this group expression, or the collective consciousness that is demonstrated here is one that was formulated almost instantly at the time, and can be said to vary from many traditional memoirs of the conflict that were composed afterwards, usually from diary records, rather than during, the event itself.[25]

Of course, narrative of an event can be anybody's story, as we have already seen. It might represent a movement rather than an individual's perspective. Equally, collective consciousness may well emerge in words, not visual evidence, that is from the text as opposed to visual entries in newspaper archives. *Labour Woman* in Britain was a subscription newspaper for members of a movement, but it should be noted, at a time when working class people had much less representation.[26]

Movements and their newspapers can produce Darnton's consciousness, but it is a collective consciousness of their perception of life as this relates to their organisation's purpose and policies. Referring to the contents page in 1923, for these women subscribers to the Labour Party's newspaper for women, the articles are very thematic: poverty, housing, labour saving devices, working and factory conditions, education (at all levels), child rearing, prohibition, international affairs, and party organizational matters.[27] *Labour Woman* shows gendered awareness emerging from a whole range of topics, all of them linking politics to economic and class concerns. Chancellor Phillip Snowden's budget event in 1924, when he claimed that he had introduced a 'housewife's budget' that reduced food duties by £30 million, including tariffs on essentials such as tea and sugar, gave the newspaper an opportunity to engage with the details of gendered, working class consumerism, by promoting what the newspaper called 'the free breakfast table'.[28] This is a far cry from any obvious definition

---

25 Chapman and Ellin, 'Dominion cartoon satire as trench culture', pp. 175–192.
26 The newspaper continued until 1971. For more on the history of this newspaper, see Jane L. Chapman, 'The Struggles and Economic Hardship of Women Working Class Activists, 1918–1923', p. 110.
27 Chapman, 'The Struggles and Economic Hardship of Women Working Class Activists', pp. 120–121.
28 David Thackeray, 'From Prudent Housewife to Empire Shopper: Party Appeals to the Female Voter, 1918–1928', in Julie V. Gottlieb & Richard Toye (eds.), *The Aftermath of Suffrage. Women, Gender, and Politics in Britain, 1918–1945* (London: Palgrave Macmillan, 2013) p. 45.

of an event, unless it is traced back to the Chancellor's budget. In fact, much of the voice that emerges from *Labour women* was an economic one. The collective consciousness emerges mainly from the deliberate and energetic effort of the newspaper's editor—Dr Marion Phillips—to present a women's angle to mainstream party policies.[29] *Labour Woman* helped create a collective confidence, at a time when working women were under attack at the workplace, and under economic pressure at home.[30]

Thus, for instance, the newspaper carried a significant amount of discussion about labour-saving devices. This, of course, was in the days when working class women had to do washing by hand, on top of a twelve-hour day in the factory. Labour saving devices, which of course they could not afford at the time, were hugely attractive—the women's acquisitional dream. Other themes include government neglect of the unemployed, and the consequential changes of policies and politics that they hoped for. Motherhood constituted a high-profile collective consciousness, exemplified by a frontpage feature, 'What children did in the election'.[31]

Although these were all themes, not clearly connected to an event, from the standpoint of organized labour, nevertheless, and from the newspaper's perspective this claim needs to be qualified—in that the newspaper also focused on events that highlighted regular editorial themes. Thus, there were also major events, such as mass strikes. Miners' strikes in Britain have always been significant events. The obvious angle for *Labour Woman* was 'What the miners' strike meant to women'. This was in 1920. Here there was a direct connection between an event and news as it affected the newspapers readership, but the relationship between event and theme is clear. Readers own debates

---

29   Jane L. Chapman, 'The Struggles and Economic Hardship of Women Working Class Activists', p. 120.
30   Ibid., p. 124.
31   Ibid. For more on the political and social history of this period from a women's perspective, see inter alia, Pat Thane, 'The Women of the British Labour Party and Feminism, 1906–45', in Harold L. Smith (ed.), *British Feminism in the Twentieth Century* (Aldershot: Edward Elgar, 1990), pp. 47–65; Marion Phillips & Grace Tavener, *Women's Work in the Labour Party; Notes for Speakers' and Workers' Classes* (London: The Labour Party, 1923); Martin Pugh, *Women and the Women's Movement in Britain Since 1914* (Basingstoke: Palgrave Macmillan, 1992); Susan Kingsley Kent, *Making Peace: The Reconstruction of Gender in Interwar Britain* (Princeton: Princeton University Press, 1993); Pamela M. Graves, *Labour Women: Women in British Working-Class Politics 1918–1939* (Cambridge: Cambridge University Press, 1994); Jane L. Chapman, *Gender, Citizenship and Newspapers: Historical and Transnational Perspectives* (Basingstoke: Palgrave Macmillan, 2013); Kathleen Canning & Sonya O. Rose, 'Gender, Citizenship and Subjectivity: Some Historical and Theoretical Considerations', *Gender and History*, 13/3 (2001), pp. 427–443.

provided a certain comfort from the hostile anti-trade union environment, exemplified by articles such as 'What the Miners' Strike Means to Women' for instance.[32]

Therefore, it is not possible to examine the relationship between events and news without considering the motivation for publishing such special interest newspapers. The theoretical roots for this contention, of course, are best illustrated by Benedict Anderson in his concept of imagined communities—much quoted, although devised originally in his study on nineteenth century nationalism.[33] What scholarship has drawn upon the most from Anderson's now seminal idea is the suggestion that the newspaper brings together diverse people who may be dispersed geographically but nevertheless will be reading the same newspaper. The act of reading of a newspaper is a collective one, but geographically separated, as an imagined community—in the way that Hegel had drawn a comparison with daily prayers. 'Reading the morning newspaper is the realist's morning prayer. One orients one's attitude towards the world either by God or by what the world is. The former gives as much security as the latter, in that one knows how one stands'. In essence (and although the newspaper was a weekly, not a daily), *Labour Woman*'s imagined community was a dystopian one in which the dream was to build a better future for all by escaping the constraints of pecuniary struggle. This very simple yet basic motivation for reader security, in this case, provides a humbling reminder that ordinary female voices had to prioritise everyday efforts to survive.[34]

6 Japan in the Aftermaths of World Conflict

Finally, and to state the obvious, a fruitful analysis of the role of events can be found in the study of the Second World War. Illustrative examples are sometimes neglected, and so are the momentous events of Hiroshima and Nagasaki, the atomic bombing of which brought an end to the Second World War in the Far East.

Keiji Nakazawa was six years old when the atomic bomb fell. He lost his father, his brother, and his sister. His mother, who was heavily pregnant the day the bomb fell, gave birth the same day. His mother, her new-born baby and

---

32 November 1920, LSE DS/329.
33 Benedict Anderson, *Imagined Communities: Reflections on the origins and Spread of Nationalism*, (London & New York: Verso, 1991); Georg Wilhelm Friedrich Hegel, *Miscellaneous Writings*, transl. Jon Bartley Stewart (Northwestern University Press, 2001), p. 247.
34 Jane L. Chapman, 'The Struggles and Economic Hardship of Women Working Class Activists', p. 125.

Keiji were forced to roam the streets. They were treated as outcasts, 'hibakusha' survivors who were disabled, physically mutilated, and burned by the atomic fallout. In fact, they were disowned by fellow compatriots. The neglected voice of the estimated 80,000 hibakusha meant that their collective consciousness was a quiet one, a hidden one, as victims from the bomb were ignored or discriminated against during the decade after the war.[35]

Nakazawa's illustrative account *Barefoot Gen* and *I Saw It* comprised 10 volumes of comic strip reality-based childhood memoirs, a story of survival that was banned in Japanese schools until recently. As a source it provides a hugely detailed memoir of childhood (itself a neglected perspective in historical record) that certainly represents a collective consciousness, even if society's attitudes towards the event meant that the neglected voices, like that of the Holocaust, articulated experiences many people preferred to forget.

How do we get impact? One way of achieving this is when events are combined with analysis of collective consciousness, according to Darnton's theory, and by building on the theory of Sewell who says that culture changes structures. This is what makes events so theoretically important.

In turn, collective consciousness can be evidenced by sources that may be unpredictable. They can be obscure, or composed by minorities as neglected voices, but they still provide a narrative and as such can be construed as 'news' in the wider sense of the word. Such examples can be found in newspaper coverage of riots, for instance, or as rumours, or in less predictable material such as cartoons, comic strips, songs, posters, or graffiti drawings. These all have their own sort of news, or thematic narrative that can contribute to a collective consciousness. This is necessary if we, as scholars, are to analyse the event in context.

The historical record of events can be fragile when it is open to interpretation, but it can still contribute towards changing structures as an impact that amounts to a collective act of creativity. By investigating newspaper examples in a way that extends beyond the straightforward connection to events and narrative, we can end up with impact as added value.

Small acts of contemporary recording—for example one article on a controversial topic such as divorce—can contribute to collective consciousness. First World War soldier cartoons are a further example of a collective consciousness that has maybe been overlooked. What unites such sources is collective

---

[35] Asai Motofumi & Richard H. Minear (trans.), '*Barefoot Gen,* Japan and I: The Hiroshima Legacy: An interview with Nazawawa Keiji', *International Journal of Comic Art*, 10/2 (2008), pp. 308–327; Nazawawa Keiji *Barefoot Gen: a Cartoon Story of Hiroshima, Vol. 1* (Last Gasp of San Francisco) (2004).

consciousness. This manifests a shared perception of belonging, according to Benedict Anderson. Imagined communities of newspaper readers help to crystallize perceptions of events. Studying newspapers as a source reminds us that a shared perception of events may or may not have been achieved at the time, through a specific imagined community of readers.

There is an equation that emerges: impact equals collective consciousness produced by events plus the narrative created by neglected voices in society. Events + narrative + neglected voices = collective consciousness. Historians can reinterpret the impact that emerged from the time, and by identifying it can recreate aspects of it. These considerations apply to different periods of history, in different contexts, and/or different countries.

If basic structures are created or enhanced by the above, the argument tends to move in the direction of Foucault's notion of the archaeology of knowledge.[36] We create a constructed view, a constructed perception of events, of narratives. The more detailed and specific the analysis becomes, the closer the scholar monitors, and the closer the criticism or underlying ideology also becomes. Gradually that creation becomes more and more apparent. From this dialectic process, eventually another story emerges that needs to be told.

Very often this other (new) story is far more important than the first that we appear to be seeing. When the scholar tries to address these questions, there is a sighting in a way, of a much more creative story, or a story that inspires or prompts creativity. This has happened through an analysis of past events in newspapers (news) in a way that the former construction could not. Yet the question remains—what is the contribution of the event to this process? Indeed, what is the event that may have acted as a catalyst for changing structures? The fact that these questions arise is a testimony to the power of events to contribute to collective consciousness—which is the real impact factor, and the real added value for the writing of neglected voices from the past. In turn, this is a tribute to the significance of newspaper study as a means of understanding the past.

---

36 Michel Foucault, *The Archaeology of Knowledge*, A. M. Sheridan Smith (trans.) (London and New York: Routledge, 2002), originally published in 1969.

Index

Act of Union (1801)   221, 243
Act on Extraordinary Measures (1938)   286
Adriatic Sea   23, 50
Africa   44
African Telegraph   420
Ahab (king of Israel)   154
Ahmed, Muhammad   270
Alba Iulia   34
Albert of Flanders, archduke   18, 24
Albornoz y Tapies, Pedro   108
Alfred the Great (king)   274
Algiers   51
Allen, Gladys   366
Althorpe   136
American Catholic Press   401
American Historical Association   418
Amsterdam   30, 46, 162, 163, 166, 167, 170, 223, 363
Anderson, Benedict   244, 425, 427
Angelo, Tonno d'   82
Anglo-American   245
Anglo-Irish   6, 245, 401
Anglo Irish Bank   406
Anglo-Saxon   287, 293–294
Anglo-Saxon Review   280
Anne Royal (ship)   47
Anschluss   282, 283, 286–289, 290
Antoine, Simeon   167
Antoinette, Marie   9, 222
Antwerp   25, 27, 28, 46, 48, 51, 354, 397
Anzacs   422
appendicitis   389
Aquino, Bartolomeo d'   82
Arafat, Yasser   408
Arblaster, Paul   51
Arendt, Hannah   283, 416
Argoll, Samuel   54
Argyll Fencibles   221
Aristotle   67
armada (various)   24, 30, 50, 152
Armistice Day   388
Armour, G. D.   359, 378
Arne, Thomas   217
Arpaia   132
Arthur (legendary king)   274

Ashmead, Captain   250
Asquith, H. H.   369
Assarino, Luca   84
Association for the Prevention of Intemperance   394
Athenian Gazette   128
Atripalda   70
Australia   358, 363, 382
Austria   16, 21, 28, 32, 72, 281, 282, 283, 286–289, 290
Avaux de Pomponne, count of   163
Avellino   63, 70

Bacchi, Pietro (Petrus Bacchus)   92, 94
Baden-Powell, Robert (colonel)   275, 277–279
Bagg, James   42
Baker, Keith   400
Balfour, Arthur   368
ballads   128, 129, 322
Ball, Charles   267
Ballina Herald   394–395
Ballylahan   394
Ballypatrick   216
Baltimore   350, 388
Bambocccianti, school of   97
Banville, John   402
Barbancon, duke of   176
Barbier, Fréderic   2
Barcelona   104, 106
Barnsley   379
Barnstaple   136
Barr (character)   315
barracks   219, 320
Barrett, Paul   381
Barrile, Antonio   82
Bartoli, Cosimo   27
Basile, Felice   80, 82
Bassa, Ibrahim   15
Basta, Giorgio   16
Bath   379
Battle of White Mountain (1620)   284
Baumann, Zygmunt   3
Baumer, Lewis   359, 376, 378
Bayle, Pierre   173

BBC   317, 323, 400
Beavan, Brad   278
Beck, Ulrich   3
Beijing (Peking)   195
Belcher, George   359, 376
Belfast   214, 314, 386, 389
Belfast Telegraph   317, 400
Belgium   287, 288, 362, 369
Belgrade   15
Bellanger, Claude   173
Belloc, Hilaire   364
Bembo, Pietro   38
Benavides Dávila y Corella, Francisco (Viceroy, conde de Santiesteban)   64
Benedict XIII (pope)   101, 106, 189
Beneš, Edvard   292
Benevento   6, 63, 66, 68, 69, 70, 100, 101
Bengal   189, 195
Beraldi, Claudio   78
Bergen op Zoom   26
Bernardis, Paolo de   103
Bernstein, Theodore M.   397, 398
Beuttler, Edward   358, 359
Bible
    Book of Lamentations   146, 156
        Old Testament   67
        Psalms   91, 129, 155, 160, 161
Billericay   373
Birmingham Daily Post   273, 279
Blacam, Aodh de   401
Blackheath   366
Blanfort   197
Blasamo, Bartolomeo   82
Bloom, Leopold (character)   396
Boccaccio, Giovanni   88
Boers   270, 275, 276, 280
Bohemia   28, 286
Bohm, Steffen   381
Bolger, Mary   386
Bombay (Mumbai)   265
Bond, James (character)   303, 314
Bonis, Novello de (printer)   103, 115, 117
Bonner, Packie   405
booksellers   165, 167, 175, 181, 191, 231, 235
Booy, David   153, 154
Bordeaux   170, 214
Bossuet, Jacques-Bénigne   167
Boston   249, 252, 254, 351
Boston Gazette   397

Boston Pilot   344
Boston Spy   252
Boylan, Bonra   204
Brahe, Tycho   40
Braudel, Fernand   22
Brazil   23, 44, 50
Breda   44, 45, 46
Breda, siege of   42
Breen, Joe   401, 402, 408, 411
Brennan, Pat   402
Brescia   67, 237
Bretislav I   293
Brett, Reginald   270, 271
Brewer, John   249
Briggs, Asa   2
Bright, John   266
Bristol   44
Britain   6, 7, 87, 189, 190, 191, 192, 206, 217, 221, 242–256, 261–280, 281–297, 303, 308, 312, 313, 314, 317, 353–380, 382, 397, 398, 407, 416, 418, 420, 421, 422, 423, 424
Brock, Henry M.   359
Brockley Park, Co. Laois   330
Brook, Ricardo   359
Broomhall, Susan   135
Brophy, John   401
Browne, Vincent   404
Brown, Jessie   267
Brown, Mathew   202
Brown, Mr   294
Bruges   18, 19
Bruno, Giordano   40
Brussels   25, 28, 50, 51, 176
Bryan, Robert   194
Buchan, John   364
Bullock   200
Buragna, Giovan Battista   96
Burc, Tomas a   196
Burc, Uilliam a   196
Burke, Peter   2, 38
Butler, Samuel   4
Buttimer, Neil   198
Buzzacarino, Giovanni Battista   82
Byrne, Gay   409
Byron, Ellen   395

Cadiz   5, 41–56
Caird, Mona   421

Cairo 270
Calais 42, 354
Calaresu, Melissa 226
Cambridge University 148
Cameron, Euan 3
Campanella, Tommaso 96
Campbell, Colin 268
Camus, Jean-Pierre 229
Canale, Giovanni 103
Candia (Crete) 130
Canissa (Nagykanizsa) 24, 31, 32
Čapek, Karel 284, 285, 295
Capuchins 163, 164
Caravaggio, Michelangelo Merisi da 97
Cardiff 358, 360, 367, 419
Cardiff, Mr 214
Cari 197
Carlos, John (photographer) 405
Carlow 220
Carmel, California 405
Carolus, Johann 162
Carr, E. H. 417
Carrick-on-Suir 6, 9, 208, 212–223
Carter, Cornelius 190, 192
Cartoons 7, 8, 277, 325, 353–380, 416, 422, 426
Castle, Frank (character) 314
Castle Hedingham 366
Castlerea 329
Catholic Church 7, 66, 73
Catholicism 5, 7, 20, 26, 46, 51, 66, 67, 101, 143, 146, 147, 149, 151, 162, 154, 155, 161, 167, 171, 172, 173, 191, 198, 199, 238, 284, 330, 333, 343, 400, 401, 406
Cavallo, Camillo (printer) 101, 117
Cavenoch, Brion 202
Cawnpore (Kanpur) 265, 266, 269, 273
Cecere, Domenico 63
Cecil, Edward (1st Viscount Wimbledon) 53–55
Ceinglen, Gabriel de 166, 169
Cennamo, president 82
Censorship of Publication Act (1929) 394
Ceretto 132
Cerquozzi, Michelangelo 97
Cerreto Sannita 63, 101
Chamberlain, John 45
Chamberlain, Neville 281, 287, 288, 289, 290, 292

Charles I 43, 144, 145, 149, 154, 155, 161
Charleville 196
Chaucelier, Mr 172
Chaucer, Geoffrey 203
Chester 201
Chesterton, G. K. 364
Chiari, Pietro 237
Chicago 345
Chomsky, Noam 8
Churchill, Winston 270, 276
Chytilová, Věra 305, 306
Ciamberlano, Luca 110
Cicero, Marcus Tullius 22
Cirillo, Antonio 103
Civitella Licinio 63
Clementis, Vlado 290
Clement VII 21
Clifden, Thomas (viscount) 382
Clonmel 214, 216
Clonmore 213
Coady, Michael 406
Colbert, Jean-Baptiste 167
Colenso 277
Colerus, Johannes 92
Collingwood, R. G. 417
Cologne 25, 27, 28, 31, 34, 46, 368
comics 310, 314–315, 422, 426
Como, David 87
Concina, Cosimo 27
Connacht 204
Connacht Tribune 407
Connaught Telegraph 400
Connecticut 250, 336
Connecticut Courant 255
Constantinople 15, 21, 197
Conway, Edward 42, 53
Coole Park (Co. Galway) 333
Coote, Chidley 149, 158
Cope, Joseph 149, 153
Córdoba 50, 108, 118, 119
Cork (city and county) 199, 204, 215, 216, 217, 219, 220, 250, 352, 388
Cornwall 42
Cornwallis, Charles 397
Cortona, Pietro da 108, 110
Coul., Den. 202
Courtney, W. L. 364
Cove 250
Coventry 354

Cranford, James   147, 149, 150
Cremona   35, 117
Crete. *See* Candia
Crilly, George   401
Crimea   263
Crimean War   262, 267
Cromwell, Oliver   93, 274
Crossley, Frederick W.   382
Cúilín   196
Cunningham, John   407
curia   65, 69, 70, 72, 73
Cybo, Alerano (cardinal)   59, 64, 66, 68, 69, 71, 72
Czechoslovakia   7, 281–296, 297–309

Dáil Éireann   311, 392, 401
Daily Graphic   355, 360
Daily Herald   355, 359
Daily Mail   263, 276, 359, 362, 383, 398
Daily Mirror   355, 359, 406
Daily News   269, 272
Daladier, Édouard   381
Dalkey Island   200
Dalton, Nancy   209, 211
Danube   288, 293
Danzig   191, 288
Darnton, Robert   8, 225, 418, 420
Davis, Lennard J.   235
Dawk's Newsletter   123
Declaration of Independence (1776)   243
Defoe, Daniel   236
Delumeau, Jean   3
Deptford   366
Derrida, Jacques   8, 417
Derry Journal   385
Derry Now   317
De Telegraaf   356, 363, 365
De Vivo, Filippo   226
Deza, cardinal   20
Diderot, Denis   240
Disraeli, Benjamin   266
Dodd, Mr Justice   387
Donnelly, Johnny (character)   312–313
Dooley, Brendan   56
Dooley, Chris   408
Doria, prince   30
Dover, castle   42
Dowd, J. H.   359

Doyle, Francis   208–209
Doyle, James   202
Drda, Jan   291
Dresden   354
Dublin   6, 136, 144, 149, 159, 187–206, 214, 215, 216, 217, 220, 221, 247, 248, 249, 250, 251, 252, 254, 335, 386, 393, 394, 396, 398, 399, 400, 401, 403, 405
  King's Inns Library   188
  National Library of Ireland   188, 330, 350
  Royal Irish Academy   188
  St Patrick's Cathedral   187
  Trinity College Library   188
Dublin Bay   200
Dublin Daily Post and General Advertiser   192
Dublin Evening Post   254
Dublin Gazette   194
Dublin Impartial News Letter   193
Dublin Journal   251
Dublin Postboy   193
Dubreuil, Jean Tronchin   167, 168, 169, 174, 175, 176, 180, 181
Ducháček, Ivo   285
Duggan, Hugh (character)   315
Duggan, Mathew   202
Duggan, Patrick (piper)   202
Dunkettle   388
Dunkirk   18, 354
Dunston, Patrick   149
Dunton, John   123, 128, 191
Dupont, Mr   294
Durazzo, Marcello (Cardinal)   64, 72
Düsseldorf   368
Dyson, Will   358–363

Eastwood, Clint   405
Edge, Selwyn   384
Eduard, Philipp   30
Egan, William G.   350
Eliot, T. S.   7
El País   407
Eltham   366
England   5, 23, 26, 28, 43, 51, 120–139, 146, 149, 151, 152, 154–158, 176, 177, 195, 197, 198, 200, 201, 220, 221, 228, 250, 269, 275, 280, 287, 289, 292, 356, 364, 369, 422
engraving   76, 91, 92, 108, 110, 112, 228

Ennis, Garth   314
Essex   195, 366, 369, 373
Euronews Project (University College Cork)   5
Evelyn, John   41, 135, 136, 137
Evening Herald   394, 403, 410
Evening Mail   401
Evening News   355, 359, 373
Evening Telegram   345, 346

Fabian, Robert   203
Fabri, Palamède (sieur de Valavez)   50
Falkland, Lord   53
Fanning, Michael   390
Faoite, Seamus de   401
Farrs, Mr   395
Faulkner, George   197
Fawkes, Guy   265
Fearon, Percy Hutton   359
Fee, Noel   401
Fegan, Gerry (character)   313
Ferrara   126, 132
Ferrazza, Federico   412
Fielding, Henry   236, 237
Filomarino, Ascalnio (cardinal)   98
Fingleton, Michael   406
First World War   7, 284, 353–356, 358, 373, 383, 416, 418, 419, 420, 422, 426
Fitzgerald, Eoin   199
FitzPatrick, Séan   406
Flanders   16, 18, 24, 28, 36, 37, 42, 47, 137
Fleet Street (London)   279, 363
Flers-Courcelette   374
Florence   15, 16, 27, 28, 35, 40, 104, 114–116
Flying Post   131, 192, 196
Flynn, Gerald   406, 407
folklore   1, 225, 342, 347
Fontainebleau, Edict of   172, 173
football   298, 308, 309, 323, 343, 405
Fortnightly Review   364, 421
Foucault, Michel   427
Foxe, John   144–147, 150–152, 158, 160–161
Foxrock   386
Frederick v   42
Free State (Ireland)   390
Free Trade Crisis (1779)   243
French, John   202
French Revolution   222, 223

Frezza, Giovanni Girolamo   111
Fugger, Octavian Secundus   30
Fujian   44

Gaelic Athletic Association (GAA)   334
Gaelic League   7, 9, 329, 330, 333, 334, 335, 338, 339, 345, 347, 351
Galanti, Giuseppe Maria (jurist)   240
Galway   350, 407
Galway Observer   407
Galway, University of   9, 330, 350
Ganges   265
Garda Síochána (Irish police)   405, 409
Garst, Robert E.   397–398
Garzadori, Coriolano   31
Gayot de Pitaval, François   227
Gazette d'Amsterdam   162, 163, 165–169, 173–178, 181
Gazette de Leyde   162, 174
Gazette de Paris   163
Gazette de Rotterdam   167, 168, 169, 175, 177, 178, 181
Geere, Michael   54
General Advertiser   192
Gennaro, St   106
Genoa   23, 25, 27, 28, 30, 33, 37, 71
George I   200
George II   200
George, Lloyd   369, 372
Georgetown University   332
Germany   36, 37, 146, 147, 149, 153, 155, 156, 162, 197, 281, 286, 288, 289, 290, 353, 354, 356, 358, 362, 365, 372, 381, 415, 419
Gestrich, Andreas   78
Gesù Nuovo. *See* Naples – Gesù Nuovo
Ghent   19, 373
Ghezzi, Pier Leone   110, 111
Gilbert, Martin   378
Ginzburg, Carlo   319
Giovannini, Baccio   27
Giraffi, Alessandro   85
Giron, Fernando   49, 50
Gladfelder, Hal   236
Gladstone, William   270–275
Glasgow Herald   266
Glenholmes, Evelyn   405
Goldoni, Carlo   237

Good Friday Agreement   310, 311, 316–320, 322, 323
Gordon, Charles (general)   263, 269–274, 276
Gotha-IV (bomber)   354
Grady, Claire   400, 401, 403, 404, 410
Granada   100, 104, 108
Granard   409
Grave, Charles   358, 359
Gravina   100
Gray, Tony   399
Grayzel, Susan   358, 376, 378
Graz   15, 25, 27, 28, 32, 33, 34, 35
Great Britain   221, 251
Great Depression   416
Great Famine (1846–1849)   204
Great Yarmouth   353
Greensmith, John (printer)   148
Greenwich   366
Gregorian calendar   46, 51, 206
Gregory, Adrian   362
Gregory, Lady (Isabella Augusta Persse)   333
Gresham's Law   5
Greuter, Johann Friederich   110
Grey, Edward   369
Grindelwald Fluctuation   44
Guardia Sanframondi   63
Guicciardini, Francesco   27
Gustavus Adolphus   55

Habermas, Jürgen   8, 76, 77, 79, 80
Habsburgs   17, 44, 284
Hackett, Miss   212
Hague Peace Conference (1907)   354
Hake, A. Egmont   274
Hall, Stuart   418
Hamburg   52, 191
Hamilton, Ian   278
Hand, James   202
Harari, Yuval Noah   54
Hardin, John   203
Harmsworth, Alfred (Lord Northcliffe)   383, 398
Harris, John   418
Harrison, Charles   359
Hartford (Conneticut)   336
Hart, Frank   359
Harvard   332

Harwood, Colonel   55
Haselden, W. K.   359
Hastings, Battle of (1066)   293
Hatfield, Maid of   127
Havelock, Henry (general)   261, 267, 268, 273
Hayes, Will   222
Hayes, William   208
Hearn, Stephen   212
Hearst, William Randolph   398
Hearty, Kevin   316
Heidegger, Martin   4
Heidelberg   146, 368
Heinsius, Anthoine   167, 180
Henderson, William John   393
Henlein, Konrad   290, 291, 292
Henry III (Holy Roman Emperor)   293
Hepnarová, Olga   301–303
Hepworth, Cecil   392
Herick, Robert   203
Herman, David   81
Herman, Edward S.   8
Hermestain, general of Schiavonia   32
Hesse, Hermann   7
Hewlett, Rose   44
Hickling, P. B.   359
Higgins, Daniel Irwin   391
Hippisley, John   42, 46, 51
Hiroshima   425
Hitler, Adolf   281, 288–291, 392
Hobbes, Thomas   4
Hoborn Turnstile   197
Hobson, J. A.   262
Hogarth, William   229
Holden, P. J.   314
Holland   24, 25, 34, 137, 163, 166, 223
Holland, Clive   356
Hollar, Wenceslaus   147
Holyhead   136
Holy Roman Empire   176, 228
Howell, James   86, 87
Howth   200
Hrad (the Castle)   284, 285, 292
HTML   411
Hughes, Frances Gertrude   388
Hughes, John   217
Hulík, Štěpán   304
Hull   373, 379
Hull Packet   266

Hungary 28, 32, 33, 188, 191
Hurly, John 202
Husák, Gustáv 299
Hutchinson, Will 215
Hyde, Douglas 7, 9, 190, 329–352
Hyde, Nuala 335
Hyde, Úna 335

Iberia 6
Illinois 387
Illustrated London News 262
Independent Chronicle 254
India 189, 195, 261, 264, 265
Indies 20, 30, 49
Infelise, Mario 1
Innocent XI 59, 64, 66, 68, 69, 70, 73
International Herald Tribune 403
Ireland 7, 8, 9, 43, 53, 54, 143–145, 147–149, 151–154, 156–161, 188–189, 191, 197, 201, 203–205, 208–209, 213, 214, 216–218, 220–221, 242–245, 246–247, 249–250, 252–255, 312, 314, 322, 329–330, 333–335, 339, 341–342, 345–346, 350–351, 358, 381–383, 387, 388, 390, 393–395
Ireland – Munster 40
Irish Automobile Club 386
Irish Civil War 383
Irish Daily Independent 334
Irish Daily Star 405, 406
Irish Independent 317, 351, 398, 399, 403, 408, 409
Irish Language 213, 329, 330, 333, 334, 343, 347
Irish Omnibus Company (IOC) 391
Irish Press (newspaper) 399, 401, 402, 407, 408
Irish Press Group 404
Irish Tourist Development Association 382–383
Irish Wheelman 383
Isle of Dogs 366
Israel 146
Israelites 67, 146, 152, 157
Israel, Jonathan 92
Istituto Nazionale di Geofisica e Vulcanologia (INGV) 62
Italy 6, 15, 40, 62, 89, 95, 100, 112, 120, 136, 405, 407

Jamaica 133, 135, 137
Jankovic, Vladimir 121
Japan 40, 415, 425
Jennis, Gurnell Charles 359
Jeremiah (prophet) 146
Jhansi Fort 266, 267
Jode the Younger, Pieter 91–92
John, Radek 306
Jones, Evan T. 44
Jones, H. A. 379
Jones, Henry 149
Jonson, Ben 203
Jordan, Claude 162, 167, 169, 174
Julianstown 386
Jülich-Cleves-Berg and Burgau, Sibylle of 21

Kalmre, Eda 319
Kavanagh, John 391
Kennion, Patrick 202
Kenny, Ivor 400, 407
Kepler, Johannes 40
Kerry News 391, 392
Khartoum 6, 263, 270–275
Kierans, John 406
Kilkenny 212, 214, 216
Killeen, Terence 396
Kimberley 275, 279
Kingsborough, Edward King, viscount 219
Kinsale 54
Kladderadatsch (satirical German magazine) 420
Kley, Heinrich 353
Klíma, Josef 306
Knock 395
Koblenz 368
Konrád, Edmund 294
Koopmans, Joop W. 134
Koselleck, Reinhardt 76
Krofta, Kamil 288
Kromschröder, Gerhard 307
Kuhn, Thomas 88
Kuiken, Jeffrey 410
Kurtz, Lucy Cometina 335
Kuwait 408
Kvaček, Robert 286

L'Estrange, Colonel   218
La Barlotta   19
Labour Party (Britain)   416, 423
Labour Woman   417, 423, 424, 425
Ladysmith   275, 276, 278
Ladysmith Day   279
La Font, Alexandre de   166, 169, 171, 172, 173, 174, 180, 181, 182
La Font, Anthony de   167, 169, 174, 180
La Locomotion Automobile (magazine)   383
la Repubblica   407
La Rochelle   173
Lasswell, Harold   8
Lavenir, Catherine Bertho   2
Lawlor, Dr   331
Lawrence, Henry   268, 273
Lazarus of Bethany   96
League of Nations   286, 287
Leckey, Edward   267
Leeds Mercury   273
Leger, William   53–55
Leicester Chronicle   273
Leiden   166, 170, 173, 178
Leinster Leader   391
Leninism   299, 307
Lennox-Boyd, Alan   287–288
Lennox, Charlotte   237
Leopoldov   309
Letitia, Gironimo   82
Leuuis, Seamus   196
Lewin, Frederick George   359
Liberal Party (Britain)   416
Lidgate, Jane   203
Lidové noviny (*People's News*)   283, 285, 287, 288, 291–295
Liège   354
Liffey river   187
Lille   354
Lima   73, 105, 120, 128, 133, 189, 196
Limerick, Co.   196, 199, 332
Limerick Leader   399–400
Lisbon   23, 24, 42, 43, 53, 62, 104, 108
Little Bray   399
Little Ice Age   42
Liverpool   214, 368
Liverpool Mercury   265

Loewenstein, Bedřich   285, 296
London   5, 41, 44, 46, 53, 143, 144, 147, 148, 149, 170, 189, 190, 191, 195, 197, 200, 202, 217, 234, 246, 247, 248, 249, 250, 251, 252, 254, 269, 272, 274, 290, 292, 355, 356, 363, 364, 366, 367, 369, 370, 372, 376, 379, 408
  Royal Opera, Covent Garden   217
  St Paul's Churchyard   146
  Theatre Royal, Drury Lane   217
London Chronicle   249
London Evening Post   249
London Gazette   120, 123, 124, 131, 132, 137
London Indepdenent   408
London Opinion   355
Long Turkish War   17
Lord Northcliffe. *See* Hamsworth, Alfred
Los Angeles   340, 343, 344
lottery (beneficiata)   65, 71, 72, 74
Louis XIV   172, 173, 176, 180
Love, Thomas (Sir)   54
Lovett, Ann   409
Low Countries   43, 44, 46, 48, 50, 51, 52, 53
Low, Harry   378
Lubrano, Cesare   82
Lucknow   6, 261, 267, 269, 273, 276, 280
Lucky Rock   384
Ludlow machine   399
Luhmann, Niklas   77, 78, 83
Luttrell, Narcissus   133, 135
Lützen   55
Lynch, Kathleen   153
Lyon   124, 126, 127, 173

Macaulay, Thomas   265
Mac Caithil, Eoin   196
Mac Cruitín, Aodh Buidhe   194
MacDonald, Donald   277–278
Macerata   110
Mackay, Anson W.   44
Mafeking   6, 275, 278, 279, 280
Mafeking Mail   276, 277, 278
Magill (current affairs magazine)   402
Magrath, Colonel   384
Mahdi   270, 271, 274, 280
Maher, Captain   251
Manchester Guardian   267

Maria, Henrietta (Queen)   53
Marlowe, Lara   403
Marseille   176
Martin, Edward   333
Marxism   299
Marx, Maarten   410
Maryland, Virgina   250
Masaniello (Tommaso Aniell D'Amalfi)   81, 88–94, 97–98
Masaryk, Jan (ambassador)   292
Masaryk, Tomáš Garrigue   284, 285
Massachusetts Bay Colony   249, 251
Matyáš, Jindřich Thurn (count)   52
Mayo, Co.   400
Mayo News   400
McCann, Fiona   312
McCarthy, Thomas   217
McDonald, Dearbhail   406
McDonald, Frank   402
McGilloway, Brian   315
McGlinchey, Dominic   312
McGlinchey, Marisa   318
McGreevy (character)   312–313
McKay, Margaret   385
McMahon, Johnny   407
McQuaid, John Charles   400
MCS. *See* Mercalli-Cancani-Sieberg scale
McShane, Clay   381
Meath, earl of   187
Mecredy, Richard J.   383–384, 390
Medici Archive Project   36
Medicis   15, 16, 20, 21, 27, 33, 39
Memphis, Tennessee   350, 387
Mercalli-Cancani-Sieberg scale (MCS)   63
merchants   30, 135, 136, 175, 181, 235, 267, 362, 392
Mercurius Britannicus   44
Meroz   157
Metz   368
Mezzogiorno   77, 89
Middle East   22
Milan   25, 27, 28, 36, 37
Milford Haven   216
Millar, Stephen R.   323
Miller, D. A.   236
Mills, A. Wallis   359
Mirabello, counsellor   82

Mitelli, Giuseppe Maria   110
Modern History or a A monethly account of all considerable Occurences   128, 133
Mons   18
Montesa   108
Moors   51
Moravia   286
Morley, Brendan   403, 404
Morley, John   279
Morning Post   276
Moro, Domenico   230
Moro, Lunardo   49, 50
Morrow, George   359
Morrow, John H.   354
Morton, Thomas (Sir)   55
Mount Bolton   213
Moxham, Noel   1
Muddiman, Henry   122
Mukharji, Projit Bihari Mukharji   267
Mulholland, Mark   312
Mullane, Catherine   388
Munich Agreement   7, 281, 282, 291, 293, 294
Munster   40, 204, 215
Munter, Robert   190, 191
Münzer, Jan   287
Muratori, Ludovico Antonio   238
Murcia   106
Murphy, Bryan   9, 222
Murphy, Mrs   223
Murphy, William Martin   398
music   1, 7, 201, 217–218, 310, 311, 320, 322–325, 331
Muslims   51
Mussolini, Benito   281, 291
Muti Papazzurri, Giovanni   59

Naas   220
Naboth   154
Naccarella, Ciommo   82
Naclerio, Andrea   82
Nádasdy, Ferencz   33
Na Fianna   319
Nagasaki   425
Nagykanizsa. *See* Canissa
Nakazawa, Keiji   425–426
Namur   176, 177
Nantes, Edict of   20, 165, 171–174, 180

Naples 6, 60, 63–67, 69–71, 74, 75–99, 101–104, 114, 115, 123, 124, 125, 128, 131, 133, 138, 230, 237, 240
    Gesù Nuovo (church) 102
    Piazza del Mercato 80, 97
    Santa Caterina a Formello (convent) 103
    Santa Chiara (royal chapel) 102
    Santi Apostoli convent 102
Napoleonic Wars 41, 268
Narveson, Kate 153
Nassau, Maurice of 18
National Assembly (France) 222
Neapolitan Revolution 4, 5, 75–99
Nelson, Horatio (1st viscount) 220
Neri, Filippo 6, 68, 100–119
Neville, Stuart 313
Newbridge, Co. Kildare 391
New Cultural History 417, 422
New England Chronicle 252
New IRA 311
News of the World 358, 360
New World 23, 42
New York 249, 250, 251, 252, 330, 332, 333, 335, 344, 351, 353, 420
New York Gazette 250, 251, 255
New York Journal 251, 252, 398
New York Post 405
New York Times 397
New York World 398
New Zealand 358, 415, 422
Ní Bhroin, Úna 187
Niccolini, Giovanni 27
Nieuwe Tijdinghen 51, 397
Nieuwpoort 18, 19, 26
Nile 220, 271, 273
Nîmes 172
Ní Ógáin, Úna 331, 332, 334, 335, 338, 339, 340
Ní Ó Nodhlaig, Ú 331
Norcia 106, 108
North, Frederick (2nd Earl of Guildford, Lord) 254
North Sea 41
Norton, Peter D. 381–382, 385, 387, 388
Norwich 148
Nouveau journal universel 162, 167, 168, 169
Nouvelles extraordinaires de divers endroits 166, 167–173, 175, 178–181
Nowland, Moses 199

Nussbaum, Martha 3

O'Conor, Charles 191
O'Donoghue, D. J. 190
O'Reilly, Fr 199
Oakland 339, 341, 342, 349
Oakland City University 341
O Beaglaoich, Conchobhar 194
O'Brien, Edna 312
O'Brien, Mark 398
Ó Buachalla, Brendan 197
Occleve, Thomas 203
Ó Cofaigh, Éamon 381–382
O'Connor, T. P. 398
O'Donnell, Brendan 406
O'Donnell McFall, Daniel 388, 389
Ó Fallamhain, C. S. 330
Ó Giolláin, Diarmuid 319
O'Kane, Maggie 409
Ó Neachtain, Sean 187
Ó Neachtain, Tadhg 6, 188, 191, 192, 194, 201, 204–206
O'Neill, Mr. 217
operetta 217
Ó Raifteiri, Antoine 333
O'Reilly, Emily 409
O'Reilly, John Boyle 344
O'Riordan, Dick 404, 407, 411
Orsini, Vincenzo Maria (archbishop of Benevento) 68, 100
Orzoff, Andrea 285
Osnabrück 200
Ostend 18, 19, 24, 354
O'Toole, Fintan 410
Ottomans 17, 20, 25, 32
Oxford 127, 364

Palermo 84, 195
Palestinian Liberation Organisation (PLO) 408
pandemic 310, 383
Papal States 64–66, 69, 70
Paris 9, 27, 46, 97, 163, 167, 171, 172, 175, 176, 178, 190, 191, 193, 222, 247, 383, 403
Parissien, Steven 381
Parker, Geoffrey 19
Parliament (Ireland) 221

Parliament (England/Britain after 1707) 47, 124, 127, 143, 145, 149, 152, 154, 155, 157, 158, 160, 247, 254, 271, 287, 368, 369
Parliament (Ireland) 221, 401
Parrino, Domenico Antonio (publisher) 67, 101
Partition (of Ireland) 390
Partridge, Bernard 359, 361
Pátečníci (Friday Men) 284
Patoillat, Marie 166–167
Patten, L. 359
Peacey, Jason 48
Pears, Charles 359
Pegram, Fred 359
Pelaschiar, Laura 312
Pennsylvania Evening Post 251
Pennsylvania Journal 248, 255
Penryn 42
Pepys, Samuel 41
perestroika 7, 298, 306, 307, 308
Peroutka, Ferdinand 285, 287
Perry, Miss 386
Persia 21
Perspectives (magazine of the American Historical Association) 418
Peru 20, 120, 131, 138, 189, 196
Peter, St 91, 195
Pětka (The Five) 284, 285
Pettegree, Andrew 128, 397
Philadelphia 250, 251, 252
Philastrius, Bishop of Brescia 67
Philip II 26, 73
Philip IV 51
Phillips, Marion 424
Pignatelli, Antonio (Archbishop) 64, 66, 68, 70
Pioneer Association 400
Pius V 4
plague 23, 197, 198, 204
plays 217
Plumstead 366
Plymouth 47, 53, 54, 55
Pocile, Andrea 84
Poland 28, 188, 191, 284
police 236, 304, 317, 318, 319, 389, 405, 409
Port Royal (Jamaica) 135, 136
postcards 347, 348
Power, Frank 272
Power, Miss 206

Power, Patrick 208
Prague 25, 27, 28, 281, 289, 290, 295, 301, 303, 304, 305, 308
Prague Spring (August 1968) 298
Pratt's (subsidiary of Irish American Oil) 390
Preston 202
printers 44, 101, 103, 108, 112, 148, 151, 165, 167, 191, 192, 235, 246, 248, 252, 253, 402
privateers 192
propaganda 8, 163, 180, 224, 301, 304, 305, 320, 380
prostitution 66
Protestantism 26, 31, 47, 51, 127, 130, 143–147, 149–161, 171–173, 190–192, 199, 205, 284, 330
providentialism 61, 62, 154
Provisional Irish Republican Army (PIRA) 312–314, 316–318, 323
Public Advertiser 251
publishers 44, 45, 51, 67, 145, 162, 163, 165, 166, 167, 169, 170, 171, 174, 181, 191, 231, 232, 233, 237, 240, 288, 331
Pue's Occurrence 385
Pulitzer, Joseph 398
Punch (magazine) 262, 355, 358–361, 368, 369, 371, 372, 374, 376–379
Puntal (fort) 48, 49, 50, 53
Purcell, John 222

Quarlos, Francis 203
Queen Elizabeth, the Queen Mother 407
Queenstown (Co. Cork), now Cobh 335
Quester, Matthew de 51
Quin, Martin 21
Quinn, John 330, 331–334, 336, 337, 343

radio 303, 410
Rádl, Otto 295
Raemaekers, Louis 356–358, 360, 361, 363–366
Rafferty, Pauline 312
railways 275, 382, 384
Rampaigne, Dorothy 159, 160
Rampaigne, Zachariah 159
Rancière, Jacques 89
Randall, David 45, 123, 130
Randolph, Thomas 203
Rathmines 393

Ratra (Co. Roscommon)   335
Raven-Hill, Leonard   360, 361, 368
Ray, John   137
Raymond, Joad   1, 44, 124
Recueil des nouvelles   168, 169, 175, 176
Redmond, Bill   401
refugees   143, 165, 166, 168
Regina, John Baptist   102
Reinisch, Dieter   319
Renaudot, Eusèbe II   165, 177
Renaudot, Théophraste   163, 168
Reni, Guido   110
Reutlingen   196
Reynolds's Newspaper   264, 269
Reynolds, Frank   360, 379
R-Giant (bomber)   354
Rhine   46, 288, 293
Rice, Seán   411
Richardson, Samuel   237
Richelieu, Armand Jean du Plessis (1st duke of, cardinal)   163
Rider, Ebenezer   191, 192
Riney, Imelda   406
Riney, Liam   406
Ripka, Hubert   285
Ritchie, John   263–264
Rivington's Royal Gazette   252
Robbe-Grillet, Alain   403
Roberti, Abbot Giambattista   239–240
Robert of Gloucester   203
Robin, Corey   4
Robinson, William Heath   358, 360, 361
Roma/Romani   309
Romania   405
Rome   16, 21, 27, 30, 31, 36, 37, 59, 60, 64, 69, 70, 74, 93, 100, 104, 170, 189, 199, 396
Rosa, Hartmut   3
Roscommon, Co.   187, 218, 329, 335
Ross, Charles D.   42
Rosset, François de   229
Rothwell, John (junior)   146
Rothwell, John (senior)   146
Rountree, Harry   359, 360
Roworth, Wassying   97, 98
Royal Gazette   252
Royal Irish Constabulary   389
RTÉ (Irish State Broadcaster)   317, 406
Rubens, Peter Paul   46, 50, 51, 52

Rubiès, Jean-Paul   226
Rudé právo (Red Justice)   282, 283, 285, 286, 288, 290, 291, 301, 302, 303
Runciman, Walter   283, 289, 290, 291, 293
Russell, John   55
Russell, William Howard   262
Ryan, Cornelius   213, 214
Ryan, James   6, 208, 209, 223
Ryan, John   213
Ryan, Stephen   408

Saeiler, Cotton   381
Sahib, Nana   265
Salamanca   104
Salisbury Plain   422
San Francisco   330, 333, 339–343, 346–351
San Francisco Call   339, 342, 343
San Francisco Examiner   342, 346, 347
San Francisco Leader   340
San Jose Mercury News   411
Sanlúcar de Barrameda   52, 54
Sannio   59, 63, 64, 65, 68, 71, 73, 74, 100, 101, 105, 106, 112
Santissima Annunziata, Daughters of   80
Santis, Tommaso de   83, 90
Saoradh   311
Sarnelli, Pompeo   103
SAS   407
Sausse, James   214, 216
Savoy   17, 35, 178
Sawbridge, Lord Mayor   252
Schudson, Michael   2, 5
Schuth, Anne   410
Scilly, Islands of   54, 124
Scotland   127, 130, 137, 152, 158, 191
Scouts   278, 388
Seaver, Paul   153
Senegal   420
Seoighe, Mainchin   399
Sequens, Jiří   304
Serbia   287
Seven Years War   247
Severall Proceedings in Parliament   124
Seville   24, 104, 106, 108
Sewell, William H.   8, 417, 426
Shagan, Ethan   145
Shalvey, Declan   314
Shapiro, Barbara   120, 121, 122, 125, 130

Sheffield Pals 418
Shepard, Ernest H. 359, 360
Shepperson, Claude Allin 360
Shirer, William L. 292
Shrivastava, K. M. 401
Sicily, Kingdom of 73, 74, 195
Silicon Valley 411
Silva, Fabrizio 80
Sinn Féin (RSF) 311, 323
Skene, Alexander (captain) 266
Skene, Margaret 266
Sligo 219
Sling 422, 423
Sluis 24
Small Press Acts (1933 and 1934) 286
Smyczek, Karel 308
Smyllie, R. M. ('Bertie') 399
Smyrna 132, 136, 138
Snowden, Phillip 423–424
social media 3, 347
sociology 1, 61
Solomon (king of Israel) 155, 161
Somerset 195, 197
Somme 374
South African War 262, 263, 275
Soviet Union 281, 282, 295, 306, 315
Spada, Virginio 97
Spain 24, 26, 30, 42, 43, 46–52, 100, 104, 106, 108, 112, 176, 198, 407
Spanish-American War 398
Sparta Prague 308
Spenser, Edmund 203
Spinola, Ambrogio 52
Spinola, Federico 24
Spinoza, Baruch 92
Spire versus Carew (legal case) 387
Spitters, Martijn 410
Sportelli, Gennaro 67
Stalinism 302
Stamp Act (1765) 243, 247–251
Stampa, Giorgio Loraine 360, 378
Staniforth, Joseph Morewood 360, 361, 367, 369, 370, 375
Starr, Freddie 405
States of Holland and Zeeland 34
Status (women's magazine) 402
Stead, W. T. 263, 271, 398
Steel, Flora Annie 266

Stefani, Gaetano de 83, 91
Steklý, K. 298
Stiele, Caspar 120
Stirling Castle 137
St Malo 176
Stöber, Rudolf 2
St Patrick's College, Maynooth 333
St Petersburg 189, 197
Strachey, Lytton 272
Strasbourg 162, 170, 368
Stronge, Humphrey 281
Stuart, Charles Edward ('The Young Pretender') 197
Stuart, Elizabeth 42, 52
Stuarts 42, 43, 45, 46, 48, 53, 198
Sturmabteilung (SA) 392
Stuttgart 368
St Vincent de Paul 407
submarines 362, 365
Sudan 270, 271, 272
Sudetenland 281, 289, 290
Suez 268
Sullivan, Edmund Joseph 360
Sullivan, Frank J. 340, 341, 350
Sunday Business Post 408
Sunday Star 335
Sunday Tribune 404, 405, 408, 409
Swabia 197
Sweden 191, 381
Swift, Jonathan 201
Switzerland 28

Tallaght Echo 401
Tatars 15
Telegram (newspaper) 345
Telegram (messaging service) 310
telegrams 268, 269, 272, 275, 279
television 297, 300, 303, 304, 322
Temple, John 150
Tennant, Harold 'Jack' 369
Tesař, Jan 281
The Athenian Mercury 123, 137
Theatre 217
The Belfast Telegraph 317, 400
The Chronicles of the New Zealand Expeditionary Force 422
The Daily Telegraph 364, 421
The Domestick Intelligence 126

The Dublin Daily Advertiser 191
The Dublin Intelligence 190
The Flying Post 131, 192, 196
The Freeman's Journal and National Press 218, 396
The Friendly Intelligence 130
The Guardian 317
The Hague 46, 52, 191
The Irish Independent 317, 351, 398, 399, 408, 409
The Irish News 317
The Irish Times 317, 387, 388, 392, 393, 399, 401, 402, 408, 411
The Irish World 344
TheJournal.ie 317
The Motor News 384, 386
The Nationalist 406
The Orange Gazette 132
The Pall Mall Gazette 271, 273, 274, 279, 398
Therberton, Suffolk 375
The Times 261, 264, 265, 266, 268, 272, 278, 317, 355, 419
The True Domestic Intelligence 137
The Washington Times 335
The Wolfe Tones 322
Thirty Years War 42, 44, 46, 47, 146, 147
Thomas, John (printer) 148
Thompson, James 262, 269
Threlkeld, Caleb 203
Ticonderoga 251
Tilimon 18
Tipperary 6, 9, 208, 214, 216, 406
Tiverton 197
Toledo 59, 105
Toman, Ludvík 306
Tomás Lucas, José 108
Torcy, Colbert de 165
Toronto 9, 338
Tracey, Michael 390, 391
Transylvania 16, 24, 28, 34, 35
Treaty of Alliance and Friendship (1924) 287
Treaty of Paris (1763) 247
Treviso 103
True Protestant Mercury 127, 130
tuberculosis 389
Tulira 333
Turin 104, 178, 179

Turkey 188, 358
Turner, Patricia A. 319
Twain, Mark 342
Twomey, Brendan 194
typhoid 389
Tyrell, Dr (coroner) 385

Ua Baoidhillean, Bonaventura 204
Uitlander Crisis 276
Ulster 143
Umbria 106
United Provinces 18, 26, 44, 52, 223
United States of America 343, 350, 382, 385, 387, 388
University College Dublin (UCD) 351
Urry, John 381
USS Maine 398, 399
Uxbridge 127

Valavez. *See* Fabri, Palamède
Valencia 33, 100, 104, 105, 106, 108
Vallicella 108, 110
van Coehoorn, Menno 176
van Gelder, Johannes 166
van Swoll, Cornelius 163, 164, 166
Varadkar, Leo 347
Varsenare 369
Vaul (fictitious) 158, 159
Velasco, Luigi di 19
Velvet Revolution (November 1989) 309
Venice 16, 21, 23, 27, 46, 48, 237
Ventry 54
Verhoeven, Abraham 51, 397
Vermij, Rienk 121, 125
Versailles, Treaty of 419, 420
Versé and Genevois, Noël Aubert de 167, 169
Vervins, Peace of 20
Vesuvius 66, 97, 106, 125, 132
Vienna 16, 24, 25, 28, 32, 33, 34, 37
Vietnamese 309
Villiers, George (1st duke of Buckingham) 43, 51, 53, 55
Vincent, Philip 146, 155, 156, 159
Vinegar Hill 219
Vivo, Filippo di 226
Voltaire (François-Marie Arouet) 62
von Clausewitz, Carl 41

von Mansfeld, Ernst (count)   42
von Schwarzenberg, Adolf   33
von Wittelsbach, Maria Anna   21
von Zeppelin, Ferdinand (count)   353

Walker, Jack   358, 360, 361
Wallerstein, Emmanuel   23
Wallington, Nehemiah   5, 143–161
Walsh, Joe (Fr)   406
Walsh, Leo   401
Ward, Henry   199
Warneford, R. A. J.   372, 373
War of Independence   383
War of Jenkin's Ear   198
War of the Grand Alliance   171, 173, 174, 175, 176, 180
Warsaw Pact   298
Washington Post   335
Waterford   6, 8, 53, 207, 208, 214–217
weather   41, 43, 44, 46, 47, 49, 52, 54, 126, 188, 192, 194, 200, 201, 204, 336, 368
Weekly Mercury   251
Wells, H. G.   353
Wenceslaus I, Duke of Bohemia   293
Wentworth, Thomas   154
Werner, Annie   393
Western People   391
West Indies   136
Westminster Review   421
Westport   401
Whalley's News-Letter   191
White, Robert W.   318, 320

Whiting, Sophie A.   316
Wicklow, Co.   196
Wilde, Oscar   329
Wilhelm II, Kaiser   353
William, George   270
William III   167, 177, 254
Wilson, David   360
Wilson, Mr   222
Wired Italia (magazine)   411–412
Wolseley, Garnet (general)   272
Women's Civic League   388
woodcuts   147, 228
Woods, Thomas   213
Woolf, D. R.   121, 123
World Cup (football)   405
Wotton   137

Yeats, Jack Butler   359
Yeats, W. B.   329
Yorke, Peter (Fr)   330, 331–335, 339, 340, 342, 343, 349
Yorkshire Post   372
Yorktown   397
Younge, Dr   209–210

Zachariah (father of John the Baptist)   155
Zagorin, Perez   89
Zavaglios, Giovanni   82
Zeebrugge   354
Zeppelins   353, 354, 356, 362, 364–369, 372–376, 378, 379
Zika, Charles   135